DOMESDAY BOOK

Norfolk

History from the Sources

DOMESDAY BOOK

A Survey of the Counties of England

LIBER DE WINTONIA

Compiled by direction of

KING WILLIAM I

Winchester
1086

DOMESDAY BOOK

general editor

JOHN MORRIS

33

Norfolk

edited by

Philippa Brown

from a draft translation prepared by

Marian Hepplestone, Janet Mothersill and Margaret Newman

(Part One)

PHILLIMORE
Chichester
1984

1984
Published by
PHILLIMORE & CO. LTD.
London and Chichester
Head Office: Shopwyke Hall,
Chichester, Sussex, England

ISBN 0 85033 478 0 (case)
ISBN 0 85033 479 9 (limp)

Printed in Great Britain by
Titus Wilson & Son Ltd.,
Kendal

NORFOLK

(Part One)
Introduction

The Domesday Survey of Norfolk
(to Landholder XI, Bishop Osbern)

(Part Two)

The Domesday Survey of Norfolk
(Landholder XII, Godric the steward to
LXVI, Annexations)

Notes
Index of Persons
Index of Places
Maps and Map Keys
Systems of Reference
Technical Terms

History from the Sources

General Editor: John Morris

The series aims to publish history
written directly from the sources
for all interested readers, both
specialists and others. The first
priority is to publish important
texts which should be widely
available, but are not.

DOMESDAY BOOK

The contents, with the folio on which each county begins, are:

1	Kent	I	1	20	Bedfordshire		209
2	Sussex		16	21	Northamptonshire		219
3	Surrey		30	22	Leicestershire		230
4	Hampshire		37	23	Warwickshire		238
5	Berkshire		56	24	Staffordshire		246
6	Wiltshire		64	25	Shropshire		252
7	Dorset		75	26	Cheshire		262
8	Somerset		86	27	Derbyshire		272
9	Devon		100	28	Nottinghamshire		280
10	Cornwall		120	29	Rutland		293
11	Middlesex		126	30	Yorkshire		298
12	Hertfordshire		132	31	Lincolnshire		336
13	Buckinghamshire		143		Claims, Yorkshire		373
14	Oxfordshire		154		Lincolnshire		375
15	Gloucestershire		162		Yorkshire, summary		379
16	Worcestershire		172				
17	Herefordshire		179	32	Essex	II	1
18	Cambridgeshire		189	33	Norfolk		109
19	Huntingdonshire		203	34	Suffolk		281

Supplementary volume (35) BOLDON BOOK

Domesday Book is termed *Liber de Wintonia* (The Book of Winchester) in column 332c

INTRODUCTION

The Domesday Survey

In 1066 Duke William of Normandy conquered England. He was crowned King, and most of the lands of the English nobility were soon granted to his followers. Domesday Book was compiled 20 years later. The Saxon Chronicle records that in 1085

> at Gloucester at midwinter ... the King had deep speech with his counsellors ... and sent men all over England to each shire ... to find out ... what or how much each landholder held ... in land and livestock, and what it was worth ... The returns were brought to him.[1]

William was thorough. One of his Counsellors reports that he also sent a second set of Commissioners 'to shires they did not know, where they were themselves unknown, to check their predecessors' survey, and report culprits to the King.'[2]

The information was collected at Winchester, corrected, abridged, chiefly by omission of livestock and the 1066 population, and fair-copied by one writer into a single volume, now known as Domesday Book Volume I, or DB. The task of abridgement and codification was not complete by the time work stopped at the death of King William. The remaining material, the commissioners' circuit returns for Norfolk, Suffolk and Essex, which there had not been time to reduce, was left unabridged, copied by several writers, in a second volume, smaller than the first, usually now referred to as Domesday Book Volume II or Little Domesday Book or LDB, which states that 'the Survey was made in 1086'. The surveys of Durham and Northumberland, and of several towns, including London, were not transcribed, and most of Cumberland and Westmorland, not yet in England, was not surveyed. The whole undertaking was completed at speed, in less than 12 months, though the fair-copying of the main volume may have taken a little longer. Both volumes are now preserved at the Public Record Office. Some versions of regional returns also survive. One of them, from Ely Abbey,[3] copies out the Commissioners' brief. They were to ask

> The name of the place. Who held it, before 1066, and now?
> How many *hides*?[4] How many ploughs, both those in lordship and the men's?
> How many villagers, cottagers and slaves, how many free men and Freemen?[5]
> How much woodland, meadow and pasture? How many mills and fishponds?
> How much has been added or taken away? What the total value was and is?
> How much each free man or Freeman had or has? All threefold, before 1066,
> when King William gave it, and now; and if more can be had than at present.

The Ely volume also describes the procedure. The Commissioners took evidence on oath 'from the Sheriff; from all the barons and their Frenchmen; and from the whole Hundred, the priests, the reeves and six villagers from each village'. It also names four Frenchmen and four Englishmen from each Hundred, who were sworn to verify the detail.

---

[1]Before he left England for the last time, late in 1086. [2]Robert Losinga, Bishop of Hereford 1079-1095 (see *E.H.R.* 22, 1907, 74). [3]*Inquisitio Eliensis*, first paragraph. [4]A land unit, reckoned as 120 acres. [5]*Quot Sochemani*.

The King wanted to know what he had, and who held it. The Commissioners therefore listed lands in dispute, for Domesday Book was not only a tax-assessment. To the King's grandson, Bishop Henry of Winchester, its purpose was that every 'man should know his right and not usurp another's'; and because it was the final authoritative register of rightful possession 'the natives called it Domesday Book, by analogy from the Day of Judgement'; that was why it was carefully arranged by Counties, and by landholders within Counties, 'numbered consecutively ... for easy reference'.[6]

Domesday Book describes Old English society under new management, in minute statistical detail. Foreign lords had taken over, but little else had yet changed. The chief landholders and those who held from them are named, and the rest of the population was counted. Most of them lived in villages, whose houses might be clustered together, or dispersed among their fields. Villages were grouped in administrative districts called Hundreds, which formed regions within Shires, or Counties, which survive today with minor boundary changes; the recent deformation of some ancient county identities is here disregarded, as are various short-lived modern changes. The local assemblies, though overshadowed by lords great and small, gave men a voice, which the Commissioners heeded. Very many holdings were described by the Norman term *manerium* (manor), greatly varied in size and structure, from tiny farmsteads to vast holdings; and many lords exercised their own jurisdiction and other rights, termed *soca*, whose meaning still eludes exact definition.

The Survey was unmatched in Europe for many centuries, the product of a sophisticated and experienced English administration, fully exploited by the Conqueror's commanding energy. But its unique assemblage of facts and figures has been hard to study, because the text has not been easily available, and abounds in technicalities. Investigation has therefore been chiefly confined to specialists; many questions cannot be tackled adequately without a cheap text and uniform translation available to a wider range of students, including local historians.

Previous Editions

The text has been printed once, in 1783, in an edition by Abraham Farley, probably of 1250 copies, at Government expense, said to have been £38,000; its preparation took 16 years. It was set in a specially designed type, here reproduced photographically, which was destroyed by fire in 1808. In 1811 and 1816 the Records Commissioners added an introduction, indices, and associated texts, edited by Sir Henry Ellis; and in 1861-1863 the Ordnance Survey issued zincograph facsimiles of the whole. Texts of individual counties have appeared since 1673, separate translations in the Victoria County Histories and elsewhere.

[6]*Dialogus de Scaccario* 1,16.

This Edition

Farley's text is used, because of its excellence, and because any worthy alternative would prove astronomically expensive. His text has been checked against the facsimile, and discrepancies observed have been verified against the manuscript, by the kindness of Miss Daphne Gifford of the Public Record Office. Farley's few errors are indicated in the notes.

The editor is responsible for the translation and lay-out. It aims at what the compiler would have written if his language had been modern English; though no translation can be exact, for even a simple word like 'free' nowadays means freedom from different restrictions. Bishop Henry emphasized that his grandfather preferred 'ordinary words'; the nearest ordinary modern English is therefore chosen whenever possible. Words that are now obsolete, or have changed their meaning, are avoided, but measurements have to be transliterated, since their extent is often unknown or arguable, and varied regionally. The terse inventory form of the original has been retained, as have the ambiguities of the Latin.

Modern English commands two main devices unknown to 11th century Latin, standardised punctuation and paragraphs; in the Latin, *ibi* ('there are') often does duty for a modern full stop, *et* ('and') for a comma or semi-colon. The entries normally answer the Commissioners' questions, arranged in five main groups, (i) the place and its holder, its hides, ploughs and lordship; (ii) people; (iii) resources; (iv) value; and (v) additional notes. The groups are usually given as separate paragraphs.

In both volumes of the MS, chapters were numbered 'for easy reference'. In the larger volume, sections within chapters are commonly marked, usually by initial capitals, often edged in red. In LDB (representing an earlier stage of the Inquiry's codification) sections are at first usually introduced by a paragraph mark, while red edging is reserved for chapter and Hundred headings; further on, however, the system of paragraphing the text becomes more haphazard and it is thus not always followed in the present translation. Owing to the less tabulated nature of the entries in LDB for Norfolk and Suffolk it is not possible to maintain throughout the translation of these two counties the sub-paragraphing that the late John Morris employed in the translation of other counties in the series. Maps, indices and an explanation of technical terms are also given. Later, it is hoped to publish analytical and explanatory volumes, and associated texts.

The editor is deeply indebted to the advice of many scholars, too numerous to name, and especially to the Public Record Office, and to the publisher's patience. The draft translations are the work of a team; they have been co-ordinated and corrected by the editor, and each has been checked by several people. It is therefore hoped that mistakes may be fewer than in versions published by single fallible individuals. But it would be Utopian to hope that the translation is altogether free from error; the editor would like to be informed of mistakes observed.

The maps are the work of Jim Hardy.

The preparation of this volume has been greatly assisted by a generous grant from the Leverhulme Trust Fund.

This support, originally given to the late Dr. J. R. Morris, has been kindly extended to his successors. At the time of Dr. Morris's death in June 1977, he had completed volumes 2, 3, 11, 12, 19, 23, 24. He had more or less finished the preparation of volumes 13, 14, 20, 28. These and subsequent volumes in the series were brought out under the supervision of John Dodgson and Alison Hawkins, who have endeavoured to follow, as far as possible, the editorial principles established by John Morris.

Conventions

★ refers to note on discrepancy between MS and Farley text

[ ] enclose words omitted in the MS ( ) enclose editorial explanation

NORFULC.

.I	Wiłłm Rex.	
.II.	Epc̄ baiocenſis.	
.III.	Com de maurit̃.	
.IIII.	Com Alanus.	
.V.	Com Euſtachi̇.	
.VI.	Com Hugo.	
.VII.	Rob̃ malet.	
.VIII	Wiłłm de War̃.	
.VIIII	Rog̃ bigot.	
.X.	Wiłłm Epc̃.	
.XI	Osb̃t epc̃.	
.XII.	Godric dapifer.	
.XIII	Hermer deferer	
.XIIII.	Abb̃ de Sco̅ . E.	
.XV.	Abb̃ de eli.	
.XVI.	Abb̃ Sc̃i B̃ (de ramesio.)	
.XVII	Abb̃ de Hulmo̅.	
.XVIII.	Scs Stephan	
.XVIIII.	Wiłłm de eſcois.	
.XX.	Radulf de bellofago̅.	
.XXI.	Rainald fili Juon.	
.XXII.	Radulf de Toenio.	
XXIII.	Hugo de monte forti.	
XX̃. (IIII)	Eudo dapifer̃.	

.XXV.	Walter Giffart̃.
XXVI.	Rog̃ pictauienſis.
XXVII.	Iuo Talleboſc.
XXVIII	Rad de Limeſio.
XXVIIII	Eudo fili Spiruwic̃.
XXX	Drogo debeuraria.
XXXI	Rad bainard
XXXII	Rannulf pipeteł.
XXXIII	Rob̃ grenon.
XXXIIII	Petr̃ Valonienſis.
XXXV.	Rob̃ fili Corbutioñ.
XXXVI	Rannulf fr ilgeri̇
XXXVII	Teheł britto.
XXXVIII	Rob̃ de uerli.
XXXVIIII	Hunfrid fili albici̇.
XL	Hunfrid de bohu̇.
XLI	Radulf defelgeres.
XLII	Giſleb̃t fili Richeťl.
XLIII	Roger de ramis.
XL̃. (IIII.)	Iuikeł . prb̃r.
XLV	Coleb̃t . pr.
XLVI	Edmund fili pagani.
XL̃ (VII.)	Iſaac.
XLṼ (III)	Touu̇.

.XLV̄ (IIII)	Iohs nepos . Walerani̇
L	Roger fili renardi.
LI	Berner arbaliſtar̃.
LII	Giſleb̃t arbaliſtar̃.
LIII	Radulf arbaliſtar̃.
LIIII	Rob̃t arbaliſtar̃.
LV	Radbeł artifex.
LVI	Hagȯ.
LVII	Radulf fili Hagoñ.
LVIII	Vlcheteł .
LVIIII	Aluredus.
LX	Aldit.
LXI	Goduin Haldeṅ.
LXII	Starcolf.
LXIII	Etdric ancipitar̃.
LXIIII	De libis hoib̃ reg.
	Ad nulla firma ptinent̃
LXV	De dominic̃ hoib̃ reg̃
LXVI	De inuaſionib̃

LIST OF LANDHOLDERS IN NORFOLK

I King William
II The Bishop of Bayeux
III The Count of Mortain
IV Count Alan
V Count Eustace
VI Earl Hugh
VII Robert Malet
VIII William of Warenne
IX Roger Bigot
X Bishop William
XI Bishop Osbern
XII Godric the steward
XIII Hermer of Ferrers
XIV The Abbot of
    Saint E(dmund)
XV The Abbot of Ely
XVI The Abbot of
    St. B(enedict) of
    Ramsey
XVII The Abbot of Holme
XVIII St. Stephen of Caen
XIX William of Écouis
XX Ralph of Beaufour
XXI Reynald son of Ivo
XXII Ralph of Tosny
XXIII Hugh de Montfort
XXIV Eudo the steward

XXV Walter Giffard
XXVI Roger of Poitou
XXVII Ivo Tallboys
XXVIII Ralph of Limésy
XXIX Eudo son of Spirwic
XXX Drogo of Beuvrière
XXXI Ralph Baynard
XXXII Ranulf Peverel
XXXIII Robert Gernon
XXXIV Peter of Valognes
XXXV Robert son of Corbucion
XXXVI Ranulf brother of Ilger
XXXVII Tihel the Breton
XXXVIII Robert of Verly
XXXIX Humphrey son of Aubrey
XL Humphrey of Bohun
XLI Ralph of Fougères
XLII Gilbert son of Richere
XLIII Roger of Raismes
XLIV Judicael the priest
XLV Colbern the priest
XLVI Edmund son of Payne
XLVII Isaac
XLVIII Tovi

XLIX John nephew of Waleran
L Roger son of Rainard
LI Berner the crossbowman
LII Gilbert the crossbowman
LIII Ralph the crossbowman
LIV Robert the crossbowman
LV Rabel the engineer
LVI Hagni
LVII Ralph son of Hagni
LVIII Ulfketel
LIX Alfred
LX Aldith
LXI Godwin Haldane
LXII Starculf
LXIII Edric the falconer
LXIV King's free men belonging
    to no estate
LXV The King's men in lordship
LXVI Annexations

.I. *FREDEBRVGE* . H̃ . 7 dim . Maſincham teñ Herold
t . r . e . III . car træ . Tñc . IIII . uill . Quando rog recep . III .
& m̃ ſimil . ſemp . I . bor . Tñc . IIII . ſer . P̃ 7 m̃ . I . 7 VII . acr p̃ti .
Tñc . II . car in dnio . p̃ 7 m̃ . I . ſilua . X . por . Hic jacent . XXV .
ſoc . III . car træ . 7 XX . acr . Tñc 7 p̃ . VI . car . 7 dim . M̃ . III . 7 d̃ .
ſemp VII . por . 7 LXIIII . ou . Tc 7 p̃ ual . XL . ſol . m̃ . X . lib . De
hoc Manerio dé ſñt . XXV . ſoc . quj aderant t . r . e . cũ omi con
ſuetudiñe . XX . ho꞉ ten& . Wido angeuin & hñt . II . car træ .
7 LVIII . ac . 7 quarta parte uni acre . Et W . de Warenna . IIII .
q̃ hñt . CXX . ac . 7 dim . Et Rog bigot . I . qui ħt . XV . acr . Et W .
de ſoies . I . de . X . acr . Sñt & de hoc manerio ablati . XIIII . libi
hoés 7 XII . uill quos ten& . Rad baign . hoc totũ ħt . I . mill in loñ .
& dim in lato & de XX . ſol ꞉ reddit XVI . d̃ in gelto .

[H̃ . de dochinge ꞉ Sutmere tenuit Herold tepr reg ꞉ ē . Tñc
III . car . in dnio . p̃ 7 m̃ . II . Tñc XXI . uill . p̃ 7 m̃ XIX ꞉ ſemp . II . bor .
7 VI . ſer . 7 . I . car hom . ſemp . III . r . 7 . I . añ . 7 . III . por . 7 LXXXVII .
ou . Hic jacent . XXXI . ſoc . XVI . acr . I . car . Et XV . ſoc ꞉ uñ quiſq
LX . acr VIII . car . 7 . I . car . & dim poſſ& reſtaurari ꞉ Et . I . ſoc .
XIIII ac . Et . I . ſoc LX . ac . tc . I . car ꞉ Et tigeſwella . I . bereuuita
ſep . I . car . 7 dim . inđ . 7 XIIII . uill ꞉ 7 VI . bor . 7 . IIII . ſer . 7 XVI . ac
p̃ti . ſilua . LX . por . m̃ . I . mol . ſemp . I . car . homũ . Et . IIII . ſoc . II .
car træ . II . car . Et . II . ſoc . V . acr . Et ꞉ I . ſoc . LX . ac . II . bou . Et
. I . ſoc . đ quarta parte . uni acre . In bereuuita . CCLX . ou . 7 XI .
por . 7 . II . añ . & . V . r . Et . I . car træ . qđ ten . I . lib ho . t . r . e .

Hoc totũ ual tc . VII . lib . p̃ . XX . m̃ . XXX . [Et . IIII . ſoc . IIII . ac træ .
t . r . e . qđ p̃ qua | uenit . 7 p̃q Rog hoc man recep̃ . Brũm p̃poſit
R . bigot tulit de hoc manerio . & m̃ ten& . Rog . Et I . ſoc . LX ac .
dim car . Stanho tenuit Aluric lib ho Subſtigando . t . r . e . I . car
træ . Tñc . I . car . p̃ 7 m̃ . II . boues . 7 I . bor . 7 ual XVI . ſol . 7 jac&
in phacham .

[LAND OF THE KING]

FREEBRIDGE Hundred and a half

1 Harold held MASSINGHAM before 1066, 3 c. of land.

Then 4 villagers, when Roger acquired it 3, now the same;
always 1 smallholder. Then 4 slaves, later and now 1.

Meadow, 7 acres. Then 2 ploughs in lordship; later and now 14.
Woodland, 10 pigs.

Here appertain 25 Freemen, 3 c. of land and 20 acres. Then
and later 6½ ploughs, now 3½. Always 7 pigs; 64 sheep.

Value then and later 40s; now £10.

25 Freemen are missing from this manor who were there before
1066 with all customary dues. Guy of Anjou holds 20 of them;
they have 2 c. of land and 58 acres, and the fourth part of 1 acre;
William of Warenne 3, who have 120½ acres; Roger Bigot 1, who
has 15 acres; William of Écouis 1, at 10 acres. 14 free men and 12
villagers have also been taken from this manor, whom Ralph
Baynard holds.

All this has 1 mile in length and ½ in width, at 20s it pays 16d
in tax.

The Hundred of DOCKING

2 Harold held SOUTHMERE before 1066.

Then 3 ploughs in lordship; later and now 2.

Then 21 villagers, later and now 19. Always 2 smallholders;
6 slaves.

1 men's plough. Always 3 cobs; 1 head of cattle; 3 pigs; 87 sheep.

Here appertain 31 Freemen, 16 acres; 1 plough. Also 15
Freemen, 60 acres each; 8 ploughs; 1½ ploughs could be restored.
Also 1 Freeman, 14 acres. Also 1 Freeman, 60 acres; then 1
plough.

Also 1 outlier, TITCHWELL; always 1½ ploughs there.

14 villagers; 6 smallholders; 4 slaves.

Meadow, 16 acres; woodland, 60 pigs. Now 1 mill; always 1
men's plough.

Also 4 Freemen, 2 c. of land; 2 ploughs. Also 2 Freemen, 5 acres.
Also 1 Freeman, 60 acres; 2 oxen. Also 1 Freeman, at ¼ of 1 acre.

In the outlier 260 sheep; 11 pigs; 2 head of cattle; 5 cobs.

Also 1 c. of land which 1 free man held before 1066.

Value of all this then £7; later 20; now 30.

Also 4 Freemen, 4 acres of land, before 1066, which Brown,
Roger Bigot's reeve, took from this manor after the King came
and after Roger acquired the manor; Roger holds them now. Also
1 Freeman, 60 acres; ½ plough.

Aelfric, a free man, held STANHOE under Stigand before 1066, 1 c.
of land. Then 1 plough; later and now 2 oxen.

1 smallholder.

Value 16s. It appertains in Fakenham.

⁋ *WANELVNT . H̄* . Saham ten̄ rex e . iii . car̄ træ 7 xlv . acr̄.

Tn̄c xliii . uill . Poſt . ix . m̄ . iiii . m̄ . xi . bor . ſep . i . ſer . Tn̄c 7 p

i . car̄ in dn̄io . m̄ . ii . Tn̄c xii . car̄ hom . p 7 m̄ . iii . xl ac p̄ti . ſilu

dcc . 7 xxx . por . ſemp . i . mol . tc . iii . r̄ . m̄ . ii . Tn̄c . iii . an̄ . m̄ . viii .

tc xxviii . por . m̄ xx . 7 m̄ lx oū . 7 xl cap̄s . Huic manerio jacebā

t . r . e . xlvi . ſoc cū omi 9ſuetudine . p 7 m̄ xxxi . iii . car̄ træ

xxvii . acr̄ . xl ac p̄ti . Tn̄c 7 p xii car̄ . m̄ . viii . ſilu . c . por .

De iſtis homib; h̄t Rainald fili iuonis . xv . & Berner arbat .

ii . ⌐ & In Griſtuna xviiii . ſoc . i . car̄ træ . t . r . e . tc . iiii . car̄ .

p 7 m̄ . iii . 7 . ii . ac p̄ti . & In Caſteſtuna . iiii . lib̄i hoes Heroldi .

cciiii . ac træ . & ſnt additi huic manerio poſtquā rex aduen̄ .

ſuo p̄|cepto . Tc . iii . car̄ & dim . 7 m̄ ſimilit . vi . ac p̄ti . ⌐ &

in Breccles . viii . lib̄i hoes . heroldi f . ii . car̄ træ . tc . v . car̄ . p 7 m̄

iii . Hii ſnt additi tepr . r . Will . ii . bor . xx ac p̄ti . & in Greſtuna

ii . lib̄i hoes heroldi . vii . acr̄ . Totū ual t . r . e . xii . lib̄ . & red

debat dimidiū die mellis . & conſuetudines mellis . 7 m̄ reddit

xx lib̄ ad penſu . ⌐ Et lib̄i hoes heroldi ual . t . r . e . liii . ſol .

m̄ ſnt in firma de xx . lib̄ . Totū h̄t . i . leug 7 dim in long

110 b

& i . leug in lat̄ . & reddit de gelto de xx . ſol . ii . ſol . 7 vi . d̄ .

⌐ In Breccles xxv ac̄ . ſemp dim car̄ . v . ſoc in Sabam & ppofit

de ſaham uendidit t . r . Willi p uhū frenū . Eudoni honīti

comitis Rad̄ . & jacuer inelinc g̃ham ad firma Rad̄ . & te

nebat eos ea die qua forisfecit . & Rob̄t blund quandiu

habuit mifteriū habebat ex eis x . ſol . 7 viii . d̄ . m̄ iterum

in ſaha & ñ reddn̄t cenſum ad godric . ⌐ & in caſtetuña

. i . ſoch . x . ac træ . dim car̄ . 7 ſimili modo reddebat

. v . ſol . 7 . iiii . den . ⌐ Totum breccles hab & . i . leug

longi . 7 dim lati . 7 . xi . d̄ . de gelđo . In eadem

. i . lib̄ in Saham xxvi . acr̄ . 7 . ii . acr̄ p̄ti . & dim car̄ . & ual

ii . ſol . Rex 7 Comes ſocam .

WAYLAND Hundred

3 King Edward held SAHAM (Toney), 3 c. of land and 45 acres.
Then 43 villagers, later 9, now 4. Now 11 smallholders; always
1 slave.
Then and later 1 plough in lordship, now 2. Then 12 men's
ploughs, later and now 3.
Meadow, 40 acres; woodland, 730 pigs; always 1 mill. Then 3
cobs, now 2. Then 3 head of cattle, now 8. Then 28 pigs,
now 20. Now 60 sheep; 40 goats.
Before 1066, 46 Freemen appertained to this manor with all
customary dues, later and now 31; 3 c. of land and 27 acres;
meadow, 40 acres. Then and later 12 ploughs, now 8.
Woodland, 100 pigs. Reynold son of Ivo has 15 of these men
and Berner the Crossbowman 2.

4 Also in GRISTON before 1066, 19 Freemen, 1 c. of land. Then 4
ploughs, later and now 3. Meadow, 2 acres.
Also in CASTON 4 free men of Harold's. 204 acres of land were
also added to this manor after the King came, by his command.
Then 3½ ploughs, now the same. Meadow, 6 acres.

5 Also in BRECKLES 8 free men, of Harold's jurisdiction, 2 c. of land.
Then 5 ploughs, later and now 3. These added, after 1066, 2
smallholders and 20 acres of meadow. And in GRISTON 2 of
Harold's free men and 7 acres.
Value of the whole before 1066 £12, and it paid ½ a day's
honey, and the customary honey dues; now it pays £20 by
weight.

6 Also Harold's free men's value before 1066, 53s; now they are in
the revenue at £20. The whole has 1½ leagues in length and 1   110 b
league in width, of a 20s tax, it pays 2s 6d.

7 In BRECKLES 25 acres, always ½ plough; 5 Freemen in SAHAM
(Toney); the reeve of Saham sold them for 1 bridle after 1066 to
Eudo, Earl Ralph's man; they appertained in (Little) Ellingham,
in Ralph's revenue; he held them on the day of his forfeiture.
Also Robert Blunt had 10s 8d from them as long as he held
office; now (they are) in Saham (Toney) again; they do not pay
tribute to Godric.

8 Also in CASTON 1 Freeman, 10 acres of land; ½ plough; it paid
5s 4d in the same way.

9 The whole of BRECKLES has 1 league in length and ½ in width; tax
of 11d.
In the same (place) 1 free (man) in SAHAM (Toney), 26 acres;
meadow, 2 acres; ½ plough;
value 2s.
The King and the Earl (had) the jurisdiction.

In brécles . quarta pars unī
acræ . & quedam confuetudo in paſtura hoc jacuit in ſaħa
in tēpore . r . e . 7 m̃ ſimiliꞇ . ſ; Godꞇic eam reuocat ad fe
udum comitis radulſi in Stou . dicens. q̇t̃ ipſe eam tenueriꞇ
duobʒ annis antequa forisfacer& . & duobʒ annis poſtea,
ex hoc offert quida famul regis de Stou portare judi
tiū.

Feorhou . H̄ . & dimidiū . Himcha tenuit Rex .E . H . car
træ . 7 xxv . acr . ſemp . lx . uiłt . tc xviʔi . bor . 7 dim̃ . m̃
xxviiii . ſemp . i . car in dnio . tc xv . car hom . m̃ . xx.
xliii . ſoc . m̃ . xx . de reliquis ħt Wiłt . de War . xiʔ .
& comes alan . iii . & eudo ſiħ clama hoc inde accep.
viii . quos m̃ ħt . Rad de bellafago . Et iłi ex . ħnt

111 a
i . car træ . 7 un ex eis ħt . iii . bor . Semp . ii . car . 7 viii . ac p̃ti.
Totū ual tc ꞏ vii lib 7 dim̃ blancas ccſuetudine . xxx . ſoł.
& iii . ſextarios mełt . m̃ xii . lib ad penſu . 7 xxx ſoł de
gerſuma . 7 . iii . ſextarios mełt cu eade cſuetudine & ħt
dim̃ in longo . & dim̃ in lato . & xiii . đ . 7 . i . oboħ de gelto.
Mittefort . H̄ . 7 dim̃ . Infloctħoʒ . xł . ac . 7 . iii . bor . 7
. i . acr p̃ti . 7 e in p̃tio de hinha . *Infloctħoʒ* xxx . ac træ
i . lib ho . 7 . i . acr & dim̃ p̃ti . tc . dim̃ car . 7 . ii . bor .
In Riſinga . & in Ocſelea . iii . bor . xii . ac træ . & . e . in p̃tio
de haincha.

H̄ . de Galgov . In Fachenha . ten Herold . t . r . e . ii . car
træ . Semp . v . uiłt . 7 . xx . bor . 7 . iiii . ſer . Semp in dnio.
ii . car . 7 homu . iiii . car . Silua ad xii . por . v . ac p̃ti . iii . moł.
dim̃ ſalina . Semp . iii . r̃ . 7 xx . por . 7 cc . oů .

10 In BRECKLES the ¼ of 1 acre, and a customary due in pasture; this
    appertained in SAHAM (Toney) before 1066, now the same; but
    Godric claims it as part of Earl Ralph's Holding in STOW (Bedon),
    stating that he had held it himself for two years before he
    forfeited, and for two years afterwards. A member of the King's
    household at Stow (Bedon) offers to undergo judicial ordeal
    on this.

FOREHOE Hundred and a half
11 King Edward held HINGHAM, 2 c. of land and 25 acres.
        Always 60 villagers. Then 18½ smallholders, now 29.
        Always 1 plough in lordship. Then 15 men's ploughs, now 20.
        43 Freemen, now 20.
        William of Warenne has 12 of the rest, Count Alan 3, and Eudo
    son of Clamahoc received 8 there, whom Ralph of Beaufort has
    now. These 20 have 1 c. of land; one of them has 3 smallholders. 111 a
        Always 2 ploughs; meadow, 8 acres.
    Value of the whole then £7½ blanched, and in customary dues,
    30s and 3 sesters of honey; now £12 by weight, premium 30s and
    3 sesters of honey, with the same customary dues. It has ½
    [?league] in length and ½ in width, tax of 13½d.

MITFORD Hundred and a half
12 In FLOCKTHORPE 40 acres; 3 smallholders; meadow, 1 acre. It is in
    the valuation of Hingham.

13 In FLOCKTHORPE 30 acres of land; 1 free man; meadow, 1½ acres.
    Then ½ plough; 2 smallholders.

14 In (Wood) RISING and in *OCSELEA* 3 smallholders, 12 acres of land.
    It is in the valuation of Hingham.

The Hundred of GALLOW
15 In FAKENHAM Harold held 2 c. of land before 1066.
        Always 5 villagers; 20 smallholders; 4 slaves.
        Always in lordship 2 ploughs; 4 men's ploughs; woodland for
            12 pigs; meadow, 5 acres; 3 mills; ½ salt-house. Always 3
            cobs; 20 pigs; 200 sheep.

ptinent . i . beruita . Alatorp . de . i . car̄ træ . Sep . iii . bor.
7 . i . ſer . 7 in dn̄io . i . car . 7 hou . ii . bou . ii . ac̄ p̄ti ; & alia
beruita . Torpaland . de . i . car̄ træ . 7 . i . car . 7 . i . ſer . Adhuc
i . beruita . de . ii . car̄ træ . in Kreic . Semp . x . uiłł . Tnc̄ xi . bor.
m̄ . iiii . Sep in dn̄io . i . car . Tnc̄ hou . iii . car . m̄ . i . dim . ac̄ .
p̄ti . Sep . i . r̄ . 7 xxx . por . 7 lxxx . ou . & . iiii . ſoc̄ . de vi .
ac̄ . 7 . i . car . 7 At beruita ſtanhou . de . i . car̄ træ . Sep . iiii .
uiłł . Tnc̄ . i . car in dn̄io . m̄ . ii . hou . In eſtanbȳrda . iii .
lib̄i hoēs . 7 In barſha . i . 7 in ſnaringa . iii . lib̄i hoēs . 7
int hos hoēs . iii . ac̄ tre . Semp . i . car . hoc totu̅ uał.

111 b

t . r . e . viii . lib̄ . m̄ . xliii . Fagenham . hab̄ . vii . quar̄ . in long.
& dim in lat̄ . 7 xii . đ . ingelt . 7 ſtabȳrda hab̄ . iii . qr̄ in long
& . ii . in lat̄ . 7 . xii . đ . ingelt . Adhuc . i . beruita . Kateſtuna de
. i . car̄ tre . Semp . iii . bor . 7 . i . car̄ . ii . ac̄ p̄ti . 7 viii . ou . app̄tia
ta eſt ſup̄ius . In nortuna . eccł̄a . viii . ac̄r . 7 vi . đ .

Ħ DE BRODERCROS . In dontuna . i . beruita de . i . car̄ træ . tc̄
vi . bor . m̄ . iiii . Tc̄ . ii . ſer . Sep in dn̄io . i . car . Tnc̄ hou̅m . i . car.
m̄ . dim . iiii . ac̄ p̄ti . i . moł . Sep . i . r̄ . 7 lx . ou . 7 xvi . ſoc̄ . de . i .
car̄ træ . Semp . v . bor . Tnc̄ . viii . car . p . iii . m̄ . i . app̄tiata . ē .
cu̅ facenha . 7 hab̄ . i . liu̅ . in long . & đ in lat̄ . 7 xiii . đ . ingelt .

⌐ In nortuna . i . beruita . jac& ad facenha . dim car̄ træ . Sep
. i . bor . 7 dim car . đ ac̄ p̄ti . Sep . i . r̄ . 7 . i . por . 7 vii . ſoc̄ . de
xx . ac̄r . 7 . i . car . 7 hab̄ . iii . qr̄ in long . 7 . ii . 7 đ . in lat̄ . 7
vi . đ . 7 obolu̅ in gelt .

16 To this manor belong
1 outlier, ALETHORPE, at 1 c. of land.
   Always 3 smallholders; 1 slave.
   In lordship 1 plough; the men, 2 oxen; meadow, 2 acres.
Also another outlier, THORPLAND, at 1 c. of land. 1 plough;
   1 slave.
Further, 1 outlier at 2 c. of land in CREAKE.
   Always 10 villagers. Then 11 smallholders, now 4.
   Always 1 plough in lordship. Then 3 men's ploughs.
     Now meadow, 1½ acres. Always 1 cob; 30 pigs; 80 sheep.
Also 4 Freemen at 6 acres; 1 plough.
Another outlier, STANHOE, at 1 c. of land.
   Always 3 villagers.
   Then 1 plough in lordship, now 2 men's [ploughs].
In STIBBARD 3 free men.
Also in BARSHAM 1 [?free man] and in (Little) SNORING 3 free
men; among these men 3 acres of land. Always 1 plough.
Value of all this before 1066 £8; now 43. Fakenham has 7   **111 b**
furlongs in length and ½ in width, 12d in tax. Stibbard has 3
furlongs in length and 2 in width, 12d in tax.
Further, 1 outlier, CASTON, at 1 c. of land.
   Always 3 smallholders;
   1 plough; meadow, 2 acres; 8 sheep.
It has been assessed above.
In (Pudding) NORTON a church, 8 acres;
[value] 6d.

   The Hundred of BROTHERCROSS
17 In DUNTON 1 outlier, at 1 c. of land.
   Then 6 smallholders, now 4. Then 2 slaves.
   Always 1 plough in lordship. Then 1 men's plough, now ½.
     Meadow, 4 acres; 1 mill. Always 1 cob; 60 sheep.
Also 16 Freemen at 1 c. of land;
   always 5 smallholders.
   Then 8 ploughs, later 3, now 1.
It is assessed with Fakenham. It has 1 league in length and ½ in
width, and 13d in tax.

18 In (Pudding) NORTON 1 outlier appertains to Fakenham, ½ c.
of land.
   Always 1 smallholder.
   ½ plough; meadow, ½ acre. Always 1 cob; 1 pig.
Also 7 Freemen, at 20 acres; 1 plough.
It has 3 furlongs in length, 2½ in width, 6½d in tax.

H̄.de holt. Holt ten̄. rex. E. II. car trǣ. Sep̄ xx. IIII. uil̄.
& xxIIII. bor. 7. II. ſer. ſemp idnio. I. car. poſſ& reſtaurari.
Sep̄ hou. xI. car. Silua. ad lx. por. vi. ac̄ p̄ti. v. mol. Sep̄
I. r̄. 7. I. mercatu. 7. ꝉ. porc. 7 xx. por. m̄ lxxxx. ou. Eſt
&iam. I. beruita. Claia. de. II. car trǣ. Semp. xxIIII. uil̄.
& xxI. bor. Tnc̄. II. ſer. m̄. IIII. Sep̄ in dn̄io. I. car. & aꝉ
poſſ& reſtaurari. 7 hou. xII. car. I. ac̄ p̄ti. Sep̄. vII. por.
m̄. c. xl. ou. Adhuc. I. beruita. in eſnuterle. de. I. car trǣ.
Sep̄ vII. uil̄. 7. I. bor. Sep̄ hou. I. car. Tc̄ ual ual. xx
lib̄. 7. I. noc̄te mellis. 7 c. ſol de c̄ſuetudine. m̄. l. libras.

112 a

ad numeru. 7 holt 7 claia hab̄. II. luig in long. 7. I. ilat. &. II. ſol. IIII
ingelt. huic manerio p̄tinebant. t. r. e. vIII. libi hoes de. III. car
trǣ & dim. m̄ ten& Walter Gifard. p̄ libatione regis. ſic̄ hoes ſui
dicn̄t. 7 Adhuc p̄tinebat huic man̄. I. lib̄ ho. xxIII. ac̄. m̄ hugo
comes ten& eos. / Huic man̄ jacet. I. beruita in henepſteda. de
xxx. ac̄. Semp. v. bord. 7. I. car. & houm. d̄. car. Silua ad
vi. por. Sep̄ vIII. por. Tnc̄. v. ſol. 7 IIII. d̄. m̄ xxxIII. ſol. 7. IIII. d̄.
& hab& . I. leug. i lon. 7. I. inlat. 7 vII. d̄ ingelt.
/ In bathele. I. lib̄ ho. de. II. car trǣ. Sep̄ x. bor. Tnc̄. II. ſer. m̄. null.
Tnc̄. II. car in dn̄io. m̄. I. Semp houm. I. car. Silua ad xxx. por.
IIII. ac̄ p̄ti. 7 II. ſoc̄. de xx ac̄ tre. 7 dim. car. I. acr p̄ti. Sep̄ ual
xx. ſol. 7 hab̄. I. leu in long. & d̄ in lat. 7 vi. d̄ 7 obolu in gelt.
/ In burſtuna. v. ſoc̄ p̄tinent ad holt. de xx ac̄ trǣ. 7. I. car.
Silua ad x. por. 7 ual xII. ſol. 7 hab̄. I. leug in long. 7 dim in
lat. 7 xIII. d̄ in gelt. qui cunq; ibi teneat.

The Hundred of HOLT

19 King Edward held HOLT, 2 c. of land.
   Always 24 villagers; 24 smallholders; 2 slaves.
   Always 1 plough in lordship; [?another] could be restored.
   Always 11 men's ploughs.
   Woodland for 60 pigs; meadow, 6 acres; 5 mills. Always 1 cob;
      1 market; 1 pig. Now 20 pigs; 90 sheep.
There is also 1 outlier, CLEY (next the Sea), at 2 c. of land.
   Always 24 villagers; 21 smallholders. Then 2 slaves, now 4.
   Always 1 plough in lordship; another could be restored;
      12 men's ploughs.
   Meadow, 1 acre. Always 7 pigs. Now 140 sheep.
Further 1 outlier, in BLAKENEY, at 1 c. of land.
   Always 7 villagers; 1 smallholder.
   Always 1 men's plough.
Value then £20, 1 night's honey and 100s in customary dues;
now £50 at face value. Holt and Cley have 2 leagues in length   112 a
and 1 in width, 2s 4[d] in tax.
   Before 1066, 8 free men belonged to this manor, at 3½ c. of
land; now Walter Gifford holds them by livery of the King, so
his men state. Further, there belonged to this manor 1 free man,
23 acres; now Earl Hugh holds them.

20 1 outlier in HEMPSTEAD appertains to this manor, at 30 acres.
   Always 5 smallholders.
   1 plough; ½ men's plough.
   Woodland for 6 pigs; always 8 pigs.
[Value] then 5s 4d; now 33s 4d. It has 1 league in length and 1
in width, 7d in tax.

21 In BALE 1 free man, at 2 c. of land.
   Always 10 smallholders. Then 2 slaves, now none.
   Then 2 ploughs in lordship, now 1; always 1 men's plough.
   Woodland for 30 pigs; meadow, 4 acres.
   Also 2 Freemen, at 20 acres of land; ½ plough; meadow, 1 acre.
Value always 20s. It has 1 league in length and ½ in width,
6½d in tax.

22 In BRISTON 5 Freemen belong to Holt, at 20 acres of land.
   1 plough. Woodland for 10 pigs.
Value 12s. It has 1 league in length and ½ in width, 13d in tax,
whoever holds there.

⌐In huneworda . iii . ſoc de . xvi . aē . 7 . i . aē p̃ti . 7 . i . caŕ . i . moł.
Tnc̄ uał xl . đ . m̄ . xi . ſoł . 7 hab̃ . i . leu . 7 . ii . quaŕ . in lon . 7 dim̄
in lat̃ . 7 xii . đ . in gelt . quicuq̃ ibi teneat.

⌐In ſtodeia . i . ſoc̃ . de . ii . aē . 7 đ . 7 redd . ii . oras . ⌐ In baiafelda
ix . ſoc̃ . de xx . aē . & hab̃ . tre . ii . caŕ ⁓ 7 m̄ . 7 quarta
pars de . i . moł . 7 uał . x . ſoł . 7 viii . đ . 7 hab̃ . i.
leug in long̃ . & đ in lat̃ . 7 viii . đ . ingelt.

⌐In glaforda . iii . ſoc̃ . de xx . aē . 7 . i . ca̋.
7 . i . aē p̃ti . 7 uał . iiii . ſoł . 7 hab̃

112 b

viii . quaŕ in long̃ . 7 . iii . in lat̃ . & vi . đ . & obolu ingelt̃.

⌐In neutuna . iii . ſoc̃ 7 đ de xii . aē træ . 7 uał . xvi . đ.

⌐In guneſtorp . đ caŕ træ quā ten̄ Aluuin̄ . t . r . e . iiii . bor . Silua
ad . iiii . por . i . aē p̃ti . Sep . i . caŕ . & đ . Tnc̄ uał . xx . ſoł . m̄ . xl.
Huic man additu ⁓ hoc de tra . Almeri epi . 7 hab̃ . i . leug i lon̄.
7 . iiii . q̃r . i lat̃ . & vi . đ . 7 obolu in gelt . Totũ holt redđ.
lxvi . lib̃ . ad numerũ . ⌐ In ſcarnetuna jac& . i . beruit 7 ptin&
ad facenha . de . i . caŕ træ . 7 ix . bor . Sep in dn̄io . i . caŕ Tnc̄
hoũm . i . caŕ . Tnc̄ . xxx ou . m̄ . lx . 7 iii . ſoc̃ . de . vi . aē . 7 hab̃
in long̃ . vii . quaŕ 7 vi . in lat̃ . 7 x . đ . ing̃ . Ad holt . eſt additũ
. i . lib̃ ho Ketel p̃ morte regis . e . inmerſtona Guert . de xxx
. aē . 7 . i . bor . 7 dim̄ caŕ . 7 uał . ii . oras.

H̃ . de holt . gunetorp . i . caŕ træ ptin& in cauſtune . tc̃ . xi.
bor . m̄ . vi . ſep . i . caŕ in dn̄io . ſep . i . caŕ hou . filua . iiii . por.
ii . aē . p̃ti . ii . por . xxiiii . ou . hoc totũ ptin& incaſtune.

⌐In Scartune . viii . ſoc̃ . 7 vi . bor . qđ ptin& in holt . 7 hi arant
. ii . caŕ . tc̃ . uał . xx . ſoł . t . r . e . m̄ xl.

23 In HUNWORTH 3 Freemen, at 16 acres.
　　Meadow, 1 acre; 1 plough; 1 mill.
Value then 40d; now 11s. It has 1 league and 2 furlongs in length
and ½ [league] in width, 12d in tax, whoever holds there.

24 In STODY 1 Freeman, at 2½ acres. It pays 2 orae.

25 In BAYFIELD 9 Freemen, at 20 acres; they had, and have now, 2 c.
of land.
　　¼ of 1 mill.
Value 10s 8d. It has 1 league in length and ½ in width, 8d in tax.

26 In GLANDFORD 3 Freemen, at 20 acres.
　　1 plough; meadow, 1 acre.
Value 4s. It has 8 furlongs in length and 3 in width, 6½d in tax. 　　112 b

27 In *NEUTUNA* 3 Freemen and a half, at 12 acres of land.
Value 16d.

28 In GUNTHORPE ½ c. of land which A(i)lwin held before 1066.
　　4 smallholders.
　　Woodland for 4 pigs; meadow, 1 acre.
　　Always 1½ ploughs.
Value then 20s; now 40.
　　This has been added to this manor from the land of Bishop
A(e)lmer. It has 1 league in length and 4 furlongs in width, 6½d
in tax.
The whole of Holt pays £66 at face value.

29 One outlier appertains in SHARRINGTON. It belongs to Fakenham,
at 1 c. of land.
　　9 smallholders.
　　Always 1 plough in lordship. Then 1 men's plough.
　　Then 30 sheep, now 60.
　　Also 3 Freemen, at 6 acres.
It has 7 furlongs in length and 6 in width, 10d in tax.
　　1 free man, Ketel, has been added to Holt after the death of
King Edward (belonging) in MORSTON, (the manor of) Gyrth,
at 30 acres.
　　1 smallholder. ½ plough.
Value 2 orae.

　The Hundred of HOLT
30 GUNTHORPE. 1 c. of land belongs in Cawston.
　　Then 11 smallholders, now 6.
　　Always 1 plough in lordship; always 1 men's plough.
　　Woodland, 4 pigs; meadow, 2 acres; 2 pigs; 24 sheep.
　　All this belongs in Cawston.

31 In SHARRINGTON, which belongs in Holt,
　　8 Freemen and 6 smallholders. These men plough 2 c.
Value then 20s before 1066; now 40.

⌐*GRENEHOV*. H̄. Wiſtune ten̛. rex . e . xii . car̛ træ . xxvi.
uiłł . tc̛ 7 m̄ . tc̛ xxiiii . bor . m̄ . xvii . tc̛ 7 m̄ . i . car̛ in dn̄io . tc̛
hou . x . car̛ . 7 p̄ 7 m̄ . vii . xx . por . ſilua . viii . ac̛ p̄ti . i . moł
ſemp . i . r̛ . m̄ . xx . por . qn̄ recep̄ null̛ . m̄ . cl.
xxx . ou̅ . tc̛ xviiii . ſoc . ſemp . xlv . ac̛ træ.
ſemp . iiii . car̛ . 7 . i . moł . iii . bor.

113 a

tc̛ . vał . x . lib̄ . 7 vi . ſext̄ mellis . 7 đ . 7 xl . i . ſoł . de conſuetudine
m̄ . xxiii . lib̄ ad penſu . 7 ht̛ . i . leug . in long̛ . 7 . i . in lat̛ . 7 vii.
đ de gelt redđ.

⌐Hohttune . i . beruita jac& huic man̛ . iiii . car̛ træ . ſemp
v . uiłł . 7 v . bor . ſep . i . car̛ in dn̄io . tc̛ . iii . car̛ hom̛ . p̄ 7 m̄ . ii.
paſtura mille ouiu̅ . iii . ac̛ p̄ti . ii . moł . & ht̛ dim̄ leu̅ in long̛.
& dim̄ in lat̛ . 7 redđ . iiii . đ . degelt . ⌐Holcha . beruita
jac& huic man̛ . iii . car̛ træ . ſ; eſt uaſtata . 7 . iii . car̛ poſſent
ibi . ee̅ . ⌐Huerueles . alia beruita . que jac& huic man̛ . đ car̛
træ . ſet nichil . e . ibi . ſ; . i . car̛ . poſſ& ibi ee̅ . & hab& . iiii . q̄r̄.
in long̛ . 7 . iiii . in lat̛ . 7 vi . đ . de gelto.

⌐Et Egemere ał beruita . de dim̄ car̛ træ . & nichil . e . ibi aliud.
ſ; i . car̛ . poſſ& . ee̅ . 7 ht̛ dim̄ leug̛ long̛ . & dim̄ latit̛ . 7 vi . đ.
de gelto . ⌐Inguelle . 7 in guarha . i . car̛ træ . ſ; i . car̛ poſſ& . ee̅.

⌐Et inſtinekai . dim̄ car̛ træ . ⌐& in hindringaha . dim̄ car̛
træ . ſ; i . car̛ poſſ& . ee̅ . ⌐Galſingaha . ten̛ herald . t . r . e . iii
car̛ tre . beruita i faganha . tc̛ 7 p̄ xiii . uiłł . 7 m̄ . vi . tc̛ 7 p̄.
vii . bor . m̄ v . ſemp . i . car̛ in dn̄io . ſep . ii . car̛ hom̛ . ſilua.
x . por . i . ac̛ p̄ti . 7 dim̄ . ii . moł . ſep . ii . r̛ . ſep . v . an̄ . tc̛ xii.
porc̛ . m̄ xiiii . tc̛ . xxiiii . ou̅ . m̄ xl . 7 viiii . ſocemans . de . i.
car̛ træ . jacent huic man̛ . ii . bor . dim̄ ac̛ p̄ti . & dim̄ moł.
tc̛ . iii . car̛ . 7 p̄ 7 m̄ . ii . hoc totu̅ ÷ ap̄pciatu̅ in facenham.

(North) GREENHOE Hundred

32 King Edward held WIGHTON, 12 c. of land.
> Then and now 26 villagers. Then 24 smallholders, now 17.
> Then and now 1 plough in lordship. Then 10 men's ploughs,
> later and now 7.
> 20 pigs' woodland; meadow, 8 acres; 1 mill. Always 1 cob.
> Now 20 pigs, when acquired none. Now 180 sheep.
> Then 19 Freemen; always 45 acres of land; always 4 ploughs;
> 1 mill; 3 smallholders.

Value then £10, 6½ sesters of honey, 41s of customary dues;   113 a
now £23 by weight. It has 1 league in length and 1 in width, it
pays tax of 7d.

33 HOUGHTON (St. Giles), 1 outlier, appertains to this manor, 4 c.
of land.
> Always 5 villagers; 5 smallholders.
> Always 1 plough in lordship. Then 3 men's ploughs, later and
> now 2.
> Pasture, 1,000 sheep; meadow, 3 acres; 2 mills.
It has ½ league in length and ½ in width, it pays tax of 4d.

34 HOLKHAM, an outlier, appertains to this manor, 3 c. of land, but
it is waste. 3 ploughs could be there.

35 QUARLES, another outlier which appertains to this manor, ½ c. of
land, but nothing is there, but 1 plough could be there.
It has 4 furlongs in length and 4 in width, tax of 6d.

36 Also EGMERE, another outlier, at ½ c. of land. Nothing else is there
but 1 plough could be.
It has ½ league in length and ½ in width, tax of 6d.

37 In WELLS (next the Sea) and in WARHAM, 1 c. of land but there
could be 1 plough.

38 Also in STIFFKEY ½ c. of land.

39 Also in HINDRINGHAM ½ c. of land but there could be 1 plough.

40 Harold held WALSINGHAM before 1066, 3 c. of land, an outlier in
(the lands of) Fakenham.
> Then and later 13 villagers, now 6. Then and later 7
> smallholders, now 5.
> Always 1 plough in lordship; always 2 men's ploughs.
> Woodland, 10 pigs; meadow, 1½ acres; 2 mills. Always 2 cobs;
> always 5 head of cattle. Then 12 pigs, now 14. Then 24
> sheep, now 40.
> Also 9 Freemen, at 1 c. of land.
To this manor appertain 2 smallholders. Meadow, ½ acre; ½ mill.
> Then 3 ploughs; later and now 2.
All this is assessed in Fakenham.

⌐In Holcha.ɪ.car̄ tre.quã tenuit Æluin.ɪ.lib̄ ho.t.r.e.

& ptin& ad guiſtune.ɪɪɪ.bor.7 vɪɪ ſok.tc 7 ſemp.ɪɪ.car̄.int om̄s
7 illu q̄ hab̄t̄ tram./ In dallinga.ten̄ Vnſpac.ɪ.car̄ træ.t.r.e.
7.e.beruita in holt.xɪ.bor.ſemp.ɪɪ.ſer.vɪ.ac̄ p̄ti.ſep.ɪ.car̄ in
dn̄io.7 ſep.ɪɪ.car̄ hou.vɪɪɪ.ſoc.de xxɪɪɪɪ.ac̄ træ.ɪɪɪɪ.acr̄
p̄ti.ſep.ɪ.car̄.tc 7 p.ɪ.eq̄.ſemp.ɪɪɪ.animalia.7 vɪɪɪ.pors.
xx.ou.tc ual.x.ſol.m̄.ɪɪɪɪ.lib̄.& h̄t dim leug in longo.
& dim in laṭit.7 de gelt.ɪɪ.ſol.Et in guarha.dim car̄
træ.ɪ.ac̄ p̄ti.7 ual.ɪɪ.ſol.7 dim.hoc totu ptin& in Holt.
Soca & ſacha de grenehou hund̄ ptin& ad Wiſtune man̄
reḡ.quicuq̄ ibi teneat 7 h̄t rex & comes.

H̄.DE WALESHA.In Mothetuna.ɪɪɪ.lib̄i ho᷄es xxxvɪɪ.ac̄
træ.7.ɪɪɪɪ.ac̄ 7 dim p̄ti.7 dim̄ car̄.7 Val.ɪɪ.ſol.7 vɪɪɪ.d.
In baſtwic.ɪ.lib̄ ho.xxx.ac̄ træ.7.ɪɪ.ac̄ p̄ti.7 dim car̄.7 ual
xvɪ.d.& Waleſa.H̄.redd̄ xl.ſol.regi.7 xx.ſol comiti.

FLETWEST.H̄./ In marcha.ɪɪ.lib̄i ho᷄es.ɪ.gert.alt heroldi
comdat.de lx.ac̄ tre.7 vɪ.ac̄ p̄ti.tc.ɪ.car̄.p 7 m̄ dim.
Tnc 7 p.ɪɪɪɪ.ſol.m̄.vɪ.ſol.7 vɪɪɪ.d.7 ſn̄t incenſu ormeſbei.
⌐In clepeſbei.ɪ.lib̄ ho᷄ gerti com̄d.t.r.e.de xx.ac̄ træ.7.ɪɪɪɪ.
ac̄ p̄ti.& ɪɪɪ.lib̄i ho᷄es ſub eo.xvɪɪ.ac̄ træ.7.ɪɪɪ.ac̄ p̄ti.Sep̄
.ɪ.car̄.Semp ual.ɪɪ.ſol.7 vɪ.d.in cenſu ormeſbei.
⌐In clepeſbei.ɪ.lib̄ ho᷄ reḡ.de xx.ac̄ træ.Sep dim car̄.7 ɪɪɪ.
ac̄ p̄ti.Semp ual.ɪɪ.ſol.

41 In HOLKHAM 1 c. of land which A(i)lwin, a free man, held before
1066. It belongs to Wighton.   113 b
   3 smallholders; 7 Freemen.
   Then and always 2 ploughs between all and him who has
the land.

42 In (Field) DALLING Ospak held 1 c. of land before 1066. It is an
outlier in (the lands of) Holt.
   11 smallholders; always 2 slaves.
   Meadow, 6 acres. Always 1 plough in lordship; always 2 men's
     ploughs.
   8 Freemen, at 24 acres of land; meadow, 4 acres; always 1
     plough. Then and later 1 horse. Always 3 head of cattle;
     8 pigs; 20 sheep.
Value then 10s; now £4. It has ½ league in length and ½ in width,
tax of 2s.
Also in Warham ½ c. of land; meadow, 1 acre.
Value 2½s. All this belongs in Holt.
The full jurisdiction of (North) Greenhoe Hundred belongs to
Wighton, the King's manor, whoever holds there and the King
and the Earl have it.

The Hundred of WALSHAM
43 In MOULTON (St. Mary) 3 free men, 37 acres of land.
   Meadow, 4½ acres. ½ plough.
Value 2s 8d.

44 In (Wood)BASTWICK 1 free man, 30 acres of land.
   Meadow, 2 acres. ½ plough.
Value 16d. Also Walsham Hundred pays 40s to the King and 20s
to the Earl.

WEST FLEGG Hundred
45 In MARTHAM 2 free men, 1 (under the patronage of) Gyrth, the
other under the patronage of Harold, at 60 acres of land; 6 acres
of meadow.
   Then 1 plough, later and now ½.
[Value] then and later 4s; now 6s 8d. They are in the tribute of
Ormesby.

46 In CLIPPESBY 1 free man under the patronage of Gyrth before
1066, at 20 acres of land; meadow, 4 acres. Also 3 free men
under him, 17 acres of land; meadow, 3 acres.
   Always 1 plough.
Value always 2s 6d. In the tribute of Ormesby.

47 In CLIPPESBY 1 free man of the King's, at 20 acres of land.
   Always ½ plough; meadow, 3 acres.
Value always 2s.

⌐ In Wintretuna . ɪ . lib̄ hŏ . de vɪɪ .
ac̓ træ . 7 v . bor . Semꝑ dim̄ car̓ . Semꝑ uaɫ . vɪɪɪ . đ . Et . e̓ .

114 a

in ꝑtio orbeſlci .

⌐ *HEINE*ſtede . *H̄* . In framingahā 7 intreuſſa tenent duo
burgenſes norwici . xɪɪ . ac̓ træ̓ . Sep̓ uaɫ . ɪɪ . ſoɫ .
H̄NDREṬ . dim̄ . *H̄ . DE DICE* . ⌐ Watlingeſeta . ten̓
R . E . ꝑ m̓ . v . car̓ træ . Tnc̄ xx uiɫɫ . poſtea & m̊ . xxɪɪɪɪ .
Sep̓ xxv . borđ . Semp xɪx car̓ hou̓ . Tnc̄ ſilua xx . por .
m̊ nichil . 7 ɪx . ac̓ p̄ti . & . ɪ . lib̄ hŏ de xx . ac̓ træ̓ . 7 . ɪ . borđ
ſub eo . Semp . ɪ . car̓ . 7 ɪɪɪ . ac̓ p̄ti . ⌐ In borſtuna . vɪ . ſoc̓ .
de . xʟ . ac̓ træ̓ . 7 ſep̓ . ɪ . bor . Tnc̄ . ɪ . car̓ . 7 dim̄ . p̄ 7 m̊ . ɪ .
& . ɪɪ . ac̓ p̄ti . ht̄ . ɪ . leug in long̓ . & dim in lat̓ . & de gelto .
vɪɪ . đ . Hoc append& addice in ſutfulc & ibi ap̄p̄tiat̓ .
Tota ſoca 7 ſaca iſtius dim̄ hund̄ . p̄t tram̄ ſc̄i Edmundi .
& de illa ſc̄s dim̄ . 7 rex alia medietate̓ p̄t tram̄ ulfiet .
& p̄t tram̄ ſtigandi . 7 de om̄ib₂ alijs ſoca fuit in hund̄ .
T . R . E .

H̄ . DE ENŜFORD . Folſha̓ . tenuit . E . Rex . xɪɪ . car̓
træ̓ . 7 . ɪɪɪ . ac̓ . tc̄ . xxx . uiɫɫ . p̄ . 7 m̊ . xxx . ɪɪɪ . tc̄ 7 p̄ ea⸵
xxxvɪɪɪ . borđ . m̊ xʟ . ɪɪɪɪ . 7 xʟ ac̓ p̄ti . tc̄ 7 p̄ . ɪɪ . carr̓ .
in dn̄io . m̊ . ɪɪɪ . tc̄ 7 p̄ xvɪɪɪ . car̓ hom̓ . m̊ . xx . ſilua . ad
cccc . pors . tc̄ 7 p̄ . ɪ . moɫ . m̊ . ɪɪ . . ɪ . eccɫa . xvɪ . ac̓r . Qn̄do
recep̄ . ɪ . r . m̊ . ɪɪ . tc̄ . ɪɪɪ . an̓ . m̊ xɪɪ . tc̄ xʟvɪɪ . pors . m̊ . ʟ .
7 m̊ . ʟx . ou̓ . ſemp . ʟ . cap̓ . tp̄r r . e . xxx . ſoc̓ . m̊ . xx . ɪɪɪɪ .
ɪ . ac̓ træ̓ . 7 x . ac̓ . ſemp . v . car̓ . 7 v . ac̓ 7 dim p̄ti . Et vɪ .
de his ten& m̊ Walter̓ gifard . Tnc̄ uaɫ xɪɪɪ . lib̄ . ad

114 b

numeru̓ . 7 xɪɪɪ . ſextarios mellis cum conſuetudine . & xxɪɪɪ .
lib̄ ad penſu̓ . m̊ . 7 xɪ . lib̄ . 7 x ſoɫ . blancas ꝑ melle . 7 ht̄ . ɪ . leu̓
in long̓ . 7 . ɪ . in lato . 7 redđ . vɪɪɪ . đ . 7 Obolu̓ in gelto regis .

48 In WINTERTON 1 free man, at 7 acres of land.
5 smallholders. Always ½ plough.
Value always 8d. It is in the valuation of Ormesby.

HENSTEAD Hundred
49 In FRAMINGHAM and in TROWSE 2 Norfolk burgesses hold 12 acres of land.
Value always 2s.

The Hundred of the Half-Hundred of DISS
50 King Edward held *WATLINGESETA* as a manor, 5 c. of land.
Then 20 villagers, later and now 24; always 25 smallholders.
Always 19 men's ploughs.
Then woodland, 20 pigs, now nothing. Meadow, 9 acres.
Also 1 free man, at 20 acres of land, and 1 smallholder
under him. Always 1 plough. Meadow, 3 acres.

51 In BURSTON 6 Freemen, at 40 acres of land.
Always 1 smallholder.
Then 1½ ploughs, later and now 1.
Meadow, 2 acres.
It has 1 league in length and ½ in width, tax of 7d.
This appertains to Diss in Suffolk and is assessed there (as is)
the whole of the jurisdiction of this Half-Hundred, except St.
Edmund's land, and of that the Saint (has) half and the King the
other half, (and) except Wulfgeat's land and except Stigand's
land; and of all other (lands) the jurisdiction was in the Hundred
before 1066.

The Hundred of EYNSFORD
52 King Edward held FOULSHAM, 12 c. of land and 3 acres.
Then 30 villagers, later and now 33. Then and later 38
smallholders, now 44.
Meadow, 40 acres. Then and later 2 ploughs in lordship,
now 3. Then and later 18 men's ploughs, now 20.
Woodland for 400 pigs. Then and later 1 mill, now 2. 1 church,
16 acres. When (King William) acquired (it) 1 cob, now 2.
Then 3 head of cattle, now 12. Then 47 pigs, now 50.
Now 60 sheep; always 50 goats.
Before 1066 30 Freemen, now 24; 1 acre of land and 10
acres; always 5 ploughs; meadow, 5½ acres. Walter Gifford
now holds 6 of these.
Value then £13 at face value and 13 sesters of honey with

customary dues; and £23 by weight now and £11 10s blanched
for the honey. It has 1 league in length and 1 in width; it pays
8½d in the King's tax.

ı . eccła . xxıı . acr̃ . Huic manerio adjunċti ſnt . ıı . libi
hões p radulfu̅ taliboſc . t . r . W . hoc teſtat̃ hundred
. xıııı . aċ træ . ſep dim̃ car̃ . 7 . ı . aċ p̃ti . ſep val̃ . ıııı . ſol.

⌐In Witewella . ı . beruita que jac& in cauſtona . ten̄
herald . t . r . e . ı . car̃ træ . tc̄ . x . bor . m̅ . vıı . ſemp . ı . car̃
in dn̄io . tc̄ . ı . car̃ hou̅ . m̅ null̃ . ſilua . xx . por . 7 v . aċ.
p̃ti . Et e̅ in p̃tio de caſtona.

⌐In Branteſtuna . ıııı . libi hões . L . ıı . aċ træ . 7 ı . car̃ & dim̃.
7 vıı . aċ p̃ti . Silua . vı . por . 7 ſnt in p̃tio de cauſtona.

H̅ . de *Taverham* . Intauerha̅ . ten̄ herold . t . r . e.
ı . car̃ træ & . ıı . aċ . 7 dim̃ . beruita . in Caueſtuna . ſep
ıı . uilł . 7 . ıııı . bor . ſemp . ı . car̃ in dn̄io . 7 dim̃ car̃ hom̃.
x . aċ . p̃ti . Silua . x . por . ſemp . ı . moł . 7 dim̃ . ſemp . ıı . r̃.
hoc . e̅ . in p̃tio de caueſtuna . Huic manerio jacebant.
t . r . e . xııı . ſoc̄ . ıı . car̃ træ . 7 xx . ı . aċ . hos ten̄& Galter
gifart . ⌐In felethorp . ıııı . libi hões . c . aċ træ . ſemp vıı.
bor . 7 . ıı . car̃ . 7 v . aċ p̃ti . Silua . ıııı . por . 7 ual̃ . x . ſoł.
Rex 7 Comes ſoca̅.

1 church, 22 acres.
After 1066 2 free men were attached to this manor by Ralph Tallboys so the Hundred testify; 14 acres of land.
　　Always ½ plough; meadow, 1 acre.
Value always 4s.

53　In WHITWELL Harold held 1 outlier before 1066 which appertains in Cawston, 1 c. of land.
　　Then 10 smallholders, now 7.
　　Always 1 plough in lordship. Then 1 men's plough, now none.
　　Woodland, 20 pigs; meadow, 5 acres.
It is in the valuation of Cawston.

54　In BRANDISTON 4 free men, 52 acres of land. 1½ ploughs.
　　Meadow, 7 acres; woodland, 6 pigs.
They are in the valuation of Cawston.

The Hundred of TAVERHAM
55　In TAVERHAM, Harold held before 1066 1 c. of land and 2½ acres, an outlier in (the lands of) Cawston.
　　Always 2 villagers; 4 smallholders.
　　Always 1 plough in lordship; ½ men's plough.
　　Meadow, 10 acres; woodland, 10 pigs; always 1½ mills.
　　　Always 2 cobs.
This is in the valuation of Cawston. Before 1066 13 Freemen appertained to this manor, 2 c. of land and 21 acres; these Walter Gifford holds.

56　In FELTHORPE 4 free men, 100 acres of land.
　　Always 7 smallholders.
　　2 ploughs;
　　meadow, 5 acres; woodland, 4 pigs.
Value 10s. The King and the Earl (have) the jurisdiction.

ERPINCHAM SVD . H̄ . Cauſtituna ten̄ . herold.
t.r.e.xɪ.car̄ træ . 7 xxxx . ac̄ . Tn̄c 7 p̄ . xxxvɪ . uiłł.
m̄ . xxx.v . Tn̄c 7 p̄ xxvɪ . bor . m̄ . xxx.ɪɪɪɪ . tc̄ 7 p̄ . vɪ . ſer.

115 a

modo . ɪɪɪɪ . Tn̄c 7 p̄ . ɪɪɪɪ . car̄ in d̄nio . m̄ . ɪɪɪ . & d̄ue poſſnt reſ
taurari . Tn̄c 7 p̄ xxvɪ . car̄ . hom̄ . m̄ xvɪ . & alie poſſent
reſtaurari . xx . ac̄ p̄ti . Tn̄c ſilua . M̄.D.por . m̄ . M̄ . ſemp . ɪɪ .
mol . Tn̄c . ɪɪɪɪ . r̄ . m̄ . ſimilit̄ . Tn̄c xx . an̄ . 7 m̄ . ſemp xL . por.
7 Lx . oū . 7 L . cap̄ . 7 v . uaſa apū . & . x . ſoc̄ . t . r . e . ex hoc h̄r
Rainald̄ filius Iuonis . ɪɪ . & . W . epc̄ . ɪɪ . & comes alanus . ɪ .
& Godric̄ . ɪɪ . ad feudū regis quē tenebat comes Rad̄ con
forisfecit . & W . de War̄ . ɪɪ . & Roḡ bigot . ɪ . & adhuc
tenebat in Cauſtuna herold̄ . t . r . e . Marſam & Blikelinga.
& xx . ɪɪɪ . ſoc̄ . & hec duo maneria ten̄& Wiłł epc̄ . & erfaſt
tenuit . & Galt̄ Gifart ten̄& xxvɪ . ſoc̄ . q̄s tenuit bodin
anteceſſor ſuus . Tenebat &iam herold̄ . v . ſoc̄ . huic ma
nerio . quos tenuit Rad̄ comes . m̄ Godric̄ ad feudū regis.
Tn̄c uał . xxx lib̄ . m̄ xL . ad numerū . & h̄r . ɪɪ . leug in lonḡ.
7 . ɪɪ . in lat̄ . qui cūq̄ ibi teneat . & vɪɪ . d̄ de gelto . huic
&iam manerio ſep jacebat . ɪ . beruita . Oulſtuna . ɪ . car̄
træ . ſemp ɪx . bord̄ . ſemp . ɪ . car̄ in d̄nio . 7 . ɪ . car̄ hom̄ . 7
ɪɪɪ . ac̄ p̄ti . ſilua . Lx . pors . m̄ . ɪ . r̄ . 7 vɪɪɪ . por . 7 . ɪɪɪɪ . ſoc̄.
7 dim̄ . & medietatē huj dimidij tenebat . R . q̄n foris
fec̄ . c.x. ac̄ . 7 uał xv . d̄ . ɪ . car̄ træ . 7 xL ac̄ . ſemp . ɪ . uiłł.
& ɪɪ . car̄ . 7 . ɪ . ac̄ p̄ti . & eſt in p̄tio de cauſtuna . Vn̄u ex
illis . ɪɪɪɪ . ſoc̄ uendidit p̄poſit de Gauſtuna . x . ſoł . 7 Ra
dulf̄ eū tenebat q̄n foris fec̄ . 7 hab̄ xɪɪɪ . ac̄ . 7 uał xvɪ . d̄.

SOUTH ERPINGHAM Hundred

57 Harold held CAWSTON before 1066, 11 c. of land and 40 acres.
Then and later 36 villagers, now 35. Then and later 26
smallholders, now 34. Then and later 6 slaves, now 4.
Then and later 4 ploughs in lordship, now 3, and 2 could be
restored. Then and later 26 men's ploughs, now 16, and
others could be restored.
Meadow, 20 acres. Then woodland, 1,500 pigs, now 1,000;
always 2 mills. Then 4 cobs, now the same. Then and now
20 head of cattle. Always 40 pigs, 60 sheep; 50 goats;
5 beehives.
Also 10 Freemen before 1066; whereof Reynold son of Ivo
has 2, Bishop William 2, Count Alan 1, Godric 2 as part of
the King's Holding which Earl Ralph held when he forfeited,
William of Warenne 2, and Roger Bigot 1.

Further Harold held before 1066 (in the lands of) Cawston
MARSHAM and BLICKLING. Also 23 Freemen. These two manors
Bishop William holds and Erfast held. Walter Gifford also holds
26 Freemen whom his predecessor Bodin held. Also Harold held
5 Freemen in this manor whom Earl Ralph held; now Godric
holds them as part of the King's Holding.
Value then £30; now 40 at face value. It has 2 leagues in length
and 2 in width, whoever holds there, tax of 7d.

Also 1 outlier, OULTON, has always appertained to this manor, 1 c.
of land.
Always 9 smallholders.
Always 1 plough in lordship; 1 men's plough.
Meadow, 3 acres; woodland, 60 pigs. Now 1 cob; 8 pigs.
Also 4 and a half Freemen. R(alph) held a moiety of this half
when he forfeited, 110 acres.
Value 15d.
1 c. of land and 40 acres.
Always 1 villager. 2 ploughs; meadow, 1 acre.
It is in the valuation of Cawston.
The reeve of Cawston sold one of these 4 Freemen (for) 10s.
Ralph held him when he forfeited; he has 13 acres.
Value 16d.

& ex eifdē . foc̄ . R . qn̄ forisfec̄ erat faifit de uno 7 h̄t

115 b

v . acr̄ . 7 ual v111 . đ . Huic manerio addit̄ eſt . 1 . lib̄ hō ſc̄i

benedic̄ti . LXXXIIII . ac̄ træ . t . r . W . femp . 111 . uiſt̄ . tc̄ 7 p̄

1 . car̄ . m̄ . 11 . boū . 7 ual . v . ſol̄ . In Matelaſc . xxx . acr̄ træ .

ten̄ herold . 7 ual . v . ſol̄ . In Stratuna LX . ac̄ træ bereuuita

in cauſtuna femp . v1 . bor . & 1 . car in dn̄io . Tnc̄ . 7 p̄ . 1 . car

m̄ dim̄ . hoc ē in p̄tio de cauſtuna . In Colebei . 11 . libī hōes

11 . car̄ træ . femp v111 . borđ . Tnc̄ v1 . car̄ . m̄ . 11 . 7 v111 . acr̄

p̄ti . Tnc̄ filua x11 . m̄ v111 . m̄ . 1 . mol̄ . 7 . 1 . foc̄ . 1 . ac̄ . In Wic

mara . 1 . lib̄ hō heroldi . xxx . acr̄ . Tnc̄ . 1 . car̄ . m̄ dim̄ .

& dim̄ ac̄ p̄ti . Tnc̄ ual xxv . ſol̄ . m̄ . xx . hanc tram ca

lupniat̄ Drodo de beureria . ad ſuū feudū quia hanfrid

eā tenuit . & h̄t . v11 . qr̄ in long . 7 v . 7 dim̄ . in lat . 7 11 . đ .

7 . 1 . ferdinc de ḡ .

Tonſteda . H̄ . In felminchā . 1 . lib̄ hō . Oſfort . v1 . ac̄ træ .

& ual v1 . đ .

⌐ Eaſt . H̄ . de flec . Ormeſbȳ . ten̄ Guert . t . r . e . 111 . car̄ .

træ . 7 xxx . ac̄ . q̄s ac̄ tenebat de ſco benedic̄to ; femp

1111 . uiſt̄ . 7 . 111 . bor . 7 . 11 . car̄ . in dn̄io . & dim̄ car hom̄ .

xv1 . ac̄ p̄ti . 7 . 111 . r̄ . 7 . 1111 . an . 7 v1 . por . 7 Tnc̄ . m̄ . ccc .

LXXX1 . ou . & LXXX . foc̄ . 1111 . car̄ træ . 7 xLv1 . ac̄ . 7 . 111 .

bor . Tnc̄ xxx111 . car̄ . p̄ 7 m̄ xx111 . xv1 . ac̄ p̄ti . Ex his

foc̄ tenet Ricard . 111 . de dono arfaſti epi . 7 h̄t dim̄ car̄

træ . Tnc̄ totū ual . x . lib̄ m̄ xx1 . ad numerū . & . 1 . leuḡ

& dim̄ in long . 7 . 1 . leuḡ in lat . 7 . 111 . ſol̄ . 7 v111 . đ de ḡ .

R(alph) also had possession of one of these same Freemen when
he forfeited; he has 5 acres.   115 b
Value 8d.
1 free man of St. Benedict's was added to this manor, 84 acres of
land after 1066.
   Always 3 villagers.
   Then and later 1 plough; now 2 oxen.
Value 5s.

In MATLASK Harold held 30 acres of land. Value 5s.

In STRATTON (Strawless), an outlier in (the lands of) Cawston, 60
acres of land.
   Always 6 smallholders.
   1 plough in lordship. Then and later 1 plough, now ½.
This is in the valuation of Cawston.

In COLBY 2 free men, 2 c. of land.
   Always 8 smallholders.
   Then 6 ploughs, now 2.
   Meadow, 8 acres. Then woodland, 12 [pigs], now 8. Now 1 mill.
   Also 1 Freeman, 1 acre.

In WICKMERE 1 free man of Harold's, 30 acres.
   Then 1 plough, now ½.
   Meadow, ½ acre.
Value then 25s; now 20.
   Drogo of Beuvrière claims this land as part of his Holding
because Humphrey held it. It has 7 furlongs in length and 5½ in
width, tax of 2¼d.

TUNSTEAD Hundred
58 In FELMINGHAM 1 free man, Asford, 6 acres of land.
    Value 6d.

The Hundred of EAST FLEGG
59 Gyrth held ORMESBY before 1066, 3 c. of land and 30 acres which
    he held from St. Benedict.
       Always 4 villagers; 3 smallholders.
       2 ploughs in lordship; ½ men's plough.
       Meadow, 16 acres; 3 cobs; 4 head of cattle; 6 pigs. Then (and)
          now 381 sheep.
       Also 80 Freemen, 4 c. of land and 46 acres. 3 smallholders.
          Then 33 ploughs, later and now 23. Meadow, 16 acres.
          Richard holds 3 of these Freemen by the gift of Bishop
          Erfast. He has ½ c. of land.
    Value of the whole then £10; now 21 at face value. (It has) 1½
    leagues in length and 1 league in width; tax of 3s 8d,

qui cūq̄ ibi teneat . In Ronha . IIII . ſibi hoés . Guerd . xxvIII

ac̄ . 7 dim̄ car̄ . II . ac̄ p̄ti . 7 . III . ſol . 7 redd̄ ſemp . III . ſol in

Ormeſbei . Rex 7 Comes ſoca.

⌐CLAVELINGA . H̄ . Kildincham . II . liḃi hoés . Guerd . xxxv.

ac̄ . 7 dim̄ car̄ . 7 . I . ac̄ p̄ti . Hoc eſt inp̄cio de Gorleſtuna Sti

gand̄ . ſoca . Oms ecclæ in p̄tio c̄ manerijs.

H̃ de NORWIC . In noruic erant tēp̄r regis . e . ꟽcccxx.

burgenſes . Quoꝝ un erat ita dn̄ic regis . ut non poſſ& rece

dere nec homagiū facere ſine licentia ipſi . cui erat nom̄ ēd

ſtan . hic habebat xvIII . ac̄ træ . 7 xII . p̄ti . & . II . eccĺas in burgo

7 ſexta parte̅ tciæ . 7 uni æcclæ ptinebat . una manſura in burgo

7 vi . ac̄ p̄ti . hoc ten̄ Roḡ bigot de dono regis . & de . ꟽ ccxxx

vIII . habebant Rex 7 comes ſoca 7 ſaca 7 c̄ſuetudine . 7 ſup . L.

habebat Stigand̄ ſoca 7 ſaca 7 c̄omdatione̅ . & ſup xxxII.

habebat herold̄ ſoca 7 ſaca 7 c̄omendatione̅ . Quoꝝ un erat

ita ei dn̄ic ut n̄ poſſ& recedǣ nec homagiū facere ſine li

centia ipſi . Int totū habebant oms . LXXX . ac̄ træ 7 xx ac̄

& dim̄ p̄ti . & de iſtis erat una mulier ſoror ſtigandi . xxxII.

ac̄ træ . 7 int eos oms habebant dim̄ mol̄ . 7 quarta parte̅

uni molini . 7 adhuc habent . & adhuc xII . ac̄ & dim̄ p̄ti.

★ quas tulit eis Wihenoc . m̄ hab& Rainald̄ fili̅ iuonis . &

adhuc . II . ac̄ p̄ti . que jacebant ad ecclam omium̄ ſcoꝝ

illas &ia tulit Wihenoc 7 m̄ h̄t Rainald̄ . E̅ &ia in burgo

queda̅ eccĺa ſci martini . quā ten̄ Stigand̄ . t . r . e . ĩ . xII.

acr̄ . træ . eam h̄t m̄ Wiĺts de noiers ad feudū ſtigandi.

Tenebat etia̅ Stigand̄ una ecclam̄ ſci Michael . Cui adja

cent . cxII . ac̄ træ . 7 vi . p̄ti . 7 . I . car̄ . hoc ten̄& Wiĺt epc̄.

ſ; n̄ de epiſcopatu . & burgenſes tenebant xv ecclas . q̄bꝝ

ptinebant in elemoſina ꞉ CLXXXI . ac̄ træ . 7 p̄ti . Et ecclam̄

ſce trinitatis tenebant . t . r . e . xII . burgenſes . m̄ ep̄s

de dono regis . Wiĺti . Rex 7 c̄ . habebant . CLXXX . ac̄ træ.

Abbas h̄t medietate̅ æcclæ Sci Laurentij . 7 . I . dom̄ . de

ſco edmundo . Hoc erat totū tēp̄r reḡ . e . Modo ſn̄t in

burgo . ꝟcLxv . burgenſes anglici & conſuetudines red

dn̄t . & ccccLxxx bordarij . q̄ p̄pt pauperie̅ nulla̅ red

dn̄t conſuetudine̅ . Et in illa t̄ra quā tenebat St . gand

whoever holds there.

In RUNHAM 4 free men of Gyrth's, 28 acres.
½ plough; meadow, 2 acres.
[Value] 3s; it has always paid 3s in Ormesby. The King and the Earl (have) the jurisdiction.

CLAVERING Hundred
60 GILLINGHAM. 2 free men of Gyrth's, 35 acres.
½ plough; meadow, 1 acre.
This is in the valuation of Gorleston. Stigand (had) the jurisdiction. All the churches (are) in the valuation with the manors.

The Hundred of NORWICH
61 Before 1066 there were 1,320 burgesses in Norwich. One of them belonged to King Edward, his lord, to such an extent that he cannot withdraw or do homage without his permission. His name was Edstan. This man had 18 acres of land and 12 [acres] of meadow, 2 churches in the Borough and one-sixth of a third. To one church belonged one dwelling in the Borough and 6 acres of meadow. Roger Bigot holds this of the King's gift. The King and the Earl had the full jurisdiction and customary dues of 1,238 [burgesses], Stigand [had] the full jurisdiction and patronage over 50, and Harold had the full jurisdiction and patronage over 32. One of these belonged to him, his lord, to the extent that he could not withdraw or do homage without his permission. In total, they all had 80 acres of land and 20½ acres of pasture. One of them was a woman, Stigand's sister, 32 acres of land. Amongst them all they had ½ mill and ¼ of 1 mill and they have it still. Further (they had) 12½ acres of meadow which Wihenoc took   116 b from them; now Reynold son of Ivo has them. Further (they had) 2 acres of meadow which appertained to the church of All Saints; Wihenoc also took them and now Reynold has them. A certain church of St. Martin is also in the Borough, which Stigand held before 1066; then 12 acres of land, now William of Noyers has it as part of Stigand's Holding. Stigand also held the church of St. Michael to which are attached 112 acres of land, 6 [acres]of meadow and 1 plough. Bishop William holds this, but (it is) not of his Bishopric. The burgesses held 15 churches to which 181 acres of land and meadow belonged in alms. Before 1066, 12 burgesses held the church of the Holy Trinity, now the Bishop (holds it) of the King's gift. King William and the Earl had 180 acres of land. The Abbot had half of the church of St. Laurence and 1 house from St. Edmund. This was all before 1066. Now there are 665 English burgesses in the Borough and they pay customary dues; also 480 smallholders who, because of their poverty, pay no customary dues. Also on the land which Stigand

t.r.e.manent m̃ ex illis ſupioribƺ xxxviiii.burg.

& in eade ſnt ix.manſure uacuæ.& in illa t̃ra de qua

herolð habebat ſoca.ſnt xv.burg 7 xvii.manſure

uacue.que ſnt in occupatione caſtelli.& in burgo

cLxxxx.manſure uacue in hoc qð erat in ſoca reg

7 comitis.7 Lxxxi.in occupatione caſtelli.In burgo

ſnt adhuc.L.dom.de quibƺ n̄ h̃t rex ſuam

conſuetudine.Ex his h̃t Rainalð ho Rogi bigot.ii.

117 a

domos;7.ii.manſuras.& Rob baro.ii.dom.& abba.i.dom.

7 Rabel.ii.dom.7.ii.manſure;Et.ii.manſure.quas

tenent;ii.femine.7 Aſcolf unglic.i;dom.7 Teodbald

ho abbis.ſci.E.i.dom.7 burghard.i.dom.7 Wala.i.dom.

7 Wills ho herui b.i.dom.7 Meinard uigil.i.dom.7 Me

★ inburgenſes.i;dom.7 Herui deb.i.dom.7 Rad arbalis

tari.ii;dom;7;i.manſura.7 Hereberd foſſator.iii.

dom.7 Roger Peteuin.ii.dom.7 Meinard ho ab de

ſco Bened.i;dom;7 petr ho abb Sci.e.i.mans.7 Euer

win burgenſis.i.dom.7 Baldeuuin.i.dom.7 Wills.

.i.anglic.i.dom.7 Gerard uigil.i.dom.Rodbt lorimar

i.manſura.7 Hildebrand lorimari.i.dom.7 Godwin

burgenſis.i.dom.7 Wills.ho Herm.i.dom.7 Gisbt uigil

i.dom.7 fulbt quida ſacdos herm.i;dom.7 Walter

★ i.dom.7 Reinold fili iuonis.i.dom.7 Richard de ſentebor.

.i.dom.7 Hugo ho W.de ſcoies.i.dom.

Et hoes epi.x.dom.7 in ppria curia epi xiiii.manſure.

quas dedit W.rex.Æ.adpncipale ſede epiſcopat.7

Gisbt arbaliſtari.i.dom.7.ii.maſure.7 Wills de

ſcoies.i.dom.& Meinard.i.dom.abbas de eli.i.manſura.

Et in burgo tenent burgenſes.xliii.capellas.7 Tota

hec Willa reddebat.t.r.e.xx.lib regi.7 comiti.

x.lib.7 pt hoc xxi.ſot.7.iiii.ð pbendarios.7 vi.

ſextarios mellis;7.i.urſu.7 vi.canes ad urſum.

117 b

7 Modo Lxx.lib penſu regis.7 c.ſot ad numeru.de ger

ſuma regine;7 i.aſturcone.7 xx.lib blancas comiti.

7 xx ſot gerſuma adnumeru.Gi

Et ecclam ſcoƺ Simonis 7 Iude ten Almar eps.t.r.e.

p erfaſt.m̃.Wills huic adjacent.iii.partes uni

mot.7 dim ac pti;7.i;manſura.& n̄.e.de epiſcopatu;

ſ; de patrimonio Almari epi.In burgo.h̃t.ii.ac pti.de

epiſcopatu.7 Val;xx.ſot.

held before 1066, 39 of the above-mentioned burgesses now dwell and on the same (land) there are 9 empty dwellings. Also on the land of which Harold had the jurisdiction, there are 15 burgesses and 17 empty dwellings which are in the occupation of the castle premises. Also in the Borough there are 190 dwellings empty in this (area) which was in the King's and the Earl's jurisdiction and 81 in the occupation of the castle. Further, there are in the Borough 50 houses from which the King does not have his customary dues; of these Reynold, Roger Bigot's man, (has) 2 houses and 2 dwellings; Robert Baron 2 houses; Abba 1 house; Rabel 2 houses and 2 dwellings; also 2 dwellings which 2 females hold; Ansculf Unlike 1 house; Theobald, the Abbot of St. E(dmund)'s man, 1 house; Burghard 1 house; Wala 1 house; William, Hervey de Vere's man, 1 house; Maynard the Watchman 1 house; the lesser burgesses 1 house; Hervey de Vere 1 house; Ralph the Crossbowman 2 houses and 1 dwelling; Hereberd the Ditcher 3 houses; Roger of Poitou 2 houses; Maynard, the Abbot of St. Benedict's man, 1 house; Peter, the Abbot of St. E(dmund)'s man, 1 dwelling; Everwin a burgess 1 house; Baldwin 1 house; William an Englishman 1 house; Gerard the Watchman 1 house; Robert the Lorimer 1 dwelling; Hildebrand the Lorimer 1 house; Godwin a burgess 1 house; William, Hermer's man, 1 house; Gilbert the Watchman 1 house; Fulbert a certain priest of Hermer 1 house; Walter 1 house; Reynold son of Ivo 1 house; Richard of Saint-Clair 1 house; Hugh, William of Écouis's man, 1 house. Also the Bishop's men 10 houses, and in the Bishop's own court 14 dwellings which King William gave to E(rfast) for the principal seat of the Bishopric; Gilbert the Crossbowman 1 house and 2 dwellings; William of Écouis 1 house and Maynard 1 house; the Abbot of Ely 1 dwelling. Also in the Borough the burgesses hold 43 chapels.

Before 1066 all this town paid £20 to the King and £10 to the Earl, and besides this except 21s 4d (to certain) pensioners, 6 sesters of honey, 1 bear and 6 dogs for the bear; now £70 by the King's weight and a premium to the Queen of 100s at face value, 1 goshawk and £20 blanched to the Earl and 20s premium at face value to G(odwin?). Also Bishop A(e)lmer held the church of St. Simon and St. Jude before 1066, later Erfast, now William (holds); ¾ of 1 mill, ½ acre of meadow and 1 dwelling are attached to this and it is not of the Bishopric but of Bishop A(e)lmer's patrimony. In the Borough (William) has 2 acres of meadow (which are) of the Bishopric.
Value 20s.

1 . car træ . 7 XVI . acr de paſtura . 7 VII . ac pti . ſubſti
gando . m̃ Rainald fili iuonis . tc 7 p . 1 . car . m̃ . 11 .
ſep ual . xxx . ſot . De burſenſibȝ qui manſer in burgo
de norwic . abier 7 manent in beccles villa abbis . S . edm̃ .
xxii . 7 vi . in humilgar . H̃ . & dimiſer burgu . 7 intorp
reg . 1 . 7 intra Rog bigot . 1 . 7 ſub W . de noies . 1 . 7 Ricard
de ſeꝗ cler . 1 . Iſti fugientes 7 alii remanentes omino
ſnt uaſtati parti ꝓpt forisfacturas . R . comitis . parti
ꝓpt arſura . parti ꝓpt geltu regis parti p Walerannu .
In hoc burgo ſi uult eꝑc poteſt habe . 1 . monetariu .
In burgo erat queda uaſta dom̃ hanc accep Rannulf
fili Walti . de dono regis . Et Walter diaco . 1 . dom̃ .
ht in burgo ſ; n̄ fuit . t . r . e . 7 . 11 . ac pti de ſco ſepulchro
abſtuler . 11 . hoes . R . comitis . p rehabuit pſbit cceſſu
uice comitis . Radulf comes tenuit xiiii . ac træ . 7 . 1 . ac .
& dim pti . p tenuit Aluuard de niwetuna .

118 a

TERRA burgenſiu . In Hundret de Humiliat . ſemp LXXX . ac .
& xiiii . bor . 7 . 1 . car . 7 . 111 . ac pti . 7 ual xiii . ſot . 7 . 1111 . d̄ .

Franci de Norwic . In nouo Burgo . xxxvi . burgenſes ; 7 vi .
anglici . & ex annua conſuetudine reddebat un quiſque
1 . d̄ pt forisfacturas . de hoc toto habebat rex . 11 . partes;
& comes tciam . Modo xli . burgenſes franci in dnio regis
& comitis . & Rog bigot ht . L . & Rad de bellafago . xiiii .
& hermer viii . & Rob arbaliſtari ; v . & Fulcher ho abbis .
1 . & iſac . 1 . & Rad uiſo lupi . 1 . & in piſtrino comitis . 111 . habet;
Rob Blund . & Wimer . 1 . manſura uaſta .
Tota hec tra burgenſiu erat in dnio comitis Rad & conceſſit
ea regi in comune ad faciendu burgu . int ſe & rege . ut teſ
tat uice comes . & oms tre iſte ta militu qua burgenſium .
reddnt regi ſua conſuetudine . Eſt & in nouo burgo queda
eccta qua fec Radulf comes . & ea dedit ſuis capellanis .
Modo ea ten& qda ſacdos uice comitis de dono regis nomine
Wala . 7 ual . LX . ſot . & quandiu Rodb blund comitatu ten .
habuit inde uno q̃qꝫ anno ; 1 . uncia auri .

62 Before 1066 Ewicman held 1½ c. of land, 16 acres of pasture and 7 acres of meadow under Stigand; now Reynold son of Ivo (holds).
Then and later 1 plough, now 2.
Value always 30s.

63 Of the burgesses who dwelt in the Borough of Norwich 22 left and dwell in Beccles, the Abbot of St. Edmund's town and 6 (dwell) in Humbleyard Hundred and they have quitted the Borough; also in THORPE (St. Andrew), the King's (manor), 1, on the land of Roger Bigot 1, under William of Noyes 1, and Richard of Saint-Clair (has) 1. Those fleeing and the others remaining have been utterly devastated partly because of Earl R(alph)'s forfeitures, partly because of fires, partly because of the King's tax, partly by Waleran.

64 In this Borough the Bishop can if he wishes have 1 moneyer. A certain house in the Borough had been unoccupied; this Ranulf son of Walter received of the King's gift. Also Walter the Deacon has 1 house in the Borough but it was not there before 1066. Two of Earl R(alph)'s men took 2 acres of meadow from St. Sepulchre, later the priest regained it by grant of the Sheriff. Earl Ralph held 14 acres of land and 1½ acres of meadow; later Alward of Newton held.

65 LAND OF THE BURGESSES   118 a
In the Hundred of HUMBLEYARD
   Always 80 acres and 14 smallholders.
   1 plough. Meadow, 3 acres.
Value 13s 4d.

66 THE FRENCHMEN OF NORWICH
In the new Borough 36 burgesses, 6 Englishmen; of his annual customary due each man paid 1d besides forfeitures. Of all this the King had 2 parts and the Earl the third. Now (there are) 41 French burgesses in the King's and the Earl's lordship. Also Roger Bigot has 50, Ralph of Beaufour 14, Hermer 8, Robert the Crossbowman 5, Fulcher the Abbot's man 1, Isaac 1, Ralph Visdeloup 1, and in the Earl's bakehouse Robert Blunt has 3 and Wymer 1 unoccupied dwelling.
All this land of the burgesses was in Earl Ralph's lordship and he granted it to the King in common for the founding of the Borough between himself and the King, as the Sheriff testifies. All these lands both of the men-at-arms and of the burgesses pay their own customary dues to the King. In the new city there is also a certain church which Earl Ralph founded and he gave it to his chaplains. Now a certain priest, Wala by name, holds it of the King's gift.
Value 60s.
As long as Robert Blunt held the county he had 1 ounce of gold from there once a year.

EST H̄. de *FLEC*. *GERNEMWA*. teñ. Rex . E . Semp

LXX . burgenses . Tñc ual cu duabʒ partibʒ ſoche de tribʒ
hundretis . XVIII . liƀ ad numeru . 7 pars comitis . IX . liƀ .
ad numeru . M̄ due partes regis . XVII . liƀ . 7 XVI . ſoł .

118 b

7 . IIII . đ . blancas . & pars comitis . X . liƀ blancas . & uicecomes
hͨt . IIII . liƀ . 7 . I . accipite͛ træ . de gerſuma has . IIII . liƀ . dant
burgenſes gratis 7 amiticia . / In ead habuit . t . r . e . Ailmar
epͨc qdā eccła ſci Benedicti eande m̄ hͨt . W . epͨc . de epiſcopatu
7 ual XX . ſoł . Totu reddit XII . đ . de gelto .

H̄ DE *TETFOD* . In tetford . e . I . eccła Sce marie qua
tenebat Stigand archiepͨc . M̄ tenent filij arſaſti
epi . huic eccłæ adjacent ; ſep IIII . eccłæ Sci petri . Sci jol̄is .
S martini . S margarite . 7 VI . car træ dimidia bouata min̄ .
Tñc . II . car . m̄ . I . Sep . V . burgenſes . & due manſure uacue
7 XII . ac p̃ti . Et . III . car poſſint reſtaurari . 7 . II . car remanent
in paſture . ſep XXXV . oues . 7 ual . XL . ſoł .

/ T̄re regis intetford vł t aqua uerſ *NORFOLC* . e una leugata
træ ilongo & dim in lat de qua rex hͨt duas partes . de his
aute duabʒ partibʒ tcia pars inconſulatu jac & . De ſupiori
leugata . R . bigot tcia parte . Tota hec t̄ra medietas arabił
e . alta inpaſtura . In hac t̄ra hͨt rex . I . car . 7 . IIII . bor . 7 . I .
ſer . 7 . I . equū . Et de duobʒ molendinis hͨt rex duas partes .
& conſul tciam . Hͨt etia rex de tcio mol duas partes . 7
de his . II . partibʒ comes hͨt tcia . De alia parte uerſuſ Suth-
folc . e dim leu træ in longo 7 dim in lato de hac t̄ra tcia
pars e ad comitatu . IIII . ac p̃ti . Tota hæc t̄ra arabił . e .
7 . IIII . car poſſent arare . In burgo aute erant . ᴅᴄᴄᴄᴄxliii
burg tp̃r r . e . de his hͨt rex omem cſuetudine . De iſtis

119 a

hominibʒ erant . XXX . VI . ita dn̄ice regis : e . ut n̄ poſſent ee

The Hundred of EAST FLEGG

67 King Edward held YARMOUTH. Always 70 burgesses.
Value then with 2 parts of the jurisdiction of 3 Hundreds £18 at
face value, the Earl's part £9 at face value; now the King's 2 parts
£17 16s 4d blanched, the Earl's part £10 blanched and the   118 b
Sheriff has £4 and 1 hawk of the land for a premium. The
burgesses give these £4 gladly and with friendship.

68 In the same before 1066 Bishop A(e)lmer had a certain church of
St. Benedict; now Bishop William has it from the Bishopric.
Value 20s. The whole pays tax of 12d.

THETFORD Hundred

69 In THETFORD there is 1 church of St. Mary which Archbishop
Stigand held; now the sons of Bishop Erfast hold it. Always
attached to this church have been the 4 churches of St. Peter,
St. John, St. Martin and St. Margaret, 6 c. of land less ½ bovate.
Then 2 ploughs, now 1.
   Always 5 burgesses.
   2 empty dwellings; meadow, 12 acres. Also 3 ploughs can be
restored; 2 c. [of land] remain in pasture; always 35 sheep.
Value 40s.

70 Of the King's land in THETFORD beyond the water towards Norfolk
there is 1 league of land in length and ½ in width of which the
King has 2 parts moreover the third part of these two parts lies
in the Earldom. Roger Bigot (has) the third part of the above-
mentioned league; all this land is half arable, the other (half) in
pasture. On this land the King has 1 plough, 3 smallholders,
1 slave and 1 horse. Also of 2 mills the King has 2 parts and the
Earl the third (part). The King also has 2 parts of a third mill and
of these 2 parts the Earl has a third. Of the other part towards
Suffolk there is ½ a league of land in length and ½ in width;
a third part of this land belongs to the Earldom; meadow, 4 acres.
All this land is arable; 4 ploughs can plough it.
Moreover in the Borough there were 943 burgesses before 1066;
of these the King has all the customary dues. 36 of these same   119 a
men belonged to King Edward, their lord, to such an extent that

hoēs cujlib& ſine licentia regis. Alii oms potant ēe hoēs
cujlib&. ſ; ſep̄ tam̄ c̄ſuetudo regis remanebat p̄t herigete.
M̄ ſnt ꝺccxx. burḡ. 7 ccxxiiii. manſure uacuæ. De iſtis
burḡ. xxi. ht. vi. car̄. 7 lx acr̄. qd teńent de rege 7 ē in ſokā
Sci edmundi. Pt hoc ht. ii. burḡ. i. mol̄. Hoc totū ſup̄i ua
lebat tep̄r. r. e. xx. lib̄ adnumerū. 7 ad op̄ c̄ſul x. l̄. ad num̄.
M̄. reddit regi. l. lib̄ ad penſū. 7 Comiti. xx. lib̄ blancas. 7 vi.
lib̄ ad numerū. Reddit etiā m̄ regi: xl. lib̄. de moneta. 7
ſep̄ xvi. ſol̄. ad ii. p̄bendarios. Reddebat etiā tep̄r. r. e.
iiii. ſeſtarios mellis. 7 xl. ꝺ. 7 x. pelles capnas. 7 iiii. coria
bouina. / In burgo ht abb̄ Sci edmundi. i. eccłam. 7. i.
domū libæ. / Abbas de eli. iii. æccłas. 7. i. domū. libæ. 7. ii.
manſuras inconſuetudine in unā. e. dom̄. / Et ep̄c. xx. domos
lib̄. 7. i. mol̄. 7 dim̄ eccłam. R. bigot. i. dom̄ libam. 7. i. monas
teriū. 7. ii. bor. ad monaſtiū;

119 b

Terre Regis qvǎ Godric Servat.

H̄. DE GRENEHOV. DE xiiii. letis. Sparle. teń. rex
Ædward. & hoc maneriū fuit de regno. S; rex edward
dedit radulfo comiti. Tnc 7 p̄ xxxii. uilł. m̄. xx. m̄. iii. bord̄
Tnc 7 p̄. ii. ſer. m̄ vi. Tnc 7 p̄. i. car̄ in dńio. m̄. iiii. Tnc int
hoēs. x. car̄. & p̄. m̄. iii. Tnc. i. mol̄. m̄. ſimił. Silua. ad lx. por̄.
Tnc. vi. an̄. 7. ii. r̄. 7 lx. porc̄. 7 clxxx. oues. 7. i. lib̄ ho. ꝺ. car̄.
7 hæc tra hab&. i. leug in lonḡ. & dim̄ in lat̄. Huic manerio jac&
. i. beruita. que uocat̄ paggraua. Tnc 7 p̄ xiii. uilł. m̄. xi.
Tnc 7 ſep̄. ii. bor. Sep. ii. ſer. Tnc. i. car̄. & qn Godric recep̄
. i. & m̄. Tnc. ii. 7 ſemp. i. car̄. homū. Sep. i. mol̄. Tnc. ii. an̄.
7 xii. por. 7 xxxvi. oues. 7 Iſta tra dim̄ leu in lonḡ. 7 v. qr̄ in
lato. Eſt &iam adhuc. alt beruita que uocat̄ Acra. Sep̄ vi.
uilł. Tnc 7 p̄. ii. hoēs. m̄. iiii. m̄. i. car̄. Tnc 7 p̄ uilł. iii. car̄.

they could not be anyone else's men without the King's permission. All the others could be anyone else's men but always the customary dues remained the King's except for heriot. Now there are 720 burgesses and 224 empty dwellings; 21 of these burgesses have 6 c. and 60 acres which they hold from the King. It is in St. Edmund's Jurisdiction. Besides this 2 burgesses have 1 mill.

Value of all the above-mentioned before 1066 £20 at face value and for the Earl's use £10 at face value; now it pays £50 by weight to the King and to the Earl £20 blanched and £6 at face value. Now it also pays to the King £40 from the mint; always 16s to 2 pensioners. Before 1066 it also paid 4 sesters of honey and 40d, 10 goat skins and 4 ox hides.

The Abbot of St. Edmund's has 1 church in the city and 1 house (which are) free. The Abbot of Ely (has) 3 churches and 1 house (which are) free and 2 dwellings by custom in one (of which) is his house.

The Bishop also (has) 20 houses (which are) free, 1 mill and ½ church; Roger Bigot (has) 1 house (which is) free, 1 monastery and 2 smallholders (belonging) to the monastery.

LAND OF THE KING OF WHICH GODRIC HAS CUSTODY   119 b

The Hundred of (South) GREENHOE

71   Of 14 leets. King Edward held SPORLE. This manor was royal but King Edward gave it to Earl Ralph.

> Then and later 32 villagers, now 20. Now 3 smallholders.
>> Then and later 2 slaves, now 6.
> Then and later 1 plough in lordship, now 4. Then and later
>> 10 ploughs between the men, now 3.
> Then 1 mill, now the same. Woodland for 60 pigs. Then 6 head
>> of cattle; 2 cobs; 60 pigs; 180 sheep.
> Also 1 free man, ½ c. [of land].

This land has 1 league in length and ½ in width.

1 outlier which is called PALGRAVE appertains to this manor.
> Then and later 13 villagers, now 11. Then and always 2
>> smallholders; always 2 slaves.
> Then 1 plough and when Godric acquired it 1, also now.
>> Then 2 and always 1 men's plough.
> Always 1 mill. Then 2 head of cattle; 12 pigs; 36 sheep.

This land (is) ½ league in length and 5 furlongs in width.

Further, there is also another outlier which is called (South) ACRE.
> Always 6 villagers. Then and later 2 men; now 4.
> Now 1 plough. Then and later the villagers (had) 3 ploughs,

ṁ . 11 . Sep̄ . 11 . moł . 7 Iſta . 1 . leug in longo . & diṁ in lato.

Alia beruita pichenhā . Tnc̄ xiiii . uiłł . & qn̄ recep̄ . 1 . ṁ . iiii . bor.

Tnc̄ . iii . ſer . ṁ . 11 . Tnc̄ in dnīo . 11 . caŕ . 7 p̄ . 1 . ṁ . 11 . Tnc̄ int hoēs.

iiii . caŕ .´ Silua ad vi . porc̄ . Sep̄ . 1 . moł . viii . ac̄ p̄ti . 7 . viii . ſochem.

in hac tṙa . & int eos . tc̄ v . caŕ . 7 p̄ . iii . 7 xxiiii . trǽ . ṁ . v . caŕ.

Semp̄ . 1 . moł . iiii . ac̄ p̄ti . Tnc̄ . 11 . an̄ . 7 xii . pors . 7 . 1 . ŕ . xx . oues.

xx . cap̄ . 7 hec´ diṁ leu in longo . 7 v . quaŕ in łatit . in ſparłe

& in pagraua xviii ꝺ . qn̄do hundret ſcotabat . xx . ſoł.

7 in Acra vi . ꝺ . & in pichenhā . xii . ꝺ . qui cuq̣ ibi teneat.

hoc totū mā ſimul uał . t . r . e . x . lib̄ . 7 qn̄ . G . recep̄ . xxii.

120 a
ṁ xxiiii . lib̄ . 7 11 . ſoł . pt iſtas reddit de gerſuma . lx . ſoł.

⌠ Nieutuna ten̄ Oſmund . t . r . e . 7 p̄ . R . ṁ e in manu regis . Tnc̄
viii . uiłł . 7 p̄ qn̄ . G . recep̄ . viii . ṁ . 11 . Tnc̄ 7 p̄ . vii . bor . ṁ . xi . Sep̄
iiii . ſer . Sep̄ in dnīo . 11 . caŕ . Tnc̄ 7 p̄ . vi . caŕ hom . ṁ . 11 . & ꝺ.
Sep̄ . 11 . moł . Sep̄ diṁ ſaline . 7 libi manſer . vi . libi hoēs . & qn̄.
G . recep̄ inuen ix . an̄ . 7 . 1 . ŕ . xxx . por . xxx . oues . 7 v . quaŕ
in long . 7 v . in łat . 7 ix ꝺ redꝺ in gelto . Tnc̄ uał . iiii . lib̄ ;
ṁ ; viii ,

⌠ Cleia ten̄ . 11 . libi hoēs & p̄ . R . ṁ . e ´ in manu regis . Tnc̄ . x.
uiłł . & p̄ . ṁ viii . Sep̄ vii . bor . Sep̄ . iiii . ſer . Tnc̄ . iiii . in dnīo
caŕ . p̄ . iii . boū . ṁ . 11 . caŕ . Tnc̄ v . caŕ hom . 7 p̄ . iiii . ṁ . iii.
& ibi manent vi . libi hoēs ſep̄ . Coputati ſnt ſupius . Sep̄ . 11.
moł . Silua ad xx . por . viii . ac̄ p̄ti . 7 G . inuenit lx . ou . 7 xiiii.
ꝺ . redꝺ ingelt . & ħt . 1 . leu in longo . & ał in lato . Tnc̄ uał
vi . lib̄ . 7 p̄ . iiii . ṁ . c . ſoł.

now 2.

Always 2 mills.

This (land has) 1 league in length and ½ in width.

Another outlier (is) PICKENHAM.

Then 14 villagers. When (Godric) acquired it 1, now 4 smallholders. Then 3 slaves, now 2.

Then 2 ploughs in lordship, later 1, now 2. Then 4 ploughs between the men.

Woodland for 6 pigs. Always 1 mill; meadow, 8 acres.

Also 8 Freemen (are) on this land; between them then 5 ploughs, later 3; 24 [acres] of land; now 5 ploughs. Always 1 mill; meadow, 4 acres. Then 2 head of cattle; 12 pigs; 1 cob; 20 sheep; 20 goats.

This (land has) ½ league in length and 5 furlongs in width; in Sporle and in Palgrave 18d, when the Hundred paid 20s scot-tax; in (South) Acre 6d, and in Pickenham 12d, whoever holds there.

Value of all this manor together before 1066 £10; when G(odric) acquired it 22, now £24 2s. Besides these it pays premium of 60s. 120 a

72 Osmund held NEWTON before 1066; later R(alph); now it is in the King's hand.

Then 8 villagers, later when G(odric) acquired it 8, now 2. Then and later 7 smallholders, now 11; always 4 slaves.

Always 2 ploughs in lordship. Then and later 6 men's ploughs, now 2½.

Always 2 mills; always ½ salt-house.

6 free men dwelt there.

When G(odric) acquired it he found 9 head of cattle; 1 cob; 30 pigs; 30 sheep.

(It has) 5 furlongs in length and 5 in width, it pays 9d in tax.

Value then £4; now 8.

73 Two free men held (Cockley) CLEY; later R(alph); now it is in the King's hand.

Then and later 10 villagers, now 8. Always 7 smallholders; always 4 slaves.

Then 4 ploughs in lordship; later 3 oxen; now 2 ploughs. Then 5 men's ploughs, later 4, now 3.

6 free men have always dwelt there; they are accounted for above.

Always 2 mills; woodland for 20 pigs; meadow, 8 acres. G(odric) found 60 sheep.

It pays 14d in tax. It has 1 league in length and another in width.

Value then £6; later 4; now 100s.

⌐ Holm tenuit . Godriꝯ . m̄ . rex . Tnc dim̄ car̄ tr̄e . Tnc . v . bor.
m̄ . IIII . Tnc . I . car̄ . m̄ . d̄ . Silua ad xx . por . Semp . II . partes
. I . mol̄ . II . ac̄ p̄ti . Tnc ual̄ . x . fol̄ . m̄ xv . fol̄ . ⌐ 7 inpichenhā ten̄
I . lib̄ hō LX ac̄ . t . r . e . & p̄qua rex uenit in ista patria dedit.
R . com̄ . ꝓpofito hundret 7 p uicecomites regis ten̄ ille adhuc
eā tram . 7 ual̄ xvi . d̄ . ⌐ 7 In eade uilla ten̄ quidā lib̄ hō
xII . ac̄ . 7 al̄ lib̄ hō ten̄ . III . ac̄ . de foca regis . ap̄ptiati ſnt
fup̄i . In acra . uilt dim̄ car̄ tr̄æ . 7 . I . car̄ . 7 ē incenfu . de hundr.

⌐ Gildecros . H̄ . In Gnateſhala . I . lib̄ hō . de xxx . ac̄ tr̄æ.

120 b

& jac& in Kenmohala . 7 . II . uilt . 7 . I . ac̄ p̄ti . fem̄p dim̄ mol̄.
& dim̄ car̄ . 7 xxIIII . ac̄ træ totū ē in p̄cio de cheninchala.

Lawendic . H̄ . Horninghetoft . tenuit aluriꝯ lib̄ hō
t . r . e . III . car̄ træ . tc̄ . vII . uilt . p̄ 7 m̄ . v . femp . III . bord̄.
7 . II . fer . 7 . IIII . ac̄ p̄ti . Tnc . II . car̄ in dnio . p̄ 7 m̄ . I . car̄ . 7 dim̄
7 dim̄ poffet reftaurari . Tc̄ . I . car̄ hom̄ . p̄ & m̄ dim̄ . 7 dim̄
poff& reftaur̄ . filua . ccc . por . 7 dim̄ pifc . femp . I . animal̄.
7 xx . pors . 7 cLx . oū . 7 xx . cap̄ . & . Ix . foc̄ . 7 . II . bor . I . car̄
træ . 7 dim̄ ac̄ p̄ti . filua xL . por . tc̄ . II . car̄ . p̄ 7 m̄ . I . 7 alia
poff& reftaurari . de his nouē foc̄ habuit Stigand focam.
t . r . e . ſ; Rad̄ eā inuafit 7 idō h̄t God̄.

74 Godric held HOLME (Hale), now the King (holds). Then ½ c. of land.
Then 5 smallholders, now 4.
Then 1 plough, now ½.
Woodland for 20 pigs. Always two-thirds of 1 mill; meadow,
2 acres.
Value then 10s; now 15s.

75 In PICKENHAM 1 free man held 60 acres before 1066. After the
King came into that country Earl Ralph gave it to the reeve of
the Hundred and he still holds the land through the King's sheriffs.
Value 16d.
In the same village a certain free man, 12 acres; and another free
man holds 3 acres of the King's jurisdiction. They are assessed
above.
In (South) ACRE a villager, 12 c. of land; 1 plough. It is in the
Hundred's tribute.

GUILTCROSS Hundred
76 In KNETTISHALL 1 free man, at 30 acres of land. It appertains in   120 b
Kenninghall.
2 villagers.
Meadow, 1 acre. Always ½ mill; ½ plough; 24 acres of land.
The whole is in the valuation of Kenninghall.

LAUNDITCH Hundred
77 Aelfric, a free man, held HORNINGTOFT before 1066, 3 c. of land.
Then 7 villagers, later and now 5. Always 3 smallholders;
2 slaves.
Meadow, 4 acres. Then 2 ploughs in lordship, later and now
1½ ploughs, ½ could be restored. Then 1 men's plough,
later and now ½, ½ could be restored.
Woodland, 300 pigs; ½ fishery. Always 1 head of cattle;
20 pigs; 160 sheep; 20 goats.
Also 9 Freemen and 2 smallholders, 1 c. of land.
Meadow, ½ acre; woodland, 40 pigs. Then 2 ploughs, later
and now 1; and another could be restored.
Stigand had the jurisdiction of these 9 Freemen before 1066
but Ralph annexed it and so Godric has it.

Et Chiptena tenueŕ Aluric .& Alfeŕ. iii . caŕ tŕæ . femp
ii . boŕ . 7 iii . ac pti . Tnc . ii . caŕ in dnio . p̄ 7 m̄ nulla fed
iiii . poſſent reſtaurari . & ix . foc . dim caŕ tŕæ . 7 . i . ac pti .
femp . i . caŕ . Totu uat tc . iiii . lib . p̄ vi . lib . m̄ . vii . ad nu
meru . de his ix . foc Stigand foca habuit . t . r . e . 7 Rad
anteq forisfaceŕ& eā inuafit . & tenuit eā . ido ten&
Godric . Totu horningetoft . ht . viii . quaŕ in longo .
7 v . in lato . 7 . iiii . d . de gelto .

Ruhham . i . caŕ & dim tŕæ . tenuit aluin . i . lib ho . t .
r . e . tc vii . uitt . p̄ 7 m̄ . iii . femp . iii . fot . tc . iii . caŕ in dnio .
p̄ 7 m̄ nulla . 7 . iiii . poſſnt reſtaurari . tc . i . caŕ hom . p̄
7 m̄ nulla . ſ; poſſ& reſtaurari . fep . xii . por . 7 xxx . ou .
Hic jacent femp xiiii . foc . i . caŕ 7 dim tŕæ . 7 . ii . uitt .

121 a

& iiii . borď . tnc . ii . caŕ 7 dim . p̄ 7 m̄ . ii . 7 dim poſſ& reſtauŕ . totu
fuit de foca ſtigandi . & de fuis manfibʒ t . r . e . p̄ totu habuit
Rad . m̄ ht Godric . Tnc 7 p̄ uat xl fot . m̄ lx . & ht . vii . qŕ in lon .
& vi . in lat . & xx ď . de gelti

In Wefenhā . iiii . libi hoes . i . caŕ tŕæ . 7 . i ac pti . femp . ii . boŕ .
7 . ii . caŕ . Stigand foca . t . r . e . m̄ . W . de noiers in meleham .
hoc e inptio de efparlea . In Mulcham . & in Britringa .
i . caŕ tŕæ . 7 xii . ac . qua ten aluin . i . lib ho m̄ ten& queda
uidua . tc . ii . caŕ m̄ nulla . & . i . foc xxiiii . ac tŕæ Sep dim
caŕ . 7 . iii . foc . xv . acŕ . 7 dim caŕ . t . r . e . totu hoc uat tc
xx . fot . m̄ nichil reddit quia nichil ht 7 tc Godric p ea
cenſum reddit .

FEORHOV . H . Chineburlai tenuit hakene . t . r . e .
ii . caŕ tŕæ . Tc . x . uitt . m̄ . xiiii . Tnc . viii . boŕ . m̄ xii . femp
iiii . fot . 7 fep . ii . caŕ ſ; Godric n recep n . v . boues . fep . viii .
caŕ hom . Silua . x . por . Semp . i . mot . 7 xii . ac pti . femp
viii . por . 7 xx . ou . Tnc x . foc . m̄ xvii . Tnc xxx . ac tŕæ .

Aelfric and Alfhere also held KIPTON, 3 c. of land.
  Always 2 smallholders.
  Meadow, 3 acres.
  Then 2 ploughs in lordship, later and now none, but 4 could
    be restored.
  Also 9 Freemen, ½ c. of land. Meadow, 1 acre; always 1 plough.
Value of the whole then £4; later £6; now 7 at face value.
  Stigand had the jurisdiction of these 9 Freemen before 1066.
Ralph before he forfeited annexed it and held it, so Godric holds.
The whole of Horningtoft has 8 furlongs in length and 5 in width,
tax of 4d.

78 ROUGHAM, 1½ c. of land. A(i)lwin, 1 free man, held it before 1066.
  Then 7 villagers, later and now 3; always 3 slaves.
  Then 3 ploughs in lordship, later and now none, 4 could be
    restored. Then 1 men's plough, later and now none, but it
    could be restored.
  Always 12 pigs, 30 sheep.
  14 Freemen have always appertained here, 1½ c. of land.
    2 villagers; 4 smallholders.   121 a
    Then 2½ ploughs, later and now 2, ½ could be restored.
The whole was of Stigand's jurisdiction and of his manors before
1066; later Ralph had the whole; now Godric has it.
Value then and later 40s; now 60. It has 7 furlongs in length
and 6 in width, tax of 20d.

79 In WEASENHAM, 4 free men, 1 c. of land; meadow, 1 acre.
  Always 2 smallholders.
  2 ploughs.
Stigand (had) the jurisdiction before 1066; now William of
Noyers (has it) in Mileham. This is in the valuation of Sporle.

80 In MILEHAM and in BITTERING 1 c. of land and 12 acres which
Alwin, 1 free man, held; now a certain widow holds it.
  Then 2 ploughs, now none.
  Also 1 Freeman, 24 acres of land. Always ½ plough.
  Also 3 Freemen, 15 acres and ½ plough before 1066.
Value of all this then 20s; now it pays nothing because it has
nothing. Then Godric pays tribute for it.

  FOREHOE Hundred
81 Hagni held KIMBERLEY before 1066, 2 c. of land.
  Then 10 villagers, now 14. Then 8 smallholders, now 12;
    always 4 slaves.
  Always 2 ploughs, but Godric did not receive anything
    except 5 oxen; always 8 men's ploughs.
  Woodland, 10 pigs. Always 1 mill; meadow, 12 acres.
    Always 8 pigs; 20 sheep.
  Then 10 Freemen, now 17. Then 30 acres of land,

m̄ xL . ſemp . ii . car̄ . Tnc̄ uaƚ totū lx . ſoƚ . m̄ . vii . liƀ blancas.
& ht . v . qr̄ in longo . 7 . iiii . in lato ; & . xiii . đ . 7 . i . obolū de
gelto . P̄t hoc jacent huic manerio . in Kaᴙletuna . xvi . liƀi
hoes . lx . ac̄ træ ſemp . ii . car̄ . 7 ſnt in ſupiori p̄tio & hoᴢ
viiii . erant ſochemani Stigandi . t . r . e . S; rađ comes eos
om̄s habebat p̄q̄ forisfacer&.

⌐ Boethorp tenuit . Hakene . t . r . e . ii . car̄ træ . tc̄ . x . uiƚƚ.

121 b
m̄ . xiiii . ſemp . iii . ſer . 7 . ii . car̄ in dn̄io 7 . ii . car̄ houm . ſiluā xvi.
porc̄ . 7 . x . ac̄ p̄ti . ſep . i . moƚ . 7 vii . por . 7 xvi . ou . Huic manerio
jacent . ii . ſoc̄ . iiii . ac̄ træ . totū uaƚ . xl . ſoƚ . m̄ . vi . liƀ albas.
& ht . iii . qr̄ in lato . 7 . iii . in longo . 7 vi . đ . 7 . i . obolū de gelto.

⌐ In Congrethorp . tenuit Bondo liƀ ho . t . r . e . xx . ac̄ træ.
ſemp . i . bor . & ē in ſupiori p̄tio . ⌐ In Runhala . i . car̄ træ.
tenuit hakene . 7 . ii . bor . 7 . i . ſoc̄ . 7 . i . moƚ . hoc eſt bereuita
in ſuatinga ; & ē . in p̄tio . & huic bereuuite jacent . vii.
liƀi hoes . xxiiii . ac̄ træ . 7 dim car̄ . 7 ē in eodē p̄tio.

⌐ H̄ de Mitteforda . Cranaworda tenuit Ulf . t . r . e . ii.
car̄ træ . Sēp . xiii . uiƚƚ . 7 . iii . bor . Tnc̄ . ii . ſer̄ . m̄ nuƚƚ.
Sēp in dn̄io . ii . car̄ 7 houm . ii . car̄ . Silua ad . cc . por.
viii . ac̄ p̄ti . Semp . i . moƚ . ii . an . xv . por . xx . oues . 7 xx . c̄ap.
& xiiii . ſoc̄ . de xl . ac̄ træ . Semp . ii . car̄ . Tnc̄ uaƚ . c . ſoƚ . m̄ . x.
liƀ . 7 x . ſoƚ . de gerſom . & ht . i . leu in lon . 7 dim in lat . 7 xv . đ.
de gelt.

now 40; always 2 ploughs.

Value of the whole then 60s; now £7 blanched. It has 5 furlongs in length and 3 in width, tax of 13½d.

Besides this, there appertained to this manor in CARLETON (Forehoe) 16 free men, 60 acres of land. Always 2 ploughs. They are in the above-mentioned valuation. 9 of them were Stigand's Freemen before 1066, but Earl Ralph had all of them before he forfeited.

82   Hagni held BOWTHORPE before 1066, 2 c. of land.
        Then 10 villagers, now 14; always 3 slaves.   121 b
        2 ploughs in lordship; 2 men's ploughs.
        Woodland, 16 pigs; meadow, 10 acres. Always 1 mill; 7 pigs,
            16 sheep.
        2 Freemen appertain to this manor, 4 acres of land.
Value of the whole 40s; now 6 white pounds. It has 3 furlongs in width and 3 in length, tax of 6½d.

83   In CROWNTHORPE Bondi, a free man, held 20 acres of land before 1066.
        Always 1 smallholder.
It is in the above-mentioned valuation.

84   In RUNHALL Hagni held 1 c. of land.
        2 smallholders. 1 Freeman.
        1 mill.
This outlier is in (the lands of) Swathing and is in (its) valuation.
        7 free men appertain to this outlier, 24 acres of land; ½ plough.
It is in the same valuation.

    The Hundred of MITFORD
85   Ulf held CRANWORTH before 1066, 2 c. of land.
        Always 13 villagers; 3 smallholders. Then 2 slaves, now none.
        Always 2 ploughs in lordship; 2 men's ploughs.
        Woodland for 200 pigs; meadow, 8 acres; always 1 mill.
            2 head of cattle; 15 pigs; 20 sheep; 20 goats.
        Also 14 Freemen, at 40 acres of land. Always 2 ploughs.
Value then 100s; now £10; premium of 10s. It has 1 league in length and ½ in width, tax of 15d.

In ſuatinga ten . Hagaña lib hō . t . r . e . ɪɪ . car̄ træ.
Sep . ɪx . uiłł . 7 xɪ . bor . 7 . ɪɪɪɪ . ſer . Tñc . ɪɪ . car̄ iñ dñio . p̄ 7 m̄
dim . 7 tote poſſent reſtaurari . Tñc . ɪɪ . car̄ houm̄ . m̄ . ɪ . 7
ał poſſñt reſtaurari . Tñc ſilua ad ʟx . por . m̄ xʟ . v̄ . ac̄ p̄ti.
ɪɪ . moł . Tñc 7 m̄ . xxx . por . 7 xxx . ou . 7 vɪ . cap̄ . Huic mañ
jacent . xɪɪɪ . ſoc . in eade uiłła manent . v̄ . 7 In thuſtuna . ɪɪɪɪ.
7 in turſtaneſtuna . ɪɪɪɪ . int̄ totu h̄t . ɪ . car̄ træ . Tñc . v̄ . car̄.
m̄ . ɪɪɪ . Tñc uał . c . ſoł . m̄ . vɪ . lib . 7 xɪɪɪ . ſoł . 7 . ɪɪɪɪ . d̄ . 7 h̄t
vɪɪ . qr̄ . in lon . 7 vɪ . in lat . q̄cuq̄ ibi tenent . 7 xɪɪ . d̄ de gelt.

122 a

Flokethorp . tenuit hakena lib hō . t . r . e . ɪɪ . car̄ træ . Semp̄
xɪɪ . uiłł . tc̄ vɪ . ſer . m̄ . ɪɪɪ . 7 xɪɪ . bor . Tñc ſilu ʟx por . m̄ . xʟ.
& x . ac̄ p̄ti . ſemp̄ . ɪ . moł . Tñc . ɪɪɪ . car̄ iñ dñio . p̄ 7 m̄ . ɪɪ . 7 . ɪ.
poſſ̄ & reſtaur̄ . Tñc . ɪɪɪɪ . car̄ hom̄ . m̄ . v̄ . 7 xɪɪ . por . 7 xxvɪ.
ou . 7 ʟxxx . cap̄ . Huic manerio jac̄ & . ɪ . bereuuita Mantates-
tona . xxx . ac̄ træ . tc̄ . ɪ . car̄ . & alia bereuuita . xxx . ac̄ tre . tc̄
. ɪ . car̄ . 7 xxɪɪ . ſoc . ɪ . car̄ træ . 7 vɪ . ac̄ p̄ti . Tñc . v̄ . car̄ . m̄ . ɪɪɪ . & dim.
Totu uał . tc̄ . c . ſoł . m̄ . x . lib blancas . & h̄t . ɪ . leu in long . 7 dim
in lato . & xxvɪɪɪ . d̄ . de gelto . In Craneworda & in Scipdham.
xxx . ac̄ træ . tenuit . ɪ . ſoc . de Stou . 7 vɪɪɪ . ac̄ p̄ti . ſilu . ɪɪɪ . por.
& uał . ɪɪ . ſoł . & Rob̄ blund eos habuit . S; Godric nuq̄ habuit.

H̄ . DE BRODERCROS . Reineha qua ten Vluiet . t . r . e.
ɪɪ . car̄ træ . Sep̄ xɪ . bor . 7 . ɪɪ . ſer . Tñc . ɪɪ . car̄ . 7 p̄ d̄ . m̄ . ɪ.
Tñc houm̄ . ɪ . car̄ . 7 p̄ d̄ . m̄ ſimił . Silua ad x . por . ɪɪɪɪ . ac̄ p̄ti.
. ɪ . moł . Semp̄ . ɪ . r̄ . 7 . ɪɪɪ . añ . 7 xɪɪɪɪ . por . 7 ʟxɪɪɪ . ou . & . ɪ . be
ruita . helgetuna . de dim car̄ træ . Semp̄ . ɪɪ . bor . 7 dim car̄.
7 . ɪ . ſer . 7 . ɪ . moł . ɪ . ac̄ p̄ti . ɪ . piſc̄ . 7 . ɪ . ſalin . 7 . ɪ . r̄ . 7 . ɪɪ . animał.
7 xʟɪɪ . ou . Iacent in hoc mañ . xvɪ . ſoc . de . ɪ . car̄ træ . Tñc

121 b, 122 a

86 In SWATHING Hagni, a free man, held 2 c. of land before 1066.
   Always 9 villagers; 11 smallholders; 4 slaves.
   Then 2 ploughs in lordship; later and now ½, all could be
       restored. Then 2 men's ploughs, now 1, the others could
       be restored.
   Then woodland for 60 pigs, now 40. Meadow, 5 acres; 2 mills.
       Then and now 30 pigs; 30 sheep; 6 goats.
   13 Freemen appertain to this manor; 5 dwell in the same
       village, 4 in *Thustuna*, and in Thuxton 4. In total they have
       1 c. of land. Then 5 ploughs, now 3.
   Value then 100s; now £6 13s 4d. It has 7 furlongs in length and
   6 in width, whoever holds there, tax of 12d.

87 Hagni, a free man, held FLOCKTHORPE before 1066, 2 c. of land.   122 a
   Always 12 villagers. Then 6 slaves, now 3; 12 smallholders.
   Then woodland, 60 pigs, now 40. Meadow, 10 acres; always
       1 mill.
   Then 3 ploughs in lordship, later and now 2, and 1 could be
       restored. Then 4 men's ploughs, now 5.
   12 pigs; 26 sheep; 80 goats.

   1 outlier, MANSON, appertains to this manor, 30 acres of land.
   Then 1 plough.

   Also another outlier, 30 acres of land. Then 1 plough.
   22 smallholders, 1 c. of land.
   Meadow, 6 acres.
   Then 5 ploughs, now 3½.
   Value of the whole then 100s; now £10 blanched. It has 1 league
   in length and ½ in width, tax of 28d.

   In CRANWORTH and in SHIPDHAM 1 Freeman of Stow (Bedon) held
   30 acres of land. Meadow, 8 acres; woodland, 3 pigs.
   Value 2s.
   Robert Blunt had them but Godric never had (them).

   The Hundred of BROTHERCROSS
88 RAYNHAM which Wulfgeat held before 1066, 2 c. of land.
   Always 11 smallholders; 2 slaves.
   Then 2 ploughs, later ½, now 1. Then 1 men's plough, later ½,
       now the same.
   Woodland for 10 pigs; meadow, 4 acres; 1 mill. Always 1 cob;
       3 head of cattle; 14 pigs; 63 sheep.

   Also 1 outlier, HELHOUGHTON, at ½ c. of land.
   Always 2 smallholders. ½ plough. 1 slave.
   1 mill; meadow, 1 acre; 1 fishery; 1 salt-house; 1 cob;
       2 head of cattle; 42 sheep.
   16 Freemen appertain in this manor, at 1 c. of land. Then

II . car 7 d̄ . 7 p̄ . II . m̄ . II . 7 VI . bor . Silua ad . IIII . por . 7 . II . ac̄
p̄ti . 7 in hælgatuna . VI . ſoc . de dim̄ car̄ træ . Semp . II . bor.
Tnc̄ . II . car . p̄ d̄ . m̄ . I . II . ac̄ p̄ti . Tnc̄ ual̄ XL . ſol̄ . m̄ . VI . lib̄.
7 reinhā ht̄ . I . leu in lonḡ . 7 III . quar̄ . in lat̄ . 7 XX . d̄ in gelt.
7 helgetuna . ht̄ . IIII . qr̄ in loñ . 7 . III . in lat̄ . 7 X . d̄ ingelt.

H̄ . de GRENEHOGA . Stiuecai . teñ Toka ingrenehoga.

122 b

ht̄ . I . car̄ træ . 7 d̄ . ſemp . XI . bor . tc̄ VI . ſer . 7 p̄ 7 m̄ . III . ſemp.
car̄ & dim̄ in dñio . tc̄ . I . car̄ houm̄ . p̄ . I . car̄ hou . m̄ . d̄ . V . anim̄.
XII . porc̄ . cc . ou . Silua . VIII . por . II . ac̄ p̄ti . 7 djm̄ mol̄.
& huic uille jac & . I . beruita . guella . t . r . e . I . car̄ træ
ſ; godric̄ nil inueñ . IIII . bord . tc̄ dim̄ car̄ . p̄ . 7 m̄ . I . boue.
7 . IIII . ſokem̄ . VIII . ac̄ træ . ſemp dim̄ car̄ . 7 huic manerio
adjacent XIII . ſocm̄ . XL ac̄ træ . t . r . e . d̄ . car̄ . 7 m̄ . Tnc̄ ual̄
IIII . lib̄ m̄ reddit . VI . lib̄ . & ſtiuecai . I . beruita . q̄ p̄tin &
ad heleſhā . IIII . bord . t . r . e . I . car̄ . 7 qm̄ ḡ . recep̄ . 7 m̄ . d̄.
car̄ . d̄ ac̄ p̄ti . hoc totu p̄tin & ad heleſhā . & ap̄p̄tiatur.
Snaringa . teñ Ketel . t . r . e . m̄ . rex . III . car̄ træ . tnc̄
7 m̄ . I . uill̄ . 7 XX . II . bord . tc̄ VIIII . ſer . m̄ VIII . tc̄ . III . car̄ in dñio.
p̄ & m̄ . II . ſep̄ . III . car̄ houm̄ . tc̄ 7 m̄ . ſilua . VIII . por . VIII . ac̄
p̄ti . II . mol̄ . ſemp . XXX . pors . p̄ & m̄ . CLXXX . ou.

2½ ploughs, later 2, now 2. 6 smallholders. Woodland for
4 pigs; meadow, 2 acres.

Also in Helhoughton 6 Freemen, at ½ c. of land.
    Always 2 smallholders.
    Then 2 ploughs, later ½, now 1.
    Meadow, 2 acres.
Value then 40s; now £6. Raynham has 1 league in length and 3
furlongs in width, 20d in tax. Helhoughton has 4 furlongs in
length and 3 in width, 10d in tax.

The Hundred of (North) GREENHOE
89 Toki held STIFFKEY in (North) Greenhoe. It has 1½ c. of land.   122 b
    Always 11 smallholders. Then 6 slaves, later and now 3.
    Always 1½ ploughs in lordship. Then 1 men's plough, later
      1 men's plough, now ½.
    5 head of cattle; 12 pigs; 20 sheep; woodland, 8 pigs;
      meadow, 2 acres; ½ mill.

90 An outlier, WELLS (next the Sea), appertains to this village, 1 c. of
    land before 1066 but Godric found nothing.
    4 smallholders.
    Then ½ plough; later and now 1 ox.
    Also 4 Freemen, 8 acres of land. Always ½ plough.
    13 Freemen are attached to this manor, 40 acres of land.
    Before 1066 and now ½ plough.
    Value then £4; now it pays £6.

91 Also STIFFKEY an outlier which belongs to Aylsham.
    4 smallholders.
    1 plough before 1066; when Godric received it and now ½
      plough.
    Meadow, ½ acre.
    All this belongs to Aylsham and is assessed (there).

92 Ketel held (Great) SNORING before 1066, now the King (holds).
    3 c. of land.
    Then and now 1 villager; 22 smallholders. Then 9 slaves,
      now 8.
    Then 3 ploughs in lordship, later and now 2; always 3 men's
      ploughs.
    Then and now woodland, 8 pigs; meadow, 8 acres; 2 mills.
    Always 30 pigs. Later and now 180 sheep.

⌐Turesfort . ɪ . beruita . ptin& ad hanc uillā . xʟ . ac træ . 7 poſt
7 m̄ . ɪ . car . ɪ . bor . ɪɪ . ac p̄ti . ɪ . mol . xxvɪɪ . ſokem̄ . jacent huic
man̄ . ɪ . car træ . ſemp . ɪɪɪɪ . car . & intureforde . v . ſok . ʟx ac
træ . ſemp đ . car . 7 ɪɪɪ . libi hoes . ɪɪɪ . car træ . ſemp . ɪ . car .
tc uał . vɪɪɪ . liƀ . m̄ . reddit xɪ . liƀ . x . ſoł . 7 vɪɪɪ . đ . de gerſum .
7 ht . ɪ . leu long . & dim lat . 7 xxɪɪɪɪ . đ de gelto .

⌐BLAFELDA . H̄ . Cantelai . R . ſtalre . ten . t . r . e . ɪɪɪɪ . car
træ . & . ɪɪɪ . ac . 7 alfi de eo . Semp . ɪɪɪɪ . uiłt . tc xxx . ɪɪɪ . bor.
7 p̄ ſimił . m̄ xʟ . ɪɪ . tc . ɪɪɪɪ . ſer . p̄ . ɪɪɪ . 7 m̄ . ɪɪ . Tnc ɪɪɪ . car .
in đnio . p̄ 7 m̄ . ɪɪ . Semp vɪɪɪ . car homū . Silua . ʟx . porc .

123 a

& xʟ . ac p̄ti . m̄ . ɪ . ſał . Semp . ɪ . r̄ . 7 . ɪɪɪ . an̄ . Semp . vɪ . por.
Semp . cccc . ou . & ibi ſnt . x . ſoc de ʟx . ac træ . 7 . ɪɪɪɪ . ac p̄ti .
Semp . ɪɪ . car . Tnc uał vɪɪ . liƀ . p̄ vɪɪɪ . m̄ x . liƀ . blanc . 7 x . ſoł.
de gerſu . Et ht . ɪ . leug in longo . 7 . ɪ . in lato . & de gelto .
xx . đ . ⌐ & in limpeho . t . r . e . xvɪ . libi hoes alfi ſub . R . co
mite . ɪ . car træ 7 xɪɪɪ . ac p̄ti . 7 . ɪ . bor . Sep . ɪɪɪ . car . & dim .
& ht . ɪ . leug in long . & x . quar in lato . & de gelto . xx . đ .
⌐In hafingehā . vɪ . libi hoes . R . ſtalre . & de uno habuit ſoca
t . r . e . ʟxx . ac træ un ht . v . bor . Int oes . v . ac p̄ti . 7 dim
tc . ɪɪɪ . car . m̄ . ɪ . car . 7 dim . ht . ɪ . leug in long . 7 . ɪɪɪɪ . qr .
in lat . Et de gelto vɪ . đ . 7 . ɪɪɪ . ſoł . & de iſtis . ɪɪ . uiłt .
t . r . e . erat ſoca reg . teſtim hund . Sed . R . tenuit
ex quo fuit comes . m̄ ten& godric in manu regis .
Infrietorp ɪx . libi hoes ſup . v . habuit . R . ſoca . t . r . e . 7 ſup
ɪɪɪɪ . rex . Sed ex quo R . fuit comes habuit eam . ʟx ac
træ . hi oes ſnt apptiati in xɪɪɪ . liƀ . Semp . ɪ . car 7 dim .

93   THURSFORD, an outlier, belongs to this village, 40 acres of land. Later and now 1 plough.

    1 smallholder.

    Meadow, 2 acres; 1 mill.

    27 Freemen appertain to this manor, 1 c. of land.

      Always 4 ploughs.

    Also in Thursford 5 Freemen, 60 acres of land. Always ½ plough.

    Also 3 free men, 3 c. of land. Always 1 plough.

  Value then £8; now it pays £11 10s, premium of 8d.

  It has 1 league in length and ½ in width; tax of 24d.

  BLOFIELD Hundred

94   R(alph) the Constable held CANTLEY before 1066, 4 c. of land and 3 acres and Alsi (held) from him.

    Always 4 villagers. Then 33 smallholders, later the same, now 42. Then 4 slaves, later 3, now 2.

    Then 3 ploughs in lordship, later and now 2. Always 8 men's ploughs; woodland, 60 pigs; meadow, 40 acres. Now 1 salt-house. Always 1 cob; 3 head of cattle. Always 6 pigs; always 400 sheep.

    Also 10 Freemen are there, at 60 acres of land.

    Meadow, 4 acres. Always 2 ploughs.

  Value then £7; later (£)8; now £10 blanched, premium of 10s.

  It has 1 league in length and 1 in width, tax of 20d.

123 a

95   Also in LIMPENHOE before 1066, 16 free men of Alsi's under Earl R(alph), 1 c. of land.

    Meadow, 13 acres.

    1 smallholder.

    Always 3½ ploughs.

  It has 1 league in length and 10 furlongs in width, tax of 20d.

96   In HASSINGHAM 6 free men of R(alph) the Constable's; he had the jurisdiction of 1 before 1066. 70 acres of land.

    1 (free man) has 5 smallholders.

    Among them all 5½ acres of meadow.

    Then 3 ploughs, now 1½.

  It has 1 league in length and 4 furlongs in width, tax of 6d and 3s.

    The jurisdiction of these 2 villages was the King's before 1066 by witness of the Hundred. But R(alph) held it from the time he became Earl; now Godric holds in the King's hand.

97   In FREETHORPE 9 free men. R(alph the Constable) had the jurisdiction over 5 before 1066, the King over 4 but from the time he became Earl, R(alph) had it. 60 acres of land.

  All these are assessed in the £13.

    Always 1½ ploughs.

Inſtromeſſaga . II . libi hões . R . ſtalre cu ſoca 7 ſaca . de
LXXXII . ac træ . Silua . IIII . por . 7 ſemp . IIII . bor . Semp
I . car . int ſe 7 hões . & in eade ali lib hõ . R . ſtalre . ad
ſoca reg xxx . ac træ . 7 VIII . ac p̃ti . Semp ual . VIII . ſol.

In blingeha . I . lib hõ . R . ſtalre cu ſoca . de xxx . ac træ.
7 x . ac libæ træ p̃tinentis ad ecclam . 7 v . ac . p̃ti . 7 dim
Adhuc in blingeha : III . libi hões 7 dim . ſemp un . R.
ſoca . Sup . II . 7 dim Rex . XLII . ac træ 7 . IIII . acr p̃ti.

123 b

Semp . I . car . In plumeſtede . II . libi hões . t . r . e . I . car træ.
& xxx . ac . 7 dim . 7 . I . bor . ſemp . & ſub eis . XVIII . ſoc.
& VII . ac p̃ti . Tnc 7 p . II . car . m̃ . IIII . Silua . VI . por.

In Witona . IIII . libi hões . de LX . ac træ . 7 XI . ac . p̃ti.
Sep . I . car . De iſtis ÷ ſoca in hund . adtciu d̃ . & reddit
VIII . ſol.

In plumeſteda . I . lib hõ . x . ac træ . In bucanaha . I . lib
hõ . de VIII . ac træ . & hi oms libi hões ſnt apptiati in
XIII . lib . de lut ſoca de Waleſſam . In plumeſteda . I . beru
ita . 7 ten edric . t . r . e . dim car træ . 7 jac & in ettuna.
Semp . III . bor . Semp . I . car . int totu . 7 . III . ac . p̃ti . Et
eſt in p̃tio ettune.

In plumeſt . I . lib hõ . v . ac træ . Rex h̃t ſoca.

98 In STRUMPSHAW 2 free men of R(alph) the Constable's with full
jurisdiction, at 82 acres of land.
> Woodland, 4 pigs.
> Always 4 smallholders.
> Always 1 plough between him and the men.

Also in the same another free man of R(alph) the Constable's,
30 acres of land.
> Meadow, 8 acres.

Value always 8s.

99 In (North) BURLINGHAM 1 free man of R(alph) the Constable's
with jurisdiction, at 30 acres of land, and 10 acres of free land
which belong to the church.
> Meadow, 5½ acres.

Further, in Burlingham 3½ free men, always R(alph) (had) the
jurisdiction over 1 and the King over 2½. 42 acres of land.
> Meadow, 4 acres. Always 1 plough.   123 b

100 In PLUMSTEAD 2 free men before 1066, 1 c. of land and 30½ acres.
> Always 1 smallholder and under them 18 Freemen.
> Meadow, 7 acres. Then and later 2 ploughs, now 4.
> Woodland, 6 pigs.

101 In WITTON 4 free men, at 60 acres of land.
> Meadow, 11 acres. Always 1 plough.

Jurisdiction of these is in the Hundred to the third penny; it
pays 8s.

102 In PLUMSTEAD 1 free man, 10 acres of land.

103 In BUCKENHAM 1 free man, at 8 acres of land.
All these free men are assessed in the £13 of the outlying
jurisdiction of (South) Walsham.

104 In PLUMSTEAD 1 outlier. Edric held it before 1066, ½ c. of land.
It appertains in Eaton.
> Always 3 smallholders.
> Always 1 plough among the whole.
> Meadow, 3 acres.

It is in the valuation of Eaton.
In Plumstead 1 free man, 5 acres of land. The King has the
jurisdiction.

HEINESTEDE . H̄ . | Hou tenuit alnoht . I . lib̃ hō ſtigan
di . archiepi . t . r . e . p̃ . I . car tr̃æ . Tnc̃ XII . uill̃ . 7 p̃ . XI.
7 m̃ ſimilit̃ . Semp . I . bord̃ . Tnc̃ . VI . ſer . p̃ 7 m̃ . III . Tnc̃
II . car in dñio p̃ 7 m̃ . I . Semp . III . car . hou . Silua . XL.
porc̃ . 7 . II . ac̃ p̃ti . Semp . IIII . an̄ . 7 XLI . porc̃ . 7 LXXX . ou.
Tnc̃ uat̃ XL ſot̃ p̃ 7 m̃ . LX . Hou ht̃ . VI . quar in long̃ . 7 . IIII.
in lato . Et de gelt . XII . d̃ . | Scoteſſa ten ide alnoht . t . r . ẽ.
p̃ . I . car tr̃æ . poſt . II . bor . m̃ . III . Tnc̃ . I . car in dñio . p̃
7 m̃ . II . boues . | & in eade ten ide alnoht . II . libos hoes.
& medietate alioʒ . IIII . comdation . & ten int̃ ſe XXXII.
ac̃ tr̃æ . 7 . I . car . Ex his tenuit . R . comes . III . integros c̃ tr̃æ

124 a

XII . ac̃ 7 dim̃ . qn̄ ſe forisfec̃ . m̃ ten& aitard hō . R . bigot . &
reclamat ex feudo epi baiocenſis . S; iſte aitard . n̄ ht̃ ab anteces
ſore ſuo n̄ in uno dim̃ comdat . teſte hundret.

| Inſtoches . I . lib̃ hō . alnoht . comd de v . ac̃ . tr̃æ . | In ſuterlingẽ
ha . III . libi hoes & dim alnot comd de XLV . ac̃ tr̃e . ſemp.
I . car̃ . 7 v . ac̃ p̃ti . 7 ſub eis . v . bor . | In Rokelunda . II . libi hoes
altnoth comd XXIIII . ac̃ tr̃æ 7 ſemp . II . bou . 7 . II . ac̃ p̃ti.
| In alta ſcoteſſa . I . lib̃ hō . 7 duo dim̃ alnoth . comd . de XL . ac̃.
7 . II . bor . 7 . IIII . ac̃ p̃ti . Int̄ oc̃s . I . car̃.
| In ailuertuna . II . libi hoes . t . r . e . I . & dim altnoth . 7 dim̃
aluredi comd hos ten̄ . R . com qn̄o ſe forisfecit . p̃ godric
in manu regis . m̃ ten& aitard hō . R . bigot . medietate
uni . 7 XV ac̃ . 7 reclamat ad feudu epi . baioc̃ . Int̄ hoes
XXXIII . ac̃ tr̃æ . 7 ſemp . II . bord̃ . Semp . I . car̃ . 7 . III . ac̃ p̃ti.

HENSTEAD Hundred

105 Alnoth, 1 free man of Archbishop Stigand's, held HOWE before
1066, as 1 c. of land.
> Then 12 villagers, later 11, now the same. Always 1
> smallholder. Then 6 slaves, later and now 3.
> Then 2 ploughs in lordship, later and now 1. Always 3
> men's ploughs; woodland, 40 pigs; meadow, 2 acres.
> Always 4 head of cattle; 41 pigs; 80 sheep.

Value then 40s; later and now 60.

Howe has 6 furlongs in length and 4 in width, tax of 12d.

106 Alnoth also held SHOTESHAM before 1066, as 1 c. of land.
> Later 2 smallholders, now 3.
> Then 1 plough in lordship; later and now 2 oxen.

Also in the same this Alnoth held 2 free men and a moiety of
another 4 in patronage. Between them they hold 32 acres of land
and 1 plough. Of these Earl Ralph held 3 whole with (their) land,
12½ acres, when he forfeited; now Aitard, Roger Bigot's man,   124 a
holds them and claims them back out of the Bishop of Bayeux's
Holding but this Aitard has nothing from his predecessor except
the patronage in (respect of) one half(-freeman) (as) the Hundred
testify.

107 In STOKE (Holy Cross) 1 free man under the patronage of Alnoth,
at 5 acres of land.

108 In SURLINGHAM 3½ free men under the patronage of Alnoth, at
45 acres of land. Always 1 plough.
> Meadow, 5 acres.
> 5 smallholders under them.

109 In ROCKLAND (St. Mary) 2 free men under the patronage of
Alnoth, 24 acres of land. Always 2 oxen.
> Meadow, 2 acres.

110 In the other SHOTESHAM 1 free man and 2 halves under the
patronage of Alnoth, at 40 acres.
> 2 smallholders.
> Meadow, 4 acres.
> Among them all 1 plough.

111 In YELVERTON 2 free men before 1066, 1½ under the patronage
of Alnoth and ½ under Alfred. Earl R(alph) held these when he
forfeited; later Godric (held them) in the King's hand; now
Aitard, Roger Bigot's man, holds a moiety of one. 15 acres. He
claims him back as part of the Bishop of Bayeux's Holding.
33 acres of land between the men.
> Always 2 smallholders.
> Always 1 plough;
> meadow, 3 acres.

⌐In porringelanda . ɪɪ . libi hŏes alnoth comdat de xɪɪɪ . ac
trǽ . Semp . ɪ . car̄ . ɪ . ac p̄ti.

⌐In ſcoteſſa . ɪ . lib hŏ de x . ac trǽ . tnc dim car̄ . p̄ 7 m̄ nichil.
Scoteſſam ual . t . r . e . xxx . ſoł . p̄ 7 m̄ . xx . ſoł . & om̄s iſti
libi hŏes ualent . xʟ . ſoł . ſ; t . r . e . n̄ erat in cenſu ſcoteſſa.
R . blond adcenſau . ⌐Inaietuna . ɪ . b̄euita Wiſlingehá
ten edric̄ . t . r . e . de ʟxxx . ac trǽ . Sep . ɪɪ . bord . Tnc̄ . ɪ.
car̄ in dn̄io . p̄ 7 m̄ dim . ɪɪɪɪ . ac̄ p̄ti.

⌐In kerkebei xɪɪ . hŏes ſequentes faldá edrici ʟxxx . ac̄
trǽ . 7 . ɪɪɪ . ac̄ p̄ti . Semp . ɪ . car̄ 7 dim . ⌐In rokelonda.

124 b

. ɪ . lib̄ hŏ edrici . t . r . e . comendat de xv . ac̄ trǽ . & ſub eo . v.
libi hŏes . de xxɪɪɪ . ac̄ trǽ . ɪɪɪ . ac̄ p̄ti . 7 ſemp dim car̄.

⌐Inſtoches . ɪɪ . ſoc̄ . edrici . xxx . ac̄ trǽ . 7 . ɪ . ac̄ p̄ti . ſemp dim
car̄ . ⌐Inſaiſelingahá . ɪ . ſoc̄ edrici com̄d . t . r . e . de xxx.
ac̄ tre . ɪ . ac̄ p̄ti . Semp dim car̄.

⌐In kerkebei . ɪ . lib hŏ edrici . t . r . e . xxx . ac̄ trǽ . 7 . ɪɪ . bor̄.
7 . ɪɪɪɪ . ac̄ p̄ti . Semp dim car̄ . ⌐In kerkebei . ɪ . lib hŏ.
edrici . t . r . e . de . vɪ . ac̄ . 7 ſemp . ɪɪ . bou

⌐In Wiſinlingahá . ɪ . lib̄ hŏ edrici com̄d . & in brabretuna
ɪɪɪ . 7 in rokelunda . ɪ . de . ɪɪɪɪ . 7 dim habuit edric̄ co
m̄dat̄ . t . r . e . 7 Ulketel de uno . 7 dim . 7 alured tantu
com̄d d dim . pq̄ W . rex coq̄ſiuit anglia & . R . tenuit
om̄s quando ſe foriſfec̄ . 7 p̄ Godric̄ in miniſteriu reg.
hoc teſtatur hundret . m̄ aitard de uals . 7 reuocat
ad feudu ep̄i baiocenſis . de tenetura aluredi anteceſ
ſoris ſui & hund defic̄ ei . q̄d n̄ p̄tin ad anteceſſorè
ſuu . Ten iſti oès xʟ . ac̄ trǽ . 7 . ɪɪɪ . ac̄ p̄ti . Tnc̄ . ɪɪ . car̄.
& p̄ . ɪɪ . m̄ . ɪ . & dim.

112 In PORINGLAND 2 free men under the patronage of Alnoth, at 13 acres of land.
> Always 1 plough;
> meadow, 1 acre.

113 In SHOTESHAM 1 free man, at 10 acres of land. Then ½ plough, later and now nothing.
Value of Shotesham before 1066, 30s; later and now 20s. Value of all these free men 40s but before 1066 Shotesham was not in the tribute but R(obert) Blunt made it so.

114 In (the land of) EATON Edric held 1 outlier, WHITLINGHAM, before 1066, at 80 acres of land.
> Always 2 smallholders.
> Then 1 plough in lordship, later and now ½.
> Meadow, 4 acres.

115 In KIRBY (Bedon) 12 men who seek Edric's fold, 80 acres of land.
> Meadow, 3 acres; always 1½ ploughs.

116 In ROCKLAND (St. Mary) 1 free man under the patronage of Edric   124 b before 1066, at 15 acres of land. Under him 5 free men, at 23 acres of land.
> Meadow, 3 acres; always ½ plough.

117 In STOKE (Holy Cross) 2 Freemen of Edric's, 30 acres of land.
> Meadow, 1 acre; always ½ plough.

118 In SAXLINGHAM 1 Freeman under the patronage of Edric before 1066, at 30 acres of land.
> Meadow, 1 acre; always ½ plough.

119 In KIRBY (Bedon) 1 free man of Edric before 1066, 30 acres of land.
> 2 smallholders.
> Meadow, 4 acres; always ½ plough.

In KIRBY (Bedon) 1 free man of Edric before 1066, at 6 acres. Always 2 oxen.

120 In WHITLINGHAM 1 free man under the patronage of Edric; in BRAMERTON 3; in ROCKLAND (St. Mary) 1. Edric had the patronage of 4½, Ulfketel of 1½ and Alfred had the patronage only of ½ after King William had conquered England. Also R(alph) held them all when he forfeited and later Godric (held) in the King's service. This the Hundred testify. Now Aitard of Vaux (holds them) and he claims them as part of the Bishop of Bayeux's Holding from the tenure of his predecessor Alfred. The Hundred does not support him because they did not belong to his predecessor. All these men hold 40 acres of land and 3 acres of meadow.
> Then 2 ploughs, later 2, now 1½.

In treus . I . ſoc ſtigandi archiepi . t . r . e . de . x . acr.
træ 7 dim . qñdo . R . ſe forefec . ten eu . m̃ aitardus
de uals reclamat ad feudu epi baiocenſis ab aluredo
anteceſſore ſuo cuj fuit comd̃ tantu p̃ qua rex . W.
uen in anglica tra in p̃tio . e . iſtoʒ.

/ In holueſtuna aitard̃ ſimilit ht̃ . I . dim lib hom̃.

125 a
VIII . ac træ . 7 dim ac p̃ti . & de VI . homibʒ integris . & de
VI . dimidijs quos aitard̃ reclamat ad feudu epi baiocſis
ual . t . r . e . x . ſol quando Godric recep̃ miſteriu xxx.
VI . ſol . m̃ aitard̃ ht̃ . XIII . ſol . 7 VIII . d̃.

/ Newotona teñ . I . liba femina ſub ſtigando . p̃ . I . car̃ træ.
Semp VIII . uiłł . 7 VIII . bord̃ . Semp . I . car in dñio.
Tñc . IIII . car hoū . p̃ . I . & dim . m̃ . II . car hoū . 7 XL.
ac p̃ti . m̃ . x . an̄ . Tñc . II . por . m̃ . III . 7 v . ou.

/ Intreus VI . ſoc . p̃tinentes iſti man de LVI ac . 7 . II . bor.
& v . ac p̃ti . 7 . I . mol . Semp . I . car & dim . Tñc ual
totu . xx . ſol . p̃ 7 m̃ . xxx . Hoc man fuit ad cenſu in
miniſteriu . G . p̃ . xxx . ſol . ſed . G . n̄ habuit eos . quia re
uocat ipſa reg addefenſore ht̃ . III . quar̃ in long 7 . IIII.
quar̃ in lat̃ . 7 VIII . d̃ de gelt.

/ Inſtokes XII . ac træ . teñ . I . lib ho . In kerkebei . IIII.
ac træ . hoc p̃tin& ad aietona / In ſaſilingaha . I . lib
ho heraldi comd̃ . t . r . e . de xxx . ac træ . Semp . III.
bord̃ . Tñc . I . car . in dñio . m̃ dim . 7 . I . ſoc . I . ac træ
hanc tram ſeruauit godric dapifer in manu regis
Sed tra n̄ reddit ei cenſu.

DĪM H̄ . HERSAM . / Radanahalla . teñ . Rada . I.
lib ho edrici comd̃ . t . r . e . II . car̃ træ . Tñc . xxx.
uiłł . p̃ 7 m̃ . x . Semp . VI . bord̃ . Tñc . IIII . ſer . p̃ . II.
7 m̃ . I . Semp . II . car in dñio . Tñc . VI . car hominū.
p̃ 7 m̃ . II . & dim . Tñc ſilua . LX . por . m̃ . xx . 7 VIII . ac p̃ti.

121 In TROWSE 1 Freeman of Archbishop Stigand's before 1066, at 10½ acres of land. When R(alph) forfeited, he held him; now Aitard of Vaux claims him as part of the Bishop of Bayeux's Holding by his predecessor Alfred under whose patronage only he was after King William came to England. He is in the valuation of those men.

122 In HOLVERSTON Aitard has likewise 1 half of a free man, 8 acres   125 a of land; meadow, ½ acre. Also with 6 whole men and 6 halves whom Aitard claims as part of the Bishop of Bayeux's Holding. Value before 1066 10s; when Godric took office 36s; now Aitard has 13s 8d.

123 1 free woman held NEWTON under Stigand, as 1 c. of land.
    Always 8 villagers; 8 smallholders.
    Always 1 plough in lordship. Then 3 men's ploughs, later 1½,
       now 2 men's ploughs.
    Meadow, 40 acres. Now 10 head of cattle. Then 2 pigs, now 3;
       5 sheep.

124 In TROWSE 6 Freemen who belong to this manor, at 56 acres.
    2 smallholders.
    Meadow, 5 acres; 1 mill.
    Always 1½ ploughs.
Value of the whole then 20s; later and now 30.
    This manor was at tribute in G(odric)'s (term of) office for 30s but G(odric) did not have them because she vouches the King as her warrantor. It has 3 furlongs in length and 4 furlongs in width, tax of 8d.

125 In STOKE (Holy Cross) 1 free man holds 12 acres of land.

126 In KIRBY (Bedon) 4 acres of land. This belongs to Eaton.

127 In SAXLINGHAM 1 free man under the patronage of Harold before 1066, at 30 acres of land.
    Always 3 smallholders.
    Then 1 plough in lordship, now ½.
    Also 1 Freeman, 1 acre of land. Godric the Steward had
      custody of this land in the King's hand, but the land does
      not pay tribute to him.

  EARSHAM Half-Hundred
128 Rada held REDENHALL. 1 free man under the patronage of Edric before 1066, 2 c. of land.
    Then 30 villagers, later and now 10; always 6 smallholders.
      Then 4 slaves, later 2, now 1.
    Always 2 ploughs in lordship. Then 6 men's ploughs, later and
      now 2½.
    Then woodland, 60 pigs, now 20. Meadow, 8 acres;

Semp . ɪ . moͭ . Semp . vɪ . aṅ . 7 xxx . por . xɪɪ . cap̅ . Tnͨ uaͭ
ʟx . foͭ . p̊ 7 m̅ . vɪɪɪ . liƀ . blanc . 7 hͭ . ɪ . leug & dim̅ in lon
go & dim̅ . 7 ɪɪɪ . pcas . in lato . Et de gelto . x . đ.

⌐ Inradanahalla . ɪɪ . liƀi hoͤes de . c . aͨ . Sep̅ . ɪ . car̅ . eps
W . calupniaͭ . xx aͨ . de iſtis . x . 7 hunđ teſtaͭ . & agneli
ten ʟxxx . aͨ.

⌐ In aldeƀga xv . liƀi hoͤes Rade 7 ulmari t . r . e . comͩ
đ ʟx . aͨ træ . Semp . ɪɪɪ . car̅ . 7 . ɪɪɪ . aͨ p̅ti . ⌐ Inſtereſtuna
xɪɪ . liƀi hoͤes ɪx rade comͩ . t . r . e . 7 . ɪ . Waſtret . 7 . ɪ.
ulmari 7 . ɪ . comunis aƀbi de ſco edmundo . 7 de eli . Int
oͤes . ʟx . aͨ træ . Sep̅ . ɪɪɪ . car̅ . xɪɪɪ . aͨ p̅ti.

⌐ Inredanahalla . xx . liƀi hoͤes rade comͩ . de ʟxxx . aͨ træ.
Iſti hoͤes tͨ uaͭ . ɪɪɪɪ . liƀ . m̅ . vɪɪɪ . R . comes ad cenſau p̊
iuo talleboſc . Semp . v . car̅ . 7 . ɪɪɪɪ . aͨ p̅ti.

In eadͤ . ɪ . liƀ hoͦ edrici comͩ . ɪ . car̅ træ . Semp . ɪɪ . uiłt.
7 vɪɪɪ . borđ . Tnͨ 7 p̊ . ɪɪ . car̅ in duͥo . m̅ . ɪ . Semp ɪɪ . car̅
hoů . Silua . xx . por . 7 . ɪɪɪ . aͨ p̅ti . Et ſub eo . v . liƀi hoͤes.
& dim̅ de xx . aͨ træ . Sep̅ . ɪɪ . car̅ . Tnͨ uaͭ . xx . foͭ.
tep̅r comitis R . reddñt hoͤes ſui 7 iudikello . xxx . foͭ.
ſ; ipſe erat quieͭ de aula . quia erat ancipitrari
comitis . p̊q R . ſe forisfeͨ & fuit in manu regis ſub . G.
ſ; nichil reddidit . & reclamat regeͤ defenſoͤre.

H̃ 7 dim̅ de fredrebruge . ⌐ In eaſtwninͤ . ɪɪ.
car̅ træ . tep̅r regis e . bereuita ineſparlea

always 1 mill. Always 6 head of cattle; 30 pigs; 12 goats.
Value then 60s; later and now £8 blanched.

It has 1½ leagues in length, ½ (league) and 3 perches in width; tax of 10d.

In REDENHALL 2 free men, at 100 acres. Always 1 plough. Bishop W(illiam) claims 20 acres; to 10 of these the Hundred also testifies. Agneli holds 80 acres.

129 In ALBURGH 15 free men under the patronage of Rada and Wulfmer before 1066, at 60 acres of land. Always 3 ploughs; meadow, 3 acres.

130 In STARSTON 12 free men; 9 under the patronage of Rada before 1066, 1 of Wihtred, 1 of Wulfmer, 1 common to the Abbot of St. Edmund and (to the Abbot) of Ely. Among them all 60 acres of land. Always 3 ploughs; meadow, 13 acres.

131 In REDENHALL 20 free men under the patronage of Rada, at 80 acres of land.
Value of these men then £4, now 8.
Earl R(alph) leased them out; later Ivo Tallboys.
Always 5 ploughs; meadow, 4 acres.

In the same 1 free man under the patronage of Edric, 1 c. of land.
Always 2 villagers; 8 smallholders.
Then and later 2 ploughs in lordship, now 1. Always 2 men's ploughs; woodland, 20 pigs; meadow, 3 acres.
Also under him 5½ free men, at 20 acres of land. Always 2 ploughs.
Value then 20s.

In the time of Earl R(alph) his men and Judichael paid 30s but he was exempt from the hall because he was the Earl's falconer; after R(alph) forfeited he was in the King's hand under G(odric) but he paid nothing and vouches the King his warrantor.

The Hundred and a Half of FREEBRIDGE
132 In EAST WINCH 2 c. of land. Before 1066 (it was) an outlier in (the lands of) Sporle.

126 a

p.i.7 m.femp.i.car houm. Quando Godric recep hoc man
inuen xxiiii.ou.7 ix por.7 m fimilit.7.i.pifc. Huic træ
jacent fep xiii.foc.liiii.ac træ.7 viii.ac pti.femp.i.car
& dim.7.i.fat.7 dim.7 x.ac pti. Hoc totu apptiatu.e.in
efparlai. Tota ht dim leu in lon.7.iiii.qr in lat.7 red
dit.viii.d.de xx.fot de gelto.

Wdetuna ten Goduin lib ho.t.r.e.tc.ii.car in dnio.p.
7 m.i. Tnc xxiiii.uilt.p 7 m.xv.fep dim car.7 ii.foc.
xxv.ac pti.tnc.xx.fot.p 7 m xiiii. hic jacent xxii.foc.
xii.ac træ dim car.qn recep.i.r.7.iiii.uac.7 x.porc.
& c.xx.ou.m fimit. Tnc uat.iiii.lib.p 7 m.ix lib.& xx
fot.de gerfuma. Tota ht dim leug in long 7 in lat.qui cuq ibi
teneat.& reddit xii.d de.xx.fot de gelto.

H.de Smetheduna In holm.ten.t.r.e.i.lib ho xl ac.7.iii.bor.
7.i.car.7 uat.x.fot.fcs.ben.foca.

WENELVNT.H. Stou ten Alfere.t.r.e.v.car in dnio.p 7 m.
.ii. Tnc 7 p xv.ii.uilt.m.xvi.Sep.ii.bord. Tnc 7 p.x.fer.m.
vii.xxx.ac pti.femp.v.car hou.filua.x.por.femp.i.mot.
fep.ii.an.7 xxviii.por.xl ou. In kateftuna.i.foc xl.ac.
foca in Saha.& tra jacet in Stuo 7 in cenfu. Huic manerio
jacent xxviiii.foc.iii.car træ 7 xxxvi.ac. Tnc uat.x.lib.
Qndo recep.xii.lib.7 xiii.fot.7.iiii.d.& Godric eu dedit
p xiii.lib.7 xiii.fot.7.iiii.d.7 xx.fot de gerfuma.quan
diu habebat foca.m pq amifit foca reddit.vii.lib.& fup
fochemanos quos amifit fnt.vii.lib.

Always 11 villagers.

Meadow, 24 acres.

Then 2 ploughs in lordship, later and now 1; always 1 men's
plough.

When Godric acquired this manor he found 24 sheep and 9 pigs, now the same. 1 fishery.

13 Freemen have always appertained to this land, 54 acres of land; meadow, 8 acres. Always 1½ ploughs; 1½ salt-houses; meadow, 10 acres.

All this is assessed in Sporle.

The whole has ½ league in length and 4 furlongs in width, of a 20s tax it pays 8d.

133 Godwin, a free man, held WOOTTON before 1066. Then 2 ploughs in lordship, later and now 1.

Then 24 villagers, later and now 15.

Always ½ plough.

Also 2 Freemen; meadow, 25 acres. Then 20 salt-houses, later and now 14.

22 Freemen appertain here. 12 acres of land; ½ plough.

When he acquired it 1 cob, 4 cows, 10 pigs and 120 sheep; now the same.

Value then £4; later and now £9, premium of 20s.

The whole has ½ league in length and in width, whoever holds there, of a 20s tax it pays 12d.

The Hundred of SMETHDON

134 In HOLME (next the Sea) 1 free man held 40 acres before 1066.

3 smallholders. 1 plough.

Value 10s. St. Benedict (has) the jurisdiction.

WAYLAND Hundred

135 Alfhere held STOW (Bedon) before 1066. 5 ploughs in lordship, later and now 2.

Then and later 17 villagers, now 16; always 2 smallholders.

Then and later 10 slaves, now 7.

Meadow, 30 acres. Always 5 men's ploughs; woodland, 10 pigs.

Always 1 mill. Always 2 head of cattle; 28 pigs; 40 sheep.

In CASTON 1 Freeman, 40 acres. The jurisdiction is in Saham (Toney). The land appertains in Stow (Bedon) and in its tribute.

29 Freemen appertain to this manor, 3 c. of land and 36 acres. Value then £10; when he acquired it £12 13s 4d; Godric gave it for £13 13s 4d and a premium of 20s as long as he had the jurisdiction; now after he lost jurisdiction it pays £7, and upon the Freemen whom he lost are £7.

126 b

Aluric lib ho . ii . car træ . femp . iiii . uilt . 7 . ii . bord . T . iiii . s.
xx . ac p̃ti . femp . ii . car in dñio . 7 . ii . car 7 dim hom . filua . c . porc.
7 . i . car poff& . ee . in dñio . fep . xii . animal . 7 xxiiii . por . 7
xxxvii . ou . xxx . iiii . cap̃ . & v . foc . de . ii . ac & dim . Tnc 7 p
ual . iiii . lib m̃ . iiii . lib blancas . 7 . iiii . fot . Huic manerio
jacebant . vi . foc ea die qua Rad forisfec qui reddebant xvi.
fot robto blundo . 7 m̃ fnt in Saham tefte . hund . Totu ht
. i . leug . 7 dim in longo 7 in lat & x d de gelto . 7 totu Stou
ht . ii . leug in long & dim in lat & de gelto . x . d . 7 . i . obolu.
& . i . ferding.

In Brecchles . ten . i . lib ho t . r . e . i . car træ . Tnc . iii . uilti.
p 7 m̃ . ii . femp . i . fer . iiii . ac p̃ti . Tnc . ii . car in dñio . p & m̃.
dim . femp . i . car hom . 7 . i . car 7 dim poff& . ee . Hoc e bere
uita de fparlea . & . e . inptio de Sparlea.

In Greftuna Lxxx . ac træ . ten . i . liba femina . t . r . e . fep
i . uilt . tnc . v . bord . fep . i . fer . vi . ac p̃ti . femp . i . car . in
d . filu . xxiiii . por . femp xii . por . 7 xi . ou . & hoc bere
wita & e apciatu in efparle.

Serpeham . H̄ . Bvcham tenuit Rad comes . t . r . e.
iii . car . træ . 7 m̃ . iiii . 7 dim . Tnc 7 p ix uilt . tc xxiiii.
m̃ xv . m̃ xxviii . bord . 7 tc xii . ac p̃ti . m̃ . xx . tc . i . car.
in dñio . p 7 m̃ . ii . femp . iii . car hom . Tnc filua . cxx . porc.
m̃ Lx . Hic jacent xxi . foc . ii . car træ . 7 x . ac p̃ti . 7 . i . bor.
femp . iii . car . filua . x . por . femp . iiii . animalia . xii . por.
7 Lxviii . ou . & xliii . foc . x . car træ Lx ac p̃ti . filu xxxx . por.

127 a

femp . xii . uilt . & xlvi . bor . Tnc xxiiii . car . p 7 m̃ xvi . 7
ii . mot . & inpdictis xliii . fochemanis habuer alij hoes
comdatione . f; rad eos oms addidit huic manerio tempr
regis Witti . Totu ual tc vi . lib & xiii . fot . 7 . iiii . d . & duos;
fextarios melt . p 7 m̃ . xxxii . lib blancas . 7 xiii . fot . & iiii
d . & xx . fot de gerfuma adnumeru . Totu ht . i . leu in lon
& . i . leug in lato . & xviiii . d de gelto.

136 Aelfric, a free man, held (Little) ELLINGHAM before 1066, 2 c. of   126 b
land.
    Always 4 villagers; 2 smallholders. Then 4 slaves.
    Meadow, 20 acres. Always 2 ploughs in lordship; 2½ men's
      ploughs; woodland, 100 pigs. 1 plough could be in lordship.
      Always 12 head of cattle; 24 pigs; 37 sheep; 34 goats.
    Also 5 Freemen at 2½ acres.
Value then and later £4; now £4 blanched 4s.
    6 Freemen appertained to this manor on the day that Ralph
forfeited who paid 16s to Robert Blunt. Now they are in (the
lands of) Saham (Toney), the Hundred testify.
    The whole of Stow (Bedon) has 2 leagues in length and ½ in
width, tax of 10¾d.

137 In BRECKLES 1 free man held 1 c. of land before 1066.
    Then 3 villagers, later and now 2; always 1 slave.
    Meadow, 4 acres. Then 2 ploughs in lordship, later and now ½;
      always 1 men's plough; 1½ ploughs could be there.
This is an outlier of Sporle and is in the valuation of Sporle.

138 In GRISTON 1 free woman held 80 acres of land before 1066.
    Always 1 villager. Then 5 smallholders; always 1 slave.
    Meadow, 6 acres. Always 1 plough in lordship; woodland,
      24 pigs. Always 12 pigs; 11 sheep.
This outlier is also assessed in Sporle.

SHROPHAM Hundred
139 Earl Ralph held BUCKENHAM before 1066, 3 c. of land, now 4½.
    Then and later 9 villagers. Then 24, now 15, now 28
      smallholders.
    Then meadow, 12 acres, now 20. Then 1 plough in lordship,
      later and now 2; always 3 men's ploughs. Then woodland,
      120 pigs, now 60.
    21 Freemen appertain here, 2 c. of land; meadow, 10 acres.
    1 smallholder. Always 3 ploughs; woodland, 10 pigs.
    Always 4 head of cattle; 12 pigs; 68 sheep.
    Also 43 Freemen, 10 c. of land; meadow, 60 acres; woodland,
      40 pigs. Always 12 villagers; 46 smallholders. Then 24   127 a
      ploughs, later and now 16. 2 mills. Other men had the
      patronage of the said 43 Freemen but Ralph added all of
      them to this manor after 1066.
Value of the whole then £6 13s 4d and 2 sesters of honey; later
and now £32 blanched 13s 4d, premium of 20s.
    The whole has 1 league in length and 1 league in width, tax
of 19d.

Effebei tenuit Rađ . t . r . e . ı . cař trǽ . femp . ıı . uiłł . 7 . ı . bor.
tńc . ıııı . fer . p̄ 7 m̊ . ıı . 7 ııı . ać p̄ti . femp . ı . cař in dńio . 7 . ıı.
boū houm . femp vı . oū . Semp̄ ual& . xx . fol . blancas.
Rudham . teń . x . lib̄ ho . t . r . e . fub eroldo . ı . cař trǽ . 7 . ıııı.
uiłł . 7 . ıı . ać p̄ti . femp . ı . cař in dńio . femp dim̄ cař homū.
& xıııı . oū . & tc̄ ual . xx . fol . p̄ 7 m̊ . x . fol . blanc̄.

Culuerteftuna tenuit lib̄ ho . t . r . e . fubftigando . ı . cař
& dim̄ trǽ . femp . v . uiłł . 7 . ı . fer . & . v . ać p̄ti tc̄ in dńio
ıı . cař . p̄ 7 m̊ . ı . bos . Tńc . ı . cař houm . p̄ nichil m̊ dim̄.
femp . ı . mol̄ . 7 . ı . pifc̄ . femp̄ ual xl fol . Totū ht̄ . ıı . leug.
in lon̄ . & in lat . quicūq ibi teneat & vıı . đ . de gelto.
Totū hunđ reddit . xl & ptin& ad mifteriū Godrıcı.

Gillecros . H̄ . Cheninkehala tenuit Rex . E . v . cař trǽ
femp xxıııı . uiłł . 7 xxıııı . bor . 7 xıı . ać p̄ti . 7 . ı . mol̄ . filu.
ccc . por . Tńc . ı . cař in dńio . p̄ 7 m̊ . ıı . tńc xıı . cař hom̄
p̄ 7 m̊ xı . & . ı . poff& reftaurari . femp̄ . ı . ř . & xıı . foc̄.
c . ać trǽ . 7 xvııı . ać p̄ti . 7 . ıı . mol̄ . femp . ııı . cař . & . ı.
127 b
lib̄ ho . ı . cař trǽ . 7 . ıı . uiłł . 7 . ııı . borđ . filua xxıııı . porc̄.
fep . ı . cař . & dim̄ cař hom̄ . & herlinga . ı . bereuuita fep
jac& huic manerio . ı . cař tre . 7 . ııı . uiłł . 7 . ıııı . bor.
& v . ać p̄ti . Tńc . ı . cař in dńio & poff& reftaurari . p̄ dim̄
& . ııı . cař hom̄ . m̊ . ıı . & tcia poff& reftaurari . Totū uale
bat tēpr̄ . r . e . x . lib̄ . 7 v . fextarios mellis . p̄ . xxvı . lib̄.
m̊ xxıııı . lib̄ blancas . 7 vı . lib̄ ad numerū . & gerfuma.
Totū Chemkehala ht̄ . ı . leug 7 dim̄ in long 7 dim̄ in lato.
& . xxv . đ . de gelto.

127 a, b

140 Ralph held ASHBY before 1066, 1 c. of land.
    Always 2 villagers; 1 smallholder. Then 4 slaves, later and now 2.
    Meadow, 3 acres. Always 1 plough in lordship; the men, 2 oxen.
    Always 6 sheep.
Value always 20s blanched.

141 1 free man held ROUDHAM before 1066 under Harold, 1 c. of land.
    4 villagers.
    Meadow, 2 acres. Always 1 plough in lordship; always ½ men's
        plough; 14 sheep.
Value then 20s; later and now 10s blanched.

142 A free man held KILVERSTONE before 1066 under Stigand, 1½ c.
of land.
    Always 5 villagers; 1 slave.
    Meadow, 5 acres. Then 2 ploughs in lordship, later and now
        1 ox. Then 1 men's plough, later nothing, now ½. Always
        1 mill; 1 fishery.
Value always 40s.
    The whole has 2 leagues in length and in width, whoever holds
there, tax of 7d. The whole Hundred pays 40(s). It belongs to
Godric's office.

GUILTCROSS Hundred
143 King Edward held KENNINGHALL, 5 c. of land.
    Always 24 villagers; 24 smallholders.
    Meadow, 12 acres; 1 mill; woodland, 300 pigs. Then 1 plough
        in lordship, later and now 2. Then 12 men's ploughs, later
        and now 11, and 1 could be restored. Always 1 cob.
    Also 12 Freemen, 100 acres of land; meadow, 18 acres. 2 mills;
        always 3 ploughs.
    Also 1 free man, 1 c. of land.   127 b
    2 villagers; 3 smallholders.
    Woodland, 24 pigs. Always 1 plough; ½ men's plough.

Also 1 outlier, HARLING, has always appertained to this manor,
1 c. of land.
    3 villagers; 4 smallholders.
    Meadow, 5 acres. Then 1 plough in lordship, and it could be
        restored; later ½ (plough). 3 men's ploughs, now 2, and the
        third could be restored.
Value of the whole before 1066 £10 and 5 sesters of honey; later
£26; now £24 blanched and £6 at face value, also a premium.
    The whole of Kenninghall has 1½ leagues in length and ½ in
width, tax of 25d.

⌐Cuidenham tenuit Godinc lib hŏ.de q̃ abbas s̃ci eadmun
di hab cm̃d tantũ.t.r.e.i.car træ.semp.ii.uill̃.7.ii.bor.
7.iii.ac p̃ti.7.i.mol̃.Tnc dim car̃ in dñio.p̃ & m̃.i.semp
hominũ.ii.bou.sep.i.r̃.7 vi.porc.xvi.ou.Tnc ual xv.sol.
p̃ 7 m̃.xxx.Hanc t̃ram tenuit idẽ Godric tres annos
de abb̃e.pq̃ rex.W.uenit.Hanc eandẽ abstulit ei God
uin auund rad comitis injuste.Soca.t.r.e.in ᴋening
—hehala regis.Totũ ht̃.v.quar̃ in lon.7.iiii.quar̃ in lat̃
& xvii.d̃.7.i.ferding.de gelto.

⌐Gerboldesh̃a ten.i.lib hŏ Aluric.t.r.e.p̃ m̃.ii.car̃ træ
semp.iii.bord.7.i.ser.7.iiii.ac p̃ti.tnc.ii.car̃ in dñio.
p̃ 7 m̃.i.car̃ & dim.& dim poss̃& restaurari.Tnc dim
7 p̃.7 m̃ simil̃.7 viii.por.&.iii.soc.xvi.ac træ.semp
dim car̃.Tnc ual xxx.sol̃.p̃ 7 m̃.xL.

⌐In Gatesthorp.i.lib hŏ.t.r.e.i.car̃ tre tnc.vi.uill̃.
128 a
m̃.viii.semp.v.bor.7.ii.ser.7 viii.ac p̃ti.semp.i.car̃ in dñio.
7.ii.car̃ hom̃.& v.soc.xx.ac træ.semp.i.car̃.filua.xii.por.
tc ual.xx.sol̃.m̃ xL.Tot̃ hundret reddit.xx.& tota soca in
inkeninghehala.totũ Gatesthor.ht̃ dim leũ in lon.& dim
in lato.7 vii.d̃ de gelto.

H̃ DE GALGOV.In bũmeha ten Vlf.t.r.e.iii.car̃ træ
Tnc xx.bord.m̃ xvi.Tnc.xii.ser.m̃.viii.Tnc.iii.car̃.
in dñio.p̃ 7 m̃.ii.Tnc homũ.i.car̃.p̃ 7 m̃ nichil̃.Silua.ad.iiii.
por.ii.mol̃ & dim.Tnc vii.r̃.7 m̃.7 xL por.7 b.c.oues.i.
salina.Est.i.beruita.huic man de.i.car̃ træ.Tnc.i.car̃.p̃
null̃.m̃.i.7 Alia beruita.de.i.car̃ træ.Tnc.i.car̃.7 p̃ null̃.

127 b, 128 a

144 Goding, a free man, held QUIDENHAM of whom the Abbot of St.
Edmund had patronage only before 1066, 1 c. of land.
   Always 2 villagers; 2 smallholders.
   Meadow, 3 acres. 1 mill. Then ½ plough in lordship, later and
      now 1; the men, always 2 oxen. Always 1 cob; 6 pigs;
      16 sheep.
Value then 15s; later and now 30.
   The same Godric held this land (for) 3 years from the Abbot
after King William came. Godwin, Earl Ralph's uncle, took this
away from him unjustly. Jurisdiction before 1066 (was) in
Kenninghall (a manor) of the King. The whole has 5 furlongs in
length and 4 furlongs in width, tax of 17¼d.

145 Aelfric, 1 free man, held GARBOLDISHAM before 1066, as a manor,
2 c. of land.
   Always 3 smallholders; 1 slave.
   Meadow, 4 acres. Then 2 ploughs in lordship, later and now
      1½ ploughs, and ½ could be restored. Then ½ [?men's
      plough], later and now the same. 8 pigs.
   Also 3 Freemen, 16 acres of land; always ½ plough.
Value then 30s; later and now 40.

146 In GASTHORPE 1 free man before 1066, 1 c. of land.
   Then 6 villagers, now 8. Always 5 smallholders; 2 slaves.   128 a
   Meadow, 8 acres. Always 1 plough in lordship; 2 men's ploughs.
   Also 5 Freemen, 20 acres of land. Always 1 plough; woodland,
      12 pigs.
Value then 20s; now 40.
   The whole Hundred pays 20[s] and the whole jurisdiction (is)
in Kenninghall. The whole of Gasthorpe has ½ league in length
and ½ in width, tax of 7d.

   The Hundred of GALLOW
147 In BURNHAM (Overy) Ulf held 3 c. of land before 1066.
   Then 20 smallholders, now 16. Then 12 slaves, now 8.
   Then 3 ploughs in lordship, later and now 2. Then 1 men's
      plough, later and now nothing.
   Woodland for 4 pigs; 2½ mills. Then 7 cobs; 40 pigs; 600
      sheep; 1 salt-house.
There is 1 outlier (belonging) to this manor, at 1 c. of land. Then
1 plough, later nothing, now 1.
Also another outlier, at 1 c. of land. Then 1 plough, later nothing,

m̃ . I . Huic man̂ ptinent . xxx . foc̃ . de . I . car̂ træ . Tñc . II . car̂ .
7 p̃ null . m̃ . I . Totu hoc ualuit . t . r . e . vIII . lib̃ . 7 p̃ qñ Ra
dulf comes eū tenuit . xx . III . lib̃ . 7 xIII . fol̃ . 7 . IIII . d̃ . m̃ . xx . lib̃ .
ad numerū . 7 in eade uilla . I . lib̃ hõ Ketel . de xx . ac̃ . 7 alia . lib̃
hõ . Oia . de xxx . ac̃ .

⌈ H̃ . de holt . In merſtuna . I . lib̃ hõ de xxx . ac̃ tre . 7 . I . bor .
& dim̃ car̂ . 7 ual̃ . II . oras . ipfe fuit hõ Guer . t . r . e . 7 jac& in
ſtiuekeia .

Erpingehã NORTH . H̃ . ⌈ In bethea teñ feiard̃ bar . t . r . e .
I . lib̃u hoẽm . com . R . addidit adeileſfam . xxx . ac̃ træ . Sep̃
I . uilt ptinens in eileſfa . I . bord̃ . uni ac̃ . 7 . I . foc̃ . I . ac̃ . Sep̃
I . car̂ . ap̃tiati ſñt in eileſfa . De NORTERPINGEHÃ H̃ . ht rex
foca 7 faca p̃t tram feiardi . bar .

H̃ Waleſfam . Waleſa tenuit elflet . I . lib̃a femina . t . r . e .

128 b
IIII . car̂ træ . Semp . IIII . uilt . tñc xvIII . bord̃ . p̃ 7 m̃ . xxIII . Semp
II . fer . & . II . car̂ in dñio . tc̃ . IIII . car̂ hoũm . p̃ & m̃ . II . xL . ac̃
p̃ti . Silua xv . porc̃ . Semp . II . añ . 7 xvIII . porc̃ . 7 xx . oũ . & xxII .
foc̃ de Lxxx ac̃ træ 7 x . ac̃ p̃ti . tc̃ . v . car̂ . p̃ 7 m̃ . IIII . Iſti adja
c& . I . beruiuita modetuna . I . car̂ træ . Semp . II . bord̃ . & I . car̂ .
& . I . ac̃ p̃ti . & . III . foc̃ de xvIII . ac̃ træ . & dim̃ car̂ . Hoc totũ
tñc ual̃ . c . fol̃ . 7 p̃ xI . lib̃ . 7 m̃ . xII . lib̃ . 7 xIII . fol̃ . 7 . IIII . den .
blanc̃ . 7 xx . fol de gerſuma adcõpot . & ht . I . leu in longo .

7 . I . in lato . & de gelto . IIII . fol .

now 1.

    30 Freemen belong to this manor, at 1 c. of land. Then 2
        ploughs, later nothing, now 1.

Value of all this before 1066 £8; later when Earl Ralph held it
£23 13s 4d; now £20 at face value.

    In the same village a free man, Ketel, at 20 acres. Also another
(female) free man, Oia, at 30 acres.

The Hundred of HOLT

148 In MORSTON 1 free man, at 30 acres of land.

    1 smallholder. ½ plough.

Value 2 orae.

    He was Gyrth's man before 1066. It lies in (the lands of)
Stiffkey.

NORTH ERPINGHAM Hundred

149 In (East) BECKHAM Siward Bairn held 1 free man before 1066.
Earl Ralph added (him) to Aylsham. 30 acres of land.

    Always 1 villager appertaining in Aylsham; 1 smallholder, of
        1 acre.

    Also 1 Freeman, 1 acre; always 1 plough.

They are assessed in Aylsham. The King has the full jurisdiction
of North Erpingham Hundred except for the land of Siward Bairn.

WALSHAM Hundred

150 Alflæd, a free woman, held WALSHAM before 1066, 4 c. of land.   128 b

    Always 4 villagers. Then 18 smallholders, later and now 23;
        always 2 slaves.

    2 ploughs in lordship. Then 4 men's ploughs, later and now 2.

    Meadow, 40 acres; woodland, 15 pigs. Always 2 head of cattle;
        18 pigs; 20 sheep.

    Also 22 Freemen, at 80 acres of land; meadow, 10 acres. Then
        5 ploughs, later and now 4.

1 outlier, MOULTON (St. Mary), is attached to this (manor), 1 c. of
land.

    Always 2 smallholders.

    1 plough.

    Meadow, 1 acre.

    Also 3 Freemen, at 18 acres of land; ½ plough.

Value of all this then 100s; later £11; now £12 13s 4d blanched,
and premium of 20s by reckoning.

    It has 1 league in length and 1 in width, tax of 4s.

v . car træ . Sep xxiii . uilł . tñc xxxviii . borđ . p̄ . xxx . m̄.

xxxviii . tñc . iii . ſer . Sep . iii . car m̄ dñio . tc 7 p̄ . x . car hou.

m̄ . xii . L . ač . & dim p̄ti . Silua ad xL . por . p̄ & m̄ . i . moł . Sep

iii . r̄ . 7 . ii . an . & xx . porč . c . 7 xx . ou . p̄ xi . uaſa apũ . m̄ . xv.

& . iiii . ſoč . đ dim car træ . Semp . i . car . iiii . ač p̄ti . tc uał

viii . lib . & p̄ xii . m̄ xiiii . lib . & xiii . ſol . 7 . iiii . đ . & de iſtis

ſñt . Liii . ſol . ad copot 7 reddit alias blancas . & m̄t . i . leug

in longo . 7 . i . in lato . & de gelto . ii . ſol.

⌐Halfriate teñ . R . comes . t . r . e . vi . car træ . Semp . vi . uiłł.

tc 7 p̄ xLvi . borđ . m̄ . L . tñc . iii . ſer . tñc . iiii . car m̄ dñio.

p̄ 7 m̄ . iii . tñc vii . car hou . p̄ 7 m̄ ix . xxx . ač p̄ti . 7 . i . ſalm̄.

Sep . ii . r̄ . 7 vii . animał . 7 xiii . por . ccLx ou . & xiii . ſoč.

de dim car træ . 7 xv . ač tre . Sep . ii . car . & dim . vi . ač p̄ti.

Tñc uał viii . lib . p̄ ix . 7 m̄ x . lib . blanč . & xL ſol de cſuet.

adnum̄ . 7 xx . ſol . de gers . & m̄t . i . leug m̄ longo . 7 . i . m̄

lato . & de gelto . ii . ſol 7 p̄t ou p̄ſcript . p̄tm̄ huic man̄ . ь . cc.

129 a

ou . & redđ . c . ſol.

⌐In fiſcele teñ . R . comes ueť . t . r . e . xxv ſoč . i . car træ . xxx

ač p̄ti . un exiſtis ÷ de ſoca reg nom̄æ vfward . Sep iii . car.

& dim . & m̄t viii . quar in long . & v . in lat . & de gelt . x . đ.

⌐In uptune . xxvii . ſoč . i . car træ . & dim . 7 xxxv . ač . p̄ti.

Semp . iii . car . m̄t . i . leu in long . & . i . in lato . & de gelto . ii . ſol.

Sup hos om̄s habuit Rex 7 comes . ſoca . 7 ſaca p̄t vii . quos

m̄t com̄d in ſoca . & int has duas fiſcele 7 optune xxv . ſoč.

Lx . ač træ . 7 xiii . ač p̄ti . Semp dim car in optune . i . ſoč . xii . ač.

uał . ii . ſol . De iſtis . e . ſoca in hunđ.

151 Earl R(alph) the Elder held ACLE before 1066, 5 c. of land.
> Always 23 villagers. Then 38 smallholders, later 30, now 38.
> Then 3 slaves.
> Always 3 ploughs in lordship. Then and later 10 men's ploughs,
> now 12.
> Meadow, 50½ acres; woodland for 40 pigs; later and now 1 mill.
> Always 3 cobs; 2 head of cattle; 20 pigs; 120 sheep. Later
> 11 beehives, now 15.
> Also 4 Freemen, at ½ c. of land. Always 1 plough; meadow,
> 4 acres.

Value then £8; later 12; now £14 13s 4d; 53s of this is by
reckoning and it pays the rest blanched.
> It has 1 league in length and 1 in width, tax of 2s.

152 Earl R(alph) held HALVERGATE before 1066, 6 c. of land.
> Always 6 villagers. Then and later 46 smallholders, now 50.
> Then 3 slaves.
> Then 4 ploughs in lordship, later and now 3. Then 7 men's
> ploughs, later and now 9.
> Meadow, 30 acres; 1 salt-house. Always 2 cobs; 7 head of
> cattle; 13 pigs; 260 sheep.
> Also 13 Freemen, at ½ c. of land and 15 acres of land. Always
> 2½ ploughs; meadow, 6 acres.

Value then £8; later 9; now £10 blanched and 40s in customary
dues at face value, premium of 20s.
> It has 1 league in length and 1 in width, tax of 2s. Besides the
sheep mentioned above, 700 sheep belong to this manor. It   129 a
pays 100s.

153 In FISHLEY Earl R(alph) the Elder held 25 Freemen before 1066,
1 c. of land; meadow, 30 acres. One of these, Wulfward by name,
is of the King's jurisdiction. Always 3½ ploughs.
> It has 8 furlongs in length and 5 in width, tax of 10d.

154 In UPTON 27 Freemen, 1½ c. of land; meadow, 35 acres. Always
3 ploughs.
> It has 1 league in length and 1 in width, tax of 2s. The King
and the Earl had the full jurisdiction over all these except 7
whom (the Earl) had in patronage in the jurisdiction.
> Between these 2 (villages), Fishley and Upton, 25 Freemen,
> 60 acres of land; meadow, 13 acres. Always ½ plough in Upton.
> 1 Freeman, 12 acres.

Value 2s. The jurisdiction of these is in the Hundred.

In Waleſſa . I . lib hō gerti . t . r . e . I . car træ . Semp . III . borđ.
& dim car . xx . ac p̃ti . Silua . vII . porc . dim ſalina . & xvII . ſoc.
I . car træ . 7 . I . car & dim . xII . ac p̃ti . & in eadē . I . lib hō de
xxx . ac træ . 7 . II . bor . & ipſe 7 hōes h̃t . I . car . 7 dim . ſemp
& vIII . ac p̃ti . & ſub eo s̃ . vI . ſoc . de vI . ac træ . III . ac p̃ti . tnc
. I . car . p̃ 9 7 m̃ . dim . Et in eadē xI ſoc . de . xvI . ac træ . II . ac p̃ti.
& ſemp . I . car.

In pankesford . III . ſoc . I . car træ . xIx . ac . 7 xII . ac p̃ti . 7 Ix . borđ
tnc . I . car . p̃ 9 & m̃ . II . In randuorda . vII . ſoc . L . ac træ . 7 vIII . ac.
p̃ti . 7 ſemp . I . car . De iſtis . e . ſoca in hunđ . 7 pankesforda 7 randu
orda h̃t . I . leug in longo . 7 dim in lato . & de gelto . xvI . đ.

In baſtuic . I . ſoc . de xxvII . ac træ . 7 . III . ac p̃ti . Semp . I . car.

In hemelingetun . vI . ſoc . de . xxx . ac træ . II . ac p̃ti . Semp . II . car.
In eadē . II . ſoc . 7 I . hoɼ i̇ ſoca hunđ . dim car træ . 7 . I . borđ.
vI . ac p̃ti . & hn̄t ſub eis . vII . ſoc . de xx ac træ . I . ac p̃ti . Semp
129 b
. I . car . & dim int oēs . & h̃t . I . leug in long . 7 dim in latituđ.
& đ gelto . xvI . đ . Inmodetuna . x . ſoc . II . car . træ . 7 . v . borđ.
xx . ac p̃ti . & ſemp . IIII . car . & h̃t . vIII . quar . in longo . & v.
in lato . & de gelto . xv . đ . 7 obol.

In Wichhatun . I . ſoc . I . car træ . 7 . v . borđ . 7 . IIII . ac p̃ti . ſemp
I . car . & h̃t . vI . quar . in long . 7 v . in lato . & de gelto . x . đ . 7 obl.
rex hab ſoca . e . & R . quando ſe forisfec̃.

In redahā . III . ſoc . de xL ac tre . 7 vII . borđ . 7 vI . ac p̃ti . 7 ſub
eis . vI . ſoc . de xx . ac træ & int oms . I . car ſemp.

155 In (South) WALSHAM 1 free man of Gyrth's before 1066, 1 c. of
land.
Always 3 smallholders. ½ plough.
Meadow, 20 acres; woodland, 7 pigs; ½ salt-house.
Also 17 Freemen, 1 c. of land. 1½ ploughs; meadow, 12 acres.
Also in the same (village) 1 free man, at 30 acres of land.
2 smallholders. He and the men have always had 1½ ploughs.
Meadow, 8 acres.
Also under him there are 6 Freemen, at 6 acres of land;
meadow, 3 acres. Then 1 plough, later and now ½.
Also in the same 11 Freemen, at 16 acres of land; meadow, 2
acres. Always 1 plough.

156 In PANXWORTH 3 Freemen, 1 c. of land and 19 acres; meadow,
12 acres.
9 smallholders.
Then 1 plough, later and now 2.

157 In RANWORTH 7 Freemen, 50 acres of land; meadow, 8 acres.
Always 1 plough. The jurisdiction of these is in the Hundred.
Panxworth and Ranworth have 1 league in length and ½ in width,
tax of 16d.

158 In (Wood)BASTWICK 1 Freeman, at 27 acres of land; meadow, 3
acres. Always 1 plough.

159 In HEMBLINGTON 6 Freemen, at 30 acres of land; meadow, 2 acres.
Always 2 ploughs.
In the same 2 Freemen. One of these is in the Hundred's
jurisdiction, ½ c. of land.
1 smallholder. Meadow, 6 acres.
Also they have under them 7 Freemen, at 20 acres of land;
meadow, 1 acre. Always 1½ ploughs among them all.   129 b
It has 1 league in length and ½ in width, tax of 16d.

160 In MOULTON (St. Mary) 10 Freemen, 2 c. of land.
5 smallholders.
Meadow, 20 acres; always 4 ploughs.
It has 8 furlongs in length and 5 in width; tax of 15½d.

161 In WICKHAMPTON 1 Freeman, 1 c. of land.
5 smallholders.
Meadow, 4 acres; always 1 plough.
It has 6 furlongs in length and 5 in width, tax of 10½d.
King Edward had the jurisdiction, and R(alph) when he forfeited.

162 In REEDHAM 3 Freemen, at 40 acres of land.
7 smallholders.
Meadow, 6 acres.
Under them 6 Freemen, at 20 acres of land. Between them all
1 plough always.

Inmodetuna . VII . libi hoes . In Wichatuna . I . foc . de LVI . ac trae.
& hñt . II . car . IIII . ac pti . & fñt in foca hundret . & isti oms
cu aliis qui fñt in alio hund redd . VIII . lib . blanc . 7 c . fot
de confuet ad numer 7 xx . fot de gerfuma . Sup oms istos
ḍ falda comitis requirebant habebat comes foca 7 faca.
fup alios oms . Rex 7 comes.

FLEC West . H̃. ⌐ In martha . I . buita . xxx . ac trae . 7 ptin&
in castra . & . III . foc de xv . ac trae . 7 . III . ac pti . ⌐ & in burc . xx.
acr . apptiatu ÷ totu in castra . ⌐ In clepesbe . I . lib ho de . IIII . ac
& dim trae . ⌐ In Rotholfuesbei . I . lib ho . de xv . ac trae . In Win
tretuna . I . lib ho . x . ac trae . apptiatu ÷ cum libis hoib; in
Waleffam.

DIM HUNDRET DE dice . ⌐ Wineferthinc ten algar
lib ho heroldi . t . r . e . p m̃ . VI . car tre . Sep VIII . uilt . 7
femp xx . bord . Tnc 7 p . IIII . fer . m̃ . II . Semp . II . car in dnio
& . IIII . car houm . Tnc filua . cc . L . por . p 7 m̃ . cc . 7 IX . ac pti.

130 a

Semp . II . equi in aula . 7 VI . añ . Sep XIIII . porc . 7 XIIII . cap.
& in eade . v . libi hoes algari comdati tantu . t . r . e . de XL . ac.
Semp . I . car . & . I . ac pti.
⌐ In borftuna . IIII . libi hoes algari . t . r . e . comdati tantu de
XL ac de trae &. I . bor . Semp . I . car . & . III . ac pti.
⌐ In gerfinga t . r . e . VIII libi hoes algari comd tantu . de . LX . ac
trae 7 IIII . bor fep . Tnc . III . car inf oes . p 7 m̃ . I . & dim . 7 . II.
ac pti . ⌐ In fimplinga . I . integer lib ho edrici . t . r . e . de
XII . ac trae . Sep . I . car . In eade . II . foc . d xvi . ac tre . fep dim car.
hoc calupniat fcs . e . 7 Hundret testat . f; R . com tenebat
qñdo fe forisfec . De his calupniat . fcs e . XIIII . ac .

163 In MOULTON (St. Mary) 7 free men. In WICKHAMPTON 1 Freeman, at 56 acres of land. They have 2 ploughs. Meadow, 4 acres. They are in the Hundred's jurisdiction.

All these with others who are in another Hundred pay £8 blanched, 100s in customary dues at face value, premium 20s.

The Earl had the full jurisdiction over all those who sought the Earl's fold; the King and the Earl (had it) over all the others.

WEST FLEGG Hundred

164 In MARTHAM, 1 outlier, 30 acres of land. It belongs in Caister.

Also 3 Freemen, at 15 acres of land; meadow, 3 acres.

165 In BURGH (St. Margaret) 20 acres. The whole is assessed in Caister.

166 In CLIPPESBY 1 free man, at 4½ acres of land.

167 In ROLLESBY 1 free man, at 15 acres of land.

168 In WINTERTON 1 free man, 10 acres of land. He is assessed with the free men in (South) Walsham.

The Half-Hundred of DISS

169 Algar, Harold's free man, held WINFARTHING, as a manor before 1066, 6 c. of land.

Always 8 villagers; always 20 smallholders. Then and later 4 slaves, now 2.

Always 2 ploughs in lordship; 4 men's ploughs.

Then woodland 250 pigs, later and now 200. Meadow, 9 acres.
    Always 2 horses at the hall; 6 head of cattle. Always 14   130 a
    pigs; 14 goats.

Also in the same 5 free men under the patronage only of Algar before 1066, at 40 acres. Always 1 plough; meadow, 1 acre.

170 In BURSTON 4 free men under the patronage only of Algar before 1066, at 40 acres of land.

1 smallholder.

Always 1 plough; meadow, 3 acres.

171 In GISSING 8 free men under the patronage only of Algar before 1066, at 60 acres of land.

Always 4 smallholders.

Then 3 ploughs between them all, later and now 1½.

Meadow, 2 acres.

172 In SHIMPLING 1 whole free man of Edric's before 1066, at 12 acres of land. Always 1 plough.

In the same 2 Freemen, at 16 acres of land; always ½ plough.

St. E(dmund) claims this and the Hundred testifies to it but Earl R(alph) held it when he forfeited. Of these St. E(dmund) claims 14 acres.

falla . ii . liɓi hões algari comᷠ cũ tra . xxxv . aꝯ́ træ . 7
i . aꝯ́ p̃ti . Silua . iiii . porꝭ . Sẽp . i . car̃.

⌐ In fceluagra . i . uilt . xv . aꝯ́ træ . Semp dim car̃ . 7 . ii . borᵭ.
Silua . v . porꝭ . 7 . ii . aꝯ́ p̃ti . Tñc uat Wineferthinc . xl.
fot . p̃ 7 m̃ viii . liɓ . 7 . iii . fot . 7 . iiii . ᵭ . blanꝯ́ . & iſti oms
liɓi cũ foꝯ́ qno G . recep̃ . 7 m̃ reddñt . vii . liɓ . f; amplı
ñ poffñt redᵭ tantũ . Wineferthinc ht́ . i . leug in longo.
& dim in lato . & de gelto . ix . ᵭ.

⌐ Ferfeuella teñ alsı tegñ regis . e . p . ii . car̃ træ . Sẽp . v.
bor . Tñc 7 p̃ . iii . fer . m̃ . i . Semp . ii . car̃ in dñio . Tñc
. i . car̃ 7 dim hou . p̃ 7 m̃ . i . ⌐ In borſtuna . i . beruiuita ᵭ.
i . car̃ træ ptinens in ferfeuella . femp . ii . uilt . 7 . i . bor.

130 b

Tñc dim car̃ in dñio p̃ nichil . m̃ . dim.

⌐ In ferfeuella xiii . foꝯ́ lx aꝯ́ træ . Semp . iii . car̃ . ⌐ In eadem
iii . liɓi hões alfi . t . r . e . lxxx . aꝯ́ træ . 7 . iii . borᵭ . Tñc 7 p̃
iii . car̃ . m̃ . i . & dim.

⌐ In borſtuna . xi . liɓi hões alfi . t . r . e . de xxx . aꝯ́ træ . Sẽp
. i . car̃ . 7 . i aꝯ́ p̃ti . ⌐ In brefingahã . vii . liɓi hões alfi comᵭ.
de xxx . aꝯ́ træ . Tñc . iii . car̃ p̃ & m̃ . ii . Silua . vi . porꝭ.
7 . ii . aꝯ́ p̃ti . Ferfeuella cũ beruiuita . 7 borſtuna . Tñc uat
lx fot . p̃ vii . liɓ . 7 vi . fot . 7 viii . ᵭ . inꞇ cenfu 7 cᷓfueꞇ.
m̃ uat xii . liɓ . 7 vi . fot . & viii . blanꝯ́ . & de his xii . liɓ
dat liɓi hoes . c . fot . 7 vi . 7 vii . ᵭ . ht́ ferfeuella . viii . q̃r̃
in long̃ . 7 . iiii . in lat̃ . & de gelto . vii . ᵭ . Borſtuna hꞇ
viii . q̃r̃ in longo . 7 . iiii . in lato . & de gelto . xii . ᵭ.

⌐ In Simplinga . i . dim liɓ hõ de . iiii . aꝯ́ træ . In feruella
jac& foca . & faca . t . r . e . de oĩbȝ q̃ miñ ht́ quã
xxx . aꝯ́ . De illis qui ht́ . xxx . aꝯ́ . jac& foca 7 faca
in hunᵭ . 7 de Wineferthinc . qno Radulꝼ forefeꝯ́
habuit eam.

173 In TIVETSHALL 2 free men under the patronage of Algar with land, 35 acres of land; meadow, 1 acre. Woodland, 4 pigs; always 1 plough.

174 In SHELFANGER 1 villager, 15 acres of land. Always ½ plough.
2 smallholders.
Woodland, 5 pigs; meadow, 2 acres.
Value then of Winfarthing 40s; later and now £8 3s 4d blanched.
All (were) free with jurisdiction when G(odric) acquired it; now they pay £7 but they cannot pay so much any longer.
Winfarthing has 1 league in length and ½ in width, tax of 9d.

175 Alsi, King Edward's thane, holds FERSFIELD, as 2 c. of land.
Always 5 smallholders. Then and later 3 slaves, now 1.
Always 2 ploughs in lordship. Then 1½ men's ploughs, later and now 1.

176 In BURSTON, 1 outlier, at 1 c. of land, which belongs in Fersfield, always 2 villagers; 1 smallholder.
Then ½ plough in lordship, later nothing, now ½.   130 b

177 In FERSFIELD 13 Freemen, 60 acres of land. Always 3 ploughs.
In the same 3 free men of Alsi's before 1066, 80 acres of land.
3 smallholders.
Then and later 3 ploughs, now 1½.

178 In BURSTON 11 free men of Alsi's before 1066, at 30 acres of land.
Always 1 plough; meadow, 1 acre.

179 In BRESSINGHAM 7 free men under the patronage of Alsi, at 30 acres of land.
Then 3 ploughs, later and now 2.
Woodland, 6 pigs; meadow, 2 acres.
Value of Fersfield with an outlier and Burston, then 60s; later £7 6s 8d between tribute and customary dues; value now £12 6s 8(d) blanched and of this £12 the free men give 100s and 6(s) 7d.
Fersfield has 8 furlongs in length and 4 in width, tax of 7d.
Burston has 8 furlongs in length and 4 in width, tax of 12d.

180 In SHIMPLING 1 half a free man at 4 acres of land.

181 In Fersfield before 1066 appertained the full jurisdiction of all those who had less than 30 acres. Of those who had 30 acres and of Winfarthing the full jurisdiction appertained in the Hundred; when Ralph forfeited he had it.

LOTHINGA. H̄. ⌐Bedingahá teñ hagane

tegñ regis 7 ſtigandi cõmdat. t. r. e. ꝑ. ii. car̄ træ.

Tñc. iiii. uiłł. ꝑ 7 m̄. ii. Tñc. iiii. borđ. ꝑ 7 m̄. v.

Semp. iii. ſer. Tñc v. car̄. in dñio. ꝑ 7 m̄. i. & dim̄.

Tñc. ii. car̄ 7 dim̄ hou. ꝑ. 7 m̄. i. Silua. xx. porc̄.

131 a

& viii. ac̄ ꝑti. Semp. i. eq in aula. 7. i. añ. 7 ſemp xiiii. porc̄

Intepr̄. R. e. adjacebant huic man̄. vi. ſoc̄ cū omi c̄ſuet.

ꝑ & m̄. xxvi. De quibꝣ addidit. R. comes. xx. cū ſoca falde

Int oes lxxx. Tñc. v. car̄. ꝑ 7 m̄. iiii. ⌐ In eade. v. libi hoes

de. iii. huit hagane cõmđ. 7 algar de. ii. & in uidetuna.

i. lib ho goduini. cõmđ. Int oes. i. car̄ 7 dim̄ træ. 7 xii. borđ.

Sep int oes. v. car̄. 7. iiii. ac̄ ꝑti. Tñc totū uał. iiii. lib

ꝑ 7 m̄. viii. blanc̄. 7 xx. ſoł. ad numerū. de gerſuma.

De his viii. lib dant hi vi. libi hoes xxvii. ſoł. 7. iiii. đ.

h̄t. i. leug in long & dim̄ in lat. & de gelto xi. đ. qcuq

ibi teneat. Sup hos libos habebat Rex. e. ſoca. ſed R. com.

tenuit injuſte qño ſe foreſec.

Siſlanda teñ Ketel lib ho eduini cõmđ tantū ꝑ m̄. ii. car̄.

træ. Semp. iii. bor. 7. i. ſer. Tñc. ii. car̄ in dñio. ꝑ 7 m̄

nulla. Semp dim̄ car̄ hou. Silu. iiii. por. 7 v. ac̄ ꝑti. Tñc

i. moł. ꝑ nułł. Tñc. xiii. ſoc̄. ꝑ 7 m̄. ix. 7 dim̄. 7 rex. e. ſoca.

xxvi. ac̄ træ. Semp. ii. car̄. Tñc uał. xx. ſoł ꝑ 7 m̄. xl. blanc̄.

7 h̄t viii. quar̄ in longo. 7 vii. in lat. 7 xi. ꝑcas. & de gelto.

viii. đ. In mundaha. dim̄ ecc̄ła de. x. ac̄.

⌐ In Wodetuna. ii. libi hoes xii. ac̄. 7 ꝑtiñ ad etona 7 ibi

appt̄iat̄. In ſcoteſſa. x. ac̄. 7 jac& in bedingaham.

LODDON Hundred

182 Hagni, a thane under the patronage of the King and Stigand, held
BEDINGHAM before 1066, as 2 c. of land.

>Then 4 villagers; later and now 2. Then 4 smallholders, later
and now 5; always 3 slaves.

>Then 5 ploughs in lordship, later and now 1½. Then 2½ men's
ploughs, later and now 1.

>Woodland, 20 pigs; meadow, 8 acres. Always 1 horse at the   131 a
hall; 1 head of cattle; always 14 pigs.

>Before 1066, 6 Freemen were attached to this manor with all
customary dues; later and now 26, of whom Earl R(alph)
added 20 with fold-rights. Among them all 80 [?acres of
land]. Then 5 ploughs, later and now 4.

In the same 5 free men. Hagni had the patronage of 3 and Algar
of 2.

Also in WOODTON 1 free man under the patronage of Godwin.
Between them all 1½ c. of land;

>12 smallholders.

Always among them all 5 ploughs; meadow, 4 acres.
Value of the whole then £4; later and now £8 blanched, premium
of 20s. These 6 free men give 27s 4d of this £8.

It has 1 league in length and ½ in width, tax of 11d, whoever
holds there. King Edward had the jurisdiction over these free
men but Earl R(alph) held it unjustly when he forfeited.

183 Ketel, a free man under the patronage only of Edwin, held
SISLAND, as a manor, 2 c. of land.

>Always 3 smallholders; 1 slave.

>Then 2 ploughs in lordship, later and now none. Always ½
men's plough; woodland, 4 pigs; meadow, 5 acres. Then
1 mill, later none.

>Then 13 Freemen, later and now 9½. King Edward (had) the
jurisdiction. 26 acres of land. Always 2 ploughs.

Value then 20s; later and now 40 blanched.

It has 8 furlongs in length and 7 (furlongs) and 11 perches in
width, tax of 8d.

In MUNDHAM ½ church, at 10 acres.

184 In WOODTON 2 free men, 12 acres. It belongs to Eaton and is
assessed there.

In SHOTESHAM 10 acres. It appertains in Bedingham.

⌠ Salla teñ Goduiñ auuncuł

Rađ comitis . t . r . e . iii . car træ . ſemp . vii . uiłł . tñc

vi . borđ . p̄ & m̄ . viii . ſemp . ii . S . tñc . iii . car in dñio.

131 b

p̄ & m̄ . ii . ſemp . iii . car hom . 7 vi . ac p̄ti . ſilua . c . porſ.

Sẽp . ii . r̄ . 7 x . añ . 7 xxx . porc̄ . 7 xxx . oũ . Et ix . ſoc̄.

7 dim̄ . xlvi . ac̄ træ . 7 dim̄ ac̄ p̄ti . ſemp . i . car & dimiđ.

Et vi . liƀi hoēs . i . car træ 7 dim̄ . 7 vi . borđ . 7 vi . ac̄ p̄ti.

ſilua . xvi . porc̄ . tñc vi . car . p̄ 7 m̄ . iiii . tñc uał . iiii . liƀ.

p̄ . c . ſoł . m̄ . x . liƀ blancas . 7 xx . ſoł . de gerſuma adnum̄.

7 ħt . i . leug in lonḡ . 7 dim̄ in lato . 7 redđ . vi . đ 7 obolũ

in geldũ regis quicũq̄ ibi ten& . Soca in folſa regis mane

rio . de iſtis ſoca mannis.

⌠ Tẏrninga teñ Vłf . i . liƀ ho . t . r . e . i . car træ . ſemp . vi.

uiłł . 7 ix . borđ . 7 . i . ſer . ſemp . ii . car in dñio . 7 . i . car

7 dim̄ hoũm . 7 x . ac̄ p̄ti . ſilua . lx . por . 7 dim̄ moł.

7 . iiii . r̄ . 7 xx . añ . 7 xvi . por . 7 l . oũ . Et vi . ſoc̄ . xvi.

ac̄ træ . ſemp . i . car 7 dim̄ . ſup ſocam . Soca iñfolſa rẽg.

Tñc 7 p̄ . uał . lx . ſoł m̄ . c . ſoł . blancas . 7 x . ſoł gſuma

ad num̄ . 7 ħt . v . quar . in lonḡ . 7 vi . in lat . 7 redđ . v . đ.

in geldũ regis.

⌠ In Wittcingehā . iii . liƀi hoēs . i . car træ 7 dim̄ . ſemp

ii . uiłł . 7 ix . borđ . ſemp . iiii . car . 7 ix . ac̄ p̄ti . tñc uał

xx . ſoł . m̄ . xxx . ſoł blancas.

⌠ $\tilde{H}$. de Taureſham . Sproweſtuna tenuit edricus

t . r . e . iii . car træ . Tñc . i . uiłł . Tñc vi . bor . m̄ . v . Tñc

i . car in dñio p̄ 7 m̄ dim̄ . Tñc . ii . car hom . p̄ 7 modo.

i . & alie poſſent reſtaurari . Silua . vi . por . Hic jacent

. ii . liƀi hoēs . in caṭetvna . lx . acr̄ . Tñc . ii . car . p̄ 7 . m̄ . i.

132 a

& In Beſetuna . vi . liƀi hoēs . xxx . ac̄ træ . Tñc . ii . car . p̄

7 m̄ . i . & . ii . ac̄ p̄ti .

The Hundred of EYNSFORD

185 Godwin, Earl Ralph's uncle, held SALL before 1066, 3 c. of land.
Always 7 villagers. Then 6 smallholders, later and now 8;
always 2 slaves.
Then 3 ploughs in lordship, later and now 2. 3 men's ploughs; 131 b
meadow, 6 acres; woodland, 100 pigs. Always 2 cobs;
10 head of cattle; 30 pigs; 30 sheep.
Also 9 Freemen and a half, 46 acres of land; meadow, ½ acre.
Always 1½ ploughs.
Also 6 free men, 1½ c. of land.
6 smallholders.
Meadow, 6 acres; woodland, 16 pigs. Then 6 ploughs, later
and now 4.
Value then £4; later 100s; now £10 blanched, premium of 20s at
face value.
It has 1 league in length and ½ in width, it pays 6½d in the
King's tax, whoever holds there. The jurisdiction over these
Freemen is in Foulsham, the King's manor.

186 Ulf, 1 free man, held THURNING before 1066, 1 c. of land.
Always 6 villagers; 9 smallholders; 1 slave.
Always 2 ploughs in lordship; 1½ men's ploughs.
Meadow, 10 acres; woodland, 60 pigs; ½ mill; 4 cobs; 20 head
of cattle; 16 pigs; 50 sheep.
Also 6 Freemen, 16 acres of land. Always 1½ ploughs upon
the jurisdiction. The jurisdiction is in Foulsham, the King's
manor.
Value then and later 60s; now 100s blanched, premium 10s at
face value.
It has 5 furlongs in length and 6 in width, it pays 5d in the
King's tax.

187 In WITCHINGHAM 3 free men, 1½ c. of land.
Always 2 villagers; 9 smallholders.
Always 4 ploughs; meadow, 9 acres.
Value then 20s; now 30s blanched.

The Hundred of TAVERHAM

188 Edric held SPROWSTON before 1066, 3 c. of land.
Then 1 villager. Then 6 smallholders, now 5.
Then 1 plough in lordship, later and now ½. Then 2 men's
ploughs, later and now 1, and others could be restored.
Woodland, 6 pigs.
Here appertain 2 free men in Catton, 60 acres. Then 2 ploughs,
later and now 1.

189 Also in BEESTON (St. Andrew) 6 free men, 30 acres of land. 132 a
Then 2 ploughs, later and now 1. Meadow, 2 acres.

&. 11 . borđ . Tńc . 11 . car . p̃ . 7 m̃ . 1 . hoc eſt totũ inptio de
Ettuna . / In Racheitha . 111 . libi hões . 111 . car trǣ . 7 . 1111 .
uilł . 7 . x11 . borđ . tńc . 1111 . ſerú . Tńc . v . car . p̃ 7 m̃ . 1111.
& v11 . ac p̃ti . Tńc ual . xx . ſoł . m̃ . LX . & h̃t . 1 . leug . in lon̄ .
& v111 . quar in lat . 7 xv . đ de gelto . Hic jacent 1x . libi
hões in Beſetuna de xL . ac . ſemp . 1 . car . & ſnt in eodem
p̃tio . Rex 7 comes ſocam . 7 Beſtuna h̃t . dim̄ leug̃ in
lon̄g . 7 . v . quar in lato . & reddit . x . đ . in geldũ regis.

/ *ERPINGHAMSVD . H̃* . Eleſham tenuit Guert . t . r . e .
xv1 . car trǣ . Tńc . xx . uiłł . p̃ 7 m̃ . x1 . Tńc 7 p̃ Lxxxv111.
borđ . m̃ . Lxv . Tńc 7 p̃ . 11 . s̃ . m̃ . 111 . Tńc v1 . car in dn̄io
p̃ 7 m̃ . 1 . 7 v1 . poſſunt fieri . x11 . ac p̃ti . Tńc ſilua . cccc.
porc . p̃ 7 m̃ . ccc . Semp . 11 . mol . ſemp v11 . porc . 7 v1 . ou .
& v11 . cap . Tńc 7 p̃ . Lx . ſoc . m̃ . xLv1 . 7 h̃t . 1 . car trǣ . 7 dim̄.
7 . x1111 . borđ . Tńc xxx . car . p̃ 7 m̃ xx1111 . 7 v1111 . ac p̃ti.
ſilua . x11 . por . ſemp . 11 . mol . 7 v1 . car .
Huic man̄ jac& . 1 . beruita . Scipedana . 1 . car trǣ . 7 ſep̃
1111 . uiłł . Tńc . 1111 . borđ . p̃ 7 m̃ . 11 . ſemp . 1 . car in dn̄io .
7 . 1 . car hom̄ . 7 dim̄ ac p̃ti . Silua . v111 . porc .
& Brundala jac& huic manerio . xxx . ac trǣ . Tńc . 1 .
car . 7 . 11 . ac p̃ti . Tńc ual . x11 . lib̄ . p̃ . xxv . lib̄ . blanc .
m̃ xx1x . lib blancas . & xx . ſoł de gerſuma . & h̃t . 11 .
leug̃ in lon̄g . 7 . 11 . in lat . & . xx . đ de gelto . hic . 1 . lib̄ hõ .

132 b

v . acr . 7 ual xv1 . đ . h̃ . . tenuic hunfriđ nepos Rañ .
fris ilgeri . ſ; hunđ . ea derationaū regi . & ex hoc dedit
uadẽ 7 tam̄ ſuus antec̃ eam tenuit .

/ Saxthorp teñ Goduin . t . r . e . 11 . car trǣ . ſemp . x . uiłł .
7 x . borđ . 7 . 11 . ſer . ſemp . 11 . car in dn̄io . Tńc 7 p̃ . 111 . car
hom̄ . m̃ . 11 . 7 . 1111 . ac p̃ti . Silua . Lx . por . Tńc . 1 . mol .

190 Also in WROXHAM 2 free men, 60 acres of land.
   2 smallholders.
   Then 2 ploughs, later and now 1.
All this is in the valuation of Eaton.

191 In RACKHEATH 3 free men, 3 c. of land.
   3 villagers; 12 smallholders. Then 4 slaves.
   Then 5 ploughs, later and now 4. Meadow, 7 acres.
Value then 20s; now 60. It has 1 league in length and 8 furlongs in width, tax of 15d.
   Here appertain 9 free men in Beeston (St. Andrew) at 40 acres; always 1 plough.
   They are in the same valuation. The King and the Earl (have) the jurisdiction. Beeston (St. Andrew) has ½ league in length and 5 furlongs in width, it pays 10d in the King's tax.

SOUTH ERPINGHAM Hundred
192 Gyrth held AYLSHAM before 1066, 16 c. of land.
   Then 20 villagers, later and now 11. Then and later 88
      smallholders, now 65. Then and later 2 slaves, now 3.
   Then 6 ploughs in lordship, later and now 1, 6 could be (there).
      Meadow, 12 acres. Then woodland, 400 pigs, later and now
      300; always 2 mills. Always 7 pigs; 6 sheep; 7 goats.
   Then and later 60 Freemen, now 46. They have 1½ c. of land;
      14 smallholders.
   Then 30 ploughs, later and now 24. Meadow, 9 acres;
      woodland, 12 pigs. Always 2 mills; 6 ploughs.
1 outlier, SHIPDHAM, appertains to this manor, 1 c. of land.
   Always 4 villagers. Then 4 smallholders, later and now 2.
   Always 1 plough in lordship; 1 men's plough; meadow, ½ acre;
      woodland, 8 pigs.
BRUNDALL also appertains to this manor, 30 acres of land.
   Then 1 plough; meadow, 2 acres.
Value then £12, later £25 blanched; now £29 blanched, premium of 20s. It has 2 leagues in length and 2 in width, tax of 20d.
   Here 1 free man, 5 acres;   132 b
value 16d.
   Humphrey, nephew of Ranulf brother of Ilger, held this, but the Hundred adjudged it to the King and he gave pledge of this; and yet his predecessor held it.

193 Godwin held SAXTHORPE before 1066, 2 c. of land.
   Always 10 villagers; 10 smallholders; 2 slaves.
   Always 2 ploughs in lordship. Then and later 3 men's ploughs,
      now 2. Meadow, 4 acres; woodland, 60 pigs. Then 1 mill,

p̄ 7 m̃ . II . ſemp . IIII . r̃ . 7 xx . an̄ . 7 L . porc̃ . 7 L . cap̃ . & xv
ſoc̃ . & dim̃ . xL . ac̃ træ . 7 . III . car̃ . 7 . II . ac̃ p̃ti . ſilua xII . porc̃.
& . I . liƀ ho̅ . xxx . ac̃ træ . ſep . I . car̃ . ſilua . IIII . porc̃ . 7.
I . ac̃ p̃ti . & . I . beruita Matelaſc . I . car̃ træ . 7 dim̃ ſep
vII . uiłł . 7 . I . car̃ in dñio . 7 . I . car̃ hom̃ . ſilua . xx .
porc̃ . & . xv . ſoc̃ . I . car̃ træ & dim̃ . 7 . II . ac̃ p̃ti . ſilua.
xx . porc̃ . ſemp . IIII . car̃ . tc̃ uał . IIII . liƀ . p̄ . vI.
m̃ . x . liƀ blancas . & xx . ſoł de gerſuma . & h̃t.
I . leug in long̃ . & alia in lat̃ . 7 xII . đ . de gelt̃.
& Matelaſc h̃t . III . quar̃ in long̃ . 7 . II . in latit̃.
& . III . đ de gelto.

Manictuna ten̄ . Goduin̄ . t . r . e . II . car̃ tre.
tñc vI . uiłł . p̄ . v . m̃ . IIII . ſemp . x . bor . tc̃ . II . ſer̃.
p̄ 7 m̃ . I . tc̃ . II . car̃ in dñio . p̄ & m̃ . I . tñc . III . car̃.
hom̃ . p̄ 7 m̃ . II . 7 . II . ac̃ p̃ti . Tñc ſilua . Lx . porc̃.
p̄ 7 m̃ . xxx . ſemp . II . moł . 7 . II . r̃ . 7 xIIII . porc̃.
& vIII . ou̅ . 7 xL cap̃ . 7 v . ſoc̃ . xx . IIII . ac̃ træ . ſep
I . car̃ . ſilua . IIII . por̃ . Tñc uał . Lx . ſoł . p̄ Lxxx.
m̃ . c . blancas 7 xvI . đ . 7 xx . ſoł . de gerſuma.

133 a
& h̃t . I . leug in long̃ . & . IIII . quar̃ in lat̃ . & . III . đ . 7 . III.
ferding̃ . de g̃ . In belaga . II . ſoc̃ ſci ƀened̃ . xxx . IIII . ac̃ træ
& in Bernes wrde . I . ſoc̃ ejuſde . xvI . ac̃ . ſemp . III . bord̃.
7 . I . car̃ . 7 dim̃ . 7 . III . ac̃ p̃ti . Hos ſoc̃ tenebat Raduł qndo
foriſfecit . Modo Godric̃ ad feudu regis . & e̅ in p̃tio de Ælſa
ham . In Scotohou̅ . I . ſoc̃ . ſci ƀened̃ . xLIII . acr̃ . ſemp . II . bord̃.
eodem modo de iſto ut de alijs.

In Crachefort . I . liƀ ho̅ Guert̃ . I . car̃ træ . ſemp . III . bord̃.
tñc . I . car̃ & dim̃ . m̃ . I . 7 . II . ac̃ p̃ti . m̃ . I . moł . & hoc e̅ in
p̃tio . de aileſham . & h̃t . IIII . quar̃ 7 dim̃ in lonḡ . 7 . IIII.
quar̃ in lato . 7 . IIII . đ . de g̃ . In V.trincham . I . liƀ ho̅ Guert̃
. I . car̃ træ . ſemp . v . bord̃ . 7 . II . car̃ . 7 . I . ac̃ p̃ti . Silua . v . por̃.

later and now 2. Always 4 cobs; 20 head of cattle; 50 pigs; 50 goats.

Also 15 Freemen and a half, 40 acres of land.

3 ploughs; meadow, 2 acres; woodland, 12 pigs.

Also 1 free man, 30 acres of land.

Always 1 plough; woodland, 4 pigs; meadow, 1 acre.

Also 1 outlier, MATLASK, 1½ c. of land.

Always 7 villagers.

1 plough in lordship; 1 men's plough; woodland, 20 pigs.

Also 15 Freemen, 1½ c. of land.

Meadow, 2 acres; woodland, 20 pigs; always 4 ploughs.

Value then £4, later 6, now £10 blanched, premium of 20s. It has 1 league in length and another in width, tax of 12d. Matlask has 3 furlongs in length and 2 in width, tax of 3d.

194 Godwin held MANNINGTON before 1066, 2 c. of land.

Then 6 villagers, later 5, now 4. Always 10 smallholders.

Then 2 slaves, later and now 1.

Then 2 ploughs in lordship, later and now 1. Then 3 men's ploughs, later and now 2. Meadow, 2 acres. Then woodland, 60 pigs, later and now 30. Always 2 mills; 2 cobs; 14 pigs; 8 sheep; 40 goats.

Also 5 Freemen, 24 acres of land.

Always 1 plough; woodland, 4 pigs.

Value then 60s; later 80; now 100 blanched 16d, premium of 20s. It has 1 league in length and 4 furlongs in width, tax of 3¾d.   133 a

In BELAUGH 2 Freemen of St. Benedict's, 34 acres of land.

In (Little) BARNINGHAM 1 Freeman of the same, 16 acres.

Always 3 smallholders.

1½ ploughs; meadow, 3 acres.

Ralph held these Freemen when he forfeited. Now Godric has them as part of the King's Holding. It is in the valuation of Aylsham.

In SCOTTOW 1 Freeman of St. Benedict's, 43 acres.

Always 2 smallholders.

This man (is held) in the same way as the others.

195 In CRACKFORD 1 free man of Gyrth's, 1 c. of land.

Always 3 smallholders.

Then 1½ ploughs, now 1. Meadow, 2 acres. Now 1 mill. This is in the valuation of Aylsham. It has 4½ furlongs in length and 4 furlongs in width, tax of 4d.

In ITTERINGHAM 1 free man of Gyrth's, 1 c. of land.

Always 5 smallholders.

2 ploughs; meadow, 1 acre; woodland, 5 pigs.

in eodẽ p̃tio & tota ht̃ . I . leu in long̃ . & dim in lato . & v.

den̄ . & oboł de gelt . In Heuincham . I . lib̃ ho p̃r . xL . ac̃

tr̃æ in elemofina & cantat una q̃q̃ ebdomada . tres

miſſas . femp . I . car̃ . 7 . I . acr̃ p̃ti . filua . x . porc̃ . 7 uał . v.

fol . 7 . IIII . đ . & . I . foc̃ . vIII . ac̃ . 7 uał xx . đ . Hunc tenuit

Leuſtan antec̃ tiħeli . t . r . e . & rađ eu ten q̃do forisfec̃ .

& . e de foca de cauſtuna . m̃ eu tenet Godric̃ . Sed tarałđ

ho Wiłłi de War̃ eu faifiu fup regẽ 7 tenuit p tres

annos . m̃ de rationat ÷ fup eu . & reddit turałđ . v.

fol de catallo regis & dedit uadẽ de juſtitia facienda.

Tonſteda . H̃ . In Wittuna . I . p̃r xxx . ac̃ in elemofina

femp . Ix . foc̃ . de xII . ac̃ tr̃æ . femp . II . car̃ . 7 . II . ac̃ p̃ti.

133 b

ex hoc cantat . III . miſſas p rege & regina . 7 tñc redđ

II . fol . & totu ht̃ . I . leug in long̃ . & dim in lat̃ . 7

x . đ de gelto . quicq̃ ibi teneat.

⌐H̃ . de hapincha . H̃apefburc tenuit edric̃ . t . r . e .

xIII . car̃ tr̃æ . femp . xxI . uiłł . 7 xx . borđ . Semp . III .

fer . 7 . III . car̃ in dñio . Tñc . Ix . car̃ hom̃ . p 7 modo

vII . x . ac̃ p̃ti . filua . xvI . porc̃ . 7 . IIII . an̄ . 7 xvIII . por .

7 . cc . oũ . & xxI . foc̃ . LxxxvI . ac̃ . Tñc . v . car̃ . p 7 m̃ .

IIII . & xII . libi ħoes de quib; habuit . edric̃ c̃mdati

onẽ tan̄tu . IIII . car̃ tr̃æ . 7 vIIII . uiłł . 7 Ix . bor . 7 dim̃ .

7 . I . fer . dim̃ car̃ ex iſtis inuafit . edric̃ ħo comitis alani.

& dedit uadẽ . Tñc . x . car̃ . p 7 m̃ vIIII . Iſtos libos

ħoes addidit Rađ comes huic manerio . 7 in eodem

ſñt adcenfati . m̃ ; & tenebat eos q̃do foris fecit.

Tñc totum uał . vII . lib̃ . 7 libi ħoes . xL . fol . Et tẽp̃r

Radulfi . totu uał . x . lib̃ . m̃ . xvI . blancas . & xx fol .

de gerfuma . & ht̃ . I . leug & dim̃ in long̃ 7 ſimiliter

in lat̃ quicq̃ ibi teneat . & xxx . đ . de gerfuma.

Hanc tram calupniat̃ rob̃ malet & dicit qđ pat̃ fu

ea tenuit q̃do iuit in marefc̃ . 7 hoc teſtat̃ hundret

& tam̃ n tenebat ea die q̃ fuit mortuus.

In the same valuation. The whole has 1 league in length and ½ in width; tax of 5½d.

In HEVINGHAM 1 free man, a priest, 40 acres of land in alms and he sings 3 masses in any one week.

Always 1 plough; meadow, 1 acre; woodland, 10 pigs. Value 5s 4d.

Also 1 Freeman, 8 acres; value 20d.

Leofstan, the predecessor of Tihel, held this (Freeman) before 1066, and Ralph held him when he forfeited. (This Freeman) is of the jurisdiction of Cawston. Now Godric holds him. But Thorald, William de Warenne's man, took possession of him against the King and held (him) for three years. Now it has been adjudged against him, and Thorald pays 5s for (him as) the King's chattel and has given pledge to do justice.

TUNSTEAD Hundred

196 In WITTON 1 priest, 30 acres in alms.

Always 9 Freemen, at 12 acres of land.

Always 2 ploughs; meadow, 2 acres.

For this he sings 3 masses for the King and Queen. Then he paid 2s. The whole has 1 league in length and ½ in width, tax of 10d, whoever holds there.   133 b

The Hundred of HAPPING

197 Edric held HAPPISBURGH before 1066, 13 c. of land.

Always 21 villagers; 20 smallholders; always 3 slaves.

3 ploughs in lordship. Then 9 men's ploughs, later and now 7. Meadow 10 acres; woodland, 16 pigs; 4 head of cattle; 18 pigs; 200 sheep.

Also 21 Freemen, 86 acres.

Then 5 ploughs, later and now 4.

Also 12 free men of whom Edric had the patronage only, 4 c. of land.

8 villagers; 9 smallholders and a half; 1 slave.

Edric, Count Alan's man, annexed ½ c. of these and gave pledge.

Then 10 ploughs, later and now 9.

Earl Ralph added these free men to this manor, and they are now leased out in the same. He held them when he forfeited. Value of the whole then £7; the free men 40s. The value of the whole was £10 in the time of Ralph, now £16 blanched, premium 20s.

It has 1½ leagues in length and the same in width, whoever holds there, premium of 30d.

Robert Malet claims this land and says that his father held it when he went into the marsh, and the Hundred testifies to this; and yet he did not hold it on the day when he died.

$\tilde{H}$. de Hapinga . Lofincham . tenuit Goduiṁ tegñ
t . r . e . III . caŕ . 7 xxx . aċ . femp̄ xv . uiłł . 7 xvi . bor .
7 vi . fer . Tnċ . II . caŕ in dñio . p̄ 7 ṁ . I . femp . III . caŕ hoṁ .

134 a
7 xII . ac p̄ti . Silua . x . porċ . 7 . II . ŕ . 7 . III . an . 7 vII . por .
& xx . ou . & vIII . libi hoès . c . aċ . femp . II . caŕ . 7 . II . acŕ
p̄ti . Tnċ uał Lx foł . 7 libi hoès . x . foł . p̄ totū . IIII . libi

★ hoès . ṁ . vI . blancas . 7 xx . foł . de gerfuma . ad numerū .

★ & hŧ . I . leu . & diṁ in long . & x đ . 7 oboł de gelto . Rex
& comes focam . Hemfteda . II . caŕ tre 7 dim . fep . x . bor .
Tñc . I . caŕ in dñio . p̄ 7 ṁ . II . femp . I . caŕ hoṁ . 7 xv . acŕ
p̄ti . 7 . II . an . 7 xIII . porċ . 7 cLx . ou . & xxx . vI . foċ . cvIII .
acŕ . femp . vI . caŕ . & xvI . libi hoès . II . caŕ træ . femp . III .
bor . 7 vI . caŕ . 7 xIIII . aċ p̄ti . Tnċ uał . L . foł . & libi hoès
xL . foł . p̄ 7 ṁ . vIII . liƀ blancas . 7 xx . foł de gerfuma
ad numerū . & hŧ . I . leu in long . 7 ał in lat . 7 xvIII . đ .
de gelt .

⌐ Pallinga tenuit goduiñ . t . r . e . III . caŕ træ . femp . vIIII .
uiłł . 7 xIIII . bor . femp . I . caŕ in dñio . 7 . I . caŕ hoṁ .
xx . ac p̄ti . 7 xIIII . eque filuatice . 7 . II . ŕ . 7 xx . III . por .
7 Lxxi . ou . Tñc uał . IIII . liƀ . p̄ 7 ṁ . vI . blancas . & hŧ
vIII . quar . & xII . perċ . 7 vIII . quar in lat . 7 vII . đ .
& obolum de gelt .

⌐ Eaſt . $\tilde{H}$. DE FLEC . Caſtre tenueŕ Lxxx liƀi hoès
t . r . e . 7 ṁ fimił . IIII . caŕ træ . Tnċ xxII . caŕ . & ex
hoc toto fecit . R . comes maneriū . ṁ . I . caŕ in dñio .
& xxI . houṁ . II . aċ p̄ti . femp dim moł . 7 xxxvIIII .
fał . 7 . III . ŕ . 7 vIII . an . 7 xII . porċ . 7 ccc . Lx . ou . Tñc
uał . vIII . liƀ . p̄ . x . ṁ xIIII . & tam hŧ abbas fċi bened .

134 b
ex hoc manerio . vI . libras . & hŧ . I . leu in long . & c . perċ .
& . I . leu in lat . 7 xL . IIII . đ . de g . qui cuq̄ ibi teneat .
hoc liƀatū . e . p̄ efcangio de tra de cornualia c̄ omŧ con
fuetudine ut godric dicit .

The Hundred of HAPPING

198 Godwin, the thane, held LESSINGHAM before 1066, 3 c. and 30
acres.
> Always 15 villagers; 16 smallholders; 6 slaves.
> Then 2 ploughs in lordship, later and now 1. Always 3 men's
> ploughs; meadow, 12 acres; woodland, 10 pigs; 2 cobs; 134 a
> 3 head of cattle; 7 pigs; 20 sheep.
> Also 8 free men, 100 acres.
> Always 2 ploughs; meadow, 2 acres.

Value then 60s, and the free men 10s; later the whole £4 now 6
blanched, premium 20s at face value.
It has 1½ leagues in length, tax of 10½d. The King and the
Earl have the jurisdiction.

199 HEMPSTEAD, 2½ c. of land.
> Always 10 smallholders.
> Then 1 plough in lordship, later and now 2. Always 1 men's
> plough; meadow, 15 acres; 2 head of cattle; 13 pigs;
> 160 sheep.
> Also 36 Freemen, 108 acres.
> Always 5 ploughs.
> Also 16 free men, 2 c. of land.
> Always 3 smallholders.
> 6 ploughs; meadow, 14 acres.

Value then 50s and the free men 40s; later and now £8 blanched,
premium of 20s at face value.
It has 1 league in length and another in width, tax of 18d.

200 Godwin held PALLING before 1066, 3 c. of land.
> Always 9 villagers; 14 smallholders.
> Always 1 plough in lordship; 1 men's plough; meadow, 20 acres;
> 14 wild mares; 2 cobs; 23 pigs; 71 sheep.

Value then £4; later and now 6 blanched.
It has 8 furlongs and 12 perches [in length] and 8 furlongs in
width, tax of 7½d.

The Hundred of EAST FLEGG

201 80 free men held CAISTER before 1066, now the same. 4 c. of land.
> Then 22 ploughs. Earl R(alph) made a manor of all this. Now
> 1 plough in lordship; 21 men's [ploughs]; meadow, 2 acres.
> Always ½ mill; 39 salt-houses; 3 cobs; 8 head of cattle;
> 12 pigs; 360 sheep.

Value then £8; later 10, now 14, and yet the Abbot of St.
Benedict's has £6 out of this manor. It has 1 league in length 134 b
and 100 perches and 1 league in width, tax of 44d, whoever
holds there. This was delivered by exchange for land in Cornwall
with every customary due as Godric states.

Malteby̌ tenuit Wiſtan . lib̄ hō . Rađ . Stalra . I . car̄
træ 7 dim̄ . Semp . VII . uiłł . 7 . II . borđ . 7 . II . ſeꝛ . 7 . I . car̄
7 dim in dn̄io . 7 . I . car̄ hom̄ . IIII . ac̄ p̄ti . m̄ dim̄ moł . 7 ſep̄
VII . ſał . 7 VII . anim̄ 7 . II . por . 7 c . XXII . ou . & XVI . lib̄i hōes
& dim̄ em̄đ tantū . LXXX . ac̄ træ . Sēp . IIII . car̄ . 7 . II . ac̄ .
7 dim̄ p̄ti . 7 . IIII . ſał . 7 XIIII . lib̄i hōes quos addidit . R.
comes . 7 ht̄ . II . car̄ tre . 7 L . ac̄ . 7 VII . borđ . 7 dim̄ . ſemp
VIIII . car̄ . X . ac̄ p̄ti . 7 VI . ſał . 7 dim̄ . 7 quarta pars uni.
Rex & comes de toto ſep̄ ſoca . & om̄s iſti lib̄i hōes uał
XXX . ſoł . tc̄ ꝛ m̄ . LIII . 7 VII . đ . & M . tnc uał XL . ſoł . 7 p̄ .
L . m̄ LXVI . 7 VI . đ . & ht̄ . I . leu in lonḡ . 7 VIII . quaꝛ in lat̄
& . II . ſoł . de ḡ.

★ Romhā . teñ . II . lib̄i hōes . t . r . e . uñ fuit hō edric̄i
de laxefelda . & alt̄ Radulfi ſtalra ; 7 ſemp . I . car̄ træ.
& dim̄ . 7 X . uiłł . 7 . I . car̄ in dn̄io . 7 . I . car̄ hom̄ . XVI . ac̄
p̄ti . 7 X . ſał . in dn̄io . I . r̄ . 7 . I . an̄ . 7 . c . I . ou . 7 IX . porc̄.
& XI . ſoc̄ . 7 dim̄ . de dim̄ car̄ træ . ſemp . III . car̄ . 7 . II . ac̄
p̄ti . 7 . II . ſał . & dim̄ . & XI . lib̄i hōes 7 dim̄ . de dim̄ car̄
træ . 7 V . ac̄ . Tnc . IIII . car̄ . p̄ 7 m̄ . III . & . III . ac̄ p̄ti.
& . II . ſał . ſemp uał . X . ſoł . Rex 7 comes ſocam . 7 m̄.

135 a
uał . tnc . XXX . ſoł . p̄ . L . m̄ . LXXXX . ſoł blancas . 7 XX . ſoł.
de gerſuma . & ht̄ . X . qr̄ in lonḡ . 7 VII . in lat̄ . 7 . II . ſoł
de gelto . q̄cuq̄ ibi teneat . In Trukebei . VI . lib̄i hōes.
Rađ ſtalra . XL . ac̄ . ſep̄ . I . car̄ . 7 dim̄ ſał . 7 . IIII . ac̄ prati.
& uał IX . ſoł . in vt ſoca de Walſam . Rex 7c . ſoca ;

Humiliart . H̄ . Ettuna tenuit . Edric̄ de laxefelda.
antec̄ Rob̄ malet . t . r . e . I . car̄ træ . ſemp . II . borđ.

202 Wistan, a free man of Ralph the Constable's, held MALTBY, 1½ c.
of land.

Always 7 villagers; 2 smallholders; 2 slaves.

1½ ploughs in lordship; 1 men's plough; meadow, 4 acres.

Now ½ mill. Always 7 salt-houses; 7 head of cattle; 2 pigs;
122 sheep.

Also 16 and a half free men under patronage only, 80 acres of land.

Always 4 ploughs; meadow, 2½ acres; 4 salt-houses.

Also 14 free men whom Earl R(alph) added. They have 2 c. of
land and 50 acres.

7 smallholders and a half.

Always 9 ploughs; meadow, 10 acres; 6½ salt-houses and
¼ of one.

The King and the Earl (have) always (had) the jurisdiction of
the whole.

Value of all those free men then 30s; now 53(s) 7d. Value of the
manor then 40s; later 50, now 66(s) 6d.

It has 1 league in length and 8 furlongs in width, tax of 2s.

203 2 free men held RUNHAM before 1066; one was the man of Edric
of Laxfield, the other of Ralph the Constable. Always 1½ c. of
land.

10 villagers.

1 plough in lordship; 1 men's plough; meadow, 16 acres;
10 salt-houses in lordship; 1 cob; 1 head of cattle;
101 sheep; 9 pigs.

Also 11 Freemen and a half, at ½ c. of land.

Always 3 ploughs; meadow, 2 acres; 2½ salt-houses.

Also 11 free men and a half, at ½ c. of land and 5 acres.

Then 4 ploughs, later and now 3. Meadow, 3 acres;
2 salt-houses.

Value always 10s.

The King and the Earl (had) the jurisdiction [then] and now.

Value then 30s, later 50; now 90s blanched, premium of 20s.   135 a

It has 10 furlongs in length and 7 in width, tax of 2s, whoever
holds there.

204 In THRIGBY 6 free men of Ralph the Constable's, 40 acres.

Always 1 plough; ½ salt-house; meadow, 4 acres.

Value 9s in the outlying jurisdiction of (South) Walsham.

The King and the Earl (have) the jurisdiction.

HUMBLEYARD Hundred

205 Edric of Laxfield, predecessor of Robert Malet, held EATON
before 1066, 1 c. of land.

Always 2 smallholders.

Tnc . ii . car in dnio . p nichil . m . i . 7 xii . ac pti . filua
vi . por . 7 . i . mot . & m . vi . an . 7 vi . pors . 7 vi . oues.
7 x . foc . lxxx . ac . femp . ii . car . 7 . iiii . ac pti . i . æccla
xiiii . acr . 7 ual xiiii . d . & . iiii . libi hoes in Stokes.
fub edrico cmdatione tantum . xlv . ac . femp . i . car.
7 . iii . ac pti . & quarta pars molendini.

Et in erlham . i . lib ho uluiet noe . i . car træ & dim
femp . i . uilt . & . iiii . bord . femp . i . car in dnio . 7 . i.
car hom . xvi . ac pti . m . i . uilt . ht &iam ide uluiet
fubfe . x . libos hoes . de lxxx . ac tre . femp . ii . car.
Tnc ual totu . iiii . lib . & qdo Rob blund tenebat.
fimilit . m . vii . lib . & libi hoes m . lx . fot . & ht . i . leu.
in long . 7 . i . in lat . 7 vii . d . 7 . i . ferding . de gelt.
& Erlham ht . i . leug in long . 7 . i . quar . & . i . leug
in lato . 7 viii . d . 7 . i . ferding de g.

In Erlham . iii . libi hoes xl . ii . ac . femp . i . bor . 7 . i.
car . 7 . i . ac pti . tc ual . iiii . fot . m . v . & jac& in bowethorp.

135 b

i . eccla . xiiii . ac . & . i . ac & dim pti . & ual xv . d.

DEPWADE . H . In Carletuna . iiii . ac . & dim . & . e . inptio
de howa.

GNAVERINGA . H . Rauerincha . ten Olf ho antecef
foris Robti malet . iii . car træ . femp . i . uilt . 7 . ii . bor.
Tnc . ii . car in dnio . p 7 m . i . vi . ac pti . xiii . pors . 7 . cc.
ou . & x . libi hoes foca falde . & cmd . lx . iiii . ac & dim
tnc . iiii . car . p . ii . m . ii . car . & dim . & . iii . ac pti . &
iii . foc . iiii . ac . Tnc ual . xxx . fot . m lx . blancas.
In eade . i . lib ho ketelfiedai . vii . ac . 7 i . mares . 7 ual.
xii . d.

135 a, b

Then 1 plough in lordship, later none, now 1. Meadow, 12
acres; woodland, 6 pigs; 1 mill. Now 6 head of cattle;
6 pigs; 6 sheep.
Also 10 Freemen, 80 acres.
Always 2 ploughs; meadow, 4 acres.
1 church, 14 acres;
value 14d.
Also 4 free men in STOKE (Holy Cross) under Edric in patronage
only, 45 acres.
Always 1 plough; meadow, 3 acres; ¼ of a mill.

206 Also in EARLHAM 1 free man, Wulfgeat by name, 1½ c. of land.
Always 1 villager; 4 smallholders.
Always 1 plough in lordship; 1 men's plough; meadow,
16 acres.
Now 1 villager.
The same Wulfgeat has under him 10 free men, at 80 acres of
land. Always 2 ploughs.
Value of the whole then £4; when Robert Blunt held it the same;
now £7; and the free men now 60s.
It has 1 league in length and 1 in width, tax of 7¼d.
Earlham has 1 league and 1 furlong in length and 1 league in
width, tax of 8¼d.

In EARLHAM 3 free men, 42 acres.
Always 1 smallholder.
1 plough; meadow, 1 acre.
Value then 4s; now 5.
It appertains in Bowthorpe.
1 church, 14 acres; meadow, ½ acre;   135 b
value 15d.

DEPWADE Hundred
207 In CARLETON (Rode) 4½ acres. It is in the valuation of Howe.

CLAVERING Hundred
208 Ulf, the man of the predecessor of Robert Malet, held
RAVENINGHAM, 3 c. of land.
Always 1 villager; 2 smallholders.
Then 2 ploughs in lordship, later and now 1. Meadow, 6 acres;
13 pigs; 200 sheep.
Also 10 free men in fold-rights and patronage, 64½ acres.
Then 4 ploughs, later 2, now 2½. Meadow, 3 acres.
Also 3 Freemen, 4 acres.
Value then 30s; now 60 blanched.
In the same 1 free man, Ketel Friday, 7 acres; 1 marsh.
Value 12d.

TRE Stigandi epi quas cuſtodit . W . de noiers in

manu regis . H̄ . de metheduna . Huneſtaneſteda
ten Stigand . t . r . e . tnc . II . car i̇d . qn̄ . W . recuſ
I . 7 dim . 7 m̄ ſimił . ſemp xvi . uiłł . 7 . IIII . bord́ . Tnc . III .
ſer . p̄ 7 m̄ . I . 7 vIII . ac̄ p̄ti . Tnc . II . car hom̄ . p̄ 7 m̄ . I . 7
dim . tc̄ . I . moł . dim . piſc̄ . Tnc . I . r̄ . 7 m̄ ſimił . 7 . II . an̄ .

136 a
7 xIIII . porc̄ . 7 xL . IIII . ou̇ . & . IIII . ſoc̄ . Lx . ac̄ . Tnc uał .
Lxx . ſoł . p̄ 7 m̄ . cx . Hic jacebat te̅pr reḡ . e . I . li̅ba femina
xxx . ac̄ træ . p̄ habuit Rad́ comes tribʒ annis anteq̄ foris
facer& . 7 qno foris fecit . p̄ tenuit Ro̅b blund́ . 7 Godric
adfirma de xxx . ſoł . cu̇ alia t̄ra . Iteru̇ adjacent illa
ſiuuard̄ huic manerio . 7 n̄ reddit Godrico firmam .
& . III . ſoc̄ ſc̄i . b̄ . addidit . W . de noiers . de . IIII . ac̄ træ .
Totu̇ ht̄ . I . leu̇ in lonḡ & dim̄ in lat̄ . 7 reddit . vI . d . de
xx . ſoł . quicuq̄ ibi teneat .

⌐ Grimeſhou . H̄ . Methelwalde . ten Stigand́ . t . r . e .
xx . car træ . Tnc̄ xxvIII . uiłł . p̄ xxIIII . m̄ . xvIII . Tnc̄
IIII . bord́ . p̄ . vIII . m̄ xIII . ſemp xx . IIII . ſer . xxx . ac̄
p̄ti . tnc vI . car in dn̄io . p̄ 7 m̄ v . Tnc xxIII . car . hou̇ .
p̄ . xIII . m̄ . vII . ſemp . II . moł 7 dim . vII . piſc̄ . in dn̄io . IIII .
r̄ . xII . an̄ . LxxxIIII . porc̄ . o̅ . ccc . ou̇ . xxvII . uaſa apu̇ .
Hic ſemp jac& . I . beruita . Wetinga ſemp . III . uiłł . 7 . I . bor .
7 . III . ſer . 7 . I . ac̄ p̄ti . Tnc . II . car in dn̄io . p̄ 7 m̄ . I . tnc . I .
car . houm̄ . ſemp . II . r̄ . Inſeltwella Lx ac̄ træ . & in ted-
forda dim car træ . 7 v . bord́ . t . r . e . m̄ . III . & . II . manſure
ſ̄nt uacuæ . & . I . eccł́a . & . I . eccł́a ſc̄e elene c̄ una car træ
7 . I . uiłł . 7 . I . car poſſ& . ēe .

LANDS OF BISHOP STIGAND OF WHICH WILLIAM DE NOYERS HAS CHARGE
IN THE KING'S HAND

The Hundred of SMETHDEN

209 Stigand held HUNSTANTON before 1066.

> Then 2 ploughs in lordship; when W(illiam) acquired it 1½; now the same.
>
> Always 16 villagers; 4 smallholders. Then 3 slaves, later and now 1.
>
> Meadow, 8 acres. Then 2 men's ploughs, later and now 1½. Then 1 mill; ½ fishery. Then 1 cob, now the same. 2 head of cattle; 14 pigs; 44 sheep.   136 a
>
> Also 4 Freemen, 60 acres.

Value then 70s; later and now 110.

1 free woman appertained here before 1066, 30 acres of land.

Later Earl Ralph had it for 3 years before he forfeited, and when he forfeited; later Robert Blunt held it. Godric (held it) at revenue for 30s with other land. Again Siward has attached it to this manor and it does not pay revenue to Godric.

> W(illiam) de Noyers added 3 Freemen of St. Benedict's, at 4 acres of land.
>
> The whole has 1 league in length and ½ in width, at 20s it pays 6d, whoever holds there.

GRIMSHOE Hundred

210 Stigand held METHWOLD before 1066, 20 c. of land.

> Then 28 villagers, later 24, now 18. Then 4 smallholders, later 8, now 13. Always 24 slaves.
>
> Meadow, 30 acres. Then 6 ploughs in lordship, later and now 5. Then 23 men's ploughs, later 13, now 7. Always 2½ mills; 7 fisheries in lordship; 4 cobs; 12 head of cattle; 84 pigs; 800 sheep; 27 beehives.

Here always appertained 1 outlier, WEETING.

> Always 3 villagers; 1 smallholder; 3 slaves.
>
> Meadow, 1 acre. Then 2 ploughs in lordship, later and now 1. Then 1 men's plough; always 2 cobs.

In FELTWELL 60 acres of land.

In THETFORD ½ c. of land.

> 5 smallholders before 1066, now 3; 2 dwellings are empty. 1 church.
>
> Also 1 church of St. Helen with 1 c. of land.
>
> > 1 villager.
> >
> > 1 plough could be (there).

& In Halingheia . ɪ . lib ho̅ . xxx . ac̅ . ɪ . car̅ . & in Wella
ɪɪɪ . bor . & in toto manerio . vɪɪɪ . car poſſent . e̅e̅ . Tnc̅
ual̅ xx . lib̅ . m̅ . xxx . Et ht̅ . ɪɪ . leug in longo . 7 dim̅ i lat̅.

& reddit . ɪɪ . ſol̅ . 7 . ɪ . obolum . de xx . ſol de gelto . & . ɪɪɪɪ .
libi hoes jacent huic manerio . t . r . e . m̅ ht̅ . W . de uuar̅.

⌐ Crokeſtuna te̅n . Stigand̅ . t . r . e . ſemp̅ . v . car̅ tre . Tnc̅
vɪɪɪ . uilt̅ . p̅ . ɪɪɪɪ . m̅ nulł m̅ . ɪɪɪɪ . bord̅ . Tnc̅ . v . ſer̅ . p̅ . ɪɪɪɪ .
m̅ . nulł . Tnc̅ . ɪɪɪ . car̅ . ind̅ . p̅ 7 m̅ . ɪɪ . Tnc̅ . ɪɪ . car̅ homu̅ .
tc̅ . ɪ . mol̅ . que̅ poſt cepit . Rad̅ . comes . t . r . W . 7 . ɪɪɪ . ac̅ .
pt̅i . ſemp̅ . ɪ . r . vɪ . an̅ . xvɪɪɪɪ . porc̅ . ccxv . ou̅ . Hic jace
bant . t . r . e . xvɪɪ . ſoc̅ . de h̅ hab̅ W . de War̅ . xvɪ . & Rad̅ .
de toeni . tnc ual̅ . x . lib̅ . m̅ ual̅ xl . ſol̅ . ſ; reddit . c . ſol̅ .
& . ɪɪɪ . car̅ poſſent e̅e̅ . Totu̅ ht̅ . ɪ . leug 7 dim in lat̅ . 7 .
ɪ . in lat̅ . & reddit xɪɪ . d̅ . de xx . ſol̅ . de gelto .

Lawendic . H̄ . Meleham te̅n Stigand̅ . t . r . e . x .
car̅ træ . ſemp̅ xx . uilt̅ . 7 xlɪɪɪɪ . bord̅ . Tnc̅ . vɪ . ſer̅ .
p̅ & m̅ . ɪ . 7 x . ac̅ pt̅i . ſemp̅ . ɪɪ . car̅ . in dnio . 7 . ɪ . car̅ poſſ&
reſtaur̅ . Tnc̅ . xxɪɪɪɪ . car̅ hom̅ . p̅ & m̅ . xvɪɪɪɪ . 7 . v .
poſſent reſtaurari . ſilua . ꝏ . por . ſemp̅ . ɪ . mol̅ . 7 . ɪ . ſal̅ .
& . ɪɪɪ . ſoc̅ . ɪ . car̅ træ . 7 . ɪ . acr̅ . tc̅ & p̅ xɪɪ . uilt̅ . m̅ . ɪɪɪɪ .
ſemp̅ . x . bor . & ɪɪɪɪ . ac̅ pt̅i . Tnc̅ . ɪ . car̅ in dnio . p̅ 7 m̅
dim̅ . 7 dimidia poſſ& reſtaurari . Tnc̅ . ɪɪɪɪ . car̅ hou̅ .
p̅ 7 m̅ . ɪɪ . & alie poſſent reſtaurari . tnc ſilua . c . por .
m̅ . l . & . ɪɪɪɪ . ſoc̅ . xxx . ac̅ tre . 7 . ɪ . bor . ſemp̅ . ɪ . car̅ .
& . ɪɪɪɪ . ac̅ pt̅i . & . ɪ . ſoc̅ . ɪ . car̅ træ . & . ɪ . ſoc̅ . vɪɪɪ . acr̅ .
int totu̅ . x . bord̅ . 7 v . ac̅ pt̅i . Tnc̅ . ɪɪ . car̅ in dnio . p̅
& m̅ . ɪɪɪ . m̅ . ɪ . car̅ hom̅ . ſilua . x . porc̅ . & . vɪɪ . ſoc̅ . xl .

ac̅ træ . 7 . ɪ . bord̅ . & . ɪɪɪɪ . ac̅ pt̅i . ſemp̅ . ɪɪ . car̅ in dnio . ſemp̅ . ɪ . r̅:

In HILGAY 1 free man, 30 acres. 1 plough.

In UPWELL 3 smallholders.

In the whole manor (there) could be 8 ploughs.

Value then £20, now 30.

It has 2 leagues in length and ½ in width, it pays 2s ½d of a
20s tax.

Also 4 free men appertained to this manor before 1066, now W(illiam) of War(enne) has (them).

211 Stigand held CROXTON before 1066. Always 5 c. of land.

Then 8 villagers, later 4, now none. Now 4 smallholders.

Then 5 slaves, later 4, now none.

Then 3 ploughs in lordship, later and now 2. Then 2 men's ploughs. Then 1 mill, which later Earl Ralph took after 1066. Meadow, 3 acres. Always 1 cob; 6 head of cattle; 19 pigs; 215 sheep.

Here appertained 17 Freemen before 1066, of these W(illiam) of War(enne) has 16 and Ralph of Tosny [1].

Value then £10; value now 40s but it pays 100s.

There could be 3 ploughs. The whole has 1½ leagues in length and 1 league in width, it pays 12d of a 20s tax.

LAUNDITCH Hundred

212 Stigand held MILEHAM before 1066, 10 c. of land.

Always 20 villagers; 44 smallholders. Then 6 slaves, later and now 1.

Meadow, 10 acres. Always 2 ploughs in lordship, and 1 plough could be restored. Then 24 men's ploughs, later and now 19, and 5 could be restored. Woodland, 1,000 pigs; Always 1 mill; 1 salt-house.

Also 3 Freemen, 1 c. and 1 acre of land.

Then and later 12 villagers, now 4; always 10 smallholders. Meadow, 4 acres. Then 1 plough in lordship, later and now ½, and ½ could be restored. Then 4 men's ploughs, later and now 2, and the others could be restored. Then woodland, 100 pigs, now 50.

Also 4 Freemen, 30 acres of land.

1 smallholder.

Always 1 plough; meadow, 4 acres.

Also 1 Freeman, 1 c. of land; 1 Freeman, 8 acres.

In all, 10 smallholders.

Meadow, 5 acres. Then 2 ploughs in lordship, later and now 3.

1 men's plough; woodland, 10 pigs.

Also 7 Freemen, 40 acres of land.

1 smallholder.

Meadow, 4 acres; always 2 ploughs in lordship. Always 1 cob;

7 XIII . añ . 7 XXIIII . porc . 7 XXX . ou . 7 . L . cap . Huic manerio
femp jac& . I . beruita Licham . IIII . car træ . femp IX . uitt . 7
XI . bord . 7 v . fer . 7 . IIII . ac pti . femp . II . car in dñio . tnc .
7 p̃ IX . car hom . m̃ . v . & alie poffent reftaurari . & . II . foc .
IIII . ac træ 7 dim . femp . I . r̃ . 7 . I . añ . 7 XVI . porc . 7 CIIII .
ou . & XX . cap . ⌐ Iac& eiam alia beruita . Dumha . IIII .
car træ . Tnc XVIIII . uitt . p̃ & m̃ . x . femp VIII . bord .
tnc & p̃ . II . fer . m̃ nullus . filua . XX . por . 7 . I . ac pti . Et
VIII . foc . XXXIIII . ac træ . 7 . I . bord . 7 . I . ac pti . tc . I . car .
& dim . p̃ 7 m̃ . I . In dñio . femp . I . car & dim poff& reftau
rari . & tnc . I . car 7 dim hom . p̃ . I . m̃ dim . 7 . I . poffet
reftaur . femp . II . añ . 7 VIII . por . 7 VI . ou . In hac bereu -
uita . femp dim mercatu . & intedfort . dim ac træ .
& . II . foc . XL . ac træ . 7 . II . bor . femp . I . car . Totu hoc
uat tepr . r . e . XXX . lib . p̃ 7 m̃ . LX . lib blancas . & ht
III . leug in lon . 7 . I . inlato . & XXVII . d̃ . de gelto . de
XX . fot qui cq̃ ibi tram habeat.
⌐ In Britringa . VII . ac filuæ . 7 . I . ac træ . in qua fñt . IIII .
bord . hoc reuocat Godric ad feudu radulfi comitis.
& queda femina que hoc tenuit . t . r . e . uult ferre
judiciu qd diffolutu ∹ auadimonio . hoc ten& fiuuard
in uadimonio . ⌐ In kertlinga . II . foc . XVII . ac træ . 7
. I . ac pti . t . r . e . dim car m̃ nichil . & hoc . e . in ptio
⌐ de mutha.

13 head of cattle; 24 pigs; 30 sheep; 50 goats.

1 outlier, LITCHAM, has always appertained to this manor, 4 c. of land.

    Always 9 villagers; 11 smallholders; 5 slaves.

    Meadow, 4 acres; always 2 ploughs in lordship. Then and later 9 men's ploughs, now 5, and the others could be restored.

    Also 2 Freemen, 4½ acres of land.

        Always 1 cob; 1 head of cattle; 16 pigs; 104 sheep; 20 goats.

Another outlier, DUNHAM, also appertains there, 4 c. of land.

    Then 19 villagers, later and now 10; always 8 smallholders.

        Then and later 2 slaves, now none.

    Woodland, 20 pigs; meadow, 1 acre.

    Also 8 Freemen, 34 acres of land.

        1 smallholder.

        Meadow, 1 acre. Then 1½ ploughs, later and now 1.

        In lordship always 1 plough, and ½ could be restored. Then 1½ men's ploughs, later 1, now ½, and 1 could be restored.

        Always 2 head of cattle; 8 pigs; 6 sheep.

In this outlier always ½ market.

    Also in THETFORD ½ acre of land.

    Also 2 Freemen, 40 acres of land.

        2 smallholders.

        Always 1 plough.

Value of all this before 1066 £30; later and now £60 blanched.

    It has 3 leagues in length and 1 in width; [it pays] 27d of a 20s tax, whoever has the land there.

213 In BITTERING 7 acres of woodland and 1 acre of land in which are 4 smallholders.

    This Godric claims as part of the Holding of Earl Ralph. A certain woman who held it before 1066 is willing to undergo judicial ordeal that it has been released from pledge. Siward holds this in pledge.

214 In KIRTLING 2 Freemen, 17 acres of land.

    Meadow, 1 acre. Before 1066 1 plough, now nothing. This is in the valuation of Mileham.

Feorhou . H̃ . Wimundhã tenuit Stigand tepr . r . e.
IIII . car̃ træ . Semp . LX . uill̃ . & L . borð . 7 VIII . ſer . ſemp
IIII . car̃ in dnio . tnc LX car̃ hom . m̃ XXIIII . hanc con
fuſione fec Rad de Warr . anteq̃ foris facer& . &cṛ̃is poſ
ſent reſtaurari . Tñc ſilua . c . por . m̃ . LX . 7 LX . ac̃ p̃ti.
ſemp . II . mol̃ . & . I . piſc . ſemp . II . r̃ . 7 XVI . an̄ . 7 L . por.
& XX . IIII . ou . Huic manerio jacebant . t . r . e . LXXX
VII . ſoc . m̃ tantum XVIII . 7 ht̃ . XXX . ac̃ træ . ſemp
I . car̃ . & adhuc . I . ſoc . I . car̃ træ . ſemp . IIII . uill̃ . 7.
X . borð . & . I . mol̃ . ſilua XVI . porc̃ . & . IIII . ac̃ p̃ti.
Hoc maneriũ cũ tota ſoca ualebat . t . r . e . c ſoca . XX.
lib̃ . M̃ . LX . & ht̃ . II . leug in long̃ . 7 . I . in lat̃ . 7 VI . ſol̃.
7 VIII . ð de gelto . Ex his ſokemanis qui abbati ſñt
ht̃ Will̃s de uuar . LV . 7 ht̃ ſub ſe . LVII . borð . int̃ totũ
ht̃ . V . car̃ træ . & XII . ac̃ p̃ti . 7 tepr . r . e . habebant . XX.
car̃ . m̃ . XIII . & dim̃ mol̃ . ſemp ual x . lib̃ . & Radulf̃
de bellafago . habet . x . ſoc . II . car̃ træ . 7 XXXII . bor.
ſemp . VII . car̃ . 7 XII . ac̃ p̃ti . 7 . I . mol̃ . 7 dim̃ . & comes
alan . I . ſoc̃ . I . car̃ træ 7 dim̃ . 7 XIII . borð . 7 . III . car̃ . 7
IX ac̃ p̃ti . & . I . mol̃ . 7 ual XXX . ſol̃ . ⌐ & Rog̃ . bigot
. II . ſoc . XL . V . ac̃ træ . 7 VI . borð . 7 . II . car̃ . 7 . II . ac̃
p̃ti . tnc ſilua . LX . por . m̃ . XVI . 7 ual . VII . ſol̃ . 7 VI . ð.

⌐ BLAWEFELLE . H̃ . Torp ten ſtigand archiepc̃.
t . r . e . III . car̃ træ . Tñc XXIIII . uill̃ . p̃ XX . III . m̃ XXII.

& V . borð . ſemp . tnc 7 p̃ . II . ſer . m̃ . I . tc . II . car̃ in dnio
p̃ 7 m̃ . I . Semp . IIII . car̃ houm . Silua ad . Ꝏ . cc . por . & XL . ac̃

215 Stigand held WYMONDHAM before 1066. 4 c. of land.
     Always 60 villagers; 50 smallholders; 8 slaves.
     Always 4 ploughs in lordship. Then 60 men's ploughs, now
          24; Ralph Wader made this undoing before he
          forfeited, and they could all be restored. Then woodland
          100 pigs, now 60. Meadow, 60 acres. Always 2 mills;
          1 fishery. Always 2 cobs; 16 head of cattle; 50 pigs;
          24 sheep.
     87 Freemen appertained to this manor before 1066, now only 18.
     They have 30 acres of land.
          Always 1 plough.
     Further 1 Freeman, 1 c. of land.
          Always 4 villagers; 10 smallholders;
          1 mill; woodland, 16 pigs; meadow, 4 acres.
Value of this manor with all jurisdiction before 1066 [£.], with
(the) jurisdiction (worth) £20; now 60.
     It has 2 leagues in length and 1 in width, tax of 6s 8d.
     Among these Freemen who have been taken away William of
Warenne has 55. They have under them
     57 smallholders.
     In all they have 5 c. of land.
     Meadow, 12 acres. Before 1066 they had 20 ploughs, now 13.
          ½ mill.
Value always £10.
Also Ralph of Beaufour has 10 Freemen, 2 c. of land.
     32 smallholders.
     Always 7 ploughs; meadow, 12 acres; 1½ mills.
Also Count Alan (has) 1 Freeman, 1½ c. of land.
     13 smallholders.
     3 ploughs; meadow, 9 acres; 1 mill.
Value 30s.
Also Roger Bigot (has) 2 Freemen, 45 acres of land.
     6 smallholders.
     2 ploughs; meadow, 2 acres. Woodland, then 60 pigs, now 16.
Value 7s 6d.

BLOFIELD Hundred
216 Archbishop Stigand held THORPE (St. Andrew) before 1066, 3 c.
     of land.
          Then 24 villagers, later 23, now 22; 5 smallholders always. 138 a
               Then and later 2 slaves, now 1.
          Then 2 ploughs in lordship, later and now 1. Always 4 men's
               ploughs; woodland for 1,200 pigs; meadow, 40 acres.

p̃ti . tnc̄ 7 m̃ . 1 . r̃ . ſemp . 11 . añ . 7 xiii . por . Semp xxxvi.
cap̃ . Sep xxvi . ſoc̄ . de . 11 . car̃ tr̃æ . uñ ht̃ . iii . bord̃ . Semp
iiii . car̃ & dim̃ 7 de uno iſtoʒ habuit . R . co̅mes . dim̃ de
xxx . ac̃ tr̃æ . & ſoca̅ ſtigandi . & quando R . ſe forisfecit.
habuit hoc̃ & ſoca̅ . 7 p̃ R . blund̃ . ad cenſum . m̃ . W . de
noiers in cenſu de torp . Tnc̃ ual xii . lib̃ . 7 . 1 . ſext̃ meſt.
& . 11 . m̃ . alleciu̅ . p̃ & m̃ xxx . lib̃ . blanc̃ . & ht̃ . iii . leug̃.
in long̃ . 7 . 1 . leu̅ 7 . iii . quar iñ lat & de gelto . viii . đ.
Et in eade̅ . iii . ſoc̄ 7 dim̃ . cu̅ ſoca & ſaca . de xxxii . ac̃ tr̃æ
7 . iiii . ac̃ p̃ti . Semp int hoes . 1 . car̃ m̃ ten& goduin halden
ex dono co̅mit R . & hundret teſtat̃ ſ; ptinent in torp
cu̅ c̃ſuet . Adhuc . c . xl . ou̅ . Sep ual xxiiii . đ.

FlecWeſt . H̄ . Somertuna . tenuit archiſti . 1 . lib̃um
hoe̅m đ . 1 . car̃ tr̃æ . Semp . xii . uiſt . 7 xi . bord̃ . 7 vi . acr̃
& dim̃ p̃ti . 7 . 1 . ſat & dim̃ . Semp . 1 . car̃ in dñio . 7 . 1 . car̃
& dim̃ hou̅ . 7 ſemp . iii . r̃ . tnc̃ viii . añ . 7 ſemp ; & c . xl . v . ou̅.
& . 11 . uaſa apu̅ . Adhuc ſ̃nt ibi xix . ſoc̄ . 7 . 1 . car̃ tr̃æ . 7 . iii.
car̃ . Sep ual . xx . ſol . & hanc tram ten W de noiers
in firma de meleha̅ . 7 ſoca . ÷ in hund . & potuit ea̅
uendere ſine licentia ſtigandi Richard̃ punat̃ ad cenſau̅.

⌐Heineſt̃ . H̄ . ⌐ Hameringahala . 1 . b̃wita de . 1 . car̃
tr̃æ ptinens in torp . Tnc̃ xvi . uiſt . p̃ 7 m̃ . viii . Tnc̃.

138 a

Then and now 1 cob. Always 2 head of cattle; 13 pigs; always
36 goats.
Always 26 Freemen, at 2 c. of land. One has
3 smallholders.
Always 4½ ploughs.
Of one of them Earl R(alph) had a half, at 30 acres of land,
and the jurisdiction of Stigand; and when R(alph) forfeited he
had the man and the jurisdiction; and later R(obert) Blunt at
tribute; now W(illiam) of Noyers in the tribute of Thorpe (St.
Andrew).
Value then £12 and 1 sester of honey and 2,000 herrings; later
and now £30 blanched.
It has 3 leagues in length and 1 league and 3 furlongs in width,
tax of 8d.
Also in the same 3 Freemen and a half with the full jurisdiction,
at 32 acres of land.
Meadow, 4 acres; always 1 plough among the men.
Now Godwin Haldane holds them from the gift of Earl R(alph)
and the Hundred testifies to it, but they belong in Thorpe with
the customary dues.
Further 140 sheep.
Value always 24d.

WEST FLEGG Hundred
217 Archbishop Stigand held SOMERTON; 1 free man, at 1 c. of land.
Always 12 villagers, 11 smallholders.
Meadow, 6½ acres; 1½ salt-houses. Always 1 plough in
lordship; 1½ men's ploughs. Always 3 cobs. Then 8 head
of cattle. Always, 145 sheep; 2 beehives.
Further there are 19 Freemen, 1 c. of land.
3 ploughs.
Value always 20s.
W(illiam) of Noyers holds this land in the revenue of Mileham.
The jurisdiction is in the Hundred. He (the 1 free man) could sell
it without the licence of Stigand. Richard Poynant leased it.

HENSTEAD Hundred
218 1 outlier, ARMINGHALL, at 1 c. of land, belonging in Thorpe (St.
Andrew).
Then 16 villagers, later and now 8.

Tc̄ . ıı . ſeꝛ m̄ . null̄ . Semp . ııı . borđ . Tnc̄ . ı . car̄ 7 dim̄ in dn̄io.
p̄ 7 m̄ . ı . Tnc̄ . ıııı . car̄ hom̄ . p̄ 7 m̄ . ıı . Silua . vııı . poꝛ.
7 xıı . ac̄ p̄ti . Tnc̄ . ı . mol̄ . p̄ 7 m̄ null̄ quia eudo clamahoc
abſtulit t . r . W . m̄ ten& . R . de belfago . ſucceſſoꝛ ſuus.
teſte hundret . & reddit xx . ıııı . ſol̄ . In ƀwita s̄ . ıııı . ſoc̄.
de xx . ac̄ træ . Semp . ı . car̄ . ht̄ v . quar̄ in lonḡ . & . ııı.
in lato . & de gelto vııı . đ.

Hersam dimiđ . H̄ . Herſam tenuit ſtigand̄ . t .
r . e . p . ııı . car̄ træ . Tnc̄ 7 p̄ xxı . uill̄ m̄ xxv . Semp
xxıııı . borđ . & ſemp . v . ſeꝛ . Tnc̄ . ııı . car̄ in dn̄io . p̄
7 m̄ . ıı . Tnc̄ xvı . car̄ hou . p̄ & m̄ xıı . Tnc̄ ſilua . ccc.
porc̄ . p̄ 7 m̄ . cc . xx . ac̄ p̄ti . Semp . ıı . mol̄ . 7 ſemp . ııı.
equi in aula . & . ı . an̄ . Tnc̄ xL . porc̄ . 7 m̄ ſimilit̄ . Sep
xxx . cap̄ . 7 . xı . ſoc̄ . de . ı . car̄ træ . 7 . ıııı . borđ . Tnc̄
ıııı . car̄ . p̄ & m̄ . ııı . Silua xL . poꝛ . 7 xıı . ac̄ p̄ti . Tnc̄
ual̄ xı . liƀ . p̄ & m̄ xL . liƀ . blanc̄ . cu omıƀȝ que ad
jacent ht̄ . ı . leuḡ 7 dim̄ in longo . 7 ı . leuḡ in lato.
& de gelto . vı . đ.

[In dentuna . xıı . ſoc̄ . de his . habebat Stigand ſoc̄
in erſa . & habebant Lx . ac̄ . & de . ıııı . ſc̄s edmund̄
habebat ſoca . & habebant . xL . ac̄ . qđ nec dare nec
uendere poterat tram ſuā extra eccl̄am . ſ; Roḡ
bigot . addidit i erſam ꝓpt c̄ſuet . quia ſoca erat
in hund̄ . Semp . v . car̄ . int oēs . [In aldeƀga xv .

xv . liƀi hoēs . de tredeci habebat antec̄ eudonis filiȷ.
ſpiruwic com̄đ de . ıı . ſc̄s edmund̄ Int̄ oēs de Lxxx
ac̄ træ . 7 . ıııı . ac̄ p̄ti . Semp int oēs . v . car̄ . 7 ht̄ . ı . leuḡ
in lonḡ 7 v . qꝛ in lato . & de gelto . x . đ . S; plures ibi
tenent . [In redanaha . vıı . liƀi hoēs ſtigandi com̄đ
t . r . e . de Lx . ac̄ træ . 7 . ıı . bor̄ . tc̄ . ııı . car̄ . p̄ 7 m̄ . ıı.
Silua . ıııı . porc̄ . 7 . ıı . ac̄ p̄ti .

Then 2 slaves, now none; always 3 smallholders.

Then 1½ ploughs in lordship, later and now 1. Then 4 men's
ploughs, later and now 2. Woodland, 8 pigs; meadow, 12
acres. Then 1 mill, later and now none, because Eudo
Clamahoc took it away after 1066, and now R(alph) of
Beaufour his successor holds it, as the Hundred testifies.

It pays 24s.

In the outlier are 4 Freemen, at 20 acres of land.

Always 1 plough.

It has 5 furlongs in length and 3 in width, tax of 8d.

EARSHAM Half-Hundred

219 Stigand held EARSHAM before 1066, as 3 c. of land.

Then and later 21 villagers, now 25. Always 24 smallholders;
always 5 slaves.

Then 3 ploughs in lordship, later and now 2. Then 16 men's
ploughs, later and now 12. Then woodland, 300 pigs, later
and now, 200. Meadow, 20 acres; always 2 mills. Always
3 horses at the hall; 1 head of cattle. Then 40 pigs, now the
same; always 30 goats.

Also 11 Freemen, at 1 c. of land. 4 smallholders.

Then 4 ploughs, later and now 3. Woodland, 40 pigs; meadow,
12 acres.

Value then £11; later and now £40 blanched. With everything
that is attached to it, it has 1½ leagues in length and 1 league in
width, tax of 6d.

220 In DENTON 12 Freemen. Stigand had the jurisdiction of 9 of these
in Earsham and they had 60 acres; St. Edmund had the
jurisdiction of 4 and they had 40 acres, so that they could
neither grant nor sell their land outside the church. But Roger
Bigot added them to Earsham on account of the customary dues,
because the jurisdiction was in the Hundred.

Always 5 men's ploughs among them all.

221 In ALBURGH 15 free men. The predecessor of Eudo son of
Spirwic had the patronage of 13, St. Edmund of 2. At 80 acres
of land among them all;

meadow, 4 acres. Always 5 men's ploughs among them all.

It has 1 league in length and 5 furlongs in width, tax of 10d.

But more hold there.

222 In REDENHALL 7 free men under the patronage of Stigand before
1066, at 60 acres of land.

2 smallholders.

Then 3 ploughs, later and now 2. Woodland, 4 pigs; meadow,
2 acres.

In ſtereſtuna xv ſoc ſtigandi ptinentes ad erſam cu
ſoca . tent . LXXX . ac træ . 7 . 11 . ac p̄ti . 7 vi . bord . Semp
viii . car int oes . ⌐ In eade xv . ſoc de quibƷ ſcs edmund
t . r . e . habuit comd . ſ; tra eoƷ omino erat in eccla
ſ; ſoca 7 ſaca in herſa . 7 R . bigot ido addidit qno ten
man herſam tempr ſtigandi . Int oes LX . ac træ . 7 . 1 . ac
p̄ti . Semp . 111 . car .

⌐ In riueſſalla . x . libi hoes ſtigandi . t . r . e . d̄ . LX . ac .
& . 111 . bord . Semp . 111 . car . Silua . vi . por . 7 . 11 . acr
p̄ti . ⌐ In torp . xx . libi hoes . 11 . ſtigandi fuer comend .
& habebant   ac træ . t . r . e . 7 xviii . ſci edmundi
comd . 7 n̄ poterant reddere ſine licentia ſci . ſ; ſoca
7 ſaca in herſa . Semp vi . car int oes . Silua . 1111 . pors
7 . 1111 . ac p̄ti . ht dim leug in longo . 7 v . quar in
lat . & de gelto vi . d̄ . ⌐ In brodiſo . xxviii . libi hoes
v . ſtigandi cu dim car træ . t . r . e . 7 xxiii . ſci edm
de c . 7 xL . ac . ſ; nec dare nec uendere poterant

139 b
ſine licentia ſtigandi . qui ſoca habebat . Tnc inf oes . viii . car
m̄ . vii . ſilua . xii . porc . vi . ac p̄ti . ht vii . quar in long . 7
v . quar in lato . & . 1111 . pcas . & de gelto . vi . d̄ . Soca 7 ſaca
de omibƷ iſtis fuit ſtigandi . t . r . e . Iſti oes libi reddebant
ſtigando . t . r . e . xL . ſol . Si n̄ redderent . eſſent forefacti
de . 1111 . lib . m̄ reddnt xvi . lib ad numeru in herſam
ubi Richard pugnat eos adcenſauit . t . r . e . habuit
ſtigand ſoca & ſaca . de hoc dim hundreto . pt torp .
ſci edmundi . 7 pt pulha ſcæ aldredre in herſam . Qno
R . ſe forefec . habuit ſoca 7 ſaca de radahalla & de comen
datis ſuis . Qndo Reimund Girald diſceſſit habuit ſoca
de ſua tra . p R . pictauenſis ſucceſſor ejus . de tra u qua
ſcs edmund ht in hoc dim hund tenuit ſocam ; In pre
leſtuna de tinuit Warenger ad feudu Rogi de ramis

223 In STARSTON 15 Freemen of Stigand's belonging to Earsham with the jurisdiction. They hold 80 acres of land;
meadow, 2 acres.
6 smallholders.
Always 8 ploughs among them all.
In the same 15 Freemen of whom St. Edmund had the patronage before 1066. But their land was entirely in the church, but the full jurisdiction was in Earsham, and R(oger) Bigot therefore added them when he held the manor of Earsham in the time of Stigand. 60 acres of land among them all.
Meadow, 1 acre; always 3 ploughs.

224 In RUSHALL 10 free men of Stigand's before 1066, at 60 acres.
3 smallholders.
Always 3 ploughs; woodland, 6 pigs; meadow, 2 acres.

225 In THORPE (Abbots) 20 free men: 2 under the patronage of Stigand, and they had 100 acres of land before 1066; 18 (were) under the patronage of St. Edmund and they could not give up (their land) without permission of the Saint, but the full jurisdiction (was) in Earsham.
Always 6 ploughs among them all; woodland, 4 pigs, meadow, 4 acres.
It has ½ league in length and 5 furlongs in width; tax of 6d.

226 In BROCKDISH 28 free men: 5 of Stigand's with ½ c. of land before 1066; and 23 of St. Edmund's, at 140 acres; but they could neither grant nor sell (their land) without the permission of   139 b
Stigand who had the jurisdiction.
Then 8 ploughs among them all, now 7. Woodland, 12 pigs; meadow, 6 acres.
It has 7 furlongs in length, 5 furlongs and 4 perches in width, tax of 6d.
The full jurisdiction of all these was Stigand's before 1066. All these free (men) paid Stigand 40s before 1066. If they did not pay they forfeited £4. Now they pay £16 at face value in Earsham, where Richard Poynant leased them out. Before 1066 Stigand had the full jurisdiction of this Half-Hundred, except Thorpe (Abbotts) (which was) of St. Edmund, and Pulham (which was) of St. Etheldreda in (the lands of) Earsham. When R(alph) forfeited he had the full jurisdiction of Redenhall and of (the men) under his patronage. When Raymond Gerald departed he had the jurisdiction of his own land, (as did) later his successor, R(oger) of Poitou; but indeed of the land which St. Edmund had in this Half-Hundred (St. Edmund) held the jurisdiction. In Billingford, Warenger retained as part of the Holding of Roger of Raismes.

⌐In redanahalla & in dentuna . ɪɪ . libi hoes ſtigandi cu̅
ſoca . xxɪɪɪ . ac tɼæ . Semp di̅m caɼ . & di̅m ac p̃ti . ap
p̃tiatu̅ eſt cu̅ alijs.

LOTHNINGA . H̃ . ⌐Dicingaha . ɪ . beruuita in erſa
de . ɪɪɪ . caɼ tɼæ qua ſtigand . t . r . e . Tnc ɪx uiłł . p̃
& m̃ vɪɪɪ . Tnc v . borđ . p̃ & m̃ . ɪɪɪɪ . Tnc . ɪɪɪɪ . ſeɼ.
p̃ 7 m̃ . ɪɪ . Tnc . ɪɪ . caɼ in dn̅io . p̃ . ɪ . m̃ . ɪɪ . Semp . ɪɪɪɪ .
caɼ hom̃ . Silua . c . porc̃ . 7 xvɪɪɪ . ac p̃ti . Tnc . ɪɪ . mot
p̃ & m̃ . ɪ . Semp xlvɪɪɪ . porc̃ . 7 lx . ɪɪɪɪ . ou̅ . 7 lv . cap̃.
& xxɪɪ . ſoc̃ . ſnt ibi de . ɪ . caɼ tɼæ 7 dim . Semp int oes.

140 a

vɪɪɪ . caɼ . Silua . ɪɪɪɪ . por . & ɪx ac p̃ti . 7 . ɪ . mot app̃tiatu
eſt in herſam . & h̃t . ɪ . leu̅g . 7 . ɪɪɪɪ . quaɼ in longo . 7 ɪx
in lato . 7 vɪɪɪ . đ de gelto . q̃cuq̃ ibi teneat

⌐In mundaha . vɪɪ . libi hoes p̃tinentes iſti b̃wite . De his
vɪɪ . fueɼ . ɪɪɪ . ſtigandi . 7 . ɪɪ . eduini comend . 7 . ɪ . algari
& ɪ . tohli uicecomitis . Int oes lx . ac tɼæ . Semp . ɪɪɪ . caɼ.
Quatuor ex his calunniatur Rob̃ filius corbutionis
exlib̃atione regis xxɪɪɪɪ . ac tɼæ teſte hund . f̃ p̃ ea
addidit eos . R . bigot . in erſam . 7 h̃t lɪɪ . ac̃ . Rex
& c̃ ſoca app̃t ſnt in erſam.

⌐Inſilinga ten̅ . ɪ . lib̃ ho̅ . ſubſtigando . ɪ . caɼ tɼæ p̃qua
rex Wiłł uenit in anglia addidit ipſe ſtiga . b̃wita
in ſtotes . Semp . ɪ . uiłł . Tnc . ɪɪ . borđ . p̃ 7 m̃ . ɪɪɪ . borđ.
Tnc 7 p̃ . ɪ . caɼ in dn̅io . m̃ . ɪ . 7 dim . Semp dim caɼ hou̅m
& . ɪ . ac dim p̃ti . Semp . ɪ . eq in aula m̃ . ɪɪɪ . porc̃ . & xxɪ.
ſoc̃ t . r . e . p̃ 7 m̃ xɪɪ . & h̃t xxɪɪɪɪ . ac tɼæ . Semp . ɪ . caɼ.
dim ac p̃ti . & e̅ inp̃tio de toſtes . Tn̅c uał xl ſoł . m̃ red
dit . ɪɪɪɪ . lib̃ . 7 x . ſoł . intoſtes . 7 h̃t . ɪ . leu̅g in long . 7 . ɪ.
in lato . & de gelto xvɪ . đ.

H̃ de taureham . Horſteda tenuit Stingand . t . r . e.
ɪɪɪɪ . caɼ tɼæ . Tnc xvɪɪɪɪ . uiłł . p̃ 7 m̃ xvɪ . ſemp . ɪx . boɼ.

227 In REDENHALL and in DENTON 2 free men of Stigand's with
jurisdiction, 23 acres of land:
Always ½ plough; meadow, ½ acre.
It is assessed with the others.

LODDON Hundred
228 DITCHINGHAM, 1 outlier, in (the lands of) Earsham, at 3 c. of land,
which Stigand held before 1066.
Then 9 villagers, later and now 8. Then 5 smallholders, later
and now 4. Then 4 slaves, later and now 2.
Then 2 ploughs in lordship, later 1, now 2. Always 4 men's
ploughs; woodland, 100 pigs; meadow, 18 acres. Then
2 mills, later and now 1. Always 48 pigs; 64 sheep; 55 goats.
Also there are 22 Freemen, at 1½ c. of land.
Always 8 ploughs among them all; woodland, 4 pigs; meadow, 140 a
9 acres; 1 mill.
It is assessed in Earsham. It has 1 league and 4 furlongs in length
and 9 [furlongs] in width, tax of 8d, whoever holds there.

229 In MUNDHAM 7 free men belonging to this outlier. Of these 7, 3
were under the patronage of Stigand, 2 under the patronage of
Edwin, 1 of Algar, and 1 of Toli, the Sheriff. Among them all 60
acres of land.
Always 3 ploughs.
Robert son of Corbucion claims 4 of these of the King's livery,
24 acres of land, as the Hundred testifies; but afterwards R(oger)
Bigot added them to Earsham, and he has 52 acres. The King and
the Earl (have) the jurisdiction. It is assessed in Earsham.

230 1 free man held in SEETHING under Stigand, 1 c. of land. After
King William came to England Stigand himself added it as an
outlier in (the lands of) Toft (Monks).
Always 1 villager. Then 2 smallholders, later and now 3
smallholders.
Then and later 1 plough in lordship, now 1½. Always ½ men's
plough; meadow, 1½ acres; always 1 horse at the hall. Now
3 pigs.
Before 1066 21 Freemen, later and now 12; they have 24 acres
of land. Always 1 plough; meadow, ½ acre.
It is in the valuation of Toft (Monks).
Value then 40s; now it pays £4 10s in Toft (Monks).
It has 1 league in length and 1 in width, tax of 16d.

The Hundred of TAVERHAM
231 Stigand held HORSTEAD before 1066, 4 c. of land.
Then 19 villagers, later and now 16; always 9 smallholders.

Tñc.viii.ſ.p̄ 7 m̃.iiii.ſemp.ii.caȓ in dñio.tñc x.
caȓ hom̃.p̄ 7 m̃.vi.7 xii.acȓ p̃ti.ſilua ʟx.por.ſemp
iii.moɫ.7.i.ȓ.7.ii.añ.7 vii.por.7 xx.oũ.Tñc.xxx.caƥ.

140 b

m̃.xʟ.7 ſemp.i.uaſa apum.Tñc jacebant huic manerio
xviii.ſoc de.iii.caȓ træ.qui fueȓ libati robto blacardo.
m̃ ſnt adfeudum Rog̃ pictauenſis

In Staningehalla.i.lib ho.i.caȓ træ.7.iiii.uiɫɫ.7.iiii.
bord.&.ii.caȓ.n.ii.moɫ.ſilua.xx.por.hoc jac& in
horſteda.& totum.e.in p̃cio de Mulham;& horſteda.
ht̄.i.leug in long.7 aɫ in laɫ.7 xv.đ de gelto.

In Cattuna.xiii.ſoc.i.caȓ træ.ſemp.iii.bord.Tñc.
iii.caȓ.p̄ 7 m̃.ii.ſilua xii.porc.& ht̄.i.leug.in long
& v.quaȓ in laɫ.7 viii.đ.7.iii.ferdins de gelto.hoc.e.
inptio de thorp.

In Sproweſtuna.cxʟ ac̄ træ.tñc.iii.caȓ.p̄ & m̃.ii.
&.iiii.acȓ p̃ti.Silua.iiii.porc.& ht̄.i.leug in long.
& viii.quaȓ in laɫ.7 xv.đ de gelto qui cq̄ ibi teneat.
Hoc etiam.e.in p̃cio de torp.In belaga.i.caȓ terre.
xxiiii.ac̄.quã teñ Stigand.ſemp.ii.bor.7 viii.ac̄
p̃ti.Tñc.i.caȓ.& e in p̃tio de hoſteda.

Humiliart.H̄.Lakemhã tenuit Stigand.t.r.e.
bereuuita intorp.ii.caȓ træ.ſemp xi.uiɫɫ.7.ii.ſoc
iiii.ac̄.Tñc.ii.caȓ in dñio.p̄ 7 m̃.i.7.i.eccɫa.de
xiii.ac̄.in elemoſina.Tñc.iii.caȓ hom̃.p̄ & m̃.ii.
& iii.caȓ poſſent reſtaurari.vii.ac̄ p̃ti.ſemp.i.moɫ
hoc e in p̃tio de torp.& ht̄.ii.leug in long.& vii.
quaȓ in laɫ.7.iii.đ.7.iii.ferding.de g.

Then 8 slaves, later and now 4.

Always 2 ploughs in lordship. Then 10 men's ploughs, later
and now 6. Meadow, 12 acres; woodland, 60 pigs. Always
3 mills; 1 cob; 2 head of cattle; 7 pigs; 20 sheep. Then 30
goats, now 40; always 1 beehive.   140 b

Then 18 Freemen appertained to this manor at 3 c. of land,
who were delivered to Robert Blanchard; now they are part of
the Holding of Roger of Poitou.

232 In STANNINGHALL 1 free man, 1 c. of land.
4 villagers; 4 smallholders.
2 ploughs; 2 mills; woodland, 20 pigs.
This appertains in Horstead, and the whole is in the valuation
of Mileham. Horstead has 1 league in length and another in width,
tax of 15d.

233 In CATTON 13 Freemen, 1 c. of land.
Always 3 smallholders.
Then 3 ploughs, later and now 2. Woodland, 12 pigs.
It has 1 league in length and 5 furlongs in width, tax of 8¾d.
This is in the valuation of Thorpe (St. Andrew).

234 In SPROWSTON 140 acres of land.
Then 3 ploughs, later and now 2. Meadow, 4 acres; woodland,
4 pigs.
It has 1 league in length and 8 furlongs in width, tax of 15d,
whoever holds there. This also is in the valuation of Thorpe
(St. Andrew).

235 In BELAUGH 1 c. of land and 24 acres which Stigand held.
Always 2 smallholders.
Meadow, 8 acres. Then 1 plough.
It is in the valuation of Horstead.

HUMBLEYARD Hundred
236 Stigand held LAKENHAM before 1066, an outlier in (the lands of)
Thorpe (St. Andrew), 2 c. of land.
Always 11 villagers.
2 Freemen, 4 acres.
Then 2 ploughs in lordship, later and now 1. 1 church at 13
acres in alms. Then 3 men's ploughs, later and now 2, and
3 ploughs could be restored. Meadow, 7 acres; always 1 mill.
This is in the valuation of Thorpe (St. Andrew). It has 2 leagues
in length and 7 furlongs in width, tax of 3¾d.

⌐Depwade . H̃ . Ta Coluestuna tenuit Stigand̃ p̔ ḃuinita
in Wimundha . v . car̂ træ . ſemp xvi . uiſt . 7 xxi . bord . 7 vi .
ſer̂ . 7 . iiii . car̂ in dñio . Tñc xiiii . car̂ hom . p̔ 7 m̂ . v . xii . ac̃ p̃ti .
Silua . xx . por . 7 ſemp . i . moł . 7 . iiii . r . 7 xvi . an̂ . 7 l . por .
7 lxxx . ou . 7 xv . cap̃ . & . v . ſoc . xii . acr̂ . ſemp dim̃ car̂ . &
viii . liḃi hões . i . car̂ træ . 7 . ii . uiſt . 7 viii . bord . Tñc . iii . car̂ .
p̔ 7 m̂ . ii . viii . ac̃ p̃ti . Tñc uał . x . liḃ . m̂ . xx . blancas . & h̃t
i . leug̃ 7 dim̃ in long̃ . 7 dim̃ in lato . 7 x . d̄ . 7 obolum deg̃ .

⌐CLAVERINCA . H̃ . Toſt ten̂ . Stigand̃ . p̔ manerio . t . r . e .
iiii . car̂ træ . 7 xx . ac̃ . ſemp xiiii . uiſti . 7 xviii . bord .
7 viii . ſer . 7 . iii . car̂ in dñio . 7 viii . car̂ . 7 xx ac̃ p̃ti .
Silua . lxxx . por . 7 . i . r . 7 . iiii . an̂ . 7 xx . porc̃ . 7 c . ou .
& v . ſoc̃ . i . car̂ træ . & dim̃ . ſep . v . car̂ . 7 viii . p̃ti .
& hadeſcou . i . berewita . ccxx . ac̃ træ . ſemp vii . uiſt .
& . iiii . bord . 7 tñc . ii . car̂ in dñio . p̔ 7 m̂ . ii . 7 iiii . ac̃ p̃ti .
Tñc . i . car̂ . m̂ dim̃ . 7 c . oues . & . iiii . ſoc̃ . lxxx . ac̃ . Tñc
iii . car̂ . p̔ 7 m̂ . ii . 7 iiii . ac̃ p̃ti . Tñc uał . x . liḃ . m̂ xxiiii .
blancas . & h̃t . i . leug̃ in long̃ . 7 . ii . quar̂ . 7 x . perc̃ .
Et . i . leug̃ in lat̄ . 7 x . d̄ . 7 . iii . ferd̄ . de gelt .

1

DEPWADE Hundred

237 Stigand held TACOLNESTON as an outlier in (the lands of) Wymondham, 5 c. of land.

    Always 16 villagers; 21 smallholders; 6 slaves.

    4 ploughs in lordship. Then 14 men's ploughs, later and now 5.

      Meadow, 12 acres; woodland, 20 pigs. Always 1 mill;

      4 cobs; 16 head of cattle; 50 pigs; 80 sheep; 15 goats.

    Also 5 Freemen, 12 acres.

      Always ½ plough.

    Also 8 free men, 1 c. of land.

      2 villagers; 8 smallholders.

      Then 3 ploughs, later and now 2. Meadow, 8 acres.

  Value then £10; now 20 blanched.

  It has 1½ leagues in length and ½ in width, tax of 10½d.

CLAVERING Hundred

238 Stigand held TOFT (Monks) as a manor before 1066, 4 c. of land and 20 acres.

    Always 14 villagers; 18 smallholders; 8 slaves.

    3 ploughs in lordship; 8 (men's) ploughs; meadow, 20 acres;

      woodland, 80 pigs; 1 cob; 4 head of cattle; 20 pigs;

      100 sheep.

    Also 5 Freemen, 1½ c. of land.

    Always 5 ploughs; meadow, 8 acres.

  Also 1 outlier, HADDISCOE, 220 acres of land.

    Always 7 villagers; 4 smallholders.

    Then 2 ploughs in lordship, later and now 2. Meadow, 4 acres.

      Then 1 plough, now ½. 100 sheep.

    Also 4 Freemen, 80 acres.

      Then 3 ploughs, later and now 2. Meadow, 4 acres.

  Value then £10; now 24 blanched.

  It has 1 league , 2 furlongs and 10 perches in length and 1 league in width, tax of 10¾d.

Stoutuna . tenuit . S . p̄ berewita . t . r . e . in erſam.
ıı . car̄ træ . 7 . ııı . borđ . Tnc . ıı . car̄ . in đnio . p̄ 7 m̄ . ı.
ſemp dim̄ car̄ hom̄ . xıı . ac̄ p̄ti . ſilua . ıııı . porc̄.
& . ı . moł . & . ıı . r̄ . 7 . ıııı . an̄ . & . ıııı . por . & xxx.
ſoc̄ . ııı . car̄ træ . ſemp vııı . car̄ . 7 xvı ac̄ p̄ti . & iu

141 b

eadem . ı . æccła . lxv . ac̄r . 7 . ııı . bor̄ . & dim̄ moł . 7 xıı . ſoc̄.
xxv . ac̄r . ſemp . ııı . car̄ . 7 vı . ac̄ p̄ti . Iacent &iam in Stou
tuna . x . ſoc̄ . ıı . car̄ træ 7 dim̄ . ſemp vı . borđ . 7 vıı . car̄ 7 dim̄.
& vııı . ac̄r p̄ti . Silua . xvı . porc̄ . & xxı . ſoc̄ . in lerpſtuna
c . xx . ac̄r . Tnc . vııı . car̄ . m̄ . v . 7 v . ac̄ p̄ti . & vııı . libi hoēs.
additi ſnt huic manerio . 7 ht̄ xıı . ac̄r ; & dim̄ car̄.
In Elinchā . v . ſoc̄ . xv . ac̄r . 7 dim̄ car̄ . 7 . ı . eccła . xxıııı . ac̄.
In kildinchā . xıı . libi hoēs . ııı . car̄ træ . 7 ıx . borđ . Tnc̄
vııı . car̄ . m̄ . v . xıı . ac̄ p̄ti . ſilua . vııı . por . & . ı . æccła . xxx
ac̄r libē træ . Ex his fuere . ıx . antecefforis . Rađ de bella
fago c̄md . t . r . e . & un̄ alwi deted & un̄ & dim̄ ābbis
de ſc̄o eadmundo . & dimiđi Stigandi . In Eade . ıııı . libi ho
mines xv . ac̄ . 7 dim̄ car̄ . Stigand̄ habuit ſoca . t . r . e.
& ſnt additi in cenſu de erſam . & totū hoc eſt incenſu.
de erſam . tota Stoutuna ht̄ . ıı . leuḡ in lonḡ . 7 . ı . leū
in lat̄ . 7 v . ſoł . 7 . ıııı . đ . de gelto . quicuq̣ ibi teneat.
In Rauincha . ııı . libi hoēs . xxx . ac̄ træ . 7 . ı . car̄ 7 dim̄
ac̄ p̄ti . & e inp̄tio de toft . In Eade . lx . ac̄ træ . ı . lib̄ ho
quas habebat inwadiatas de pluribȝ hoibȝ ſemp . ı . car̄
7 xxvıı . bor . ı . ac̄ p̄ti . 7 uał xx . ſoł.

239 S(tigand) held STOCKTON as an outlier, before 1066, in (the lands of) Earsham, 2 c. of land.

   3 smallholders.
   Then 2 ploughs in lordship, later and now 1. Always ½ men's plough; meadow, 12 acres; woodland, 4 pigs; 1 mill; 2 cobs; 4 head of cattle; 4 pigs.
   Also 30 Freemen, 3 c. of land.
   Always 8 ploughs; meadow, 16 acres.
   Also in the same 1 church, 65 acres.   141 b
   3 smallholders.
   ½ mill.
   Also 12 Freemen, 25 acres.
   Always 3 ploughs; meadow, 6 acres.
Also in Stockton appertain 10 Freemen, 2½ c. of land.
   Always 6 smallholders.
   7½ ploughs; meadow, 8 acres; woodland, 16 pigs.
Also 21 Freemen in *IERPSTUNA*, 120 acres.
   Then 8 ploughs, now 5. Meadow, 5 acres.
Also 8 free men have been added to this manor; they have 12 acres; ½ plough.
In ELLINGHAM, 5 Freemen, 15 acres. ½ plough.
   Also 1 church, 24 acres.
In GILLINGHAM 12 free men, 3 c. of land.
   9 smallholders.
   Then 8 ploughs, now 5. Meadow, 12 acres; woodland, 8 pigs.
   Also 1 church, 30 acres of free land.
Of these 9 were under the patronage of the predecessor of Ralph of Beaufour before 1066, 1 of A(i)fwy of Thetford, 1 and a half of the Abbot of St. Edmund's, and a half of Stigand.
In the same 4 free men, 15 acres. ½ plough.
Stigand had the jurisdiction before 1066. They have been added in the tribute of Earsham, and all this is in the tribute of Earsham.
The whole of Stockton has 2 leagues in length and 1 league in width, tax of 5s 4d, whoever may hold there.

240 In RAVENINGHAM 3 free men, 30 acres of land.
   1 plough; meadow, ½ acre.
It is in the valuation of Toft (Monks).
In the same 1 free man, 60 acres of land which he had pledged from many men.
   Always 1 plough.
   27 smallholders.
   Meadow, 1 acre.
Value 20s.

Inturuertuna . ɪ . lib hō . xx . ac . & dim car . 7 . ɪ . ac p̃ti.
7 ual . ɪɪ . ſol . ╱ In eadē . ɪɪ . libi hões . x . ac . 7 . ɪɪ . bord.
& dim car . 7 . ɪ . ac p̃ti . 7 ual xvɪ . d . In Turuertuna.
ɪ . lib anteceſſoris Radulfi de bellafago . 7 h̃t vɪɪɪ . ac . 7
╱ ual xɪɪ . d.

142 a

Terre epĩ Baiocensis . H̄ . & dim . de fredrebrnge.

In torp . ɪɪ . libi hões . t . r . e . lx ac træ . ſemp . ɪ . uilt . 7 . ɪ . bord.
& . ɪ . ac p̃ti . ſemp . ɪ . car . 7 ual . vɪ . ſol . 7 vɪɪɪ . d . un ex h̃ hõibʒ
fuit cõmdat tantu anteceſſori Rog bigot . hoc totu jac&
in neſteſha . Totu torp . vɪɪɪ . quar in long . 7 . ɪɪɪɪ . in lat . &
reddit . vɪɪɪ . d . de xx . ſol de gelto.

╱ Grimeſtuna ten Stigand . t . r . e . ɪɪɪ . car træ . Tnc xvɪ . uilt.
p̃ & m̃ . vɪɪɪ . ſemp . xɪɪɪ . bord . tnc . ɪ . ſer . xxvɪɪɪ . ac p̃ti.
Tnc . ɪɪ . car in dnio . p̃ 7 m̃ . ɪ . Tnc . ɪ . car houm . p̃ 7 m̃ dim
& . ɪɪɪ . mol . ſemp . ɪ . r . Tnc . ɪɪɪ . an . m̃ . ɪɪɪɪ . ſemp lx ou . Hic
jacent . xɪɪɪɪ . ſoc . ɪ . car træ . ſemp . ɪ . car . Tnc 7 p̃ ual . c.
ſol . m̃ . vɪɪ . lib . Tota Grimeſtuna h̃t . ɪ . leug 7 dim in long.
& in lat . 7 reddit . ɪɪ . ſol . de xx . ſol de gelto.

╱ Herpelai ten Stigand . t . r . e . p̃ . ɪ . bereuuita . inſneſha.
ɪɪ . car træ ſemp . ɪɪ . uilt . 7 . ɪx . bord . Tnc . ɪɪ . car in dnio
m̃ . ɪ . Et . v . ſoc . xɪɪ . ac træ . Tnc . ɪɪ . car houm . m̃ . ɪ . 7 dim.

.II.

241 In THURLTON 1 free man, 20 acres.
    ½ plough; meadow, 1 acre.
Value 2s.
In the same 2 free men, 10 acres.
    2 smallholders.
    ½ plough; meadow, 1 acre.
Value 16d.
In THURLTON 1 free (man) of Ralph of Beaufour's predecessor; he
has 8 acres.
Value 12d.

LANDS OF THE BISHOP OF BAYEUX

The Hundred and a Half of FREEBRIDGE
1 In (Gayton) THORPE 2 Freemen before 1066, 60 acres of land.
    Always 1 villager; 1 smallholder.
    Meadow, 1 acre; always 1 plough.
Value 6s 8d.
    One of these men was under the patronage only of the
predecessor of Roger Bigot. All this appertains in Snettisham.
The whole of (Gayton) Thorpe (has) 8 furlongs in length and 4 in
width, it pays 8d of a 20s tax.

2 Stigand held GRIMSTON before 1066, 3 c. of land.
    Then 16 villagers, later and now 8; always 13 smallholders.
        Then 1 slave.
    Meadow, 28 acres. Then 2 ploughs in lordship, later and now 1.
        Then 1 men's plough, later and now ½. 3 mills; always 1
        cob. Then 3 head of cattle, now 4. Always 60 sheep.
    14 Freemen appertain here, 1 c. of land.
        Always 1 plough.
Value then and later 100s; now £7.
    The whole of Grimston has 1½ leagues in length and in width;
it pays 2s of a 20s tax.

3 Stigand held HARPLEY before 1066 as 1 outlier in (the lands of)
Snettisham, 2 c. of land.
    Always 2 villagers; 9 smallholders.
    Then 2 ploughs in lordship, now 1.
    Also 5 Freemen, 12 acres of land.
    Then 2 men's ploughs, now 1½.

Tnc ual xL.fol.m̄.Lxxx.hoc ten& hugo de portu.

Snettefham.ten Stigand.t.r.e.viii.car trǽ.fep

xx.uilt.7 xii.bord.Tnc vi.fer.p̄ 7 m̄.iii.& xxx.ac
p̄ti.Tnc.iiii.car in dn̄io.p̄ 7 m̄.ii.Tnc vi.car hoūm.
p̄ 7 m̄.iiii.7 v.mol.7.i.fal.7.i.pifc.filua.c.porc.fep.iiii.
r̄.7 xxxviii.porc.7 ccccxL.oū.Et vi.foc.ii.car trǽ.7
x.uilt.7 vi.bord.7.i.fer.7 x.ac p̄ti.& dim̄ mol.7.i.pifc.
& in Scernebruna.i.foc.v.ac.Huic manerio jacet.i.bere
uita Flicha.vii.car trǽ 7 dim̄.femp xviii.uilt.7 xiiii.bor.
7.iii.fer.7 viii.foc.7.iiii.mol.Tnc.iii.car in dn̄io.
p̄ 7 m̄.ii.femp.v.car homū.Jac& &iam.i.bereuita.
in uetuna.i.car & dim̄.7 vi.uilt.7.iii.bord.7.ii.fer.
&.ii.car in dn̄io.Semp.ii.car hom̄.7 xx.ac p̄ti.7.ii.
foc.xvi.ac trǽ.7 dim̄ car.femp.i.r̄.7 vii.ou.Et adhuc
.i.bereuita.Rifinga.iii.car trǽ.femp.xii.uilt.7 xxx.
viii.bord.tc.iiii.fer.m̄.iii.7 xiiii.ac p̄ti.femp.ii.car.
in dn̄io.7.ii.car hou.Et.vii.fochem.xxiiii.ac trǽ.
femp.i.car.7.iii.mol.7 xii.fal.7.i.pifc.Et.iii.foc.
Lx.ac.trǽ.femp.i.car.7.i.foc.Lx.ac.7.i.car.7 xxvi.
bord.7.i.car.7 viii.ac p̄ti.7.i.mol.7.i.fal.Et inreiduna.
.i.foc.i.car trǽ.femp xxv.bord.7.ii.fer.7 vi.ac p̄ti.
&.i.car in dn̄io.7 dim̄ car hoūm.7.ii.fal.Et viii.foc.
.ii.car trǽ.7 xvi.ac.7 v.bord.7.ii.car.7.i.fal.7 dim̄.
Totū ual.t.r.e.L.lib.p̄ 7 m̄ Lxxx.lib.& c.fol.Totū
ht.ii.leug & dim̄ in long.& dim̄ leug in lat quicq̄
ibi teneat.7 reddit.iiii.fol.de xx.fol de gelto regis.

2

Value then 40s; now 80.
    This Hugh of Port holds.

4 Stigand held SNETTISHAM before 1066, 8 c. of land.
    Always 20 villagers; 12 smallholders. Then 6 slaves, later   142 b
       and now 3.
    Meadow, 30 acres. Then 4 ploughs in lordship, later and now 2.
       Then 6 men's ploughs, later and now 4. 5 mills; 1 salt-house;
       1 fishery; woodland, 100 pigs. Always 4 cobs; 38 pigs;
       440 sheep.
    Also 6 Freemen, 2 c. of land.
       10 villagers; 6 smallholders; 1 slave.
       Meadow, 10 acres; ½ mill; 1 fishery.
And in SHERNBORNE 1 Freeman, 5 acres.
1 outlier, FLITCHAM, appertains to this manor, 7½ c. of land.
    Always 18 villagers; 14 smallholders; 3 slaves; 8 Freemen.
    4 mills. Then 3 ploughs in lordship, later and now 2. Always
       5 men's ploughs.
There appertains also 1 outlier, (West) NEWTON, 1½ c. [of land].
    6 villagers; 3 smallholders; 2 slaves.
    2 ploughs in lordship. Always 2 men's ploughs; meadow,
       20 acres.
    Also 2 Freemen, 16 acres of land.
       ½ plough. Always 1 cob; 7 sheep.
Further 1 outlier, (Castle) RISING, 3 c. of land.
    Always 12 villagers; 38 smallholders. Then 4 slaves, now 3.
    Meadow, 14 acres. Always 2 ploughs in lordship; 2 men's
       ploughs.
    Also 7 Freemen, 24 acres of land.
       Always 1 plough; 3 mills; 12 salt-houses; 1 fishery.
    Also 3 Freemen, 60 acres of land; always 1 plough.
    Also 1 Freeman, 60 acres; 1 plough.
       26 smallholders.
       1 plough; meadow, 8 acres; 1 mill; 1 salt-house.
And in ROYDON 1 Freeman, 1 c. of land.
    Always 25 smallholders; 2 slaves.
    Meadow, 6 acres; 1 plough in lordship; ½ men's plough;
       2 salt-houses.
    Also 8 Freemen, 2 c. of land and 16 acres.
       5 smallholders.
       2 ploughs; 1½ salt-houses.
Value of the whole before 1066 £50; later and now £80 and 100s.
    The whole has 2½ leagues in length and ½ league in width,
whoever holds there, it pays 4s of a 20s King's tax.

/ $\bar{H}$. dedochinge . Dochinge . ı . car̃ træ ten̄ . ı . lib̃ ho᷎ Sub̃
ſtigando . ſemp dim̄ car̃ . ııı . bor . hoc e in p̃tio de ſneteſha.
Inſtanho xıı . lib̃i hoe᷎s Sub ſtigando . t . r . e . tn̄c . ıııı . car̃
træ . 7 . ıııı . car̃ tn̄c . p̃ 7 m̃ . ııı . In̄ Stoffta . ıııı . car̃ træ . ten̄
. ı . lib̃ ho᷎ ſub ſtigando . t . r . e . ıı . car̃ in dn̄io . tc 7 p̃ . 7 m̃ . ı.
ſemp vııı . uilt . 7 v . bord̃. Hoc e in p̃tio de Sneteſha . hoc
totũ Stoffta ht̃ . ı . leũ in long̃ . 7 . ıııı . quar̃ . in lat̃ . 7 reddit
x . d̃ de xx . ſot de gelto . Et totũ Stanho . ht̃ . ı . leũ in long̃
& . ıııı . quar̃ in lat̃ . & reddit xıııı . d̃ . 7 . ı . obolũ . de xx . ſot.
de gelto.

/ $\bar{H}$. GRENEHOV . In Warha᷎ . ten̄ Stigand᷎ . ıı . ſoc̃ de dim̃
car̃ træ . ſemp dim̄ car̃ . 7 ſemp uat . xxx . denar̃.

/ HEINESTEDE . $\bar{H}$. Infra᷎mingaha᷎ ten̄& . Rog̃ bigot
lx . ac̃ træ . qm ten̄ Goduin ſub ſtigando . t . r . e . Tn̄c
ıııı . bord̃ . 7 m̃ . vıı . Tn̄c . ıı . car̃ . p̃ . ı . 7 dim̃ . m̃ . ıı . in dn̄io.
Semp . ııı . bou̅ hom̃ . & . ıııı . ſoc̃ . 7 dim̃ . de xvı . ac̃ træ . 7 . ıııı.
ac̃ p̃ti . Sep̃ ar̃ cu᷎ . ııı . bou̅ & in alũtuna . ı . ſoc̃ 7 dim̃ de xvı
ac̃r . Semp ar̃ cu᷎ . ııı . bou̅ . Et in holueſtuna . ııı . ſoc̃ . 7 . ıı . dim̃
de xvı . ac̃ træ . ſemp dim̄ car̃ . 7 in kerkebei . ıı . ſoc̃ . 7 dim̃.
de xıı . ac̃ . Sep̃ ar̃ cu᷎ . ııı . bou̅ . ſemp . ı . eq̃ in aula . Tn̄c
vııı . por . m̃ xxvııı . 7 vı . uaſa apu̅ . Tn̄c 7 p̃ uat xx . ſot.
m̃ xl . / In ſcoteſſa᷎ . ten̄ alured̃ . ı . lib̃ ho᷎ ſubſtig̃ . t . r . e.
xıı . ac̃ . 7 . ııı . ſoc̃ . de xx . ac̃ træ . 7 . ı . ac̃ p̃ti . Semp . ı.
car̃ . Et in porringalanda . ı . lib̃ ho᷎ . 7 . ı . ſoc̃ . de xx . ı . ac̃.

143 a

Semp dim̄ car̃ . / In bra᷎bretuna . ıı . ac̃ 7 dim̃ træ . apptiati ſnt
in Kiningaford . Holueſtuna ht̃ . ıııı . quar̃ in long̃ . 7 . ııı . in
lat̃ . & de gelto . vııı . d̃.

The Hundred of DOCKING
5 1 free man under Stigand held DOCKING, 1 c. of land.
    Always ½ plough.
    3 smallholders.
    This is in the valuation of Snettisham.
In STANHOE 12 free men under Stigand before 1066; then 4 c. of land.
    Then 4 ploughs, later and now 3.
In (Bircham) TOFTS 1 free man under Stigand held 4 c. of land before 1066.
    Then 2 ploughs in lordship, and later and now 1.
    Always 8 villagers; 5 smallholders.
This is in the valuation of Snettisham. All this (Bircham) Tofts has 1 league in length and 4 furlongs in width, it pays 10d of a 20s tax. The whole of Stanhoe has 1 league in length and 4 furlongs in width, it pays 14½d of a 20s tax.

(North) GREENHOE Hundred
6 In WARHAM Stigand held 2 Freemen, at ½ c. of land.
    Always ½ plough.
Value always 30d.

HENSTEAD Hundred
7 In FRAMINGHAM Roger Bigot holds 60 acres of land which Godwin held under Stigand before 1066.
    Then 4 smallholders, now 7.
    Then 2 ploughs, later 1½, now 2 in lordship. The men, always
        3 oxen.
    Also 4 Freemen and a half, at 16 acres of land; meadow, 4 acres.
        They have always ploughed with 3 oxen.
And in YELVERTON 1 Freeman and a half, at 16 acres.
    They have always ploughed with 3 oxen.
And in HOLVERSTON 3 Freemen and 2 halves, at 16 acres of land.
    Always ½ plough.
And in KIRBY (Bedon) 2 Freemen and a half, at 12 acres.
    They have always ploughed with 3 oxen; always 1 horse at the
        hall. Then 8 pigs, now 28. 6 beehives.
Value then and later 20s; now 40.

8 In SHOTESHAM Alfred, 1 free man under Stigand, held 12 acres before 1066.
    Also 3 Freemen, at 20 acres of land;
        meadow, 1 acre. Always 1 plough.
And in PORINGLAND 1 free man and 1 Freeman, at 21 acres.
    Always ½ plough.

9 In BRAMERTON 2½ acres of land. They are assessed in Cringleford.
    Holverston has 4 furlongs in length and 3 in width, tax of 8d.

H̄. DE ENFORD. ⌈ In Weſtuna . teñ Stigand . t . r . e . 1 . bereuita.
L . ac̃ træ . 7 xx . ac̃ . ſemp . vi . borđ . ſemp dim car . & e inṕtio
de Sneteſha.

⌈ *ERPINCHAM SVD . H̄.* In Wicmera . 11 . libi hões . xxx . ac̃
træ . ſemp . 111 . borđ . & dim car . 7 . 1 . ac̃ ṕti . 7 uat . 1111 . ſot.
hoc ten& tihel de helion.

HVMILIART . H̄. In Krigelforda . 1 . car træ . teñ aluređ
pr̃ lib ho Stigandi . ſemp . 111 . uitt . 7 . 1 . car iñ dñio . & dim
car hom . viii . ac̃ ṕti . ſemp . 1 . mot . & xyii . ſoc̃ . 1 . car træ.
ſemp . 111 . car . 1111 . ac̃ ṕti . & . 111 . libi hões . 7 dim . emdati tantũ
t . r . e . Li . ac̃ . ſemp . 1 . car . 7 . H . ae ṕti , 7 tres partes . molenđ.
& . 1111 . ſoc̃ . vii . acr 7 dim ſubiſtis . Tñc uat . xx . ſot . m̃ . xL.
hoc ten& Rog̃ bigot . & ht̃ dim leug̃ 7 . 11 . quar iñ long̃.
& vi . quar iñ lat . & xi . đ de gelto . qui cuq̃ ibi teneat.
In Florenduna . 11 . lib̃ 7 dim Stigandi . xxv . acr . Tñc dim.
car . 7 . 1 . ac̃ ṕti . 7 uat . 11 . ſot . hoc ten& Rog̃ bigot.

.III. **T**ERRE COMITIS . R . DE **M**AVRITANIO . Erṕiñ
gaha nort . *H̄.* In Ruſtuna teñ Vlnoth . t . r . e . 1 . car̃
tre . ſemp . 11 . uitt & dim . & v . bor . 7 . 1 . car iñ dñio . 7 . 1 . car . 7
dim hou . ſilua . viii . porc̃ . 7 11 . ac̃ ṕti . ſep . 1 . mot . tñc . 1 . r̃ . 7 m̃.
7 . 111 . añ . tñc . v . por . 7 m̃ xx . oū . 7 xii . cap̃ . ſep uat xx . ſot.
& ht̃ ix quar iñ long̃ . 7 v . in lato . 7 x . đ 7 obolũ . in gelto.

EYNSFORD Hundred

10 In WESTON (Longville) Stigand held 1 outlier before 1066, 50 acres of land;
> [meadow] , 20 acres.
> 6 smallholders.
> Always ½ plough.

It is in the valuation of Snettisham.

SOUTH ERPINGHAM Hundred

11 In Wickmere 2 free men, 30 acres of land.
> Always 3 smallholders.
> ½ plough; meadow, 1 acre.

Value 4s. Tihel of Hellean holds this.

HUMBLEYARD Hundred

12 In CRINGLEFORD Alfred the priest, a free man of Stigand, held 1 c. of land.
> Always 3 villagers.
> 1 plough in lordship; ½ men's plough; meadow 8 acres; always 1 mill.
> Also 17 Freemen, 1 c. of land.
>> Always 3 ploughs; meadow, 4 acres.
> Also 3 free men and a half under patronage only before 1066, 51 acres.
>> Always 1 plough; meadow, 2 acres; ¾ of a mill.
> Also 4 Freemen, 7½ acres under them.

Value then 20s; now 40.
> Roger Bigot holds this. It has ½ league and 2 furlongs in length and 6 furlongs in width, tax of 11d, whoever holds there.

In FLORDON 2 free (men) and a half of Stigand's, 25 acres.
> Then ½ plough; meadow, 1 acre.

Value 2s.
> Roger Bigot holds this.

3   LANDS OF COUNT R(OBERT) OF MORTAIN

NORTH ERPINGHAM Hundred

1 In ROUGHTON Wulfnoth held 1 c. of land before 1066.   144 a
> Always 2 villagers and a half; 5 smallholders.
> 1 plough in lordship; 1½ men's ploughs; woodland, 8 pigs; meadow, 2 acres; always 1 mill. Then 1 cob and now.
> 3 head of cattle. Then 5 pigs. Now 20 sheep; 12 goats.

Value always 20s.
> It has 9 furlongs in length and 5 in width, 10½d in tax.

$\mathcal{T}$ONESTEDA . $\bar{H}$. Clareia ten̄ comes herold . t . r . e . dim̄
car̄ tre . ſemp . III . bor . 7 . I . car̄ . 7 . I . ac̄ p̄ti . 7 ual̄ VI . ſol̄.

$\bar{H}$. DE GRENEHOV . TERRE Alani comitis . Suafha̅ . p̄tinuit   .IIII.
ad regione̅ & Rex E . dedit ; R . comiti . Tn̄c XII . uilt̄ . 7 p̄ VIII.
& m̄; Tn̄c . XX . VI . bord̄ . 7 ſep . qn̄o recep̄ . III . ſer̄ ; 7 m̄ . tn̄c
in dn̄io . I . car̄ ; 7 qn̄o recep̄ . II . m̄ . IIII . 7 XII . libı̄ hoes mane̅b
ibi . Sep int hoes . VIII . car̄ . Silua ad XIII . por . 7 . I . mot̄ 7 dim̄.
7 . I . piſc̄ . I . r̄ . inuen̄ tc̄ . m̄ . II . Sep . IIII . an̄ . Tn̄c XII . porc̄ . 7 m̄.
Semp . CC . oues . 7 ht̄ . I . leū ı̄n longo . & at̄ in lato . 7 ad get̄ redd̄.
XVI . d̄ . Tn̄c ual̄ . VIII . lib̄ . 7 p̄ XVI . 7 m̄ ; 7 p̄t iſtas . XX . ſot̄.
Hec t̄ra recep̄ ꝑ . II . man̄.
⌐ Nereforda ten̄ phanceon . qua̅ ten̄ Alfahc̄ . t . r . e . Tn̄c
VIII . uilt̄ . 7 ſemp . Semp XII . bord̄ . Tn̄c . III . ſer̄ . qn̄o recep̄
& m̄ . I . Tn̄c in dn̄io . III . car̄ . & p̄ . II . m̄ . III . Tn̄c hm̄ VI . car̄;
& qn̄o recep̄ ; 7 m̄ . v́ . 7 . IIII . libı̄ hoes ibi tenuer . I . car̄ tr̄æ
7 . car̄ . 7 . I . mot̄ 7 dim̄ . 7 . I . piſc̄ . VIII . ac̄ p̄ti . 7 qn̄o recep̄.
inuen̄ . III . r̄ . m̄ . II . Tn̄c nult̄ an̄ . m̄ VII . tn̄c XVI . porc̄ . m̄ XXXV.
144 b
Tn̄c . c . oues . VI . mı̄n . m̄ LXXX 7 VI . 7 v . uaſa apū . 7 ht̄ . I . milłe
in lonḡ . 7 VIII . quar̄ in lato . 7 XVIII . d̄ . redd̄ in gelto . Tn̄c ual̄.
. IIII . lib̄ . 7 p̄ . 7 m̄ . c . ſot̄.
⌐ In Fulenduna ten̄& ribald̄ . qua̅ ten̄ . Alt̄ſtan̄ . dim̄ car̄ tr̄æ . Sep
I . carr̄ . ſemp . I . mot̄ . I . ac̄ p̄ti . ap̄tiata . e̅ . cū ſuafha̅ . 7 in eade̅
uilla . II . libı̄ hoes tenent . I . car̄ tr̄æ . & ſub ipſis . v . bord̄ . 7 . I . ſer̄.
7 . II . car̄ . IIII . ac̄ p̄ti . Tn̄c ual̄ . XX . ſot̄ . m̄ . XL . ſot̄ . menſurata . e̅.
ad t̄ram . W . de Wa.
⌐ In Sculatorpa . XV . ac̄ . 7 reddit . XX . d̄.

144 a, b

TUNSTEAD Hundred
2 Earl Harold held *CLAREIA* before 1066, ½ c. of land.
 Always 3 smallholders.
 1 plough; meadow, 1 acre.
Value 6s.

LANDS OF COUNT ALAN

4

The Hundred of (South) GREENHOE
1 SWAFFHAM belonged to the realm and King Edward gave it to
 Earl R(alph).
  Then 12 villagers, later and now 8. Then and always 26
   smallholders. When he acquired it and now 3 slaves.
  Then 1 plough in lordship, when he acquired it 2, now 4.
  12 free men dwelt there.
  Always 8 ploughs among the men; woodland for 13 pigs;
   1½ mills; 1 fishery. 1 cob was found then, now 2; always
   4 head of cattle. Then and now 12 pigs; always 200 sheep.
  It has 1 league in length and another in width, it pays 16d
 towards tax.
 Value then £8; later and now 16, and besides these 20s.
  This land was acquired as 2 manors.

2 Phanceon holds NARFORD which Alfheah held before 1066.
  Then and always 8 villagers; always 12 smallholders. Then 3
   slaves, when he acquired it and now 1.
  Then 3 ploughs in lordship, later 2, now 3. Then 6 men's
   ploughs, when he acquired it and now 5.
  Also 4 free men held 1 c. of land there.
  A plough; 1½ mills; 1 fishery; meadow, 8 acres.
  When he acquired it he found 3 cobs, now 2. Then no head of
   cattle, now 7. Then 16 pigs, now 35. Then 100 sheep less 6, 144 b
   now 86. 5 beehives.
  It has 1 mile in length and 8 furlongs in width, it pays 18d
 in tax.
 Value then £4; later and now 100s.

3 In FOULDEN Ribald holds ½ c. of land which Alstan held.
  Always 1 plough; 1 mill; meadow, 1 acre.
 It is valued with Swaffham.
 In the same village 2 free men hold 1 c. of land. Under these
  5 smallholders; 1 slave.
  2 ploughs; meadow, 4 acres.
 Value then 20s; now 40s.
  It is measured with the land of W(illiam) of Wa(renne).

4 In SCULTHORPE 15 acres. It pays 20d.

⌐In pagraua ten̄ edric̄

dim̄ car̄ træ.Tn̄c.vɪ.borđ.& m̄.tc̄.ɪ.car̄ 7 đ. 7 m̄.Tn̄c ual.

& ſemp.x.ſol.⌐In pikenha ten& Ribalđ q̄ ten̄ Goduin̄.ɪɪ.car̄.

træ.tn̄c 7 ſemp.vɪ.uiłł.7.ɪɪɪ.borđ.7.ɪɪ.ſer̄.7.ɪɪ.car̄.7 uiłł

ɪɪɪ.car̄.Silua.ad x.porc̄.vɪɪɪ.ac̄ p̄ti.ɪ.mol̄.ɪ.piſc̄.7 vɪ.libi

hoes ibi manent ſemp.& ht̄.ɪ.car̄.Tn̄c ual.xxx.ſol̄.m̄.ʟx.s̄.

⌐ 7 In alt picheha ten̄ iđe.ɪx.libi hoes.t.r̄.e.ɪɪɪ.car̄.m̄ vɪɪ.libi

hoes & ht̄.v.car̄.7.ɪɪ.borđ.x.ac̄ p̄ti.7 ht̄ x.quar̄ in longo.

7 vɪ.in lato.7 de gelto.redđ.xɪɪ.đ.Tn̄c ual.xʟ.ſol̄.m̄.ʟ.ſol̄.

7 in crſſingaha ten& .ɪ.   Ł.x.ac̄.apptiat̄.e.ſupi.

⌐LAVENDIC.H̄.In Mulha dim̄ car̄ træ.7 vɪ.ac̄ in Stan

felda.quā ten& fili almari.|ɪɪ.ſoc̄ Stigandi.t.r.e.ſep

ɪɪɪ.borđ.7.ɪɪ.ac̄ p̄ti.ſemp.ɪɪ.car̄.ſilua.ad xx.porc̄.

7 ual.x.ſol̄.

FEORHOV.H̄.Coteſeia ten̄ guert.t.r.e.ɪɪɪɪ.car̄ træ.

ſemp.vɪɪɪ.uiłł.7 vɪɪɪ.borđ.Tn̄c.ɪɪɪɪ.ſer̄.m̄.ɪ.ſemp.ɪɪ.

145 a

car̄ in dn̄io.7 v.car̄ hom̄.Silua.x.por̄.7 vɪ.ac̄ p̄ti.ſemp.ɪɪ.mol̄.

ſemp.xɪɪɪɪ.an̄.&.ɪ.parc̄ beſtiis.7 xxvɪɪ.por.7 xɪɪɪ.cap̄.

Huic manerio jac&.ɪ.bereuita Bauenburc.ɪɪ.car̄ træ.ſep.vɪ.

uiłł.7 vɪ.borđ.7.ɪɪ.ſer̄.tc̄.ɪ.car̄ in dn̄io.m̄.ɪɪ.ſemp.ɪ.car̄

hom̄.7.ɪɪɪɪ.ac̄ p̄ti.ſemp.ɪ.mol̄.In torp.ɪ.car̄ træ bereuita

huic manerio.ſemp.ɪɪɪɪ.uiłł.7.ɪɪɪ.borđ.7.ɪ.car̄ in dn̄io.

& dim̄ car̄ hom̄.7.ɪɪɪɪ.ac̄ p̄ti.ſemp.ɪ.mol̄.

5 In PALGRAVE Edric held ½ c. of land.
  Then and now 6 smallholders.
  Then and now 1½ ploughs.
Value then and always 10s.

6 In PICKENHAM (South) Ribald holds 2 c. of land which Godwin
  held.
  Then and always 6 villagers; 3 smallholders; 2 slaves.
  2 ploughs; the villagers, 3 ploughs; woodland for 10 pigs;
    meadow, 8 acres; 1 mill; 1 fishery.
  Also 6 free men have always dwelt there. They have
    1 plough.
Value then 30s; now 60s.

7 In the other PICKENHAM the same man holds
  9 free men before 1066, 3 ploughs. Now 7 free men and they
    have 5 ploughs; 2 smallholders.
  Meadow, 10 acres.
  It has 10 furlongs in length and 6 in width, it pays tax of 12d.
Value then 40s, now 50s.
In (Great)CRESSINGHAM he holds 1 villager, 10 acres. It is assessed
above.

LAUNDITCH Hundred
8 In MILEHAM ½ c. of land, and 6 acres in STANFIELD which the son
  of A(e)lmer holds, which 2 Freemen of Stigand held before 1066.
  Always 3 smallholders.
  Meadow, 2 acres. Always 2 ploughs; woodland for 20 pigs.
Value 10s.

FOREHOE Hundred
9 Gyrth held COSTESSEY before 1066, 4 c. of land.
  Always 8 villagers; 8 smallholders. Then 4 slaves, now 1.
  Always 2 ploughs in lordship; 5 men's ploughs; woodland,   145 a
    10 pigs; meadow, 6 acres; always 2 mills. Always 14 head
    of cattle; a park for beasts of chase; 27 pigs; 13 goats.
1 outlier, BAWBURGH, appertains to this manor, 2 c. of land.
  Always 6 villagers; 6 smallholders; 2 slaves.
  Then 1 plough in lordship, now 2. Always 1 men's plough;
    meadow, 4 acres; always 1 mill.
In (Honingham)THORPE 1 c. of land, an outlier in (the lands of)
this manor.
  Always 4 villagers; 3 smallholders.
  1 plough in lordship; ½ men's plough; meadow, 4 acres; always
    1 mill.

Huic manerio jacent xl.iiii.foc̃.iii.car̃ træ.Tñc.xii.car̃.
m̃.viii.7.iiii.poffent reftaurari.In bereforda.vii.foc̃.7
dim̃.ac̃ træ.7.ii.car̃ 7 vi.libi.uilt.7.v.bor̃.7 dim̃ mol̃.
7.ii.ac̃ p̃ti.Tñc uat.xx.lib̃.m̃.xl.v.& ht̃.vii.quar̃ in
long.7 vi.in lato.7 xiii.đ.7.i.obolũ de gelto.
& Bauenbuc̃.v.quar̃ in long.7.iiii.in lato.7 viii.đ.7.i.
obolũ de gelto.   Et thorp.v.qr̃ in long.7.iiii.in lat̃.
7 vi.đ.7.i.obolũ de gelto.Et t̃ra fochemano₂ ht̃.vi.qr̃.
in long.& v.in lato.7 xiii.đ.7.i.obolũ de gelto.& hoc̃
eft eftuna.& hunincham quã ten& quidã de ift foc̃.
ht̃ vi.quar̃ in long.& v.in lato.

╱ WRanplincham.xv.ac̃ træ.ten̄.i.foc̃.Guert.femp
.i.car̃.7.i.uilt.7 dim̃ mol̃.7 uat.xx.fot.Ex hoc̃ calup
niatur Godric̃.dim̃ domũ.ad feudũ regis.& hoc̃ tes
tat̃ hunđ.

╱ In Brandim.vi.foc̃ & dim̃.xii.ac̃ træ.7.i.car̃.hoc̃ ē
in p̃tio.de cofteseia.In Runhal iiii.foc̃.x.ac̃.dim̃ car̃.

145 b

In Carletuna.iii.foc̃.x.ac̃.7 dim̃ car̃.In hunichã.i.foc̃.
xxx.ac̃r̃.7.i.car̃.7.iiii.uilt.7.iii.borđ.Hoc̃ totu.ē.in p̃tio
de Cofteseia.╱ In Waranplicha.ii.foc̃.iiii.ac̃ træ.
╱ Inmerlingeforda.ii.foc̃ xvi.ac̃.dim̃ car̃.╱ In Toketorp.ten&
enifam mufar.xxx.ac̃.que fñt adidē maneriũ.femp.i.car̃.
7 iiii.uilt.& quarta pars mol̃.7 uat.xx.fot.

145 a, b

44 Freemen appertain to this manor, 3 c. of land.
Then 12 ploughs, now 8, and 4 could be restored.

In BARFORD 7 Freemen and a half, 46 acres of land.
2 ploughs.
6 free villagers; 5 smallholders.
½ mill; meadow, 2 acres.
Value then £20; now 45.
It has 7 furlongs in length and 6 in width, tax of 13½d. And
Bawburgh has 5 furlongs in length and 4 in width, tax of 8½d.
(Honingham) Thorpe (has) 5 furlongs in length and 4 in width,
tax of 6½d. The land of the Freemen has 6 furlongs in length and
5 in width, tax of 13½d. This is Easton; and HONINGHAM which a
certain one of these Freemen holds, has 6 furlongs in length and
5 in width.

10 1 Freeman of Gyrth's holds WRAMPLINGHAM, 15 acres of land.
Always 1 plough.
1 villager.
½ mill.
Value 20s.
Of this Godric claims ½ of a house as part of the King's
Holding, and the Hundred testifies to this.

11 In BRANDON (Parva) 6 Freemen and a half, 12 acres of land.
1 plough.
This is in the valuation of Costessey.
In RUNHALL 4 Freemen, 10 acres. ½ plough.
In CARLETON (Forehoe) 3 Freemen, 10 acres. ½ plough.   145 b
In HONINGHAM 1 Freeman, 30 acres.
1 plough.
4 villagers; 3 smallholders.
All this is in the valuation of Costessey.

12 In WRAMPLINGHAM 2 Freemen, 4 acres of land.

13 In MARLINGFORD 2 Freemen, 16 acres. ½ plough.

14 In *TOKETORP* Enisant Musard holds 30 acres which were added
(to) the manor.
Always 1 plough; 4 villagers; ¼ of a mill.
Value 20s.

In eade̅ . I . car̄ træ 7 dim quā tenuit . . . . . toke subſtigando m̄ Ribald
p m̄ . ſemp . VII . uillt . 7 . III . bord̄ . 7 . II . car̄ in dn̄io . 7 . I . car̄ hom̄ .
m̄ . I . mot̄ . X . ac p̄ti . ſemp . V . an̄ . 7 . II . porc̄ . Tn̄c ual̄ . XX . ſot .
m̄ . XXX .

Ⅰ Mitteforde . H̃ . Intodeneham . X . ſoc̄ Guert . in Coteſeia
t . e . r . XXXXII . ac træ . 7 . III . ac p̄ti . ſemp . I . car̄ & dim . 7 ſn̄t in
p̄tio de coſteſeia . In appetorp . I . ſoc̄ Guert . XXX . ac træ .
ſemp . II . bor . 7 . I . car̄ . 7 . III . ac p̄ti . Silua XV . porc̄ . In eode̅
p̄tio . In lacheſha . II . ſoc̄ . ejde̅ XXIIII . ac træ . ſep dim car̄ .
In eode̅ p̄tio . In Baskenea XII . ac træ . I . ſoc̄ ejde̅ in eode̅ p̄tio .
Inflochethor . I . ſoc̄ . heroldi in Coſteſeia . XXX . ac træ . 7 . II . ſer .
7 . I . car̄ . 7 . II . ac p̄ti . 7 ual̄ . V . ſot .

Ⅰ Weſtfelda ten̄& faeicon . quā ten̄ . S . A . t . r . e̅ . I . car̄ træ .
Semp VIII . uillt . 7 VIII . bord̄ . Sémp in dn̄io . I . car̄ . 7 houm̄ . II .
car̄ III . ac p̄ti . I . mot̄ . Tn̄c ual̄ . LX . ſot . m̄ . XL . ſot . 7 ht̄ . VI .
quar̄ in long . 7 VI . in lato . 7 VI . d̄ de̅ gelt .

Ⅰ H̃ . DE BRODECROS . In cideſtna ten̄ . Alfah . t . r . e . III . car̄
træ . Semp XIIII . bord̄ . Semp in dn̄io . III . car̄ . 7 houm̄ . II . car̄ .

146 a

IIII . ac p̄ti . Semp . I . r̄ . Tn̄c . IIII . por . m̄ XVI . Tn̄c XL . ou .
m̄ . c . Tn̄c ual̄ . LX . ſot . m̄ ſimilit̄ . 7 hab̄ . X . quar̄ in long .
& VIII . in lat̄ . 7 XIII . d̄ in gelt . Ide̅ ten̄& .

Ⅰ In rudeha eſt . beruita . huic man̄ dim car̄ træ . 7 dim car̄
& eſt in p̄tio ſcideſtn̄ . & ten̄& ide̅ .

In the same 1½ c. of land which Toki held under Stigand (and) Ribald (holds) now as a manor.

Always 7 villagers; 3 smallholders.

2 ploughs in lordship; 1 men's plough. Now 1 mill; meadow, 10 acres. Always 5 head of cattle; 2 pigs.

Value then 20s; now 30.

MITFORD Hundred

15 In (East)TUDDENHAM 10 Freemen of Gyrth's in Costessey before 1066, 42 acres of land.

Meadow, 3 acres; always 1½ ploughs.

They are in the valuation of Costessey.

In *APPETHORP* 1 Freeman of Gyrth's, 30 acres of land.

Always 2 smallholders.

1 plough; meadow, 3 acres; woodland, 15 pigs.

In the same valuation.

In YAXHAM 2 Freemen of the same, 24 acres of land.

Always ½ plough.

In the same valuation.

In *BASKENEA* 12 acres of land; 1 Freeman of the same.

In the same valuation.

In FLOCKTHORPE 1 Freeman of Harold's, in (the lands of) Costessey; 30 acres of land.

2 slaves.

1 plough; meadow, 2 acres.

Value 5s.

16 Phanceon holds WESTFIELD which S(t.) E(theldreda) held before 1066, 1 c. of land.

Always 8 villagers; 8 smallholders.

Always 1 plough in lordship; 2 men's ploughs; meadow, 3 acres; 1 mill.

Value then 60s; now 40s.

It has 6 furlongs in length and 6 in width, tax of 6d.

The Hundred of BROTHERCROSS

17 In SYDERSTONE Alfheah held 3 c. of land before 1066.

Always 14 smallholders.

Always 3 ploughs in lordship; 2 men's ploughs; meadow, 146 a
4 acres; always 1 cob. Then 4 pigs, now 16. Then 40 sheep, now 100.

Value then 60s; now the same.

It has 10 furlongs in length and 8 in width, 13d in tax. He also holds.

In RUDHAM there is an outlier to this manor, ½ c. of land.

½ plough.

It is in the valuation of Syderstone. He also holds.

⌐*H̄. DE HOLT*.In bruningaha ten& Gausfrid̃ . q̃ tenuit
Turber . lib̃ ho̅ . t . r . e . & fuit com̃dat heroldo . **xxx** . ac̃.
Semp . I . uill̃ . 7 . I . bord̃ . 7 . I . car̃ . Silua ad . III . porc̃ . II . ac̃
p̃ti . Tñc ual̃ . x . fol̃ . m̃ . v . fol̃.

⌐ 7 In bathele . I . lib̃ ho̅ . de dim̃ car̃ træ heroldi . 7 . I . bord̃.
Sep dim̃ car̃ . Sep ual̃ . III . fol̃ . & ten& Ide.

⌐*H̄. DE GRENEHOV*.Indallinga . ten̄ alan̄ comes.
I . fokem̃ . de d̃ car̃ træ . 7 hic fuit ho̅ heraldi . t . r . e . fep
VI . bord̃ . II . ac̃ p̃ti . fep dim̃ car̃ . fep ual̃ . VII . fol̃ . Idē ten̄.
& ignarha . 7 i holkha . 7 in guella ten& ~~alan̄ comes~~ Ribald de comite.
XI . fokm̃ . de . II . car̃ træ . 7 VI . bord̃ . I . ac̃ p̃ti . tñc ual̃ . XL.
fol̃ . 7 m̃ . & ibi calupniatur edui p̃pofit regis . I . homem
de xxx . ac̃ . 7 hoc teftat hundret.

⌐Holt . *H̄* . Huneuurde tenuit Aleftan . t . r . e . 7 m̃ . de . A.
comite . xxx . ac̃ træ . VIII . uill̃ . filua . III . por . dim̃ ac̃ p̃ti.
II . mol̃ . tc̃ . II . car̃ . habebant m̃ . car̃ 7 d̃ . hoc totu̅ appre
tiatu̅ . e̅ . in faxiorp . Idē ten& . Ri.

ERPINGEHAM NORT . *H̄* .Inmatingeles ten̄ eftan . I . lib̃
ho̅ eral . t . r . e . XVI . ac̃ træ . Semp . II . bor . 7 . cu̅ . II . bo̅
146 b
apptiata e̅ infaftorp . Idē ten& . ⌐Infutfelle . ten̄ Gun̄ . I . lib̃ ho̅
radftarle . t . r . e . dim̃ car̃ træ . Semp . IIII . bord̃ . 7 dim̃ ca̅ in
dñio . & dim̃ hom̃ . 7 dim̃ ac̃ p̃ti . ⌐Ingunetune . I . foc̃ . de xII . ac̃
træ . I . ac̃ . 7 dim̃ p̃ti . Semp ual̃ . VI . fol̃.

The Hundred of HOLT

18 In BRININGHAM Geoffrey holds what Thorbern, a free man who was under patronage to Harold, held before 1066, 30 acres.
Always 1 villager; 1 smallholder.
1 plough; woodland for 3 pigs; meadow, 2 acres.
Value then 10s; now 5s.

19 In BALE 1 free man of Harold's, at ½ c. of land.
1 smallholder.
Always ½ plough.
Value always 3s. He also holds.

The Hundred of (North) GREENHOE

20 In (Field) DALLING Count Alan holds 1 Freeman, at ½ c. of land. He was Harold's man before 1066.
Always 6 smallholders.
Meadow, 2 acres; always ½ plough.
Value always 7s. He also holds.

In WARHAM and in HOLKHAM and in WELLS (next the Sea) Ribald holds from the Count 11 Freemen, at 2 c. of land.
6 smallholders.
Meadow, 1 acre.
Value then and now 40s.
Edwy, the King's reeve, claims 1 man here at 30 acres, and this the Hundred testifies.

HOLT Hundred

21 Alstan held HUNWORTH before 1066, and now (he holds) from Count A(lan). 30 acres of land.
8 villagers.
Woodland, 3 pigs; meadow, ½ acre; 2 mills. Then they had 2 ploughs, now 1½.
All this is assessed in Saxthorpe. Ri(bald) also holds.

NORTH ERPINGHAM Hundred

22 In MATLASK Estan, 1 free man of Harold's, held 16 acres of land before 1066.
Always 2 smallholders with 2 oxen.
It is assessed in Saxthorpe. He also holds.   146 b

23 In SUFFIELD Gunni, 1 free man of Ralph the Constable's, held. ½ c. of land before 1066.
Always 4 smallholders.
½ plough in lordship; ½ men's (plough); meadow, ½ acre.

24 In GUNTON 1 Freeman, at 12 acres of land;
meadow, 1½ acres.
Value always 6s.

⌐Inmatelefc ubi comes alan̄.ten̄ caḷupniat̄.ı.ho᷉ regis.xvı.ac̄
trae offerendo juditiu᷉ ı̄ bellu᷉ con̄t hund̄.qd̄ teſtat̄ eos comiti.
f; quida᷉ ho᷉ comitis uult p̄bareˆqd̄ hund̄ ueru᷉ teſtatur.
ı̄ juditio.ı̄ bello.Ribald̄ ten̄&

FLECWEST. H̄. Somertuna ten̄& Wihunmard̄.qm
tenuit.Alfric̄.t.r.e.ho᷉ heraldi.ııı.car̄ trae.Tn̄c.ıııı.uill.
p̄ 7 m̄.ıı.Semp̄ xı.bord̄.Tn̄c.vı.ſer̄.p̄ 7 m̄.ıı.Semp̄.ııı.
car̄ in dn̄io ſemp̄.ı.car̄ 7 dım̄.homu᷉.7 xxx.ac̄ p̄ti.7.ı.
ſal̄ & dım̄.7 ıx.libı hōes.ıı.car̄ trae.Semp̄.ııı.r̄ in aula.
7.ıı.an̄.tc̄ xıı.por.m̄.xx.ıııȷ.tc̄.c.oū.m̄.cc.Semp̄.x.por.
& xx.ac̄ p̄ti.& duo dım̄ ex iſtis fuer̄.ſc̄i Ben̄.de hulmo.
& godram inuafit tēpr̄.R.comitis.Sēp̄.ııı.car̄.7 ad
huc ſn̄t ibi.vıı.ſoc̄ LXvıı.ac̄ trae.Sēp̄.ı.car̄ & dım̄.
Tn̄c 7 p̄ hoc totu᷉ ual̄.v.lib̄.m̄ ıx.lib̄.cu᷉ ſoc̄ d̄.ſn̄t in
hund̄.7 ht̄.ı.leug in longo.7 vııı.qr̄.7 x.in lato.&
de gelt.xxx.d̄.⌐Inmartha.ıı.libı hōes 7 dım̄.de.vı.
ac̄ trae.7 xx.ac̄.in dn̄io.Semp̄ dım̄ car̄.⌐In repes.
.ı.lib̄ ho᷉ 7 dım̄.x.ac̄ trae.Sēp̄ dım̄ car̄.Ap̄p̄tiati ſn̄t
in ſomertuna.⌐In baſtuic̄.ıı.libı hōes p̄tinētes
in ſomertuna.xıı.ac̄.ı.ac̄ p̄ti.

147 a
H̄ de *ENSFORDA*.⌐Weſtuna.xx.ſoc̄.ı.car̄ trae.7 xvı.
bord̄.In̄t oms.t.r.e.vııı.car̄.p̄ 7 m̄.v.7.ıııı.ac̄ prati.
7 ſn̄t iſti ſoc̄ in p̄tio de coſteſei.Soca infolſa regis.t.r.e.
m̄ ten̄&.A.quia tenuit Bad̄ comes.

25 In MATLASK, where Count Alan holds, 1 man of the King's claims 16 acres of land by offering judicial ordeal or battle against the Hundred which testifies that they (belong) to the Count. But a certain man of the Count's is willing to prove that the Hundred testifies the truth, either by judicial ordeal or by battle. Ribald holds.

WEST FLEGG Hundred
26 Wymarc holds SOMERTON which Aelfric, Harold's man, held before 1066. 3 c. of land.
> Then 4 villagers, later and now 2; always 11 smallholders.
> > Then 6 slaves, later and now 2.
> Always 3 ploughs in lordship. Always 1½ men's ploughs; meadow, 30 acres. 1½ salt-houses.
> Also 9 free men, 2 c. of land.
> > Always 3 cobs at the hall, 2 head of cattle. Then 12 pigs, now 24. Then 100 sheep, now 200. Always 10 pigs; meadow, 20 acres.
> Two halves of these were of St. Benedict of Hulme and Godram annexed (them) in the time of Earl R(alph).
> > Always 3 ploughs.
> Further there are 7 Freemen, 67 acres of land.
> > Always 1½ ploughs.
Value of all this then and later £5; now £9 with the Freemen who are in the Hundred.
> It has 1 league in length and 8 furlongs and 10 [perches] in width, tax of 30d.

27 In MARTHAM 2 Freemen and a half, at 6 acres of land and 20 acres in lordship.
> Always ½ plough.
In REPPS 1 free man and a half, 10 acres of land.
> Always ½ plough.
They are assessed in Somerton.
In BASTWICK 2 free men belonging in Somerton, 12 acres; meadow, 1 acre.

The Hundred of EYNSFORD   147 a
28 WESTON (Longville), 20 Freemen, 1 c. of land.
> 16 smallholders.
> Among them all before 1066 8 ploughs, later and now 5.
> Meadow, 4 acres.
These Freemen are in the valuation of Costessey. The jurisdiction was in the King's (manor of) Foulsham, before 1066; now A(lan) holds because Earl Ralph held.

Ling tē Alfah . i . lib hō . t . r . e . iii . car træ . ſemp xv.
uill . 7 . ii . ſer . ſemp . ii . car in dñio . tnc . iii . car hou . p 7 m̄
ii . 7 viiii . ac p̄ti . ſilua . ccc . porc . 7 . i . mol . 7 v . ſoc . xx . iiii.
ac træ . ſemp . i . car . 7 . ii . ac p̄ti . Et in tudenha dim̄ ſoc.
xii . ac træ . 7 . ii . ac p̄ti . ſemp dim̄ car . Et in Baldereſwella
. i . ſoc . xxx . ac træ . tnc 7 p̄ . i . car . m̄ . n̄ . Et . i . ac p̄ti . tnc
tnc ual . iiii . lib . p̄ . x . lib . m̄ . c . ſol . 7 ht . i . leug in long.
7 . in lato . 7 redd . iiii . ď . 7 obolū de gelto regis.
Belega . ten& Gingom̄ quā ten Rad comes . t . r . e . iiii.
car træ . ſemp . ix . uill . 7 vii . bord . ſemp . ii . car in dñio.
tc . iiii . car hou . p̄ 7 m̄ . ii . 7 vi . ac p̄ti . ſilua . xxx . por.
& . i . mol . m̄ . i . r̄ . tnc viii . an̄ . m̄ . xii . tnc xxxv . porc
m̄ . xl . ſemp . c . ou̅ . m̄ . iii . uaſa apū . 7 xii . ſoc . ii . car træ.
tnc vi . car . p̄ . iii . m̄ . ii . ſilua . xxx . porc . Et . i . lib hō
xxx ac træ . ſemp . i . car . 7 . i . ac p̄ti . Hic jac& . i . bereuita.
que dr̄ . Bec . i . car træ . ſemp . i . car . 7 . i . ac p̄ti . Tn̄c 7 p̄
ual . iii . lib . m̄ . c . ſol . 7 ht . i . leug in long . 7 dim̄ in lat.
7 reddit . iiii . ď . 7 obol̄ de gelt.
Foxle . ten& Godric quā ten Lord . i . lib hō . t . r . e.
m̄ alan 7 Godric de eo . iii . car træ . ſemp x . uill.

147 b
7 . iii . de his manent inbec . 7 xx . i . bord . 7 . ii . de his manent in billingeforda . tc . ii . ſer . ſep iii . car in dñio . 7 tnc
v . car homū . p̄ 7 m̄ . iii . 7 . iii . ac p̄ti . ſilua . ccc . pors . qn̄o
recep̄ . ii . r̄ . m̄ . i . m̄ . xiiii . an̄ . tc xxx . por . m̄ . xxii . tc xl
ou̅ . m̄ . c . tnc lx . cap̄ . m̄ . nulla . tc v . uaſa apū . m̄ . vii . Et . ii.
ſoc in eade uilla 7 in Baldereſwella . xii . 7 ht . xl . viii . ac træ.
ſemp . ii . car . 7 dim̄ . Silua . x . por . Tn̄c ual . c . ſol . p̄ viii . lib.
m̄ . x . lib . & ht . i . leug in longo . & dim̄ in lato . 7 redd . viii.
ď . 7 obolū ingeltū regis . Baldereſuuella . ht vi . quar
in long . 7 vi . in lat . 7 viii . ď . 7 . i . obolū de gelto quiſquis
ibi teneat p̄t m̄ſura de foxſe.

147 a, b

4

29 Alfheah, 1 free man, held LYNG before 1066, 3 c. of land.
Always 15 villagers; 2 slaves.
Always 2 ploughs in lordship. Then 3 men's ploughs, later
and now 2. Meadow, 9 acres; woodland, 300 pigs; 1 mill.
Also 5 Freemen, 24 acres of land.
Always 1 plough; meadow, 2 acres.
In (East) TUDDENHAM half a Freeman, 12 acres of land;
meadow, 2 acres. Always ½ plough.
In BAWDESWELL 1 Freeman, 30 acres of land.
Then and later 1 plough, now none. Meadow, 1 acre.
Value then £4; later £10; now 100s.
It has 1 league in length and in width, it pays King's tax of 4½d.

30 Wigwin holds BYLAUGH which Earl Ralph held before 1066,
4 c. of land.
Always 9 villagers; 7 smallholders.
Always 2 ploughs in lordship. Then 4 men's ploughs, later
and now 2. Meadow, 6 acres; woodland, 30 pigs; 1 mill.
Now 1 cob. Then 8 head of cattle, now 12. Then 35 pigs,
now 40; always 100 sheep. Now 3 beehives.
Also 12 Freemen, 2 c. of land.
Then 6 ploughs, later 3, now 2. Woodland, 30 pigs.
Also 1 Freeman, 30 acres of land.
Always 1 plough; meadow, 1 acre.
Here lies 1 outlier which is called BECK, 1 c. of land.
Always 1 plough; meadow, 1 acre.
Value then and later £3; now 100s.
It has 1 league in length and ½ in width, it pays tax of 4½d.

31 Godric holds FOXLEY which Lord, 1 free man, held before 1066.
Now Alan (holds) and Godric from him. 3 c. of land.
Always 10 villagers and 3 of these dwell in Beck; 21   147 b
smallholders and 2 of these dwell in Billingford. Then
2 slaves.
Always 3 ploughs in lordship. Then 5 men's ploughs, later and
now 3. Meadow, 3 acres; woodland, 300 pigs. When he
acquired it 2 cobs, now 1. Now 14 head of cattle. Then 30
pigs, now 22. Then 40 sheep, now 100. Then 60 goats, now
none. Then 5 beehives, now 7.
Also 2 Freemen in the same village, and
in BAWDESWELL 12, and they have 48 acres of land.
Always 2½ ploughs; woodland, 10 pigs.
Value then 100s; later £8; now £10.
It has 1 league in length and ½ in width, it pays 8½d towards
the King's tax. BAWDESWELL has 6 furlongs in length and 6 in
width, tax of 8½d, whoever holds there. (It is) outside the
measurement of Foxley.

147 a, b

⌐In Sueningatuna ten& anſchitill’ quã teñ Turbern.
ı.liƀ hõ.t.r.e.dim car̃ træ.tñc vııı.ſoc.p̃ 7 m̃.v.ſemp
.ı.car̃ in dñio.Tñc.ıı.car̃ hom.p̃ 7 m̃.ı.7.ıııı.ac̃ p̃ti.
ſilua.v.por.7 val xx.ſol.

H̃.de taVERHÃ.⌐In Tauerhã teñ Turƀt.ı.liƀ hõ.
t.r.e.ı.car̃ træ.ſemp.ııı.uiħ.7.ııı.bor.ſemp.ı.car̃ i dño
& dim car̃ homũ.7 v.ac̃ p̃ti.ſilua.v.por.tñc ual.xx.ſol
7 m̃.& ten& haimer̃.⌐In Feletorp.lxxx.ac̃.7 vııı.ac̃
træ.7 xx.liƀi hoẽs.ſep.ıı.car̃.7.ııı.ac̃ p̃ti.ſilua xıı.porc̃.
& ẽ in p̃tio de coſteſeia.Soca Regis & comitis.7 hħ.x.qr̃.
in long.7 v.in lat.7 reddit vııı.đ.7 obolũ ing̃.
In Atebruge.ııı.liƀi hoẽs ſub Guerd xxx.ac̃.Tñc.ı.car̃.
m̃ dim.7.ıı.ac̃ p̃ti.7 ual.ıııı.ſol.

148 a

⌐ERPINCHÃMSVD.H̃.Saſtorp.teñ adſtan.ſub heroldo
t.r.e.m̃ ten& Ribald.ı.car̃ træ.Tñc 7 p̃.xx.uiħ.m̃.vııı.
Semp.vııı.borđ.7.ı.car̃ in dñio.Tñc.ııı.car̃ homũ.p̃
7 m̃.ıı.7.ı.ac̃ p̃ti.Silua.xxx.porc̃.ſep.ı.mol.7 dim.Sep
ıııı.ſoc̃ xxvııı.ac̃ træ.& dim car̃.Tñc ual.xx.ſol.
m̃ xxx.⌐In Scotohou.ı.liƀ hõ xıı.ac̃ træ.7 ual xıı.đ.Idc̃.
⌐Tonſteda.H̃.Ordeſteda teñ Sc̃s beneđ.t.r.e.ıı.car̃
træ.ſemp.ıııı.uiħ.Tñc 7 p̃.v.bor.m̃ x.ſemp.ı.car̃ in dñio.
7.ı.car̃ hom.7.ıı.ac̃ p̃ti.ſilua.vı.por.ſemp ual xx.ſol.

32 In SWANNINGTON Ansketel holds what Thorbern, 1 free man, held
before 1066, ½ c. of land.
   Then 8 Freemen, later and now 5.
   Always 1 plough in lordship. Then 2 men's ploughs, later and
      now 1. Meadow, 4 acres; woodland, 5 pigs.
Value 20s.

The Hundred of TAVERHAM
33 In TAVERHAM Thorbert, 1 free man, held 1 c. of land before 1066.
   Always 3 villagers; 3 smallholders.
   Always 1 plough in lordship; ½ men's plough; meadow, 5 acres;
      woodland, 5 pigs.
Value then and now 20s. Haimer holds.

34 In FELTHORPE, 80 acres and 8 acres of land, 20 free men.
   Always 2 ploughs; meadow, 3 acres; woodland, 12 pigs.
It is in the valuation of Costessey. The jurisdiction (is) the King's
and the Earl's. It has 10 furlongs in length and 5 in width, it
pays 8½d in tax.
In ATTLEBRIDGE 3 free men under Gyrth, 30 acres.
   Then 1 plough, now ½; meadow, 2 acres.
Value 4s.

SOUTH ERPINGHAM Hundred   148 a
35 Athelstan held SAXTHORPE under Harold before 1066, now Ribald
holds; 1 c. of land.
   Then and later 20 villagers, now 8; always 8 smallholders.
   1 plough in lordship. Then 3 men's ploughs, later and now 2.
      Meadow, 1 acre; woodland, 30 pigs; always 1½ mills.
   Always 4 Freemen, 28 acres of land;
      ½ plough.
Value then 20s; now 30.

36 In SCOTTOW 1 free man, 12 acres of land.
   Value 12d. He also (holds).

TUNSTEAD Hundred
37 St. Benedict held WORSTEAD before 1066, 2 c. of land.
   Always 4 villagers. Then and later 5 smallholders, now 10.
   Always 1 plough in lordship; 1 men's plough; meadow, 2 acres;
      woodland, 6 pigs.
Value always 20s.

Dilhá 7 inpancforda . L . ac tráe . I . foc . Radulfi Stalra . Tñc
III . uilt . 7 m̃ . III . Tñc . III . bord . m̃ . II . 7 dim̃ . femp . I . car̃ .
7 . I . ac p̃ti . Tñc ual VIII . fot . m̃ . v.

H̃ . De Hapinga . Hikelinga teñ . Goduin lib̃ hõ edrici de
Laxefelda . t . r . e . 7 m̃ ten& GVihumar . III . car̃ tráe 7 dim̃ .
fep IX . uilt . 7 XI . bord . tñc . III . fer̃ . m̃ . I . femp . II . car̃ in dñio .
tñc . II . car̃ 7 dim̃ hom̃ . m̃ . III . I . eccta . XX . ac̃ . 7 ual . XX . d̃ .
Silua . LX . por . XXIIII . ac̃ p̃ti . 7 . I . r̃ . 7 v . eque filuaticæ .
7 . IIII . añ . tñc . XII . por . m̃ . XXIIII . tc . c . oũ . m̃ . CC . 7 . II . uafa
apũ · & IX foc̃ . I . car̃ tráe . Tñc . I . car̃ . 7 dim̃ . m̃ . II . 7 . I . ac̃ . 7
dim̃ p̃ti . & in Stanhá XI . libi hoẽs . c . ac tráe c̃mdatione tantũ
& dim̃ foca ; & rex alia medietate fochæ . Tñc . II . car̃ . m̃ . I .
7 . II . ac̃ p̃ti . & in Ludhá . VII . libi hoẽs . dim̃ car̃ tráe . Rex
& comes foca . femp . I . car̃ . 7 . I . bord .

⌠ In Hinchá . IIII . libi hoẽs XII . ac̃ . Rex . 7 c . foca . fep dim̃ car̃ .
148 b
Totũ hoc ual . t . r . e . XL . fot . 7 p̃ fimil . m̃ . VIIII . lib̃ .
⌠ In eade tenuit edric̃ hõ edrici de laxefelda . t . r . e . III .
car̃ tráe . femp . IX . uilt . 7 XIIII . bord . tñc . IIII . fer̃ . m̃ . II . fep
II . car̃ in dñio . Tñc . II . car̃ 7 dim̃ hom̃ . m̃ . II . filua LX . por .
XXIIII . ac̃ p̃ti . tñc . II . r̃ . m̃ . I . 7 VI . añ . 7 VII . por . 7 CCC . L . oũ .
& XL . IIII . cap̃ . 7 VII . foc̃ . XXXV . ac̃ . femp . I . car̃ . 7 dim̃ ac̃ p̃ti . Ide .

148 a, b

(In) DILHAM and in PANXWORTH 50 acres of land, 1 Freeman of Ralph the Constable's.

> Then 3 villagers, now 3. Then 3 smallholders, now 2 and a half.
> Always 1 plough; meadow, 1 acre.

Value then 8s; now 5.

The Hundred of HAPPING

38 Godwin, a free man of Edric of Laxfield's, held HICKLING before 1066; now Wymarc holds. 3½ c. of land.

> Always 9 villagers; 11 smallholders. Then 3 slaves, now 1.
> Always 2 ploughs in lordship. Then 2½ men's ploughs, now 3.
> 1 church, 20 acres;

value 20d.

> Woodland, 60 pigs; meadow, 24 acres; 1 cob; 5 wild mares;
>> 4 head of cattle. Then 12 pigs, now 24. Then 100 sheep,
>> now 200. 2 beehives.
> Also 9 Freemen, 1 c. of land.
> Then 1½ ploughs, now 2. Meadow, 1½ acres.

Also in STALHAM 11 free men, 100 acres of land in patronage only, and half the jurisdiction, the King (has) the other half of the jurisdiction.

> Then 2 ploughs, now 1. Meadow, 2 acres.

Also in LUDHAM 7 free men, ½ c. of land. The King and the Earl have the jurisdiction.

> Always 1 plough.
> 1 smallholder.

39 In INGHAM 4 free men, 12 acres. The King and the Earl (have) the jurisdiction.

> Always ½ plough.

Value of all this before 1066 40s; later the same; now £9.   148 b

In the same Edric, Edric of Laxfield's man, held 3 c. of land before 1066.

> Always 9 villagers; 14 smallholders. Then 4 slaves, now 2.
> Always 2 ploughs in lordship. Then 2½ men's ploughs,
>> now 2. Woodland, 60 pigs; meadow, 24 acres. Then 2
>> cobs, now 1. 6 head of cattle; 7 pigs; 350 sheep; 44 goats.
> Also 7 Freemen, 35 acres.
> Always 1 plough; meadow, ½ acre.

He also (holds).

In Stalha . iii . libi hões xv . ac̃ trǣ . de quibɏ habuit edric̃.
com̃d . 7 dimid̃ foca . & Rex & comes alia medietate . Tñc
7 p̃ ual . c . fol . m̃ . vi . lib̃ . 7 ten& ide . Hec duo maneria
calupniat̃ Rob̃ malet q̃d̃ edric̃ fuus anteceffor habuit
com̃datione tantu . t . r . e . illoɏ qui tenebant . & dicit
q̃d̃ pat̃ fuus ex eis faifit fuit . & hoc teftat̃ Rog̃ bigot.
& ht̃ hoc man . ii . leu̇ 7 dim̃ in long̃ . 7 xii . p̃c̃ ; & in lato.
. i . leu̇ & x . perc̃ & xv . d̃ de gelt . q̃cq̃ ibi teneat.
In Wacftaneſt ii . libi hões . un fuit ho edrici . & alt̃ hõ ed̃.
7 fci Bened̃ . c . lxi . ac̃ trǣ . femp . xiii . bord̃ . 7 . ii . car̃ 7 dim̃.
7 xviii . ac̃ p̃ti . 7 . iiii . libi hões . x . ac̃ trǣ . 7 dim̃ car̃ . Tñc
ual̃ xx . fol̃ . m̃ xxxv . i . eccl̃a . xx . ac̃ . 7 ual̃ xvi . d̃.
Hincham teñ edric̃ . hõ . G . de Laxafelda . i . car̃ trǣ . Tñc.
iii . uilt̃ . p̃ 7 m̃ . ii . femp . vi . bord̃ . 7 . i . car̃ in dñio . filůa.
vi . porc̃ . 7 . iiii . ac̃ p̃ti . 7 . vii . equǣ filuatice . 7 . vi . an̆ . 7 . xii.
porc̃ . 7 lx . cap̃ . 7 xvi . libi hões . cm̃datione tantu . i . car̃
trǣ . 7 xx . ac̃ . femp . ii . bord̃ . 7 . iii . car̃ . Tñc ual̃ maner̃.
xii . fol̃ . & libi hões xii . fol̃ . 7 m̃ fimilit̃ . & ht̃ xi . q̃r̃

149 a

in long̃ . 7 vii . in lat̃ . qui cq̃ ibi teneat . & xi . d̃ . 7 . i . ferding de g̃.
In Waɛtaneſhã lxxx . ac̃ trǣ teñ ide edric̃ lib̃ hõ . femp xii . bord̃.
& i . car̃ in dñio . tñc 7 p̃ . i . car̃ hom̃ . m̃ dim̃ . 7 vi . ac̃ p̃ti . 7 vi . por̃ . 7 . ii . anim̃.
& c . ou . femp ual̃ x . fol̃ . i . eccl̃a xviii . ac̃ . 7 ual̃ . xviii . d̃ . Huic ad
didit edric̃ . ii . foc̃ fci benedi̇ɛti . t . R . comitis . 7 ht̃ . iii . ac̃ . 7 dim̃.

In STALHAM 3 free men, 15 acres of land, of whom Edric had the patronage and half the jurisdiction, the King and the Earl the other half.
Value then and later 100s; now £6. He also holds.

Robert Malet claims these 2 manors because Edric, his predecessor, had the patronage only, before 1066, of those who held (there), and he states that his father had possession of them; and this Roger Bigot testifies. This manor has 2½ leagues and 12 perches in length and 1 league and 10 perches in width, tax of 15d, whoever holds there.

40 In WAXHAM 2 freemen; one was a man of Edric's, the other a man of Edric's and of St. Benedict's. 161 acres of land.
Always 13 smallholders.
2½ ploughs; meadow, 18 acres.
Also 4 free men, 10 acres of land; ½ plough.
Value then 20s; now 35.
1 church, 20 acres;
value 16d.

41 Edric, a man of G. of Laxfield's, held INGHAM, 1 c. of land.
Then 3 villagers, later and now 2; always 6 smallholders.
1 plough in lordship; woodland, 6 pigs; meadow, 4 acres;
7 wild mares; 6 head of cattle; 12 pigs; 60 goats.
Also 16 free men in patronage only, 1 c. of land and 20 acres.
Always 2 smallholders.
3 ploughs.
Value of the manor then 12s, and the free men 12s; now the same.
It has 11 furlongs in length and 7 in width, whoever holds   149 a
there, tax of 11¼d.

42 In WAXHAM the same Edric, a free man, held 80 acres of land.
Always 12 smallholders.
1 plough in lordship. Then and later 1 men's plough, now ½.
Meadow, 6 acres; 6 pigs; 2 head of cattle; 100 sheep.
Value always 10s.
1 church, 18 acres;
value 18d.
Edric added 2 Freemen of St. Benedict's to this in the time of Earl R(alph). They have 3½ acres.

7 ual . vi . đ . & viii . libi hões cm̄d tantū LXXX . ac̄ træ . tnc 7 p̄ . ii . car.

m̄ . i . car̄ . & dim̄ . 7 . iii . ac̄ p̄ti . 7 ual . v . fol . hoc totū tenebat edric

q̄no Rađ . forisfec̄ . Rex 7 comes foca.

H̄ . 7 dim̄ de clachelofa . In Bȳcham ten& Ribald . LX . ac̄ . træ . t.

r . e . tc̄ . i . car̄ . m̄ dim̄ . femp ual . v . fol . In Stoches . ten& idē . iii . libos.

hões . de vii . ac̄ . t . r . e . 7 ual xii . đ.

Fredrebruge hund 7 dim̄ . In ilfinghetuna . i . car̄ tre . ten Rolf

lib hō . tempr̄ . r . e . femp . vi . borđ . 7 . ii . libi Hões . ii . acr̄ . & dim̄.

femp . i . car̄ . 7 . iii . faline 7 dim̄ . 7 xvi . ac̄ p̄ti . 7 ual xx . fol . Hanc

tr̄am habuit epc̄ baioc̄ ea die q̄ comes Rađ forisfec̄ . dimidia.

m̄ ht comes alan in fua parte . 7 iuo taillebofc . libauit.

In eadē ten& Gausfrid . i . libm hom̄e . i . car̄ træ . 7 vii . borđ.

femp . i . car̄ E . i . lib hō . 7 dim̄ . x . ac̄ træ . 7 . i . falina . xii . ac̄ p̄ti.

totū ual xx . fol.

In mildetuna ten& ribald . ii . car̄ træ tenuit comes Radulf̄

femp . iii . uilt . 7 . i . pr̄ . 7 . iii . borđ . femp . ii . car̄ . 7 xviii . ac̄ p̄ti.

Tnc̄ . i . pifc̄ . 7 ual xx . fol . In Waltuna ten turchill . t . r . e.

. i . car̄ femp . vi . uilt . & . i . borđ . 7 . i . car̄ in dn̄io . dim̄ car̄ hom̄ . 7 . i.

mol̄ . & ual xx . fol . Idē . In Wica 7 bowefeia . dim̄ car̄ træ . ten vluiet

149 b

lib hō . t . r . e . vii . borđ . ix ac̄ p̄ti . dim̄ car̄ . dim̄ mol̄ . dim̄ falina.

7 ual v . fol . tenet Idē . Tota Waltuna . i . leu in long . & dim̄ in lat̄.

& reddit xviii . đ . de xx . fol . de gelto.

Value 6d.

Also 8 free men under patronage only, 80 acres of land.

Then and later 2 ploughs, now 1½ ploughs. Meadow, 3 acres.
Value 5s.

Edric held all this when Ralph forfeited. The King and the Earl have the jurisdiction.

The Hundred and a Half of CLACKCLOSE

43 Ribald holds in BEECHAMWELL, 60 acres of land before 1066.

Then 1 plough, now ½.
Value always 5s.

He also holds in STOKE (Ferry) 3 free men, at 7 acres before 1066.
Value 12d.

FREEBRIDGE Hundred and a Half

44 In ISLINGTON Rolf, a free man, held 1 c. of land before 1066.

Always 6 smallholders. Also 2 free men, 2½ acres.

Always 1 plough; 3½ salt-houses; meadow, 16 acres.
Value 20s.

The Bishop of Bayeux had this land on the day that Earl Ralph forfeited; now Count Alan has half in his share. Ivo Tallboys delivered it.

In the same Geoffrey holds 1 free man, 1 c. of land.

7 smallholders.

Always 1 plough.

Also 1 free man and a half, 10 acres of land.

1 salt-house; meadow, 12 acres.

Value of the whole 20s.

45 In MIDDLETON Ribald holds 2 c. of land (which) Earl Ralph held.

Always 3 villagers; 1 priest; 3 smallholders.

Always 2 ploughs; meadow, 18 acres. Then 1 fishery.
Value 20s.

In (East) WALTON Thorkell held 1 c. [of land] before 1066.

Always 6 villagers; 1 smallholder.

1 plough in lordship; ½ men's plough; 1 mill.
Value 20s. He also (holds).

In (ASH)WICKEN and BAWSEY Wulfgeat, a free man, held ½ c. of land before 1066.

7 smallholders.

Meadow, 9 acres; ½ plough; ½ mill; ½ salt-house.
Value 5s.

He also holds. The whole of (East) Walton (has) 1 league in length and ½ in width, it pays 18d of a 20s tax.

149 b

$\bar{H}$. *SCEREPHAM*. In Baconſtorp. ten& torſtin dim̄ car̄ træ.

q̄ ten̄ Chetelbern lib̄ hō. t. r. e. ſemp. iii. bord̄. 7. ii. ac̄ p̄ti. ſilua.

iiii. por. ſemp. i. car̄ 7 ual̄ x. ſol. ſoca tep̄r, r. e. in bucha.

Gillecros. $\bar{H}$. In herlinga ten& anſchittil̄. iiii. car̄ træ. qm

ten̄ Vlchetel lib̄ hō. t. r. e. tn̄c xv. uil̄. p̄ & m̄ xiii. ſemp. iiii.

bord̄. tn̄c. ii. ſer̄. p̄ 7 m̄. i. viii. ac̄ p̄ti. ſemp. ii. car̄ in dn̄io. tn̄c

vii. car̄ hom̄. p̄ vi. m̄. iiii. ſemp. i. mol̄. tn̄c. v. piſc̄. m̄. i. piſc̄.

7 dim̄. 7. iiii. ſochem̄. dim̄ car̄ træ. Soca in keninchala. ſep. i.

bord̄. 7. iiii. ac̄ p̄ti. Tn̄c 7 p̄. ii. car̄. m̄. i. ſemp. i. r̄. m̄. iiii. an.

7 xx. por. ſemp lxx. oues. Tn̄c ual̄. vi. l̄b̄. p̄. vii. lib̄. m̄. c. ſol.

totū h̄t. i. leū & dim̄ in lon.&. i. leug in lato. quicq̄ ibi teneat.

& xx. vii. d̄ de gelto.

Dim̄. *HVNDRET. DE HERSA*. ⌐ In aldeb̄ga. xii. ac̄ træ. 7 dim̄

ac̄ p̄ti.& p̄tin& in romborc. ⌐ *DICE DIMI*. $\bar{H}$. Sceluagra ten̄ colo

lib̄ hō aſgeri ſtalre. t. r. e. p̄ man̄. m̄ ten& herucus. ii. car̄ træ.

Sep. ii. uil̄. 7 xv. bord̄. Tn̄c 7 p̄. ii. ſer̄. m̄. i. Semp. ii. car̄

in dn̄io. 7. ii. car̄ houm. Silua. xl. porc̄. 7. iii. ac̄ p̄ti. &. i. ſoc̄.

de. iiii. ac̄. Semp ual̄. xx. ſol.

⌐ In ſceluagra ten̄ modepheſe lib̄a femina algari. ii. car̄ træ. Sep

iii. uil̄. & xv. bord̄. Semp. ii. car̄ in dn̄io. 7. ii. car̄ houm. 7. i. ſoc̄.

de. iiii. ac̄. Silua ad xl. por. 7. iii. ac̄ p̄ti. Semp ual̄. xl. ſol.

150 a

Sceluagra h̄t. i. leug in longo. 7 dim̄ in lato. & de gelto. ix. d̄.

SHROPHAM Hundred

46 In BACONSTHORPE Thurstan holds ½ c. of land which Ketelbern, a free man, held before 1066.
    Always 3 smallholders.
    Meadow, 2 acres; woodland, 4 pigs; always 1 plough.
  Value 10s.
    The jurisdiction (was) in Buckenham before 1066.

GUILTCROSS Hundred

47 In HARLING Ansketel holds 4 c. of land which Ulfketel, a free man, held before 1066.
    Then 15 villagers, later and now 13; always 4 smallholders.
    Then 2 slaves, later and now 1.
    Meadow, 8 acres; always 2 ploughs in lordship. Then 7 men's ploughs, later 6, now 4; always 1 mill. Then 5 fisheries, now 1½ fisheries.
    Also 4 Freemen, ½ c. of land. The jurisdiction (is) in Kenninghall.
    Always 1 smallholder.
    Meadow, 4 acres. Then and later 2 ploughs, now 1; always 1 cob. Now 4 head of cattle; 20 pigs; always 70 sheep.
  Value then £6; later £7; now 100s.
    The whole has 1½ leagues in length and 1 league in width, whoever holds there, tax of 27d.

The Half Hundred of **EARSHAM**

48 In Aldburgh 12 acres of land; meadow, ½ acre.
    It belongs in Rumburgh.

DISS Half-Hundred

49 Colo, a free man of Asgar the Constable's, held SHELFANGER before 1066 as a manor; now Hervey holds 2 c. of land.
    Always 2 villagers; 15 smallholders. Then and later 2 slaves, now 1.
    Always 2 ploughs in lordship; 2 men's ploughs; woodland, 40 pigs; meadow, 3 acres.
    Also 1 Freeman, at 4 acres.
  Value always 20s.

50 In SHELFANGER Modgifu, a free woman of Algar, holds 2 c. of land.
    Always 3 villagers; 15 smallholders.
    Always 2 ploughs in lordship; 2 men's ploughs.
    1 Freeman, at 4 acres.
    Woodland for 40 pigs; meadow, 3 acres.
  Value always 40s.
    Shelfanger has 1 league in length and ½ in width; tax of 9d.   150 a

$\bar{H}$. DE HAPINGA. In Hapeſburc . II . libi hoes . c . ac͛
træ . t . r . e . ex ħ . c . acris erant . LX in dnio hapeſburc . qno . R . foris
fec͛ . ſ; edric͛ eas inuaſit . 7 reuocat Warant iuone͛ taileſboſc . 7 ſuos
ſocios . & ex hoc dedit uade͛ . & ħt͛ . v . borđ . & . I . car͛ . 7 LX . ac͛ . 7 uat . VI.
ſot . & XL ac͛ . uat . IIII . ſot . In ludha͛ ten edric͛ liħ ho edrici.
de delaxefelda . t . r . e . LX . ac͛ træ . 7 . IIII . borđ . 7 dim car͛ . 7 . II . ac͛.
& dim p͛ti . & XI libi hoes LXXX . ac træ.
In Catefelda . I . liħ ho͛ . v . acr͛ . 7 uat . VI . đ . In lvdha͛ . I . car͛ træ . XVIIII.
ſoc . ſci ben . t . r . e . 7 hoc inuaſit edric͛ ho comitis alani . tp͛r . R.
comitis & erat inde ſeiſit quando faĉta . e͛ . diuiſio traru͛ int rege͛
& comite͛ . 7 ħt͛ . I . car͛ 7 dim . IIII . ac p͛ti . 7 uat . x . ſot . In pallinga
. I . liħm hom . de XXX . ac træ inuaſit idê edric͛ t . R . comitis . 7 ħt
dim͛ car͛ . 7 uat . II . ſot.

$\bar{H}$. de humiliart . Hederſeeta . ten͛ Olf͛ teinn . t . r . e . m͛ ten&
Ribald . III . car͛ træ . ſemp . VIII . uitt . 7 VII . borđ . Tnc͛ . III . ſer . p͛
7 m͛ . II . ſep . II . car id . & dim car homu . Silua . XL porc . XII . ac
p͛ti . Tnc͛ VII . r͛ . m͛ . I . ſep . v . an͛ . 7 v . porc͛ 7 LXXVII . ou͛ . 7 VII.
uaſa apiu͛ . I . eccła . de LX . ac͛ . 7 uat . v . ſot . & at eccła . VIII . ac͛ . 7
uat . VIII . đ . 7 LXXX . ſoc . III . min͛ . IIII . car͛ træ . Tnc͛ x . car.
7 p͛ 7 m͛ . VII . x . ac͛ p͛ti . I . mot͛ . 7 . II . libi hoes comdati . tantu͛ . de
LX . ac͛ træ . 7 R . com͛ ſoca͛ . ſep . I . uitt . 7 v . borđ . 7 . II . car͛ . 7 v.
ac͛ p͛ti . Tnc͛ 7 p͛ uat . VIII . liħ . m͛ . x . 7 ħt . I . leu͛ in lon͛ . 7 dim in
lat͛ . 7 XXVI . đ . 7 . III . ferding͛ de gelt.

The Hundred of HAPPING

51 In HAPPISBURGH 2 free men, 100 acres of land, before 1066. Of these 100 acres 60 were in the lordship of Happisburgh when R(alph) forfeited, but Edric annexed them and vouches to warranty Ivo Tallboys and his associates, and gave pledge of this.

He has 5 smallholders, 1 plough and 60 acres.

Value 6s. And the 40 acres, value 4s.

In LUDHAM Edric, a free man of Edric of Laxfield's, held 60 acres of land before 1066.

4 smallholders.

½ plough; meadow, 2½ acres.

Also 11 free men, 80 acres of land.

In CATFIELD 1 free man, 5 acres.

Value 6d.

In LUDHAM 1 c. of land, 19 Freemen of St. Benedict's before 1066. Edric, a man of Count Alan's, annexed this in the time of Earl R(alph) and he had possession when division of the lands was made between the King and the Earl.

It has 1½ ploughs; meadow, 4 acres.

Value 10s.

In PALLING the same Edric annexed 1 free man, at 30 acres of land, in the time of Earl R(alph). He has ½ plough.

Value 2s.

The Hundred of HUMBLEYARD

52 Ulf, a thane, held HETHERSETT before 1066; now Ribald holds. 3 c. of land.

Always 8 villagers; 7 smallholders. Then 3 slaves, later and now 2.

Always 2 ploughs in lordship; ½ men's plough; woodland, 40 pigs; meadow, 12 acres. Then 7 cobs, now 1. Always 5 head of cattle; 5 pigs; 87 sheep; 7 beehives.

1 church, at 60 acres of land;

value 5s.

Also another church, at 8 acres;

value 8d.

Also 80 Freemen less 3, 4 c. of land.

Then 10 ploughs, later and now 7. Meadow, 10 acres; 1 mill.

2 free men under patronage only, at 60 acres of land. Earl R(alph) (had) the jurisdiction.

Always 1 villager; 5 smallholders.

2 ploughs; meadow, 5 acres.

Value then and later £8; now 10.

It has 1 league in length and ½ in width; tax of 26¾d.

hó heroldi . xxx . ac̃ . 7 . ɪɪɪɪ . borđ . ſep dim̃ car̃ . 7 . ɪɪɪ . ac̃ p̃ti . & tcia
pars . ɪ . moł . 7 . ɪɪ . liƀi hóes . & dim̃ . cm̃datione tantu . Rex 7 c . ſocã .
7 hñt xɪɪɪɪ . ac̃ . ſemp . ɪ . car̃ . 7 uał . v . ſoł . Iierlha . ɪ . liƀ hó .
edrici . anteceſſoris . R . malet . de xxx . ac̃ . 7 v . borđ . ſep . ɪ . car̃ .
7 . ɪɪɪɪ . ſoc̃ de xv . ac̃ t̃re . ſep dim̃ car̃ . 7 . ɪ . moł . 7 vɪɪɪ . ac̃ p̃ti .
Tñc uał . vɪɪɪ . ſoł . m̃ . xɪɪ . ┌ In Florenduna . ɪ . liƀ hó Wert . vɪɪ .
ac̃r . 7 . ɪ . uiłt de v . ac̃ . 7 . ɪɪ . boues . & é inp̃tio de coſteſeia .
In Cringaforda . ten& R . bigot . ɪ . liƀm̃ hom̃ Stigandi . xv . ac̃r .
7 . ɪɪ . borđ . & . ɪɪ . liƀi hóes vɪɪ . ac̃ 7 dim̃ . ſemp dim̃ car̃ . 7 . ɪ . ac̃r
& dim̃ p̃ti . & octaua pars moł . 7 uał . ɪɪɪ . ſoł .

┌ DEPWade . H̃ . In Carletuna xɪɪɪɪ . liƀi hóes . Lxxxxv . ac̃r .
Tñc . ɪ . car̃ 7 dim̃ . m̃ . ɪɪ . 7 . ɪɪ . ac̃ p̃ti . In ᴋekilinctuna . ɪɪɪ . liƀi hóes
Lxxɪɪɪ . ac̃ . 7 . ɪɪɪ . borđ . Tñc . ɪɪ . car̃ . p̃ 7 m̃ . ɪ . car̃ . 7 dim̃ . 7 . ɪɪɪɪ . ac̃
p̃ti . In Waketuna . ɪɪ . liƀi hóes xxvɪɪɪ . ac̃ t̃ræ . tc̃ dim̃ car̃ . 7 . ɪɪ .
liƀi hóes . xx . ac̃ . 7 dim̃ car̃ . 7 . ɪɪ . ac̃ 7 dim̃ p̃ti . In Tibhã . ɪ . liƀ hó .
xxx . ac̃ . 7 . ɪ . ac̃ p̃ti . In Oſlactuna . ɪ . ſoc̃ . vɪ . ac̃ . In muletuna .
vɪ . liƀi hóes . Lvɪɪ . ac̃ . 7 dim̃ car̃ . 7 . ɪɪɪ . ac̃ p̃ti . In eſtratuna . vɪɪɪ .
liƀi hóes . c . ac̃ . 7 . ɪ . car̃ . 7 . ɪ . ac̃ p̃ti . In Taſeburc . vɪ . ſoc̃ . xxɪ . ac̃ .
7 . ɪ . ac̃ p̃ti . & dim̃ car̃ . Vñ ex his fuit hó anteceſſoris Rogi bigot .
& comes . R . tenebat eũ qnõ forisfec̃ . In Tuanetuna . ɪɪ . ſoc̃ . vɪɪ .
ac̃ . 7 dim̃ car̃ . In Mildeltuna . ɪ . liƀ hó . 7 dim̃ xɪɪ . ac̃ 7 dim̃ . 7 .
dim̃ car̃ . 7 . ɪɪ . ac̃ p̃ti . Hoc totũ ÷ in̄ p̃tio de · **Coſteſeia.**

53 In DUNSTON 1 free man of Harold's, 30 acres.
    4 smallholders.
    Always ½ plough; meadow, 3 acres; one third of 1 mill.
    Also 2 free men and a half in patronage only: the King and the
       Earl (have) the jurisdiction. They have 14 acres.
    Always 1 plough.
Value 5s.
In EARLHAM 1 free man of Edric's, the predecessor's of R(obert)
Malet, at 30 acres.
    5 smallholders.
    Always 1 plough.
    Also 4 Freemen, at 15 acres of land.
    Always ½ plough; 1 mill; meadow, 8 acres.
Value then 8s; now 12.

54 In FLORDON 1 free man, Gyrth. 7 acres. 1 villager, at 5 acres;
    2 oxen. It is in the valuation of Costessey.

55 In CRINGLEFORD R(oger) Bigot holds 1 free man of Stigand's,
    15 acres.
    2 smallholders.
    Also 2 free men, 7½ acres.
    Always 1 plough; meadow, 1½ acres; one-eighth of a mill.
Value 3s.

DEEPWADE Hundred
56 In CARLTON (Rode) 14 free men, 95 acres.
    Then 1½ ploughs, now 2. Meadow, 2 acres.
In KETTLETON 3 free men, 73 acres.
    3 smallholders.
    Then 2 ploughs, later and now 1½ ploughs. Meadow, 4 acres.
In WACTON 2 free men, 28 acres of land. Then ½ plough.
    Also 2 free men, 20 acres; ½ plough; meadow, 2½ acres.
In TIBENHAM 1 free man, 30 acres; meadow, 1 acre.
In ASLACTON 1 free man, 6 acres.
In MOULTON (St. Michael) 6 free men, 57 acres; ½ plough;
    meadow, 3 acres.
In STRATTON 8 free men, 100 acres; 1 plough; meadow, 1 acre.
In TASBURGH 6 Freemen, 21 acres; meadow, 1 acre; ½ plough.
    One of these was the man of Roger Bigot's predecessor, and
Earl R(alph) held him when he forfeited.
In SWANTON 2 Freemen, 7 acres; ½ plough.
In MIDDLETON 1 free man and a half, 12½ acres; ½ plough;
    meadow, 2 acres.
All this is in the valuation of Costessey.

In Maringatorp . ı . lıb̄ hō . xxx . ııı . ac̄ . 7 vıı . bord̄ . 7 . ı . car̄ .

151 a

&. ıı . ac̄ p̄ti . 7 ual̄ . ıııı . fol̄ . In Stratuna . ı . lıb̄ hō . xxv . ac̄ . 7 dım̄ car̄ .
&. ı . ac̄ p̄ti . 7 ual̄ . ıı . fol̄ . In eade̋ . ı . lıb̄ hō Lxxxxı . ac̄ . 7 . ııı . uıl̄l . 7 v . bord̄ .
tn̄c . ı . car̄ . 7 dım̄ . m̄ . ı . 7 . ıııı . ac̄ p̄ti . In eade̋ vıı . foc̄ . xxvıı . ac̄ .
In eade̋ xv lıb̄i hoēs xvıı . ac̄ . & dım̄ car̄ . 7 ual̄ . vııı . fol̄ . & v̋ . pars mol̄ .
Tota Stratuna h̄t . ıı . leű . 7 vı . q̋r̄ in lonḡ . ı . leuḡ . 7 . ıııı . q̋r̄ in lat̄ .
7 xxv . d̄ . de gelt . In Tafeburc . ı . lıb̄ hō . xxx . ac̄ . 7 dım̄ car̄ . 7 . ıı . ac̄
p̄ti . ual̄ . ıı . fol̄ . / Claueringa . H̄ . In Thuruertuna . ı . lıb̄ hō . x . ac̄ .
7 . ıı . foc̄ . ıııı . ac̄ . 7 ual̄ xvı . d̄ .

T̄ERRE Comitis Euftachij . Fredrebruge hundret & dım̄ .   .V.
Mafincha̋ tenuit Orgar̋ lıb̄ hō . t . r . e . ıııı . car̄ træ . femp . v .
uıl̄l . 7 v . bord̄ . 7 . ıı . ac̄ p̄ti . Tn̄c 7 p̋ . ıı . car̄ in dn̄io . m̄ . ııı . femp . ı . car̄
hoūm & quarta pars fal̄ . Hic jac̄&: . ı . foc̄ . xıı . ac̄ træ . Tn̄c xxıııı . oű .
m̄ . cc . Lx . 7 xx . ııı . porc̄ . Tn̄c 7 p̋ ual̄ . xx . fol̄ . m̄ . L . Et xx . focm̄ .
heroldi . in marfinghara . de . ıı . car̄ 7 dım̄ . femp v . bord̄ . Tn̄c 7 p̋
vı . car̄ . m̄ . ııı . 7 ual̄ . L . fol̄ . Ifti hoēs fuer̄ lı̄bati fic tenebat eos
herold̄ . M̄ hoc totū tenet Wido angeuin̋ . Tota h̄t . ı . leuḡ in lonḡ
& dım̄ in lato . 7 reddit . vııı . d̄ . de gelto de xx fol̄ .
/ Anemere tenuit orgar̋ lıb̄ hō . t . r . e . ıı . car̄ træ . fep . ı . uıl̄l :
7 vı . bord̄ . tn̄c . ıııı . fer̄ . 7 . ııı . part̄ . uni acre̋ . fep . ıı . carr̄
in dn̄io . & dım̄ car̄ hoūm . 7 . ı . pifc̄ . 7 dım̄ fal̄ . Tn̄c xı . porc̄:

150 b, 151 a, b

In MORNING THORPE 1 free man, 33 acres.
    7 smallholders; 1 plough; meadow, 2 acres.   151 a
Value 4s.
In STRATTON 1 free man, 25 acres; ½ plough; meadow, 1 acre.
Value 2s.
In the same 1 free man, 91 acres.
    3 villagers; 5 smallholders.
    Then 1½ ploughs, now 1. Meadow, 4 acres.
In the same 7 Freemen, 27 acres.
In the same 15 free men, 17 acres; ½ plough.
Value 8s; and one-fifth of a mill.
    The whole of Stratton has 2 leagues and 6 furlongs in length
and 1 league and 4 furlongs in width, tax of 25d.
In TASBURGH 1 free man, 30 acres; ½ plough; meadow, 2 acres.
Value 2s.

CLAVERING Hundred
57 In THURLTON 1 free man, 10 acres. Also 2 Freemen, 4 acres.
Value 16d.

5   LANDS OF COUNT EUSTACE

FREEBRIDGE Hundred and a Half
1 Ordgar, a free man, held MASSINGHAM before 1066, 4 c. of land.
    Always 5 villagers; 5 smallholders.
    Meadow, 2 acres. Then and later 2 ploughs in lordship, now 3.
        Always 1 men's plough; ¼ of a salt-house.
    1 Freeman appertains here, 12 acres of land.
        Then 24 sheep, now 260. 23 pigs.
Value then and later 20s; now 50.
Also 20 Freemen of Harold's, in Massingham, at 2½ c. [of land].
    Always 5 smallholders.
    Then and later 6 ploughs, now 3.
Value 50s.
    These men were delivered just as Harold held them. Now Guy
of Anjou holds all this.
    The whole has 1 league in length and ½ in width, it pays 8d
of a 20s tax.

2 Ordgar, a free man, held ANMER before 1066, 2 c. of land.
    Always 1 villager; 6 smallholders. Then 4 slaves.
    [Meadow], three parts of 1 acre. Always 4 ploughs in lordship;
        ½ men's plough; 1 fishery; ½ salt-house. Then 11 pigs,   151 b

m̃ . vııı . Tñc . c . ou̇ . m̃ . lxxx . Tnc 7 p̃ uaƚ . xl . foƚ 7 m̃ . Et vı . libi . ħ.
de . ı . car̃ træ . 7 . ıı . borđ . femp . ı . car̃ . 7 . ı . faƚ . 7 uaƚ xv . foƚ . 7 . ıııı.
đ . hos liƀos hões reclamat de dono regis . Tota ħt dı̃m leug in lon.
7 v . qr̃ in lato . & reddit . ıııı . đ . 7 obolu̇ de xx . foƚ de gelto . Et in
foc̃ de xxx acr̃ quė ten ofmund de liƀatione . 7 . ı . foc̃ de vııı . acr̃.
7 uaƚ . v . foƚ.

H̄ . de dochinge . Frenge . ı . car̃ træ ten orgar̃ liƀ hõ . t . r . e . 7.
ı . car̃ in dñio . femp . ııı . car̃ houm . 7 . ıııı . uilƚ . 7 vı . botđ . ı . ac̃ p̃ti.
m̃ xvı . porc̃ . tnc . c . ou̇ . m̃ . c:vı . Tñc 7 p̃ uaƚ xl . foƚ . m̃ . lx.
Et . ı . liƀ hõ . ı . car̃ 7 dim̃ træ . t . r . e : Tnc . ı . car̃ 7 dı̃m . p̃ 7 m̃.
ı . car̃ . 7 vıı . borđ . Et . ı . foc̃ . xxx . ac̃ . & uaƚ . xx . foƚ . Et . ı . focm̃.
xv . ac̃ . totu̇ ħt dı̃m leug in long . 7 dı̃m in lat . qui cu̇q̃ ibi teneat.
& reddit xxvıı . đ . de xx . foƚ de gelto.

H̄ . de ensford . ⌐ Wit cingehȧ tenuit godwin̄ . ı . liƀ hõ . t . r . e.
ıı . car̃ træ . femp . ıı . uilƚ . 7 xvııı . borđ . 7 ıııı . fer . femp . ıı . car̃
in dñio . 7 . ııı . car̃ houm . 7 . ııı . ac̃ p̃ti . 7 . ıı . moƚ . 7 . ıı . r̃ . 7 xıı.
an̄ . 7 xx . ıııı . pors . 7 lxxx . ou̇ . 7 . ıııı . uafa apu̇ . 7 vııı . foc̃.
de xx . ac̃ træ . de quiƀz . e . foca in folfa . f; comes ten & . fep . ıı . car̃.
7 . ı . ac̃ p̃ti . Tnc 7 p̃ vaƚ . c . foƚ . m̃ . vıı . liƀ.

Humiliart . H̄ . In Neilanda . xı . liƀi hões ftigandi . l . ac̃ . fep
ı . car̃ 7 dı̃m . 7 v . ac̃ p̃ti . 7 uaƚ . x . foƚ.

now 8. Then 100 sheep, now 80.
Value then, later and now 40s.
Also 6 free men, at 1 c. of land.
2 smallholders;
Always 1 plough; 1 salt-house.
Value 15s 4d.
These free men he claims of the King's gift. The whole has ½
league in length and 5 furlongs in width, it pays 4½d of a 20s tax.
Also 3 Freemen, at 30 acres which Osmund holds by livery.
Also 1 Freeman, at 8 acres.
Value 5s.

The Hundred of DOCKING
3 Ordgar, a free men, held FRING before 1066, 1 c. of land.
1 plough in lordship; always 3 men's ploughs.
4 villagers; 6 smallholders.
Meadow, 1 acre. Now 16 pigs. Then 100 sheep, now 106.
Value then and later 40s; now 60.
Also 1 free man, 1½ c. of land, before 1066.
Then 1½ ploughs, later and now 1 plough.
7 smallholders.
Also 1 Freeman, 30 acres.
Value 20s.
Also 1 Freeman, 15 acres.
The whole has ½ league in length and ½ in width, whoever
holds there, it pays 27d of a 20s tax.

The Hundred of EYNSFORD
4 Godwin, 1 free man, held WITCHINGHAM before 1066, 2 c. of land.
Always 2 villagers; 18 smallholders; 3 slaves.
Always 2 ploughs in lordship; 3 men's ploughs; meadow,
3 acres; 2 mills; 2 cobs; 12 head of cattle; 24 pigs; 80 sheep;
4 beehives.
Also 8 Freemen, at 20 acres of land, of whom the jurisdiction
is in Foulsham; but the Count holds.
Always 2 ploughs; meadow, 1 acre.
Value then and later 100s; now £7.

HUMBLEYARD Hundred
5 In NAYLAND 11 free men of Stigand's, 50 acres.
Always 1½ ploughs; meadow, 5 acres.
Value 10s.

DepWade . H̄ . Torp . ten̅ teinn̅ Stigandi . iii . caŕ træ . ſemp
xii . uiłł . Tnc̅ . x . borđ . m̄ . xv . Tnc̅ . iiii . ſeŕ . m̄ . iii . ſemp̄ . iii .
caŕ in dn̅io . tnc . vii . caŕ . m̄ . v . xxx . ac p̄ti . ſilua . xxx . porc̅ .

152 a

tnc̅ . i . r . tn̅c xvi . an̄ . Tnc̅ xŁ . porc̅ . m̄ . xvii . Tnc̅ xx . iiii . ou̅ .
tn̅c xxiiii . cap̄ . m̄ xŁ . 7 viii . uaſa apu̅ . Tnc̅ uał . c . ſoł . m̄ . vi . liƀ
& h̄t . i . leug 7 dim̄ . in lonḡ . 7 v . quaŕ in lat̄ . 7 vi . đ . 7 . iii . ferđ deg̅ .

TERRE HVGONIS COMĪTIS . SCEREPHAM HVNDRET̄ .

ṠCERΞPHAM ten̄& Ricarđ . qua^(de vernof.)^rten̄ Anaut liƀ ho̅ . t . r . e . ii .
caŕ træ . Semp̄ . iiii . uiłł . 7 xiii . borđ . 7 . ii . ſeŕ . 7 xx . ac p̄ti . ſemp̄
ii . caŕ in dn̅io . 7 . i . caŕ hom̄ . 7 . ii . moł . & de duoƀȝ molinis .
quartas partes . Tnc̅ . i . an̄ . m̄ . ii . Tnc̅ . x . porc̅ . m̄ . vi . Tnc̅ xxx
ou̅ . m̄ . xxviiii . 7 . ii . ſoc̄ . i . ac træ . 7 quarta pars uni acræ . Tnc̅
uał . Lx . ſoł . 7 m̄ ſimilit̄ . ſ; reddit . Lxxx . Totu̅ h̄t . i . leug in lon̅ .
& dim̄ in lat̄ . 7 xviii . đ de gelto . Soca reg̅ inbucha tep̄r . r . e .
7 ſemp donec Walter̄ dedoł habuit de dono Radulfi . ut Godric̄
dicit . In Snetretuna xŁ . ac̅ træ tenuit iđe . 7 i . borđ . 7 dim̄ ac̅
p̄ti . tn̅c dim̄ caŕ .

H̄ . de Holt . In Wabrunna ten̄ Hagan̄ . t . r . e . m̄ ten̄& Ranulf̄ .
ii . caŕ træ . Semp̄ ix . uiłł . 7 xxx . borđ . 7 . v . ſeŕ . Sep̄ in dn̅io
. ii . caŕ . 7 houm̄ . iiii . Silua ad . x . por . iii . ac p̄ti . ii . moł . Tnc̅
viii . an̄ . m̄ . x . tnc xxvi . por . m̄ . xxviii . Tnc̅ . Lx . ou̅ . m̄ . xŁ .
viii . Tnc̅ . xŁvii . cap̄ . m̄ xxxvi . Tnc̅ uał . iiii . liƀ . m̄ vii . 7 haƀ .
. i . leug . 7 . iii . quaŕ in lonḡ . 7 . i . leug in lat̄ . 7 xviii . đ . in gelt .

.VI.

DEPWADE Hundred
6 A thane of Stigand's held (Ashwell) THORPE, 3 c. of land.
>Always 12 villagers. Then 10 smallholders, now 15. Then
>>4 slaves, now 3.
>Always 3 ploughs in lordship. Then 7 [men's] ploughs, now 5.
>>Meadow, 30 acres; woodland, 30 pigs. Then 1 cob. Then
>>16 head of cattle. Then 40 pigs, now 17. Then 24 sheep.
>>Then 24 goats, now 40. 8 beehives.
>Value then 100s; now £6.
>It has 1½ leagues in length and 5 furlongs in width, tax of 6¾d.

152 a

6   **LAND OF EARL HUGH**

SHROPHAM Hundred
1 Richard of Vernon holds SHROPHAM, which Anand, a free man,
held. 2 c. of land.
>Always 4 villagers; 13 smallholders; 2 slaves.
>Meadow, 20 acres. Always 2 ploughs in lordship; 1 men's
>>plough; 2 mills and the fourth parts of 2 mills. Then 1 head
>>of cattle, now 2. Then 10 pigs, now 6. Then 30 sheep,
>>now 29.
>Also 2 Freemen, 1 acre of land and the fourth part of 1 acre.
>Value then 60s; now the same, but it pays 80.
>The whole has 1 league in length and ½ in width, tax of 18d.
The jurisdiction (was) the King's in Buckenham before 1066, and
always until Walter of Dol had (it) of the gift of Ralph, as Godric
says.
The same held 40 acres of land in SNETTERTON.
>1 smallholder.
>Meadow, ½ acre; then ½ plough.

The Hundred of HOLT
2 In WEYBOURNE before 1066 Hagni held, and now Ranulf holds,
2 c. of land.
>Always 9 villagers; 30 smallholders; 5 slaves.
>Always 2 ploughs in lordship; 4 men's [ploughs]; woodland
>>for 10 pigs; meadow, 3 acres; 2 mills. Then 8 head of cattle,
>>now 10. Then 26 pigs, now 28. Then 60 sheep, now 48.
>>Then 47 goats, now 36.
>Value then £4, now 7.
>It has 1 league and 3 furlongs in length and 1 league in width,
tax of 18d.

⌠In kellinga teñ Osgot̕ . t . r . e . iii . car̕ træ̕ . Tnc̕ . ii . uiłł . m̕ . i .
152 b

Tnc̕ xiii . borđ . m̕ . xxii . Tnc̕ . iiii . ser̕ . m̕ . vi . Tnc̕ 7 p̕ in dnĩo
iii . car̕ . m̕ . ii . Tnc̕ 7 p̕ houm̕ . iiii . car̕ . m̕ . ii . car̕ . i . ac̕ p̕ti . Sep
i . r̕ . Tnc̕ . iii . an̕ . m̕ . iiii . Tnc̕ xi . porc̕ . m̕ . v . Tnc̕ xl . ou̕ . m̕ xviii .
Tnc̕ uał xl . soł . m̕ . lx . soł . 7 hab̕ . i . leug̕ & đ in long̕ . 7 . i . in łat̕ .
7 xviii . đ in gelt . Idẽ teñ & .

LOTHNINGA . *H̄* . Hedenaha̕ teñ & Warinc̕ . qua̕ tenuit
algar̕ teinñ stigandi . t . r . e . p̕ m̕ . ii . car̕ træ̕ . Semp̕ v . uiłł .
& ix . borđ . Tnc̕ . vi . ser̕ p̕ 7 m̕ . nułł . Tnc̕ . iii . car̕ in dnĩo .
p̕ nulla . m̕ . ii . Tnc̕ 7 p̕ . i . car̕ 7 dim̕ houm̕ . m̕ . ii . 7 xii . acr̕
p̕ti . Tnc̕ . i . mol̕ . 7 m̕ . ii . an̕ . m̕ . xii . porc̕ . m̕ xl . cap̕ . & sub eo
xx . libi hoes com̕đ . dim car̕ træ̕ . Tnc̕ . iii . car̕ . p̕ nulla .
m̕ . iiii . 7 . iiii . ac̕ p̕ti . ⌠ In sithinga ix libi hoes . 7 . iiii . dim̕
stigandi . t . r . e . 7 Galter̕ dedol abstulit 7 addidit ad ennaha̕
7 ht̕ dim car̕ træ̕ . Tnc̕ . i . car̕ . p̕ . nuł̕ . m̕ . i .
In Wdetuna . ii . libi hoes 7 dim̕ . de quibʒ Alger̕ habuit
com̕đ . dim car̕ træ̕ . Sep̕ . ii . uiłł . 7 . i . borđ . Tnc̕ . i . car̕ .
p̕ nichil . m̕ dim̕ . 7 . i . ac̕ p̕ti . Tnc̕ 7 p̕ totu̕ uał xl . soł .
m̕ . iiii . lib̕ . Soca stigandi . 7 ht̕ . i . leug̕ in long̕ . 7 . i . in łat̕ .
& de gelto viii . đ .

Depwade . *H̄* . Fundehala teñ & Roger̕ bigot̕ . qua̕ teñ
Burkart teinñ . t . r . e . ii . car̕ træ̕ . semp̕ xi . uiłł . 7 xi . bor̕ .
tnc̕ . iiii . ser̕ . m̕ . iii . Sep̕ . ii . car̕ in dnĩo . 7 . iiii . car̕ hom̕ .
xx . ac̕ p̕ti . | Eccł in . xxiiii . ac̕ libe træ̕ Silua xiii . por̕ . m̕ . i . r̕ . 7 ix . an̕ . 7 xxx . porc̕ .
7 xlviii . ou̕ . 7 xlviii . cap̕ . 7 . i . soc̕ . i . ac̕ . Tnc̕ uał xl . soł .

3 In KELLING before 1066 Osgot held 3 c. of land.
   Then 2 villagers, now 1. Then 13 smallholders, now 22.
     Then 4 slaves, now 6.
   Then and later 3 ploughs in lordship, now 2. Then and later
     4 men's ploughs, now 2 ploughs. Meadow, 1 acre; always
     1 cob. Then 3 head of cattle, now 4. Then 11 pigs, now 5.
     Then 40 sheep, now 18.
Value then 40s; now 60s.
   It has 1½ leagues in length and 1 in width, tax of 18d. He also
holds.

LODDON Hundred
4 Waring holds HEDENHAM which Algar, a thane of Stigand's, held
   before 1066 as a manor, 2 c. of land.
     Always 5 villagers; 9 smallholders. Then 6 slaves, later and
     now none.
     Then 3 ploughs in lordship, later none, now 2. Then and later
     1½ men's ploughs, now 2. Meadow, 12 acres. Then 1 mill.
     Now 2 head of cattle; now 12 pigs; now 40 goats.
     Also 20 free men in patronage under him, ½ c. of land.
     Then 3 ploughs, later none, now 4. Meadow, 4 acres.

5 In SEETHING 9 free men and 4 halves of Stigand's before 1066.
Walter of Dol took them away and added them to Hedenham.
They had ½ c. of land.
     Then 1 plough, later none, now 1.
In WOODTON 2 free men and a half of whom Algar had the
patronage, ½ c. of land.
     Always 2 villagers; 1 smallholder.
     Then 1 plough, later nothing, now ½. Meadow, 1 acre.
Value of the whole then and later 40s; now £4.
     Stigand's jurisdiction. It has 1 league in length and 1 in width,
tax of 8d.

DEPWADE Hundred
6 Roger Bigot holds FUNDENHALL which Burghard, a thane, held
   before 1066, 2 c. of land.
     Always 11 villagers; 11 smallholders. Then 4 slaves, now 3.
     Always 2 ploughs in lordship; 4 men's ploughs; meadow,
     20 acres.
     (Belonging) to the church 24 acres of free land. Woodland,
     13 pigs. Now 1 cob; 9 head of cattle; 30 pigs; 48 sheep;
     48 goats.
     Also 1 Freeman, 1 acre.
Value then 40s.

In Eade. 11. car træ ten Aluric lib ho Stigandi. Semp. v. uilt. 7 xvi.
bord tnc vi. fer. m̄. 1111. femp. 11. car in d̄nio. Tnc. 1111. car hom.
p̄ 7 m̄. 111. & xx ac p̄ti. Silua. xxx. porc. Sep. 1. mot. 7. 111. fochem
x11. ac. Tnc uat lx. fot. & hic ptin&. una bereuita eilanda. xxx.
ac. tnc. 1. uilt. femp. 1111 bord. 7. 1. car in d̄nio. 7 dim car hom.
1. ac p̄ti. Silua. x11. porc. Huic manerio addidit Galter de Dol.
11. libos hoes. qui fnt in habetuna. un Stigandi 7 alt Guertd.
7 hnt. xc. ac. fep. v. uilt. 7 v11. bord. Tnc. 111. fer. Tnc. 111. car. 7
dim. m̄. 11. 7 xv11. ac p̄ti. Addidit &iam. 111. libos hoes. v111. ac.
Tnc uat. x11. fot. In habetuna. 1. eccta. xv. ac. Ex hoc toto
fec̄ Galter de dol. 1. maneriu. & totu fimul uat. 1x. lib. 7
hab&. 1. leu & dim in long. & dim in lat. 7. 1111. d̄. & obot
de gelto. Rog bigot ten& de comite. & Habetuna. 1. leu
in long. 7 v. quar in lato. 7 v1. d̄. 7. 111. ferd de gelt.

CLAVELINGA. H̄. Kerkebey. ten̄. 1. teinn Stigandi.
Ofmund Anteceffor. R. de belfago. t. r. e. 1. car træ. m̄
ten& Warinc. 1. bord. tnc 7 p̄. 1. car. 7. 111. ac p̄ti. filua
111. por. &. 1111. libi hoes c̄mend xv. ac. 7 dim car. 7 uat
xv. fot. In Rauincha. 1. lib ho regis. e. xxx. ac. 7. 1. bor.
& uat. v. fot.

.VII.

TERRE ROBERTI MALET.

Fredrebruge. Hundret 7 dim. Gloreftorp. tenuit
Goduin lib ho. 11. car træ. t. r. e. Tnc 7 poftea. v111. uilt.
m̄. 111. Tnc 7 p̄. 111. bord. m̄. v. femp. 111. feruos. 7 xxx
acr p̄ti. Semp. 11. car in d̄nio. Tnc dim car homum
& m̄; Silua. v111. porc. &. 11. mot. Hic jacent x111.
fokeman. de xl. ac træ. quando recep. 11. r̄. m̄. 1. fep
v111. porc. tnc xx. ou. 7 uat lx fot.

In the same Aelfric, a free man of Stigand's, holds 2 c. of land. 153 a
Always 5 villagers; 16 smallholders. Then 6 slaves, now 4.
Always 2 ploughs in lordship. Then 4 men's ploughs, later and
   now 3. Meadow, 20 acres; woodland, 30 pigs; always 1 mill.
Also 3 Freemen, 12 acres.
Value then 60s.
Here belongs 1 outlier, NAYLAND, 30 acres.
   Then 1 villager; always 4 smallholders.
   1 plough in lordship; ½ men's plough; meadow, 1 acre;
      woodland, 12 pigs.
Walter of Dol added to this manor 2 free men who are in
Hapton, 1 Stigand's, the other Gyrth's. They have 90 acres.
   Always 5 villagers; 7 smallholders. Then 3 slaves.
   Then 3½ ploughs, now 2. Meadow, 17 acres.
   He also added 3 free men, 8 acres.
Value then 12s.
In HAPTON 1 church, 15 acres.
   Out of all this Walter of Dol made 1 manor.
Value of the whole together £9.
   It has 1½ leagues in length and ½ in width, tax of 4½d. Roger
Bigot holds from the Earl. Hapton (has) 1 league in length and
5 furlongs in width, tax of 6¾d.

CLAVERING Hundred
7 1 thane of Stigand's, Osmund, the predecessor of R(alph) of
Beaufour, held KIRBY (Cane) before 1066, 1 c. of land. Waring
now holds.
   1 smallholder.
   Then and later 1 plough. Meadow, 3 acres; woodland, 3 pigs.
   Also 4 free men under patronage, 15 acres; ½ plough.
Value 15s.
In RAVENINGHAM 1 free man of King Edward's, 30 acres.
   1 smallholder.
Value 5s.

7   **LAND OF ROBERT MALET**   153 b

FREEBRIDGE Hundred and Half
1 Godwin, a free man, held GLOSTHORPE, 2 c. of land, before 1066.
   Then and later 8 villagers, now 3. Then and later 3 smallholders,
      now 5; always 3 slaves.
   Meadow, 30 acres; always 2 ploughs in lordship. Then and now
      ½ men's plough; woodland, 8 pigs; 2 mills.
   13 Freemen appertain here, at 40 acres of land.
   When he acquired it, 2 cobs, now 1; always 8 pigs. Then 20
      sheep.
Value 60s.

Jac& etiam . I . beruita p̄ manerio heufeda . t . r . e . I . car̄
træ tnc 7 p̄ . VII . uiłł . m̄ . v . femp XII . bord̄ . 7 . III . fer.
7 XL acr̄ p̄ti . 7 . I . car̄ in dn̄io . 7 . II . bou houm . 7 . I . moł.
Silua XVI . porc̄ . 7 . I . fał & dimid̄ . tnc . I . r̄ . 7 modo ;
7 XIIII . porc̄ . XXX . ou . 7 L . cap̄ . Huic bereuuite jaceꝏ
III . foc̄ . X . ac̄ træ . 7 uał XXX . foł . Hec duo maneria
ħt . II . leug in long . 7 . IIII . qr̄ in łat̄ . d̄ cuq̄ ibi teneat.
& redd̄ XII . d̄ . de XX . foł de gelto.

SCERPHAM . H̄ . Culuerfteftuna ten̄ edric̄ . t . r . e.
II . car̄ træ . Semp . IIII . uiłł . 7 . I . bord̄ . 7 . IIII . fer.
v . ac̄ p̄ti . 7 . II . car̄ in dn̄io . Tnc 7 p̄ . I . car̄ . m̄ dim.
Semp . I . moł . 7 . I . pifcatio . Hic jac& . I . foc̄ regis . LX . ac̄ træ.
unde fuus antec̄ habuit com̄d̄ tantu & tra clamat de
dono regis . Tnc 7 p̄ . I . car̄ . m̄ . II . bou . 7 . II . ac̄ pti.
Semp . II . r̄ . 7 . IIII . an . tc̄ . CCC . ou . m̄ . CCC . XII . minus.

154 a

Tnc XVI . porc̄ . m̄ . III . Tnc 7 p̄ uał . LX . foł . m̄ . LXXX . &. I.
car̄ pofſ& ēē ; Gałt de cadomo ten& de . R.

HEINESTEDE . H̄ . In fafilingaba tenuit edric̄ anteceffor
R . Malet . II . foc̄ & dim̄ de LXVI . ac̄ træ . m̄ ten& Walter.
Tnc IX . bord̄ . Modo XIII . Semp . III . car̄ & dim̄ inter
ōes . 7 . III . ac̄ p̄ti . & octaua pars molendini . & Subeis
. I . foc̄ . de . VI . ac̄ træ . Semp dim̄ car̄ . Tunc uał . XXX
foł . m̄ reddit . L . Soł.

In Scoteffam ten̄ ulketel . I . łib ho . edrici com̄d . t . r . e.
de XXX acr̄ træ . Tnc . I . bord̄ . p̄ 7 m̄ . II . Tnc dim̄
carr̄ . nec p̄ . nec m̄ . Semp uał . v . folid̄ . 7 . IIII . d̄ . Id̄ē.

2 There appertains also 1 outlier, BAWSEY, as a manor before 1066, 1 c. of land.

 Then and later 7 villagers, now 5. Always 12 smallholders; 3 slaves.

 Meadow, 40 acres; 1 plough in lordship; the men, 2 oxen; 1 mill; woodland, 16 pigs; 1½ salt-houses. Then and now 1 cob. 14 pigs; 30 sheep; 50 goats.

 3 Freemen appertain to this outlier, 10 acres of land.

Value 30s.

 These two manors have 2 leagues in length and 4 furlongs in width, whoever holds there, it pays 12d of a 20s tax.

SHROPHAM Hundred

3 Edric held KILVERSTONE before 1066, 2 c. of land.

 Always 4 villagers; 1 smallholder; 4 slaves.

 Meadow, 5 acres; 2 ploughs in lordship. Then and later 1 plough, now ½. Always 1 mill; 1 fish pond.

1 Freeman of the King's appertains here, 60 acres of land whereof his predecessor had the patronage only and he claims the land of the King's gift.

 Then and later 1 plough, now 2 oxen. Meadow, 2 acres. Always 2 cobs; 4 head of cattle. Then 300 sheep, now 300 less 12. Then 16 pigs, now 3.   154 a

Value then and later 60s; now 80.

 There could be 1 plough. Walter of Caen holds from R(obert).

HENSTEAD Hundred

4 In SAXLINGHAM Edric, the predecessor of R(obert) Malet, held 2 Freemen and a half, at 66 acres of land; now Walter holds.

 Then 9 smallholders, now 13.

 Always 3½ ploughs among them all; meadow, 3 acres; one-eighth of a mill. Also under them

1 Freeman, at 6 acres of land.

 Always ½ plough.

Value then 30s; now it pays 50s.

5 In SHOTESHAM Ulfketel, 1 free man under the patronage of Edric, held before 1066, at 30 acres of land.

 Then 1 smallholder, later and now 2.

 Then ½ plough, but not later or now.

Value always 5s 4d. He also (holds).

DIMID HVNDRET HERSAM. In Scotoford . ten&
humfridvs . quã tenuit . ı . liɓ hõ edrici comd d xlııı
ac̃ træ . & Semp . ıı . uiℓℓ . 7 . ıı . borđ . Semp inter
homes . ı . carr̃ . Silua . xv . por . 7 . ııı . ac̃ p̃ti . Semp
uaℓ . x . foℓ.

DICE DIMID . H̄. Geffinga tenuit alftan liɓ hõ
edrici comd tantu . lx . ac̃r̃ træ . m̃ ten& Wiℓℓm̃.
Semp . ıııı . borđ . Semp . ı . carr̃ in dnio . 7 dim̃
carr̃ homum̃ . 7 . ıı . ac̃r̃ p̃ti . Tnc̃ 7 poftea uaℓ
vııı . foℓ . m̃ xv.

∫ In borftuna ten& Galter̃ quã tenuit aculf̃
liɓ homo edrici comd tantu xxvı . ac̃r̃ . 7 . ıı.
borđ . Semp . ı . carruca . 7 . ıı . ac̃r̃ p̃ti . 7 . ı . fõc̃.

154 b
de . ıı . ac̃r̃ træ . Semp uaℓ& vııı . foℓ.
∫ In torp . tenuit edric̃ foc̃ fub edrico antec̃ maℓet
lxxx . ac̃ . m̃ ten& huɓt̃ . Semp . ııı . uiℓℓ . 7 . ııı . borđ.
Semp . ı . car̃ in dnio . Semper . ıı . car̃ houm̃ . 7 vı.
ac̃r̃ prati . & inteluetuna . ıı . liɓi hoẽs ejdem xıııı.
ac̃r̃ træ . Semp dim car̃ . tnc̃ totu uaℓ . x . foℓ . p̃ 7 m̃
xx . Soca regis . Torp ħ ııı . quar̃ in longo . 7 . ııı.
in latitudõẽ . & de gelto . ııı . đ.
In borftuna tenuit moithar liɓ hõ edrici . xxx . ac̃
træ . ıııı . borđ . tnc̃ . ı . car̃ in dnio . m̃ dim . In eadem
. ıııı . liɓi hoẽs fub eode de xxvı . ac̃ træ . Sep̃ dim car̃.
& . ıı . ac̃ı prati . Tnc̃ 7 p̃ uaℓ vııı . foℓ . m̃ xv.
∫ Frifa tenuit edric̃ fub edrico p . ı . car̃ træ . m̃ ten&
huɓt̃ . Tnc̃ 7 p̃ . ı . uiℓℓ . m̃ . ıı . Tnc̃ 7 p̃ . ı . borđ . m̃ . ıı.
Semp . ı . car̃ in dnio . Sep̃ . ar̃ hoẽs cũ . ıı . boũ . . 7
ıııı . ac̃ p̃ti . m̃ . ı . moℓ . Tnc̃ 7 p̃ uaℓ . x . m̃ . xv . ħ . v . qr̃.
in longo . 7 . ıııı . in lato . 7 ııı . đ . de . g.

EARSHAM Half-Hundred

6 In SHOTFORD Humphrey holds what 1 free man under Edric's patronage held before 1066, at 43 acres of land.
Always 2 villagers; 2 smallholders.
Always 1 plough among the men; woodland, 15 pigs; meadow, 3 acres.
Value always 10s.

DISS Half-Hundred

7 Alstan, a free man under the patronage only of Edric, held GISSING, 60 acres of land. Now William holds.
Always 4 smallholders.
Always 1 plough in lordship; ½ men's plough; meadow, 2 acres.
Value then and later 8s; now 15.

8 In BURSTON Walter holds what Acwulf, a free man under the patronage only of Edric, held, 26 acres.
2 smallholders.
Always 1 plough; meadow, 2 acres.
Also 1 Freeman, at 2 acres of land.   154 b
Value always 8s.

9 In THORPE (Parva) Edric, a Freeman under Edric the predecessor of Malet, held 80 acres. Now Hubert holds.
Always 3 villagers; 3 smallholders.
Always 1 plough in lordship; always 2 men's ploughs; meadow, 6 acres.
Also in THELVETON 2 free men of the same, 14 acres of land.
Always ½ plough.
Value of the whole then 10s; later and now 20.
The King's jurisdiction. Thorpe (Parva) has 4 furlongs in length and 3 in width, tax of 3d.

10 In BURSTON Morcar, a free man of Edric's, held 30 acres of land.
4 smallholders.
Then 1 plough in lordship, now ½.
In the same 4 free men under the same, at 26 acres of land.
Always ½ plough; meadow, 2 acres.
Value then and later 8s; now 15.

11 Edric held FRENZE under Edric for 1 c. of land. Now Hubert holds.
Then and later 1 villager, now 2. Then and later 1 smallholder, now 2.
Always 1 plough in lordship; the men have always ploughed with 2 oxen; meadow, 4 acres. Now 1 mill.
Value then and later 10[s], now 15.
It has 5 furlongs in length and 4 in width, tax of 3d.

In regadona tenuit . I . lib ho edrici comd xx . acr
træ . m ten& Galter . Semp dim car . 7 . I . ac pti . Tnc
& p ual . II . fol . 7 vI . d . m . III . fol.

In fimplingaha . II . libi hoes ejufdem . comd tantu.
xv . ac træ . Tnc dim car . m . I . bos . Semp ual xvI d.

In teluetaham . II . libi hoes ejufde cmd . vIII . ac træ
m ten& Galter . Tnc 7 p dim car . m nichil . Sep

155 a

ual& xvI . d . / Infemera . I . lib ho fub edrico comd
tantu xL . acr . 7 fub eo . III . bord . Semp . I . car inter
hoes . Silua . IIII . por . 7 . II ac pti . Semp ual vIII . fol . Ide.

In geffinga . dim lib ho edrici comd tantu . de xI . acr.
& fub eo . I . bord . & ual xII . d . & ten& Wilt.

In borftuna . I . lib ho lefrici de torenduna comd xx . ac
m ten& . R . mal& ex dono regine . femp . II . bord.
7 fubeo . I . lib . vI . ac . fep dim car . fep ual III . folid.
7 m ten& mat Robti malet.

LOTHNINGA . H̃ . Wodetona tenuit ulketel . I . lib
ho edrici comd . p xxx . acr . & ten& Galter . Semp
v . bord . Tnc . II . car . p . I . 7 m . II . Semp dim car.
houm . Silua . IIII . por . 7 . I . ac pti . m . vII . porc . m
xL ou . & ibi fnt vIII . libi hoes . ulketelli . comd
t . r . e . xxx . ac træ . Int hoes . femp . I . car . Tnc
7 p ual xx . fol . modo . xxx . ht . I . leug in longo.
& dim in lato . & de gelto xv . d . Soca in hund.

12 In ROYDON 1 free man under the patronage of Edric held 20 acres
of land. Now Walter holds.
   Always ½ plough; meadow, 1 acre.
Value then and later 2s 6d; now 3s.

13 In SHIMPLING 2 free men under the patronage only of the same,
15 acres of land.
   Then ½ plough; now 1 ox.
Value always 16d.
In THELVETON 2 free men under the patronage of the same, 8
acres of land. Now Walter holds.
   Then and later ½ plough, now nothing.
Value always 16d.   155 a
In SEMERE 1 free man under Edric in patronage only, 40 acres.
   3 smallholders under him.
   Always 1 plough among the men; woodland, 4 pigs; meadow,
      2 acres.
Value always 8s. He also (holds).
In GISSING half a free man under the patronage only of Edric,
at 11 acres. 1 smallholder under him.
Value 12d. William holds.

14 In BURSTON 1 free man under the patronage of Leofric of
Thorndon, 20 acres. Now Robert Malet holds of the Queen's gift.
   Always 2 smallholders.
   Also under him 1 free (man), 6 acres.
      Always ½ plough.
Value always 3s. Now the mother of Robert Malet holds.

   LODDON Hundred
15 Ulfketel, a free man under the patronage of Edric, held WOODTON,
   as 30 acres. Walter holds.
   Always 5 smallholders.
   Then 2 ploughs, later 1, now 2. Always ½ men's plough;
      woodland, 4 pigs; meadow, 1 acre. Now 7 pigs, now
      40 sheep.
   Also there were 8 free men under the patronage of Ulfketel
   before 1066, 30 acres of land.
      Always 1 plough among the men.
Value then and later 20s; now 30.
   It has 1 league in length and ½ in width; tax of 15d. The
jurisdiction (is) in the Hundred.

H̃ DE TAVERHAM. ⌐HOSFORDA teñ edric̅

. I . lib̅ hō . t . r . e . II . cař træ & dim . tñc 7 p̃ .

v . uilt . m̃ . VII . femp v . borđ tc̃ 7 p̃ . II . cař in dñio .

m̃ . I . tñc 7 p̃ . I . cař hou̅m . m̃ dim . 7 . IIII . ac̃ p̃ti . Tnc̃

& p̃ . filua . CLX . ⌐ m̃| . LX . 7 . I . mot̅ . femp . I . ř . tñc . III .

añ . m̃ . IIII : 7 m̃ XVII . por . tñc . XXX . ou̅ . m̃ . LXXXXII .

7 m̃ . XV . uafa apiu . Et tñc 7 p̃ . XX . II . foc . m̃ XXI .

155 b

cař tre . 7 . II . ac̃r p̃ti . Tñc 7 p̃ . I . cař & dim . m̃ . I . de duob₂

foc . ht̅ rex 7 comes Soca . 7 fup alios . VI . forisfacturas .

Tñc 7 p̃ vat̅ . III . lib̅ . m̃ cx . fot̅ . & ht̅ . I . leug 7 dim in lug̅ .

& . I . in lat̅ . & reddit XVII . deñ . in gelto regis .

& . I . ferding .

Horfha̅ tenuit idem edric̃ . I . lib̅ hō . t . r . e . IIII .

cař træ . tñc 7 poftea XII . uilt̅ . m̃ XVI . femp IX borđ .

tñc 7 p̃ . II . cař in dñio . m̃ . I . femp . I . cař homu̅ . 7 dim̅

ac̃r p̃ti . Tñc 7 p̃ . filua . CLX por . m̃ . LX . 7 . II . mot̅ .

femp . I . ř . tñc . II . anim̅ . m̃ . IIII . tñc VI . por . modo

XVIII . tñc X . cap̃ . m̃ XXXV . Et XIX . focem . I . cař træ .

femp . I . carr̅ . De trib₂ rex 7 comes foca . 7 fup alios

VI . forisfacturas . tñc 7 p̃ uat̅ . III . lib̅ . m̃ . IIII . lib̅ .

7 X . fot̅ . & ht̅ . I . leug 7 dim in long . 7 . I . in latitudo̅e

& reddit XVII . đ . 7 . I . ferding . Et in Boofetuna . II .

lib̅i hōes . 7 In Sprotuna . III . & hñt LXIIII . ac̃ træ

& . I . borđ . femp . I . cař . 7 . I . ac̃ p̃ti . 7 uat̅ . VI . fot̅ . Rex

& comes Soca̅ .

⌐ Tonfteda . H̃ . Baketuna teñ& Rob̅tus

quam tenuit edric̃ . t . r . e . III . carr̅ tre

Tñc XIIII . uilt̅ . m̃ X . 7 . III . borđ . Tñc . IIII .

fer . m̃ . III . femp . III . cař in dñio . Tñc . V . cař

hom̅ . p̃ 7 m̃ . I . XIIII . ac̃ p̃ti . Silua . LX . pors .

femp . II . mot̅ . modo . II . ř . 7 . I . añ . tñc VIII .

156 a

. pors . m̃ . XIII . Tñc CLXXX ou̅ . m̃ . L . 7 XVI . cap̃ .

The Hundred of TAVERHAM

16 Edric, 1 free man, held HORSFORD before 1066, 2½ c. of land.
Then and later 5 villagers, now 7; always 5 smallholders.
Then and later 2 ploughs in lordship, now 1. Then and later
1 men's plough, now ½. Meadow, 4 acres. Woodland, then
and later 160 pigs, now 60. 1 mill; always 1 cob. Then 3
head of cattle, now 4. Now 17 pigs. Then 30 sheep, now 92.
Now 15 beehives.
Also, then and later 22 Freemen, now 21, [ ] c. of land.   155 b
Meadow, 2 acres. Then and later 1½ ploughs, now 1.
The King and the Earl have the jurisdiction of 2 Freemen, and
over the others the 6 forfeitures.
Value then and later £3; now 110s.
It has 1½ leagues in length and 1 in width; it pays 17¼d in the
King's tax.

17 The same Edric, 1 free man, held HORSHAM (St. Faith) before
1066, 3 c. of land.
Then and later 12 villagers, now 16; always 9 smallholders.
Then and later 2 ploughs in lordship, now 1. Always 1 men's
plough; meadow, ½ acre. Woodland, then and later 160 pigs,
now 60. 2 mills; always 1 cob. Then 2 head of cattle, now 4.
Then 6 pigs, now 18. Then 10 goats, now 35.
Also 19 Freemen, 1 c. of land.
Always 1 plough.
Of 3 the King and the Earl (have) the jurisdiction, over the
others 6 forfeitures.
Value then and later £3; now £4 10s.
It has 1½ leagues in length and 1 in width; it pays 17¼d.
In BEESTON (St. Andrew) 2 free men, and in SPROWSTON 3, and
they have 64 acres of land.
1 smallholder.
Always 1 plough; meadow, 1 acre.
Value 6s.
The King and the Earl (have) the jurisdiction.

TUNSTEAD Hundred

18 Robert holds BACTON which Edric held before 1066, 3 c. of land.
Then 14 villagers, now 10. 3 smallholders. Then 4 slaves, now 3.
Always 3 ploughs in lordship. Then 5 men's ploughs, later and
now 1.
Meadow, 14 acres; woodland, 60 pigs; always 2 mills. Now
2 cobs, 1 head of cattle. Then 8 pigs, now 13. Then 180   156 a
sheep, now 50. 16 goats.

& XXVIII . ſoċ . CLXX 7 VIII . aćr . Tnċ 7 p̊ . x . carr̊.

modo VIIII . & dim̊ . & XIIII . libi hoés . 7 dimiḋ.

II . car̊ træ . 7 XXXIII . aċ . ſemp XI . borḋ . Sep̊.

x . car̊ 7 dim̊ . 7 v . aċ p̊ti . Semp ual̊ . c . x . ſol̊.

& libi hoés . ual̊ XL . ſol̊ . & hẗ . I . leug̊ in long̊.

& . I . leug̊ in lato . 7 xv . ḋ . de gelt.

In Dilham . I . car̊ træ ten edriċ . t . r . e . Tnċ VIIII.

borḋ . modo . IIII . Semp . I . car̊ in dn̊io . 7 VI . aċr̊

prati . 7 . I . ṙ . m̊ VII . porċ . 7 . II . ſoċ . 7 dim̊ . L . aċ.

Semp . II . borḋ . 7 . II . aċ p̊ti . Tnċ ual̊ XXX . ſol̊.

m̊ . XXX . v . & hẗ XI . quar̊ in long̊ . 7 VI . in laẗ.

7 IX . ḋ de gelt.

Dep Wade . H̃ . Frietuna . I . lib̊ ho̊ de quo ſuus

anteceſſor habuit com̊ḋ . t . r . e . XXX . aċr̊ . 7.

II . borḋ . m̊ . dim̊ car̊ . & dim̊ aċr̊ prati . 7 ual̊.

VII . ſol̊ . 7 ten& Garin̊ coċ.

⌐ In Herdeuuic . I . uilt̊ . de v . aċr̊ . & e in p̊tio

de eia . In frietuna . I . lib̊ ho̊ . de quo habuit

ſuus anteceſſor . com̊ḋ tant̊ . t . r . e . 7 hẗ . xv . aċ.

& . II . borḋ . & dim̊ car̊ . 7 ual̊ . IIII . ſol̊ . 7 . III . ḋ.

156 b

T̃ræ Wiĺĺ de WARENNA . H̃ DE ENSFORDA.

⌐ Stinetuna . Rardulfus ten& . quam tenuit Wither . I.

lib̊ ho̊ . t . r . e . III . car̊ træ . ſep̊ . IX . uilt̊ . XXXVIIII . bor.

7 III . ſ . ſep̊ . III . cã in dõio . 7 . VIII cã . hõu̇ . 7 IIII . aċ p̊ti . filu̇ . c . por.

7 . I . mol̊ . ſep̊ . II . r . 7 . XX . an̊ . 7 . xL . por . 7 . cxx . ou̇ . 7 XXVII.

ċap̊ . 7 . III . uaſa apu̇ . I . eccleſia . XIIII . aċ . Et . XIIII . ſoċ . LXXX . aċ.

Also 28 Freemen, 178 acres.
Then and later 10 ploughs, now 9½.
Also 14 free men and a half, 2 c. of land and 33 acres.
Always 11 smallholders.
Always 10½ ploughs; meadow, 5 acres.
Value always 110s; and the free men value 40s.
It has 1 league in length and 1 league in width, tax of 15d.

19 In DILHAM Edric held 1 c. of land before 1066.
Then 9 smallholders, now 4.
Always 1 plough in lordship; meadow, 6 acres; 1 cob. Now
7 pigs.
Also 2 Freemen and a half, 50 acres.
Always 2 smallholders.
Meadow, 2 acres.
Value then 30s; now 35.
It has 11 furlongs in length and 6 in width, tax of 9d.

DEPWADE Hundred
20 FRITTON: 1 free man of whom his predecessor had the patronage
before 1066, 30 acres.
2 smallholders.
Now ½ plough; meadow, ½ acre.
Value 7s. Warin Cook holds.

21 In HARDWICK 1 villager, at 5 acres. It is in the valuation of Eye.
In FRITTON 1 free man of whom his predecessor had the patronage
only before 1066. He has 15 acres.
2 smallholders.
½ plough.
Value 4s 3d.

8   LANDS OF WILLIAM OF WARENNE   157 a

The Hundred of EYNSFORD
1 Randolph holds STINTON which Wither, 1 free man, held before
1066, 3 c. of land.
Always 9 villagers; 39 smallholders; 3 slaves.
Always 3 ploughs in lordship; 8 men's ploughs; meadow,
4 acres; woodland, 100 pigs; 1 mill. Always 2 cobs; 20 head
of cattle; 40 pigs; 120 sheep; 27 goats; 3 beehives.
1 church, 14 acres.
Also 14 Freemen, 80 acres.

sép . IIII . caŕ . filu̅ . x . por . 7 . I . ac̅ p̃ti . 7 . I . bor . duos ex h̷ foc̅ tenebat

R . qn̅do forisfec̅ . & habebaɴ duo decim . ac̅ . & ual̅ . xx đ.

int̅ totu̅ . tc̅ ual̅ . c . fol̅ m̊ . VII . lib̷ . & ht̅ . I . leug̅ in long̅ . 7 dim̊

in lato . 7 . redđ . XI . đ . ingeldu̇ regis . ⌐Kerdeſtuna . ten̊

Godwinus . I . lib̷ hõ . t . r . e . m̊ id . R . II . caŕ t̃re . sép.

XVI . vilt̷ . 7 . XX . bor . tc̅ . II . f . sép . II . caŕ in dñio . 7 . III.

caŕ hõu̅ . 7 . VIII . ac̅ p̃ti . filu̅ . XL . por . tc̅ . II . ṙ . m̊ . nut̷:

tc̅ . IIII . an̊ . m̊ . VI . tc̅ . XL . por . m̊ . VII . 7 . m̊ . LX . ou̇.

7 XXIIII . cap̊ . 7 dim̷ . ecc̄la . VII . Et . I . foc̅ . v . ac̅ t̃rǣ.

Et . I . lib̷ hõ . XXX . ac̅ t̃rǣ ; & dim̷ . I . p̃ſbit̷ . VII . ac̅ t̃rǣ.

sép int̅ om̅s . I . caŕ . sép ual̅ . c . fol̅ . Et . I . lib̷ hõ addit̊

huic maneŕ . t . r . W . XLV ; ac̅ t̃rǣ . 7 . VI . bor . sép

int̅ fe . 7 . hõẽs . I . caŕ . 7 . dim̷ . 7 . I . ac̅ 7 . dim̷ . p̃ti . filu̅ . x . por.

7 quartā parte̅ uni̇ mot̷ . 7 . ual̅ . XX . fol̅ . 7 hoc totu̅

. e̊ p̷ eſcan̅g de . II . maneris delaq̅s . 7 . ht̅ . I leug̅ in longo.

7 dim̷ in lato . 7 redđ . XV . đ . ingeltu̇ regis q̄cq̨ ibi

teneat.

157 a

⌐Hac forda . turolđ . tenet . ⌐Wither . I . lib̷ hõ｜ᵖ . I . caŕ t̃rǣ.

7 dim̷ . sép . VI . vilt̷ . 7 . x . bor . 7 . I . f . sép . II . cã in dñio . 7 . III.

caŕ hõu̅ . 7 . IIII . ac̅ p̃ti . filu̅ . LX . por . Et . I . foc̅ . XI . ac̅ t̃rǣ.

7 . dim̷ . caŕ . I . mot̷ . qn̊ . rec̅ . IIII . r . m̊ . III . 7 . x . an̊ . 7 . XL . por.

7 LX . ou̇ . m̊ . v . uaſa apu̇ . 7 . I . ecc̄la . IX . ac̅ . 7 . II . ac̅ p̃ti.

sép ual̅ . L . fol̅ . 7 ht̅ . v . quaŕ in long̅ . 7 . III . in lato . 7 redđ.

. IIII . đ . q̄cq̨ ibi teneat . hoc ÷ p̃ian̅g delaq̅s.

Always 4 ploughs; woodland, 10 pigs; meadow, 1 acre. 1 smallholder.

R(alph) held 2 of these Freemen when he forfeited, and they had 12 acres.

Value 20d.

In total, value then 100s, now £7.

It has 1 league in length and ½ in width, it pays 11d towards the King's tax.

2 Godwin, 1 free man, held KERDISTON before 1066, now R(andolph) also (holds); 2 c. of land.

    Always 16 villagers; 20 smallholders. Then 2 slaves.

    Always 2 ploughs in lordship; 3 men's ploughs; meadow, 8 acres; woodland, 40 pigs. Then 2 cobs, now none. Then 4 head of cattle, now 6. Then 40 pigs, now 7. Now 60 sheep; 24 goats.

    ½ church, 7 acres.

    Also 1 Freeman, 5 acres of land.

    Also 1 free man, 30 acres of land.

    Also half of 1 priest, 7 acres of land.

    Always 1 plough among them all.

Value always 100s.

1 free man was added to this manor after 1066, 45 acres of land. 6 smallholders.

    Always between himself and the men 1½ ploughs; meadow, 1½ acres; woodland, 10 pigs; ¼ of 1 mill.

Value 20s.

All of this is by exchange for 2 manors of Lewes. It has 1 league in length and ½ in width, it pays 15d towards the King's tax, whoever holds there.

3 Thorold holds HACKFORD which Wither, 1 free man, held, 1½ c. of land.   157 b

    Always 6 villagers; 10 smallholders; 1 slave.

    Always 2 ploughs in lordship; 3 men's ploughs; meadow, 4 acres; woodland, 60 pigs.

    Also 1 Freeman, 11 acres of land.

    ½ plough; 1 mill. When he acquired it 4 cobs, now 3. 10 head of cattle; 40 pigs, 60 sheep. Now 5 beehives.

Value always 50s.

It has 5 furlongs in length and 3 in width, it pays 4d whoever holds there. This is by exchange of Lewes.

.v.libi hões.7 In Tẏrninga.i.liƀ hõ.de.i.caŕ terræ.int
oms.ſep.iii.caŕ 7 dim.7.ii.ac̄.p̄ti.filu.viii.poŕ.tc̄.
val.xx.ſol.m̂.xxx.Eſt p̄ eſcãg de laquiſ. ſ Ille
de tirninga fuit incenſu de ſalla regis.t̄.R.comitis.
7.ſub.R.blundo.7.i.anno ſub.Godrico.m̂.tene&.
.W.de W̱aŕ.7 hoc teſtat hund.qđ fuit.liƀ hõ.t.r.æ.
ſ Helſinga.Wimerus.tene&.| Loca.p̄ maneŕ.i.liƀ hõ.
t.r.æ.ii.cã træ.ſep.vi.vilt.tc̄.xii.bor.m̂.x.
tc̄.iiii.S.tc̄ 7 p̄.iii.caŕ in dñio.m̂.ii.tc̄.iiii.caŕ hõu.
p̄.7 m̂.iii.7 vii.ac̄.p̄ti.filu.ccc.7.ii.molt.ſep.ii.r.
7.x.an̄.7 tc̄.xl.por.m̂.xiiii.ſep.xl.ou.7.xii.uaſa
apū.7.i.eccła.xviii.ac̄.7.i.ac̄ p̄.ſep.Val.iiii.liƀ.
hoc ÷ de feudo fretherici.7 ht̄.i.leuḡ in lonḡ.7 dm̂
in lato.7.i.uirgata.7 redd.viii.đ.7 obolu.in geldu
regis.

ſ H̄ de TAVERHA. ſ In Tauerha ide ten.
Toca.p̄ man.i.liƀ ho.t.r.æ.i.caŕ tre.ſep.vi.vilt.

7.vi.bor.7.i.ſ.tc̄ 7 p̄.i.caŕ.in dñio.m̂.ii.tc̄ 7 p̄.i.caŕ.
7.dim.hõu.m̂.ii.7.x.ac̄ p̄ti.filu.v.por.7.quartã
parte uni.molt.quarta pars.eccłæ.iii.ac̄.7.ii.runc.
tc̄.iiii.an̄.m̂.vii.tc̄.viii.por.m̂.xl.tc̄.xl.ou.
m̂.ccc.tc̄ 7 p̄.val.xxx.ſol.m̂.xl.ſol.hoc c̄.
de feudo fretherici.7.ht̄.i.leuḡ.7 dm̂ in lonḡ.7.i.
leuḡ.in lato.7 redd.xvii.đ.7 fertingu ingeldum
regis.q̇c̄q̇ ibi ten&.

ERPINCHAM SUD.H̄.In Cokeres hala.ten&
turoldus.quã ten.xvi.ſoc̄.Stigand.7.Rađ Stalra.cx.
ac̄.træ.ſep.iii.ƀor.i.eccłe.x.ac̄.7.v.caŕ.7.viii.ac̄.p̄ti.

4 In (Wood) DALLING 5 free men. And in THURNING he also (holds); 1 free man, at 1 c. of land.

>Always 3½ ploughs among them all; meadow, 2 acres; woodland, 8 pigs.

Value then 20s; now 30.

>It is by exchange of Lewes.

5 The man of Thurning was in the tribute of the King's (manor of) Sall in the time of Earl R(alph), and under R(obert) Blunt, and for 1 year under Godric, and now he is held by W(illiam) of Warenne. This the Hundred testifies, that he was a free man before 1066.

6 Wymer holds ELSING, which Lokki, 1 free man, held as a manor before 1066. 2 c. of land.

>Always 6 villagers. Then 12 smallholders, now 10. Then 4 slaves.

>Then and later 3 ploughs in lordship, now 2. Then 4 men's ploughs, later and now 3. Meadow, 7 acres; woodland, 300 [pigs] ; 2 mills. Always 2 cobs; 10 head of cattle. Then 40 pigs, now 14. Always 40 sheep; 12 beehives.

>Also 1 church, 18 acres; meadow, 1 acre.

Value always £4.

>This is of the Holding of Frederic. It has 1 league in length and half [a league] and one rod in width, it pays 8½d towards the King's tax.

The Hundred of TAVERHAM

7 In TAVERHAM Toki, 1 free man, held as a manor before 1066, 1 c. of land.

>Always 6 villagers; 6 smallholders; 1 slave. 158 a

>Then and later 1 plough in lordship, now 2. Then and later 1½ men's ploughs, now 2. Meadow, 10 acres; woodland, 5 pigs; ¼ of 1 mill. ¼ of a church, 3 acres. 2 cobs. Then 4 head of cattle, now 7. Then 8 pigs, now 40. Then 40 sheep, now 300.

Value then and later 30s; now 40s.

>This is of the Holding of Frederic. It has 1½ leagues in length and 1 league in width, it pays 17¼d towards the King's tax, whoever holds there.

SOUTH ERPINGHAM Hundred

8 In COLTISHALL Thorold holds what 16 Freemen of Stigand's and of Ralph the Constable's held, 110 acres of land.

>Always 3 smallholders.

>(Belonging) to 1 church, 10 acres.

>5 ploughs; meadow, 8 acres.

tc̄ . uaɫ . xxx . foɫ . m̄ . xl . Rađ dedit Sc̄o benedicto
fuá parte̓ . fochæ c̄uxore fuo . ut dicit abbas . & totū
hī . i . leuḡ . in lonḡ . 7 . dim̓ . in laī . 7 . de geldo . xii . đ.
İn Mortosſt . iđn̄io . ii . libi̓ hoēs . dim̄ . cař . træ . sēp . viii.
b̄or . 7 . iii . cař . 7 . iiii . ac̄ p̄ti . 7 . i . moɫ . tc̄ . uaɫ . xx . foɫ.
m̄ . xx . Rex 7 comes foca̓ . In Vlīrinchā . i . lib hō.
heroldi . xv . ac̄ . sēp . iii . bor . 7 . i . cař . 7 . i . ac̄ p̄ti . filu̓ . iiii.
por . 7 . dim̄ . moɫ . 7 . uaɫ . iii . foɫ . In Wicmar& . i . libá.
fem̄ . heroldi . xxiiii . ac̄ tře . 7 . iii . bōr . sēp . i . cař . 7 . i . ac̄
7 . dim̓ . p̄ti . 7 . vaɫ . v . foɫ . In Bernincham . ii . libi hoēs.
heroldi . xxx . ac̄ . træ . sēp . v . bor . 7 . ii . cař . & īcia
pars . moɫ . 7 . ii . ac̄ . p̄ti . filu̓ . xx . por . 7 . uaɫ . xiii . foɫ.
7 . iiii . đ . 7 . i . eccɫe . ix . ac̄ . . In Maninctuna . ii.

158 b
libi Rađ ſtalra . xvii . ac̄ tře . sēp̓ . i . cař . filu̓ . iii . por.
7 . vaɫ . v . foɫ . In Vrminclanda : turoldus . i . lib hm̄.
viii . ac̄ . træ . i . cař . 7 . vaɫ . xi . đ . In Corpeſtih . ii . libi
hoēs . xiiii . ac̄ træ . sēp . i . c̄ař . 7 . uaɫ . xi . đ.
Iu Tatituna . ii . libi hoēs . Gued . xvi . ac̄ . sēp . i . cař.
7 . i . ac̄ p̄ti . 7 . uaɫ . xvi . đ . Soca in Aileſhā . t̓ . r . e.

Value then 30s; now 40.

Ralph gave his part of the jurisdiction with his wife to St. Benedict as the Abbot says. The whole has 1 league in length and half in width, tax of 12d.

In MORTOFT 2 free men in lordship, ½ c. of land.

Always 8 smallholders.

3 ploughs; meadow, 4 acres; 1 mill.

Value then 20s; now 20.

The King and the Earl (have) the jurisdiction.

In ITTERINGHAM 1 free man of Harold's, 15 acres.

Always 3 smallholders.

1 plough; meadow, 1 acre; woodland, 4 pigs; ½ mill.

Value 3s.

In WICKMERE 1 free woman of Harold's, 24 acres of land.

3 smallholders.

Always 1 plough; meadow, 1½ acres.

Value 5s.

In (Little) BARNINGHAM 2 free men of Harold's, 30 acres of land.

Always 5 smallholders.

2 ploughs; one-third of a mill; meadow, 2 acres; woodland, 20 pigs.

Value 13s 4d.

Also (belonging) to 1 church, 9 acres.

In MANNINGTON 2 free (men) of Ralph the Constable's, 17 acres   158 b
of land. Always 1 plough; woodland, 3 pigs.

Value 5s.

In IRMINGLAND Thorold holds 1 free man, 8 acres of land.

1 plough.

Value 11d.

In CORPUSTY 2 free men, 14 acres of land. Always 1 plough.

Value 11d.

In TUTTINGTON 2 free men of Gyrth's, 16 acres.

Always 1 plough; meadow, 1 acre.

Value 16d.

The jurisdiction was in Aylsham before 1066.

In Crakeforda . ten& Turold . x . ac̄ . q̄d ten̄ lib̄ ho Guert . ad ailefsā.
sēp . dim̄ . car̄ . 7 . ual . III . fol̄ . In Brantuna . id̄ . III . foc̄.
.... heroldi . foc̄ in caupſtuna . VI . ac̄ . sēp.
I . car̄ . | 7 . ual̄ . III . fol̄ . hos foc̄ tenuit hoinfridus
de sc̄o otmaro ad feudū sui anteceſſoris . 7 . hoc
teſtat̄ . hundret & drogo eos calūpniant̄ . hanc
tr̄a tenuit Ainfrid . q̄ndo forisfec̄ . & drogo poſtea . ſ;
Wil̄ls . de uuar̄ eā p̄ ill̄ . habuit . 7 . m̄ . ſimilit̄ hr̄.

/ In Erminclandā . id̄ē . I . foc̄ . heroldi . III . Cauſtuna.
. I . car̄ . tr̄æ . sēp . V . vil̄li . 7 . I . car̄ . 7 . dim̄ . 7 . IIII . ac̄
p̄ti . ſilu . LX . por . t̄cia pars mol̄ . 7 . ual . X . fol̄.

/ In hobuiſt . I . foc̄ . Rad̄ ſtalra . CLX . ac̄ . & jacet
in houetuna q̄m Rad̄ comes dedit sc̄o benedic̄to
cū uxore ſua c̄cedente rege . ut dicit abbas.
sēp . II . bor . & . I . foc̄ . 7 . dim̄ . XIII . ac̄ . tr̄æ . tc̄ . I . car̄ . X
Totū . ē . p̄ eſc̄ de laq̄s.

/ Tuneſteda . H̄ . In Paſtuna . turoldus . ten& V . libos
hoēs . I . car̄ . tr̄æ . 7 . XXX . ac̄ . sēp . I . uil̄l . 7 . XIX .

159 a
bor . sēp . V . car̄ . 7 . II . boū . ſilu . VI . por . 7 . II .
ac̄ . p̄ti . tc̄ . I . mol̄ . I . eccl̄e . I . ac̄ . 7 . ual . XL . fol̄.
Soca sc̄i benedic̄ti.

(left margin, marked with ✕)
✕
7 . dim̄ . m̄ . I . sēp
dim mol̄ . IIII . ac̄
p̄ti . val̄ . V . fol̄ . 7
. IIII . d̄ In ead̄.
. II . foc̄ sc̄i benedicti-
✕
. clav . ac̄ . tr̄æ . ſep
. I . uil̄l . 7 . II . bor.
tc̄ . II . car̄ . m̄ . I . car̄
7 . dim̄ . Val . X . fol̄
hoc fuit libatū p̄ . I . car̄ . tr̄æ.

In CRACKFORD Thorold holds 10 acres which a free man of Gyrth's held as part of (the lands of) Aylsham.

Always ½ plough.

Value 3s.

In BRAMPTON he also (holds); 3 Freemen ...... of Harold's. The jurisdiction (is) in Cawston. 6 acres.

Always 1 plough; meadow, 1 acre.

Value 3s.

Humphrey of St. Omer held these Freemen as part of the Holding of his predecessor. The Hundred testifies to this and Drogo claims them. Humphrey held this land when he forfeited and Drogo later. But William of Warenne had it before him, and has it now likewise.

9 He also holds in IRMINGLAND; 1 Freeman of Harold's, and 3 (in) CAWSTON, 1 c. of land.

Always 5 villagers.

1½ ploughs; meadow, 4 acres; woodland, 60 pigs; one-third of a mill.

Value 10s.

10 In HAUTBOIS 1 Freeman of Ralph the Constable's, 160 acres. It appertains in Hoveton which Earl Ralph gave to St. Benedict with his wife, with the King's consent as the Abbot says.

Always 2 smallholders;

1 Freeman and a half; 13 acres of land.

Then 1½ ploughs, now 1. Always ½ mill; meadow, 4 acres.

Value 5s 4d.

Also 2 Freemen of St. Benedict's, 175 acres of land.

Always 1 villager; 2 smallholders.

Then 2 ploughs, now 1½ ploughs.

Value 10s.

This was delivered as 1 c. of land.

The whole is by exchange of Lewes.

TUNSTEAD Hundred

11 In PASTON Thorold holds 5 free men, 1 c. of land and 30 acres.

Always 1 villager; 19 smallholders.

Always 5 ploughs; 2 oxen; woodland, 6 pigs; meadow, 2 acres. Then 1 mill.

159 a

(Belonging) to 1 church, 1 acre.

Value 40s. St. Benedict's jurisdiction.

Ⱶ Wituna . i . liƀ . hō . xxx . aꞓ . sēp . x . ƀor . 7 . ii . eaꞃ.
7 . iiii . foꞓ . xx . aꞓ . sēp . i . caꞃ . 7 . ii . aꞓ p̄ti . 7 . i . eccłe.
x . aꞓ . tꞓ . uał . xv . foł . m̄ . xx . ex hō habuit.
Almaꞃ . epꞓ . t . r . e . 7 Wiłłi . medietate᷈ . & . W . malet.
fimiliꞇ aliā medietatem.
In Walfam . ii . liƀi hōēs . cv . aꞓ . sēp . i . eaꞃ . uiłłs.
7 . iiii . ƀor . & . ii . foꞓ . sēp . iiii . caꞃ . 7 . dim̄ . 7 . iii . aꞓ.
7 . dim̄ . p̄ti . filu᷈ . iiii . por . sēp . i . moł . tꞓ . uał . xxx.
foł . modo . xl . Sꞓs . Benedictus . foca᷈ habuit.
7 cōmendatione᷈ . t . r . æ.
In Riftuna . iiii . foꞓ . Stigandi . x . aꞓ . sēp . dim̄.
caꞃ . & . ē . i̇ ptio . de coleetes hala . hoc ē de efcañg de laꞅs.
In ƀtuna . i . liƀ hō . xvi . aꞓ . 7 uał . ii . foł . sꞓs benedict̊.
foꞓ . t . r . æ . 7 ꝑ eode᷈ fcañg . Ex hoc toto fuit
foca sꞓi benedicti . M̊ eā teneat . W . cꞇꞃa.

Ⱶ EAST H̄ . de flec . In philebeẏ . turołd ten᷈&
. i . liƀm h᷈m Eftgari . t . r . æ . i . caꞃ . trӕ᷉ . 7 . ix . aꞓ.
tꞓ . i . uiłł . sēp . iii . ƀor . 7 . i . caꞃ . in dn̄io . 7 . dim̄᷈.
★ caꞃ . hōm . 7 . ii . aꞓ . p̄ti . tꞓ . iii . foł . m̄ . ii . ~~tꞓ . uał.~~
tꞓ . uał . viii . foł . m̄ . xvi . hoc . ē . de efcangio delaꞅs.
159 b
Ⱶ Dep Wade H̃ . In Carletuna . xxx . aꞓ . tꞃӕ.
tenuit Almaꞃ . liƀ hō . t̊ . r . æ . fub . Stigando . 7 . sēp.
. i . ƀor . 7 dim̄᷈ . 7 . i . feꞃ . 7 . i . aꞓ p̄ti . 7 . i . caꞃ . 7 uał . v . foł.
hoc ē de dono regis om̄s eccłe sꞇ . ap̄p̄tiatæ ꞓ manerijs.
Ⱶ HVNDRET . DE CLACLELOSA In marham ten̄ Radulfu᷉
dim̄ caꞃ terræ . . . . quā tenuit sꞓa adelꝺ . t . r . e . Semp . iii . borꝺ.
& . i . caꞃ᷉ . & . iiii . aꞓ p̄ti . Tꞓ uał . xx . foł . & p᷉ . modo xxvi . foł . &
Ⱶ viii . ꝺ.

12 WITTON, 1 free man, 30 acres.
> Always 10 smallholders; 2 ploughs.
> Also 4 Freemen, 20 acres.
>> Always 1 plough; meadow, 2 acres.
> (Belonging) to 1 church, 10 acres.

Value then 15s; now 20.
Of this Bishop A(e)lmer had a moiety before and after 1066.
W(illiam) Malet likewise the other moiety.
In (North) WALSHAM 2 free men, 105 acres.
> Always 1 villager; 4 smallholders; 2 Freemen.
> Always 4½ ploughs; meadow, 3½ acres; woodland, 4 pigs;
>> always 1 mill.

Value then 30s; now 40.
> St. Benedict had the jurisdiction and the patronage before 1066.
In (Sco) RUSTON 4 free men of Stigand's, 10 acres.
> Always ½ plough.
It is in the valuation of Coltishall. This is of the exchange of Lewes.
In BARTON (Turf) 1 free man, 16 acres.
Value 2s.
> St. Benedict (had) the jurisdiction before 1066. It is by the same exchange.
> Of all this the jurisdiction was St. Benedict's. Now W(illiam) is to hold it, with the land.

The Hundred of EAST FLEGG
13 In FILBY Thorold holds 1 free man of Estgar's before 1066, 1 c. of land and 9 acres.
> Then 1 villager; always 3 smallholders.
> 1 plough in lordship; ½ men's plough; meadow, 2 acres.
>> Then 3 salt-houses, now 2.

Value then 8s; now 16.
This is of the exchange of Lewes.

DEPWADE Hundred   159 b
14 In CARLETON (Rode) A(e)lmer, a free man, held 30 acres of land under Stigand before 1066.
> Always 1 smallholder and a half; 1 slave.
> Meadow, 1 acre; 1 plough.

Value 5s.
> This is of the King's gift. All the churches are assessed with the manors.

The Hundred of CLACKCLOSE
15 In MARHAM Ralph holds ½ c. of land .... which St. Etheldreda held before 1066.
> Always 3 smallholders.
> 1 plough; meadow, 4 acres.

Value then and later 20s; now 26s 8d.

ↁ In Phinchā tenuit lib hō ad sochā abbis de rameseia . ii .
car terræ . t r . e . m̄ ten& hugo . Tc̄ xxiiii . libi hoes . & modo 7 . vi . bord .
& . iiii . ser . & . x . ac̄ p̃ti . Semp . ii . car̄ in dn̄io . Tc̄ dim̄ car̄ hom̄ . M̊ . i.
Semp ual . lx . sol . In eadē . uill . semp viii . libi hoes/ qd̃ ten&. w. & . xi . bord
& . v . ser . semp . ii . car̄ in dominio . & dim̄ car̄ hom̄ . xvi . ac̄ p̃ti . Quan -
do recep̄ . cc . ou̅s . xx . minus . & mo c . Semp . vi . an̄ . xxiiii . porc̄ .
& . iiii . runc̄ . Tc̄ ual xl . sol . P̃ & modo lx . In ead . uilla . ten̄
Wiłłm̄ . brant . ii . car̄ . terræ . quas tenuit . i . liba femina . t . r . e .
Semp . ii . libi hoes . & . iiii . bord . & iiii . seru . 7 xvi . ac̄ p̃ti . Semp
ii . car̄ in dn̄io . & xx . ou̅s . & . iii . porc̄ . & ual . xxx . sol . In ead uill
xii . ac̄ . & ual . xii . d . Totū hoc maneriū phinchā . ht̄ . i . leuga
in longo . & dim̄ in lato . quicūq̣ ibi teneat . qn̄ hund̄ . 7 dim̄ reddit
xx . sol . de gelto ✗ & hæc uilla xvi . d .
ↁ In hidlingheia . xxii . ac̄ . qd̄ ten̄ . t . r . e . viii . oes . & ual . vii . sol .
& viii . d . S̃7 hund̄ testatur qd̄ fuit aduic̄tū monacho꞉
de sc̄o benedic̄to .

160 a

ↁ In Winebotesham . i . car̄ terræ & dim̄ . & . i . car̄ & dim̄ . 7 x . ac̄ p̃ti .
7 ual xl sol . 7 hanc terrā tenuer̄ xxiii . libi hoes ad soca sc̄i ben̄ .
ↁ In danefella ten& hugo . ii . car̄ tr̄æ . 7 iiii . ac̄ . quas tenuit Al -
uric̄ lib hō . t . r . e . semp . ii . car̄ in dominio . 7 . xii . bord . 7 viii . libi
hoes . xl . ac̄ terræ . Tc̄ 7 p̃ . i . car̄ . modo . i . 7 xii . ac̄ p̃ti . semp ht̄
. i . piscaria . Tc̄ ual lx . sol . m̄ . xl . hoc reclam̄ . p̃ escanḡ . Tota
ht̄ . i . lḡ in longo . & dim̄ in lato . 7 reddit . viii . d . de gelto .

16 In FINCHAM a free man held at the jurisdiction of the Abbot of
Ramsey 2 c. of land before 1066; now Hugh holds.
  Then and now 24 free men; 6 smallholders; 4 slaves.
  Meadow, 10 acres; always 2 ploughs in lordship. Then ½ men's
    plough, now 1.
Value always 60s.
In the same village always 8 free men. This W(illiam) holds.
  11 smallholders; 5 slaves.
  Always 2 ploughs in lordship; ½ men's plough; meadow,
    16 acres. When he acquired it 100 sheep less 20, now 100.
    Always 6 head of cattle; 24 pigs; 4 cobs.
Value then 40s; later and now 60.
In the same village William Brant holds 2 c. of land which 1 free
woman held before 1066.
  Always 2 free men; 4 smallholders; 4 slaves.
  Meadow, 16 acres. Always 2 ploughs in lordship; 20 sheep;
    3 pigs.
Value 30s.
In the same village 12 acres; value 12d.
  All this manor of Fincham has 1 league in length and ½ in
width, whoever holds there, when the Hundred and Half pays a
20s tax, this village (pays) 16d.

17 In HILGAY 22 acres which 8 men held before 1066.
Value 7s 8d.
  But the Hundred testifies that it was for the supplies of the
monks of St. Benedict.
In WIMBOTSHAM 1½ c. of land.   160 a
  1½ ploughs; meadow, 10 acres.
Value 40s.
  23 free men held this land at the jurisdiction of St. Benedict.

18 In DENVER Hugh holds 2 c. of land and 3 acres which Aelfric, a
free man, held before 1066.
  Always 2 ploughs in lordship.
  12 smallholders; 8 free men, 40 acres of land.
  Then and later 1 plough, now 1. Meadow, 12 acres. It has
    always had 1 fishery.
Value then 60s; now 40.
  This he claims by exchange. The whole has 1 league in length
and ½ in width, it pays tax of 8d.

In ead̄.ıı.car̄ terræ.&.ıı.car̄.ten̄ Wiłł.quas tenuit.ı.lib̄ hō
hoſmunt.t.r.e.ſemp.vıııı.uiłł.&.ı.ſeru.&.vııı.ac̄ p̄ti.&.ıı
piſcar̄. In dane fæla ten̄.id̄.ıııı.lib̄o.hōes Lxx.ı.ac̄ qd̄ ten̄
oſmund̄.de.H̄.habuit ant̄.hem̄.com̄d̄ tant̄.7 h̄t ſemp.dim̄
car̄ In eadē uillā.v.lib̄ h̄.7.dim̄.xxx.vı.ac̄.ſemp.dim̄.car̄.
hos tenuit oſmundus com̄ tn̄tū 7 ſc̄s b̄ h̄t ſocā de duo hoeb̄z
In ead̄.ııı.libi h̄.qd̄ ten̄& idē oſmundus.ıı.ac̄.tr̄æ.&.ıı
bord̄.hoc totū uał xL.ſoł.

★ In derham.ı.lib̄.xxx.ac̄.ſemp dim̄ car̄.In forh̄a.ıı.lib̄ hōes
ııı.ac̄.ter̄re.In dunh̄a.xxx.ac̄ qd̄ ten̄.ıx.libi hōes ſemp dim̄.car̄.
&.uał.xıı.ſoł.7 ıııı.d̄.de h̄ ıx hōib̄z h̄t ſc̄s benedict̄ com̄d̄ & ſocā
& Wiłłm de War̄ rect̄ p̄ eſcagio

  In utuuella.vı.bord̄.& ſt̄ ap̄tiati.

HVND̄ & dim̄.fredrebruge.Waltuna.ten̄ Tōhe lib̄ hō
t.r.e.M ten̄ ſc̄s petrus.ıııı.car̄ terræ.ſemp.ıx.uiłł.Tc̄ Lxııı.
bōrd̄.modo.Lx.vı.Tc̄ xıııı.ſeru.modo.vııı.&.c.ac̄ p̄ti.Tc̄
.vı.car̄ in dn̄o.P̄ nulla.modo.v.ſemp.vı.car̄ hom̄.Tc̄.ı.ſalina

160 b

& dim̄.modo.vıı.Tc̄.xıııı.runc.M̄.vııı.Tc̄ xxxvı.equæ modo
nułł.Tc̄ xxıııı.an̄.Modo.xx.ııı.Tc̄.c.porc̄.modo.c.xıııı.Tc̄.
bcc.ous.modo.bccc.huic.man̄ jacent.vı.ſoc̄.ı.car̄.terræ.&.x.
ac̄.&.xxx.ac̄ prati.ſemp xvıı.bord̄.&.ııı.car̄ & dim̄.& vıı.ſa-
linæ.Tot̄ uał xvıı.lib̄.&x.ſoł.Tota h̄t.ıııı.lḡ in lonḡ.&.ıı.
qr̄ in lato.qui cūq̄ ibi teneat.& redit.ıı.ſoł de gelto de xx.ſoł.
hoc ē de feudo fedrici.

In the same William holds 2 c. of land and 2 ploughs which 1 free man, Osmund, held before 1066.

Always 8 villagers; 1 slave.

Meadow, 8 acres; 1 fishery.

In Denver he also holds 4 free men, 71 acres, which Osmund held. Of these the predecessor of Hermer had the patronage only. He has always had ½ plough.

In the same village 5 free men and a half, 36 acres.

Always ½ plough.

These Osmund held in patronage only. St. B(enedict) has the jurisdiction of 2 men.

In the same 3 free men which Osmund also held, 2 acres of land.

2 smallholders.

Value of all this 40s.

19 In (West) DEREHAM 1 free (man), 30 acres; always ½ plough.

In FINCHAM 2 free men, 3 acres of land.

In DOWNHAM (Market) 30 acres which 9 free men hold.

Always ½ plough.

Value 12s 4d.

Of these 9 men St. Benedict has the patronage and the jurisdiction and William of Warenne claims them by exchange.

20 In OUTWELL 6 smallholders: they have been assessed.

FREEBRIDGE Hundred and Half

21 Toki, a free man, held (West) WALTON before 1066, now St. Peter holds; 4 c. of land.

Always 9 villagers. Then 63 smallholders, now 66. Then 14 slaves, now 8.

Meadow, 100 acres. Then 6 ploughs in lordship, later none, now 5; always 6 men's ploughs. Then 1½ salt-houses, now 7. 160 b Then 14 cobs, now 8. Then 36 mares, now none. Then 24 head of cattle, now 23. Then 100 pigs, now 114. Then 700 sheep, now 800.

6 Freemen appertain to this manor, 1 c. and 10 acres of land; meadow, 30 acres. Always 17 smallholders; 3½ ploughs; 7 salt-houses.

Value of the whole £17 10s.

The whole has 4 leagues in length and 2 furlongs in width, whoever holds there, of a 20s tax it pays 2s. This is of the Holding of Frederic.

ACRE ten& Toche lib hō . t . r . e . ~~i . æcelia xxx~~ . ac̄ . III . car̄ in
dominio . & . VIII . car̄ hom . semper . II . uill . Tc̄ XL . II . borđ . m̄
XL . VIII . Tc̄ . VIII . serū . modo . III . & . VIII . ac̄ p̄ti . & . II . mot . & dim̄
salin . 7 I . piscaria . Tc̄ . VI . runc̄ . modo . I . Tc̄ VIII . an̄ . modo . XI .
Tc̄ XL . V . porc̄ . modo LXX . Tc̄ . c . LX . ōus . modo . ɔXL . huic terræ .
jacent . II . libi hoēs . I . car̄ terræ . & . VIII . borđ . Tc̄ . II . car̄ . modo
. I . 7 VIII . ac̄ p̄ti . Tc̄ ual . c . sol . modo . IX . lib . & illi duo libi hōes
XX . sol . Tota h̄t . I . lḡ . & . X . ptic̄ . & . I . lḡ . in lat . & . IIII . pedes &
dim̄ . & reddit . VIII . đ . de . XX . sol de gelto . Eccliæ . XXX . ac̄ .

╱ In Gaituna . XVI . libi h̄ . II . car̄ tr̄e . 7 XI . borđ . semp . III . car̄ . &
ual XL . sol . hoc h̄t ꝑ escāgo .

╱ In gaituna ten̄ Radulfus . I . car̄ terræ . quā tenuit Alueua
liba femina . t . r . e . semp . IIII . uill . & . II . borđ . & . I . serū . sēp
I . car̄ in dominio . & . VIII . ac̄ p̄ti . & . I . salina & dim̄ . Et . III .
libi hoēs & dim̄ . LX . ac̄ . & . I . car̄ . & . III . ac̄ p̄ti . 7 ual . XXX .
sol . istud ꝑ manerio .

╱ In Grimestuna . I . car̄ terræ . ten̄ Alueua . liba femina .

161 a

t . r . e . XI . borđ . & . VII . libi homines . de . IIII . ac̄ terræ . XII . ac̄ p̄ti
semp . I . car̄ in dn̄io . & . VII . libi hoēs . dim̄ car̄ . Totū ual . XX . sol .
In eadē . II . lib h̄ . I . car̄ terræ 7 . I . car̄ . & . XIIII . borđ . Et . XII . libi
hoēs . XII . ac̄ terræ . semp . I . car̄ . & . X . ac̄ p̄ti . Totū ual XX . sol .
In eađ . I . lib hō . I . car̄ terræ semp . XIII . borđ . & . I . molin̄ . Et
VI . libi hoēs . IX . ac̄ . 7 X . ac̄ p̄ti . Tc̄ & p . I . car̄ . in dn̄io . modo
dim̄ . & . illi . VI . libi hoēs . dim̄ car̄ . Totū ual . XXX . sol .

22 Toki, a free man, held (Castle) ACRE before 1066.
3 ploughs in lordship; 8 men's ploughs.
Always 2 villagers. Then 42 smallholders, now 48. Then
8 slaves, now 3.
Meadow, 8 acres; 2 mills; ½ salt-house; 1 fishery. Then 6 cobs,
now 1. Then 8 head of cattle, now 11. Then 45 pigs, now
70. Then 160 sheep, now 540.
2 free men appertain to this land, 1 c. of land.
8 smallholders.
Then 2 ploughs, now 1. Meadow, 8 acres.
Value then 100s, now £9; and those 2 free men, 20s.
The whole has 1 league and 10 perches in length and 1 league
and 4½ feet in width; of a 20s tax it pays 8d.
(Belonging) to the church, 30 acres.

23 In GAYTON 16 free men, 2 c. of land.
11 smallholders; always 3 ploughs.
Value 40s.
He has this by exchange.

24 In GAYTON Ralph holds 1 c. of land which Aelfeva, a free woman,
held before 1066.
Always 4 villagers; 2 smallholders; 1 slave.
Always 1 plough in lordship; meadow, 8 acres; 1½ salt-houses.
Also 3 free men and a half, 60 acres; 1 plough; meadow, 3 acres.
Value 30s.
This (is held) as a manor.

25 In GRIMSTON Aelfeva, a free woman, held 1 c. of land before   161 a
1066.
11 smallholders. Also 7 free men, at 4 acres of land;
meadow, 12 acres. Always 1 plough in lordship; the 7 free men,
½ plough.
Value of the whole 20s.
In the same 2 free men, 1 c. of land.
1 plough; 14 smallholders.
Also 12 free men, 12 acres of land.
Always 1 plough; meadow, 10 acres.
Value of the whole 20s.
In the same 1 free man, 1 c. of land.
Always 13 smallholders; 1 mill.
Also 6 free men, 9 acres; meadow, 10 acres.
Then and later 1 plough in lordship, now ½.
Those 6 free men, ½ plough.
Value of the whole 30s.

In Cōgreham . ɪ . car̄ terræ . lib hō . xɪɪɪɪ . bord̄ . ſemp . ɪ . car̄ in
dominio . & dim car̄ hom̄ : 7 xɪɪ . libi homines . xv̄ . ac̄ . terræ
& dim . car̄ . & dim ſal . & . vɪɪɪ . ac̄ prati . & ual . xx . ſot . h̄ totū
eſt ꝓ eſc̄aḡ de laes .

/ In congheham . ɪ . car̄ terræ . ten̄ . ɪ . libū hōem̄ . xɪ . bord̄ . & . ɪ . ſer̄
& . x . ac̄ p̄ti : ſemp . ɪ . car̄ in dominio . & ı v . libi hōes . vɪɪɪ . ac̄ . terræ
dim car̄ . & . ɪ . mot̄ . 7 ual . xx . ſot ; In ead̄e . ɪ . lib hō . & in grimeſtuna . ɪɪ . libi homines . om̄s . ɪ . car̄ terræ . xɪɪɪɪ . bord̄ . inter eos
. ɪ . car̄ & dim̄ . & xv̄ . ac̄ . & xɪ . ac̄ p̄ti . 7 . vɪɪɪ . libi homines . xı . ac̄
terræ dim car̄ . & dim̄ . ſal . & ual xxɪɪ . ſot .

/ Nidlinghetuna . ɪɪ . car̄ terræ . ten̄ . ɪɪ . libi hōies . t . r̄ . e . ſemp . v
uiłł . & . vɪ . bord̄ . & . ɪɪ . ſerū . & . vɪɪɪ . ac̄ p̄ti . & . ɪɪ . car̄ . in dominio
& dim car̄ hominū . & . ɪ . molin̄ . Et Wiłłm̄ . ten̄ . ɪ . car̄ terræ
de iſta terra . Et . ɪ . lib homo . xv̄ . ac̄ . ſemp dim̄ . car̄ . Totū ual
ɪx . ſot . hoc eſt ꝑeſcagio .

/ Inmarſinchā ten̄ . W . ɪ . car̄ terræ quā tenuit Alflet . libā femina
t . r̄ . e . ſemp . ɪɪɪ . bord̄ . & . ɪ . ſerū . & . ɪ . car̄ . & ual . xv̄ . ſot .

161 b

De hŏc habuit ſuus antec̄ com̄ tm̄tū . & heroldus ſoc̄a .
& Rainaldus fili iuonis calūpniatur ad ſuū ſeudū . & Wihe-
woc inde fuit ſaiſitus . & pat̄ Rain̄ . & ıpſe Raı̄ . & h̄ teſtatur . hūdı .

/ In harpelai ten̄ Walt̄rus . ɪɪ . car̄ in dominio quæ tenuit tohæ
t . r̄ . e . 7 . ɪɪ . car̄ hominū . & . ɪɪ . uiłłi . & . x . bord̄ . Tc̄ . vɪ . ſer̄ . modo
. ɪɪɪ . & dim̄ ſal . ſemp . ɪ . runc̄ . & . ɪɪɪɪ . an̄ . Tc̄ . x . porc̄ . modo . xxx .
. Tc̄ . cɪxxx . modo . cccvɪɪɪ . hic jacent . xɪɪ . ſoc̄ . de ɪx . ac̄ . terræ .
ſemp dim car̄ . Tot̄ ual tc̄ ɪx . ſot . modo ɪxx .

Tota h̄t . in longo . & . v . qr̄ in lato . & reddit vɪɪɪ . d̄ . de . xx . ſot .
quicūq̄ ibi teneat .

26 In CONGHAM, 1 c. of land, 1 free man;
    14 smallholders. Always 1 plough in lordship; ½ men's plough;
      ½ fishery.
    Also 12 free men, 15 acres of land; ½ plough; ½ salt-house;
      meadow, 8 acres.
Value 20s.
All this is by exchange of Lewes.

27 In CONGHAM, 1 church, 1 c. of land. 1 free man is held;
    11 smallholders; 1 slave.
    Meadow, 10 acres; always 1 plough in lordship.
    Also 5 free men, 8 acres of land; ½ plough; 1 mill.
Value 20s.
In the same 1 free man and in GRIMSTON 2 free men all (hold) 1 c.
of land.
    14 smallholders. Among them 1½ ploughs; 15 acres; meadow,
      11 acres.
    Also 8 free men, 11 acres of land; ½ plough; ½ salt-house.
Value 22s.

28 In HILLINGTON 2 free men held 2 c. of land before 1066.
    Always 5 villagers; 6 smallholders; 2 slaves.
    Meadow, 8 acres; 2 ploughs in lordship; ½ men's plough;
      1 mill.
William holds 1 c. of that land.
    Also 1 free man, 15 acres; always ½ plough.
Value of the whole 60s.
    This is by exchange.

29 In MASSINGHAM W(illiam) holds 1 c. of land which Alflæd, a free
woman, held before 1066.
    Always 3 smallholders; 1 slave; 1 plough.
Value 15s.
    Of this his predecessor had the patronage only, and Harold   161 b
the jurisdiction; Reynold son of Ivo claims it as part of his
Holding, and Wihenoc had possession and Reynold's father and
Reynold himself. The Hundred testifies to this.

30 In HARPLEY Walter holds 2 ploughs in lordship which Toki held
before 1066.
    2 men's ploughs. 2 villagers; 10 smallholders. Then 6 slaves,
      now 3.
    ½ salt-house. Always 1 cob, 4 head of cattle. Then 10 pigs,
      now 30. Then 180 sheep, now 308.
    12 Freemen appertain here, at 60 acres of land. Always ½ plough.
Value of the whole then 60s, now 70.
    The whole has 1 league in length and 5 furlongs in width at
20s it pays 8d, whoever holds there.

Inananere . dim̄ . car̄ terræ . 7 . ī . car̄ . & . ᴵᴵᴵᴵ . bord̄ . qd̄ teñ . ī . liƀa
hō . t . r . e de hac non habuit n̄ com̄d tantū ſuus ante c̄ . Tot
uaɫ . v . ſoɫ . hanc tr̄a reuocat Wido qd̄ fuit liƀata ſuo auncto
Oſmundo . & comiti euſtachio . & hōes Wiɫɫi de Wareñ eos deſaiſer.

In pħlicam . ī . car̄ tr̄æ . teñ . ᴵᴵᴵᴵ . liƀi hōes . t . r . e . ſemp . v . bord̄ .
& . vɪ . ac̄ p̄ti . ſemp . ɪɪ . car̄ . & uaɫ . xx . ſoɫ . hoc reclamat p̄ eſc̄ag.

HᴠɴD . de Dochinga . Bereuuica . ɪɪ . liƀi hōes un̄ fuit
hō heroldi . & alt̄ com̄d tantū ante c̄ fredrici . qui hn̄t . ī . car̄
terræ ſemp . xɪɪ . bord̄ . ſemp . ɪ . car̄ . & dim̄ car̄ hominū . ſemp .
ī . runc̄ . Tc̄ . xxx . ou̅s . Modo . cLx . Et . ī . liƀ hō com̄d tantum
Lx ac̄ terræ . 7 . ɪɪ . bord̄ . ſemp . dim̄ . car̄ . Tc̄ uaɫ . xv . ſoɫ . modo xx.

HᴠɴD . de grimeſhou . Wiltuna tenuit Alueua . t . r . e .
ſemp . v . car̄ . in dominio . 7 xvɪ . uiɫɫi . xxɪᴵᴵᴵ . bord̄ . Tc̄ . x . ſoɫ . m̄
vɪɪɪ . xɪɪ . ac̄ p̄ti . 7 . ɪɪɪ . car̄ hominū . 7 . vɪ . piſcinæ . In dn̄io . vɪɪ.

162 a
vɪɪ . an . 7 . xxx . porc̄
xx . ac̄ . tr̄æ . ſemper
modo . x . Tot ht̄ . ī . lḡ
7 reddit xvɪɪ . d . de xx . ſoɫ

oc̄ . ou̅s . hic jacent . vɪɪɪ . ſoc̄
dim̄ car̄ . Tc̄ & p̄ uaɫ . vɪ . liƀ .
in longo . & dim̄ in late .
de gelto .

7 in hocuuella . ī . car̄ . ī dn̄o .
7 in Riſinga . ɪɪ . car̄ . ī dn̄o.

Fatwella tenuit Alueua . t . r . e . ɪɪ . car̄ in dominio . Inter
totū ſemp xvɪ . uiɫɫ . 7 xvɪɪɪ . bord̄ . 7 ɪɪɪɪ . feru . & . ɪᴵᴵᴵ . car̄ hom̄ .
& . xvɪ . ac̄ p̄ti . ſilua . cc . por̄ . xxx . cap̄ . ſemp . ɪɪ . runc̄ . & . vɪ.
an . & . xL . porc̄ . 7 . c . ou̅s . 7 xvɪɪ . uaſa apū.

In Riſinga . ɪɪ . ſoc̄ . xx . ac̄ . Tc̄ dim̄ car̄ . modo . ī . Tc̄ & p̄ uaɫ
vɪ . liƀ . modo . x.

31 In ANMER ½ c. of land; 1 plough; 4 smallholders. This 1 free man held before 1066; his predecessor had none of this except the patronage only.
Value of the whole, 5s.
   Guy claims this land because it was delivered to his uncle, Osmund, and to Count Eustace, and William of Warenne's men dispossessed them.

32 In FLITCHAM 4 free men held 1 c. of land before 1066.
   Always 5 smallholders.
   Meadow, 6 acres; always 2 ploughs.
   Value 20s.
   He claims this by exchange.

The Hundred of DOCKING
33 Simon holds BARWICK; 2 free men: 1 was Harold's man, and the other under the patronage only of the predecessor of Frederic. They have 1 c. of land.
   Always 12 smallholders. Always 1 plough; ½ men's plough; always 1 cob. Then 30 sheep, now 160.
   ½ church, 10 acres.
   Also 1 free man under patronage only, 60 acres of land.
   2 smallholders; always ½ plough.
   Value then 15s; now 20.

The Hundred of GRIMSHOE
34 Aelfeva held WILTON before 1066. Always 5 ploughs in lordship.
   16 villagers; 24 smallholders. Then 10 slaves, now 8;
   Meadow, 12 acres; 3 men's ploughs; 6 fisheries; in lordship, 7 head of cattle; 30 pigs; 200 sheep.
   8 Freemen appertain here, 20 acres of land. Always ½ plough.
   Value then and later £6; now 10.
   The whole has 1 league in length and ½ in width, of a 20s tax it pays 17d.

162 a

35 Aelfeva held FELTWELL before 1066; 2 ploughs in lordship. In HOCKWOLD 1 plough in lordship. In RISING 1 plough in lordship.
   In total 16 villagers; 18 smallholders; 4 slaves.
   4 men's ploughs; meadow, 16 acres; woodland, 200 pigs; 30 goats. Always 2 cobs; 6 head of cattle; 40 pigs; 100 sheep; 17 beehives.

36 In RISING 2 Freemen, 20 acres. Then ½ plough, now 1.
   Value then and later £6; now 10.

ꝼIn fat wella . xl . ſoc . iii . car terræ . & . xl . ac . v . car . & . viii . ac
p̄ti . & ual lxx : ſol . ⁊ . i . ſoc ſimon . i . car tr̄æ . ⁊ vii . uill . & . v . bord̄ .
& . iiii . ſeru . ⁊ . i . car in dominio . & . iii . ac p̄ti . & . i . car hom .
⁊ ual xx . ſol . ⁊ . i . æccl̄a hanc caluͤpniatur Godric ad feudum
Rad̄ qd̄ jacuit in Stohu . & inde uult un̄ h̄o Godric portare
juditiu̅ . Sup hos om̄s habuit ſc̄a Aeldreda ſoca̅ & om̄e conſuetud̄ .
⁊ comdat . ⁊ illoⱫ . vii : libi erant c̄ tr̄is ſuis ſed ſoca ⁊ comd̄ re -
manebat ſc̄æ Aeldredæ . Totu̅ fuit libatu̅ . W . p̄ eſcangio .
ꝼIn matel walde . iii . car terræ . ſemp . iiii . uill . & . i . bord . ⁊ . iiii .
ac p̄ti . Tc̄ . iiii . car . p̄ ⁊ modo . iii . Tc̄ . ual . xx . ſol . modo xl . v .
Stigandus ſoca̅ . & fuer̄ liberati p̄ eſcang̅ . Simon ⁊ Galf̄ . ii .
car terræ . ii . car . ⁊ xl ſol ual .
ꝼNorhwalde . xxxiiii . ſoc . ſce adeld̄ . v . car . terre . ſemp
vii . car̄ . & . viii . ac p̄ti . Tc̄ ual lx . ſol . modo . c . Sc̄a . A . ſoc . & comd̄

162 b
& om̄e conſuetud̄ : de ill   xxx . tantu̅ . & . iiii .
erant libi . ſoca & com̄   S . A .
ꝼIn mondefort . vii . ſoc   Sc̄æ . A . om̄i conſuetu -
dim̄ car terræ . & . i . car   & ual . x . ſol . hoc etiam
p̄ eſcāgio In ea d̄ . i . lib̄ h̄o heroldī dim̄ car terræ . ii . bord̄ . ii . ac
prati . ſemp dim̄ car & ual . x . ſol . p̄ eſcag̅ .
In Coueſtuna . i . car terræ . i . lib̄ h̄o heroldī . iiii . uill̄ . iiii . bord̄ .
Tc̄ . ii . ſeru . xii . ac p̄ti . Tc̄ & p̄ . ii . car in dn̄io . Tercia poſſ & . ec̄ .
modo . i . & . ſemp . i . car hominu̅ . & . ii . molini . & . i . piſcar̄ .
ſilua de . xv . porc̄ . & ual viii . ſol . h̄ e̅ p̄ caſtellatione aquaⱫ .
Totu̅ h̄t . v . qr̄ in longo . & . iiii . in lato . ⁊ reddit . v . den̄ .
⁊ . i . obolu̅ de . xx . ſol . de gelto .

37 In FELTWELL 40 Freemen, 3 c. of land and 40 acres.
     5 ploughs; meadow, 8 acres.
     Value 70s.
     Simon holds 1 Freeman, 1 c. of land. 7 villagers; 5 smallholders;
        4 slaves.
     1 plough in lordship; meadow, 3 acres; 1 men's plough.
     Value 20s.
        Also 1 church;
        This Godric claims as part of Ralph's Holding which lay in
     Stow (Bedon), and on this account 1 man of Godric's is willing
     to undergo judicial ordeal. Over all these St. Etheldreda had the
     jurisdiction and all customary dues and the patronage. 7 of them
     were free, with their lands, but the jurisdiction and patronage
     remained with St. Etheldreda's. All this was delivered to W(illiam)
     by exchange.

38 In METHWOLD 4 free men, 3 c. of land.
        Always 4 villagers; 1 smallholder.
        Meadow, 4 acres. Then 4 ploughs, later and now 3.
     Value then 20s; now 45.
        Stigand (had) the jurisdiction. They were delivered by exchange.
     Simon and Walter (hold) 2 c. of land; 2 ploughs.
     Value 40s.

39 NORTHWOLD, 34 Freemen of St. Etheldreda's, 5 c. of land.
        Always 7 ploughs; meadow, 8 acres.
     Value then 60s; now 100.
        St. E(theldreda) had the jurisdiction and the patronage and all
     customary dues over 30 of them only, and 4 were free. St.   162 b
     E(theldreda's) jurisdiction and patronage.

40 In MUNDFORD 7 Freemen of St. E(theldreda's), with all customary
     dues, ½ c. of land. 1 plough.
     Value 10s.
        This also (is) by exchange.
     In the same 1 free man of Harold's, ½ c. of land.
        2 smallholders.
        Meadow, 2 acres; always ½ plough.
     Value 10s. By exchange.
     In COLVESTON 1 c. of land, 1 free man of Harold's.
        4 villagers; 4 smallholders. Then 2 slaves.
        Meadow, 12 acres. Then and later 2 ploughs in lordship, a
           third could be there, now 1. Always 1 men's plough; 2 mills;
           1 fishery; woodland at 15 pigs.
     Value 8s.
        This is for the Castellany of Lewes. The whole has 5 furlongs
     in length and 4 in width, of a 20s tax it pays 5½d.

⁋In Keburna . teñ Roḡ . ıı . libo hoēs dim car̄ terre . & . vı.
ac̄ . & . ı . borđ . & . ı . ac̄ p̄ti . Semp . ı . car̄ . & . ual . ıɪɪ . soł.

⁋In Santuna . v . libi hoēs . ıı . car̄ terre Galterus . ten&
medietatē . ı . uiłł . ıɪɪ . borđ . Semp . ıɪɪ . car̄ . 7 ual . x . soł.

⁋Otrinkeehia . ı . car̄ terræ . ɪɪɪ . libi hoīes . ıɪɪ . borđ . semp . ıı.
car̄ . & . ual . v . soł . Idē . Galt . medietatē.

⁋Wetinge . ıx . libi hoēs v . car̄ terræ & dim̄ . xv . uiłł . et
xx . borđ . & . vı . ser . xɪɪɪ . ac̄ . p̄ti . semp . vı . car̄ . Siłua . de
v . porc̄ . dim . piscar̄ . & . ıı . car̄ hom̄ . semp ual . lx . soł . hoꝛ
vɪɪɪ . comdatio 7 soca fuit sc̄æ . aelđ . & de duobꝛ soca tantū
Totū ħt . ı . leuga & dim in łat . & reddit xɪɪɪɪ . đ in gelto.

⁋Otringheia . ıɪɪɪ . q̄r in longo . & . & . ıɪɪ . in łato . & reddit

163 a

in gelto . ıɪɪɪ . đ . Hoc totū ē de castæłlatione de ławes.

⁋Crane Wisse . ı . lib hō heroldi . semper . ıı . car̄ in dominio.
& . x . uiłł . & . v . borđ . 7 . ıɪɪ . seru . & . ıɪɪɪ . ac̄ p̄ti . Tc̄ & p̄ . ıɪɪɪ . car̄
& dim . hom̄ . modo . ıɪɪ . dim molin̄ . & dim piscar̄ . fiłua . x.
porc̄ . semp . ıɪɪɪ . runc̄ . Tc̄ ı vıı . añ . semp xɪɪɪ . porc̄ . Tc̄ . c . ous.
modo . c . xx . 7 vıı . uasa apū . & ual . lx . soł . In eadē ten& . id
Wiłłm . ı . libū hom̄ . S . aelđ . soc̄ & comd . ıı . car̄ tr̄e . semp . ıı . car̄
in dominio . & . ıx . uiłł . & . v . borđ . & . ıı . ser . & . ıɪɪɪ . ac̄ p̄ti,
Tc̄ & post . ıɪɪɪ . car̄ . & dim . 7 hom̄ ; m̄ . & . ıı . car̄ in dominio.
& dim mot . & dim piscar̄ . fiłua . x . porc̄ . & . ıɪɪɪ . runc̄ . & . vı.
añ . 7 xɪɪɪɪ . porc̄ . Tc̄ . c . ous . modo . c . xx . 7 vıı . uasa apum.
& ual lx . soł . Totū ħt . vıı . q̄r in longo . & . ıɪɪɪ . in łato . & reddit . vɪɪɪɪ . deñ . & . ı . obolū de gelto de . xx . soł . hoc de castel -
latione łauues.

41 In ICKBURGH Roger holds 2 free men, ½ c. of land and 6 acres.
1 smallholder; meadow, 1 acre; always 1 plough.
Value 3s.

42 In SANTON 5 free men, 2 c. of land. Walter holds a moiety.
1 villager; 3 smallholders.
Always 3 ploughs.
Value 10s.

43 OTTERING HITHE, 1 c. of land, 3 free men.
3 smallholders; always 2 ploughs.
Value 5s.
The same Walter (holds) a moiety.

44 WEETING, 9 free men, 5½ c. of land. Wazelin and Osward, 2 c. of
land, a third of the whole.
15 villagers; 20 smallholders; 6 slaves.
Meadow, 13 acres. Always 6 ploughs; woodland at 5 pigs;
½ fishery; 2 men's ploughs.
Value always 60s.
The patronage and jurisdiction of 8 of these was St.
E(theldreda's), and of 2 (St. Etheldreda had) the jurisdiction
only. The whole has 1½ leagues in width, it pays 14d in tax.

45 OTTERING HITHE, 4 furlongs in length and 3 in width, it pays 4d
in tax.   163 a
The whole of this is of the Castellany of Lewes.

46 CRANWICH, 1 free man of Harold's. Always 2 ploughs in lordship.
10 villagers; 5 smallholders; 3 slaves.
Meadow, 4 acres. Then and later 4½ men's ploughs, now 3;
½ mill; ½ fishery; woodland, 10 pigs; always 4 cobs. Then
7 head of cattle; always 13 pigs. Then 100 sheep, now 120.
7 beehives.
Value 60s.
In the same William also holds 1 free man; St. Etheldreda (has
the) jurisdiction and patronage; 2 c. of land. Always 2 ploughs
in lordship.
9 villagers; 5 smallholders; 2 slaves.
Meadow, 4 acres. Then and later 4½ men's ploughs, now 3.
2 ploughs in lordship; ½ mill; ½ fishery; woodland, 10 pigs;
4 cobs; 6 head of cattle; 14 pigs. Then 100 sheep, now 120.
7 beehives.
Value 60s.
The whole has 7 furlongs in length and 4 in width, of a 20s tax
it pays 9½d. This (is) of the Castellany of Lewes.

HVNDRET. Smetheduna . Hecham . ten& Toche lib̄ hō

t . r . e . femper . vii . caŕ in dominio . & lxx . borḋ . & vi . feru̇ . & . xii.

ac̄ p̄ti . & . vii . caŕ hom̄ . filua . c . porc̄ . & . iii . molini . & dim̄.

. i . pifcaŕ . femper . i . runc̄ . xxx . an̄ . lx . porc̄ . ɔc . ou̇s . hic jacēt

xxx.v . foc̄ . i . caŕ & dim̄ terræ . Semp . vi . caŕ . iiii . ac̄ p̄ti . Tē uȧl

xii . lib̄ . modo . xv . In eadē ten& . W . ii . caŕ terræ . quas tenuit

Alnod lib̄ homo . t . r . e . femp . xxvi . borḋ . & , ii . feru̇ . & . vi . ac̄

p̄ti . & . ii . caŕ in dominio . & . i . caŕ & dim̄ hom̄ . & dim̄ molin̄.

& . i . falina . & . i . pifcaria . & . iiii . foc̄ . ii . ac̄ Tē . xii . animal.

modo xvi . Tē . xxx . porc̄ . modo . xl . Tē lxxx . ou̇s . modo . lx .

163 b

& uȧl& l̇x . fol . Totū h̄ī . i . l̄ḡ in longo . & dim̄ in lato & redḋ.

iiii . fol . de xx . fol de gelto.

∫ In Snetefh̄a vii . foc̄ Stigandi . ii . caŕ terræ . & . xi . foc̄ . Stigand̄

xx . ac̄ . iiii . uilt̄ . xv . borḋ . riii . caŕ . & . viii . ac̄ p̄ti . & . i . molin̄.

& dim̄ . i . pifcaŕ . 7 du̇e partes uni̇ falinæ . Tē & p̄ uȧl . xxx . fol.

modo . l . hoc eft p̄ efcangio.

∫ HVNDRET . de Dochinge . Infrainghes . i . lib̄ homo

xx . ac̄ terre . & uȧl xvi . ḋ . de hoc habuit fu̇us antec̄ com̄ḋ tant̄.

Stigandus foc̄a.

∫ WANELVND . HVND̄ . Intreftun̄a . ten& hugo

. i . caŕ terræ 7 iiii . uilt̄ . 7 iiii̇ . borḋ . 7 . i . feŕ . 7 . x . ac̄ p̄ti . femp̄

. i . caŕ . & dim̄ in dominio & dim̄ caŕ hominū . & . i . lib̄ hō

xii . ac̄ . & uȧl xxx . fol . 7 hoc p̄tin& ad laues . & l̄t . x . qŕ in

longo . & dim̄ leuga in lato . & xv . den̄ . de gelto . quicūq̇ ibi

teneat ;

SMETHDON Hundred. Of Frederic's Holding.

47 Toki, a free man, held HEACHAM before 1066. Always 7 ploughs in lordship.

70 smallholders; 6 slaves.

Meadow, 12 acres; 7 men's ploughs; woodland, 100 pigs; 3½ mills; 1 fishery. Always 1 cob; 30 head of cattle; 60 pigs; 600 sheep.

35 Freemen appertain here, 1½ c. of land.

Always 6 ploughs; meadow, 4 acres.

Value then £12; now 15.

In the same W(illiam) holds 2 c. of land which Alnoth, a free man, held before 1066.

Always 26 smallholders; 2 slaves.

Meadow, 6 acres; 2 ploughs in lordship; 1½ men's ploughs; ½ mill; 1 salt-house; 1 fishery.

Also 4 Freemen, 2 acres.

Then 12 head of cattle, now 16. Then 30 pigs, now 40. Then 80 sheep, now 60.

Value 60s.   163 b

The whole has 1 league in length and ½ in width, of a 20s tax it pays 4s.

48 In SNETTISHAM 7 Freemen of Stigand's, 2 c. of land. Also 11 Freemen of Stigand's, 20 acres.

4 villagers; 15 smallholders.

4 ploughs; meadow, 8 acres; 1½ mills; 1 fishery; two-thirds of 1 salt-house.

Value then and later 30s; now 50.

This is by exchange.

The Hundred of DOCKING

49 In FRING 1 free man, 20 acres of land.

Value 16d.

Of this his predecessor had the patronage only. Stigand (had) the jurisdiction.

WAYLAND Hundred

50 In THREXTON Hugh holds 1 c. of land.

4 villagers; 4 smallholders; 1 slave.

Meadow, 10 acres. Always 1½ ploughs in lordship; ½ men's plough.

Also 1 free man, 12 acres.

Value 30s.

This belongs to Lewes. It has 10 furlongs in length and ½ league in width, tax of 15d, whoever holds there.

⁊ In Cateſtuna . III . ħbi hoēs . I . caƀ terræ . Tē . II . borđ . modo . x .
& XII . aē p̃ti . ſemp . II . caƀ . & ual XVII . ſoł . & . IIII . deñ . Suƥ
II . ħt Rex & comes ſocā & ante ceſſor joħis nepotis ſłi
Walerami de r̃tio . ħ ptin& . ađ caſtelħ de lauues . Totū ħt
. I . lg̃ in longo . & dim̃ in lato . & . XI . đ de gelto .

⁊ In tofſtes . IIII . libi homines . I . caƀ terræ & dim̃ . Tē . VII .
borđ . modo . XVII . xx . aē p̃ti . ſemp . v . caƀ . ſemp . I . Moliñ .
ſilua . VIII . porē . & ual XL . ſoł . & ħt VI . q̃r in longo . & . IIII . in
lato . & . v . đ de gelto . hoc eſt ƥ eſcagio .

164 a

⁊ In Ailincham . VI . libi hoēs ; LXXX; aē . t̃ræ . Tē : I . caƀ . m̃ . I;
& dim̃ . Tē . II . borđ . modo . III . & . in Sculetuna . VI . libi hoēs .
XXX aē terræ . Tē . I . caƀ . modo . I . caƀ & . dim̃ . ⁊ in tomeſtuna . VI
libi homines . I . caƀ terræ . Tē & ƥ . I . borđ . modo . III . XII ; aē p̃ti .
Tē . & ƥ . II . caƀ . modo . II . caƀ & dim̃ . Totū ual XLIX . ſoł . hoc ē
ƥ eſcago .

HVND . DESCEREPHAM . LVRLINGA ten& . hugo . I . caƀ
terræ & dim̃ . ſ& fuit liƀata ƥ una . caƀ . quā tenuit lib homo
t . r . ē . ſemƥ IX . borđ . & . III . libi homines . ⁊ xv . aē . t̃ræ . ⁊ . II . bou;
& . I . borđ . ſemp . II . caƀ in dominio . & . I . caƀ hominū . & . VIII .
aē p̃ti . ſemp ual& xxx . ſoł .

⁊ In Rokelun ten& ſimon . III . caƀ terræ . quā tenuit . I . lib hō Brode
t . r . e . ſemp . II . uilt . ⁊ XII . borđ . Tē . IIII . ſeru . modo . I . & . VIII .
aē p̃ti . ſemp . II . caƀ in dominio . & . I . caƀ hominum . ſilua . VI .
porē . Tē . IIII . runē . modo nult . Tē . VIII . an ; m̃ . v . Tē xxx ; porē ;
modo . xv . Tē . c . oūs . & m̃ ſimilit̃ . ⁊ in ead̃ ten& idem Simon
. VI . libos homines & dim̃ . q̃s habuit . ſoca in bucheham regis . t̃ . r̃ . ē̃ . ⁊ ʃ his . VI ; ⁊ dim̃
Ideм Brode c̃m̃ʒ tantū . lxx . aē . t̃ræ . ⁊ . IIIf . aē p̃ti . Sē̃ƥ . I . caƀ . ⁊ . ʒ . ex
⁊ poſt . ⁊ neſt donec Witt de Gaƀ . habuit . Tē & ſemp . III . liƀ . ⁊ x . ſoł .

51 In CASTON 3 free men, 1 c. of land.
  Then 2 smallholders, now 10. Meadow, 12 acres; always 2
    ploughs.
  Value 17s 4d.
  The King and the Earl have the jurisdiction over 2, and the
predecessor of John, nephew of Waleran, of the third. This
belongs to the Castle of Lewes. The whole has 1 league in length
and ½ in width, tax of 11d.

52 In ROCKLAND (St. Peter) 4 free men, 1½ c. of land.
  Then 7 smallholders, now 17.
  Meadow, 20 acres; always 5 ploughs. Always 1 mill; woodland,
    8 pigs.
  Value 40s.
  It has 6 furlongs in length and 4 in width, tax of 5d. This is
by exchange.

53 In (Little) ELLINGHAM 6 free men, 80 acres of land.   164 a
  Then 1 plough, now 1½. Then 2 smallholders, now 3.
  In SCOULTON 6 free men, 30 acres of land.
  Then 1 plough, now 1½.
  In THOMPSON 6 free men, 1 c. of land.
  Then and later 1 smallholder, now 3.
  Meadow, 12 acres. Then and later 2 ploughs, now 2½.
  Value of the whole 49s.
  This is by exchange.

  The Hundred of SHROPHAM
54 Hugh holds LARLING, 1½ c. of land, but it was delivered for 1 c.
which a free man held before 1066.
  Always 9 smallholders.
  Also 3 free men, 15 acres of land; 2 oxen, 1 smallholder.
  Always 2 ploughs in lordship; 1 men's plough; meadow, 8 acres.
  Value always 30s.

55 In ROCKLAND Simon holds 3 c. of land which 1 free man, Brode,
held before 1066.
  Always 2 villagers; 12 smallholders. Then 4 slaves, now 1.
  Meadow, 8 acres. Always 2 ploughs in lordship; 1 men's plough;
    woodland, 6 pigs. Then 4 cobs, now none. Then 8 head of
    cattle, now 5. Then 30 pigs, now 15. Then 100 sheep, now
    the same.
  In the same Simon also holds 6 free men and a half which the
same Brode also had in patronage only; 70 acres of land.
  Meadow, 4 acres; always 1½ ploughs.
  Of these 6 and a half the jurisdiction was in the King's (manor
of) Buckenham before 1066 and later, until William of Warenne
had it.
  [Value] then and always £3 10s.

V Pt hoc additi st̃ huic terræ . ix . libi homines . & dim̃ . i . car̃ . terræ
. hoc ẽ in d̃n̄o.
liiii . ac̃ . femp . ix . bord̃ . & . viii . ac̃ prati . femp vi . car̃ . & . ii . dimidios
molin̄ . hoc totũ eſt p̃ uno man̄ de laq̃s . & ual& iii . lib̃ . & . xi . ſol̃.
De iiii . 7 dimidio ex . ix : ſoca 7 com̃d erat inbucham regis . t.
                                                 or
. r . e . 7 poſt donec W . habuit 7 totũ fuit lib̃atũ t̃p̃r Radulfi
comitis . Tot̃ ht̃ . i . lg̃ in longo 7 dim̃ in lato . & . xv . d̃ de gelto.

164 b

V In Rudham . ii . lib̃i homines . t . car̃ terræ . & iii . ſoc̃ . & . v . bord̃.
& dim̃ ac̃ p̃ti . Tc̃ . i . car̃ . modo . ii . & ual x . ſol̃ Soca t̃p̃r . e . in bucham
regis & lib̃atũ ẽ . t̃ Rad̃ comitis . poſt retinuit ſoca̅.

V Inillinketuna ten̄ Will̃m . i . lib̃ hõm . i . car̃ terræ & dim̃ . ſemp
vii . uilt̃i . & . x . bord̃ . & . iiii . ac̃ . p̃ti . 7 vi . lib̃i hoẽs . xx . ii . ac̃ . terræ.
ſemp . i . car̃ in dominio . & . iii . car̃ hom̃ . Tc̃ ual xx . ſot̃ . p̃ 7 m̃
xxx . Soca in buchã . Totũ ht̃ dim̃ in longo . & . iiii . qr̃ in lato.
& . vii . d̃ . de gelto . & hoc . de caſtello delaquis

HVND̃ . DE GILDECROS . In nortuna ten̄ fulcherus
. i . car̃ terræ . quã tenuit . i . lib̃ homo . t . r . e . ſemp . vi . uilt̃ . & . ii
bord̃ . & . i . ac̃ p̃ti . Tc̃ & p̃ . i . car̃ in dominio . m̃ . i . car̃ & dimid̃.
& dim̃ . car̃ . hom̃ . dim̃ mol̃ . & . i . ſoc̃ . i . ac̃ terræ . Tc̃ & p̃ ual
xx . ſot̃ . modo xxx . hoc ẽ de caſtello de laq̃s . Soca In chenighe
hala regis . ſemp donec . W . hab̃.

V In Wica ten& Will̃ . i . car̃ terræ quã tenuit . i . liber homo . t . r . e.
ſemp . v . uilt̃ . & . x . bord̃ . & . iiii . ac̃ p̃ti . Tc̃ & p̃ . i . carr in dominio
modo . ii . ſemp . i . car̃ hominũ . modo . i . mol̃ . Tc̃ ual . xx . ſol̃.
modo . xxx . & . viii . ſoc̃ . xxx . ii . ac̃ . i . car̃ & dim̃ ſemp &

56 Besides this there were added to this land 9 free men and a half,
1 c. of land and 54 acres. This is in lordship.
Always 9 smallholders.
Meadow, 8 acres. Always 6 ploughs; 2 halves of a mill.
All this is for 1 manor of Lewes.
Value £3 11s.
Of 4 and a half of these 9 the jurisdiction and patronage was
in the King's (manor of) Buckenham before 1066 and later, until
W(illiam) had it. The whole was delivered in the time of Earl
Ralph. The whole has 1 league in length and ½ in width, tax
of 15d.

57 In ROUDHAM 2 free men, 1 c. of land.   164 b
3 Freemen; 5 smallholders.
Meadow, 1 acre; then 1 plough, now 2.
Value 10s.
The jurisdiction before 1066 was in the King's (manor of)
Buckenham and it was delivered in the time of Earl Ralph, and
afterwards he kept the jurisdiction.

58 In ILLINGTON William holds 1 free man, 1½ c. of land.
Always 7 villagers; 10 smallholders.
Meadow, 4 acres. Also 6 free men, 22 acres of land. Always
1 plough in lordship; 3 men's ploughs.
Value then 20s; later and now 30.
The jurisdiction is in Buckenham. The whole has ½ [league] in
length and 4 furlongs in width, tax of 7d. This is for the castle
of Lewes.

The Hundred of GUILTCROSS
59 In (Blo)NORTON Fulcher holds 1 c. of land which 1 free man held
before 1066.
Always 6 villagers; 2 smallholders.
Meadow, 1 acre. Then and later 1 plough in lordship, now 1½
ploughs; ½ men's plough; ½ mill.
1 Freeman, 1 acre of land.
Value then and later 20s; now 30.
This is of the castle of Lewes. The jurisdiction (was) always in
the King's (manor of) Kenninghall until W(illiam) had it.

60 In WICK William holds 1 c. of land which 1 free man held before
1066.
Always 5 villagers; 10 smallholders.
Meadow, 4 acres. Then and later 1 plough in lordship, now 2.
Always 1 men's plough; now 1 mill.
Value then 20s, now 30(s).
Also 8 Freemen, 32 acres; always 1½ ploughs.

ual.x.ſol.ħ totū fuit libatū .p.ı.car terræ.& eſt de caſtello
de laquis.Soca in Kenehala.ſemp donec.W.habuıit.

ᚠIn Benham tenuit.ı.lib ħō.Leſsi.t.r:e.ı.car.terræ.ſemp
ıx.uilt.&.vı.bord.Tc.ı.ſeru.&.xıı.ac pti.Tc & p.ı.car in dnio.
modo.ıı.ſemp.ı.car & dım hominū.ſilua de.c.porc.& ual
xʟ.ſol.&.v.ſoc teñ.ide.xxxı.ac terræ.&.ıı.ac pti.Tc.

165 a
.ı.car & dimid.Poſt & m.ı.& ual&.v.ſol.Totū hf.ı.lg & dım
in longo.&.ı.lg in lato.& xxıııı.đ.7.ı.obolū de gelto.quicūq
ibi habeat.Totū e de caſtello de laqs.

ᚠ HVNDRET; DE LAWENDIC.In Greſſenhala tenuit Toke
lib ħō.t.r.e.P fedricus.ıı.car.terræ.& dım.ſemp.x.uilt.
&.xvııı.bord.Tc.ıııı.ſeru.modo.ı.7 ıııı.ac pti.ſemp.ıı.car
in dominio.7.ıı.hom.ſilu.c.porc.Tc.ı.moliñ.modo.ıı.&
xvııı.ſoc ſemp cū oı conſuetud.ı.car terræ.ſemp.ııı.bord.
&.ıııı.ac pti.Tc.& p.ııı.car.modo.ıı.ſemp.ıı.moliñ.7.ı.
runc.Tc.x.añ.modo.xı.ſemp xxx.porc.modo.xxx.ous.
7 xxx.cap.hic jac& ſemp.ı.berewita Scerninga.dım.car
terræ.&.v.bord.&.ı.ac pti.ſemp.ı.car in dominio.7.ı.car
hominū.7 xx.porc.&.ıııı.añ.Tc totū ual xʟ.ſol.modo.
ıııı.lib.Totū ħt.vıı.qr in longo.&.ıııı.in lato.&.vıı.đ
& obolū de gelto.Wimer ten&.

ᚠIn Leceeſham id.|qd tenuit Oſchetel lib ħō.t.r.e.P fedricus.p
mañ.ıı.car terræ.Tc.vııı.bord.modo.xıı.Tc.ıııı.ſeru.
ıı.ac pti.ſemper.ıı.car in dominio.Tc.ı.car hom.modo
.ıı.ſilu.de.xxx.porc.ſemp.ı.moliñ.&.xıı.ſoc.ı.car træ
Tc.ııı.car.modo.ıı.In dnio.ıııı.runc.modo.ııı.vııı.añ.
modo.ıx.ſemp.xxıııı.porc.&.cc.ous.ſemp ual xʟ.ſol.

Value 10s.

All this was delivered as 1 c. of land, and is of the castle of Lewes. The jurisdiction (was) always in Kenninghall until W(illiam) had it.

61 In BANHAM 1 free man, Leofsi, held 1 c. of land before 1066.
    Always 9 villagers; 6 smallholders. Then 1 slave.
    Meadow, 12 acres. Then and later 1 plough in lordship, now 2.
    Always 1½ men's ploughs; woodland at 100 pigs.
Value 40s.
He also held 5 Freemen, 31 acres of land; meadow, 2 acres. Then
    1½ ploughs, later and now 1.   165 a
Value 5s.

The whole has 1½ leagues in length and 1 league in width, tax of 24½d, whoever holds there. The whole is of the castle of Lewes.

The Hundred of LAUNDITCH

62 In GRESSENHALL Toki, a free man, held before 1066, later Frederic, 2½ c. of land.
    Always 10 villagers; 18 smallholders. Then 4 slaves, now 1.
    Meadow, 4 acres. Always 2 ploughs in lordship; 2 men's
        [ploughs]; woodland, 100 pigs. Then 1 mill, now 2.
    Also 18 Freemen always with their customary dues; 1 c. of land.
        Always 3 smallholders; meadow, 4 acres. Then and later 3
        ploughs, now 2. Always 2 mills; 1 cob. Then 10 head of
        cattle, now 11; always 30 pigs. Now 30 sheep; 30 goats.
Here has always appertained 1 outlier, SCARNING, ½ c. of land.
    5 smallholders; meadow, 1 acre. Always 1 plough in lordship;
        1 men's plough; 20 pigs; 4 head of cattle.
Value of the whole then 40s; now £4.

The whole has 7 furlongs in length and 4 in width, tax of 7½d. Wymer holds.

63 In LEXHAM he also (holds) what Ulfketel, a free man, held before 1066, and later Frederic, as a manor, 2 c. of land.
    Then 8 smallholders, now 12. Then 4 slaves.
    Meadow, 2 acres; always 2 ploughs in lordship. Then 1 men's
        plough, now 2. Woodland at 30 pigs; always 1 mill.
    Also 12 Freemen, 1 c. of land. Then 3 ploughs, now 2, in
        lordship. 4 cobs, now 3. Then 8 head of cattle, now 9.
        Always 24 pigs; 200 sheep.
Value always 40s.

In Wefenhã tenueř . xii . foc̄ . Stigandi . t . r . e . ii . car̄ t̄ræ . m̄
vi . foc plus . sēp . iiii . borđ . T̄c̄ . iiii . car̄ in̄ totū qr̄ū due s̄t in dominio.
& . i . ac̄ p̄ti . femp . iii . car̄ hominū . modo . vi . añ . 7 . viii . porc̄,

165 b

7 ix . oũs . & . ii . runc̄ . T̄c̄ ual̄ . xl . fol̄ . modo lx . hoc eſt de
efcagio de noua terra . Totū ħt . i . lḡ . in longo . & dim̄ in lato .
& xx . đ de gelto . q̄cūq̄ ibi teneat . Wimer ten̄ .

In Kemeſtuna . iiii . foc̄ . i . car̄ . terræ . Subſtigando . femp . iiii .
uiłł . & . i . feru̅ . & . i . ac̄ p̄ti . T̄c̄ . iii . car̄ . P̄ 7 modo . ii . & dim̄ .
filua . x . porc̄ . femp ual̄ . xx . fol̄ .

In fraudeſhã tenueř . t . r . e . ii . libi hoes đe q̄b7 antec̄ fedrici
habuit com̄d . tantū . P̄ fedricus : modo ħt . W . 7 Giſlebtus đe eo .
. i . car̄ . & dim̄ terræ . femp . iiii . uiłłi . & . viii . borđ . T̄c̄ . ii . feru̅ . 7 iiii.
ac̄ p̄ti . femp . iii . car̄ . filu̅ . lx . porc̄ . T̄c̄ . i . molin̄ . modo . i . &
dim̄ . femp ual̄ . xxx . fol̄ .

Scernenga . tenuit fredregis lib̄ ho . t . r . e . i . car̄ terræ . &
dim̄ . femp . iiii . ulli . & . vi . borđ . iii . ac̄ p̄ti . femp . i . car̄ in đnio.
& . i . car̄ hominū . filua . de . xxx . porc̄ . femp . i . molin̄ . T̄c̄ ual̄
xx . fol̄ . modo . xxx . de feudo fedrici 7 fuus antec̄ habuit com̄
tantū . 7 fui ante ceſſores habueř foca . ipfim̄& .

In Ruhham 7 in̄ fraudeſham . ii . car̄ terræ ten̄ toke lib̄ ho
t . r . e . femp . i . uiłł . T̄c̄ . xii . borđ . modo . x . T̄c̄ . iii . feru̅ . m̄ . i .
& . i . ac̄ prati . femp . iii . car̄ in dominio . 7 . i . car̄ & dim̄ hom̄ .
filua . x . porc̄ . 7 modo dim̄ molin̄ . 7 . xvi . libi hoes . dim̄ car̄
terre . 7 . viii . ac̄ terræ . femp . i . car̄ . 7 dim̄ . T̄c̄ ual̄ . l . fol̄ . modo .
lx . hoc eſt p efcaḡ delaquis . Totū fraudehā . ħt . ix . qr̄ in longo
& . viii . in lato . & . x . đen . de gelto . q̄cūq̄ ibi teneat . W . ten̄&

165 a, b

64 In WEASENHAM 12 Freemen of Stigand's held 2 c. of land before
1066. Now 6 more Freemen. Always 4 smallholders.
  Then 4 ploughs in all, of which 2 are in lordship; meadow,
    1 acre; always 3 men's ploughs. Now 6 head of cattle;
    8 pigs; 60 sheep; 2 cobs.   165 b
Value then 40s; now 60.
  This is of the exchange of the new land. The whole has 1 league
in length and ½ in width, tax of 20d, whoever holds there.
Wymer holds.

65 In KEMPSTON 4 Freemen under Stigand, 1 c. of land.
  Always 4 villagers; 1 slave.
  Meadow, 1 acre. Then 3 ploughs, later and now 2½. Woodland,
    10 pigs.
Value always 20s.

66 In FRANSHAM 2 free men held before 1066, of whom Frederic's
predecessor, and later Frederic, had the patronage only; now
W(illiam) has it, and Gilbert from him. 1½ c. of land.
  Always 4 villagers; 8 smallholders. Then 2 slaves.
  Meadow, 4 acres. Always 3 ploughs; woodland, 60 pigs.
    Then 1 mill, now 1½.
Value always 30s.

67 He also (holds) SCARNING, Fredregis, a free man, held it before
1066; 1½ c. of land.
  Always 4 villagers; 6 smallholders.
  Meadow, 3 acres. Always 1 plough in lordship; 1 men's plough;
    woodland at 30 pigs; always 1 mill.
Value then 20s; now 30.
  (It is) of the Holding of Frederic; his predecessor had the
patronage only, and his predecessors had the jurisdiction
themselves.

68 In ROUGHAM and in FRANSHAM Toki, a free man, held 2 c. of land
before 1066.
  Always 1 villager. Then 12 smallholders, now 10. Then 3 slaves,
    now 1.
  Meadow, 1 acre. Always 3 ploughs in lordship; 1½ men's
    ploughs; woodland, 10 pigs. Now ½ mill.
  Also 16 free men, ½ c. of land and 8 acres of land. Always
    1½ ploughs.
Value then 50s; now 60.
  It is by exchange of Lewes. The whole of Fransham has 9
furlongs in length and 8 in width, tax of 10d, whoever holds
there. W. holds.

ꟻIn tītes hala . tenuer̉ . t . r . e . v . liƀi hoes̉ . ɪ . car̉ terre . m̂ ten̄ . Wimer̉

166 a

de Wiłł . femp . vɪɪ . borđ . vɪ . ac̄ . p̂ti . femp . ɪɪɪ . car̉ . & dim̂ . 7 filua
xʟ . porc̉ . 7 . ɪ . pifcar̉ . Tc̄ ual xx . foł . modo . xxx . ħ ē ‿p efcag̉ . de laᵭs.
Soca in muleħa regis.

ꟻIn Stanuelda . ɪɪ . car̉ terræ tenuer̉ . xxxɪɪɪ . liƀi hoes̉ fubſtigando
foca & com̉d . femp . v . borđ . 7 vɪ . ac̄ p̂ti . Semp inꝼ totū . x . car̉
filua ʟx . porc̉ . Tc̄ ual . xʟ . foł . modo . ʟx . hoc ē de eſc̄ . de laᵭs . Soca
in mulħa regis.

ꟻHѴnd̉ . De WANELѴND . In Greſtuna . ɪ . æcclia . 7.
x . ac̄ . terræ hoc calūpniatur . Godric jacere t͠pr . Ra . comitis.
in ſtou . & hoes de hund̉ eā teſtantur ad feudū Wiłłi . de Waren̉ &
quidā regis hō uult ferre judiciū qđ jacuit in Stou . quando foris
fecit fe rađ & uno anno p̑us . 7 uno anno p̑ea.

ꟻFEOR HOѴ . HѴNDRET . ET DIM̂ . In berham . ɪɪ . car̉ terre.
& . vɪ . ac̄ . tenebant xʟvɪɪ . li liƀ hoes̉ quando recepit . 7 modo . ʟvɪɪ.
femp . vɪɪ . borđ . & . vɪɪɪ . car̉ . & . x . ac̄ p̂ti . femp . ɪ . molin̄ . 7 dim̂ . Tc̄
ual . c . foł . modo . ɪx . liƀ . Soca in Wid-mundħa regis . Totū ħ͠ . vɪ . qr̉
in longo . & . ɪɪɪɪ . in lato . & de gelto regis . vɪɪɪ . foł . & . v . đ . q͠cq₂ ibi teneat.

ꟻIn Coletuna . ɪɪ . liƀi hoies . xxx . ac̄ terræ . & s̄ in eođ p̄tio.

ꟻIn tocheſtorp . xxɪɪɪɪ . ac̄ . terræ . & funt in eodē p̄tio

ꟻIn Walebruna . x . liƀi hoies . t . r . e . ɪ . car̉ . terræ . & xʟ . acras m̂ funt
xx . liƀi homines . femp . ɪɪɪɪ . car̉ . & . ɪɪɪ . ac̄ . p̂ti.

ꟻIn tokeſtorp . ɪɪɪ . liƀi homines . xx . ac̄ . terræ . Totū ual . ʟx . foł.

ꟻIn Wikelepuda . ɪ . liƀ hō . ɪ . car̉ . terræ . femp xvɪɪ . borđ . 7 . ɪɪɪ . car̉
& . vɪ . ac̄ p̂ti . Tc̄ ual . xx . foł . modo . xʟ.

69 In TITTLESHALL 5 free men held 1 c. of land before 1066. Now Wymer holds from William.

Always 7 smallholders.
Meadow, 6 acres. Always 3½ ploughs; woodland, 40 pigs; 1 fishery.
Value then 20s; now 30.
This is by exchange of Lewes. The jurisdiction (is) in the King's (manor of) Mileham.

70 In STANFIELD 33 free men, under Stigand by jurisdiction and patronage, held 2 c. of land.
Always 5 smallholders;
meadow, 6 acres. In all always 10 ploughs; woodland, 60 pigs.
Value then 40s; now 60.
This is of the exchange of Lewes. The jurisdiction (is) in the King's (manor of) Mileham.

The Hundred of WAYLAND

71 In GRISTON 1 church, 10 acres of land. This Godric claims appertained in Stow (Bedon) in the time of Earl Ralph. The men of the Hundred testify that it is part of the Holding of William of Warenne. A certain King's man is willing to undergo judicial ordeal that it appertained in Stow (Bedon) when Ralph forfeited and for one year before and one year after that.

FOREHOE Hundred and Half

72 In BARNHAM (Broom) 47 free men held 2 c. and 6 acres of land when he acquired it, now 57 (hold).
Always 7 smallholders;
8 ploughs; meadow, 10 acres; always 1½ mills.
Value then 100s; now £9.
The jurisdiction is in the King's (manor of) Wymondham. The whole has 6 furlongs in length and 4 in width, King's tax of 8s 5d, whoever holds there.

73 In COLTON 2 free men, 30 acres of land. They are in the same valuation.

74 In TOCHESTORP 24 acres of land. They are in the same valuation.

75 In WELBORNE 10 free men before 1066, 1 c. and 40 acres of land; now there are 20 free men. Always 4 ploughs; meadow, 3 acres.

76 In TOKESTORP 3 free men, 20 acres of land.
Value of the whole 60s.

77 In WICKLEWOOD 1 free man, 1 c. of land.
Always 17 smallholders. 3 ploughs; meadow, 6 acres.
Value then 20s; now 40.

ᚦIn morlea . ɪɪ . car̄ terræ unā tenuit . ɪ . p̄br . & aliā . v . liƀi
homines . & p̄br habebat xɪx . borð . & . t . r . e . v . car̄ . modo . ɪɪɪ .
& . v . ac̄ p̄ti . Tc̄ uaƚ . ʟx . ſoƚ . modo . xʟ . & . v . liƀi homines habe-
bāt ſub ſe . x . borð . ſemp . ɪɪ . car̄ . & . ɪɪɪɪ . ac̄ p̄ti . ᛘ uaƚ . xʟ . ſoƚ .

ᚦIn dephā . xxx . ac̄ terræ . ɪ . liƀ hō . in eadē carrucata . ſemp
v . borð . & . ɪ . car̄ . & c̄ in eoð p̄tio . Tota ſoca in hincham regis .

ᚦIn Wimundham . xxx . liƀi hoi̯es qdo recepit . modo . xʟ . ɪɪɪ .
ſemp . ɪ . car̄ terræ . Tc̄ & . p̄ . v . car̄ . modo . ɪɪ . ſemp . vɪ . borð . & .
vɪ . ac̄ p̄ti . T_otū uaƚ xʟ . ſoƚ . hoc totū c̄ de eſcago . de laquis .
de terra ſanĉtorum .

ᚦMITTEFORT . HVNDRET . In turſtaneſtuna .
x . liƀi homines p̄ dim̄ car̄ terræ . t . r . e . ſemp . ɪɪ . borð . & . v . ac̄ p̄ti .
ſemp . ɪɪ . car̄ . Tc̄ uaƚ . x . ſoƚ . modo . xx . ᛘ In mateſhala . xɪɪɪɪ . ac̄ .
terræ . ɪ . liƀ homo . & . c̄ in eð p̄tio

ᚦIn berch . vɪɪ . liƀi hoi̯es . p̄ dim̄ car̄ terræ . & . ɪɪɪ . borð . & . v . ac̄ p̄ti .
Tc̄ . ɪɪ . molin̄ . modo . ɪɪɪ . Tc̄ ſilua . vɪɪɪ . porc̄ . modo . ɪɪɪɪ . Tc̄ &
p̄ . ɪɪ . car̄ . modo . ɪ . car̄ . & dim̄ . & uaƚ . xx . ſoƚ .
.ɪ. æcclia . xɪɪ . ac̄.

ᚦIn Lettuna . ɪx . liƀi hoi̯es . t . r . e . p̄ dim̄ car̄ terræ . & . ɪɪ . borð .
& . vɪɪɪ . ac̄ p̄ti . ſilua de . vɪɪɪ . porc̄ . ſemp . ɪɪɪ . car̄ . Tc̄ uaƚ . x . ſoƚ .
modo xx . ſoƚ . ɪ . ecclia . xɪɪ . ac̄ .

ᚦIn Scipdham . xɪ . liƀi homines . p̄ . ɪ . car̄ . terræ . & . ɪɪɪ . borð . & . x .
ac̄ p̄ti . Tc̄ ſilua ʟx . porc̄ . modo xʟ . Tc̄ . v . car̄ . p̄ & modo . ɪɪɪɪ .
Tc̄ uaƚ . xxx . ſoƚ . modo . xʟ . ſoƚ . & . ɪ . lḡ in longo . & . v . qr̄ in lato .
dim' ecclia . vɪɪɪ . ac̄.
ᛘ xv . ð . de gelto . & Berc h̄t . vɪ . qr̄ in longo

& . v . in lato . & . xv . den̄ . de gelto . ᛘ Lettuna ſimiliᵗ redð . hoc totū c̄
p̄ eſcagio de laquis . In tureſtuna . ɪx . ac̄ . ɪ . liƀ hō . & uaƚ . ɪɪ . ſoƚ .
deoð ſcangio .

78 In MORLEY 2 c. of land: 1 priest held 1 and 5 free men the other.   166 b
   The priest had 19 smallholders.
   Before 1066 5 ploughs, now 3. Meadow, 5 acres.
Value then 60s; now 40.
   The 5 free men had under them 10 smallholders. Always 2
      ploughs; meadow, 4 acres.
Value 40s.

79 In DEOPHAM 1 freeman, 30 acres of land in the same c.
   Always 5 smallholders; 1 plough.
It is in the same valuation. All the jurisdiction (is) in the King's
(manor of) Hingham.

80 In WYMONDHAM 30 free men when he acquired it, now 43. Always
1 c. of land.
   Then and later 5 ploughs, now 2. Always 6 smallholders;
      meadow, 6 acres.
Value of the whole 40s.
   All this is of the exchange of Lewes of the land of the Saints.

MITFORD Hundred
81 In THUXTON 10 free men, as ½ c. of land before 1066.
   Always 2 smallholders; meadow, 5 acres; always 2 ploughs.
Value then 10s; now 20.
Also in MATTISHALL 14 acres of land, 1 free man. It is in the same
valuation.

82 In (South)BURGH 7 free men, as 1½ c. of land.
   3 smallholders; meadow, 5 acres. Then 2 mills, now 3. Then
      woodland, 8 pigs, now 4. Then and later 2 ploughs, now 1½.
   1 church, 12 acres.
Value 20s.

83 In LETTON 9 free men before 1066, as ½ c. of land.
   2 smallholders; meadow, 8 acres; woodland at 8 pigs; always
      3 ploughs.
Value then 10s; now 20s.
   1 church, 12 acres.

84 In SHIPDHAM 11 free men, as 1 c. of land.
   3 smallholders. Meadow, 10 acres. Woodland, then 60 pigs,
      now 40. Then 5 ploughs, later and now 4.
Value then 30s; now 40s.
   ½ church, 8 acres.
   (It has) 1 league in length and 5 furlongs in width, tax of 15d.
And (South)burgh has 6 furlongs in length and 5 in width, tax   167 a
of 15d. Letton pays the same. All of this is by exchange of Lewes.
In THUR(E)STUNA 9 acres, 1 free man.
Value 2s. Of the same exchange.

HVNDRET . DE DOKINGA . Stanho . i . lib̃ homo ulketel
com̃datione tantū . i . car̃ terræ . & . iii . bord̃ . Semp . i . car̃ . 7 ual̃
xx . ſol̃.

In Scernebuna . iiii . libi homines . ii . car̃ terræ . & . i . lib̃ hõ . de
xl . ac̃ . Semp . v . uill̃ . & ſemp . iii . car̃ . & ual̃ lx . ſol̃.

Mittefort . *HVNDRET .* Riſinga teñ . Alueua . t . r . e.
. i . car̃ terre . ſemp . i . car̃ in dominio . & xvi . uill̃ . & vi . bord̃ . & . v.
car̃ hom̃ . & . xv . ac̃ p̃ti . Tc̃ ſilua . cc . porc̃ . modo . c . lx . & . ibi . l̃
viii . libi hoẽs . iii . car̃ terræ . Semp . iii . car̃ . Silũ . vi . porc̃ . & . vii .
añ . & . i . runc̃ . 7 xx . porc̃ . xxx . cap̃ . Tc̃ ual̃ xl . ſol̃ . Modo . lx . Et
ht . viii . qr̃ in longo . & . vi . in lato . & . xv . d̃ de gelto.

HEINESTEDE . HVNDRET . In alinituna . i . lib̃ hõ
heraldi com̃d̃ xxx ac̃ . træ . & . iii . bord̃ . i . ac̃ p̃ti . Semp . i . car̃ . ē
ap̃ciata l̃ aca . De eſcangio.

HVND . DE GRENEHOV . In Dudelingatuna tenuer̃ . xxx
ii . libi hoĩes . iiii . car̃ terræ . & adhuc tenẽt . Semp . xv . bord̃.
ſub ipſis Semp inter eos . v . car̃ . & habt̃ . viii . qr̃ in longo . &.
iiii . in lato . 7 reddit ad gelt . xiii . d̃ . de his teñ . Oger̃ . i . car̃ tre
. i . car̃ . ſup eũ xx . ſol̃ . ~~q̃ndo . h . redd . xx . ſol̃.~~ Tc̃ ual̃ & . c . ſol̃.
modo . iiii . lib̃ . & . v . ſol̃.

In fugalduna tenuer̃ . xxiiii libi hoĩes . vi . car̃ . træ . & adhuc tenẽt

Sub Willo . 7 Willmus teñ . i . carr̃ . terræ . 7 . i . car̃ . Sup eũ 7 ual̃ . xx . ſol̃.
Tc̃ ſub ipſis . xvi . uilli . 7 xvi . bord̃ ꞇ 7 modo . Tc̃ . vii . car̃ ꞇ & ſemp . Semp
. i . moliñ . x . ac̃ p̃ti . & . ii . piſcar̃ . 7 ht̃ . i . mill̃ . in longo . & dim̃ in lato.
7 reddit . in gelt . xvi . d̃ . Tc̃ ual̃ . lx . ſol̃ . modo . c . ſol̃ 7 xx . 7 hanc
tr̃a dic̃ ſe habere ,p eſcangijs de leuis.

The Hundred of DOCKING

85 STANHOE, 1 free man, Ulketel, in patronage only. 1 c. of land.
3 smallholders; always 1 plough.
Value 20s.

86 In SHERNBORNE 4 free men, 2 c. of land; and 1 free man, at 40
acres.
Always 5 villagers; always 3 ploughs.
Value 60s.

MITFORD Hundred

87 Aelfeva held (Wood)RISING before 1066, 1 c. of land.
Always 1 plough in lordship. 16 villagers; 6 smallholders.
5 men's ploughs; meadow, 15 acres. Woodland then 200
pigs, now 160.
Also there are 8 free men, 3 c. of land.
Always 3 ploughs; woodland, 6 pigs; 7 head of cattle; 1 cob;
20 pigs; 30 goats.
Value then 40s; now 60.
It has 8 furlongs in length and 6 in width; tax of 15d.

HENSTEAD Hundred

88 In YELVERTON 1 free man under the patronage of Harold, 30 acres
of land.
3 smallholders; meadow, 1 acre; always 1 plough.
It is assessed in Acre. Of the exchange.

The Hundred of (South) GREENHOE

89 In DIDLINGTON 32 free men held 4 c. of land, and still hold it.
Always 15 smallholders under them.
Always 5 ploughs between them.
It has 8 furlongs in length and 4 in width, it pays 13d towards
tax.
Of these, Oger holds 1 c. of land and 1 plough on it.
[Value] 20s. *when the Hundred pays 20s.*
Value then 100s; now £4 5s.

90 In FOULDEN 24 free men held 6 c. of land, and still hold under
William. William holds 1 c. of land and 1 plough on it.   167 b
Value 20s.
Under those then and now 16 villagers and 16 smallholders.
Then and always 7 ploughs. Always 1 mill; meadow, 10 acres;
2 fisheries.
It has 1 mile in length and ½ in width, it pays 16d in tax.
Value then 60s; now 120s.
He says that he has this land by the exchanges of Lewes.

ꝶHildeburh Wella tenuit . t . r . e . Ofmund . m̃ . W . ꝓ mañ . de dono
regis . | Tc̃ xxii . uilł ꝿ & femp . Tc̃ . x . borđ ꝿ & femp . Tc̃ . vi . feru̇ . & . m̃ ꝿ
Semp . in dominio . iiii . car̃ . Tc̃ iñt oẽs . x . car̃ . 7 p̃ . vii . & . modo
viii . ac̃ . p̃ti . Qñ recep̃ ꝿ v . añ . in ueñ . 7 . ii . ruñc̃ . modo . fimiliſ .
7 tc̃ . xv . porc̃ . & . modo . Tc̃ . c . oũs . modo . c . 7 xx . m̃ xvii . cap̃ .
7 . v . uafa apũ . 7 . iii . moł . filua . ad xx . porc̃ . 7 hт dim̃ milł . & .
. ii . qr̃ . in longo . & . vii . in lato . & reddit ad gelt . viii đ . Tc̃ ual̃ . vi .
liɓ . modo . viii ¡

 ꝶ Et in Claia . teñ . Ofmundus . đ . car̃ terræ . Tc̃ . v . borđ ꝿ 7 modo .
Semp . i . car̃ . i ¡ ac̃ . p̃ti . Tc̃ ual̃ . x . foł . modo . xv . foł . 7 incleia
inuñ iii . runc̃ ꝿ 7 m̃ . 7 . vi . añ . 7 . xx . porc̃ . 7 . c . oũs . 7 . ii . 7 . i . uaꝰ
apũ . idẽ . W . ten&

ꝶ In bradenhã teñ qđã liɓ hõ . xxx . ac̃ . ibi femp . iii . borđ . ſ& . Ofm̃
habebat foca & faca . filua . ad . x . porc̃ . ii . ac̃ . p̃ti . Tc̃ ual̃ . v . foł .
modo . v . folidos .

ꝶ In pagraua teñ Sc̃s ricarius . i . car̃ . terre . quã tenuit qđã liɓ hõ
t . r ¡ e . Tc̃ . iiii . uilłi ꝿ 7 femper . M̊ . ii . borđ . Semp . in dominio .
¡ i . car̃ 7 femp . iñt oẽs . đ . car̃ . Tc̃ ual̃ . xx . foł . modo . xxv . foł .

ꝶ In acꝛa teñ qđã liɓ hõ ¡ i . car̃ . terræ ¡ femp . vi . uilł . & . i . borđ . & . iii ¡ ſer̃ .
168 a
 & . i . car̃ in dominio . Tc̃ iñt oẽs . iii . car̃ . modo . i . Silua ad xv . porc̃ .
Semp . dim̃ . moliñ . Tc̃ ual̃ 7 femp xx . foł . hoc ē defedo fretherici . Wimer̃ ten& .

 ꝶ In budeneia . tenueꝛ . iii . liɓi hões . i . car̃ . terræ . modo . ten& . W .
in efcangio . Semp . i . uilł . Semp . i . car̃ . Silua . ad . xii . porc̃ . ii .
ac̃ p̃ti . & quartẽ partẽ . i . moliñ . Tc̃ ual̃ xx . foł . m̃ . fimił .

91 Osmund held HILBOROUGH before 1066, now W(illiam) (holds) as a manor of the King's gift, and W(illiam) from him.

Then and always 22 villagers. Then and always 10 smallholders. Then and now 6 slaves.

Always 4 ploughs in lordship. Then 10 ploughs between them all, later and now 7. Meadow, 8 acres. When he acquired it he found 5 head of cattle and 2 cobs, now the same. Then and now 15 pigs. Then 100 sheep, now 120. Now 17 goats; 5 beehives; 3 mills; woodland for 20 pigs.

It has ½ mile and 2 furlongs in length and 7 [furlongs] in width, it pays 8d towards tax.

Value then £6; now 7.

92 And in (Cockley) CLEY Osmund held ½ c. of land.

Then and now 5 smallholders. Always 1 plough; meadow, 1 acre.

Value then 10s; now 15s.

Also in (Cockley) Cley he found 3 cobs and (the same) now. 6 head of cattle; 20 pigs; 102 sheep; 1 beehive.

W(illiam) also holds it.

93 In BRADENHAM, this free man also holds 30 acres.

There always 3 smallholders; but Osmund had the full jurisdiction.

Woodland for 10 pigs; meadow, 2 acres.

Value then 5s; now 5s.

94 In PALGRAVE St. Riquier holds 1 c. of land, of Frederic's Holding, which a certain free man held before 1066.

Then and always 4 villagers. Now 2 smallholders.

Always 1 plough in lordship; always ½ plough among them all.

Value then 20s; now 25s.

95 In (South) ACRE a certain free man held 1 c. of land.

Always 6 villagers; 1 smallholder; 3 slaves.

1 plough in lordship. Then 3 ploughs among them all, now 1.   168 a

Woodland for 15 pigs; always ½ mill.

Value then and always 40s.

This is of Frederic's Holding. Wymer holds.

96 In BODNEY 3 free men held 1 c. of land. Now W(illiam) holds it in exchange.

Always 1 villager; always 1 plough; woodland for 12 pigs; meadow, 2 acres; ¼ of 1 mill.

Value then 20s; now the same.

In pichenhā teñ Willm̄ dim̄ . car̄ . terræ . quā tenuit . Osfordus
t . r . e . Tc̄ . ii . uill⁄ & modo, Semp , i . car̄ . filua . ad . iiii . porc̄ . ii . ac̄
p̄ti . Semp . i . mol . Sēp ual . x . fol .

HVNDRET . DE GALHOu . Sculetorpa tenuit Toka de fedo
fretherici . t . r . e . iii . car̄ , trǣ . Semp xii . uill . 7 . xxx . iiii . bord̄ . Tc̄
vi . feru . modo . iii . Tc̄ . & . p̄ . iii . car̄ . m̄ . iiii . Sēp . hom . v . carr̄ .
Silua ad . xx . porc̄ . iiii . ac̄ . p̄ti . iii . moliñ . Qn̄ . recep̄ . iiii . runc̄ .
modo . vi . Tc̄ . vi . an̄ . modo . xx . Tc̄ . xl . porc̄ . modo . xx . Tc̄ . c . ous̄ . modo .
cccc . 7 xxx . foc̄ . jacent huic mañ . cū . ōi . confuetudine . manentes .
. i . car̄ . & dim̄ terræ . Semp . iiii . car̄ . 7 . ii . al⁄ . foc̄ . de . xl . ac̄ . manent
intoffas . 7 fub ipfis . xii . bord̄ . i . aē . i . ac̄ . & . dim̄ . p̄ti . Semp . ii . car̄ . i . æcclia . lx . ac̄ .
Tc̄ ual . vi . lib̄ . 7 p̄ . m̄ . x . fed fuit ad firmā . xv . lib̄ f7 ñ potuit redde⁄ .
7 ht̄ in longo . dim̄ lḡ . 7 . dim̄ in lato . 7 vi . d̄ . de gelto . 7 . xii . eque
filuatice 7 ual . xii . fol . Eccliæ lx . ac̄ .

Barfehā tenuit ka . t . r . e . iiii . car̄ terræ . Semp . x . uill . 7 xx . vi . bord̄ .
Tc̄ . iiii . feru . modo . null . Tc̄ . iiii . car̄ . in dominio . 7 p̄ . null . modo . ii .
f7 pofſ reftaurari . Tc̄ hom . v . car̄ . 7 p̄ . null . modo . iii . 7 pofſt reftaurari .
Silua ad xx . porc̄ . iii . ac̄ . p̄ti . iiii . moliñ . Tc̄ . nichil . m̄ . ii . runc̄ .
modo . iiii . an̄ . 7 . xxx . porc̄ . 7 . cc . ous̄ . 7 d̄ . 7 . vi . foc̄ dim̄ . car̄ . terræ .

168 b
iii . bord̄ . Semp . ii . car̄ . i . æccli⁄ . de . d̄ . ac̄ . Tc̄ ual . iiii . lib̄ . modo . vi ,

97 In PICKENHAM William holds ½ c. of land which Asford held before 1066.

    Then and now 2 villagers.

    Always 1 plough; woodland for 4 pigs; meadow, 2 acres; always 1 mill.

Value always 10s.

The Hundred of GALLOW

98 Toki held SCULTHORPE from Frederic's Holding before 1066, 3 c. of land.

    Always 12 villagers; 34 smallholders. Then 6 slaves, now 3.

    Then and later 3 ploughs, now 4. Always 5 men's ploughs; woodland for 20 pigs; meadow, 4 acres; 3 mills. When he acquired it 4 cobs, now 6. Then 6 head of cattle, now 20. Then 40 pigs, now 20. Then 100 sheep, now 400.

    Also 30 Freemen appertain to this manor (who) dwell (there) with all customary dues, 1½ c. of land.

    Always 4 ploughs.

    Also 2 other Freemen, at 40 acres, dwell in TOFTREES.

    Under these, 12 smallholders, 1 acre; meadow, 1½ acres; always 2 ploughs.

    1 church, 60 acres.

Value then £6; later (and) now 10. But it was at revenue (for) £15 but could not pay it. It has ½ league in length and ½ in width, tax of 6d.

    Also 12 wild mares,

value 12s.

    (Belonging) to the church, 60 acres.

99 Hugh (holds) BARSHAM (which) Toki held before 1066, 4 c. of land.

    Always 10 villagers; 26 smallholders. Then 4 slaves, now none.

    Then 4 ploughs in lordship, later none, now 2, but they could be restored. Then 5 men's ploughs, later none, now 3 and they could be restored. Woodland for 20 pigs; meadow, 3 acres; 4 mills. Then nothing, now 2 cobs. Now 4 head of cattle; 30 pigs; 200 sheep and a half.

    Also 6 Freemen, ½ c. of land.

    3 smallholders; always 2 ploughs.   168 b

    1 church, at 100 acres.

Value then £4; now 6.

& ħt dim lḡ in longo.& dim in lato.7 vi.d̄.de gelto.In ead̄ uilla.i.

liƀm hoēm de.i.car̄ terræ ꝓ mañ.7 fuit liƀata ꝓ tr̄a.Semp

xxi.bord̄.&.i.feru̅.7 manebaṭ i.ii.hallis.Tc̄.ii.car̄.7 p̄.nichil.

modo.dim̄.7 inf̄ hes.ii.car̄.7.ii.ac̄ p̄ti.ii.d̄.moliñ.Silua.ad

x.porc̄.7.vi.foc̄.de.vi.ac̄.terræ.modo.lxxx.ou̅s.7 xxx.porc̄.Tc̄

ual̄.xl.fol̄.7 p̄.m̄.l.fol̄.7 hæc terra redd.xii.d̄.de gelto.i ead̄ m̄fura.

feiner tenǁ
.i.æcclia.xii.ac̄.

Ⅴ In ead̄ villa ten.Toka ꝓ mañ.i.car̄ terræ.t.r.e̅.Sēper.iii.uill.

&.vii.bord̄.Tc̄.ii.feru̅.Tc̄.in d̄nio.i.car̄.7 p̄ nichil.modo.i.7 femp

hom.i.car̄.ii.ac̄.p̄ti.iii.7 d̄.moliñ.modo.ii.runc̄.&.iiii.añ.&.

viii.porc̄.lxxx.vi.ou̅s.7 xv.foc̄.de dim̄.car̄ terræ.7.ii.bord̄.Sēp

.i.car̄.i.ac̄ p̄ti.i.æcclia.viii.ac̄.&.dim̄ ac̄.p̄ti.

Ⅴ In fnaringes.ii.foc̄.7 in clipeftuna.iiii.7 in ketleftuna.viii.7 hn̄t

dim̄ car̄ terræ.Tc̄.iii.car̄.7 p̄ null.modo.iii.ii.ac̄.p̄ti.i.æcclia.

viii.ac̄.Tc̄ ual̄.xl.fol̄.modo.iii.liƀ.7 hæc tr̄a reddit.xii.d̄ de gelto

menfurata e̅ fupius.Id̄e ten&

Ⅴ In Waȓdenna ten lamƀtus.i.car̄ terræ qua̅ tenuer̄.ii.libi hoes

t.r.e.Semp.xvii.bord̄.Tc̄.ii.feru̅.Semp in d̄nio 7 inf̄ oēs.ii.car̄.

7 In creich.tenebat.i.ex iftis.i.aliu̅ liƀum hom.dę dim̄ car̄ terræ.

7 fub ipfis.vi.bord̄.& inf̄ eos.i.car̄.i.quaru̅.carr̄.eft in dominio.

.i.æcclia.v.ac̄.
modo.i.runc̄.&.v.porc̄.&.lx.ou̅s.Tc̄ ual̄.xx fol̄.modo.xvii.fol̄.

&.iiii.d̄.7 ħt in longo.iii.qr̄.&.ii.in lato.7 xii.d̄.in gelto.

Ⅴ In fulmoteftuna.ten&.t.r.e.Toka ꝓ mañ.ii.car̄ terræ.Semp

xx.ix.bord̄.Tc̄.ii.fer.femp in d̄nio.ii.car̄.& hom.iiii.car̄.filua

168 b

It has ½ league in length and ½ in width; tax of 6d.
In the same village 1 free man at 1 c. of land, as a manor: he was delivered for land.
Always 21 smallholders; 1 slave.
He dwelt in 2 halls. Then 2 ploughs; later nothing, now ½.
2 ploughs among the men; meadow, 2 acres; 2 half mills; woodland for 10 pigs.
Also 6 Freemen, at 6 acres of land. Now 80 sheep; 30 pigs.
1 church, 12 acres.
Value then 40s; later (and) now 50s.
This land pays tax of 12d. (It is) in the same measurement.

100 In the same village Toki held 1 c. of land as a manor before 1066. Rainer holds.
Always 3 villagers; 7 smallholders. Then 2 slaves.
Then 1 plough in lordship, later nothing, now 1. Always 1 men's plough; meadow, 2 acres; 3½ mills. Now 2 cobs; 4 head of cattle; 8 pigs; 86 sheep.
Also 15 Freemen, at ½ c. of land.
2 smallholders. Always 1 plough; meadow, 1 acre.
1 church, 8 acres. Meadow, ½ acre.

101 In (Little) SNORING 2 Freemen, in CLIPSTONE 4, in KETTLESTONE 8. They have ½ c. of land.
Then 3 ploughs, later none, now 3. Meadow, 2 acres.
1 church, 8 acres.
Value then 40s; now £3.
This land pays tax of 12d. It has been measured above. He also holds.

102 In WATERDEN Lambert holds 1 c. of land which 2 free men held before 1066.
Always 17 smallholders. Then 2 slaves.
Always in lordship and among them all 2 ploughs.
In CREAKE 1 of those held 1 other free man, at ½ c. of land.
Under these, 6 smallholders. Between them 1 plough; 1 of which ploughs is in lordship. Now 1 cob; 5 pigs; 60 sheep.
1 church, 5 acres.
Value then 20s; now 17s 4d.
It has 3 furlongs in length and 2 in width, 12d in tax.

103 In FULMODESTON Toki held 2 c. of land as a manor before 1066.
Always 29 smallholders. Then 2 slaves.
Always 2 ploughs in lordship; 4 men's ploughs; woodland

ad . xxx . pocos . xvi . ač pti . Tč . i . moliñ . Semp . i . runč . 7 . v . añ ؛ 7

xxiii ، porč . Qn̄ receꝑ . c . lxxx . ōus . m̄ nuꝉ . Tč xl . caꝑ . m̄ . nuꝉ.

m̄ . i . uas . apū . i . æcclia finę ter�**ꝥa** . Galter teñ . Tč ual xl . foꝉ.

modo . lx . foꝉ . 7 tota ħt . iiii . q̄r in longo ، 7 . iii . in lato . & reddit

xii . d . de gelto

¶ In crokeſtona teñ Toka . t . r . e . i . car terræ . Tč . iiii . libi ħoes . Tč
     . i . eccl̄ia fine tr̄a .
. i . car . & . iiii . ač . pti . & ē in p̄tio fupius . 7 ħt . ii . q̄r in longo . &
. i . in ſato . & . xii . d . de gelto . Idē teñ&

¶ In Bruneham torp . teñ . Galf . ii ، car terre quas tenuit Tocha
. t . r . e . ii . car terræ . Semp . x . uiꝉꝉ . 7 xx . ix . bord . Tč . iii . feru؛

     Semp . in dominio . ii . car . & tč hominū . v . carr.

     modo . ii . poſſ reſtaura**te** . Silua . ad̄ viii ، porč . i . ač . prati.

     Tercia parte . i . moꝉ . Tč . ii . runč . modo . vi . & . i . afin.

Tč ، iiii . añ . 7 modo . 7 xxviii . porč . 7 . ccc . xl . & . v . ōus . 7 ix . foč . jacent
     . i . ecclia . lxxt . ač .
huic mañ . de . i . car terræ . 7 ħt . ii . car . Tč ual . lx . foꝉ . 7 p̄ ، modo . iiii.

lib . 7 ħt . in longo . i . ꝉg . & d . & . i . ꝉg . in lato . 7 de xx . foꝉ . reddit . iii . foꝉ.

de gelto . quicūq، ibi teneat ;
                                 Petrus Walouienſis
¶ In reieburh . i . foč . 7 in ſtabrige . aꝉ . de xxx . ač . terre . 7 . i . car . i . ač
prati dim̄ æcclia . iii . ač . 7 ual . v . foꝉ . & . iiii . d.

HVNDRET DE BRODERCROS . In Rudchā teñ& . Rad̄ . iiii.

car terræ quas tenuit toka . t . r . e . Semp . vi . uiꝉꝉ . 7 xvi . bord.

Tč . iii . feru . modo . i . Tč . iii . car . modo . i . Semp . hom . i . carr.

iiii . ač pti . ii . moliñ . i . ſaliñ . femp . xi . añ . 7 tč . xxx . porč.
                                                      ii . ecclia lx . ač .
modo . xxviii . Tč . cccc . ōus . modo . c 7 ꝉxxx . Tč . xiiii . eq̄ . m̄ . xxii.

                                                          ꝉeque ſaluat؛

for 30 pigs; meadow, 16 acres. Then 1 mill. Always 1 cob; 169 a
5 head of cattle; 23 pigs. When he acquired it 180 sheep,
now none. Then 40 goats, now none. Now 1 beehive.
1 church without land.
Walter holds.
Value then 40s; now 60s.
The whole has 4 furlongs in length and 3 in width; it pays tax
of 12d.

104 In CROXTON Toki held 1 c. of land before 1066.
Then 4 free men.
Then 1 plough; meadow, 4 acres.
It is in the valuation above.
1 church without land.
It has 2 furlongs in length and 1 in width; tax of 12d. He
also holds.

105 In BURNHAM THORPE Walter holds 2 c. of land which Toki held
before 1066, 2 c. of land.
Always 10 villagers; 29 smallholders. Then 3 slaves.
Always 2 ploughs in lordship. Then 5 men's ploughs, now 2,
they could have been restored. Woodland for 8 pigs;
meadow, 1 acre; one-third of 1 mill. Then 2 cobs, now 6.
1 ass. Then and now 4 head of cattle; 28 pigs; 345 sheep.
9 Freemen appertain to this manor, at 1 c. of land.
They have 2 ploughs.
1 church, 80 acres.
Value then 60s and later; now £4.
It has 1½ leagues in length and 1 league in width; at 20s it pays
tax of 3s, whoever holds there.

106 In (Little) RYBURGH 1 Freeman, and in STIBBARD Peter of Valognes
(holds) another, at 30 acres of land. 1 plough; meadow, 1 acre.
½ church, 3 acres.
Value 5s 4d.

The Hundred of BROTHERCROSS
107 In RUDHAM Ralph holds 3 c. of land which Toki held before 1066.
Always 6 villagers; 16 smallholders. Then 3 slaves, now 1.
Then 3 ploughs, now 1. Always 1 men's plough; meadow,
4 acres; 2 mills; 1 salt-house; always 11 head of cattle.
Then 30 pigs, now 28. Then 400 sheep, now 180. Then
14 horses, now 22 wild mares.
2 churches, 60 acres.

⌐Huic mañ ptiñ . I . berewita bacheſtorp .¹.caɍ terræ.Semp . III.

borđ .&.I.caɍ.Semper.II.rũnc̄.&.III.añ.7.IIII.porc̄.Tc̄ LXXX.

oūs.modo.c.7 alia berewita houtuna.de.I.caɍ terræ.Semp

XIII.ſoc̄.cū ōi conſuetuđ.Semp in dñio.I.carɍ.& hominū.I.

carɍ.Tc̄.IIII.porc̄.Tc̄.LX.oūs.modo.XL.7 XXV.ſoc̄.7 In Rude-

ham jacent.huic mañ.de.I.caɍ terræ & dim̄.7 Semp inŧ eos.IIII.

caɍ.7 In houtuna.I.ſoc̄.de.XXX.ac̄.7 Sub ipſis.III.uiłł.7.III.borđ.

Semp.I.caɍ.I.æcclia.ſine tɍa.Radulfus teñ.7 in beneɯara.IIII.

ſoc̄.teñ.Rađ.de.LX.ac̄ terræ.&.III.borđ.Semp.I.caɍ.7 dim̄ ecclia

7 In Sciſterna.teñ.iđ.Rađ.IIII.ſoc̄.de.XL.ac̄.Tc̄.7 p̄.I.caɍ.m̄.đ.

7 in helgatuna.teñ.iđ.I.ſoc̄.de.XII.ac̄.& dim̄ caɍ.h̄ totū

uał.t.r.e.VIII.lib̄.m̄.x.lib̄.in dñio s̄ xx.soł.& h̄t totū

Rudehā.I.łg in longo.&.I.in lato.7.IIII.soł.7.III.đ de gelto.

h̄ŧ totū bene mara.III.qɍ in longo.7.II.in lato.&.VI.đ.& ob de gł.

⌐In Rudehā teñ Lambŧ.I.caɍ terræ quā tenuit.I.lib̄.hō.t.r.e.

Semp.I.uiłł.&.XIIII.borđ.Tc̄.III.ſerū.m̄.II Tc̄ in dñio.

II.caɍ.modo.I.Semp.hom̄.I.caɍ.dim̄ ac̄ p̄ti.Tc̄.IIII.rũnc̄.

modo.v.7.I.mulus.Tc̄.VI.añ.m̄.XI.Tc̄.XVI.porc̄.m̄.XX.Tc̄

cccc.7 L.oūs.modo.ccc.Jacent huic mañ.XVIII.ſoc̄.in eađ carɍ.

Semp.II.caɍ.Tc̄ uał XX.soł.m̄.XXX.soł.h̄ fuit ſibi libata p tɍa.

huic mañ ptin&.I.berewita.Scideſterna.de.XXX.ac̄.dim̄.carɍ.

7.III.borđ.Tc̄ uał.v.soł.&.IIII.đ.m̄ redđ.XII.soł.

⌐In tateſſete teñ Reinerus.I.caɍ terræ quā tenuit.Toka.t.r.e.

Semp.XV.borđ.7.I.ſerū.ſemp.in dominio.I.caɍ.7 hom̄.I.caɍ.I.ac̄ p̄ti.

108 To this manor belongs 1 outlier, BAGTHORPE, at 1 c. of land.
    Always 3 smallholders; 1 plough. Always 2 cobs; 3 head of cattle; 4 pigs. Then 80 sheep, now 100.

Also another outlier, HOUGHTON, (which) Simon holds, at 1 c. of land.
    Always 13 Freemen with all customary dues.
    Always 1 plough in lordship; 1 men's plough. Then 4 pigs. Then 60 sheep, now 40.

Also in RUDHAM 25 Freemen appertain to this manor, at 1½ c. of land. Always 4 ploughs between them. Also in HOUGHTON 1 Freeman, at 30 acres.
    Under these, 3 villagers; 3 smallholders. Always 1 plough.
    1 church without land.
    Ralph holds.

Also in BARMER Ralph holds 4 Freemen, at 60 acres of land.
    3 smallholders; always 1 plough. ½ church.

In SYDERSTONE Ralph also holds 4 Freemen, at 40 acres.
    Then and later 1 plough, now ½.

In HELHOUGHTON he also holds 1 Freeman, at 12 acres; ½ plough. Value of all this before 1066 £8; now £10. In lordship are 20s.
    The whole of Rudham has 1 league in length and 1 in width, tax of 4s 3d. The whole of Barmer has 3 furlongs in length and 2 in width, tax of 6½d.

109 In RUDHAM Lambert holds 1 c. of land, which 1 free man held before 1066.
    Always 1 villager; 14 smallholders. Then 3 slaves, now 2.
    Then 2 ploughs in lordship, now 1. Always 1 men's plough; meadow, ½ acre. Then 4 cobs, now 5. 1 mule. Then 6 head of cattle, now 11. Then 16 pigs, now 20. Then 450 sheep, now 300.
    18 Freemen appertain to this manor in the same c.
    Always 2 ploughs.

Value then 20s; now 30s. This was delivered to him for land.
To this manor belongs 1 outlier, SYDERSTONE, at 30 acres; ½ plough.
    3 smallholders.
Value then 5s 4d; now it pays 12s.

110 In TATTERSETT Rainer holds 1 c. of land, which Toki held before 1066.
    Always 15 smallholders; 1 slave.
    Always 1 plough in lordship; 1 men's plough; meadow, 1 acre;

ıı.molini.Tc̄.ı.runc̄.m̄.ıı.7.v.an̄.&.vı.porc̄.Tc̄.xʟ.ous.

modo.ʟxxx.ıı.æcclie.xʟ.ac̄.7 xıɪɪɪ.foc̄.p̄tin& huic man̄.

de ʟxıx.ac̄.Semp.vı.borđ.7.ıɪ.car̄.ı.ac̄.p̄ti.Tc̄ uaɫ.x.foɫ.modo.

ʟx.foɫ.7 h̄t dim̄ lḡ in longo.&.ıɪɪɪ.qr̄ in lato.7 xıɪɪ.đ.de gelto.

∨In helgetuna.ı.foc̄.de.ʟx.ac̄.Semp.vɪɪɪ.borđ.7.ı.car̄.ı.ac̄

7 dim̄ p̄ti.Tc̄.dim̄ molin̄.Silua ad.vɪɪɪ.porc̄.Semp uaɫ.v.foɫ.

H̄ terra eſt ſup̄i ſcripta de fedo.frederici.

∨In Sciraforda.ı.car̄ terræ tenuer̄.vı.liƀi hōes.t.r.e.Semp.vı.

borđ.Semp.ıɪ.car̄.ıɪ.ac̄.7 dim̄.p̄ti.Tc̄ uaɫ.x.foɫ.modo reddit

xx.7 h̄t.ıɪɪ.qr̄ in longo.7.ıɪɪ.in lato.7 ıx.đ & obolū.in gelto.h̄ ē

p̄ eſcangio de laquis.

∨In reieborh.vɪɪɪ.foc̄.ten̄ Petrus.de.ı.car̄ terræ.Semp.ı.uiɫt ı.

7.vı.borđ.7.ıɪ.car̄.Silua ad.xx.porc̄.ıɪ.ac̄ p̄ti.ı.molin̄.Semp

uaɫ.xx.foɫ.h̄ ē de fedo frederici.

∨In hamatuna.ıɪɪɪ.liƀi hōes.de.dim̄ car̄ terræ.7.ıɪɪɪ.borđ.7.ı.car̄.

.ı.æcclia.de.ı.ac̄.Tc̄ uaɫ.v.foɫ.modo.ıɪɪ.foɫ.7 h̄t.ıɪ.qr̄ in longo.7

in lato.&.ıɪɪɪ.đ.& oboɫ.de gelto.

∨HVNDRET.DE HOLT.In Wiuentona ten̄ Wiɫɫm̄.ıɪ.car̄

træ quas tenuit turgrim.t.r.e p̄ man̄.Semp.ıɪ.uiɫt.&.xx.

ıɪ.borđ.7.ı.foc̄.de.xɪɪ.ac̄.terræ.~~7 xxɪɪ.borđ~~.7.ıɪ.fer̄.7.ıɪ.car̄

in dominio.7 hom̄.ıɪ.car̄.ıɪ.ac̄.p̄ti.dim̄ molin̄.tc̄.vı.porc̄.m̄.vı.

Tc̄ ʟx.ous.m̄.xxx.7 đ.foc̄.de.ıɪ.ac̄.Tc̄ uaɫ.xʟ.foɫ.modo.ʟx.foɫ.

∨In burſtuna.xıɪɪɪ.foc̄.q̄s Toka ten̄.t.r.e.đ.car̄.terræ.7.ıɪɪ. ^{de feudo frederici ten̄.}

borđ.Semp.ıɪɪɪ.car̄.Silua ad.xx.porc̄.7 uaɫ.xvı.foɫ.

2 mills. Then 1 cob, now 2. 5 head of cattle; 6 pigs. Then 40 sheep, now 80.

2 churches, 40 acres.

Also 14 Freemen belong to this manor, at 69 acres. Always 6 smallholders; 2 ploughs; meadow, 1 acre.

Value then 10s; now 60s.

It has ½ league in length and 4 furlongs in width, tax of 13d.

111 In HELHOUGHTON 1 Freeman, at 60 acres.

Always 8 smallholders;

1 plough; meadow, 1½ acres. Then ½ mill; woodland for 8 pigs.

Value always 5s.

This land is listed above, of Frederic's Holding.

112 In SHEREFORD 6 free men held 1 c. of land before 1066.

Always 6 smallholders. Always 2 ploughs; meadow, 2½ acres.

1 church, 12 acres.

Value then 10s; now it pays 20.

It has 3 furlongs in length and 3 in width, 9½d in tax. This is by exchange of Lewes.

113 In (Great) RYBURGH Peter holds 8 Freemen, at 1 c. of land.

Always 1 villager; 6 smallholders.

2 ploughs; woodland for 20 pigs; meadow, 2 acres; 1 mill.

Value always 20s.

This is of Frederic's Holding.

114 In HEMPTON 4 free men, at ½ c. of land. 4 smallholders; 1 plough.

1 church, at 1 acre.

Value then 5s; now 3s.

It has 2 furlongs in length and in width, tax of 4½d.

The Hundred of HOLT

115 In WIVETON William holds 2 c. of land, which Thorgrim held before 1066 as a manor.

Always 2 villagers; 22 smallholders. 1 Freeman, at 12 acres of land. 2 slaves.

2 ploughs in lordship; 2 men's ploughs; meadow, 2 acres; ½ mill. Then 6 pigs, now 6. Then 60 sheep, now 30.

Also half a Freeman, at 2 acres.

Value then 40s; now 60s.

116 In BRISTON he holds of Frederic's Holding 14 Freemen whom Toki held before 1066, ½ c. of land.

3 smallholders. Always 4 ploughs; woodland for 20 pigs.

Value 16s.

HVNDRET.DE GRENE HOGA. Eſt gamera ten& Eluoſt.

.I.liƀ homo.t̄.r̄.ē.& & fuit liƀata frederio ꝓ terra ad pſiçiendū mañ.
ſuos dim̄ car̄ terræ.ſemp.III.borđ.&.I.ſoc̄.de XII.ac̄.& ē apꝑtiata
in barſahā.

꒦In holcham ten&.Galter̄ dīmidiā car̄ terræ.ſemp.I.borđ.& ꝑtiñ&
ad brunahā.& ē de feudo frederici.& ibi ē apꝑtiata.

꒦*ERPINHAM.NORTH.HVNDRET*

꒦In giningeham.teñ.Ratho.I.liƀ homo.II.car̄ terræ.Semp
XII.uiⱦi.7 XL.borđ.Tc̄.II.ſeru.modo.I.Tc̄ &.p̄.II.car̄.in dominio.
&.modo.III.Semp.IIII.car̄ hom̄.Silua ad LXXX.porc̄.XII.ac̄ p̄ti.
Tc̄ 7 poſt.II.molin.7 modo.IIII.Tc̄.II.runc̄.Tc̄.XI.equæ fiⱡuaticæ.
m̄.VII.modo.VIII.añ.Tc̄.XXX.porc̄.m̄.XL.Tc̄.XXX.oūs.modo c.LX.
Semp XXX.cap̄.7 XXIII.ſoc̄.de XLVIII.ac̄ terræ.Semp.III.car̄.
& dim̄.I.æcclia.XXVIII.ac̄.

꒦Siſtran.ten&.I.liƀ hō de ſtigando archi epō.ꝓ m̄.I.car̄ terræ.Semp
VIII.uiⱦt.&.I.ſeru.Tc̄ & poſt.I.car̄ in dominio.&.modo.II.&.I.car̄
hominū.&.v.ſoc̄.de XXI.ac̄ terræ.Semp.I.car̄.I.ac̄ & đ.p̄ti.Sēp
II.runc̄.Tc̄.III.añ.7.III.porc̄.hoc liƀaū.Waleram ad pſiciendum
manerium.gimingeham.

꒦Ranapatone.teñ.I.liƀ hō.I.car̄.terræ.Semp.X.uiⱦt.&.v.borđ.
Tc̄.I.ſeru.modo.II.Tc̄ & p̄.I.car̄ in dūio.& m̄.II.Semp.I.car̄
hom̄ II.ac̄ p̄ti.7 XIII.ſoc̄ de.III.car̄.t̄r̄e.&.I.borđ.Semp.III.
car̄ & dim̄.&.IIII.añ.&.IIII.porc̄.& fuit liƀatū ad pſiciendū
gimingehā.& giming.Tc̄ ual.XL.ſoⱡ.&.p̄.IIII.liƀ.m̄.VIII.liƀ.

꒦Siſtran ual tc̄ & p̄.XX.ſoⱡ.modo.LX.Tc̄ & p̄ ual& kanā
pat̄.XX.ſoⱡ.modo.LX.& hoc totū fuit liƀatū ꝓ uno mañ.de
.IIII.car̄ terræ.& hoc totū ħt II.lḡ in longo.&.VIII.per.&.v.
pedes.&.in lato.I.lḡ.7 XII.perc̄.7.IIII.pedes.& de gelto.v.ſoⱡ.I.deñ
quicumq̨ ibi teneat.

The Hundred of (North) GREENHOE

117 Alwold, 1 free man, held EGMERE before 1066, and it was delivered to Frederic for land to make up his manors, ½ c. of land.
  Always 3 smallholders; 1 Freeman, at 12 acres.
  It is assessed in Barsham.

118 In HOLKHAM Walter holds ½ c. of land.
  Always 1 smallholder.
  It belongs to Burnham, it is of Frederic's Holding, and it is assessed there.

NORTH ERPINGHAM Hundred

119 In GIMINGHAM Rathi, 1 free man, holds 2 c. of land.
  Always 12 villagers; 40 smallholders. Then 2 slaves, now 1.
  Then and later 2 ploughs in lordship, now 3. Always 4 men's ploughs; woodland for 80 pigs; meadow, 12 acres. Then and later 2 mills, now 4. Then 2 cobs. Then 11 wild mares, now 7. Now 8 head of cattle. Then 30 pigs, now 40. Then 30 sheep, now 160; always 30 goats.
  Also 23 Freemen, at 48 acres of land; always 3½ ploughs.
  1 church, 28 acres.

120 1 free man held SIDESTRAND from Archbishop Stigand as a manor, 1 c. of land.
  Always 8 villagers; 1 slave.
  Then and later 1 plough in lordship, now 2. 1 men's plough.
  Also 5 Freemen, at 21 acres of land. Always 1 plough; meadow, 1½ acres; always 2 cobs. Then 3 head of cattle; 3 pigs.
  Waleran delivered this to make up the manor of Gimingham.

121 1 free man holds KNAPTON, 1 c. of land.
  Always 10 villagers; 5 smallholders. Then 1 slave, now 2.
  Then and later 1 plough in lordship, now 2. Always 1 men's plough; meadow, 2 acres.
  Also 13 Freemen, at 3 c. of land; 1 smallholder. Always 3½ ploughs; 4 head of cattle; 4 pigs.
  It was delivered to make up Gimingham.
  Value of Gimingham then 40s; later £4; now £8.
  Value of Sidestrand then and later 20s; now 60.
  Value of Knapton then and later 20s; now 60.
  All this was delivered as 1 manor, at 4 c. of land. All this has 2 leagues and 8 perches and 5 feet in length, and 1 league, 12 perches and 4 feet in width, tax of 5s 1d, whoever holds there.

In torp teñ . Rað . II . car̄ . terræ . quas tenuit . I . libum hõem
de ſtigand . t . r . e . Semp . IIII . uilli . 7 XXIIII . borð . & . I . ſer . Sẽp
II . car̄ in dñio . 7 . III . car̄ hom . Silu ad . XL . porc̄ . II . ac̄ prati .
& . II . moliñ . I . uas apũ . Sẽp . II . runc̄ . & . III . añ . Tc̄ . VI . porc̄ .
modo . XI . 7 modo . L . ous̄ . Semp XX . cap̄ . & . V . ſoc̄ . de . XXXII .
ac̄ . terræ . & . hñt . I . car̄ . Tc̄ & p⁹ ual XL . ſol . 7 modo . VIII . lib̄ .

    ^{7 . I . æcclia . x . ac̄ .}

In muleſlai . teñ . griketel . I . lib̄ hõ . xxx . ac̄ . terre . 7 . II . borð . Sẽp
. I . car̄ . & adhuc teñ . Will . in eað . III . libõs hões . edri . t . r . e .
de . X . ac̄ . terræ . & . I . car̄ . Semp reddit . IIII . ſol . I . æcclia . de . XII . ac̄ .

In trunchet . III . libi hõies . uñ heroldi . alter Rað ſtalr̄ . tercius
ketelli . LXXXX . ac̄ terre . & . XIIII . borð . Semp . V . car̄ int̄ eos . I . æclia . X . ac̄ .
Silua . ad . III . porc̄ . III . ac̄ p̄ti . ſemp ual . XXX . ſol . Et adhuc
ſt ibi . VI . libi homines edrici . t . r . e . de . XXX . IIII . ac̄ terræ . & . II .
car̄ . & . II . ac̄ & dim p̄ti . Semp ual . VII . ſol . & . IIII . ð .

In repes . II . libi homines . edrici . teñ . XXX . ac̄ terræ . Sẽp . II .
uilli . II . car̄ . & . IIII . borð . Semp ual . VI . ſol .

In norrepes . I . lib̄ hõ Ketelli . de . XXX . ac̄ . terræ . Semp
. II . uilli . & . V . borð . Silua . de . V . porc̄ . Semp . I . car̄ . II . ac̄ p̄ti
II . moliñ . I . ecclia . de . XVIII . ac̄ . Semp ual . X . ſol .

171 b

In Inſiſtran . II . libi homines . unus edrici . alter . almar⁹ . de . LX . ac̄ .
terræ . ſemp . V . uilt̄ . 7 . V . borð . 7 III . car̄ . I . ac̄ p̄ti . Silua . III . porc̄ .
ſemp ual . X . ſol .

122　In THORPE (Market) Ralph holds 2 c. of land which 1 free man held from Stigand before 1066.

>　Always 4 villagers; 24 smallholders; 1 slave.

>　Always 2 ploughs in lordship; 3 men's ploughs; woodland for 40 pigs; meadow, 2 acres; 2 mills; 1 beehive. Always 2 cobs; 3 head of cattle. Then 6 pigs, now 11. Now 50 sheep; always 20 goats.

>　Also 5 Freemen, at 32 acres of land; they have 1 plough.

>　1 church, 10 acres.

Value then and later 40s; now £8.

123　In MUNDESLEY 1 free man, Grimketel, holds 30 acres of land.

>　2 smallholders; always 1 plough.

Further William holds in the same 3 free men, of Edric's before 1066, at 10 acres of land. 1 plough.

It has always paid 4s.

>　1 church, at 12 acres.

124　In TRUNCH 3 free men: 1 of Harold's, another of Ralph the Constable's, the third of Ketel's, 90 acres of land.

>　14 smallholders. Always 5 ploughs among them.

>　1 church, 10 acres.

>　Woodland for 3 pigs; meadow, 3 acres.

Value always 30s.

Further there are 6 free men, of Edric's before 1066, at 34 acres of land. 2 ploughs; meadow, 2½ acres.

Value always 7s 4d.

125　In REPPS 2 free men of Edric's hold 30 acres of land.

>　Always 2 villagers; 2 ploughs; 4 smallholders.

Value always 6s.

126　In NORTHREPPS 1 free man of Ketel's, at 30 acres of land.

>　Always 2 villagers; 5 smallholders.

>　Woodland at 5 pigs. Always 1 plough; meadow, 2 acres; 2 mills.

>　1 church, at 18 acres.

Value always 10s.

127　In SIDESTRAND 2 free men: 1 of Edric's, the other of A(e)lmer's, 171 b at 60 acres of land.

>　Always 5 villagers; 5 smallholders.

>　3 ploughs; meadow, 1 acre; woodland, 3 pigs.

Value always 10s.

ⅤIn ſutrepes 7 norhrepes . ⅤⅢ . libi homines . ⅡⅠ . aluoldi . abbis . ⅴ ra -
- thoñ degiming̅ . Ⅰ . oſbti . de . ⅩⅤⅠ . ac̅ . & hñt . ⅡⅠ . car̅ . Semp ual̅ . ⅠⅠⅠⅠ .
ſol̅ . Ⅰ . ecclia . ⅩⅡ . ac̅ . 7 tor h̅t . dim̅ lg̅ lg̅ in longo . 7 . ⅠⅠ . perc̅ .
& . ⅠⅠⅠⅠ . qr̅ . & . ⅠⅠⅠⅠ . pedes . in lato . & de gelto . ⅤⅠ . đ . & obolu̅ & fer -
ding . & h̅ tota terra fuit libata . W . p̵ . Ⅰ . mañ . ⅴ . car̅ terræ
Ⅴ G In muleſlai 7 in truchet calupniatur . R . mal& Ⅴ in torp .
ⅩⅤⅠⅠⅠⅠ . libos hoes . tres qr comdtione . 7 alio de o̅i conſuetudiñ .
Ⅴ Gerſam ten& Willm̅ . ⅡⅠ . car̅ terræ . quas tenuit Ulſtanus
. Ⅰ . lib h̅o Semp . ⅠⅠⅠⅠ . uill̅ . 7 ⅤⅠ . bord̅ . & . Ⅰ . ſeru̅ . Semp . ⅡⅠ . car̅
in dominio . 7 . ⅠⅠⅠⅠ . car̅ . hom̅ . ⅩⅠ . ſoc̅ . ⅩⅩⅩⅤ . ac̅ . 7 . Ⅰ . car̅ . ⅡⅠ . ac̅ p̅ti .
. Ⅰ . mol̅ . & iſti ptin& . Ⅰ . beruita . aldeburc . de . ⅬⅩ . ac̅ . terræ .
Semp . ⅠⅠⅠ . uilli̅ . & . ⅠⅠⅠⅠ . bord̅ . & . Ⅰ . car̅ & dim̅ in̅r eos . & in ſalhus
ⅩⅩⅩ . ac̅ . Ⅰ . uill̅ . & . Ⅰ . bord̅ . ⅩⅬ . cap̅ . 7 . ⅠⅠⅠ . ſoc̅ . ⅩⅤ . ac̅ . dim̅ car̅ . Sep̅
ual̅ . ⅠⅠⅠⅠ . lib̅ . & . h̅t . ⅤⅠⅠⅠⅠ . qr̅ . in longo . 7 ⅤⅠ . in lato . & de gelto . ⅤⅠⅠ . đ .
Et ē de feudo frederici . Et aldeburg . h̅t . ⅤⅠⅠⅠ . qr̅ in longo
7 . ⅠⅠⅠ . in lato . & de gelto . ⅴ . đ . & obolu̅ .
Ⅴ In ſurſtede . Ⅰ . dim̅ lib̅ homo đ . ⅩⅤ . ac̅ terræ . 7 . Ⅰ . bord̅ . Ⅰ . uirga
p̅ti . & dim̅ mol̅ . Semp dim̅ car̅ . Tc̅ & p̵ . ⅡⅠ . ſol̅ . 7 . ⅤⅠ . đ . & m̅
ⅠⅠⅠ . ſol̅ .
Ⅴ In Almartune ten̅ . Willm̅ . ⅡⅠ . car̅ . terræ quas tenuit Viulfus
. Ⅰ . lib̅ h̅o edrici . Semp . ⅠⅠⅠ . uilli̅ . & . ⅩⅢ . bord̅ . Tc̅ . ⅡⅠ . ſer̅ .

172 a

Tc̅ 7 . p̵ . ⅡⅠ . car̅ . in dñio . modo . Ⅰ . Semp . ⅡⅠ . car̅ hom̅ . Silua ad . ⅠⅠⅠⅠ .
porc̅ . ⅡⅠ . ac̅ & đ p̅ti . Tc̅ . Ⅰ . runc̅ . Tc̅ . ⅠⅠⅠ . añ . Tc̅ . ⅠⅩ . porc̅ . m̅ . ⅠⅠⅠ .
Tc̅ . ⅩⅬ . ous̅ . m̅ . ⅩⅤ . Tc̅ ⅬⅩ . cap̅ . dimid ecclia . Ⅹ . ac̅ . 7 duo ſoc̅
de ⅩⅩ . ac̅ terræ . dimidia . car̅ . Ⅰ . ac̅ prati . Tunc ual&
ⅩⅩ . ſol̅ . 7 p̵ 7 modo ⅩⅬ . Et hab& . ⅠⅩ . qr̅ in longo . & . ⅤⅠ .
in lato . 7 de gelto . ⅤⅠⅠⅠ . den̅ . 7 . ⅠⅠⅠ . ferding . & hoc eſt ma -
- ner̅ . de feudo frederici .

128 In SOUTHREPPS and NORTHREPPS 8 free men: 2 of Abbot Alfwold's, 5 of Rathi's of Gimingham, 1 of Osbert's, at 16 acres.
They have 2 ploughs.
Value always 4s.
1 church, 12 acres.
The whole has ½ league and 2 perches in length and 4 furlongs and 4 feet in width, tax of 6½d and half a farthing.
All this land was delivered to W(illiam) as 1 manor, 5 c. of land (belonging) in Thorpe (Market).

129 G In MUNDESLEY and in TRUNCH R(obert) Malet claims 19 free men, 3 in patronage and the others with all customary dues.

130 William holds GRESHAM, 2 c. of land, which 1 free man, Wulfstan, held.
Always 4 villagers; 6 smallholders; 1 slave.
Always 2 ploughs in lordship; 4 men's ploughs.
11 Freemen, 35 acres; 1 plough; meadow, 2 acres; 1 mill.
To this belongs 1 outlier, ALDBOROUGH, at 60 acres of land.
Always 3 villagers; 4 smallholders;
1½ ploughs among them.
Also in SALTHOUSE 30 acres.
1 villager; 1 smallholder; 40 goats.
Also 3 Freemen, 15 acres; ½ plough.
Value always £4.
It has 9 furlongs in length and 6 in width, tax of 7d. It is of Frederic's Holding.
And Aldborough has 8 furlongs in length and 3 in width, tax of 5½d.

131 In SUSTEAD 1 half of a free man, at 15 acres of land.
1 smallholder; meadow, 1 rood; ½ mill; always ½ plough.
[Value] then and later 2s 6d; now 3s.

132 In AYLMERTON William holds 2 c. of land which Wigulf, 1 free man of Edric's, held.
Always 3 villagers; 13 smallholders. Then 2 slaves.
Then and later 2 ploughs in lordship, now 1. Always 2 men's 172 a ploughs; woodland for 4 pigs; meadow, 2½ acres. Then 1 cob. Then 3 head of cattle. Then 9 pigs, now 3. Then 40 sheep, now 15. Then 60 goats.
½ church, 10 acres.
Also 2 Freemen, at 20 acres of land; ½ plough; meadow, 1 acre.
Value then 20s; later and now 40.
It has 9 furlongs in length and 6 in width, tax of 8¾d. This is a manor of Frederic's Holding.

V DE ESCANGIO.LEWES. In berningeham tenet
turoldus xxx . aċ . terræ quas tenuit . 1 . liƀ hom̄ hem.
Ketelli . t . r . e . Semp . 111 . bordarij . 7 . 1 . carr . 7 dimidia . aċ . prati . & ibi sunt . x . liƀi homines . alwini cil.
t . r . e . de . xxviii . aċ terræ . Semper . 11 . car.

V In Plumestede ten& id̄ . Turoldus . 1 . liƀum homin̄.
de . x11 . aċ . terræ . Semp . 1 . car . Silua ad . x . porc.
Tċ 7 p̄ . x . sol . modo xx . hos calumpniatur drogo
de befrerere . p̄ homagio tan̄tu.

V In Vltretune ten̄ id̄ . 1111 . bord . Semp dimidia car.
de xvi . aċ.

V In hamingeham ten& . id̄ . 111 . bord . de . xvi . aċ . & . ð.
car . & . 1 . soċ . de . 111 . aċ . appreciati . sunt . Om̄s eccliæ
de tr̄a Willmi de Warena app̄ciate sunt . cū manerijs.

HVNDRET . DE *DROS CROS* . helgatuna ten&
Willmus de Warena . de feudo frederici . 1 . liƀ homo.
id̄o qd̄ ante cessor ej̄ ita tenuit . quod non poss&

172 b

recedere a tr̄a . nisi licencia illius . & hundret hoc testat.
& quidam homo . drogonis . de bevraria franco n̄oe
calumpniatur illam ad feudū . domini sui . de dono
regis . de liƀatione . dice∫ . quod ante cessor ej̄ tenuerit.
heinfridus . scilic& tp̄r . frederi . & p̄ eū tenuit drogo 7 hund
testatur h̄ . quod ipsi tenuer̄ . sed h̄ . n̄ uid . in breue . nec liƀatore
HVNDRET . *GILHOV* . In norbarsan qd̄ ten& . W . de Warena . ten& heraldus . 11 . liƀos homines . de . 1 . car terræ
p̄tinentes ad faganahā . & . in ten& . W . s& h̄oes sui nesci-
unt qmodo . & hund testatur eos . Willemo qd̄ ex eis est
saisitus . Sed h̄o reḡ offert judiciū . qd̄ p̄tinebant . t . r . e.
ad faganaham . man̄ . regis.

OF THE LEWES EXCHANGE

133 In (North) BARNINGHAM Thorold holds 30 acres of land, which
1 free man of Ketel's held before 1066.
   Always 3 smallholders; 1 plough; meadow, ½ acre.
   Also there are 10 free men of Young A(i)lwin's before 1066, at
   28 acres of land. Always 2 ploughs.

134 In PLUMSTEAD Thorold also holds 1 free man, at 12 acres of land.
   Always 1 plough; woodland for 10 pigs.
   [Value] then and later 10s; now 20.
   Drogo of Beuvriere claims these, for homage only.

135 He also holds in WOLTERTON 4 smallholders; always ½ plough;
at 16 acres.

136 Also in BANNINGHAM 3 smallholders, at 16 acres; ½ plough. Also
1 Freeman, at 3 acres. They have been assessed.
   All the churches of the land of William of Warenne have been
assessed with the manors.

The Hundred of BROTHERCROSS

137 William of Warenne holds HELHOUGHTON, of Frederic's Holding.
   1 free man (whom he holds) in the same way as his predecessor
held him so that he could not withdraw from his land unless by   172 b
his permission, and the Hundred testifies to this. And a certain
man of Drogo of Beuvriere, Frank by name, claims it as part of
his lord's Holding, of the King's gift by delivery, saying that his
predecessor, Humphrey, held it, that is in the time of Frederic,
and after him Drogo held it. The Hundred testifies to this, that
they held, but it has not seen this in a writ nor the delivery.

GALLOW Hundred

138 In NORTH BARSHAM which W(illiam) of Warenne holds, Harold
held 2 free men, at 1 c. of land, belonging to Fakenham, and now
W(illiam) holds them; but his men do not know how, and the
Hundred testifies that they are William's, because he had taken
possession of them. But a King's man offers judicial ordeal that
they belonged before 1066 to Fakenham, a manor of the King's.

TERRA Rogeri bigoti In Tedfort ħt Roḡ in dño ꝗetam ab
omī confuetudinē. cui adjacebant. t. r̃. e. ii. car. trǣ. 7 m̃ fimiliꞇ. Sēp. ii. caꞧ in
dño. xx. borđ. ii. feꞧ. i. moꞇ. xiii. aꞇ p̃ti. 7. xxx. aꞇ trǣ. ibi ē. i. moꞇ. 7. v. aꞇ. p̃ti.
Sēp. cxxviii. oũ. tē uaꞇ. vii. liꞗ. Poſt 7 m̃. viii. De fuꝓdiꞇtis borđ. habⅇ
rex fcotũ de fuo capite tantũ. In burgo ħt. Roḡ. xxxiii. hōēs fibi cōm̃da
tos ꝗs tenuit fuus anteꞇeſſor. in ꝗꝧ nichil p̃t cōm̃dōem habuit. Hꞇ ⅇiam.
. i. moꞇ. quē tenⅇ Turſtin burgenſis. hoc reclamat de dono reḡ. ſꝗ hund
nefcit qm̃. hic moꞇ. uaꞇ. xxxii. foꞇ. i. eccꞇia.

Ⅴ Hundret ⅇ dim̃ de fedebruge. Pentelei ⅇ tenuit Hagane. t. r̃. e
ꝓ mañ. iii. caꞧ. trǣ. m̃ tenⅇ Roꞗ de uals. Sēp. xi. uiꞇꞇ. xiiii. boꞧ. vi
feꞧ. iii. caꞧ in dño. iii. caꞧ hōm̃. xx. aꞇ p̃ti. iii. moꞇ. ꝼcia pars falinǣ. huic
trē jacⅇ. i. bereuuita Waltuna. i. caꞧ. trǣ. Sēp. vi. boꞧ. ii. feꞧ. i. caꞧ in
dño. xvi. aꞇ. p̃ti. iii. runꞇ. tē. xx. equǣ. m̃. vii. Sēp. xxi. animalia
xxx. por. tē. xꞈ. oũ. m̃. Lxxxxii. vii. uáfa apũ. In eađ. x. foꞇ. Lxxii.
aꞇ. Sēp. i. caꞧ. Totũ uaꞇ. t. r̃. e. c. foꞇ. 7 qñ reꞇ; m̃. vii. liꞗ. hoc totũ
tenⅇ Roꞗ. v. q̃ꞧ. in loñ. 7. iiii. in lato. 7. viii. đ. de. gelto. Eccꞇǣ. xxx.
aꞇ. vaꞇ. ii. foꞇ. 7. viii. đ.

In Torp Lxxx. aꞇ. tenuit liꞗ hō. t. r̃. e. m̃ Idē. R. Sēp. vi. uiꞇꞇ. vi. borđ.
. iii. aꞇ p̃ti. i. caꞧ. in dño. dim̃. caꞧ. hōm̃. In eađ liꞗ hō. xx. aꞇ vaꞇ. xii. đ.
Eaſt uuininc. liꞗ hō Guꝛert. t. r̃. e Lx. aꞇ. m̃ Idē. R. Sēp. vi. uiꞇꞇ. iii. boꞧ.
. ii. caꞧ. xi. aꞇ p̃ti. Tē uaꞇ totũ. xꞈ. foꞇ. m̃. Lx.

[THETFORD Hundred]

1   In THETFORD Roger has (land) exempt from all customary dues in his lordship; to which were attached 2 c. of land before 1066, now the same. Always 2 ploughs in lordship.

      20 smallholders; 2 slaves.

      1 mill; meadow, 13 acres; 30 acres of land. 1 mill is there; meadow, 5 acres; always 128 sheep.

Value then £7; later and now 8.

      Of the above-mentioned smallholders the King has the poll-tax only.

      In the Borough Roger has in patronage to him 33 men whom his predecessor held; in whom he had nothing except the patronage. He also has 1 mill which Thurstan a burgess holds. He claims this of the King's gift but the Hundred does not know how.

Value of this mill 32s.

      1 church.

The Hundred and a Half of FREEBRIDGE

2   Hagni held PENTNEY before 1066 as a manor, 3 c. of land; now Robert of Vaux holds.

      Always 11 villagers; 14 smallholders; 6 slaves.

      3 ploughs in lordship; 3 men's ploughs.

      Meadow, 20 acres; 3 mills; one-third of a salt-house.

An outlier, (East) WALTON, appertains to this land, 1 c. of land.

      Always 6 smallholders; 2 slaves.

      1 plough in lordship.

      Meadow, 16 acres; 3 cobs. Then 20 horses, now 7. Always 21 head of cattle; 30 pigs. Then 40 sheep, now 92. 7 beehives.

      In the same 10 Freemen, 72 acres. Always 1 plough.

Value of the whole before 1066 and when he acquired it 100s; now £7.

      Robert holds all this. (It has) 5 furlongs in length and 4 in width, 8d in tax.

      (Belonging) to the church 30 acres; value 2s 8d.

3   In (Gayton) THORPE a free man held 80 acres before 1066; now R(obert) also (holds).

      Always 6 villagers; 6 smallholders.

      Meadow, 3 acres; 1 plough in lordship; ½ men's plough.

      In the same a free man, 20 acres.

Value 12d.

A free man of Gyrth's (held) EAST WINCH before 1066, 60 acres; now R(obert) also (holds).

      Always 6 villagers; 3 smallholders.

      2 ploughs; meadow, 11 acres.

Value of the whole then 40s; now 60.

ac. Ide. R. ten& : I. boꝛ. 7. I. ac. pti. tc : II. boū. m̄. III. val. III. fol. Eccliæ
: VIII. val. VIII. d.

⁊ In Mafingheham. I. lib hō. xxx. qd ten& Humfrid de cuelai. II. boꝛ.
val. XVIII. d. hanc t̃ram inuafit Aluui pq̄ rex uenit in hanc patriam.
foca jac& in mafingeham regis. ⁊ In pliceha tenuit algar de ftigando
173 b
archiepo. m̄ ten& Ranulf f Galteri. p m̄. II. car træ. tnc xx boꝛd.
m̄ XXIII. tnc III. fer. m̄ II ; tnc. II. car in dnio. 7 p. I. m̄. II. fep. I. car
houm. v. acr pti. 7. I. mol. tnc. I. r. 7 m̄ ; tnc. III. an. tnc XXVII. poꝛc
m̄ XXXII. tnc. CLXXX : ou. m̄. I. tnc 7 p. XL. f. m̄. I. fol. Tota ħt. I. mil
& d in long. & v. quar i lato. 7 reddit XVI. d. de gelt de xx fol; q
cuq̄ ibi teneat. hic jac&. I. foc : v. ac træ. & ual. II. fol. Sup hoc
maneriū & fup oms hoes q erant in eo habebat ftigand foca &
fuit libatū rogero uiuente eo. Ide. R. ten&.

⁊ Apletuna ten aba. II. car træ p m̄. de Stigando. fep xx. boꝛ. 7. II. fer.
x. acr pti. 7. II. car i dnio. 7. IIII. car | houm. tnc. I. r. tnc vI. poꝛ.
m̄ xxxv. tnc LXIII : ou. m̄ XIIII. & ual. tnc. XL. fol. m̄. L. 7 ten& ide.
. I. ectla. XII. ac. 7 ual. XII. d.

⁊ H̄. de Smetheduna : In Rincteda ten. tou& lib hō f. r. e. fep
. I. car. in dnio : 7. II. fer. 7 v. uill. femp dim car houm. 7. II. ac pti.
.7 VIII. pars. mol. &. I. r. tnc. LXXXII. oues. 7 m̄ fimil. &. IIII. fochem̄.
x. acr træ. 7. I. foc Sci Benedicti. II. ac. qui eft addit tepr. r. Willi.

4 In FLITCHAM 1 Freeman, 30 acres. R(obert) also holds 1 smallholder. Meadow, 1 acre. Then 2 oxen, now 3. Value 3s.

(Belonging) to the church, 8 [acres] ; value 8d.

5 In (Great) MASSINGHAM 1 free man, 30 [acres] which Humphrey of Culey holds. 2 smallholders. Value 18d.

A(i)lwy annexed this land after the King came to this country. The jurisdiction appertains in Massingham the King's (manor).

6 In FLITCHAM Algar held from Archbishop Stigand, now Ranulf   173 b son of Walter holds, as a manor 2 c. of land.

Then 20 smallholders, now 23. Then 3 slaves, now 2.

Then 2 ploughs in lordship, later 1, now 2. Always 1 men's plough; meadow, 5 acres; 1 mill. Then and now 1 cob. Then 3 head of cattle. Then 27 pigs, now 32. Then 180 sheep, now 1.

[Value] then and later 40s; now 1s.

The whole has 1½ miles in length and 5 furlongs in width; of a 20s tax it pays 16d, whoever holds there.

1 Freeman appertains here, 5 acres of land. Value 2s.

Stigand had the jurisdiction over this manor and over all the men who were in it and it was delivered to Roger in his lifetime. R(obert) also holds.

7 Abba held APPLETON, 2 c. of land, as a manor, from Stigand.

Always 20 smallholders; 2 slaves.

Meadow, 10 acres; 2 ploughs in lordship; 4½ men's ploughs.

Then 1 cob. Then 6 pigs, now 35. Then 63 sheep, now 14.

Value then 40s; now 50. He also holds.

1 church, 12 acres; value 12d.

The Hundred of SMETHDON

8 A free man Tovi held in RINGSTEAD before 1066. Always 1 plough in lordship.

2 slaves; 5 villagers.

Always ½ men's plough.

Meadow, 2 acres; one-eighth of a mill; 1 cob. Then 82 sheep, now the same.

Also 4 Freemen, 10 acres of land;

1 Freeman of St. Benedict, 2 acres, who was added after 1066.

totū ual tnc.x.fol.m̃.xx.Scs bened foca.7 ten& Rad ł.herluini

ꝟ In eadē.ɪ.car træ ten alftan Subftigando.t.r.e.m̃ ten& Rad de
turuauilla.tñc 7 p̃.ɪ.car.m̃.ɪɪ.boū.7.ɪɪ.ac pti.7 ual.v.fol.
In eadē.ɪ.foc.vɪ.ac.7 ual.vɪ.đ.7 ten& ide.&.ɪɪ.foc fci.ƀ.xvɪ.ac.
træ.tñc.ɪ.car.7 ual.ɪɪɪɪ.fol.Ide.Et.ɪ.liƀ hō.xx.ɪɪɪɪ.ac træ.
tñc 7 p̃.ɪ.car.m̃.ɪ.bos.7 ual.ɪɪ.fol.hoc fuit fibi liƀatū ꝑ ꝑficien
dis man.Ide.ꝟ Huneftatuna ten& Rad ł herluini.ɪɪ.car ĩ dnio.
qđ ten.ɪ.liƀ hō.t.r.e.Tñc 7 p̃.xɪɪ.uilł.m̃ vɪ.fep.vɪ.bor.tñc 7 p̃
ɪɪɪ.fer.m̃.ɪɪ.Tñc 7 p̃.vɪ.car houm.7 v.acr.m̃.v.7 dim.tñc.ɪ.mol.
m̃.ɪɪ.7.ɪ.pifc.fep.ɪ.r.tñc.ɪ.an̄.filua xL.porc.tñc xvɪ.por.m̃.
L.ɪ.Tñc.Lxxx.ou.m̃.L.v.uafa apŭ.Hic jacent.ɪɪ.foc.x.ac.Ide.

174 a

tñc 7 p̃ ual.ɪɪɪ.liƀ.m̃.ɪɪɪɪ.In eadē tenuit torn liƀ hō.t.r.e.ɪ.car.
in dnio.tñc.ɪɪɪ.uilł.m̃.ɪɪ.Tñc.ɪɪɪɪ.borđ.m̃.v.Tñc 7 p̃.ɪɪɪ.ł.7.ɪɪ.acr
7 dim ꝑti.femp dim car houm.ɪ.pifc.Tñc.ɪ.uac.Tñc xxx.ou.Et
ɪɪɪ.foc.v.ac træ.fep ual.xx.fol.Totū hť.ɪ.leug in long.7.ɪ.leu
in lato.7 reddit.xvɪ.đ.de.xx.fol.de gelto.

H̃.de Grimeſhou.In Lineforda ten.A.ɪ.foc.Lx.ac træ.Sep dim car.
7.ɪ.fer.ɪɪɪ.ac ꝑti.7 ual.xx.đ.hoc ten& Stanart.

Value of the whole then 10s; now 20.

St. Benedict (has) the jurisdiction. Ralph son of Herlwin holds.

In the same Alstan held 1 c. of land under Stigand before 1066; now Ralph of Tourleville holds. Then and later 1 plough; now 2 oxen. 2 acres of meadow.

Value 5s.

In the same 1 Freeman, 6 acres.

Value 6d. He also holds.

Also 2 Freemen of St. Benedict's, 16 acres of land. Then 1 plough.

Value 4s. He also (holds).

Also 1 free man, 24 acres of land. Then and later 1 plough, now 1 ox.

Value 2s. This was delivered to him to make up the manors. He also (holds).

9   Ralph son of Herlwin holds HUNSTANTON. 2 ploughs in lordship. 1 free man held this before 1066.

Then and later 12 villagers, now 6; always 6 smallholders; Then and later 3 slaves, now 2.

Then and later 6 men's ploughs.

5 acres, now 5½. Then 1 mill, now 2. 1 fishery; always 1 cob. Then 1 head of cattle; woodland, 40 pigs. Then 16 pigs, now 51. Then 80 sheep, now 50; 5 beehives.

2 Freemen appertain here, 10 acres.

He also (holds).

Value then and later £3; now 4.   174 a

In the same a free man, Thorn, held 1 plough in lordship before 1066.

Then 3 villagers, now 2. Then 4 smallholders, now 5. Then and later 3 slaves.

Meadow, 2½ acres. Always ½ men's plough; 1 fishery. Then 1 cow; then 30 sheep.

Also 3 Freemen, 5 acres of land.

Value always 20s.

The whole has 1 league in length and 1 league in width, of a 20s tax it pays 16d.

The Hundred of GRIMSHOE

10   In LYNFORD A., 1 Freeman, held 60 acres of land. Always ½ plough. 1 slave. Meadow, 3 acres.

Value 20d.

Stanard holds this.

WANELVND . H̃. Wadetuna tenuit aldreda liɓa femina . t . r . e.

v . car̄ træ . m̃ ten& Ranulf . f̃ . Galti . Tnc 7 p̃ . ix . uilt . m̃ . null.

Tñc 7 p̃ xi . bor . m̃ xii . ſep . iii . ſer . xxx . ac p̃ti . ſep . iiii . car i dñio.

Tñc 7 p̃ . iiii . car houm . m̃ . iii . ſilua . cccc . por . m̃ . i . mol . ſep . iii . f̃.

7 xiii . an̄ . m̃ . v . 7 xxxv . por . m̃ . xxx . 7 xvii . ou . m̃ lx . ii . hic jacent

xv . ſoc . t . r . e . m̃ . xxiii . lxxxii . ac . ſep . iiii . car . Ide ten& . . i . eccla.

xx . ac . 7 ual . xx . d . Hec uilla fuit in duobʒ man . t . r . e . unu quodq̃

ualebat . iiii . liɓ . m̃ totu ual . vii . liɓ . & h̃t . i . leu in long . 7 dim i lato.

quicq̃ ibi teneat . 7 de xx . ſol de gelto . xiii . d . 7 . i . obolu.

V In totintuna ten& Rad . f̃ . herluini . iiii . car træ . qua ten alwi . t . r . e.

tñc 7 p̃ xv . uilt . m̃ . iiii . tñc 7 p̃ . x . bord . m̃ . xvii . Tñc 7 p̃ . viii . ſer . m̃.

iiii . xx . iiii . ac p̃ti . ſep . iii . car in dñio . Tñc 7 p̃ . v . car houm . m̃ . iii.

ſilua . xxx . por . m̃ . i . mol . & ſep . iii . ſoc . lxxxv . ac . Tñc 7 p̃.

ii . car . m̃ . nichil . ſ; poſſent . ee . ſemp . i . f̃ . tñc xvii . an̄ . m̃ . xviiii . Tñc

xxx . ii . por . m̃ xii . Tñc cxl . ou . m̃ . cxl . iii . min . xx . iiii . cap̃s.

Tñc lxiii . eque . m̃ . xv . Tñc 7 p̃ ual lxxx . ſol . 7 m̃ . lx . Totum

★ h̃t . ii . leu in lat . 7 . i . in lat . qui cq̃ ibi teneat . 7 xv . d de gelto.

FLECWEST . H̃. ⌐ In ſuttuna jacent . vii . liɓi hoes . 7 ſñt in repes

7 rotholfueſbei . i . car træ . 7 ix . ac p̃ti . 7 . iii . liɓos ſub eis . vii . ac tre.

Sep . ii . car . & unu de his dim . vii . liɓis teſtat hund ſco

174 b

benedicto de holmo . & un ho . R . comitis inuaſit 7 hic dim . h̃t . vi . acr̃ træ.

Apptiati ſñt . i x liɓ . ſuttune . S; ſup eos xiiii . ſol . 7 ten& in dñio.

WAYLAND Hundred

11 Aldreda, a free woman, held WATTON before 1066, 5 c. of land;
now Ranulf son of Walter holds.
> Then and later 9 villagers, now none. Then and later 11
> smallholders, now 12; always 3 slaves.
> Meadow, 30 acres; always 4 ploughs in lordship. Then and later
> 4 men's ploughs, now 3.
> Woodland, 400 pigs. Now 1 mill. Always 3 cobs. 13 head of
> cattle, now 5. 35 pigs, now 30. 17 sheep, now 62.
> 15 Freemen appertained here before 1066, now 23, 82 acres.
> Always 4 ploughs.

He also holds.
> 1 church, 20 acres;

value 20d.
> This village was in 2 manors before 1066; value of each one was
£4. Value of the whole now £7.
> It has 1 league in length and ½ in width, whoever holds there,
of a 20s tax, 13½d.

12 Ralph son of Herlwin holds 4 c. of land in TOTTINGTON which
A(i)lwy held before 1066.
> Then and later 15 villagers, now 4. Then and later 10
> smallholders, now 17. Then and later 8 slaves, now 4.
> Meadow, 24 acres; always 3 ploughs in lordship. Then and later
> 5 men's ploughs, now 3.
> Woodland, 30 pigs. Now 1 mill.
> Always 3 Freemen, 95 acres. Then and later 2 ploughs, now
> nothing but they could be (restored).
> Always 1 cob. Then 17 head of cattle, now 18. Then 32 pigs,
> now 12. Then 140 sheep, now 140 less 3; 24 goats. Then 63
> mares, now 15.

Value then and later 80s; now 60.
> The whole has 2 leagues in length and 1 in width, whoever
holds there, tax of 15d.

WEST FLEGG Hundred

13 7 free men appertain in SUTTON. They are in Repps and Rollesby;
1 c. of land; meadow, 9 acres. 3 free (men) under them, 7 acres
of land. Always 2 ploughs. One half-a-free-man of these 7 free
(men), the Hundred testifies, (belongs) to St. Benedict of Holme; 174 b
a man of Earl R(alph) annexed him. This half-a-free-(man) has 6
acres of land.
They are assessed in the £10 of Sutton but upon them 14s (are
charged). He holds in lordship.

⌐ In oebei ten̄& Stanart quã ten̄ Ringulf̄.ɪ.lib̄ hō tepr̄ r.e.xxx.ac̄
trǣ.   Semp dim̄ car̄.vɪ.ac̄ p̄ti.⁊ vɪ lib̄i hōes ſnt ſub eo.xxx
ac̄ trǣ.ɪ.ac̄ p̄ti.Sēp dim̄ car̄.hos reclamat.R bigot ex dono reḡ.⁊ ſnt
de feudo alwi de tetfordo anteceſſoris ſui.Sēp ual̄.ɪɪɪɪ.ſol̄. ⌐ In eade
ten̄.ɪ.lib̄ hō goduin xxx.ac̄ trǣ.m̄.v.bor.ide Stanart.Semp.ɪ.car̄.
&.ɪɪɪ.lib̄i hōes ſub eo de xv.ac̄ trǣ.ɪ.ac̄ p̄ti.Sēp dim̄ car̄.Sēp ual̄.ɪɪɪɪ.ſol̄.
hos ht̄.R.bigot de feudo alui anteceſſoris ſui. ⌐ In clepeſbei.ɪ.lib̄ hō
ſci.bened̄.⁊ i omeſbei.ɪɪ.ſci bened̄ com̄dat.⁊ p̄ea ten̄ alwi.m̄.R.bigot.
ex dono reḡ.de xxxɪɪɪ.ac̄ trǣ.⁊ v.ac̄ p̄ti.⁊.ɪ.bord̄.Sēp dim̄ car̄.Sēp
ual̄.ɪɪ.ſol̄.Ide Stanart. ⌐ In thura.dim̄ lib̄ hō xxɪ.ac̄ trǣ.ɪɪɪɪ.ac̄ p̄ti.
Sēp dim̄ car̄.& ſub eo.ɪ.lib̄ hō.ɪɪɪɪ.acr̄.Sēp ual̄.ɪɪɪɪ.ſol̄.Idem.
In burc ten̄ ulketel lib̄ hō edrici com̄d.t.r.e.xxx.ac̄ trǣ.⁊.ɪɪɪ.lib̄i
hōes alwi com̄d xlv.ac̄.⁊.ɪɪɪ.ac̄ p̄ti.Sēp.ɪ.car̄.Tnc ual̄.ɪɪɪ.ſol̄.
p̄ ⁊ m̄ vɪ. ⌐ In bitlakebei.ɪ.lib̄ hō alwi.t.r.e.com̄d.xx.ac̄ trǣ.
ɪɪ.ac̄ p̄ti.⁊.ɪ.bord̄.Sēp dim̄ car̄.Semp ual̄.xx.d̄.Ide ten̄&.
⌐ In repes.vɪɪ.lib̄i hōes.ɪɪɪɪ.ſci be.ɪɪ.alwi.ɪ.almari ep̄i.com̄dat.t.r.e.
lxxx ac̄ trǣ.x.ac̄ p̄ti.Sēp.ɪ.car̄.⁊ dim̄.Sēp ual̄.vɪɪɪ.ſol̄.Ide.
⌐ In baſtuic.ɪɪ.lib̄e femine edrici ⁊ rigulfi.xɪɪɪ.ac̄.trǣ com̄d.t.r.e.
ɪ.ac̄ p̄ti.⁊ ſep ar̄ cū.ɪɪ.bou.Sēp ual̄ xvɪɪɪ.d̄.Ide ten̄&.
⌐ In othebei.ɪ.lib̄ hō.vɪ.ac̄ trǣ.ɪ.ac̄ p̄ti.cū.ɪɪ.bouib̄ʒ Sēp ual̄ vɪɪɪ.d̄.

14 In OBY Stanard holds what Ringwulf, a free man, held before 1066, 30 acres of land. Always ½ plough; meadow, 6 acres. Also 6 free men are under him, 30 acres of land; meadow, 1 acre. Always ½ plough. R(oger) Bigot claims these men of the King's gift; they are of the Holding of A(i)lwy of Thetford his predecessor.
Value always 4s.

15 In the same 1 free man, Godwin, held 30 acres of land.
 Now 5 smallholders. Stanard also (holds). Always 1 plough.
 Also 3 free men under him, at 15 acres of land; meadow, 1 acre.
  Always ½ plough.
Value always 4s. R(oger) Bigot has these men of the Holding of Alwin his predecessor.

16 1 free man in CLIPPESBY of St. Benedict's and 2 in ORMESBY under the patronage of St. Benedict; later A(i)lwy held them; now Roger Bigot of the King's gift; at 33 acres of land; meadow, 5 acres.
 1 smallholder. Always ½ plough.
Value always 2s. Stanard also (holds).

17 In THURNE half-a-free-man, 21 acres of land; meadow, 4 acres; always ½ plough.
 Also under him 1 free man, 4 acres.
Value always 4s. He also (holds).

18 In BURGH (St. Margaret) Ulfketel, a free man under the patronage of Edric, held 30 acres of land before 1066.
 Also 3 free men under the patronage of Alwin, 45 acres; meadow, 3 acres; always 1 plough.
Value then 3s; later and now 6.

19 In BILLOCKBY 1 free man under the patronage of A(i)lwy before 1066, 20 acres of land; meadow, 2 acres.
 1 smallholder. Always ½ plough.
Value always 20d. He also holds.

20 In REPPS 7 free men, 4 under the patronage of St. Benedict, 2 of A(i)lwy and 1 of Bishop A(e)lmer before 1066, 80 acres of land; meadow, 10 acres; always 1½ ploughs.
Value always 8s. He also (holds).

21 In BASTWICK 2 free women under the patronage of Edric and of Ringwulf before 1066, 13 acres of land; meadow, 1 acre. They have always ploughed with 2 oxen.
Value always 18d. He also holds.

22 In OBY 1 free man, 6 acres of land; meadow, 1 acre; with 2 oxen.
Value always 8d.

⌐In ſomertuna . ı . lıḃ hõ . xxı . aᷓc trǽ . ııı . aᷓc p̃tı . Seꝑ dım carᷓ . Tñc
uaɫ xvı . đ . p̃ 7 m̃ reddıt . xx . ıııı . Hos lıḃos dedıt rex alwıo de
tetfordo cũ t̃rıs ſuıs ſıc . R . bıgot reclamat . Repes h̃t . vıı . q̃r ın
longo . 7 v . ın lato . & de gelto . xv . đ.

HEINESTEDE . *H* . In Scoteſſa tẽ . ı . lıḃ hõ ſtigandi

175 a

comđ . t . r . e . ıı . carᷓ trǽ . ꝑ m̃ . m̃ ten& Ranuɫf f Galterı . Seꝑ . v . uıɫɫ.
7 xvıı . borđ . Semp . ıı . ſer . Tñc 7 p̃ . ıı . carᷓ ın dñıo . m̃ . ııı . Seꝑ . ıııı.
carᷓ houm̃ . Sılua . xx . por . 7 vı . aᷓc p̃tı . 7 dım moɫ . tñc . ı . eq̃ . m̃ . ıı.
tñc . xxıııı . por . m̃ xx . tñc xxıııı . caꝑ . m̃ nulla . & vı . ſoᷓc ſ̃nt ıbı
de xxxvı . aer̃ trǽ . Seꝑ . ı . carᷓ . Tñc 7 p̃ uaɫ xʟ . ſoɫ . m̃ . ıııı . lıḃ.
h̃t . ı . leug̃ 7 dım̃ ın longo . 7 dım̃ ın lato . & de gelto . xvı . đ . dım̃ ǽccɫa
xv . aᷓc uaɫ xv . đ . ⌐In Stokes tenuıt alwı de tetfordo ʟxxx aᷓc trǽ
t . r . e . m̃ ten& W . peccatu . Seꝑ . ııı . borđ . 7 ſemp . ı . carᷓ ın dñıo . 7 . ıı.
acr̃ p̃tı . & ı̃ ſıthınges . ı . uıɫɫ . de xıı . acr̃ p̃tınens huıc ſtokes . Seꝑ uaɫ
xxvı . ſoɫ . 7 vı . đ . ı . eccɫa xvııı . aᷓc . 7 uaɫ . ıı . ſoɫ.

DE ESCANGIO . TRE ISAAC . ⌐In ſutherlıngaha tẽ anſger . ı . lıḃ
hõ goduını . t . r . e . vııı . acr̃ trǽ . 7 . ıı . acr̃ p̃tı . Aıtard ten&.

⌐Adhuc ın eadẽ xxx lıḃı hões ulketel . c . ʟ . aᷓc trǽ . 7 x lıḃı hõs.
Stıgandı . ʟ . aᷓc trǽ . ſub xxx . ıſtıs . ı . borđ . 7 ſub x . lıḃıs . ıı . borđ.
Int oẽs xxx . ıı . aᷓc p̃tı . Tñc . ıııı . carᷓ habebat xxx . p̃ . ıı . 7 dım̃.
m̃ . ıııı . Tñc habebant ınt̃ x . ı . carᷓ & dım̃ . p̃ 7 m̃ . ı . Tñc hı xxx.
uaɫ xv . ſoɫ . p̃ 7 m̃ xx . ıı . ſoɫ . 7 vı . đ . Tñc hı . x . uaɫ v . ſoɫ . p̃ 7 m̃.
vııı . ſoɫ . 7 vı . đ . 7 h̃t . ı . leug̃ ı̃ longo . 7 dım̃ ın lato . & de gelto
xıx . đ . S; plures ıbı tenent .

23 In SOMERTON 1 free man, 21 acres of land; meadow, 3 acres; always ½ plough.
Value then 16d; later and now it pays 24.
 The King gave these free (men) to A(i)lwy of Thetford with their lands, so R(oger) Bigot claims.
 Repps has 7 furlongs in length and 5 in width, tax of 15d.

HENSTEAD Hundred
24 In SHOTESHAM 1 free man under the patronage of Stigand held   175 a
 2 c. of land as a manor before 1066; now Ranulf son of Walter holds.
 Always 5 villagers; 17 smallholders; always 2 slaves.
 Then and later 2 ploughs in lordship, now 3. Always 4 men's
  ploughs; woodland, 20 pigs; meadow, 6 acres; ½ mill. Then
  1 horse, now 2. Then 24 pigs, now 20. Then 24 goats,
  now none.
 Also 6 Freemen are there, at 36 acres of land. Always 1 plough.
Value then and later 40s; now £4.
 It has 1½ leagues in length and ½ in width, tax of 16d.
 ½ church, 15 acres;
value 15d.

25 In STOKE (Holy Cross) A(i)lwy of Thetford held 80 acres of land before 1066; now W(illiam) Petch holds.
 Always 3 smallholders.
 Always 1 plough in lordship; meadow, 2 acres.
Also in SEETHING 1 villager, at 12 acres, belonging to this Stoke (Holy Cross).
Value always 26s 6d.
 1 church, 18 acres;
value 2s.
Of the Exchange of Isaac's Land.

26 In SURLINGHAM Ansger, 1 free man of Godwin's held 8 acres of land before 1066; meadow, 2 acres. Aitard holds.
Further in the same 30 free men of Ulfketel, 150 acres of land and 10 free men of Stigand's, 50 acres of land.
 Under these 30, 1 smallholder and under the 10 free (men),
  2 smallholders.
 Between them all 32 acres of meadow. Then the 30 had 4
  ploughs, later 2½, now 4. Then the 10 had between them
  1½ ploughs, later and now 1.
Value of these 30 then 15s; later and now 22s 6d. Value of these 10 then 5s; later and now 8s 6d.
 It has 1 league in length and ½ in width, tax of 19d. But more hold there. He also holds.

⌐In rokelunda xɪɪɪɪ.integri liƀi

hoes ulketel.cõmđ.t.r.e.7 vɪ dimidij.Int hoes ʟxxxx ac̷ træ.

& x.ac̷ p̃ti.Sep.ɪɪ.car & dim̃.Tnc 7 p̃ ual x.sol.m̃ reddnt xx.sol.

Rokelunda ht̃.ɪ.leu ĩ longo.& dim in lato.& de gelto xvɪ.đ.

ɪ.æcc̷la xɪɪ.ac̷.7 ual vɪɪɪ.đ.7 ten& ide⌐In braƀetuna xɪɪ.liƀi

liƀi hoes.ɪx ulketelli cõmđ.ɪ.sc̷i edmundi.alt̃.ɪɪ.de feudo

175 b

Stigandi.Int x.tenent xʟ.ac̷ træ.Int.ɪɪ.de feudo stigandi.t.r.e.xxx̷

ɪɪɪ.ac̷r.træ.m̃.xv.ac̷.Int.x.ɪ.car & dim̃.semp.Int.ɪɪ.tnc dim car.

p̃ nichil.m̃.ɪ.bos.Tnc 7 p̃ ual oes.v.sol.m̃.vɪ.sol.7.ɪɪɪɪ.đ.ht̃

ɪɪɪɪ.quar in longo.7.ɪɪ.quar & dim in lato.& de gelto.x.đ.7 oƀol.

.ɪ.æcc̷la xxɪɪɪɪ.ac̷r ual.xxɪɪɪɪ.đ.Ide ten&.

⌐In Kerkebei.vɪ.integri liƀi hoes.ɪɪɪ.ulketel.sc̷i alwi de tetfordo.

quart Genred.quint alured.cõmđ.t.r.e.de xʟ.ɪ.ac̷ træ.7.ɪɪ.ac̷r

p̃ti.Semp.ɪ.car.Tnc 7 p̃ ual.v.sol.m̃.ɪɪɪ.sol.7.ɪɪɪɪ.đ.ɪ.eccla x.ac̷r

ual xɪɪ.đ.7 ten& Roƀt de curcun.⌐In eadē.ɪɪɪ.liƀi hoes.ɪ.in

teger.ɪɪ.dim stigandi cõmđ xʟvɪ.ac̷r træ.7 sub eis.ɪ.borđ.

7.ɪɪɪ.ac̷r p̃ti.Semp.ɪ.car.Tnc 7 semp ual.v.sol.ht̃ dim leug in

longo.& dim in lato.& de gelto xx.đ.quicuq̷ ibi teneat.ɪ.æcc̷la

x.ac̷r.ual xɪɪ.đ.Roƀ de curcun.ten&.⌐In framingahã.ɪ.liƀ

hõ eduini cõmdat.7 pea godrici dapiferi successoris sui.sub

comite.R.qno.R.com.se forefec.tenuit almar ep̃c.m̃.R.

bigot.Turolđ xx.ac̷r træ.in quibɀ ~~manent~~.ɪɪ.bor.Semp dim̃

car.7 dim ac̷r p̃ti.Semp ual.ɪɪ.sol.ɪ.æcc̷la.xxx.ac̷r ual.ɪɪɪ.sol.

27 In ROCKLAND (St. Mary) 14 whole free men under the patronage of Ulfketel before 1066 and 6 halves. Between the men 90 acres of land; meadow, 10 acres. Always 2½ ploughs.
Value then and later 10s; now they pay 20s.
   Rockland (St. Mary) has 1 league in length and ½ in width, tax of 16d.
   1 church, 12 acres;
value 8d.
He also holds.

28 In BRAMERTON 12 free men, 9 under the patronage of Ulfketel, and 1 of St. Edmund, the other 2 from Stigand's Holding. 10   **175 b** hold 40 acres of land among them, between the 2 from Stigand's Holding 33 acres of land before 1066, now 15 acres.
   The 10 always (had) 1½ ploughs among them; between them the 2 (had) then ½ plough, later nothing, now 1 ox.
Value of them all then and later 5s; now 6s 4d.
   It has 4 furlongs in length and 2½ furlongs in width, tax of 10½d.
   1 church, 24 acres;
value 24d.
He also holds.

29 In KIRBY (Bedon) 6 whole free men before 1066, 3 under the patronage of Ulfketel, the third of A(i)lwy of Thetford, the fourth of Genred, the fifth of Alfred, at 41 acres of land; meadow, 2 acres. Always 1 plough.
Value then and later 5s; now 3s 4d.
   1 church, 10 acres;
value 12d.
Robert of Courson holds.
In the same 3 free men, 1 whole and 2 halves under the patronage of Stigand, 46 acres of land.
   Under them 1 smallholder.
   Meadow, 3 acres; always 1 plough.
Value then and always 5s.
   It has ½ league in length and ½ in width, tax of 20d, whoever holds there.
   1 church, 10 acres; value 12d. Robert of Courson holds.

30 In FRAMINGHAM 1 free man under the patronage of Edwin and later of Godric the Steward his successor, under Earl R(alph). When Earl R(alph) forfeited, Bishop A(e)lmer held it; now R(oger) Bigot (holds).
Thorold (holds) 20 acres of land in which 2 smallholders [dwell].
   Always ½ plough; meadow, ½ acre.
Value always 2s.
   1 church, 30 acres;
value 3s.

⌐ In Wiſinlingahá ten̄ . ɪ . liƀa femina ulflet . t . r . e . ſub ſtigando
epo.c.ʟx aċ træ . Sep̄ . ɪx . bor . tn̄c . ɪ . car̄ 7 dim̄ in dn̄o . p̄ 7 m̄ . ɪ.
7 dim̄ hoūm . vɪɪɪ . acr̄ p̄ti . & xɪɪɪ . ſoċ integri . 7 . ɪɪɪ . dim̄ . xʟɪɪɪ.
aċ træ͞ . 7 . ɪɪɪ . acr̄ p̄ti . Semp . ɪ . car̄ 7 dim̄ . Tn̄c ual xx . ſol̄ . p̄ 7 m̄.
xxx . ht̄ dim̄ leug in longo 7 . ɪɪɪɪ . quar in lato . & de gelto . vɪɪ . đ.
Qui cuq̃ ibi teneat . ɪ . æccła . x . aċ ual xɪɪ . đ . hec tota tra . e͞ . de
feudo almari epī . & ten̄& ide͞ Roƀt̄.

176 a

ĐE ESCANGIO T͂RE ISAAC . ⌐ Fiſkele tenuit Genret liƀ ho͞ ſub ſtigandò

t . r . e . p̄ . ɪ . car̄ & dim̄ træ . 7 ten̄& Ranulf̄ filī Galteri . Semp . ɪɪ . uiłł.
Sep̄ . ɪɪɪɪ . borđ . Tn̄c 7 p̄ . ɪ . car̄ in dn̄io . m̄ . ɪɪ . Sep̄ . ɪ . car̄ hoūm . 7 v . aċ p̄ti.
Sep̄ . ɪ . eq in dn̄io . Tn̄c . ɪɪ . an̄ . m̄ . x . por . & xɪɪɪ . ſoċ . Manent i dim̄ car̄ pdiċte
træ . & . ɪ . liƀ ho͞ . de . ɪɪ . acr̄ liƀæ træ . Int o͞es . ſep . ɪɪɪɪ . car̄ . Tn̄c 7 p̄ ual xx . m̄
ʟ . ſol̄ . ht̄ dim̄ leug i longo . 7 . ɪɪɪɪ . quar i lato . & de gelto . x . đ . 7 oboł . ɪ . æccła
xxɪɪɪɪ . acr̄ . ual . ɪɪ . ſol̄ . hoc recepit . p̄ . ɪ . car̄ & dim̄ træ . ⌐ In framingahá
ten̄ ulchetel . ɪ . liƀ ho͞ algar comitis com̄đ . ɪ . car̄ træ . m̄ ten̄& vlchetel.
Sep̄ xxɪɪɪɪ . borđ . Sep̄ . ɪ . car̄ i dn̄io . & . ɪɪɪ . car̄ hoūm . 7 . ɪɪɪ . aċ p̄ti . Sep̄ . ɪɪ.
equi . tn̄c . ɪɪ . an̄ . m̄ . ɪɪɪ . Tn̄c xɪɪ . porċ . m̄ xvɪ . 7 . ɪɪɪɪ . uaſa apu͞ . 7 in eadem
x liƀi ho͞es ſub eo . ʟ . aċ træ . 7 . ɪɪ . aċ p̄ti . Semp . ɪɪ . car̄ . Tn̄c 7 p̄ ual . xx . ſol̄.
m̄ . ʟx . ſol̄ . 7 dim̄ leug ht̄ in longo 7 dim̄ i lato . & de gelto xɪɪɪ . đ 7 obołu.
⌐ In kerkebei . ɪɪɪɪ . liƀi ho͞es ulketel . x . acr̄ træ . 7 dim̄ acr̄ p̄ti . Sep̄ dım̄ car̄. ᵗᵉⁿ Vlchetel.
⌐ In holueſtuna . ɪɪɪ . liƀi ho͞es ejde͞ . x . aċ træ . Sep̄ ar̄ . cu͞ . ɪɪ . bou͞.

31 In WHITLINGHAM 1 free woman, Wulflet, under Bishop Stigand
held 160 acres of land before 1066.
Always 9 smallholders.
Then 1½ ploughs in lordship; later and now 1½ men's [ploughs].
Meadow, 8 acres.
Also 13 whole Freemen and 3 halves, 43 acres of land; meadow,
3 acres. Always 1½ ploughs.
Value then 20s; later and now 30.
It has ½ league in length and 4 furlongs in width, tax of 7d,
whoever holds there.
1 church, 10 acres;
value 12d.
All this land is of Bishop A(e)lmer's Holding. The same Robert
holds.

Of the Exchange of Isaac's Land   176 a
32 Genred, a free man under Stigand, held BIXLEY before 1066, at
1½ c. of land; Ranulf son of Walter holds.
Always 2 villagers; always 4 smallholders.
Then and later 1 plough in lordship, now 2. Always 1 men's
plough; meadow, 5 acres; always 1 horse in lordship. Then 2
head of cattle; now 10 pigs.
Also 13 Freemen; they dwell in ½ c. of the said land. Also 1
free man, at 2 acres of free land. Among them all always 4 ploughs.
Value then and later 20; now 50s.
It has ½ league in length and 4 furlongs in width; tax of 10½d.
1 church, 24 acres;
value 2s.
He acquired this as 1½ c. of land.

33 In FRAMINGHAM Ulfketel, 1 free man under the patronage of Earl
Algar, held 1 c. of land; now Ulfketel holds.
Always 24 smallholders.
Always 1 plough in lordship; 3 men's ploughs;
meadow, 3 acres; always 2 horses. Then 2 head of cattle, now 3.
Then 12 pigs, now 16. 4 beehives.
In the same 10 free men under him, 50 acres of land; meadow,
2 acres. Always 2 ploughs.
Value then and later 20s; now 60s.
It has ½ league in length and ½ in width; tax of 13½d.

34 In KIRBY (Bedon) 4 free men of Ulfketel's, 10 acres of land;
meadow, ½ acre. Always ½ plough. Ulfketel holds.

35 In HOLVERSTON 3 free men of the same man's, 10 acres of land.
They have always ploughed with 2 oxen.

tuna . III . libi hões ejdē . xx . ač træ . Sẽp dim car̄ I . eccła ⸱ xx . acr̄ . uał.
xx . đ . 7 ten& idē . � In porrikelanda . VII . itegri libi hões ejdē xxx . acr̄.
Sẽp dim car̄ . I . æccła . XII . acr̄ . uał XII . đ . Idē . � In scoteffā . III . libi hões⸱
ejdem XVI . ač terræ . I . ač & dim p̃ti . Sẽp ar̄ cū . II . bobȝ . Idē.
� In stokes . I . lib hō ejdē dim . XXIIII . ač terræ . Semper dim
car̄ . Idē . � In sutherlingahā . II . libi hóies ejdē . XII . ač terræ.
Semp ar̄ cū . II . bobȝ Idē ten . ⌢ In rokelunda . I . lib hō . ulketelli
de . VI . ač terræ App̃tiati s̃t oēs isti in framingahā . Idē ten.
⌢ In biskele . I . lib hō ulketelli . cōm̄d . & dim lib sub eo . de . XVII.
ač terræ . &. I . uiłł . &. I . bord̄ . 7 . I . ač p̃ti . Semp dim . car̄ . Tc uał&
xxx . đ . M̄ . IIII . soł . Idē ten . Hanc terrā Calūpniatur godricus
dapifer . p̄ homiñe suūm juditio . I . bello . Radulfū scilic& . qđ tenuit
176 b
ad feudū comitis . R . 7 hund testatur ad feudū . R . bigot . Sed
godricus reclamat istā cū medietate quæ ē i b̄ue . regis . hač recep̃.
Godric̄ . p̄ dim car̄ terræ . ⌢ In sutherlingahā . integri . II . libi 7 dim
hões Godwini sub stig̃ de . xx . ač terræ . Idē ten . ⌢ In Rokelunda . I.
integer lib &. II . dim hões godwini sub stig̃ de . xx . ač . Idē ten.
⌢ In brabretuna . ten Ranulfus filı̄ . Galteri . III . libi . &. II . dim . hões
ejd̄ . de xx . ač . Int oēs . V . ač & dim ač p̃ti . Semp . II . car̄ . Tc uał
VIII . soł . m̄ . x . Isti fuer libati ad p̃ficiendū mań . biskele.

36 In YELVERTON 3 free men of the same man's, 20 acres of land.
Always ½ plough.
   1 church, 20 acres;
value 20d. He also holds.

37 In PORINGLAND 7 whole free men of the same man's, 30 acres.
Always ½ plough.
   1 church, 12 acres;
value 12d. He also (holds).

38 In SHOTESHAM 3 free men of the same man's, 16 acres of land;
meadow, 1½ acres. They have always ploughed with 2 oxen. He
also (holds).

39 In STOKE (Holy Cross) 1 free man of the same man's, (he is) a half
(-a-free-man), 24 acres of land. Always ½ plough. He also (holds).

40 In SURLINGHAM 2 free men of the same man's, 12 acres of land.
They have always ploughed with 2 oxen. He also holds.

41 In ROCKLAND (St. Mary) 1 free man of Ulfketel's, at 6 acres of land.
   All these men are assessed in Framingham. He also holds.

42 In BIXLEY 1 free man under the patronage of Ulfketel and a half-
a-free-(man) under him, at 17 acres of land.
   1 villager; 1 smallholder.
   Meadow, 1 acre; always ½ plough.
Value then 30d; now 4s. He also holds.
   Godric the Steward claims this land by his man, that is Ralph,
by judicial ordeal or by battle, that he held it as part of the   176 b
Holding of Earl R(alph). The Hundred testify (that it is) part of
R(oger) Bigot's Holding but Godric claims this back with the half
which is in the King's writ. Godric acquired this as ½ c. of land.

43 In SURLINGHAM 2 whole free men and a half of Godwin's under
Stigand, at 20 acres of land. He also holds.

44 In ROCKLAND (St. Mary) 1 whole free man and 2 halves of
Godwin's under Stigand at 20 acres. He also holds.

45 In BRAMERTON Ranulf son of Walter holds; 3 free men and 2 halves
of the same man's, at 20 acres. Between them all 5 acres; meadow,
½ acre; always 2 ploughs.
Value then 8s; now 10.
   These men were delivered to make up the manor of Bixley.

*Ⅴ*Dɪᴄᴇ ᴅɪᴍ. Hᴠɴᴅ. Simplingahá teñ Roɓ deuais . ꝓ mañ

7 ꝓ xl . ac træ . qua teñ torɓt liɓ hõ ſtigandi . t . r . e . Tñc ix borđ . ꝓ 7 m̃ .

vii . Sep . i . caɼ i dñio . Tñc . i . caɼ houm . ꝓ 7 m̃ dim . Silua . vii . por . 7 vi : ac

ꝓti . Sep . i . eq . m̃ . iii . añ . Tñc . v . por . m̃ . xxɪɪ . Sep . ix ou . 7 . iiii . liɓi hões

liɓati ad hoc mañ ꝑficiendũ . xvi . ac træ . Tñc . i . caɼ . ꝓ 7 m̃ dim . Sep ual

xx . ſoł . hͭ v . quaɼ i long . 7 . iiii . i lato . & de gelto . v . đ . Qui cuq̇ ibi te

neat . i . æccła . x . ac ual . xii . đ . ⌠ Geſſinga teñ . i . liɓ hõ ſubſtigando . t . r . e.

xl . ii . acɼ . 7 sep . vi . borđ . Sep . i . caɼ i dñio . Sep aɼ hões cũ . ii . boũ . **Silua**

viii . porc . 7 . iiii . ac ꝓti . Tñc 7 ꝓ ual v . ſoł . m̃ . x . 7 ten& ide . ⌠ Oſmun

deſtuna ten algaɼ trec ſub edrico . t . r . e . dim caɼ træ . 7 ten& hugo

de corbun . Sep . ii . uiłł . 7 vi . borđ . Sep . i . caɼ in dñio . ſ; . ii . poſſent . ꝭꝭ .

Tñc 7 ꝓ . ii . caɼ houm . m̃ . ii . & dim . Silua xv . porc . 7 vi . acɼ ꝓti . & . i.

liɓ hõ 7 dim de xvi . acɼ . fuit liɓat ad ħ mañ ꝑficiendũ . Tñc dim caɼ

m̃ . nichil . Sep ual . l . ſoł .

Loᴛʜɪɴɢᴀ . H̃ . ⌠ In mundahá teñ aluric liɓ hõ ſub ſtigando . t . r . e .

xxx . acɼ træ . 7 ibi . ꝭ . dim borđ . m̃ . i . caɼ . Silua . iiii . por . & dim acɼ

ꝓti . Sep ual . v . ſoł . Iſte aluric ut lagaũ . 7 ꝑpoſit . reg . ulketel . ſai

ſiuit tram i manu reg . 7 rog bigot . rogaũ a rege . & conceſſit ei .

177 a

Hanc calupniatur comes alañ quod ten com . R . ad roɓort mañ ſuũ . 7 hões

hundreti audieɼ iſtu ulketel cognoſcente una uice . p . i . annũ anteq̇ . R .

ſe fore fec . 7 pea q̇ forefeciſſ& . i . uice ſimilit q̇đ iſte ulketel deſeruiebat

in roɓoro . & ad ultimũ audiuit hunđ iſtu eunđ dicente q̇đ deſeruiebat

erga Rogeɼũ bigot . hões comitis alani uno quoq̇ anno habueɼ inde . x . ſoł .

pͭ . iiii . annos ultimos 7 hoc uolñt ꝓbare q̇lib& Modo . 7 ten& Vlketel .

DISS Half-Hundred

46 Robert of Vaux holds SHIMPLING as a manor and as 40 acres of land which Thorbert, a free man of Stigand's, held before 1066.
Then 9 smallholders, later and now 7.
Always 1 plough in lordship. Then 1 men's plough, later and now ½. Woodland, 7 pigs; meadow, 6 acres; always 1 horse; now 3 head of cattle. Then 5 pigs, now 23; always 9 sheep.
Also 4 free men were delivered to make up this manor, 16 acres of land. Then 1 plough, later and now ½.
Value always 20s.
It has 5 furlongs in length and 4 in width; tax of 5d, whoever holds there.
1 church, 10 acres;
value 12d.

47 1 free man under Stigand held GISSING before 1066, 42 acres.
Always 6 smallholders.
Always 1 plough in lordship. The men have always ploughed with 2 oxen. Woodland, 8 pigs; meadow, 4 acres.
Value then and later 5s; now 10. He also holds.

48 Algar Trec held OSMONDISTON before 1066 under Edric, ½ c. of land; (now) Hugh of Corbon holds.
Always 2 villagers; 6 smallholders.
Always 1 plough in lordship but 2 could be (restored). Then and later 2 men's ploughs, now 2½. Woodland, 15 pigs; meadow, 6 acres.
Also 1 free man and a half was delivered to make up this manor. Then ½ plough, now nothing.
Value always 50s.

LODDON Hundred

49 In MUNDHAM Aelfric, a free man under Stigand, held 30 acres of land before 1066.
A half a smallholder is there.
Now 1 plough; woodland, 4 pigs; meadow, ½ acre.
Value always 5s.
This Aelfric was outlawed and Ulfketel, the King's reeve, had possession of the land in the King's hand; Roger Bigot asked for it from the King and he granted it to him. Count Alan claims 177 a this because Earl R(alph) held it as part of his manor of Rumburgh; the men of the Hundred heard Ulfketel acknowledge this on one occasion during the year before R(alph) forfeited and likewise on one occasion after he forfeited, that he, Ulfketel, was doing service in Rumburgh, and finally the Hundred heard this same man say that he was doing service to Roger Bigot. Count Alan's men had 10s from there each year except for the last 4 years and this they are willing to prove by any means. Ulfketel holds.

⌐In mundahã viii . libi hoẽs ulketelli . lx . acr̃ træ . 7 . iii . borđ . 7 ten& vlketel.
Sẽp . iii . car̃ . int̃ oẽs . Tñc ual . viii . fot . m̃ . x . hãc hab& Roger i v . car
rucatis . quas rex dedit ei . Idẽ Vlketel . In fithinga . v . borđ de . x . ac̃.
& ptinent i framingahã . ii . ecclæ xvi . acr̃ ual . ii . fot . 7 iii . bou . ⌐Inal
gamundeftuna . xiii . libi hoẽs ulketelli de . l . acr̃ træ . 7 vii . borđ.
de xii . ac̃ træ . Sẽp int̃ oẽs . iiii . car̃ . 7 . ii . acr̃ p̃ti . Tñc ual viii . fot
m̃ . x . Idẽ . ⌐In clareftona . iiii . libi hoẽs ejdẽ 7 . iii . borđ . de xiiii . acr̃.
Sẽp dim̃ car̃ . Sẽp ual . ii . fot . hoc ten& Rob de uals . ⌐In Wodetona
. i . lib hõ ejdẽ de xx . acr̃ . 7 fub eo . i . lib hõ . 7 . i . borđ . de . iiii . acr̃ . 7 sẽp
dim̃ car̃ . Sẽp ual xxx . ii . đ . i . eccla xii . ac̃ . ual xii . đ . In norfen
ten& Vlketel . i . liba femina . de viii . acr̃ . 7 ual . viii . đ . ⌐Soca 7 faca
de mundahã i hunđ . ⌐Clareftona ten fuetman lib hõ fub ftigando
t . r . e . p̃ xxx . ac̃ træ . Robt deuals . Sẽp vii . borđ . Sẽp . i . car̃ in dñio.
Sẽp arat hoẽs . cũ . ii . bobʒ 7 v . acr̃ p̃ti . i . eccla . xxx . acr̃ . ual . iii . fot.
& in eadẽ xv libi hoẽs fuetman . de xxx . acr̃ . Sẽp int̃ oẽs . i . car̃.
& . ii . ac̃ p̃ti . In eadẽ xiii . dim̃ libi hoẽs ejdẽ . l . ac̃ . Sẽp . i . car̃ . 7
i . ac̃ p̃ti . ⌐In afebei . x . libi hoẽs ejdẽ de xxx . acr̃ . femp . i . car̃.
& . ii . acr̃ p̃ti . In eadẽ vii . dim̃ libi de xxvii . acr̃ . Sẽp . i . car̃ . Idẽ.
In halgatona dim̃ lib de viii . acr̃ . Sẽp . cũ . ii . bobʒ

50 In MUNDHAM 8 free men of Ulfketel's, 60 acres of land.
    3 smallholders. Ulfketel holds.
    Always 3 ploughs among them all.
  Value then 8s; now 10.
    Roger has this in 5 c. which the King gave him. Ulfketel also
(holds).

51 In SEETHING 5 smallholders, at 10 acres. They belong in Framingham.
    2 churches, 16 acres;
  value 2s.
    3 oxen.

52 In *ALGAMUNDESTUNA* 13 free men of Ulfketel's, at 50 acres of land.
    7 smallholders, at 12 acres of land.
    Always 4 ploughs among them all. Meadow, 2 acres.
  Value then 8s; now 10. He also (holds).

53 In CLAXTON 4 free men of the same man's.
    3 smallholders, at 14 acres.
    Always ½ plough.
  Value always 2s. Robert of Vaux holds this.

54 In WOODTON 1 free man of the same man's, at 20 acres, and under
him 1 free man.
    1 smallholder, at 4 acres.
    Always ½ plough.
  Value always 32d.
    1 church, 12 acres;
  value 12d.

55 In NORTON (Subcourse) Ulfketel holds; 1 free woman, at 8 acres.
  Value 8d. The full jurisdiction of Mundham (is) in the Hundred.

56 Sweetman, a free man under Stigand, held CLAXTON before 1066,
as 30 acres of land. Robert of Vaux (holds).
    Always 7 smallholders.
    Always 1 plough in lordship. The men have always ploughed
      with 2 oxen. Meadow, 5 acres.
    1 church, 30 acres;
  value 3s.
    Also in the same 15 free men of Sweetman's, at 30 acres.
      Always among them all 1 plough; meadow, 2 acres.
    In the same 13 halves-a-free-man of the same man's, 50 acres.
      Always 1 plough; meadow, 1 acre.

57 In ASHBY (St. Mary) 10 free men of the same man's, at 30 acres.
    Always 1 plough; meadow, 2 acres.
    In the same 7 halves-a-free-man, at 27 acres. Always 1 plough.
He also (holds).

58 In HELLINGTON a half-a-free(-man), at 8 acres. Always with 2 oxen.

.ɪ.lib ejde.v.acr.Sep.ɪ.eq i aula.7.ɪɪɪ.an.7 ʟxxxx.ou.7 xɪɪɪɪ.porc.

177 b

hac ten Roger bigot de libat reg.hoc totu sep ual.ʟx.sol. ~~ibi tenent.~~

Clakestona ht.vɪ.quar in longo.7 v.in lato.& de gelto ɪx d.7 obolu.

Sed plures ibi tenent. ⌐ In mundaha.ɪ.lib ho comd alwi de tetfordo.xxx
acr træ.qua ten& Turold.ſ; nec dare nec uendere poterat sine licentia.
Sep.ɪ.uill.7.ɪ.bord.Tnc.ɪ.car.m dim.& sub eo.ɪɪ.libi hoes 7 dim.de
vɪɪɪ.acr.7.ɪɪ.ser.7.ɪɪ.ac pti.Sep.ɪ.car int oes.Tnc ual.v.sol.m.vɪɪɪ.
⌐ In affebei.ɪ.soc.de.ɪɪɪɪ.ac træ.7.ɪɪ.bou.7 ual vɪ.d.Rob. ⌐ In sithinga.
.ɪ.lib ho alwi comd de xvɪ.acr.7 ual xxɪɪɪɪ.d.& ten& Turold.
⌐ Pirenhou ten algar lib ho sub stigando.t.r.e.p dim car træ.hoc ten&
Goduin.Sep vɪ.bord.Tnc dim car i dnio.m.ɪɪ.7 dim car houm.m.ɪ.
mol.m.ɪɪ.eq i aula.7 v.an.m.ʟx.ou.&.ɪ.soc.de.ɪɪɪɪ.acr.Tnc ual
x.sol.m xx.ht.vɪɪɪ.quar i longo.7.ɪɪɪ.in lato.& vɪɪɪ.d de gelto.
Qui cuq ibi tenent.Soca in herſa. ⌐ In tortuna ten almar lib ho
sub stigando.t.r.e.p xxx.acr.hoc ten& Rob de uals.Sep.ɪɪ.bord.
Sep.ɪ.car in dnio.7.ɪɪɪɪ.ac pti.7 xvɪɪ.libi hoes.7 dim algari comd de
ʟxxx.acr.Tnc 7 p.ɪɪ.car.m.ɪ.7 dim.In eade dim lib ho.de xv.acr.
Sep dim car.ɪ.acr pti.In afebei.ɪɪ.libi hoes ejde.ɪx.acr.Sep ar cum
ɪɪ.bouib.Ide.In Karlentona.ɪɪ.libi hoes.de.v.ac træ.In mundaha.
ɪx acr in dnio.&.v.libi hoes.ejde de xɪx acr.Semp dim car.Ide.
In appletona.xxx.acr træ in dnio.7.ɪ.bord.Totu semp ual xxx.sol.
Soca in hund.Tortuna ht.x.quar i longo.7 v.in lato.& de gelto.
vɪɪ.d.7 ob.

59 In CARLETON (St. Peter) 1 free (man) of the same man's, 5 acres.
   Always 1 horse at the hall; 3 head of cattle; 90 sheep; 14 pigs.
   Roger Bigot holds this of the King's livery. 177 b
   Value of all this, always 60s.
   Claxton has 6 furlongs in length and 5 in width, tax of 9½d.
   But more hold there.

60 In MUNDHAM 1 free man under the patronage of A(i)lwy of
   Thetford, 30 acres of land which Thorold holds but he cannot
   grant or sell it without permission.
   Always 1 villager; 1 smallholder.
   Then 1 plough, now ½.
   Also under him 2 free men and a half, at 8 acres.
   2 slaves.
   Meadow, 2 acres. Always 1 plough between them all.
   Value then 5s; now 8.

61 In ASHBY (St. Mary) 1 Freeman at 4 acres of land. 2 oxen.
   Value 6d. Robert (holds).

62 In SEETHING 1 free man under the patronage of A(i)lwy, at 16 acres.
   Value 24d. Thorold holds.

63 Algar, a free man under Stigand, held PIRNHOW before 1066, as
   ½ c. of land. Godwin holds this.
   Always 6 smallholders.
   Then ½ plough in lordship, now 2. ½ men's plough.
   Now 1 mill; now 2 horses at the hall; 5 head of cattle; now
      60 sheep.
   Also 1 Freeman, at 4 acres.
   Value then 10s; now 20.
   It has 8 furlongs in length and 3 in width, tax of 8d, whoever
   holds there. The jurisdiction is in Earsham.

64 In THURTON A(e)lmer, a free man under Stigand, held before
   1066, as 30 acres. Robert of Vaux holds this.
   Always 2 smallholders.
   Always 1 plough in lordship; meadow, 4 acres.

65 In ASHBY (St. Mary) 2 free men of the same man's, 9 acres. They
   have always ploughed with 2 oxen. He also (holds).

66 In CARLETON (St. Peter) 2 free men, at 5 acres of land.

67 In MUNDHAM 9 acres in lordship. Also 5 free men of the same man's,
   at 19 acres. Always ½ plough. He also (holds).

68 In ALPINGTON 30 acres of land in lordship. 1 smallholder.
   Value of the whole always 30s. The jurisdiction (is) in the Hundred.
   Thurton has 10 furlongs in length and 5 in width, tax of 7½d.

In ſithinga . I . liƀ ho vlketelli de VI . ac . 7 ual . VI . ƌ.
Aſebei hƚ . IX . quar ̄ i longo . 7 v . in lato . & de gelto . IX . ƌ.

H̄ . de grenehou . Nereburh ten Ælwi . t . r . e . m̄ . R . vicar træ .p
man . Tnc XXXIII . uiℓℓ . & p . XX . VIII . m̄ ſimiℓ . Tnc 7 ſemp . X . borƌ.
Tnc . IIII . ſer . m̄ . III . Tnc 7 p in dn̄io . III . car . m̄ . II . Tnc & p it hoes
178 a
XI . car . m̄ . VII . XVI . acr p̄ti . III . moℓ . Qn̄ receƥ . II . r̄ . 7 m̄ ; Semp XIII . animℓ.
& XXV . porc . 7 . CC . oues . 7 . III . uaſa apu . & hab& ̄ i longo . I . m̄ . 7 X . quar in
lato . 7 qn̄ . hoc redƌ . XX . ſoℓ . tnc reddit XII . ƌ . Tnc ual VIII . liƀ . & ſemp.

⌈SCEREPHÀ . H̄ . Hocha ten edric tegn̄ . t . r . e . v . car træ . Tnc 7 p XIII . uiℓℓ.
m̄ . VII . Qn̄ rec . XI bor . 7 m̄ ſimiℓ . Tnc 7 p . VII . ſoℓ . m̄ . III . XXXVII . acr p̄ti . ſilua
c . porc . Tnc 7 p . III . car indñio . m̄ . II . tnc . III . car houm . p 7 m̄ . II . 7 . II . car
poſſent reſtaurari . & . IIII . ſoc . III . acr & dim . Tnc . CCXX . equæ ſiluaticæ m̄
nulla . tnc . v . r̄ . m̄ . II . Tnc XII . an . m̄ . II . tnc XII . porc . m̄ . VIII . Seƥ . CC . XX.
ou . m̄ . II . uaſa apu . Tnc . 7 p uaℓ . IIII . liƀ . 7 m̄ ſimiℓ . totu hƚ . I . leu . 7 dim in
long . 7 dim leug in lato . ƌcuꝗ ibi teneat . 7 XV . ƌ de gelto . In paruo hocha
ten Ailuuin dim car træ . ſemp . III . uiℓℓ . 7 . III . borƌ . 7 . II . ſer . 7 . III . acr.
p̄ti . ſemp . I . car in dñio . 7 dim car houm . 7 . I . ſoc . III . acr 7 dim . ſeƥ ual
XIII . ſoℓ . 7 . IIII . ƌ . 7 ten& Turolƌ .

69 In SEETHING 1 free man of Ulfketel's, at 6 acres.
Value 6d.
   Ashby (St. Mary) has 9 furlongs in length and 5 in width,
tax of 9d.

The Hundred of (South) GREENHOE

70 A(i)lwy held NARBOROUGH before 1066; now R(oger holds) 6 c. of
land as a manor.
   Then 33 villagers, later 28, now the same. Then and always 10
      smallholders. Then 4 slaves, now 3.
   Then and later 3 ploughs in lordship, now 2. Then and later 11
      ploughs among the men, now 7. Meadow, 16 acres; 3 mills.   178 a
      When he acquired it and now 2 cobs.
   Always 13 head of cattle; 25 pigs; 200 sheep; 3 beehives.
   It has 1 mile in length and 10 furlongs in width, when this
[Hundred] pays 20s, then it pays 12d.
Value then and always £8.

SHROPHAM Hundred

71 Edric, a thane, held HOCKHAM before 1066, 5 c. of land.
   Then and later 13 villagers, now 7. When he acquired it, 11
      smallholders, now the same. Then and later 7 slaves, now 3.
   Meadow, 37 acres; woodland, 100 pigs.
   Then and later 3 ploughs in lordship, now 2. Then 3 men's
      ploughs, later and now 2, and 2 ploughs could be restored.
   Also 4 Freemen, 3½ acres.
   Then 220 wild mares, now none. Then 5 cobs, now 2. Then 12
      head of cattle, now 2. Then 12 pigs, now 8. Always 220
      sheep; now 2 beehives.
Value then and later £4; now the same.
   The whole has 1½ leagues in length and ½ league in width,
whoever holds there, tax of 15d.

72 In LITTLE HOCKHAM A(i)lwin held ½ c. of land.
   Always 3 villagers; 3 smallholders; 2 slaves.
   Meadow, 3 acres. Always 1 plough in lordship; ½ men's plough.
   Also 1 Freeman, 3½ acres.
Value always 13s 4d. Thorold holds.

In Snetretuna . ten ide p̄ . ɪ . car tre . 7 p̄

man̄ . 7 ten& Rađ . f̄ . herluini . Semp . ɪɪ . uiłł . 7 . ɪɪɪ . bor . 7 . ɪ . ſer . vɪɪɪ . ac p̄ti.
ſep̄ . ɪ . car in dn̄io . 7 dim car hom̄ . tn̄c . ɪɪɪ . an̄ . m̄ . vɪɪ . 7 ɪx . por . tn̄c ʟx . ou.
m̄ . cʟx . 7 xɪɪɪɪ . cap̄ . 7 . ɪɪ . uaſa apu . Sep̄ uał xx . ſoł . 7 hł . ɪ . leug in long
& dim in lat . q̄cq̄ ibi teneat . 7 xvɪɪ . đ . 7 . ɪ . ferding de gelto.

┌ GILDEGROS . H . In Snareſhella ten turſtin lib ho . t . r . e . ɪɪ . car træ.
ſemp . vɪ . borđ . 7 . ɪ . ſer . 7 . ɪɪɪ . ac p̄ti . tn̄c 7 p̄ . ɪɪ . car in dn̄io . m̄ . ɪ . & alia
poſſ& reſtaurari . ſep̄ dim car hom̄ . 7 dim piſc . Tn̄c . ɪɪɪɪ . r̄ . m̄ . ɪ . tn̄c . ɪɪɪ . an̄.
m̄ . ɪɪ . tn̄c xɪɪ . por . Tn̄c ʟxxx . ou . m̄ . ʟx . Tn̄c uał xvɪ . ſoł . m̄ . xx . In
alia SNARSHELLA . ten Ailuuin . ɪ . car træ . 7 . ʟx . ac . hoc ten& Aleſtan
angł . tn̄c . ɪɪ . ſer . m̄ . ɪ . & vɪ . ſoc . de omi cſuetudine . ſ; un quiſq̄ redit
ſemp . ɪɪɪɪ . đ . in Keninchala regis ex ſumagio & vɪ . forisfacturas hł rex
ex iłł . In dn̄io ſep̄ . ɪ . car . 7 dim poſſ& reſtaurari . dim car hom̄ . tn̄c . ɪ . r̄.
ſep̄ . ɪɪɪɪ . an̄ . tn̄c . vɪɪ . por . m̄ . v . tc̄ . c . ou . m̄ . ccc . 7 v . uaſa apu . 7 uał xx . ſoł.

178 b

Totu hł . ɪ . leug in long & dim in lat & xɪ . đ . & . ɪ . obolu de gelto . ┌ Loꝑham
★ ten Oſl lib ho . t . r . e . ɪɪɪ . car tre . p̄ . man̄ . ſemp . ɪɪ . uiłł . 7 xɪɪɪ . borđ . 7 . ɪɪɪɪ.
★ ſer . 7 xɪɪ . acr p̄ti . Tn̄c 7 p̄ . ɪɪ . car in dn̄io . m̄ . ɪɪɪ . ſep̄ . ɪɪ . car hom̄ . 7 ſilua . c . por.
& xvɪɪɪɪ . ſoc . ɪ . car træ . cu omi cſuetudine . 7 xɪɪ . ac . 7 . ɪɪ . car . Tn̄c . ɪ . r̄ . m̄
. ɪ . r̄ . m̄ . ɪɪ . tn̄c . ɪ . an̄ . m̄ . xɪɪɪ . m̄ xʟ . porc . tn̄c . c . ou . m̄ . ʟx . tn̄c 7 p̄ uał
ʟx . ſoł m̄ . c . ſoł . 7 xɪɪ . ſoł .

73 In SNETTERTON the same held, as 1 c. of land, also as a manor. Ralph son of Herlwin holds.
>Always 2 villagers; 3 smallholders; 1 slave.
>Meadow, 8 acres. Always 1 plough in lordship; ½ men's plough. Then 3 head of cattle, now 7. 9 pigs. Then 60 sheep, now 160. 14 goats; 2 beehives.

Value always 20s.
>The whole has 1 league in length and ½ in width, whoever holds there, tax of 17¼d.

GUILTCROSS Hundred
74 In (Great) SNAREHILL Thurstan, a free man, held 2 c. of land before 1066.
>Always 6 smallholders; 1 slave.
>Meadow, 3 acres. Then and later 2 ploughs in lordship, now 1, and another could be restored. Always ½ men's plough; ½ fishery. Then 4 cobs, now 1. Then 3 head of cattle, now 2. Then 12 pigs. Then 80 sheep, now 60.

Value then 16s, now 20.

75 In (Little) SNAREHILL A(i)lwin held 1 c. of land and 60 acres. Alstan an Englishman holds.
>Then 2 slaves, now 1.
>Also 6 Freemen with all customary dues but each one has always paid 4d for carrying-service in the King's (manor) of Kenninghall and the King has the 6 forfeitures from them.
>Always 1 plough in lordship and ½ could be restored; ½ men's plough. Then 1 cob; always 4 head of cattle. Then 7 pigs, now 5. Then 100 sheep, now 300. 5 beehives.

Value 20s.
>The whole has 1 league in length and ½ in width, tax of 11½d.   178 b

76 Ulf, a free man, held LOPHAM as a manor before 1066, 3 c. of land.
>Always 2 villagers; 13 smallholders, 4 slaves.
>Meadow, 12 acres. Then and later 2 ploughs in lordship, now 3. Always 2 men's ploughs; woodland, 100 pigs.
>Also 19 Freemen, 1 c. of land with all customary dues; 12 acres; 2 ploughs.
>Then 1 cob, now 1 cob, now 2. Then 1 head of cattle, now 13. Now 40 pigs. Then 100 sheep, now 60.

Value then and later 60s; now 100s and 12s.

In alio Lopham tenuit alsi lib hō . t . r . e . ii.

car træ . ſemp . ii . uiłł . 7 vii . bor . 7 . iiii . ſer . 7 xi . acr p̄ti . ſemp . ii . car in
dnio . 7 dim car hom & una car poſſ& reſtaurari . ſilua . lxxx . por . &
iiii . ſoc . xiii . ac træ . 7 . ii . boū . 7 . i . lib hō . xl . ac træ . i . borđ 7 . i . acr
& dim p̄ti . ſemp dim car . ſemp . i . r . tnc . i . an . m̄ . iii . ſẽp xl por . tnc
c . oū . m̄ . lx . 7 x . uaſa apū . Soca de lībo hōe in kenichala . ∫ In nortuna
. i . car træ ten ide p̄ m̄ . t . r . e . m̄ ten& Alured angł . Seṗ . iiii . uiłł . 7
iiii . borđ . 7 . i . ac p̄ti . Tnc . ii . car i dnio . p̄ 7 m̄ . i . 7 alia poſſ& reſtaurari .
ſẽp dim car hom . & . vii . ſoc . lx . ac træ . 7 . ii . bor . 7 . i . acr p̄ti . ſep . i . car.
Hanc trā addidit Alsi in Lopham p̄ bereuita tep̄r . r . Wiłłi . & eā
habebat p̄ manerio . tep̄r . r . e . Inea . xx . oues . Lophā uał t . r . e . lx
ſoł . & nortuna . xx . ſoł . M̄ tot uał Lopham lxx . ſoł . 7 nortuū.
xxx . ſoł . Tot Lopham h̄t . i . łg in long . & . i . łg in lat . & . xxx.
iiii . đ . & . i . obolū . ∫ In benham . i . ſoc . cū oī conſuetudine . ſcē adel
drede . t . r . e . q̄ p̄ q̄ uenit . W . Rex in anglia anteceſſor . R . bigot
habuit c̄mdatione tantū . 7 h̄t . x . ac terræ . 7 uał . ii . ſoł . m̄ ten
Berardus . ∇ LAWENDIC . HVND . In Witcingkeſeta
ten Ranulfus fili Galti . iii . car terræ p̄ man ∫ . Tnc̄ 7 p̄ . viii.
uiłł . m̄ . v . Tc̄ 7 p̄ . vi . borđ . m̄ . x . Tc . iiii . ſer . xv . ac . p̄ti . ſemp
Tc̄ . iiii . car . inter totū . Quar duæ modo ſ in dnio . 7 due hom.
ſilū . de . c . porc̄ . Quarta pars piſciṅ . ſemp . ii . runc̄ . m̄ . xii . aṅ.
179 a
Tc̄ ix . porc̄ . m̄ . xxv . Tc . lx . ous . m̄ . lx . vii . m̄ . xxx . vi . cap̄ . 7 . vii.
uaſa apū . Tc̄ uał . xl . ſoł . modo . lx . De . iii . bz libis hōibz ē ſoca . in
muleha regis . Totū hŕ dim łg in long & dim in lato . & . x . đ . de gelto
q̄cuq̄ ibi teneat.

77 In the other LOPHAM Alsi, a free man, held 2 c. of land before 1066.
Always 2 villagers; 7 smallholders; and 4 slaves.
Meadow, 11 acres. Always 2 ploughs in lordship; ½ men's plough, and 1 plough could be restored. Woodland, 80 pigs.
Also 4 Freemen, 13 acres of land; 2 oxen.
Also 1 free man, 40 acres of land.
1 smallholder; meadow, 1½ acres; always ½ plough.
Always 1 cob. Then 1 head of cattle, now 3; always 40 pigs.
Then 100 sheep, now 60. 10 beehives.
Jurisdiction of the free man is in Kenninghall.

78 In (Blo) NORTON he also held 1 c. of land as a manor before 1066; now Alfred an Englishman holds.
Always 4 villagers; 4 smallholders.
Meadow, 1 acre. Then 2 ploughs in lordship, later and now 1, and another could be restored; always ½ men's plough.
Also 7 Freemen, 60 acres of land; 2 smallholders; meadow, 1 acre; always 1 plough.
Alfsi added this land to Lopham as an outlier after 1066; [   ] had it as a manor before 1066. On it 20 sheep.
Value of Lopham before 1066, 60s and of (Blo) Norton 20s.
Value of the whole of Lopham now 70s, and of (Blo) Norton 30s.
The whole of Lopham has 1 league in length and 1 league in width, [tax of] 34½d.

79 In BANHAM 1 Freeman with all customary dues of St. Etheldreda's before 1066 whom Roger Bigot's predecessor had in patronage only after King William came to England. He has 10 acres of land. Value 2s. Berard holds now.

LAUNDITCH Hundred

80 In WHISSONSETT Ranulf son of Walter holds 3 c. of land as a manor which 9 free men held.
Then and later 8 villagers, now 5. Then and later 6 smallholders, now 10. Then 4 slaves.
Meadow, always 15 acres. Then 4 ploughs between the whole, 2 of which are now in lordship and 2 (are) the men's.
Woodland at 100 pigs; ¼ of a fishery; always 2 cobs.
Now 12 head of cattle. Then 9 pigs, now 25. Then 60 sheep, now 67. Now 36 goats; 7 beehives.   179 a
Value then 40s; now 60.
The jurisdiction of 3 free men is in the King's (manor) of Mileham.
The whole has ½ league in length and ½ in width, tax of 10d, whoever holds there.

Ƒ Feor hou . *H* . Ahincham Stanart . Anglus

dim caŕ terræ tenet p̃ mań quã tenuit Aluuiñ . t . r . e . Tc̃ . v . borđ.

m̃ . vi . semp.ii . seŕ . Silu xii . porc̃ . & . iiii . ac̃ . p̃ti . semp . i . caŕ in dñio

& dim caŕ hom̃ . semp . ii . runc̃ . & . viii . ań . & . vi . porc̃ . 7 xx . oũs.

7 xvi . cap̃ . & . ii . uasa apū . &. i . soc̃ . 7 dim̃ . xxvii . ac̃ . Tc̃ uaɫ . xx . soɫ.

m̃ . xxv . *HVND* . *DE MITTEFORD* . In Jachesham tenet

Ranulfus . f . Gaɫt . xxx . ac̃ . terræ . q̃s tenuit Aldui p̃br liɓ ho . t . r . e.

7 viii . borđ semp . i . caŕ . siɫu . v . porc̃ . & . iiii . ac̃ p̃ti . 7 uaɫ . x . soɫ . & hɫ . vii.

qŕ in long . & . v . in lato . 7 . xx . đ de gelto.

HVNDRET . *DE GALGOV* . Kreich . teñ Turstiñ . fiɫ Guidonis

iiii . caŕ terræ . quas tenuit Kochaga . t . r . e . Sep . vi . uiɫt . & . xiiii . borđ.

& x . seŕu . Tc̃ . iiii . caŕ . in dñio . 7 p̃ . modo . iii . Tc̃ hom̃ . iii . caŕ . modo

ii . & possent restaurari . Silu ad xx . porc̃ . vi . ac̃ p̃ti . Semp . i . runc̃.

Tc̃ xviii . porc̃ . modo . xiii . Tc̃ . ccc . 7 xx . oũs . m̃ . cc . lx . iiii . 7 xx . v . soc̃.

de . i . caŕ . terræ . Tc̃ . vii . caŕ . m̃ . v . Tc̃ uaɫ . iiii . liɓ . m̃ . vi.

HVNĐ . *DE BRODERCROS* . In bruneh̃a teñ hũfriđ . de cuelai

. i . caŕ terræ . q̃s tenuit Kochagana . t . r . e . Tc̃ . ii . uiɫt . 7 m̃ ; Semp . x . borđ.

Tc̃ . ii . seŕu . modo . i . Semp . in dñio . i . caŕ . Tc̃ hom̃ . ii . caŕ . m̃ . i . sed potest

restaurari . M̊ . xl . oũs . Tc̃ uaɫ . xx . soɫ . m̃ . xvi . soɫ.

HVNĐ . *DE GRENE HOGA* . In gueruelei . teñ . turstiñ . fiɫ . Guidonis

. i . beruita quæ ptiñ & . i . caŕ terræ ad creic . v . borđ . semp . i . caŕ . 7 ẽ in

p̃tio de crehic;

FOREHOE Hundred

81 Stanard, an Englishman, holds HINGHAM as a manor, ½ c. of land which A(i)lwin held before 1066.

Then 5 smallholders, now 6; always 2 slaves.

Woodland, 12 pigs; meadow, 4 acres. Always 1 plough in lordship; ½ men's plough. Always 2 cobs; 8 head of cattle; 6 pigs, 20 sheep; 16 goats; 2 beehives.

Also 1 Freeman and a half, 27 acres.

Value then 20s; now 25.

The Hundred and a Half of MITFORD

82 In YAXHAM Ranulf son of Walter holds 30 acres of land which Aldwy, a priest and free man, held before 1066.

8 smallholders.

Always 1 plough; woodland, 5 pigs; meadow, 4 acres.

Value 10s.

It has 7 furlongs in length and 5 in width, tax of 20d.

The Hundred of GALLOW

83 Thurstan son of Guy holds CREAKE, 4 c. of land which Cock Hagni held before 1066.

Always 6 villagers; 14 smallholders; 10 slaves.

Then 4 ploughs in lordship, later (and) now 3. Then 3 men's ploughs, now 2, and they could be restored. Woodland for 20 pigs; meadow, 6 acres; always 1 cob. Then 18 pigs, now 13. Then 320 sheep, now 264.

Also 25 Freemen at 1 c. of land. Then 7 ploughs, now 5.

Value then £4; now 6.

The Hundred of BROTHERCROSS

84 In BURNHAM Humphrey of Culey holds 1 c. of land which Cock Hagni held before 1066.

Then and now 2 villagers; always 10 smallholders. Then 2 slaves, now 1.

Always 1 plough in lordship. Then 2 men's ploughs, now 1, but (another) could be restored.

Now 40 sheep.

Value then 20s; now 16s.

The Hundred of (North) GREENHOE

85 In QUARLES Thurstan son of Guy holds; 1 outlier which belongs to 1 c. of land at Creake.

5 smallholders. Always 1 plough.

It is in the valuation of Creake.

$\mathbb{V}$ Dalliga ten⁊ Ælsi 7 Lefstan . I . lib hō . t . r . e . m̅ . R.

uice coms̅ . II . car terræ . & hanc reuocat . ipse rogerus ⸵ mutuo illi terræ

q̃ rex dedit isaac . I . uilt . 7 . III . bord . VI . soc . XVIII . ac . terræ . VII . ac̅ p̅ti . i̅ toto

179 b

semp . III . car . 7 tc̅ ual . XXX . sot . m̅ . XL . sot

HVNDRET . DE . NORTH . ERPINGEHĀ . Hagan Worda . ten̅ . I . lib

homo Withri . t . r . e . m̅ ten̅ . R . bigot . IIII . car træ . semp . XI . uilt . & . XXX.

bord . Tc̅ . & . post . II . ser . & . m̅ . I . Tc̅ . IIII . car in dn̅io . & p̅ . II . 7 . m̅ . III . 7 semp

v . car . hom̅ . Silu ad . LX . porc . VI . ac̅ p̅ti . Tc̅ 7 p̅ . I . mot . m̅ . II . Tc̅ . I . runc̅.

7 m̅ . V . Tc̅ . XIIII . an̅ . 7 m̅ . XXIIII . Tc̅ . VII . porc . ~~Tc̅ . VII . por~~ . 7 m̅ . XL . Tc̅ . XI.

ous̅ . m̅ . c . 7 . V . Tc̅ XXX . cap̅ . m̅ . XXVI . Tc̅ . VII . uasa apu̅ . 7 modo . VIII . huic

adjac̅ . I . beuuita rostuna . I . car terre . semp . II . uilt . 7 . VIII . bord . 7 . I . seru.

semp . I . car in dominio . 7 . I . car 7 dim hom̅ . III . ac̅ p̅ti.

$\mathbb{V}$ In alabei . I . uilt . & . III . in sutstede . 7 . I . bord . de man̅ p̅dicto . In ingewrda

. I . uilt . quem ten̅ tocho de Wintretune . 7 hc̅ addit . antecet̅ . R . huic

man̅ . $\mathbb{V}$ In aldeburc . I . bord . que̅ ten̅ ulstan . t . r . e . additū similit̅.

$\mathbb{V}$ In turgaitune . II . bord . ptinentes man̅ . $\mathbb{V}$ In calatorp . I . uilt . que̅ ten̅

q̃d uuin̅ d̅ scoto hou . additū similit̅ . & hi tres additi tenent . XXXVI.

ac̅ . terræ . h̅ tot ual . t . r . e . IIII . lib . 7 . p̅ . LX . sot . & m̅ . VI . lib . & h̅t man̅

VIII . q̃r in long̅ . 7 . V . 7 d̅ in lato . 7 de gelto . IX . d̅ . & . obot . & iste Withri.

habebat sachā 7 socā . sup istā trā . 7 rex & coms̅ . VI . forisfacturas ;

86 Alsi and Leofstan, 1 free man, held (Field) DALLING before 1066,
[later] God'... and Robert, now R(oger) the Sheriff, 2 c. of land.
The same Roger claims this back by exchange of that land which
the King gave to Isaac.
  1 villager; 3 smallholders.
  6 Freemen, 18 acres of land; meadow, 7 acres.
  Always 3 ploughs in all.   179 b
Value then 30s; now 40s.

The Hundred of NORTH ERPINGHAM
87 Withri, 1 free man, held HANWORTH before 1066, now R(oger)
Bigot holds, 4 c. of land.
  Always 11 villagers; 30 smallholders. Then and later 2 slaves,
    now 1.
  Then 4 ploughs in lordship, later 2, now 3. Always 5 men's
    ploughs; woodland for 60 pigs; meadow, 6 acres. Then and
    later 1 mill, now 2. Then 1 cob, now 5. Then 14 head of cattle,
    now 24. Then 7 pigs, now 40. Then 11 sheep, now 105. Then
    30 goats, now 26. Then 7 beehives, now 8.

An outlier ROUGHTON is attached to this, 1 c. of land.
  Always 2 villagers; 8 smallholders; 1 slave.
  Always 1 plough in lordship; 1½ men's ploughs.
  Meadow, 3 acres.

In ALBY 1 villager; in SUSTEAD 3 (villagers) and 1 smallholder of
the said manor.

In INGWORTH 1 villager whom Toki of Winterton held; R(oger's)
predecessor added this man to this manor.

In ALDBOROUGH 1 smallholder, whom Wulfstan held before 1066,
was added likewise.

In THURGARTON 2 smallholders belonging to the manor.

In CALTHORPE 1 villager whom Godwin of Scottow held was
added likewise.
These 3 men who were added hold 36 acres of land.
Value of all this before 1066 £4; later 60s; now £6.
  The manor has 8 furlongs in length and 5½ in width, tax of 9½d.
This Withri had the full jurisdiction over this land; the King and
the Earl the 6 forfeitures.

$\bar{H}$. de hapinga . Suttuna ten̄ Edric̄⁹ de laxefelda . t . r . e . iii . car̄ tre.

& dim̄ . ſemp . vi . uill̄ . 7 xvii . bor . 7 . ii . car̄ in dn̄io . 7 . iii . car̄ hom̄ . ſilua . lx . por.

xxxviiii . acr̄ p̄ti . dim̄ ſalina . 7 . ii . r̄ . Tn̄c xxiii . eque filuaticæ . m̄ . vii . Tn̄c

xiii . an̄ . m̄ xxii . tn̄c ix . por . m̄ . xxiii . Tn̄c . clxxx . oũ . m̄ . cc . 7 . iiii . uaſa

ap̄ . & . ii . ſoc̄ xii . ac̄⁷ . 7 dim̄ . huic manerio jac̄& . i . beruita . Catesfelda . i . car̄

træ . ſemp . ii . bord̄ . 7 . i . car̄ i dn̄io . 7 . dim̄ car̄ hom̄ . 7 xviii . acr̄ p̄ti . ſilua

x . por . i . eccla . x . acr . & xiiii . ſoc̄ lxxv . acr̄ . ſep ii . car̄ 7 dim̄ . 7 dim̄ ac̄ p̄ti.

i . eccla . xx . acr̄ . & xxiiii . libi hões . cm̄datione tantũ . ii . car̄ træ . ſep . iiii.

car̄ . 7 xiiii . acr̄ p̄ti . Rex 7 com̄ ſoca̅ . Jac̄& &iam huic manerio . Bru

meſtada ten̄ Rob̄t . qua ten̄ edric̄ . ii . car̄ træ . ſep . ii . uill̄ . 7 . iiii . bord̄.

180 a

tn̄c 7 p̄ . i . car̄ in dn̄io . m̄ . ii . ſep . i . car̄ hom̄ . i . eccla . ix . acr̄ . Silua xvi . por . 7 viii.

acr̄ p̄ti . m̄ . i . mol̄ . 7 . i . an̄ . m̄ . x . por . 7 xl . oũ . 7 xxx . cap̄ . & xvii . libi hões.

cx . acr̄ cm̄datione tantũ . 7 ſc̄s bened̄ cm̄datione de uno . ſep . ii . bord̄.

7 . ii . car̄ . 7 . ii . acr̄ p̄ti . & ten̄& ide . In Stalham . de ix libi hões cm̄datione

edrici tantũ . 7 dimidia ſoca̅ . Rex 7 comes alia medietate . 7 hn̄t . lx . ac̄ træ

7 . i . car̄ 7 dim̄ . 7 . iii . ac̄ p̄ti . In horſheia . iiii . libi hões cm̄datione tantũ

Rex 7 comes ſoca . 7 ht̄ . l . acr̄ . 7 . i . car̄ . 7 vi . acr̄ p̄ti . Om̄s iſti libi hões ual̄ tc̄

xl . ſol̄ . m̄ lxviii . ſol̄ . 7 viii . đ . & totũ maneriu č bereuuitis tn̄c . ual̄ lxxx

ſol̄ . m̄ . vi lib̃ . 7 xi . ſol̄ . 7 . iiii . đ . m̄ totũ ſimul č libis hoib̃ ual̄ . x . lib̄ . hoc

hoc fuit de manerijs comitis Radulfi . & erat ad cenſatũ . x . lib̄ . 7 ſic dedit

eũ Rex Roḡ bigot ut ipſe dicit quando fr̄ ſuus Will̄s uenit de apulia cũ

Goisfrido ridel.

The Hundred of HAPPING

88 Edric of Laxfield held SUTTON before 1066, 3½ c. of land.
    Always 6 villagers; 17 smallholders.
    2 ploughs in lordship; 3 men's ploughs.
        Woodland, 60 pigs; meadow, 39 acres; ½ salt-house; 2 cobs.
        Then 23 wild mares, now 7. Then 13 head of cattle, now 22.
        Then 9 pigs, now 23. Then 180 sheep, now 200. 4 beehives.
    Also 2 Freemen, 12½ acres.
    1 church and 10 acres.

1 outlier, CATFIELD, appertains to this manor, 1 c. of land.
    Always 2 smallholders.
    1 plough in lordship; ½ men's plough.
        Meadow, 18 acres; woodland, 10 pigs.
    Also 14 Freemen, 75 acres. Always 2½ ploughs; meadow, ½ acre.
    1 church, 20 acres.
    Also 24 free men in patronage only, 2 c. of land. Always 4
        ploughs; meadow, 14 acres.
    The King and the Earl (have) the jurisdiction.

BRUMSTEAD also appertains to this manor. Robert holds what
Edric held, 2 c. of land.
    Always 2 villagers; 4 smallholders.
    Then and later 1 plough in lordship, now 2; always 1 men's   180 a
        plough.
    1 church, 9 acres.
    Woodland, 16 pigs; meadow, 8 acres. Now 1 mill; 1 head of
        cattle. Now 10 pigs; 40 sheep; 30 goats.
    Also 17 free men, 110 acres, in patronage only; St. Benedict
(has) the patronage of 1.
        Always 2 smallholders, 2 ploughs; meadow, 2 acres.
    He also holds.

In STALHAM 9 free men under the patronage only of Edric, and
half the jurisdiction, the King and the Earl (have) the other
moiety. They have 60 acres of land, 1½ ploughs and 3 acres of
meadow.

In HORSEY 4 free men in patronage only. The King and the Earl
(have) the jurisdiction. They have 50 acres, 1 plough and 6 acres
of meadow.

Value of all these free men then 40s; now 68s 8d.
Value of the whole manor with its outliers then 90s; now
£6 11s 4d; now value of the whole (manor) together with the
free men £10.
    This was of the manors of Earl Ralph and was leased at £10.
Thus the King gave it to Roger Bigot, so he says, when his brother
William came from Apulia with Geoffrey Ridel.

Eaſt. $\bar{H}$. de ſlec. In trikebei đ. III. libi hōes. A. xxx. I. ac̄ træ. de duobȝ
habuit ailwin cm̄đ tm̄. & de alio Guerd. 7 ſep. I. car̄. 7. II. ac̄ p̄ti. 7 ual. IIII. ſot.
In Rohađ. III. libi hōes cm̄đ tantu ailuuini. XIII. ac̄ 7 dim̄. 7 dim̄ ac̄ p̄ti.
ſep dim̄ car̄. 7. II. ſat 7 dim̄. 7 ual. XVIII. đ. In filebeẏ. IIII. libi hōes. ejđe
ſimit cxvIII. ac̄ træ. 7. I. bor̄. ſemp. II. car̄. 7. IIII. acr̄ p̄ti. 7. II. ſat 7 dim̄.
7 ual. V. ſot. hoc ten& Stanhart. In Neſſa. I. lib̄ hō xv. acr̄ qđ inuaſit ail
uin t. r. Witti. 7 Roḡ reuocat ad ſuū feudu de dono regis ſep. II. boues
7. I. acr̄ p̄ti. 7. III. part ſaline. 7 ual xvI. đ. 7 ten& iđe. In Maltebeẏ. I.
lib̄ hō ſub ailuino cm̄datione tantu. xx. ac̄ 7 dim̄ træ. ſep. III. borđ 7 dim̄.
7. II. bou. 7. I. acr̄ p̄ti. 7 I. ſat. 7 ual. VIII. đ.

Humiliart. $\bar{H}$. hethella. ten̄ Olf̄. teinn̄. t. r. e. II. car̄ træ. 7 xxx
v. ac̄. Tn̄c XII. uitt. p̄ x. m̄. XII. Tn̄c 7 p̄. VII. borđ. m̄ xI. ſemp. II. ſer.
Tn̄c. II. car̄ i dn̄io. p̄. I. m̄. II. 7. I. eccta xxx. ac̄. Tn̄c. v. car̄ hom̄. p̄
7 m̄. III. XII. acr̄ p̄ti. Silua LX. por. m̄. I. mot. Tn̄c. II. r̄. m̄. v. Tn̄c. v. an̄.
m̄. VIII. 7. III. eque ſiluaticæ. Tn̄c. XVIII. porc̄. m̄ xxv. tn̄c. I. oū. m̄.

180 b

LXXX. tn̄c. II. uaſa ap̄. & VIII. ſoc̄. xxx. ac̄ træ. tn̄c 7 p̄. I. car̄. m̄ dim̄. 7. I. ac̄
p̄ti. & ſemp. I. bereuuita. Cheſewic. de. I. car̄ træ. 7 xx. acr̄. Tn̄c. II. uitt.
p̄ 7 m̄. I. ſemp. I. ſer. Tn̄c 7 p̄. I. car̄ in dn̄io. m̄. II. 7. III. acr̄ p̄ti. ſep. I. mot.
Tn̄c ual. cvI. ſot. 7 vI. đ. P̄. vI. lib̄. m̄. VIII. & ht̄. I. leug in long. 7 vI. quar
in lat̄. 7 vI. đ. 7. III. ferđ de gelt. & Cheſewic ht̄. vI. quar in long. 7 v. qr
in lat̄. 7 vI. đ. 7 obolu. de gelt. 7 ten& Aitarđ.

The Hundred of EAST FLEGG

89 In THRIGBY half of 3 free men of A., 31 acres of land. A(i)lwin had the patronage only of 2 and Gyrth of the other.
Always 1 plough; meadow, 2 acres.
Value 4s.

90 In RUNHAM half of 3 free men under A(i)lwin's patronage only, 13½ acres; meadow, ½ acre. Always ½ plough; 2½ salt-houses.
Value 18d.

91 In FILBY 4 free men of the same man's likewise, 118 acres of land.
1 smallholder.
Always 2 ploughs; meadow, 4 acres; 2½ salt-houses.
Value 5s. Stanard holds this.

92 In NESS 1 free man, 15 acres which A(i)lwin annexed after 1066.
Roger claims it as part of his Holding of the King's gift.
Always 2 oxen; meadow, 1 acre; ¾ of a salt-house.
Value 16d. He also holds.

93 In MAUTBY 1 free man under A(i)lwin in patronage only, 20½ acres of land.
Always 3½ smallholders.
2 oxen; meadow, 1 acre; 1 salt-house.
Value 8d.

HUMBLEYARD Hundred

94 Ulf, a thane, held HETHEL before 1066, 2 c. of land and 35 acres.
Then 12 villagers, later 10, now 12. Then and later 7 smallholders, now 11; always 2 slaves.
Then 2 ploughs in lordship, later 1, now 2. Also 1 church, 30 acres. Then 5 men's ploughs, later and now 3. Meadow, 12 acres; woodland, 60 pigs. Now 1 mill. Then 2 cobs, now 5. Then 5 head of cattle, now 8. 3 wild mares. Then 18 pigs, now 25. Then 1 sheep, now 80. Then 2 beehives.   180 b
Also 8 Freemen, 30 acres of land.
Then and later 1 plough, now ½. Meadow, 1 acre.
Always 1 outlier, KESWICK, at 1 c. of land and 20 acres.
Then 2 villagers, later and now 1; always 1 slave.
Then and later 1 plough in lordship, now 2.
Meadow, 3 acres; always 1 mill.
Value then 106s 6d; later £6; now 8.
It has 1 league in length and 6 furlongs in width, tax of 6¾d.
Keswick has 6 furlongs in length and 5 furlongs in width, tax of 6½d. Aitard holds.

t . r . e . ɪɪ . car træ . m̃ ten& Rañ . f . Galt . ſemp . ɪɪɪɪ . uiſt . ⁊ xɪɪ . borđ . Tñc
ɪɪɪ . ſer . m̃ . ɪ . ſep . ɪɪ . car ı dn̄io . & . ɪ . car ⁊ dim̃ hom̃ . vɪɪɪ . ac p̃ti . ſep . ɪɪ . r̃ .
ɪ . ecc̃la xʟ . acr̃ . Tñc . ɪ . moł . m̃ . n̄ . ſ; e ı hetella . tñc . ɪ . an̄ . m̃ . ɪɪɪ . m̃ . xx . por .
⁊ ʟxxx . ou . & vɪɪɪ . ſoc . ʟx . acr̃ . ſep . ɪ . car & dim̃ . Tñc ⁊ p̃ uał . ʟ . ſoł . m̃ . ʟx .
& ħt̃ . ɪ . leu in long . ⁊ dim̃ in lat̃ . ⁊ xvɪ . đ . ⁊ obolu de gelt . q̃cq̃ ibi te
neat . ʃ Karletuna ten& Gualter̃ . quã ten Olf . ɪ . car træ . ⫽p m̃ . ſep
ɪɪ . borđ . ⁊ . ɪ . car in dn̄io . ɪɪɪɪ . ac p̃ti . Silua . ɪɪ . por . tñc . ɪ . r̃ . ⁊ uał . x
ſoł . ɪɪ . æcc̃læ . xxx . vɪɪɪ . acr̃ . In florenduna . x . ac̃ . & in Niwetuna . xv .
acr̃ de dn̄io de hathella . ſep . ɪ . car̃ . ⁊ . ɪ . moł . ⁊ uał . v . ſoł . & Floren
duna h̃& . vɪɪɪ . quar̃ in long̃ . ⁊ . v . in lato . ⁊ . ɪx . đ . ⁊ . ɪɪɪ . ferding . de ·g̃ .

ʃ Depwade . H̃ . Forneſſeta . tenuit Coleman̄ lib̃ ho̅ ſub Stigando .
ɪ . car̃ træ . tñc . ɪ . uiłt . p̃ ⁊ m̃ . ɪɪ . ⁊ . ɪ . ecc̃la xv . acr̃ . tñc vɪɪɪ . borđ . p̃ . x .
m̃ xɪɪɪɪ . ſemp . ɪɪ . car̃ in dn̄io . ⁊ . ɪɪ . car̃ hom̃ . xɪɪ . acr̃ p̃ti . tñc . ɪɪ . r̃ . m̃ v .
tñc . x . an̄ . m̃ . xɪɪ . tñc . ɪ . ou . m̃ ʟxxx . Tñc . ɪ . por . m̃ xvɪɪɪ . & . ɪɪɪ . ſoc .
xxvɪɪ . acr̃ . tñc . ɪ . car̃ . m̃ dim̃ . & . ɪ . bereuita . Oſlaɕtuna ʟxxx . ac̃ .
ſemp . vɪ . borđ . tñc . ɪɪ . car̃ ı dn̄io . ⁊ m̃ ſimił . Tñc . ɪ . car̃ hom̃ . vɪ . ac̃
p̃ti . Silua . ɪɪɪɪ . por . tñc . ɪ . r̃ . Tñc . v . an̄ . m̃ . ɪ . ⁊ . ɪ . porc̃ . & . ɪɪɪ . ſoc . vɪ .
acr̃ . tñc dim̃ car̃ . & alia bereuita . ten& Wiłtm̃ . Tuanatunati xʟ . ac̃ .
ſep . ɪɪɪ . borđ . ſemp . ɪ . car̃ ı dn̄io . & dim̃ car̃ hom̃ . ⁊ . ɪɪɪɪ . acr̃ p̃ti . ⁊ . ɪɪɪ .
an̄ . & . ɪ . ſoc̃ . ɪɪɪ . acr̃ .

95 Ulf also held KETTERINGHAM before 1066, 2 c. of land; now Ranulf son of Walter holds it.

Always 4 villagers; 12 smallholders. Then 3 slaves, now 1.

Always 2 ploughs in lordship; 1½ men's ploughs. Meadow, 8 acres; always 2 cobs. 1 church, 40 acres. Then 1 mill, now none, but it is in Hethel. Then 1 head of cattle, now 3. Now 20 pigs; 80 sheep.

Also 8 Freemen, 60 acres; always 1½ ploughs.

Value then and later 50s; now 60.

It has 1 league in length and ½ in width, tax of 16½d, whoever holds there.

96 Walter holds (East) CARLETON which Ulf held as a manor, 1 c. of land.

Always 2 smallholders.

1 plough in lordship. Meadow, 4 acres; woodland, 2 pigs.

Then 1 cob.

Value 10s.

2 churches, 38 acres.

97 In FLORDON, 10 acres and in NEWTON (Flotman) 15 acres of the lordship of Hethel. Always 1 plough; 1 mill.

Value 5s.

Flordon has 8 furlongs in length and 5 in width, tax of 9¾d.

DEPWADE Hundred

98 Coleman, a free man under Stigand, held FORNCETT, 1 c. of land.

Then 1 villager, later and now 2.

Also 1 church, 15 acres.

Then 8 smallholders, later 10, now 14.

Always 2 ploughs in lordship; 2 men's ploughs. Meadow, 12 acres. Then 2 cobs, now 5. Then 10 head of cattle, now 12. Then 1 sheep, now 80. Then 1 pig, now 18.

Also 3 Freemen, 27 acres. Then 1 plough, now ½.

Also 1 outlier, ASLACTON, 80 acres.

Always 6 smallholders.

Then 2 ploughs in lordship, now the same. Then 1 men's plough; meadow, 6 acres; woodland, 4 pigs. Then 1 cob. Then 5 head of cattle, now 1. 1 pig.

Also 3 Freemen, 6 acres. Then ½ plough.

Also another outlier, SWANTON, 40 acres. William holds.

Always 3 smallholders.

Always 1 plough in lordship; ½ men's plough. Meadow, 4 acres; 3 head of cattle.

Also 1 Freeman, 3 acres.

In kekelingetuna . II . foc . VII . ac . tc dim car.

m . II . bou . In halas . III . foc . XII . ac . tnc . I . car . m dim . tnc totu

181 a

ual . LX . fol . m . VI . lib . Tota hala dim leug in long . & . IIII . quar in lat

7 . IIII d de g . Forneffeta ht . I . leug in long . & dim in lat . 7 VI . d . &

obol . de g . & Oflactuna . I . leug in long . & dim in lat . 7 IX . d de

gelto . Et tuanatuna . XI . qr in long . 7 VI . in lat . 7 X . p . 7 XI . d

& obol de gelt . In Forneffeta . XXX . acr . ten Olf . t . r . e . femp.

I . uilt . 7 . III . bord . 7 . I . fer . Tnc 7 p . I . car i dnio . m . n . fep dim car

hom . VI . acr pti . Silua . VIII . porc . tc . I . r . tc . III . an.

In Kekilingetuna . II . foc . VI . ac . & in tuanatuna . II . foc . VI . acr.

In Waketuna . I . foc . IIII . acr . In muletuna . I . foc . X . ac . In afla

ketuna . I . foc . XXX . acr . femp . I . car . 7 . II . bord . 7 . III . ac pti . In

Tibham . II . foc . LXVI . acr . 7 VIII . bord . Tnc . II . car . m . I . car

& dim . III . acr pti . In Therftuna . II . foc . XLV . acr . tnc . I . car.

m dim . 7 . I . ac pti . In Stretuna . I . foc . XII . acr . In Sceltuna . I . foc

LX . acr . 7 XIIII . bord . 7 VI . uilt . 7 . I . fer . 7 . I . car 7 dim in dnio.

7 . II . car hom . 7 . III . acr pti . filua . VIII . pors . In hierdinc . II . foc.

XXXV . acr . 7 V . bord . fep . II . car . 7 . II . acr pti . Silua . II . pors.

In fredetuna . I . foc . VIII . acr . 7 . II . bou . Tnc ual totu . LXXX.

fol . m . c . 7 X . d . Rex 7 com foca . Stereftuna ten & Robt

de uals . qua ten Vluric Sub ftigando . II . car træ . femp . I.

uilt . tc 7 p XXVI . bord . m XXIIII . femp . II . car in dnio.

In KETTLETON 2 Freemen, 7 acres; then ½ plough; now 2 oxen.
In *HALAS* 3 Freemen, 12 acres. Then 1 plough, now ½.
Value of the whole then 60s; now £6.   181 a
    The whole of *Halas* (has) ½ league in length and 4 furlongs in
width; tax of 4d. Forncett has 1 league in length and ½ in width;
tax of 6½d. Aslacton (has) 1 league in length and ½ in width; tax
of 9d. Swanton (has) 11 furlongs in length and 6 [furlongs] and
10 perches in width; tax of 11½d.
In FORNCETT Ulf held 30 acres before 1066.
    Always 1 villager; 3 smallholders; 1 slave.
    Then and later 1 plough in lordship, now none. Always ½ men's
        plough; meadow, 6 acres; woodland, 8 pigs. Then 1 cob. Then
        3 head of cattle.
In KETTLETON 2 Freemen, 6 acres and in SWANTON 2 Freemen, 6 acres.
In WACTON 1 Freeman, 4 acres.
In MOULTON (St. Michael) 1 Freeman, 10 acres.
In ASLACTON 1 Freemań, 30 acres.
    Always 1 plough.
    2 smallholders. Meadow, 3 acres.
In TIBENHAM 2 Freemen, 66 acres.
    8 smallholders.
    Then 2 ploughs, now 1½ ploughs. Meadow, 3 acres.
In THARSTON 2 Freemen, 45 acres. Then 1 plough, now ½.
    Meadow, 1 acre.
In STRATTON 1 Freeman, 12 acres.
In SHELTON 1 Freeman, 60 acres.
    14 smallholders; 6 villagers; 1 slave.
    1½ ploughs in lordship; 2 men's ploughs. Meadow, 3 acres;
        woodland, 8 pigs.
In HARDWICK 2 Freemen, 35 acres.
    5 smallholders.
    Always 2 ploughs; meadow, 2 acres; woodland, 2 pigs.
In FRITTON 1 Freeman, 8 acres. 2 oxen.
Value of the whole then 80s; now 100(s) 10d.
    The King and the Earl (have) the jurisdiction.

99 Robert of Vaux holds THARSTON which Wulfric held under Stigand,
    2 c. of land.
    Always 1 villager. Then and later 26 smallholders, now 24.
    Always 2 ploughs in lordship.

ɪ . æccɫa . xʟ . acr̅ . 7 uaɫ . ɪɪɪ . foɫ . Tnc . ɪɪ . car̅ hom̅ . m̅ . ɪ . & . ɪ.
car̅ poſſ& reſtaurari . xɪɪ . acr̅ p̅ti . ſilua . x . por . 7 . ɪɪ . moɫ.
Tnc . ɪɪɪɪ . r̅ . m̅ . ɪɪɪɪ . an̅ . Tnc xʟ . por . m̅ . xx . Tnc . ᴋʟ . ou̅.
m̅ . ʟxxx . 7 . ɪ . uaſa apu̅ . & xxxɪɪɪ . foc̅ . ɪ . car̅ træ . Tnc̅
vɪɪɪ . car̅ . p̅ 7 m̅ . ɪɪɪɪ . 7 . ɪɪ . acr̅ p̅ti . Tnc uaɫ . v . liɓ . 7 vɪ . foɫ.
7 m̅ ſimiɫ . 7 ht̅ . ɪ . leug 7 dim in long . 7 . ɪ . quar̅ 7 dim in ɫat.
& xv . d̅ . 7 oboɫ de gelto . ʜuic manerio addidit Roɓ de uals.
vɪɪ . liɓi ho̅es . 7 dim de om̅ib₂ habuit ſuus anteceſſor c̅mdat

181 b

tantu̅ p̅t ex uno qui fuit foc̅ Stigandi . & hn̅t . ʟxxxɪɪ . acr̅ . Tnc̅ 7 p̅ . ɪɪɪ . car̅.
m̅ . ɪɪ . 7 . ɪɪɪ . acr̅ p̅ti . 7 uaɫ xɪɪɪɪ . foɫ . ʃ Hadeſtuna tenuit Ailuin de tedfort.
ɪɪ . car̅ træ . m̅ ten& Roɓt de curcun . femp . ɪ . uiɫɫ . 7 xxɪ . bord̅ . 7 . ɪɪ . fer.
tc̅ . ɪ . car̅ in dn̅io . m̅ . ɪɪ . Tnc̅ 7 p̅ . ɪɪɪ . car̅ hom̅ . m̅ . ɪɪ . vɪ . acr̅ p̅ti . Silua . vɪ.
por . femp . ɪ . moɫ . 7 . ɪ . r̅ . 7 . ɪɪɪ . an̅ . 7 xʟvɪ . por . Et xɪ . ho̅es foca falde 7 com̅d̅.
t . r . e . 7 poſſent uendere t̅ram ſ; confuetudo remanebat in manerio.
7 ht̅ xxvɪ . acr̅ . tc̅ . ɪ . car̅ . 7 dim . m̅ . ɪ . 7 . ɪ . æccɫa . xxx . acr̅ . 7 . ɪɪ . ac̅ p̅ti.
7 dim car̅ . Rex 7 comes foca . tc̅ uaɫ xʟ . foɫ . m̅ ʟxx . foɫ . 7 v . liɓi ho̅es
de duob₂ habuit . 7 . ɪ . bord̅ . Aluui com̅d̅ tantu̅ . & de t̅cio anteceſſor̅
R . malet . 7 de quarto antec̅ Rad̅ ɓlang̅ . 7 de quinto antec̅ Eudonis
fiilij ſpiruie . 7 ht̅ . xʟɪɪ . acr̅ . fep . ɪ . car̅ . 7 . ɪɪɪ . ac̅ p̅ti . 7 uaɫ . vɪ . foɫ.
Rex 7 com̅ foca . Et in hemenhala . ɪ . liɓ ho̅ Aluui . com̅d̅ tantu̅ . xxx.
acr̅ . 7 . ɪ . car̅ . 7 . ɪ . acr̅ p̅ti . ſilua . vɪɪɪ . porc̅ . 7 uaɫ . x . foɫ . 7 ten& Turoɫd̅.

1 church, 40 acres;
value 3s.

Then 2 men's ploughs, now 1, and 1 plough could be restored.
Meadow, 12 acres; woodland, 10 pigs; 2 mills. Then 4 cobs.
Now 4 head of cattle. Then 40 pigs, now 20. Then 40 sheep, now 80. 1 beehive.
Also 33 Freemen, 1 c. of land.
Then 8 ploughs, later and now 4. Meadow, 2 acres.
Value then £5 6s; now the same.

It has 1½ leagues in length and 1½ furlongs in width; tax of 15½d.

Robert of Vaux has added 7 free men and a half to this manor; of all his predecessor had the patronage only except for 1 of them who was a Freeman of Stigand's. They have 82 acres. Then and later 3 ploughs, now 2. Meadow, 3 acres.
Value 14s.

181 b

100 A(i)lwin of Thetford held HUDESTON, 2 c. of land; now Robert of Courson holds.

Always 1 villager; 21 smallholders; 2 slaves.
Then 1 plough in lordship, now 2. Then and later 3 men's ploughs, now 2. Meadow, 6 acres; woodland, 6 pigs. Always 1 mill; 1 cob; 3 head of cattle; 46 pigs.
Also 11 men in fold-rights and patronage before 1066; they could sell the land but the customary dues remained in the manor. They have 26 acres.
Then 1½ ploughs, now 1.
Also 1 church, 30 acres; meadow, 2 acres; ½ plough.
The King and the Earl (have) the jurisdiction.
Value then 40s; now 70s.

Also 5 Freemen; A(i)lwy had the patronage only of 2 and 1 smallholder, of the third R(obert) Malet's predecessor, of the fourth Ralph Berlang's predecessor and of the fifth Eudo son of Spirwic's predecessor. They have 42 acres. Always 1 plough; meadow, 3 acres.
Value 6s.
The King and the Earl (have) the jurisdiction.

101 Also in HEMPNALL 1 free man under the patronage only of A(i)lwy, 30 acres. 1 plough. Meadow, 1 acre; woodland, 8 pigs.
Value 10s. Thorold holds.

In tuanatuna . xxx . acŕ teń hardekinc liƀ hõ . t . r . e . ſep . IIII . borđ.
tc̄ . III . ſer . m̃ . ῏II . ſemp . I . caŕ in dñio . 7 dim̄ caŕ hom̄ . 7 . I . moł . 7 . III.
acŕ p̃ti . & XI . liƀi hóes ſubſe t . r . e . com̃d . XX . acŕ . tc̄ . I . caŕ 7 đ.
m̃ . I . tc̄ uał XV . ſoł . m̃ . XXIII . 7 VII . đ . hoc reclamat de dono reg.
Hoc teń& Walter.

Glauelinga . H̃̃ . Hateſcov . IX . liƀi hóes Stigandi : cXX . acŕ ، 7 . I . borđ.
ſep . II . caŕ . paſtura LXXX . ou . IX acŕ p̃ti . 7 uał XV . ſoł . & ht̄ . I.
leug in long ، 7 VIII . qŕ i lat . 7 IX . đ . 7 . I . ferđ . de g̃ . Roƀ ten.
Hals teń Aleſtan . teinń нeroldi . t . r . e . I . caŕ træ . 7 XL . acŕ.
ſep VIIII . borđ . 7 . II . caŕ in dñio . 7 . I . caŕ hem̄ . 7 V . acŕ p̃ti . ſilua.
III . porc̃ . Tnc̃ . I . ŕ . m̃ . II . tc̄ . I . an̄ . m̃ . II . Tnc̃ XIIII . porc̃ . m̃ . XXVII.
Tc̄ . X . ou . & XIII . liƀi hóes ſoca falde . 7 com̃đ XL . acŕ . Tnc̃ uał
XX . ſoł . m̃ . XL . нic Aleſtan c̃mdau ſe alwino de tedford . tep̃e
regis Wiłłi . 7 ex hoc erat ſaiſit qño rex Wiłł dedit Rogo tram
illi . ſ; hund̄ ñ uidit breue ł liƀatore qđ daret alvino . Totu

182 a
Hals hab&.XV . qrantenas   & . XIII . percas
& . VI . quarantenas in latum . & reddit oc̄to dena
rios de geldo.
Ĩɴ Hadeſcou unus ſochemanus Edrici
de LAXSEFELDA . XXX . acras . et . III . bordari
os . 7 . una carruca & dimidia . VI . acræ prati.
& . IIII . liƀos homines ſub illo . χIX . acras . tc̄
uał . X . ſolidos . modo . XIII . & . IIII . đ Ibi ē
&iam paſtura ad . L . oues.
hic ſocheman c̃õmdauit ſe Aluuino tempore
. Wiłłi . regis . & erat inde ſaiſitus quando
rex dedit terram Rogero bigoto.
Ĩ Hechingheam teń& . Turold de Rogero
quod tenuit liƀ hõ tep̃ore . e . XXVI . acŕ.
7 . I . borđ . & . I . ac̃ . p̃ti . Tc̄ . dimidia carr
modo nulla ſed poteſt reſtaurari & Vał
XVI . denarios.

102 In SWANTON Hardekin, a free man, held 30 acres before 1066.
  Always 4 smallholders. Then 3 slaves, now 2.
  Always 1 plough in lordship; ½ men's plough. 1 mill; meadow,
    3 acres.
  Also 11 free men under him in patronage before 1066, 20 acres.
    Then 1½ ploughs, now 1.
  Value then 15s; now 23(s) 7d.
  He claims this of the King's gift. Walter holds this.

  CLAVERING Hundred
103 HADDISCOE, 9 free men of Stigand's, 120 acres.
  1 smallholder.
  Always 2 ploughs; pasture, 80 sheep; meadow, 9 acres.
  Value 15s.
  It has 1 league in length and 8 furlongs in width, tax of 9¼d.
  Robert holds.

104 Alstan, a thane of Harold's, held HALES before 1066, 1 c. of land.
  and 40 acres.
  Always 9 smallholders.
  2 ploughs in lordship; 1 men's plough. Meadow, 5 acres;
    woodland, 3 pigs. Then 1 cob, now 2. Then 1 head of cattle,
    now 2. Then 14 pigs, now 27. Then 10 sheep.
  Also 13 free men under fold-rights and patronage, 40 acres.
  Value then 20s; now 40.
  This Alstan put himself under the patronage of A(i)lwin of
  Thetford after 1066. He had possession of this when King
  William gave his land to Roger but the Hundred did not see the
  writ or the deliverer that gave him to A(i)lwin.
  The whole of HALES has 15 furlongs and 13 perches [in   182 a
  length] and 6 furlongs in width, it pays tax of 8d.

105 In HADDISCOE 1 Freeman of Edric of Laxfield's, 30 acres.
  3 smallholders.
  1½ ploughs; meadow, 6 acres.
  Also 4 free men under him, 19 acres.
  Value then 10s; now 13(s) 4d.
  There is also pasture for 50 sheep. This Freeman put himself
  under the patronage of A(i)lwin after 1066 and he had possession
  there when the King gave the land to Roger Bigot.

106 Thorold holds HECKINGHAM from Roger which a free man held
  before 1066, 26 acres.
  1 smallholder.
  Meadow, 1 acre. Then ½ plough, now none, but it could be
    restored.
  Value 16d.

$\ulcorner$ *IN* Hatefcou . tenuit . I . liber . homo . I.
acr̃ . & dimid . & . I . bord . & uat . III . đ.
hunc ten& Rob de Rogo.

$\ulcorner$ *IN* Raueringham . tenuit . I . lib̃
homo . XII . acr̃ . t̃ . r̃ . e . de quo Aluuius
erat faifitus quando Rogerus recepit
t̃ram illius hoc ẽ in p̃tio de hatefcou . Idẽ . R . ten&.

182 b

In Nortuna tenuit Vlchetel lib̃ homo
XXX . acr̃ . m̃ tenent . II . homines de feudo
Vlchetelli . Sẽp . I . bor . & dimidiam carr̃.
& . I . acr̃ . prati . & . I . lib̃ homo fub . eo . I . ac̃.
Tota ht̃ . I . leug̃ in longo . & . dimid in
lato . & . XII . denar̃ . de . g̃.

$\ulcorner$ In Turuertuna . II . libi homines XXII.
ac̃ . & . I . ac̃ . p̃ti . & dimid . carrucam.
hoc ten& Rob de Rogo.

In Hethingham . I . lib̃ homo Bondo.
XXX . acr̃ . t̃re . quẽ ten& Rog̃ Sad feudũ
Vlchetelli . f; ipfe Vlchetel habuit dimidiã
commendationem de illo . tẽpore . regis . E.
& de uxore ipsi totã cõmdationem.
& Godricus dapifer eum calump
niatur quod eum tenuit quando
Radulfus comes forisfecit.
& *HVNDRET* teftatur quod
feruieẽbat Godrico fed nefciuɲ
quomodo . & hab& sẽp . I . carrucã.
& . II . ac̃ . prati . Vat . IIII . fot

$\ulcorner$ *IN* *ERPINCHAM* nord *H*und . ht̃
Rogerus . II . bord̃ . de . XV . ac̃.

$\ulcorner$ In Framincham . VIII . bord̃ . XVI . ac̃.
terræ . In bifchelai . Aluric lib̃ hõ . XXIIII . ac̃.
In Porringhelanda . I . lib̃ hõ . XXIIII . ac̃ . 7
. II . bor . & . dim̃ . 7 ualet . VIII . folidos.
Totũ ẽ in Hainefteda *HVNDRETO*.

183 a

Ifti s̃ libi hões Rog̃ bigot Fredrebruge . *H* . 7 dim̃.
In ernneftuna . I . lib̃ hõ . LX . acr̃ t̃re . quem tenet . Robt̃ de uuals.
III . bor . 7 VIII . ac̃ p̃ti . femp . dim̃ car̃ . 7 uat . V . fot . In eãdẽ tenet
idẽ . IIII . libi XL . ac̃ . 7 II . ac̃ p̃ti . t̃ . r . e . I . car̃ . m̃ . dim̃ . 7 uat.
V . fot.

107 In HADDISCOE 1 free man held 1½ acres.
   1 smallholder.
Value 3d.
   Robert holds him from Roger.

108 In RAVENINGHAM 1 free man held 12 acres before 1066; A(i)lwy
had possession of him when Roger acquired his land. This is in
the valuation of Haddiscoe. The same R(obert) holds.

109 In NORTON (Subcourse) Ulfketel, a free man, held 30 acres; now   182 b
2 men hold it from Ulfketel's Holding.
   Always 1 smallholder.
   ½ plough; meadow, 1 acre.
   Also 1 free man under him, 1 acre.
The whole has 1 league in length and ½ in width; tax of 12d.

110 In THURLTON 2 free men, 22 acres. Meadow, 1 acre; ½ plough.
Robert holds this from Roger.

111 In HECKINGHAM 1 free man, Bondi, 30 acres of land; Roger holds
him as part of Ulfketel's Holding but Ulfketel himself had half
the patronage of him before 1066 and the whole patronage of
his wife. Godric the Steward claims him because he held him
when Earl Ralph forfeited. The Hundred testifies that he did
service to Godric but they do not know in what way. He always
has 1 plough and 2 acres of meadow.
Value 4s.

   In NORTH ERPINGHAM Hundred
112 Roger has 2 smallholders, at 15 acres.

   [HENSTEAD Hundred]
113 In FRAMINGHAM 8 smallholders, 16 acres of land.

114 In BIXLEY Aelfric, a free man, 24 acres.

115 In PORINGLAND 1 free man, 24 acres.
   2 smallholders and a half.
Value 8s.
The whole is in HENSTEAD Hundred. These free men are Roger   183 a
Bigot's.

   FREEBRIDGE Hundred and a Half
116 In GRIMSTONE 1 free man, 60 acres of land; Robert of Vaux holds
   him.
   3 smallholders.
   Meadow, 8 acres, always ½ plough.
Value 5s.
In the same he also holds 4 free men, 40 acres; meadow, 2 acres.
   Before 1066, 1 plough, now ½.
Value 5s.

$\tilde{H}$.de chinga.In tigeuuella.ten.toue lib hō sub heroldo
t̃.r.e.1.car t̃ræ.m̂.tenet.Radulfus.Tc̃.1.car.in dn̄io.7 m̂
sēp.1.car.houm.7.vi.uilt.7 1.bor.7.11.ac̃ 7 dim̄.p̃ti.Tc̃ ual
xiii.fot.7.1111.d.m̂.xii.

$\tilde{H}$.de Smetheduna.In hunestuna.1111.libi hoēs.t̃.r.e.
lxv.ac̃ quos tenet.Radulfus f̃.H.Tc̃.1.car.m̂.11.boū.tc̃
ual.xvi.fot.m̂.1111.

$\tilde{H}$.Grimefhou.In mundeforda.lx.ac̃ t̃ræ.quas ten̄.1.lib
hō.sēp.1.car.7.11.bor.7.11.ac̃ p̃ti.filu ad.v.por.Tc̃ ual.7 m̂
11.fot. ⌐In eftereftuna.1.lib hō.de.lx.ac̃.quos tenet.
R.f.H.Tc̃ dim̄.car.Tc̃ ual.xxx.d.m̂.viii.d.

⌐In Stanforda.1.lib hō.lx.ac̃ t̃re.modo tenet Stanard.Tc̃ 7
p̃.dim̄ car.7.11.ac̃ p̃ti.7 ual.11.fot.7 viii.d.

$\tilde{H}$ WeneLVNT.In Greftuna.1.lib hō.xxviii.ac̃ t̃re.
dim̄ car.7 111.ac̃ p̃ti 7 ual.1111.fot.

⌐In breces.viiii.libi hoēs.c.x.ac̃.7.1.uilti.7.1.bor.7.x.
ac̃ p̃ti.sēp.11.car.7.ual.x.fot.

⌐In Saham.1.lib hō.lx.ac̃ t̃re.quē tenet.Rotb̃t.1.car
7 v.bor.7 viii.ac̃ p̃ti.filu.xv.por.7 ual.xxx.fot.

⌐In Tomeftuna.xl.ac̃ t̃re.7 dim̄.car.7 ual.111.fot.

Hundred of DOCKING
117 In TITCHWELL Tovi, a free man under Harold, held 1 c. of land
before 1066; now Ralph holds.
    Then and now 1 plough in lordship; always 1 men's plough.
    6 villagers; 1 smallholder.
    Meadow, 2½ acres.
Value then 13s 4d; now 12.

The Hundred of SMETHDON
118 In HUNSTANTON 4 free men before 1066, 45 acres; Ralph son of
H(erlwin) holds them. Then 1 plough; now 2 oxen.
Value then 16s; now 4.

GRIMSHOE Hundred
119 In MUNDFORD 60 acres of land which 1 free man holds. Always 1
plough.
    2 smallholders.
    Meadow, 2 acres; woodland for 5 pigs.
Value then and now 2s.

120 In STURSTON 1 free man, at 60 acres. R(alph) son of H(erlwin)
holds these. Then ½ plough.
Value then 30d; now 8d.

121 In STANFORD 1 free man, 60 acres of land. Stanard holds now.
Then and later ½ plough. Meadow, 2 acres.
Value 2s 8d.

WAYLAND Hundred
122 In GRISTON 1 free man, 28 acres of land. ½ plough. Meadow, 3 acres.
Value 4s.

123 In BRECKLES 9 free men, 110 acres.
    1 villager; 1 smallholder.
    Meadow, 10 acres; always 2 ploughs.
Value 10s.

124 In SAHAM (Toney) 1 free man, 60 acres of land; Robert holds him.
1 plough.
    5 smallholders.
    Meadow, 8 acres; woodland, 15 pigs.
Value 30s.

125 In THOMPSON 40 acres of land. ½ plough.
Value 3s.

$\bar{H}$. *SCEREPHAM*. In Hocham . iiii . libi hões . 7 In Serphā

v . 7 in Wilebeẏ . i . 7 In beſethorp . i . inť totum . iii . car tr̃æ.

183 b

7 . ii . ac̛ 7 dim̃ . 7 vi . bor . 7 xvii . ac̛ p̃ti . filu̇ . viii . por . sẽp . v . car . totũ

uaɫ . lxviii . foɫ . Soca in Bucham regis . In Scẽpham . i . liƀ hõ.

xxx . ac̛ tr̃e . sẽp . i . bor . 7 iii . ac̛ p̃ti . 7 dim̃ car . 7 uaɫ . iiii . foɫ . Soca

in eoɖe Bueham . In Scerpham . i . liƀ hõ . viii . ac̛ tr̃e . 7 i . ac̛ 7 dim̃.

p̃ti . 7 ii . bou̇ . 7 uaɫ . xvi . ɖ.

$\mathcal{V}$ In beſethorp . i . liƀ hõ . i . dim̃ . car tr̃e . i . uiɫɫs . 7 vii . bor . 7 vi . ac̛

p̃ti . sẽp i . car . in dñio . Tc̃ 7 p̃ . i . car . hoũm . m̃ . ii . boues . filu̇ . viii.

Tc̃ uaɫ . x . foɫ . m̃ . xx . Soca in bucham . In Rochelant dim̃ car

tr̃e . i . liƀ hõ . qu̇e tenet paganus . ii . bor . 7 iii . ac̛ p̃ti . sẽp dim̃.

car̛ . 7 uaɫ . v . foɫ . Soca in bucham .   In Bretham . iii . libi hões

i . car tr̃e qu̇ōs tenet Wiɫɫ de burnevilla . 7 iii . bor . 7 iiii . ac̛.

p̃ti . Tc̃ 7 p̃ . i . car̛ . 7 dim̃ . m̃ . i . 7 uaɫ . xxiii . foɫ . 7 viii . ɖ . Soca

in bucham.

$\vec{H}$. Gilletros . In Lopham . v . libi hões . i . car̛ tr̃e . 7 xx . ac̛.

7 v . bor . 7 v . ac̛ p̃ti . sẽp . ii . car̛ 7 dim̃ . filu̇ . xl . por . Totũ uaɫ xlviii . foɫ

7 iiii . ɖ . Soea in ĸenichala . In Guidenham . i . liƀ hõ . xxiiii . ɫ.

r . e . m̃ . iii . libi hões . ii . ac̛ p̃ti . Tc̃ dim̃ . car̛ . 7 uaɫ . ii . foɫ . Soça

in ĸeninchala . Mitte

SHROPHAM Hundred

126 In HOCKHAM 4 free men, in SHROPHAM 5, in WILBY 1 and in BESTHORPE 1; in all 3 c. of land and 2½ acres.   183 b
6 smallholders.
Meadow, 17 acres; woodland, 8 pigs; always 5 ploughs.
Value of the whole 68s.
The jurisdiction (is) in the King's (manor of) Buckenham.

127 In SHROPHAM 1 free man, 30 acres of land.
Always 1 smallholder.
Meadow, 3 acres; ½ plough.
Value 4s.
The jurisdiction (is) in the same (manor of) Buckenham.

128 In SHROPHAM 1 free man, 8 acres of land;
meadow, 1½ acres. 2 oxen.
Value 16d.

129 In BESTHORPE 1 free man, 1½ c. of land.
1 villager; 7 smallholders.
Meadow, 6 acres; always 1 plough in lordship. Then and later 1 men's plough; now 2 oxen. Woodland 8 [pigs].
Value then 10s; now 20.
The jurisdiction (is) in Buckenham.

130 In ROCKLAND ½ c. of land; 1 free man whom Payne holds.
2 smallholders.
Meadow, 3 acres; always ½ plough.
Value 5s.
The jurisdiction (is) in Buckenham.

131 In BRETTENHAM 3 free men, 1 c. of land; William of Bourneville holds them.
3 smallholders.
Meadow, 4 acres. Then and later 1½ ploughs, now 1.
Value 23s 8d.
The jurisdiction (is) in Buckenham.

GUILTCROSS Hundred

132 In LOPHAM 5 free men; 1 c. of land and 20 acres.
5 smallholders.
Meadow, 5 acres. Always 2½ ploughs; woodland, 40 pigs.
Value of the whole 48s 4d.
The jurisdiction (is) in Kenninghall.

133 In QUIDENHAM 1 free man, 24 [acres] before 1066; now 3 free men; meadow, 2 acres. Then ½ plough.
Value 2s.
The jurisdiction (is) in Kenninghall.

$\bar{H}$.Mitteford 7 dim̄.In Thurſtuna.xx.ac̕ tr̃e.1.lib hō quē
tenet Rotb̃t.1.car̕.7 iiii.ac̕.p̃ti.7 iiii.ſoc̕.7 dim̄.x.ac̕.7 ual̃
iiii.ſol̃.1.eccl̃a.xvi.ac̕ 7 ual̃.xvi.đ.

$\bar{H}$.de *GALGOV*.In creich.iiii.libi hoēs de dimidia car̕ tr̃e
quos tenet Turſtinus filus Widonis.Tc̄.1.car̕ & dim̄.m̄.ii.bou̕
7 ual̃ iii.ſol̃.

$\bar{H}$.de *BRODECROS*.In bruneham.tenet idē.ii.libi hoēs.
de.1.car̕ tr̃e Tc̄ 7 m̄.x.bor.ſep.in dñio.1.car̕.Tc̄ hoūm
.1.car̕.m̄.đ.7.ii.par̃t.de mol̃.đ.ac̕ p̃ti.Tc̄ ual̃.viii.ſol̃.m̄

184 a

xviii.ſol̃. Γ In eadem uilla.ii.libi hoēs de dim̄ car̕ tr̃e tenet
idem.Sēp.ii.bor.Sēp dim̄ car̕.Tc̄ ual̃.ii.ſol̃.m̄.xii.đ.
Γ In depedala.1.lib hō de dim̄.car̕ tr̃e.tenet idē.Sēp.iii.bor.Sēp
1.car̕.Tc̄ ual̃.xx.ſol̃.m̄.x.

Γ In reineham de fcdo ſtigand̕ ep̄i.teñ.1.lib hō dim̄ car̕ tr̃e.m̄ tenet
eadvuunus.Sēp.iiii.ſer̕.Tc̄.1.car̕.m̄.dim̄.ii.acr p̃ti.Tc̄ ual̃.x
ſol̃.m̄.v.ſol̃.In fut reinham.1.lib hō.de.xx ac̕ tr̃e quē tenet.aitard̕.
7.1.bor.Sēp.dim̄ car̕.1.ac̕ p̃ti.Tc̄ ual̃.v.ſol̃.m̄.iii.ſol̃.

$\bar{H}$.*HOLT*.In marſtuna.1.lib homo de dim̄.car̕ tr̃e.quē tenet
Turald̕.7 iiii.bor.7.1.car̕.7 ual̃.xx.ſol̃.

MITFORD Hundred and a Half

134 In *THUR(E)STUNA* 20 acres of land; 1 free man whom Robert holds.
1 plough; meadow, 4 acres.
    Also 4 Freemen and a half, 10 acres.
Value 4s.
    1 church, 16 acres;
value 16d.

The Hundred of GALLOW

135 In CREAKE 4 free men, at ½ c. of land, whom Thurstan son of
Guy holds. Then 1½ ploughs; now 2 oxen.
Value 3s.

The Hundred of BROTHERCROSS

136 In BURNHAM he also holds; 2 free men, at 1 c. of land.
    Then and now 10 smallholders.
    Always 1 plough in lordship. Then 1 men's plough, now ½.
        Two-thirds of a mill; meadow, ½ acre.
Value then 8s; now 18s.

184 a

137 In the same village 2 free men, at ½ c. of land. He also holds.
    Always 2 smallholders.
    Always ½ plough.
Value then 2s; now 12d.

138 In (Burnham) DEEPDALE 1 free man at ½ c. of land. He also holds.
    Always 3 smallholders.
    Always 1 plough.
Value then 20s; now 10.

139 In RAYNHAM 1 free man held ½ c. of land of Bishop Stigand's
Holding; now Edwin holds it.
    Always 4 slaves.
    Then 1 plough; now ½. Meadow, 2 acres.
Value then 10s; now 5s.

140 In SOUTH RAYNHAM 1 free man, at 20 acres of land, whom Aitard
holds.
    1 smallholder.
    Always ½ plough; meadow, 1 acre.
Value then 5s; now 3s.

HOLT Hundred

141 In MORSTON 1 free man, at ½ c. of land, whom Thorold holds.
    4 smallholders.
    1 plough.
Value 20s.

$\bar{H}$. DE NORTHERPINGEHAM. In Haganaworda teñ. Withri.

III. libos hões. m̃. r. bigot m̃. ħnt. I. bor. 7. LX. ac̃ tr̃e. tc̃. I. car̃
7 dim̃. 7 femp 7 III. uirgas. p̃ti. Tc̃ 7 p̊. ual. x. fol. 7 m̃. xviii.

In hametuna teñ. Withri. t̃. r. e. III. liɓ hões. 7 herold. I. m̃. teñ.
. r. bogot. fẽp. I. car̃ tr̃e. 7. I. uilts. 7. III. bor. 7 dim̃. 7 II. car̃. III.
ac̃ p̃ti. 7. I. mol̃. tc̃ 7 p̊. ual. xx. fol. m̃. xxx. 7 viii. đ.

V In futftede teñ. Withri. I. liɓum hoẽm. 7. I. teñ. Ulftan. t. r. e.
m̃. R. 7 ħñt. xxx. ac̃ tr̃e. 7. I. bor. 7 dim̃. fẽp. 7. I. car̃. I. ac̃
p̃ti 7 dim̃. 7 m̃. I. mol̃. Tc̃ 7 p̊. ual. viii. fol. 7. m̃. xii. In al
mertun&. I. liɓ. hõ. elwini. m̃. rog̃. 7 ħt. I. car̃ tr̃e. fẽp. vii. uilti.
7 vii. bor. 7. I. car̃. in dñio. 7. I. car̃. houm. 7 fub ifto. II. foc̃. xvi. ac̃
tr̃e. 7 fẽp dim̃ car̃. 7 filu. ad. IIII. por. I. ac̃ 7 dim̃ p̃ti. tc̃ 7 p̊.
ual. xx. fol. 7 m̃. xL. In felebruge. II. libi. hões gerti. 7 ħt. II.
car̃ tr̃e. fẽp. I. uilts. 7 vii. bor. 7. II. car̃ in dñio. 7. I. car̃ houm
Silua ad. Lx. por. IIII. ac̃ p̃ti. 7. ifte ħt. viii. foc̃. đ. Lxiii. ac̃
tr̃e. 7 fẽp. I. car̃ 7 dim̃. houm. Silua ad vi. por. Tc̃. 7 p̊. ual.
xL. fol. 7 m̃. IIII. liɓ. ħt dim̃ leug̃. in long̃ 7. IIII. qr̃. 7. III. perc̃.

184 b

in lato. 7 de gelto. III. đ. 7 obolum. 7 metune. v. qr̃ in longo. 7
IIII. 7 vi. perc̃ in lato. 7 de delto. v. đ.

V In greffam teñ. alward. IIII. foc̃. đ. xiii. ac̃ tr̃e femp dim̃. car̃.
I. ac̃ p̃ti. ap̃ptiati ft. cum. IIII. liɓ. In eadem uilla. I. liɓ hõi
de xxx. ac̃ tr̃e. femp. II. bor. 7 dim̃ car̃.

The Hundred of NORTH ERPINGHAM

142 In HANWORTH Withri held 3 free men; now R(oger) Bigot (holds).
Now they have 1 smallholder. 60 acres of land.
Then and always 1½ ploughs. Meadow, 3 roods.
Value then and later 10s; now 18.

143 In METTON Withri held 3 free men before 1066 and Harold 1; now
Roger Bigot holds. Always 1 c. of land.
1 villager; 3 smallholders and a half.
2 ploughs; meadow, 3 acres; 1 mill.
Value then and later 20s; now 30(s) 8d.

144 In SUSTEAD Withri held 1 free man and Wulfstan held 1 before
1066; now R(oger holds). They have 30 acres of land.
Always 1 smallholder and a half.
1 plough; meadow, 1½ acres. Now 1 mill.
Value then and later 8s; now 12.

145 In AYLMERTON 1 free man of A(i)lwin; now Roger (holds). He has
1 c. of land.
Always 7 villagers; 7 smallholders.
1 plough in lordship; 1 men's plough.
Under him 2 Freemen, 16 acres of land. Always ½ plough;
woodland for 4 pigs; meadow, 1½ acres.
Value then and later 20s; now 40.

146 In FELBRIGG 2 free men of Gyrth's. They have 2 c. of land.
Always 1 villager; 7 smallholders.
2 ploughs in lordship; 1 men's plough. Woodland for 60 pigs;
meadow, 4 acres.
Also he has 8 Freemen at 63 acres of land. Always 1½ men's
ploughs; woodland for 6 pigs.
Value then and later 40s; now £4.
It has ½ league in length and 4 furlongs and 3 perches in width, 184 b
tax of 3½d. Metton (has) 5 furlongs in length and 4 [furlongs]
and 6 perches in width, tax of 5d.

In GRESHAM Alward holds 4 Freemen, at 13 acres of land. Always
½ plough; meadow, 1 acre. They are assessed with the 4 free (men).
In the same village 1 free man, at 30 acres of land.
Always 2 smallholders;
½ plough.

alward̉.ɪɪɪ.bor.7 h̄ɫ dim̃ car̉.In b̃nigeham.ɪ.ſoꝯ d̃.xɪɪ.aꝯ̉

t̃re.tꝯ arabat cum.ɪɪ.bouib̉ m̃ cum dim̃.car̉.In ald̉ebur

ɪ.lib hõ.d̃ xxx.aꝯ t̃re quem teñ.ᴋetel.t.e.ɾ.dim̃.aꝯ p̃ti.

In Almertun&.ɪɪ.ſoꝯ quos teñ.Alward̉.de xɪɪ.aꝯ t̃re.7 ɪɪɪ.

bor.Semꝑ cum dim̃ car̉ arar̉ 7 hoc totum ē in p̃tio de felebruge

⌐ In Runetune.ɪ.lib̃um hoēm tenuit bundo.t̄.r.e.de.xxx.

aꝯ t̃re.lib̃atus fuit ꝑ uno lib̃o ſ; m̃ tenent̄.lib̃i.v.uilℏ.7.ɪɪ

bor.ſēp.ɪ.car̉.Silu̇.ad.ɪɪɪɪ.por.ɪ.aꝯ p̃ti.tꝯ 7 p̃.val̃.vɪɪɪ.

ſol.fuit ꝑ.xx.ſol.ſ; n̄ potuit redd̃e.7.ideo ē m̃.ꝑ xv.

⌐ In ruſtuna teñ.Withri.t.r.e.ɪɪ.lib̃os hoēs.de xxx.aꝯ t̃re.

Silua.ad.ɪɪ.por.dim̃ aꝯ p̃ti.tꝯ 7 p̃.ual̃.v.ſol.m̃.x.7.ɪɪɪɪ.d̃

hic teñ.edricus.ɪ.lib̃um hoē.ɪɪɪ.aꝯ d̃ n̄ poꞇant reced̃e ſine licentia

edric.ſ; hoēs rotb̃.malet calumpniatur.

⌐ In ſutfelle.ɪɪɪɪ.lib̃os hoēs 7.ɪ.de iſtis teñ.Withri.7 rex.al̃tum

7 herold̉.ɪɪ.alios.ɪɪ.car̉ t̃re.S̃ēp.x.uilℏ.7 xɪ.bor.T̃ꝯ 7 ſ̃ēp

ɪɪɪɪ.car̉ in dñio.7.ɪɪɪ.car̉ hoũm.Silua ad xɪɪ.por.ɪɪɪɪ.aꝯ p̃ti

tꝯ 7 p̃.ɪɪ.mol̃.m̃.ɪɪɪɪ.tꝯ 7 p̃.ual̃.ɪɪɪɪ.lib̃ 7.m̃.vɪ.lib̃.7 xv.

ſol.7 h̄ɫ.vɪɪɪ.qr̉.in longo.7 v.7 dim̃.in lato.7 xɪɪɪ.d̃.7

obolum de gelto.

⌐ In b̃ningeham.xvɪ.aꝯ.t̃re d̃ dñio p̃dicꞇo.Silua ad.ɪɪɪɪ.por.

⌐ In antigeham.ɪɪ.bor h̄ɫ dim̃ car̉.app̃ꞇiati s̄ɫ in ſutfelle.

In SUSTEAD Alfward holds 3 smallholders. He has ½ plough.

In (North) BARNINGHAM 1 Freeman, at 12 acres of land. Then he ploughed with 2 oxen, now with ½ plough.

In ALDBOROUGH 1 free man, at 30 acres of land, whom Ketel held before 1066; meadow, ½ acre.

In AYLMERTON 2 Freemen whom Alfward holds, at 12 acres of land. 3 smallholders. They have always ploughed with ½ plough.

All this is in the valuation of Felbrigg.

147 In RUNTON Bondi held 1 free man before 1066, at 30 acres of land. He was delivered for 1 free (man). Now 2 free (men) hold.
5 villagers; 2 smallholders.
Always 1 plough; woodland for 4 pigs; meadow, 1 acre.
Value then and later 8s; it was for 20s but could not pay and so it is now for 15.

148 In ROUGHTON Withri held 2 free men before 1066, at 30 acres of land.
Woodland for 2 pigs; meadow, ½ acre.
Value then and later 5s; now 10(s) 4d.
Edric holds 1 free man here, 3 acres. They could not withdraw without Edric's permission. But Robert Malet claims the men.

149 In SUFFIELD 4 free men; Withri holds 1 of these, the King another, Harold 2 others. 2 c. of land.
Always 10 villagers; 11 smallholders.
Then and always 4 ploughs in lordship; 3 men's ploughs.
Woodland for 12 pigs; meadow, 4 acres. Then and later 2 mills, now 4.
Value then and later £4; now £6 15s.
It has 8 furlongs in length and 5½ in width, tax of 13½d.

In (North) BARNINGHAM 16 acres of land of the said lordship.
Woodland for 4 pigs.

In ANTINGHAM 2 smallholders have ½ plough. They are assessed in Suffield.

In hoc antigeham . III . liɓi hoēs . I . fuit almari . alƚ alwoldi

185 a

ťi . unſpati . I . caŕ 7 dim̃ tře . tenent . quos tenet Torſtinus . f.
Ẃd . femp . IIII . uiłti . 7 . IIII . bor . Tē 7 p̃ . I . caŕ . 7 dim̃ . 7 . m̃ . II .
caŕ . 7 dim̃ . III . ać p̃ti . 7 . II . caŕ hoūm . ſep . tē 7 p̃ . uaƚ . xxv.
ſoƚ . m̃ . xxxvi . ſoƚ.

⫶ In aldeburc . IIII . liɓi hoēs quos tenuit ɧeroldus . t . e . r . de
dim̃ caŕ . tře . Sẽp . vi . bor . Sẽp . III . caŕ . I . ać p̃ti . I . moƚ.
7 dim̃ . tõ 7 p̃ . xv . ſoƚ . m̃ . xxx . ſ; fueŕ . ad . xl . ſ; nõn potueŕ
redde . ⫶ In turgartuŋ& . I . liɓ . ɧõ . quễ teñ iluingus de XII.
ać tře . ſemp . arat . cum dim̃ . caŕ . tē 7 p̃ . uaƚ . II . ſoƚ . m̃ . v .

⫶ In ſcepedane . I . liɓ ɧõ teñ osɓņus . t . e . r . xl . ać tře . m̃ tenet
Torſtinus . tē . III . bor . m̃ . v . ſep . I . caŕ in dñio . 7 dim̃ caŕ
hoūm . I . ać p̃ti . Silua ad . xxx . por . 7 . I . ſoç . de III . ać tře.
Tē 7 p̃ . uaƚ . vIII . ſoƚ . m̃ . x .

⫶ In ɓningeham teū . Osfert . III . liɓi hoēs . de dim̃ . caŕ ţerre.
Sẽp v . bor . tē 7 p̃ . caŕ 7 dim̃ . m̃ . II . caŕ 7 dim̃ . I . ać p̃ti.
tē 7 p̃ . uaƚ . x . ſoƚ . 7 . m̃ . L . 7 ɧ̃t x . q̃ŕ in lonḡ . 7 vi . in lato.
7 de gelto . xvi . đ.

⫶ In betham . I . liɓ ɧõ . de . Lx . ać ţeŕŕe . Semp . I . uiłts 47 III.
bor . 7 . I . caŕ in dñio . 7 dim̃ hoūm . Silu ad . v . por . ţ . ać p̃ti . 7 . I.
ſoç . de . IIII . ać teŕŕe . tē 7 p̃ . uaƚ . v . ſoƚ . 7 . IIII . đ . 7 m̃ . x . ſoƚ.

⫶ In ɓningeham . I . liɓ ɧõ . de . III . ać tře cū . II . bouibᷱ aŕ tē
7 p̃ . uaƚ . xvi . đ . m̃ . III . ſoƚ . Suꝑ oēs liɓos iſťi . Hund ɧ̃t reɈ
ſacā 7 ſocam.

150 In this ANTINGHAM 3 free men; 1 was A(e)lmer's, another Alwold's and the third Ospak's. They hold 1½ c. of land. Thurstan son of   185 a
Guy holds them.
>Always 4 villagers; 4 smallholders.
>Then and later 1½ ploughs, now 2½ ploughs. Meadow, 3 acres.
>>Always 2 men's ploughs.
Value then and later 25s; now 36s.

151 In ALDBOROUGH 4 free men whom Harold held before 1066, at ½ c. of land.
>Always 6 smallholders.
>Always 3 ploughs; meadow, 1 acre; 1½ mills.
[Value] then and later 15s; now 30; they were at 40 but they could not pay.

152 In THURGARTON 1 free man whom Ylfing holds, at 12 acres of land. He has always ploughed with ½ plough.
Value then and later 2s; now 5.

153 In SHIPDEN 1 free man (whom) Osbern held before 1066, 40 acres of land; now Thurstan holds.
>Then 3 smallholders, now 5.
>Always 1 plough in lordship; ½ men's plough. Meadow, 1 acre; woodland for 30 pigs.
>Also 1 Freeman, at 3 acres of land.
Value then and later 8s; now 10.

154 In (North) BARNINGHAM Osferth holds; 3 free men, at ½ c. of land.
>Always 5 smallholders.
>Then and later 1½ ploughs, now 2½ ploughs. Meadow, 1 acre.
Value then and later 10s; now 50.
>It has 10 furlongs in length and 6 in width, tax of 16d.

155 In (East) BECKHAM 1 free man, at 60 acres of land.
>Always 1 villager; 3 smallholders.
>1 plough in lordship; ½ men's [plough]. Woodland for 5 pigs; meadow, 1 acre.
>Also 1 Freeman, at 4 acres of land.
Value then and later 5s 4d; now 10s.

156 In (North) BARNINGHAM 1 free man, at 3 acres of land. He ploughs with 2 oxen.
Value then and later 16d; now 3s.
>The King has the full jurisdiction over all the free men of this Hundred.

H̄.*FLECWEST*. Iñ burc. teñ. 1. liƀ hō Alwi cōmd̄ tantũ
t. r. e. c. vi. ac t̄re. m̄ tenet ſtanhard. xii. ac p̄ti. Sep̄
1. uiƚƚ. viii. bor. Sep̄. 1. car in dñio. 7 dim̄ car hoũm. 7 ſuƀ
eos. xvii. liƀi. hoēs. lxxxix. ac t̄re. xii. ac p̄ti. Sem̄p. iii. car̄.

T̄c. 7 ſemp uálebat. xx. ſoƚ. hoc tenet idem.
ꟊ In Wintretúna. 1. liƀ hō de. xxi. ac t̄re. 7 dim̄ ac p̄d. Sep̄ dim̄
car̄. 7. ē in p̄tio Ailwardi de felebrúge. hoc tenet idē.

H̄. *HEINESTE*. In ſcoteſſam. iiii. liƀi hoēs ſc̄i. be. 1. uƚfi. q̄r̄t
gert cōmd̄. t̄. r. e. lx. ac t̄re. 7. i. ac p̄ti. 7. iii. bor. Sep̄. i.
car̄. 7 dim̄. T̄c uaƚ. ii. oras p̄ 7 m̄. x. ſoƚ. Hoc tenet idē.
ꟊ In ſtokes. 1. liƀ. hō gert cōmd̄. t. r. e. de. xxiiii. ac t̄re. quē
teñ. R. cōm. qm̄ ſe foreſec̄. cum dim̄ t̄ra 7 Ro. baiḡ aliam
teſte hund. m̄. tenet. Ro. bigot. 7 reuocat ad ſeudum ſuóꝛ
liƀoꝛ ex dono regis. 7 aitard. coñt dicit. Hundret qui hoc
teſtat ſ; meinard. affirmat cum hundreto. Sub eo ſep̄. iii. bor.
7 ſep̄. i. car̄. 7 adhuc ſub eo. iii. ſoc. de viiii. ac t̄re. 7. iii. partes
i. moƚ. 7. iii. ac p̄ti. T̄c uaƚ. v. ſoƚ. 7 ſep̄. 7 hoc. cognoſcit. R. bigot.
ſuſcepiſſe p̄q. R. ſe fore fecit ad ſeruandum in manu regis. 7
huc ſeruat.

WEST FLEGG Hundred
157 In BURGH (St. Margaret) 1 free man under the patronage only of
A(i)lwy held 106 acres of land before 1066; now Stanard holds.
Meadow, 12 acres.
Always 1 villager; 8 smallholders.
Always 1 plough in lordship; ½ men's plough.
Also 17 free men under them, 89 acres of land; meadow, 12
acres. Always 3 ploughs.
Value then and always 20s. He also holds this. 185 b

158 In WINTERTON 1 free man, at 21 acres of land; meadow, ½ acre.
Always ½ plough.
It is in the valuation of Aelward of Felbrigg.
He also holds this.

HENSTEAD Hundred
159 In SHOTESHAM 4 free men, [2] under the patronage of St. Benedict,
1 of Ulf and the fourth of Gyrth before 1066; 60 acres of land;
meadow, 1 acre.
3 smallholders.
Always 1½ ploughs.
Value then 2 orae; later and now 10s. He also holds this.

160 In STOKE (Holy Cross) 1 free man under the patronage of Gyrth
before 1066, at 24 acres of land. Earl R(alph) held him when he
forfeited with half the land and Ro(ger) Bigot (held) the other
(half) as the Hundred testifies; now Roger Bigot holds him and
claims him as part of the Holding of his free (men) from the
King's gift. Aitard contradicts the Hundred who testify this but
Maynard affirms it with the Hundred.
Under him always 3 smallholders.
Always 1 plough.
Further 3 Freemen under him, at 9 acres of land; ¾ of 1 mill;
meadow, 3 acres.
Value then and always 5s.
R(oger) Bigot acknowledges this to have been received, after
R(alph) forfeited, to be kept in the King's hand and he still keeps it.

In frieſtuna . I . liɓ . hõ ulſi . cõmd .   hoc te

net Ranulfus. ⫽ In framingaham . I . liɓ hõ . ulſi cõmd,

In ailuertuna . I . liɓ hõ . ſtigã hoc tenet idẽ . ⫽ In Rokelunda

IIII liɓi hõẽs ulſi hoc tenet idẽ . In ſcutherlingahã . II . dĩm.

liɓi hõẽs ulſi . hoc tenet idẽ . In braɓretuna . I . liɓ hõ ulſi cõmd.

hoc tenet idẽ Inſ oẽs . LXVIII . aċ t̃re . 7 . IIII . bor . 7 . III . aċ p̃ti.

Sẽp . I . caŕ . 7 dĩm . Tc̃ uaɫ . XVI . ſoɫ . m̃ . XX . ſoɫ . ⫽ In treus . I . liɓ.

hõ anſgot cõmd . t . r . e . XL . aċ t̃re . 7 IIII . bor . Hoc tenet idẽ.

7 . I . liɓ . hõ dĩm . ſub eo . IIII . aċ p̃ti . Tc̃ 7 p̃ . inſ oẽs . I . caŕ . m̃.

II . Tc̃ . 7 p̃ . v . ſoɫ . m̃ . VII . ſoɫ . hſ . III . qŕ . in lõng . 7 . III . qãr in

lato 7 de gelto . IX . d̃ . 7 obolum . ⫽ In ſcoteſſam . I . liɓ hõ ulſi.

cõmd . X . aċ t̃re . 7 dĩm . aċ p̃ti . Tc̃ . II . bou . m̃ . dĩm caŕ . Sẽp.

uaɫ . XVI . d̃ . idem tenet . ⫽ In ſaſilingaham . I . liɓ . hõ ulſi.

186 a

cõmd . t . e . r . XXIIII . aċ t̃re . 7 I . aċ p̃ti . Sẽp dĩm caŕ . Sẽp . uaɫ.

III . ſoɫ . hoc tenet idem . ⫽ In ailũtuna . I . liɓ hõ ſtigandi cum

ſoca . cõmd . t . r . e . de XX . aċ t̃re . modo tenet aitardus . IIII.

bor . I . aċ 7 dĩm . p̃ti . Sẽp . I . caŕ . 7 dĩm . 7 ſub eo . III . ſoc̃ . 7 dĩm . de

X . aċ . t̃re . Tc̃ 7 p̃ . uaɫ . v . ſoɫ . m̃ . XX . ⫽ In porrinkelanda . I.

liɓ hõ edrici . de XII . aċ t̃re . 7 dĩm . aċ p̃ti . Sẽp . aŕ . cum . III . bou.

Tc̃ 7 ſemp uaɫ . XII . d̃ . Hunt ailumtuna hſ . IIII . qŕ . in longo . 7 . III.

qŕ . in lato . 7 de gelto . X d̃ . 7 obolum . hoc tenet idẽ . Porringalanda

hſ v . qŕ in longo . 7 . IIII . d̃ . lato . 7 de gelto . XII . d̃.

161 In FRITTON 1 free man under the patronage of Ulf. Ranulf holds this.
In FRAMINGHAM 1 free man under the patronage of Ulf.
In YELVERTON 1 free man of Stigand's. He also holds this.
In ROCKLAND (St. Mary) 3 free men of Ulf's. He also holds this.
In SURLINGHAM 2 halves-a-free-man of Ulf's. He also holds this.
In BRAMERTON 1 free man under the patronage of Ulf. He also holds this.
Between them all 68 acres of land.
    4 smallholders.
    Meadow, 3 acres; always 1½ ploughs.
Value then 16s; now 20s.

162 In TROWSE 1 free man under the patronage of Ansgot before 1066, 40 acres of land.
    4 smallholders. He also holds this.
    1 free man (and) a half under him; meadow, 4 acres.
    Then and later between them all 1 plough, now 2.
[Value] then and later 5s; now 7s.
    It has 3 furlongs in length and 3 furlongs in width, tax of 9½d.

163 In SHOTESHAM 1 free man under the patronage of Ulf, 10 acres of land; meadow, ½ acre. Then 2 oxen, now ½ plough.
Value always 16d. He also holds.

164 In SAXLINGHAM 1 free man under the patronage of Ulf before 1066, 24 acres of land; meadow, 1 acre. Always ½ plough.   186 a
Value always 3s. He also holds this.

165 In YELVERTON 1 free man with jurisdiction under the patronage of Stigand before 1066, at 20 acres of land; now Aitard holds.
    3 smallholders.
    Meadow, 1½ acres; always 1½ ploughs.
    Under him 3 Freemen and a half, at 10 acres of land.
Value then and later 5s; now 20.

166 In PORINGLAND 1 free man of Edric's, at 12 acres of land; meadow, ½ acre. He has always ploughed with 3 oxen.
Value then and always 12d.
    'Hunt' Yelverton has 4 furlongs in length and 3 furlongs in width, tax of 10½d. He also holds this.
Poringland has 5 furlongs in length and 4½ (in) width, tax of 12d.

$\bar{H}$.dim̃.Herſam.In ſtereſtuna teñ.1.lib̃ hõ ſc̃e aldrede.t̃ r.e.

7 ſtigandi erat ſoca 7 ſaco in herſam.ſ; nec dare nec uend̃e pot̃at

t̃ram ſuam.ſine licentia ſc̃e aldrede 7 ſtigandi.dim̃ car̃ t̃re.

m̃ tenet Goduinus.7 ſub eo.111.bor.Sẽp.1.car̃ in dñio.7 v111.

libi hõẽs ſub eo.de xx.ac̃.Sẽp.111.car̃.Sẽp ual̃.x.ſol̃.m̃.R.

bigot reuocat ad feudum lib̃oƶ ſuoƶ ex dono regis.Sed hund̃

teſtat̃ qd̃.qñõ Ricard̃ punnat̃ erat p̃poſit in herſam.p̃tinebat

in herſã ſ; ille q̃.m̃ tenet.Tc̃ ſub p̃poſitus ricardi.in erſam.ab

ſtulit.7.teſte hund̃ 7 dedit cenſũ in erſã.xx.ſol̃.7.v1.d̃.uno

q̃q̃ anno de hac t̃ram.nominatim.7 de alia.ſ; hoc anno ñ

reddidit.7 W.de noiers habuit huc uſq̃ cenſum.

$\bar{H}$.LOTNINGA.In bethingahã.teñ.offo teinñ.ſtigandi

p̃.mañ.1.car̃ t̃re.t̃.r.e.m̃ tenet id̃e.Sẽp.x11.bor.7.11.

ſer̃.Sẽp.11.car̃ in dñio.7.111.car̃.hoũm.7.111.ac̃ p̃ti.Sẽp

11.eq̃.in dñio 7.1x.por.Sẽp xx.cap̃.Tc̃ ual̃.x.ſol̃.m̃.xxx.

V In ſithinga.teñ.1.lib̃.hõ ſub gert.t.r.e.xxx.ac̃ t̃re.7 11.

ſer̃.Tc̃ dim̃.car̃.m̃.1.i̓ dñio.id̃e tenet.7 ſub eo tenet id̃e

v1.libi.hõẽs.xxx.ac̃ t̃re.in ſoca ſtigandi.Sẽp.11.car̃ it̃ eos.

186 b

V In eadem.1.lib̃ hõ ſtigandi c̃omd̃.t e.R.1.car̃ t̃re.m̃ tenet

id̃e.Sẽp.1.uil̃li.7 v11.bor.Silua.x11.por.Tc̃ dim̃.car̃.

in dñio m̃.1.car̃.Sẽp.dim̃ car̃ hoũm.7.111.ac̃ p̃ti.7

1.mol̃.7 ſub eo.v111.libi hõẽs.c̃omd̃ in ſoca ſtigandi.

xx.ac̃ t̃re.7.11.ſer̃.Sẽp.1.car̃.Tc̃ totum ual̃ xx.ſol̃.

m̃.xl.

EARSHAM Half-Hundred

167 In STARSTON 1 free man of St. Etheldreda's held before 1066. The full jurisdiction was Stigand's in Earsham. But he could not grant or sell his land without the permission of St. Etheldreda and of Stigand. ½ c. of land. Now Godwin holds.

3 smallholders under him; always 1 plough in lordship.

8 free men under him, at 20 acres; always 3 ploughs.

Value always 10s.

Now R(oger) Bigot claims it as part of the Holding of his free (men) from the King's gift but the Hundred testify that when Richard Poynant was reeve in Earsham, it belonged in Earsham but he who now holds, then Richard's under-reeve in Earsham, took it away. The Hundred testify that he gave tribute in Earsham of 20s 6d in any one year expressly from this and other land but he has not paid this year. Hitherto W(illiam) of Noyers had the tribute.

LODDON Hundred

168 In BEDINGHAM Offa, a thane of Stigand's, held 1 c. of land as a manor before 1066; now he also holds.

Always 12 smallholders; 2 slaves.

Always 2 ploughs in lordship; 3 men's ploughs. Meadow, 3 acres. Always 2 horses in lordship; 9 pigs; always 20 goats.

Value then 10s; now 30.

169 In SEETHING 1 free man under Gyrth held 30 acres of land before 1066.

2 slaves.

Then ½ plough, now 1 in lordship.

He also holds.

Under him he also holds 6 free men, 30 acres of land in Stigand's jurisdiction; always 2 ploughs between them.

In the same 1 free man under the patronage of Stigand before 186 b 1066, 1 c. of land; now he also holds.

Always 1 villager; 7 smallholders.

Woodland, 12 pigs. Then ½ plough in lordship, now 1 plough.

Always ½ men's plough; meadow, 3 acres; 1 mill.

Under him 8 free men in patronage in the jurisdiction of Stigand, 20 acres of land.

2 slaves;

always 1 plough.

Value of the whole then 20s; now 40.

⫟In mundahā . ɪ . liƀ hō goduini ſub gert . t̄ . ɪ . e.
xxx . ac̄ tr̄e . m̄ . tenet id̄e . Sēp . v . bor . Sēp . dim̄ . car̄
apptiat̄ . i . xʟ . ſoł . In ead̄e . ɪɪɪ . liƀi hōes ejdem ſub gert.
xvɪ . ac̄ tr̄e . Semp . ɪ . car̄ . Sēp . uał . v . ſoł . hoc tenet id̄e.
⫟In ſithinga . ɪ . liƀ hō ſtigandi cōm̄d . xvɪ . ac̄ . Tc̄ dim̄ . car̄
m̄ . ɪ . Sēp . uał . xxxɪɪ . đ . Hoc tenet id̄e . ⫟In bron tēn.
toka . ɪ . liƀ . homo heroldi . cōm̄d . t̄ ɪ . e . xxx . ac̄ . ⁊ vɪ . ac̄
p̄ti . Tc̄ ɪ . car̄ . m̄ dim̄ . Soca in hund̄ . Sēp . uał x . ſoł.
⫟In ᴋarlentona . ɪ . liƀ hō goduini . xx . ac̄ . ⁊ . ɪɪ . bor . Sēp . dim̄
car̄ . Sēp . uał . xx . đ.

H̄ . Erpincham ſud . Alebei . ɪ . car̄ tr̄e tēn . ɪ liƀ hō.
Osfort . ꝑ mā . ſub heroldo . modo tenent . ɪɪɪɪ . ſui filii . ſemp
ɪɪɪ . uiłti . ⁊ . v . bor . Tc̄ ⁊ p̄ . ɪ . car̄ in dñio . Tc̄ ⁊ p̄ . ɪɪ . hōum . m̄.
int̄ totum . ɪɪɪɪ . ⁊ . ɪ . moł . Tc̄ ⁊ p̄ . uał . xx . ſoł . m̄ . xʟ . ⁊ ħt
vɪ . q̄r̄ . in lonḡ . ⁊ . v . in lato . đc̄q, ibi teneat . ⁊ . ɪɪɪ . đ . ⁊ obō
de gelto ; In Buc . ɪɪ . liƀi hōes . xc . ac̄ tr̄e . ſēp . ɪɪ . bor . ⁊.
ɪ . car̄ ⁊ dim̄ . ⁊ dim̄ ac̄ p̄ti . m̄ dim̄ moł . Tc̄ ⁊ p̄ . uał . xv.
ſoł . m̄ . xxv . ſoł . ⁊ . ɪɪɪɪ . đ . ⁊ ħt . ɪɪɪ . q̄r̄ in lonḡ . ⁊ . ɪɪ . in
lato . ⁊ . ɪɪ . de . gelto . In Erpincham . ɪ . liƀ hō heroldi.
xxx . ac̄ tr̄e . ſemp . ɪ . bor . ⁊ dim̄ . car̄ . ⁊ dim̄ . ac̄ p̄ti . Tc̄
⁊ p̄ . uał . ɪɪɪɪ . ſoł . m̄ . v . ⁊ . ɪɪɪɪ . đ.

170 In MUNDHAM 1 free man of Godwin's under Gyrth before 1066, 30 acres of land; now he also holds.
 Always 5 smallholders.
 Always ½ plough.
It is assessed in the 40s.
In the same 3 free men of the same man's under Gyrth, 16 acres of land; always 1 plough.
Value always 5s. He also holds this.

171 In SEETHING 1 free man under the patronage of Stigand, 16 acres. Then ½ plough, now 1.
Value always 32d. He also holds this.

172 In BROOME Toki, 1 free man under the patronage of Harold, held 30 acres before 1066; meadow, 6 acres. Then 1 plough, now ½. The jurisdiction (is) in the Hundred.
Value always 10s.

173 In CARLETON (St. Peter) 1 free man of Godwin's, 20 acres.
 2 smallholders.
 Always ½ plough.
Value always 20d.

SOUTH ERPINGHAM Hundred
174 Asford, 1 free man, held ALBY, 1 c. of land, as a manor under Harold; now his four sons hold.
 Always 3 villagers; 5 smallholders.
 Then and later 1 plough in lordship. Then and later 2 men's [ploughs], now 4 in all. 1 mill.
Value then and later 20s; now 40.
 It has 6 furlongs in length and 5 in width, whoever holds there, tax of 3½d.

175 In BURGH (next Aylsham) 2 free men, 90 acres of land.
 Always 2 smallholders.
 1½ ploughs; meadow, ½ acre. Now ½ mill.
Value then and later 15s; now 25s 4d.
 It has 3 furlongs in length and 2 in width, tax of 2[s].

176 In ERPINGHAM 1 free man of Harold's, 30 acres of land.
 Always 1 smallholder.
 ½ plough; meadow, ½ acre.
Value then and later 4s; now 5(s) 4d.

LX . ac̗ tr̅æ . modo tenet Turoldus . T̅c̅ 7 p̚ . v . bor . m̊ . II .

187 a

ſemp . I . car̗ in dn̅io . 7 dim̅ . car̗ hou̅m . Silua v . por . 7 . I . ſoc̗
I . ac̗ . T̅c̅ ual . x . ſol̅ . m̊ . xx . In Wicmera . ix . libi h̅o̅es ejuſde̅
I . car̗ tr̅e . m̊ tenet Rot̅b̅t̅ d̲e cu꞊con . ſe̅p . v . bor . 7 . II . ſer . 7
II . car̗ . 7 . I . ac̗ p̊ti . Silu̚ . x . por . T̅c̅ ual . xx . ſol̅ . m̊ . xxx . 7
vi . q̅r̅ . in long̅ . 7 IIII . in lato . 7 . VIII . d̄ . de gelto . In eade̅ .
II . libi h̅o̅es heroldi 7 almari ep̅i . xxx . ac̗ . ſe̅p . II . bor . 7 dim̅
car̗ . 7 dim̅ . ac̗ . p̊ti . T̅c̅ III . part . I . mol̅ . T̅c̅ ual . VIII . ſol̅ . m̊
XII .

H̃ Tonſteda . In felmicham . I . car̗ tr̅æ . que p̊tinent . IIII.
h̅o̅ib꙼ de Sudfelda . ſemp . VII . bor . 7 . IIII . ſoc̗ in eadem tr̅am̊
ſemp . II . car̗ . 7 . I . ac̗ 7 dim̅ . p̊ti . 7 hoc e̅ in p̅tio de Sudfelda
. In eade̅ . IIII . libi . h̅o̅es . LXXX . ac̗ ſemp . IIII . bor . 7 . II . car̗ .
7 . II . ac̗ p̊ti . 7 I . mol̅ . T̅c̅ ual . x . ſol̗ xvi . 7 . IIII . d̄ . 7 l̅t̅ . I.
leug̅ in longo . 7 . v . q̅r̅ in lato . 7 xviii . d̄ . de gelto . vnus ex iſti꙼
q̊tuor . fuit h̅o̅ antec̅ . R . malet .

V In Smalebga . III . libi h̅o̅es . I . car̗ tr̅e . ſemp . XII . bor . 7 . IIII.
ſoc̗ . T̅c̅ 7 p̚ . III . car̗ . m̊ . IIII . 7 . II . ac̗ p̊ti . ſilu̚ . vi . por . duo
ex h̅ . ſt̅ in p̅tio de antingham 7 r̅cius . ual . x . ſol . Vnus ex h̅ fuit
h̅o̅ anteceſſoris . Rob̅ . malet 7 alii . ſc̅i . benedicti . ipſemet . S꙾
b . ſocam .

177 In (Bacons)THORPE 1 free man of the same man's, 60 acres of land; now Thorold holds.

    Then and later 5 smallholders, now 2.

    Always 1 plough in lordship; ½ men's plough. Woodland,   187 a
       5 pigs.

    Also 1 Freeman, 1 acre.

Value then 10s; now 20.

178 In WICKMERE 9 free men of the same man's, 1 c. of land; now Robert of Courson holds.

    Always 5 smallholders; 2 slaves.

    2 ploughs; meadow, 1 acre; woodland, 10 pigs.

Value then 20s; now 30.

    (It has) 6 furlongs in length and 4 in width, tax of 8d.

In the same 2 free men of Harold's and Bishop A(e)lmer's, 30 acres.

    Always 2 smallholders.

    ½ plough; meadow, ½ acre. Then ¾ of 1 mill.

Value then 8s; now 12.

    TUNSTEAD Hundred

179 In FELMINGHAM 1 c. of land which belongs to 4 men of Suffield.

    Always 7 smallholders; 4 Freemen on the same land.

    Always 2 ploughs; meadow, 1½ acres.

This is in the valuation of Suffield.

In the same 4 free men, 80 acres.

    Always 4 smallholders.

    2 ploughs; meadow, 2 acres; 1 mill.

Value then 10s; now 16(s) 4d.

    It has 1 league in length and 5 furlongs in width, tax of 18d.

One of those 4 was the man of R(obert) Malet's predecessor.

180 In SMALLBURGH 3 free men, 1 c. of land.

    Always 12 smallholders; 3 Freemen.

    Then and later 3 ploughs, now 4.

    Meadow, 2 acres; woodland, 6 pigs.

Two of these are in the valuation of Antingham; the value of the third is 10s.

    One of these was the man of Robert Malet's predecessor, the others of St. Benedict's. S(t.) B(enedict has) the jurisdiction.

In dillam . ɪ . lib̄ hō . Edrici . ʟx . ac̄ tr̄e . sēp . v . bor.
7 . ɪ . car̄ . 7 . ɪ . ac̄ p̄ti . hoc ē in p̄tio de Sudfelda.

H̃ . de Hapinga . In Palinga . ɪ . lib̄ hō Guerd . ɪ . car̄ tr̄e.
sēp . v . bor . 7 . ɪ . car̄ in dn̄io 7 xxɪɪɪɪ . ac̄ p̄ti . 7 . ɪ . car̄ hom̄.
In eadē . v . hōēs xxxɪɪɪ . ac̄ quos tenet hugo de hoſdenc.
sēp . ɪ . car̄ Tc̄ ual̄ . xx . ſol̄ . m̄ . xʟ . ex iſtis . erant . ɪɪɪɪ . libi
ut non poſſent recedɇ n̄ dando . ɪɪ . ſol̄.

Γ In Wacſteneſham . dim̄ . libi . hom̄ . vɪɪ . ac̄ tr̄æ . 7 ē in eod̄ p̄tio.

187 b

In Stalham . ɪ . lib̄ ho . xv . ac̄ . hoc tenet idē Γ In bruneſtada
ɪ . lib̄ hō . xv . ac̄ . 7 In horſeia . ɪ . lib̄ hō . xɪɪ . ac̄ . Ex his non habuit
Ailwinus ſuus . anteceſ &iam cōm̄d . t̄ . r e . 7 tam̄ eos reuocat
ad ſuum feudum . ex dono regis . quia ille Ailwinus habuit
comendationē ex eis . t . r . w . Sēp . ɪ . car̄ . 7 . ɪɪɪɪ . ac̄ p̄ti.
7 ual̄ . ɪɪɪɪ . ſol̄ . Rex 7 comes ſocam.

H̃ . de Humiliart . In Carletuna . xxvɪɪ . libi . hōes . 7 dim̄.
ſub . Olfo . cōmdatione tantum 7 ſoca falde . t . r . e . 7 h̄t
ɪ . car̄ terre 7 dedim̄ . 7 x . ac̄ 7 ɪɪɪɪ . libi hōes 7 de duob꜀ ante
ceſſor Ranulfi pipelli cōm̄d . de ſcio medietatē ⁙ habuit 7 an
teceſſor eudonis dapiferi ⁙ ſimilit̄ de uno 7 de medietate alt̄i
de qb꜀ ſuus antec̄ nichil habuit 7 h̄t . ʟ . ac̄ In̄ totum h̄t . ɪɪɪɪ·
car̄ . 7 v . ac̄ p̄ti.

181 In DILHAM 1 free man of Edric's, 60 acres of land.
Always 5 smallholders.
1 plough; meadow, 1 acre.
This is in the valuation of Suffield.

The Hundred of HAPPING

182 In PALLING 1 free man of Gyrth's, 1 c. of land.
Always 5 smallholders.
1 plough in lordship; meadow, 24 acres; 1 men's plough.
In the same 5 men, 33 acres; whom Hugh of Houdain holds.
Always 1 plough.
Value then 20s; now 40.
Of those 4 were free although they could not withdraw except
by giving 2s.
In WAXHAM a half-a-free-man, 7 acres of land. It is in the same
valuation.

183 In STALHAM 1 free man, 15 acres. He also holds this.   187 b
In BRUMSTEAD 1 free man, 15 acres.
In HORSEY 1 free man, 12 acres.
His predecessor A(i)lwin did not have even the patronage of
these before 1066; however he claims them as part of his Holding
from the King's gift because A(i)lwin had the patronage of them
after 1066.
Always 1 plough; meadow, 4 acres.
Value 4s. The King and the Earl (have) the jurisdiction.

The Hundred of HUMBLEYARD

184 In (East) CARLETON 27 free men and a half under Ulf in patronage
only and fold-rights before 1066. He has 1½ c. of land and 10
acres. Also 4 free men; Ranulf Peverel's predecessor had the
patronage of 2 and a moiety of the (patronage) of the third,
Eudo the Steward's predecessor likewise (had the patronage) of
1 and a moiety (of the patronage) of the other, of these his
predecessor had nothing. They have 50 acres. In all they have 4
ploughs; meadow, 5 acres.

In Suerdeftuna . I . lib̄ hō . VIII . ac̄ . In Suer

deftuna h̄t . VI . q̄r in lonḡ . 7 v . in latō . 7 XIII . d̄ ; t̄ . e . r.

Florenduna . XV . lib̄i hōēs ſub olfo ſoca falde 7 c̄ōmdatione

tantum . In Braccles . I . lib̄ hō eodē m̄ . In̄t totum h̄t . c .

ac̄ . II . min̄ . 7 . v . bor . 7 . I . ac̄ p̄ti . ſemp . II . car̄ . In Neilanda

7 In Vrnincham . IX . lib̄ hōēs . ex hoꝛ VIII . 7 dim̄ ꞉ habuit ante ▪

-ceſſor R . c̄ōmdatione tantum . 7 ſoca falde 7 anteceſſor .

hermeri . de uno medietatem ſoca falde ꞉ 7 c̄ōm̄d tātum .

In Waſincham . VI . lib̄i hōēs . ſub antec̄ . Roḡ . ſoca falde 7 c̄ōm

datione tantum . In̄t totum h̄t . c . XXX . ac̄ . ſēp . III . car̄ .

7 I . mot̄ . 7 . I . bor . In Braccas . v . lib̄i hōēs . de quatuor ⸱ habuit

antec̄ . Roḡe . bigot dimidiā c̄ōmdatione . 7 de quinto totam .

7 antec̄ . Ran̄ . piperelli de quatuor . ſimilit̄ . 7 h̄t . c . L . ac̄ t̄re

ſēp . II . car̄ . 7 dim̄ . 7 VI . ac̄ p̄ti . In Florenduna . v . lib̄i hōēs

de H̄ habuit antecef . R . dim̄ c̄ōmdatione tātum . 7 antec̄ .

188 a

eodrici dapiſcri . ſimilit̄ . 7 hun̄t . I . car̄ t̄re ꞉ 7 . XXX . ac̄

7 . II . bor . 7 . II . ac̄ p̄ti . ſemp̄ . II . car̄ . In Eilanda IIII ꞉

lib̄ hōēs . I . car̄ t̄re . 7 . IIII . bor . ſēp . II . car̄ . 7 . IIII . ac̄ p̄ti .

de duobꝣ libis . 7 dim̄ habuit antec̄ . Roḡ . c̄ōmda . t̄ . r . e .

7 ſtigandus de uno . 7 antec̄ Hermeri . de dimidio꞉

In duneſtuna . III . lib̄i hōēs 7 dim̄ . XLIX . ac̄ . c̄ōmdatione

tantum . t̄ . r . e . ſēp . III . bor . 7 . I . car̄ . 7 II . ac̄ p̄ti .

185 In SWARDESTON 1 free man, 8 acres.
In Swardeston it has 6 furlongs in length and 5 in width, tax of 13d before 1066.

186 FLORDON, 15 free men under Ulf in fold-rights and patronage only. In BRACON ASH 1 free man in the same way. In all it has 100 acres less 2.
5 smallholders.
Meadow, 1 acre; always 2 ploughs.

187 In NAYLAND and in WRENINGHAM 9 free men. R(oger's) predecessor had the patronage only of 8 and a half of these and fold-rights and Hermer's predecessor (had) the moiety of 1 in fold-rights and patronage only.

188 In WALSINGHAM 6 free men under Roger's predecessor in fold-rights and patronage only. In all they have 130 acres.
Always 3 ploughs; 1 mill; 1 smallholder.

189 In BRACON ASH 5 free men. Roger Bigot's predecessor had half the patronage of 4 and the whole (patronage) of the fifth, Ranulf Peverel's predecessor (had the half patronage) of 4 likewise. They have 150 acres of land.
Always 2½ ploughs; meadow, 6 acres.

190 In FLORDON 5 free men. R(oger's) predecessor had half the patronage only of these and Godric the Steward's predecessor 188 a likewise. They had 1 c. of land and 30 acres.
2 smallholders.
Meadow, 2 acres; always 2 ploughs.

191 In NAYLAND 4 free men, 1 c. of land.
4 smallholders.
Always 2 ploughs; meadow, 4 acres.
Roger's predecessor had the patronage of 2 free men and a half before 1066, Stigand of 1 and Hermer's predecessor of a half.

192 In DUNSTON 3 free men and a half in patronage only before 1066, 49 acres.
Always 3 smallholders.
1 plough; meadow, 2 acres.

Manegrena . 1 . lib ħo 7 dim̃ . de hoc habuit antec̃ . Rog̃
dimid . cõm̃d . 7 antec̃ē . Godrici fimilit̃ 7 ħt . xxx . 111 . ac̃.
In Suedeftuna . viii . libi . ex trib₂ 7 dimidio habuit fuus
ant̃ . cõm̃d . tantũ t̃ . e͂ . r̃ . 7 de q̃tuor ꞉ antec̃ . Godrici.
fimilit ; 7 de dimidio antec̃ . R . piperelli fimilit̃ . Inter
totum ħt . xlv . ac̃ . 7 11 . bor . fēp . 1 . car̃ 7 dim̃ . 11 . ac̃ p̃ti.
In torp . 1 . lib ħo cõm̃d tantũ . xv . ac̃ . 7 . 11 . libi . ħoēs.
de . 1111 . ac̃ dim̃ ac̃ p̃ti . 7 dim̃ . car̃ . In Molkebteftuna
. 1 . lib ħo xxx . ac̃ . fub antec̃ Godrici cõmdatione tantũ
t̃ . e͂ . r̃ . fēp . 11 . bor . tc̃ dim̃ . car̃ . m̃ . 1 . In eadem . 1 . libã
feĩ . fub antec̃ . Godrici cõm̃d . tantũ t̃ . e . r̃ . xxx . ac̃
tr̃e 7 ex hoc erat Godricus faifitus q̃do . R . forisfecit
7 ex debito reddebat ei . v . fot . 7 q̃ ħo Rog̃ē cõm̃d
tantũ filius ejud̃e mulieris manebat in ead̃e
tr̃am cũ matre fua . 7 . ideo . Ro . reuocat dimidiã
tr̃am . 7 pat̃ ejd̃e ħõis habuit in alio loco . aliam
tr̃am libam fub anteceffore . R . cõm̃d tantũ . 7 1 illã
tr̃am tenet . Rog̃ totam . In ilt fupiorib₂ xxx . ac̃
Tc̃ . 1 . car̃ . 7 dim̃ . m̃ . 1 . 7 . 1111 . bor . 7 . 11 . ac̃ p̃ti . 7 fub fe
11 . 11 . libi ħoēs . 7 dim̃ cõm̃d . tantũ . de . xvii . ac̃ 7 dim̃.

188 b
femp . dim̃ . car̃ . Oм̃s ifti libi ħoēs . uat . t . e͂ . r̃ . viii . lib.
p̃ . x . m̃ . xv . lib . 7 v . fot . 7 v . d̃ . 7 obolum.
In Ketrincham . v . libi ħoēs dim̃ cõm̃d tantũ . fub antec̃.
Rog̃ . 7 didmidia cõm̃datione fub antec̃ Godrici . 7 ħt . 1.
car̃ . terre . 7 . xvi . ac̃ modo tenet Ranulfus . f . G . fēp
1 . bor . tc̃ 7 p̃ . 11 . car̃ . m̃ . 1 . car̃ . 7 dim̃ . 7 . 1111 . ac̃ p̃ti . 7.
uat . x . fot.

193 In MANGREEN 1 free man and a half. Of this Roger's predecessor had half the patronage and Godric's predecessor likewise. He has 33 acres.

194 In SWARDESTON 8 free (men). Of 3 and a half his predecessor had the patronage only before 1066. Of 4 Godric's predecessor likewise, and of half R(anulf) Peverel's ancestor likewise. In all it has 45 acres.
2 smallholders.
Always 1½ ploughs; meadow, 2 acres.

195 In SWAINSTHORPE 1 free man in patronage only, 15 acres.
Also 2 free men, at 4 acres; meadow, ½ acre; ½ plough.

196 In MULBARTON 1 free man under Godric's predecessor in patronage only before 1066, 30 acres.
Always 2 smallholders.
Then ½ plough, now 1.
In the same 1 free woman under Godric's predecessor in patronage only before 1066, 30 acres of land. Godric had possession of this when R(alph) forfeited and she duly paid him 5s. A certain man of Roger's in patronage only, the son of this woman, dwelt on the same land with his mother and so Roger claims half the land. The father of this man had other free land in another place under R(oger's) predecessor in patronage only. Roger holds all that 1 land.
On the above 30 acres then 1½ ploughs, now 1.
4 smallholders.
Meadow, 2 acres.
Under those 2 free men and a half in patronage only, at 17½ acres; always ½ plough.   188 b
Value of all these free men before 1066 £8; later 10; now £15 5s 5½d.

197 In KETTERINGHAM 5 free men in half patronage only under Roger's predecessor and in half patronage under Godric's predecessor. They have 1 c. of land and 16 acres. Now Ranulf son of Walter holds.
Always 1 smallholder.
Then and later 2 ploughs, now 1½ ploughs. Meadow, 4 acres.
Value 10s.

In kefewic . XIIII . libi hoēs . quos tenet

aitard . IIII . fub antec̄ . Roḡ comd tantū . 7 de v.

foca falde 7 cōmd . 7 . v . fub antec̄ . Godrici cōmdtāt

7 hn̄t . LX . ac tc̄ . I . car . 7 dim . p 7 m̄ . I . 7 dim . ac p̄ti .

In edem . IIII . libi hoēs . duo cōmd . tantū . 7 unus fub

antec̄ Godrici . fimilit̄ 7 quart . ſtigandi fimilit̄ .

7 hn̄ . I . car tr̄e . de . XXX . ac iſtius tr̄e faifitus erat

Godricus . qm̄ . R . forisfecit 7 due fue mulieres ibi

manebant m̄ eam tenet aitard . de Roḡ . II . bor̄ .

fēp . II . car . 7 VI . ac p̄ti . Tc̄ ual . in̄t totum . XV fol

m̄ . XXV . Rex . 7 comes de omībz̄ iſtis lībis hoibz̄ foca

In Colenen . I . lib hō Stigandi cōmd tantū . I . car tr̄e .

quem tenet Waregerius . femp . II . uiƚƚ . 7 x . lib hoēs

fub eo cōmd . tantū . XXIIII . ac . tc̄ . III . car . p̄ . IIII .

car 7 dim . m̄ . I . car . 7 II . boues . 7 VI . ac p̄ti .

7 . I . mol . Tc̄ ual . XX . fol . m̄ . XXX .

In Florenduna . v . libi hoēs de q̄tuor habuit

antec̄ . Roḡ . cōmd . tantum . 7 antef . Roḡ . de Rām̄ .

de q̄nto . 7 hn̄t . XV . ac . 7 dim . car 7 ual . XVI . d.

ꝟ In eadē . II . lib hoēs de uno 7 de medietat & altius ha

buit Stigandus . cōmd t . ē . R . 7 de alia medietate

189 a

habuit antec̄ Roḡ bigot cōmd tantū . t . ē . r . 7 hn̄t . XXX . ac

7 . II . bor . 7 dim car . 7 . I . ac p̄ti . 7 ual . IIII . fol . De dimidia

hac tr̄a erat Godricus faifitus ad fuum feudum qn̄ . R . foris

fecit . In Cringaforda . I . lib hō Stigandi . XV . ac . 7 . II . bor .

7 . II . libi hoēs VII . ac . 7 dim . femp . dim car . 7 . I . ac 7 dim .

p̄ti . 7 . VIII . pars mol . 7 ual . III . fol .

198 In KESWICK 14 free men whom Aitard holds; 4 under Roger's predecessor in patronage only, 5 in patronage and fold-rights and 5 in patronage under Godric's predecessor. They have 60 acres.
　Then 1½ ploughs, later and now 1. Meadow, ½ acre.
In the same 4 free men; 2 in patronage only, 1 under Godric's predecessor likewise and the fourth of Stigand's likewise. They have 1 c. of land. Godric had possession of 30 acres of this land when R(alph) forfeited and 2 of his women dwelt there. Now Aitard holds it from Roger.
　2 smallholders.
　Always 2 ploughs; meadow, 6 acres.
In total, then 15s, now 25. The King and the Earl (have) the jurisdiction of all these free men.

199 In COLNEY 1 free man under the patronage only of Stigand, 1 c. of land. Warenger holds him.
　Always 2 villagers.
　9 free men under him in patronage only, 24 acres.
　Then 3 ploughs, later 3½ ploughs, now 1 plough and 2 oxen.
　　Meadow, 6 acres; 1 mill.
Value then 20s; now 30.

200 In FLORDON 5 free men. Roger's predecessor had the patronage only of 4 and Roger of Raismes's predecessor of the fifth. They have 15 acres and ½ plough.
Value 16d.
In the same 2 free men. Stigand had the jurisdiction over 1 and a moiety of the other before 1066 and Roger Bigot's predecessor 189 a had the patronage only of the other moiety before 1066. They have 30 acres.
　2 smallholders.
　½ plough; meadow, 1 acre.
Value 4s.
　Godric had possession of half of this land as part of his Holding when R(alph) forfeited.

201 In CRINGLEFORD 1 free man of Stigand's, 15 acres;
　2 smallholders.
　Also 2 free men, 7½ acres.
　　Always ½ plough; meadow, 1½ acres; one-eighth of a mill.
Value 3s.

In Raineſtorp . dim lib hō cōm̄d . t̄ . e . r . xxx ac̓ . m̄ tenet
Wareg̃js . Tc̄ . ii . uiłłi . m̄ . i . ſep . dim̄ . car̓ . 7 . i . ac̓ p̃ti . 7 uał .
v . ſoł . In Niweſtuna . i . lib̄ hō . xv . ac̓ . 7 ii . bor . 7 uał . xvi . d̃ .
In Flórenduña . i . lib̄ hō xxx . ac̓ . tc̄ dim̄ car̓ . ex hoc habuit
antec̄ Godrici cōm̄d . 7 uał . iii . ſoł .

H̃ . Depwade . In forneſſeta . vi ́ . lib̄i . hōēs cōm̄d . ʟxxxv .
ac̓ . Tc̄ . iii . car̓ . m̄ . ii . v . ac̓ p̃ti . 7 In halſa . iiii . lib̄i . hōēs
xxxvi . ac̓ . ſep . ii . car̓ . 7 . iii . ac̓ p̃ti . In Carletuña . iii . lib̄i .
hōēs . xii . ac̓ . 7 dim̄ car̓ 7 . i . ac̓ p̃ti . In Fredetuña : iii . lib̄i hōēs
7 dim̄ . ʟxxx . ac̓ . 7 . xiii . bor . ſemp . ii . car̓ . 7 dim̄ car̓ hoūm .
7 . iii . ac̓ p̃ti . 7 . i . ecclā . xʟ . ac̓ . 7 . i . ſoc̓ 7 dim̄ ſub iłł . v . ac̓ .
In Carletuña . xvi . lib̄i hōēs . 7 dim̄ . 7 . i . car̓ terre . 7 vi . ac̓
7 x . bor . Tc̄ . iii . car̓ . m̄ . ii . 7 . v . ac̓ p̃ti 7 . ii . eccłe xxx . ac̓
In kikelingatuna . iii . lib̄i hōēs . xʟviii . ac̓ . 7 . i . car̓ . 7 . iii . ac̓ p̃ti .
In Oſlaĉtuna xi . lib̄i hōēs . ʟiiii . ac̓ Tc̄ . ii . car̓ m̄ . i . iiii . ac̓
p̃ti . de iii . bʒ ex h̄ . xi . habuit antec̄ Rotb̄ti . malet cōm̄d .
t̄ . r . e . 7 die qua . Wiłł malet mortuus eſt fuit ſaiſitus
de duobʒ Hoc tenet hugo .

202 In RAINTHORPE a half-a-free-man in patronage before 1066, 30 acres; now Warenger holds it.
  Then 2 villagers, now 1.
  Always ½ plough; meadow, 1 acre.
Value 5s.

203 In NEWTON (Flotman) 1 free man, 15 acres.
  2 smallholders.
Value 16d.

204 In FLORDON 1 free man, 30 acres. Then ½ plough. Godric's predecessor had the patronage of this man.
Value 3s.

DEPWADE Hundred

205 In FORNCETT 6 free men in patronage, 85 acres. Then 3 ploughs, now 2. Meadow, 5 acres.

206 In *HALAS* 4 free men, 36 acres. Always 2 ploughs; meadow, 3 acres.

207 In CARLTON (Rode) 3 free men, 12 acres. ½ plough; meadow, 1 acre.

208 In FRITTON 3 free men and a half, 80 acres.
  13 smallholders.
  Always 2 ploughs; ½ men's plough. Meadow, 3 acres.
  1 church, 40 acres.
    Also 1 Freeman and a half under it, 5 acres.

209 In CARLETON (Rode) 16 free men and a half, 1 c. of land and 6 acres.
  10 smallholders.
  Then 3 ploughs, now 2. Meadow, 5 acres.
  Also 2 churches, 30 acres.

210 In KETTLETON 3 free men, 48 acres. 1 plough; meadow, 3 acres.

211 In ASLACTON 11 free men, 54 acres. Then 2 ploughs, now 1.
  Meadow, 4 acres.
  Robert Malet's predecessor had the patronage of 3 of these 11 before 1066; on the day on which William Malet died he had possession of 2. Hugh holds this.

In muletuna . ix . libi hões . 7 dim.

cxl . ac . m̃ tenet Malgerus . 7 . xv . bor . Tc 7 p̃ . iiii . car.
m̃ . iii . 7 . ii . libi hoẽs . 7 dim̃ ſub iłł . xv . ac . 7 . viii . ac p̃ti.
Siłu . v . por . In muletuna . i . liƀ hõ . lx . ac idẽ tenet . 7 . vii . bor:
189 b
7 . ii . car . 7 vi . ac p̃ti . 7 . i . ecct̃a . de xv . ac . Siłu . viii . por . Tc . r:
mot : 7 ſub iſto . xiiii . libi . hoẽs . xx . ac . ſẽp . i . car . 7 . ii . ac p̃ti.
In eadem̃ . iiii . libi hõẽs . vi . ac . Tota Muletuna . hñt . i . leug̃ 7 dim̃
in long̃ . 7 dim̃ in lato . 7 . xiii . ɗ . 7 obolum de gelto.
In Tuaneſtuna . xii . libi hõẽs . cxl . ac : 7 . iiii : bor . m̃ tenet Wiłł.
Tc . v . car . p̃ . iiii . m̃ . iii . 7 . viii : ac p̃ti : In eadẽ . ſub iſtis . iiii :
libi hoẽs . 7 dim̃ . vi . ac . 7 dim̃ . car . In Waketuna . vi . libi hoẽs
7 dim̃ . lxxxvi . ac . 7 . v . bor . Tc . iii . car 7 p̃ . m̃ . ii . 7 . iiii : ac p̃ti:
In eadẽ ſub iſtis . iiii . libi hõẽs . xv . ac . In Stratuna : vii . libi : hoẽs
lx . ac Tc . 7 p̃ . iii . car m̃ . i . 7 . ii . ac p . 7 dim̃ . mot . In Sceltuna
viiii . libi . hoẽs . 7 dim̃ . 7 . iii : bor . 7 : i . ecct̃a . xvi : ac . 7 ſub iſtis
iiii . libi hõẽs . inł om̃s lix . ac . ſemp . ii . car . 7 . ii . ac p̃ti . 7 tota
Sceltuna h̃t . i . leug̃ in longo . 7 dim̃ in lato . 7 . ix . ɗ . de gelto.
hoc tenet durandus . 7 Waketuna ſimilił.
In Tibham . iii : libi hoẽs . lxviiii . ac . 7 . vii . bor . Tc 7 p̃ . ii .
car . m̃ . i : 7 dim̃ . 7 . ii . ac p̃ti . In habituna . i . liƀ homo : Stigandi
ł . r . e : xxx . ac . Tc : i : uiłłs : femp . ii : bor . 7 . i . car in dñio.
Tc dim̃ car . In eadẽ . iiii . libi : hoẽs . xxxvi . ac . 7 dim̃ : car
7 . iii : ac : p̃ti :

212 In MOULTON (St. Michael) 9 free men and a half, 140 acres. Now
Mauger holds.
    15 smallholders.
    Then and later 4 ploughs, now 3.
Also 2 free men and a half under them, 15 acres; meadow, 8 acres;
    woodland, 5 pigs.
In MOULTON (St. Michael) 1 free man, 60 acres. He also holds.
    7 smallholders.
    2 ploughs; meadow, 6 acres. Also 1 church, at 15 acres.   189 b
        Woodland, 8 pigs. Then 1 mill.
    Under this man 14 free men, 20 acres. Always 1 plough;
meadow, 2 acres.
In the same 4 free men, 6 acres.
The whole of Moulton (St. Michael) has 1½ leagues in length and
½ in width, tax of 13½d.

213 In SWANTON 12 free men, 140 acres.
    3 smallholders. Now William holds.
    Then 5 ploughs, later 4, now 3. Meadow, 8 acres.
In the same under them 4 free men and a half, 6 acres; ½ plough.

214 In WACTON 6 free men and a half, 86 acres.
    5 smallholders.
    Then and later 3 ploughs, now 2. Meadow, 4 acres.
In the same under them 4 free men, 15 acres.

215 In STRATTON 7 free men, 60 acres.
    Then and later 3 ploughs, now 1. Meadow, 2 acres; ½ mill.

216 In SHELTON 9 free men and a half.
    3 smallholders. Also 1 church, 16 acres. Under them 4 free men.
        Between them all 59 acres.
    Always 2 ploughs; meadow, 2 acres.
The whole of Shelton has 1 league in length and ½ in width,
tax of 9d.
    Durand holds this and Wacton likewise.

217 In TIBENHAM 3 free men, 69 acres.
    7 smallholders.
    Then and later 2 ploughs, now 1½. Meadow, 2 acres.

218 In HAPTON 1 free man of Stigand's before 1066, 30 acres.
    Then 1 villager; always 2 smallholders.
    1 plough in lordship. Then ½ plough.
In the same 4 free men, 36 acres.
    ½ plough; meadow, 3 acres.

In taſeburc . vii . libi . hoēs . ex . ac m̄ tenent
berard 7 aſelinus . ſēp . ii . car ; 7 . vii ; ac p̄ti ; 7 . val̄ . xxiiii . ſol̄.
In Fundahala . i . lib̄ hō . viii . ac ; 7 dim̄ . car . In̄ Tuanatuna . i . lib̄;
hō oſlac ; xxx . ac . Tē ; v . bor . m̄ . x . Tc ; iiii . s . m̄ . i . Semp ; i . car
in̄ dn̄io . 7 . i . car houm̄ . iiii . ac p̄ti . 7 . iiii . ſoc ; vi . ac . 7 dim̄ . car
7 . i . eccla . lx . ac . de liba tr̄a . elemoſina plurimoȝ . In carletuna
ii . libi hoēs . Oſlac cōmdati tantū . 7 h̄t . vii . ac . In kikelingatuna
ii . lib̄i hoēs . ii . ac . In forneſſeta ; i . lib̄ hō . ii . ac . In tanatuna
iii . libi . iiii . ac . In̄ Wachetuna ; ii . libi . i . ac . 7 dim̄ ; In Stratuna
190 a
. i . lib̄ . iiii . ac . In muletuna . iii . libi hoēs . v . ac . In tibham . ii . libi hoēs
vii . ac . In Aſlactuna . i . lib̄ hō . i . ac . In̄t totum . ii . car . 7 . ii . ac p̄ti.
In tacolueſtuna . i . lib̄ hō . Stigandi . xxv . ac . 7 . iii . bor . i . car . 7 . ii.
ac p̄ti . In fundehala . ii . lib̄ hoēs . lx . ac quos tenet osb̄tus . 7 . ii.
bor . Tc . ii . car m̄ . i . 7 dim̄ . In tibham . iii . libi hoēs . xxviii . ac.
7 i . ca 7 . i . ac p̄ti . totum ſimul Val̄ . t . e . r . x . lib̄ . m̄ . xxii . lib̄.
7 . ii . ſol̄ . 7 viiii . d̄ . Vnum ex ill̄ ſeptem de taſeburc calumpni
at̄ . Hermer . 7 quidā anglicus ſuus hō ex hoc offert judicium.
qd̄ ſuus anteceſſor erat ex eo ſaiſitus die q̄ rex . E . uiuus fuit 7 mortuus.
7 hoc cont̄ dicit totus . H̄ . i bello i judico . ex hoc dedit ille anglic̄.
uadē.

219 In TASBURGH 7 free men, 110 acres. Now Berard and Azelin hold.
   Always 2 ploughs; meadow, 7 acres.
   Value 24s.

220 In FUNDENHALL 1 free man, 8 acres. ½ plough.

221 In SWANTON 1 free man, Oslac, 30 acres.
   Then 5 smallholders, now 10. Then 3 slaves, now 1.
   Always 1 plough in lordship; 1 men's plough. Meadow, 4 acres.
   Also 4 Freemen, 6 acres; ½ plough.
   Also 1 church, 60 acres of free land, the alms of very many men.

222 In CARLETON (Rode) 2 free men under the patronage only of
   Oslac. They have 7 acres.

223 In KETTLETON 2 free men, 2 acres.
   In FORNCETT 1 free man, 2 acres.
   In SWANTON 3 free men, 4 acres.
   In WACTON 2 free (men), 1½ acres.
   In STRATTON 1 free man, 4 acres.   190 a
   In MOULTON (St. Michael) 3 free men, 5 acres.
   In TIBENHAM 2 free men, 7 acres.
   In ASLACTON 1 free man, 1 acre.
   In all 2 ploughs and 2 acres of meadow.

224 In TACOLNESTON 1 free man of Stigand's, 25 acres.
   3 smallholders.
   1 plough; meadow, 2 acres.

225 In FUNDENHALL 2 free men, 60 acres; Osbert holds them.
   2 smallholders.
   Then 2 ploughs, now 1½.

226 In TIBENHAM 3 free men, 28 acres. 1 plough; meadow, 1 acre.
   Value of the whole together before 1066 £10; now £22 2s 9d.

227 Hermer claims 1 of the 7 (free men) of TASBURGH. A certain
   Englishman, his man, offers judicial ordeal on the fact that his
   predecessor had possession of him on the day that King Edward
   was alive and dead. The whole Hundred disputes this either by
   battle or judicial ordeal. The Englishman has given pledge of this.

H̃.GNAVERINC.HATESCOV.I.lib̃.hõ.Regis.e.que p̃q̃

Wilts.uenit.Alwi⁹.fuus anteč.habuit cõm̃d.7 h̃t.XL.ac̃.m̃.tenet
turold.7.VI.bor.paftura.XL.ou.Tc̃ dim̃.car̃.m̃.I.7 VI.ac̃ p̃ti.
7.VI.libi.hões fub illo cõm̃d.Tc̃.I.car̃.m̃.I.car̃.7.IIII.ac̃ p̃ti.
Tc̃ ual.x.fol.7.m̃.fimil.Stigand̃ focam.In Ekincham.I.
lib̃ hõ Stigandi.XXX.ac̃.modo tenet.Rotb̃.de Wals.7.II.bor
7.II.libi hões.fub eo.III.ac̃ 7 dim̃.fẽp.dim̃.car̃.7 ual.IIII.fol.

H̃.de clacheflofa.In Walinghetuna.XXX.ac̃ terre teñ.

Hufgarla.lib̃ hõ t.e.r.modo tenet Hugo.fẽp ual.III.fol.
In Hulingheia.I.ac̃ 7 dim̃.teñ.lib̃.hõ tep̃r.e r.7 ual.III.d̃.
hoc tenet idẽ.In bekefwella.I.lib̃.hõ fub herolt.xx.ac̃ t̃re.
m̃ tenet.R.f.erluini.7 ual.II.fol.7.VIII.d̃.In dunham
I.lib̃.hõ.XII.ac̃.7 ual.XVI.d̃.Hoc tenet idẽ.In derham.VI.libi
hões.IX.ac̃ t̃re.7.III.bor.7 ual.x.fol.hoc tenet Hugo.In eadẽ
.I.lib̃ hõ.XVI.ac̃.7 ual.XII.d̃.hoc tenet idẽ.de hoc hab̃ fuus añt,
cõm̃d.tantum.In eadẽ.LX.ac̃ t̃ræ.q̃d.teñ Goddric lib̃ hõ.t.r.e.

190 b

m̃ tenet idẽ.de hoc habuit anteč.Rog̃.7 anteč.baig̃n.cõm̃d
cõm̃d tant̃.7 ẽ.ap̃p̃tiatum.fupius.In Strafeta.I.lib̃ hõ.VI.ac̃
t̃re.7 ual.VI.d̃.hoc tenet idẽ.

CLAVERING Hundred

228 HADDISCOE. 1 free man of King Edward's whom his predecessor A(i)lwy had in patronage after William came. He has 40 acres. Now Thorold holds.
    6 smallholders.
    Pasture, 40 sheep. Then ½ plough, now 1. Meadow, 6 acres.
    Also 6 free men in patronage under him.
        Then 1 plough, now 1 plough. Meadow, 4 acres.
Value then 10s; now the same. Stigand (had) the jurisdiction.

229 In HECKINGHAM 1 free man of Stigand's, 30 acres. Now Robert of Vaux holds.
    2 smallholders.
    Also 2 free men under him, 3½ acres. Always ½ plough.
Value 4s.

The Hundred of CLACKCLOSE

230 In WALLINGTON Huscarl, a free man, held 30 acres of land before 1066; now Hugh holds.
    Value always 3s.

In HILGAY 1 free man held 1½ acres before 1066.
Value 3d. He also holds this.

231 In BEXWELL 1 free man under Harold, 20 acres of land; now R(alph) son of Herlwin holds.
Value 2s 8d.

In DOWNHAM (Market) 1 free man, 12 acres.
Value 16d. He also holds this.

232 In (West) DEREHAM 6 free men, 9 acres of land.
    3 smallholders.
Value 10s. Hugh holds this.
In the same 1 free man, 16 acres.
Value 12d. He also holds this. His predecessor had the patronage only of this man.
In the same, 60 acres of land which Godric, a free man, held before 1066; now he also holds. Roger's predecessor and   **190 b** Baynard's predecessor had the patronage only of this man. It is assessed above.

In STRADSETT 1 free man, 6 acres of land.
Value 6d. He also holds this.

In b́ycham . teñ . alfeih . liƀ hõ.

t̄ . r . e . ıı . car̄ tr̄e . 7 . ıı . ac̄ tr̄e . xıııı . bor . modo tenet . R.
de vals . Tc̄ . ıııı . f. m̂ . ı . fēp . ı . car̄ hoūm . vı . ac̄ p̄ti . Tc̄ . ıııı . por.
m̂ . xıı . Tc̄ . lxxx . oũ . ı . min̂ . m̂ . c . ı . afin̂ . Huic manerio
femp jacent . ııı . liƀi hões . cõm̂d . tantum . lx . ac̄ . de h̄ habuit
heroldus focam . 7 ual . xl . fol . de dño iftius tr̄e tulit Wihenoc
xxx . ac̄ . iftos reclamā . de dono regis . ı . eccl̂a . xxx . ac̄ ual . ıı fol̄
7 vı . d.

H̄ 7 dim̂ . de fredrebruge . EaftWninc . ı . liƀ hõ . Guerd.
t . e . r . lx . ac̄ tr̄e . 7 . xı . ac̄ p̄ti . femp . vı . uiłt . 7 . ııı . bor.
fēp . ıı . car̄ . Tc̄ ual . xl . fol . m̂ . lx . hoc tenet . R . de vals.

191 a

Terra Eƥi Tedfordensis Ad epifc̄opatū ptinens . t̄ . r̄ . e.

Terra Wilłi Eƥi . Hund̄ de Grenehou . Crefincghahā   . X .
ten& Eƥs in dñio . ꝑ manerio 7 ꝑ . ıı . car̄ . tr̄æ . Tc̄ . vıı . uiłt . m̂ . ıııı.
m̂ . ııı . bor . Tc̄ . ıııı . fer̄ . m̂ . ı . Tc̄ . ıı . car̄ . in dñio . m̂ . ııı . Tc̄ int̄ hões . ı . car̄.
m̂ dim̂ . Silu . lx . porc̄ . vııı . ac̄ p̄ti . ıı . mol̄ . ıı . pifc̄ . Sēp . xxıı . anim̂.
7 . v . runc̄ . 7 . xvıı . porc̄ . 7 . lxxx . oũ . 7 . ı . eccl̂æ . xx . ac̄ . ual . xx . d̄

233 In BEECHAM(WELL) Alfheah, a free man, held 2 c. of land and 2 acres of land before 1066.
 14 smallholders. Now R(obert) of Vaux holds. Then 4 slaves, now 1.
 Always 1 men's plough; meadow, 6 acres. Then 4 pigs, now 12. Then 80 sheep less 1, now 100. 1 ass.
 3 free men in patronage only have always appertained to this manor, 60 acres. Harold had the jurisdiction of them.
Value 40s.
Wihenoc took 30 acres of the lordship of this land. He claims them of the King's gift.
 1 church, 30 acres;
value 2s 6d.

The Hundred and a Half of FREEBRIDGE
234 EAST WINCH. 1 free man of Gyrth's before 1066, 60 acres of land; meadow, 11 acres.
 Always 6 villagers; 3 smallholders.
 Always 2 ploughs.
Value then 40s; now 60. R(obert) of Vaux holds this.

LAND OF THE BISHOP OF THETFORD BELONGING TO 191 a THE BISHOPRIC BEFORE 1066
10   LAND OF BISHOP WILLIAM

The Hundred of (South) GREENHOE
1 The Bishop holds (Great) CRESSINGHAM in lordship as a manor, and as 2 c. of land.
 Then 7 villagers, now 4. Now 3 smallholders. Then 4 slaves, now 1.
 Then 2 ploughs in lordship, now 3. Then between the men 1 plough, now ½. Woodland, 60 pigs; meadow, 8 acres; 2 mills; 2 fisheries. Always 22 head of cattle; 5 cobs; 17 pigs; 81 sheep. Belonging to 1 church, 20 acres;
value 20d.

7 . xvii . foc . de LX . ac . 7 . iii . ac . pti . 7 . iii . car . Tc ual . vi . lib . m . ix.

7 ht . i . leug in long . 7 . dim in lat . 7 totu fimul c tenentib; in ea.

reddit . xiiii . d . qn Hund reddit . xx . fol.

/ Gaiuude tenuit Ailmar epc . t . r . e . p man . 7 . p . iii . car . træ m . ten&

Eps . in dnio . Sep . ii . car . in dnio . 7 . i . car . hom . 7 . xvi . uilt . tc . xxviii . bor.

m . xxiiii . sep . i . fer, xl . ac . pti . filu . clx . porc . i . mol . 7 . xxxii . ac . træ.

tc . xxx . fal . m . xxi . 7 . iii . foc . de . xxix . ac 7 . iiii . ac . pti . Sep . i . runc .

7 . iii . 7 . xxv . porc . cxc . ou . Tc ual . xiii . lib . m . xviii . 7 . x . fol.

Totu ht . i . leug in long . 7 . dim . in lat . 7 . reddit . xii . d . de gelt.

/ Smezeduna Hund Tornham tenuit Ailmar epc . t . r . e . p

man . m Eps ind . p . man . 7 . p . iii . car træ . 7 . sep . iii . car in dnio.

7 . iii . car hom 7 , xxi . uilt xiiii . ac pti . m . i . mol 7 . xvi . foc.

de . i . car . 7 . dim . 7 . v . bor . In dnio . ii . runc . ii . an . xxx . porc . 7

. o . ou . Tc ual . xiiii . lib . m . xvi . Totu ht . i . leug . in long . 7 . dim.

in lat . 7 . reddit . ii . fol de gelto.

/ Hund de greneshou . Stofftam tenuit Ailmar epifcopus

191 b

t . r . e . 7 . p . vi . car træ . m tenent . Ricard . 7 Heli . de epo . Sep . iii . uilt . Tc .

xix . bor . m . xv . Tc . iiii . fer . m . i . viii . ac . pti . tc . i . car . in dnio . m . iii . tc .

. ii . car . hom . m . i . Sep . xxii . porc . cclxxx . ou . Tc ual . xl . fol . m . lx.

Totu ht . i . leu in longo . 7 . dim . in lat . 7 . reddit . xvii . d . de . gelto.

Also 17 Freemen, at 60 acres; meadow, 3 acres; 3 ploughs.
   at 60 acres; meadow, 3 acres; 3 ploughs.
Value then £6; now 9.
   It has 1 league in length and ½ in width, the whole together
with the tenants in it pays 14d when the Hundred pays 20s.

[Freebridge Hundred]
2 Bishop A(e)lmer held GAYWOOD before 1066 as a manor, and as
   3 c. of land. Now the Bishop holds in lordship.
      Always 2 ploughs in lordship; 1 men's plough.
      16 villagers. Then 28 smallholders, now 24; always 1 slave.
      Meadow, 40 acres; woodland, 160 pigs; 1 mill; 32 acres of land.
         Then 30 salt-houses, now 21.
      Also 3 Freemen at 29 acres; meadow, 4 acres.
      Always 1 cob; 3 head of cattle; 25 pigs; 190 sheep.
   Value then £13; now (£)18 10s.
      The whole has 1 league in length and ½ in width, it pays tax of 12d.

SMETHDON Hundred
3 Bishop A(e)lmer held THORNHAM before 1066 as a manor; now the
   Bishop (holds) in lordship as a manor, and as 3 c. of land.
      Always 3 ploughs in lordship; 3 men's ploughs.
      21 villagers.
      Meadow, 14 acres. Now 1 mill.
      Also 16 Freemen, at 1½ ploughs; 5 smallholders.
      In lordship 2 cobs; 2 head of cattle; 30 pigs; 500 sheep.
   Value then £14; now 16.
      The whole has 1 league in length and ½ in width, it pays tax of 2s.

The Hundred of GRIMSHOE
4 Bishop A(e)lmer held (West) TOFTS before 1066, as 6 c. of land.   191 b
   Now Richard and Eli hold from the Bishop.
      Always 3 villagers. Then 19 smallholders, now 15. Then 4
         slaves, now 1.
      Meadow, 8 acres.
      Then 1 plough in lordship, now 3. Then 2 men's ploughs, now 1.
      Always 22 pigs; 280 sheep.
   Value then 40s; now 60.
      The whole has 1 league in length and ½ in width, it pays tax of 17d.

Lawendic Hund. Elmenham tenuit Ailmar epc t. r. e. p man.

7 p. VIII. car. træ. m̅ ten& Epc in dn̅io. Sep. XLI. uiłł. 7 LXIII. bor. Tc. VI. ser.

bor. m̅. IIII. XXIIII. ac. pti. sep. IIII. car. in dn̅io. 7. XVI. car hom. Tc silu.

. M̅. porc. m̅. ꝺ. sep. IIII. moł. 7. III. runc. 7. XXXII. porc. CCC. ou. XXXV. cap.

7. XXIIII. soc. de. I. car. træ. Stigand soca. t. r. e. 7 m̅ in Milham. sep.

. IIII. car. IIII. ac. pti. Silu. XXX. porc. I. moł. hic jacet sep. I. beuuita quæ uocat

Betellea. de. I. car. træ. 7. VII. uiłł. X. ac. pti. I. car. in dn̅io. 7. II. posst

restaurari. sep. II. car. hom. 7 hic jac &. I. soc. de. XXVI. ac. sep. I. car. 7.

. I. ac. 7. dim. pti. Silu. V. porc. 7. I. ecclia I est manerio de. LX. 7. I. car.

7. ual. V. soł. Tc ual totu. X. lib Post 7. m̅. XXXII. ht. I. leug in long.

7. dim. in lat. 7. redd. XX. d. de gelto. 7 biuuita ht VIII. qr in lon.

7. IIII. in lat.

Hund de brodereros. Colechirca tenuit. A. t. r. e. p man. 7 p

. II. car. træ. m̅. E. in dn̅io. Tc. I. uiłł. m̅ nułł. Sep. XII. bor. Tc. IIII. ser.

m̅. II. Sep. II. car. in dn̅io. Silu. LX. porc. IIII. ac. pti. VII. animalia. XXVII. porc.

Tc. X. ou. m̅. C. LX. cap. ecclæ. XL. ac. ual. II. soł. 7. XIIII. soc. de. LXVI. ac.

Tc. III. car. m̅. II. 7. dim. Tc ual. VI. lib. m̅. IX. ht. V. qr. in long. 7. IIII.

in lat. 7. XI. d. in gelto.

LAUNDITCH Hundred

5 Bishop A(e)lmer held (North) ELMHAM before 1066 as a manor, and as 8 c. of land. Now the Bishop holds in lordship.

Always 41 villagers; 63 smallholders. Then 6 slaves, now 4.

Meadow, 24 acres. Always 4 ploughs in lordship; 16 men's ploughs. Woodland, then 1,000 pigs, now 500. Always 4 mills. 3 cobs; 32 pigs; 300 sheep; 35 goats.

Also 24 Freemen, at 1 c. of land.

Stigand (had) the jurisdiction before 1066, and now (it is) in MILEHAM.

Always 4 ploughs; meadow, 4 acres; woodland, 30 pigs; 1 mill. Here has always appertained 1 outlier which is called BEETLEY, at 1 c. of land.

7 villagers.

Meadow, 10 acres; 1 plough in lordship; 2 could be restored; always 2 men's ploughs.

1 Freeman appertains here, at 26 acres. Always 1 plough; meadow, 1½ acres; woodland, 5 pigs.

Also 1 church is in the manor, at 60 acres; 1 plough; value 5s 4d.

Value of the whole then £10; later and now 32.

It has 1 league in length and ½ in width; it pays tax of 20d. The outlier has 8 furlongs in length and 4 in width.

The Hundred of BROTHERCROSS

6 A(elmer) held COLKIRK before 1066 as a manor, and as 2 c. of land; now the Bishop (holds) in lordship.

Then 1 villager, now none; always 12 smallholders. Then 4 slaves, now 2.

Always 2 ploughs in lordship; woodland, 60 pigs; meadow, 4 acres; 7 head of cattle; 27 pigs. Then 10 sheep. Now 160 goats.

(Belonging) to the church, 40 acres; value 2s.

Also 14 Freemen, at 66 acres. Then 3 ploughs, now 2½.

Value then £6; now 9.

It has 5 furlongs in length and 4 in width, 11d in tax.

⌐Hund de Galgou. Saxelinghaham tenuit . A . t . r . e . p man̄ . 7 p.

192 a

7 p . 1 . car . træ . m̄ ten& Eps . Sep . vii . bor . 7 . 1 . ſer . 7 . 1 . car in dn̄io . 7 . dim̄ .
car . hom̄ . 11 . ac . p̄ti . app̄tiatū e in Tornedis . 1 . ecclia . de . xii . ac . De hoc man̄ .
ten& . W . dim̄ . car . træ . 7 . 1 . car . 7 ual . xx . ſol . h̄t . vii . qr in long . 7 . v . in
lat . 7 . 11 . ſol de . gelt.

⌐Hund de Holt Tornediş tenuit Ailmar epc . p man̄ . 7 . p viii . car
træ . t . r . e . 7 m̄ Eps in dn̄io . Sep . xl . bor . 7 . viii . ſer . 7 . viii . car . in dn̄io . 7
. x . car hom̄ . Silu . l . porc . ix . ac . p̄ti . iii . mol . iiii . runc . xii . porc . c . ou.
Huic manerio ptinent . iiii . beuuitæ . hoc e Brūtuna . 7 . Saxelingh̄a . 7
Becham . 7 Hemeſteda . 7 . conputatæ ſt in Tornedis . 7 . xvi . ſoc . de . xxxvi . ac .
Sep . in̄t . eos . iiii . car . Totū ual . t . r . e . xiii . lib . m̄ reddit . xxx . lib . h̄t . 1 .
leu in long . 7 . iiii . qr . in lat . 7 . xii . d . de . g . 1 . ecclæ . xxxii . ac . ual . xxxii . d .

⌐Suanetunam tenuit . A . t . r . e . p . 11 . car . træ . 7 . jac& ad hidolfeſtunā.
Sep . viii . bor . 7 . 11 . car . in dn̄io . Tc . 111 . car . hom̄ . m̄ . 1 . 7 . 11 . poſ̄t reſtaurari.
Silu . c . porc . Tc . xiii . por . m̄ . vi . m̄ . cc . ou . Tc ual . vi . lib . m̄ . viii . 7 h̄t dim̄
leug in long . 7 . d . in lat . 7 . 111 . d . de . g.

The Hundred of GALLOW

7 A(elmer) held SAXLINGHAM before 1066 as a manor, and as 1 c.
of land. Now the Bishop holds.
    Always 7 smallholders; 1 slave.
    1 plough in lordship; ½ man's plough.
    Meadow, 2 acres.
It is assessed in THORNAGE.
    1 church at 12 acres.
    Of this manor W(illiam) holds ½ c. of land; 1 plough.
Value 20s.
    It has 7 furlongs in length and 5 in width; tax of 2s.

The Hundred of HOLT

8 Bishop A(e)lmer held THORNAGE before 1066 as a manor, and as
8 c. of land; now the Bishop (holds) in lordship.
    Always 40 smallholders; 8 slaves.
    8 ploughs in lordship; 10 men's ploughs. Woodland, 50 pigs;
        meadow, 9 acres; 3 mills; 4 cobs; 12 pigs; 100 sheep.
To this manor belong 4 outliers, that is BRINTON, SAXLINGHAM,
(East) BECKHAM, HEMPSTEAD; they are accounted in Thornage.
    Also 16 Freemen at 36 acres; always 4 ploughs between them.
Value of the whole before 1066 £13; now it pays £30.
    It has 1 league in length and 4 furlongs in width, tax of 12d.
    (Belonging) to 1 church, 32 acres;
value 32d.

9 A(elmer) held SWANTON (Novers) before 1066, as 2 c. of land. It
appertains to Hindolveston.
    Always 8 smallholders.
    2 ploughs in lordship. Then 3 men's ploughs, now 1, 2 could
        be restored. Woodland, 100 pigs. Then 13 pigs, now 6.
        Now 200 sheep.
Value then £6; now 8.
    It has ½ league in length and ½ in width, tax of 3d.

⁊Hund de grenehov . Hindringaham ten& . Ep̄s . in dn̄io . qđ tenuit
Ailm̄ . p man̄ . ⁊ . p . IIII . car træ . t . r . e . Sēp . XI . uiłł . Tc̄ . XX . bor . m̄ . XV .
Tc̄ . VIII . ſer . m̄ . VII . Sēp . IIII . car . in dn̄io . Tc̄ . V . car . hom̄ . m̄ . III . Tc̄ . ſilu . X . por .
m̄ . VIII . ſēp . I . moł . V . ac . p̄ti . XVII . porc . CLX . ou . VI . uaſa apum ⁚ ⁊
. VII . ſoc . dīm . car . træ . ⁊ . t . r . e . arabant . II . car . m̄ . I . Tc̄ uał . X . lib̄ . m̄ ⁚
reddit . XV . lib̄ . ħt . I . leu . in long . ⁊ . I . in lat . ⁊ . II . ſoł de ḡ . ⁊ in Warhā
ē . I . hō . p̄tinens huic maner . de . XII . ac . ⁊ In guuella . II . hōes .
q̄ p̄tinent huic manerio . de . XII . ac . Paſt . c . ou .

192 b

⁊Edgamerā tenuit . Ailmar . e . p man̄ . ⁊ . p . III . car . træ . t . r . e . m̄ ten&
Morel de ep̄o . Tc̄ . XIIII . uiłł . m̄ . VIII . Tc̄ . II . ſer . m̄ . null . Tc̄ . II . car . in dn̄io .
m̄ . I . Tc̄ . II . car . hom̄ . m̄ . II . bou . ⁊ . II . car . poſſt reſtaurari . ſēp . I . runc .
. I . ac . p̄ti . VIII . porc . Tc̄ . CLXXX . ou . m̄ . LXXXX . ⁊ . VII . ſoc . jacent huic .
uillæ . de . XLV . ac . Tc̄ . II . car . m̄ . I . Tc̄ uał . LXX . ſoł . m̄ . XLV . ſoł . ⁊ . IIII . đ .
⁊ . I . ſoc . q̄ ē in murlai . hō ep̄i Wiłłi . Tc̄ . arabat . I . carr . m̄ . II . bobꝫ
⁊In Torp tenuit . A . I . ſoc . ⁊ₐ . II . bor . ⁊ . p̄tin& ad langham
⁊In Locham ten& . W . de Noiers de ep̄o o . I . lib̄m hominē . quē tenuit . A . ep̄c
t . r . e . de . XXIII . ac . tre . ⁊ non potat t̄ram ſuam dare uł uend̄e . ⁊ erat in ſoca reḡ .
Tc̄ . uał . V . ſoł . m̄ . XVII . ſoł . ⁊ . IIII . đ . ⁊ . in hocham ten& . I . ſoc . de . X . ac . ⁊ p̄tin& In hidringhā .

192 a, b

The Hundred of (North) GREENHOE

10   The Bishop holds HINDRINGHAM in lordship, which A(e)lmer held
before 1066 as a manor, and as 4 c. of land.
    Always 11 villagers. Then 20 smallholders, now 15. Then 8
        slaves, now 7.
    Always 4 ploughs in lordship. Then 5 men's ploughs, now 3.
        Then woodland, 10 pigs, now 8. Always 1 mill; meadow, 5
        acres; 17 pigs; 160 sheep; 6 beehives.
    Also 7 Freemen, ½ c. of land. Before 1066 they ploughed with
        2 ploughs, now 1.
Value then £10; now it pays £15.
    It has 1 league in length and 1 in width; tax of 2s.
    In WARHAM is 1 man who belongs to this manor, at 12 acres; in
WELLS (next the Sea) 2 men who belong to this manor, at 12 acres;
pasture, 100 sheep.

11   Bishop A(e)lmer held EGMERE before 1066 as a manor, and as   192 b
3 c. of land. Now Morel holds from the Bishop.
    Then 14 villagers, now 8. Then 2 slaves, now none.
    Then 2 ploughs in lordship, now 1. Then 2 men's ploughs, now
        2 oxen, 2 ploughs could be restored. Always 1 cob; meadow,
        1 acre; 8 pigs. Then 180 sheep, now 90.
    Also 7 Freemen appertain to this village, at 45 acres.
        Then 2 ploughs, now 1.
Value then 70s; now 45s 4d.
    Also 1 Freeman, Bishop William's man, who is in MURLAI; then
he ploughed with 1 plough, now with 2 oxen.

12   In (Cock)THORPE A(elmer) held 1 Freeman; 2 smallholders; it
belongs to Langham.

13   In HOLKHAM William of Noyers holds O., 1 free man, from the
Bishop, whom Bishop A(elmer) held before 1066, at 23 acres of
land; he could not grant or sell his land; he was in the King's
jurisdiction.
Value then 5s; now 17s 4d.
    He holds 1 Freeman in Holkham, at 10 acres; he belongs in
Hindringham.

Ⅴ Walesham Hund. In Hemelintuna . xxi . soć . de . cxl . ać . t̄ræ . 7 . viii . ać.
p̄ti . T̄c . iii . caŕ . 7 . dim̄ . m̄ . ii . hoc ē ap̄p̄ciatū in blauuefelda . In Ead̄ uilł . lx . ać . t̄re . in
dn̄io.

Ⅴ ENSFORT Hund . Hidolfestunam ten& Ep̄c in dn̄io ꝑ man̄.
7 ꝑ . cc . ać . Sēp . xii . uiłłi . 7 . xxii . bord . 7 . iii . seŕ . 7 . ii . caŕ . in dn̄io . 7 . v . caŕ . hom̄.
t̄c . silu . �expⁱŕ . porć . m̄ . ccc . xii . ać . p̄ti . i . mol . Sēp . ii . runć . 7 . xx . anim̄ . 7 . xl . porć.
. xl . cap̄ . ii . uasa apū . Hic jac& . i . bereuuita . que dr̄ Nortuna . de . cc . ać.
Sēp . ix . uiłł . 7 . vi . bor t̄c . ii . seŕ . m̄ . i . Sēp . i . caŕ . in dn̄io . 7 . ii . caŕ . hominū.
. viii . ać . p̄ti . Silu . xxx . porć . 7 . i . ecc̄lia in manerio de . xxvi . ać . 7 . uał
. xx . đ . 7 . tⁱa pars ecc̄læ in bereuuita . de . ii . ać . 7 . dim̄ . 7 . uał . iiii . đ.
7 . viii . soć . de . li . ać . t̄ræ qđ ten& hugo de ep̄o . iii . bord . sēp . ii . caŕ.
       7 . iiii . ać . p̄ti . Silu . x . porć . 7 In Geghestueit . i . soć . de . xxiiii.
193 a
ać . t̄ræ 7 . ii . bor . T̄c . dim̄ . caŕ . m̄ . i . 7 In Gegeseta . ii . soć . de . ii . ać . qđ
ten& Idē hugo . T̄c uał totū . x . liƀ . m̄ . xiii . liƀ . 7 . viii . soł . 7 Hidoluestuna
ħt . i . leuḡ . in longo . 7 . i . in lat̄ . 7 . reddit . viii . đ . 7 . obolū . de . ḡ.

Ⅴ Helmingham tenuit . Ailmar ep̄c̄ . t . r . e . ꝑ manerio . 7 . ꝑ . iii . caŕ . t̄ræ . m̄
ten& Gonfrid archidiacon . de ep̄o . T̄c . viii . uiłł . m̄ . iiii . Sēp . ix . bor . T̄c . i . seŕ

WALSHAM Hundred

14 In HEMBLINGTON 21 Freemen, at 140 acres of land. Meadow 8
  acres. Then 3½ ploughs, now 2.
  This is assessed in Blofield.
  In the same village 60 acres of land in lordship.

EYNSFORD Hundred

15 The Bishop holds HINDOLVESTON in lordship as a manor, and as
  200 acres.
    Always 12 villagers; 22 smallholders; 3 slaves.
    2 ploughs in lordship; 5 men's ploughs. Woodland, then 600
      pigs, now 300. Meadow, 12 acres; 1 mill. Always 2 cobs;
      20 head of cattle; 40 pigs; 40 goats; 2 beehives.
  1 outlier appertains here which is called (Wood) NORTON, at
  200 acres.
    Always 9 villagers; 6 smallholders. Then 2 slaves, now 1.
    Always 1 plough in lordship; 2 men's ploughs; meadow, 8 acres;
      woodland, 30 pigs.
  Also 1 church in the manor, at 26 acres;
  value 20d.
    One-third of a church (is) in the outlier, at 2½ acres;
  value 4d.
    Also 8 Freemen, at 51 acres of land. This Hugh holds from the
  Bishop. 3 smallholders. Always 2 ploughs; meadow, 4 acres;
  woodland, 10 pigs.
  In GUESTWICK 1 Freeman, at 24 acres of land. 2 smallholders.   193 a
    Then ½ plough, now 1.
  In GUIST 2 Freemen, at 2 acres. This Hugh also holds.
  Value of the whole then £10; now £13 8s.
    Hindolveston has 1 league in length and 1 in width, it pays tax
  of 8½d.

16 Bishop A(e)lmer held HELMINGHAM before 1066 as a manor, and
  as 3 c. of land. Now Gunfrid the Archdeacon holds from the
  Bishop.
    Then 8 villagers, now 4; always 9 smallholders. Then 1 slave,

modo nullus . ſemp . ii . caŕ in dn̄io . ſemp . i . caŕ & dim hom̄ . & viii .

ac̄ p̄ti . & . i . molin̄ . modo . xi . porc̄ . 7 xix . ous̄ . Et xiii . ſoc̄ ten&

ii . æccliæ . x . ac̄ . & ual . viii . d.

id̄ . de xl . ac̄ . terræ . ſemp . v . caŕ . & . ii . ac̄ p̄ti . ſemp ual . iiii . lib̄ .

⁋ In Corpſtẏ xxx . ac̄ terræ tenuit Ailmarus ep̄s . t . r̄ . e . ſemp dim̄

caŕ . & . i . ac̄ p̄ti . ſilua . de . iiii . porc̄ . & ual . ii . ſol . ſocauſtuna .

HVN̄D . de Tonſteda In Suaffelda ten̄ Gonfridus . i . ſoc̄ . xx .

iiii . ac̄ terræ . & . ii . bord̄ . & dim̄ . & . i . caŕ . & ual . v . ſol . & . iiii . d̄ .

⁋ In ead̄ xxviii . ac̄ ad eccliam . ſemp . i . bord̄ . & . ii . ac̄ p̄ti . & ual .

ii . ſol . & totū ħt . i . lḡ in longo . & . iiii . qŕ in lat̄ . 7 . i . perc̄ . quicq̗

ibi teneat . & xviii . d̄ . de gelto ;

⁋ DEPWADE . HVNDRET . Stratuna ten& Walt̄

diaconus . ii . caŕ terræ . xxx ac̄ . quas . tenuit . A . ep̄s . t . r . e . Semp

vii . uilt̄ . 7 vi . bord̄ . & dim̄ . Tc̄ . ii . caŕ in dominio . modo . i . Tc̄

. ii . caŕ hom̄ . modo . i . vi . ac̄ . p̄ti . Silua de . vi . porc̄ . & ſemp . i .

molin̄ . & . i . an̄ . & . xi . porc̄ . Et xx . vi . ſoc̄ ten̄ Ranulfus 7 Galt̄

diacon̄ Rex & com̄s dim̄ ſoca̅ . & ħnt lxxx . iii . ac̄ . ſemp . ii . caŕ

ſemp ual . iiii . lib̄ . 7 . ii . ſol . ide̅ dimidiū unū ex his calumpniatur

q̇de̅ homo comitis Alani . & dic̄ qd̄ . R . eū tenuit p̅q̅ foris facer& .

ex hoc offert judiciū .

now none.

Always 2 ploughs in lordship. Always 1½ men's ploughs; meadow, 8 acres; 1 mill. Now 11 pigs; 19 sheep.

2 churches, 10 acres;

value 8d.

He also holds 13 Freemen, at 40 acres of land. Always 5 ploughs; meadow, 2 acres.

Value always £4.

17   In CORPUSTY Bishop A(e)lmer held 30 acres of land before 1066.
  Always ½ plough; meadow, 1 acre; woodland at 4 pigs.
  Value 2s. The jurisdiction is in Cawston.

The Hundred of TUNSTEAD

18   In SWAFIELD Gunfrid holds 1 Freeman; 24 acres of land.
  2 smallholders and a half.
  1 plough.
  Value 5s 4d.
  In the same 28 acres (belong) to the church.
  Always 1 smallholder.
  Meadow, 2 acres.
  Value 2s.
  The whole has 1 league in length and 4 furlongs and 1 perch in width, whoever holds there, tax of 18d.

DEPWADE Hundred

19   Walter the Deacon holds STRATTON, 2 c. of land and 30 acres, which Bishop Aelmer held before 1066.
  Always 7 villagers; 6 smallholders and a half.
  Then 2 ploughs in lordship, now 1. Then 2 men's ploughs, now 1. Meadow, 6 acres; woodland at 6 pigs. Always 1 mill; 1 head of cattle; 11 pigs.
  Ranulf and Walter the Deacon also hold 26 Freemen. The King and the Earl (have) the jurisdiction. They have 83 acres; always 2 ploughs.
  Value always £4 2s.
  A certain man of Count Alan's claims half one of these, and says that R(alph) held him before he forfeited. He offers judicial ordeal on this.

TERRA EJVSDEM DE FEVDO . Smeteduna . H̃.

Secesforda ten& Guert . t . r . e . iii . car̄ in dominio. & xv ac̄ . Tc̄ . xv.
uilł . p̃ 7 modo . v . Semp . xxxix . borđ . 7 . v . ſeru̅ . viii . ac̄ prati . Sem
p . v . car̄ hominũ . ſilua ad lx . porc̄ . iiii . moł . Semper . i . runc̄ . 7 xl
. v . porc̄ . 7 . ccc . oũs . huic mañ . jac& . i . beruita . quæ uocatur frenga.
Semp . i . car̄ in dominio . & . vii . uilł . 7 . ii . ſoc̄ . ten̅ . i . car̄ & dim̅ . 7 de
uno ſoc̄ . fecit beruita . Agelmar̄ . eps̃ . & . vii . borđ . 7 alĩ ſoc̄ . ht̅
iiii . borđ . & . i . lib̅ hō . i . car̄ in dominio . de h̃ & fecit bereuitā ſemp
vi . borđ . 7 . ii . ſerui; & alĩ lib̅ hō ſemp . i . car̄ in dominio . 7 de hoc
fecit beuita . ſemp . iiii . borđ . & . ii . ſeru̅ . &c . ii . libi hoēs . ii . car̄ t̃ræ
de h̃ & . i . bereuuita . ii . car̄ in dominio . & . v . borđ . & . ii . ſeru̅ . & . ii.
ac̄ p̃ti . 7 . t . r . e . i . molin̅ hunc inde tulit anant . ante c̄ petri
de ualoniis . h̃ totũ ual& . t . r . e . xvi . lib̅ p̃ & modo xxiiii . lib̅;
In eadē Ingulfus ten̅ . i . car̄ . terræ . quã tenuit . Guert . t . r . e . ſemp
. i . car̄ in dominio . 7 uał . x . soł . Tota ht̅ . i . lg̅ . in longo . 7 . i . lg̅ in
lato . & reddit . iiii . soł . de . xx . soł . de gelto;
Hic jacent ſemp . viii . libi homines ſoca & c̄omdatione . tantũ
. iiii . car̄ terræ . Semp . v . uilł . iiii . ac̄ p̃ti . Tc̄ iiii . car̄ . modo
iii . Tc̄ ual& xl . soł . modo . lxxx . Totũ ht̅ . i . lg̅ in longo 7 dim̅
in lato . & reddit xvii . đ . & . i . obolũ de . xx . soł . gelto.

LAND OF THE HOLDING OF THE SAME

SMETHDON Hundred

20 Gyrth held SEDGEFORD before 1066; 3 ploughs in lordship; 15 acres.

Then 15 villagers, later and now 5. Always 39 smallholders; 5 slaves.

Meadow, 8 acres. Always 5 men's ploughs; woodland for 60 pigs; 4 mills. Always 1 cob; 45 pigs; 300 sheep.

1 outlier appertains to this manor, which is called FRING.

Always 1 plough in lordship.

7 villagers.

2 Freemen hold 1½ ploughs.

Of (the lands of) 1 Freeman Bishop A(e)lmer made an outlier. (He has) 7 smallholders and the other Freeman has 4 smallholders. Also 1 free man; 1 plough in lordship. Of this he also made an outlier.

Always 6 smallholders; 2 slaves.

Also another free man; always 1 plough in lordship. Of this he also made an outlier.

Always 4 smallholders; 2 slaves.

Also 2 free men, 2 c. of land. Of this also (he made) 1 outlier.

2 ploughs in lordship.

5 smallholders; 2 slaves.

Meadow, 2 acres. Before 1066, 1 mill. This Anand the predecessor of Peter of Valognes took away.

Value of all this before 1066 £16; later and now £24.

In the same Ingulf holds 1 c. of land which Gyrth held before 1066. Always 1 plough in lordship.

Value 10s.

The whole has 1 league in length and 1 league in width; of a 20s tax it pays 4s.

8 free men have always appertained here with jurisdiction and in patronage only, 4 c. of land.

Always 5 villagers.

Meadow, 4 acres. Then 4 ploughs, now 3.

Value then 40s; now 80.

The whole has 1 league in length and ½ in width; of a 20s tax it pays 17½d.

Ⅴ Scerpham . *HVNDRET* . In eccles . ten& . Rad̄ . com̄s . t .

r . e . ɪɪɪɪ . car̄ p̄ tenuit Radulfus comes fili ej . P̄ ea ailmarus.

ep̄s de utroq̔ P̄ ea Arf ep̄s . M̄ ten& . Willm̄ ep̄s . femp . xɪɪ . uiłł.

& . xɪ . bord̄ . Tc̄ . v . feru . modo . ɪɪ . xx . ac̄ . p̄ti . filua . c . porc̄ . femp . ɪɪ.

car̄ in dominio . Tc̄ . v . car̄ hom̄ . modo . ɪɪɪɪ . femp . ɪ . molin̄ . m̄.

ɪɪɪ . an̄ . & . vɪɪ . porc̄ . c . lxxx . ou̅s . Tc̄ uał . c . foł . modo . lx . Totū hɬ

ɪ . lḡ in longo . & . ɪɪɪɪ . qr̄ in lato . & vɪɪ . d̄ . de gelto . han̄ terrā habuit

. A . ep̄s in tp̄r utroroq̔ 7 hundret nefcit q̔m̄ . & nūq̔ fuit de

epifcopatu . tefte hund̄.

H . DE HOLT . In Langaham ten& . Guert . ɪɪɪɪ . car̄ terræ

t . r . e . Semp . xxx . ɪ . uiłł . 7 . ɪɪɪɪ . bord̄ . & . v . feru . Semp . in dominio.

ɪɪɪɪ . car̄ . 7 hom̄ vɪɪɪ . car̄ . vɪ . ac̄ . p̄ti . ɪ . molin̄ . Semp . ɪ . runc̄.

& . ɪ . an̄ . & . xvɪ . porc̄ . & . lx . ou̅s . 7 xvɪɪ . foc̄ . de . lxxx . ac̄ terræ

& . ɪɪɪɪ . car̄ . Tc̄ uał& . vɪɪɪ . lib̄ . modo reddit . xx . lib̄ . 7 hɬ . ɪ . lḡ in
<small>7 ɪɪ . æccliæ . xvɪ . ǣ . 7 uał . xvɪ . d̄.</small>

longo . 7 . ɪ . lḡ in lato . & . ɪɪ . foł de gelto . Ablate ſɬ de h̄ manerɪ

lx . ac̄ . m̄ . tenet eos petrus de ualonis.

Ⅴ *ERPINGEHAM NORT . HVND* . In gune tune quā

emit Almar̄ . t . r . e . ad epifcopatū ten̄ die qua fuit mortuus . ɪɪ.

car̄ terræ . vɪɪɪ . uiłł . femp . vɪ . bord̄ . Semp . ɪ . car̄ in dominio . ɪɪ.

car̄ hom̄ . ɪɪɪɪ . ac̄ . & dim̄ p̄ti . Tc̄ . ɪ . molin̄ . 7 m̄ . ɪ . Semp . ɪ . runc̄.

& . ɪ . an̄ . & . ɪɪ . porc̄ . & . vɪɪ . foc̄ . dim̄ . car̄ tr̄æ . 7 . ɪ . bord̄ . ɪ . moł . dim̄

ac̄ p̄ti . femp . ɪɪ . car̄ . Tc̄ uał . xx . foł . modo . ɪɪɪɪ . lib̄ . hɬ dim̄ lḡ in

longo . 7 vɪ . qr̄ in lato . & de gelto . vɪ . d̄ . 7 . ɪɪɪ . ferding . De has ten& . Willm̄

denuers . ɪ . car̄ . terræ . & . ɪ . car̄ . fup eū . 7 uał . xɪɪ . foł . in eod̄ p̄tio.

SHROPHAM Hundred
21 In ECCLES Earl Ralph held 4 c. [of land] before 1066; later Earl
Ralph his son held; later Bishop A(e)lmer from both; later Bishop
Erfast; now Bishop William holds.
Always 12 villagers; 11 smallholders. Then 5 slaves, now 2.
Meadow, 20 acres; woodland, 100 pigs. Always 2 ploughs in
lordship. Then 5 men's ploughs, now 4. Always 1 mill.
Now 3 head of cattle; 7 pigs; 180 sheep.
Value then 100s, now 60.
The whole has 1 league in length and 4 furlongs in width,
tax of 7d. Bishop A(elmer) had this land in the time of both; the
Hundred does not know in what way. It never was (land) of the
Bishopric, as the Hundred testifies.

The Hundred of HOLT
22 In LANGHAM Gyrth held 4 c. of land before 1066.
Always 31 villagers; 4 smallholders; 5 slaves.
Always 4 ploughs in lordship; 8 men's ploughs. Meadow, 6 acres;
1 mill. Always 1 cob; 1 head of cattle; 16 pigs; 60 sheep.
Also 17 Freemen, at 80 acres of land; 4 ploughs.
2 churches, 16 acres;
value 16d.
Value then £8; now it pays £20.
It has 1 league in length and 1 league in width, tax of 2s.
60 acres were taken from this manor; now Peter of Valognes
holds them.

NORTH ERPINGHAM Hundred
23 In GUNTON, which A(e)lmer bought before 1066 for the Bishopric,
he held on the day he died, 2 c. of land.
8 villagers; always 6 smallholders.
Always 1 plough in lordship; 2 men's ploughs. Meadow, 4½
acres. Then 1 mill, now 1. Always 1 cob; 1 head of cattle;
2 pigs.
Also 7 Freemen, ½ c. of land; 1 smallholder.
1 mill; meadow, ½ acre; always 2 ploughs.
Value then 20s; now £4.
It has ½ league in length and 6 furlongs in width, tax of 6¾d.
Of these William of Noyers holds 1 c. of land and 1 plough on it.
Value 12s in the same valuation.

*V*In ſcepedane tʹwita Gunetune . ı . car̓ terræ . Semp ııı . uilt . ııı.
bord . Tc̄ . ı . car̓ in dominio . modo . dim̄ . Semp . ı . car̓ . hom̄ . Silua
vı . porc̓ . ı . ac̄.p̓ti . Tc̄ ualʹ . x . ſolʹ . modo . v . ſolʹ & . ıııı . đ . & h̓t in lon -
go dim̄ lḡ . & . ıııı . qr̓ . in lato . Et de gelto . vı . đ.

HVND . DE WALESSAM. In begetuna . ten̄ ep̄s Almarus
p̓ ep̄tionē . t . r . e . cū ſoca & ſaca de comite algaro de bor . & de
ſequentib3 faldam . ııı . car̓ terræ . Tc̄ . xL . bord̓ . modo xxıx . Sēp
ıı . car̓ in dominio . Tc̄ . v . car̓ hominū . 7 dim̄ . modo . v . xvı . ac̄ p̓ti.
modo . ı . runc̓ . modo . xvı . porc̓ . modo . c . xL . ous̄ . c̃ . v . ſoc̓ . de . xxx.
. ıı . ac̄ terræ . & . ıx . ſoc̄ . de . L . ac̄ . terræ . & . vııı . ac̄ . terræ . Semp
. ı . car̓ . Tc̄ totū ualʹ . vı . libʹ . modo . vıı . libʹ . 7 xııı . ſolʹ.& . ıııı . đ . &
h̓t dim̄ lḡ in longo . 7 dim̄ in lato . & de gelto . xıı . đ . ı . æcclı̓a . vıı.
ac̄ . ualʹ . vıı . đ.

HVND . DE GRENEHOV. In hoccham ten̄ . Witt de noers . de W
ep̄s . ı . libum hominē . quē ten̄ . A . ep̄s . t . r . e . xxııı . ac̄ terre . ſ7
non poterat terrā ſuā dare nec uendere . & erat in ſoca regis
Tc̄ ual& . v . ſolʹ . modo reddit xxıı . ſolʹ . 7 ıııı . đ . 7 in hoccham
ten& . ı . ſoc̓ . de . x . ac̄ . terræ . & ptin& in dregeham.

H̄. de *WALASSAM.* In Walaſſam . ı . libum hoc̄em . de . xvııı . ac̄ q̓s
ille libʹ homo . dedit ſc̄o beneđ . de holmo . ſ7 eruaſtus ep̄s inde abſtulit.
modo ten& . W . ep̄s . & ual& . ıııı . ſolʹ.

24 In SHIPDEN, an outlier of Gunton, 1 c. of land.
Always 3 villagers; 3 smallholders.
Then 1 plough in lordship, now ½; always 1 men's plough;
woodland, 6 pigs; meadow, 1 acre.
Value then 10s; now 5s 4d.
It has ½ league in length and 4 furlongs in width; tax of 6d.

The Hundred of WALSHAM
25 In BEIGHTON Bishop A(e)lmer held before 1066 through purchase
from Earl Algar with full jurisdiction of the smallholders and of
those seeking the fold. 3 c. of land.
Then 40 smallholders, now 29.
Always 2 ploughs in lordship. Then 5½ men's ploughs, now 5.
Meadow, 16 acres. Now 1 cob; now 16 pigs; now 140 sheep.
Also 5 Freemen, at 32 acres of land. Also 9 Freemen, at 50
acres of land and 8 acres of land. Always 1 plough.
Value of the whole then £6; now £7 13s 4d.
It has ½ league in length and ½ in width, tax of 12d.
1 church; 7 acres;
value 7d.

The Hundred of (North) GREENHOE
26 In HOLKHAM William of Noyers holds from Bishop W(illiam), 1 free
man whom Bishop A(elmer) held before 1066; 23 acres of land.
But he could not grant or sell his land. He was in the King's
jursidiction.
Value then 5s; now it pays 22s 4d.
Also in Holkham he holds 1 Freeman, at 10 acres of land. He
belongs to Hindringham.

The Hundred of WALSHAM
27 In (South) WALSHAM 1 free man (is held), at 18 acres which that
free man granted to St. Benedict's of Holme, but Bishop Erfast
took them away from there. Now Bishop W(illiam) holds.
Value 4s.

HVNDRET . BLAFELDA . H̃ . In blafelda ten& **Almarus**
ẽps . t . r . e . 11 . car̋ terræ . Semp . ix . uilł . & . 11 . ferù . Semp . 11 . car̋
in dominio . & dim̄ car̋ hom̄ . Silua . viii . porc̃ . 7 . 1111 . ac̃ p̋ti.

195 a

Semp . 11 . runc̋ . & . 11 . an̄ . modo . xi . porc̋ . & . 111 . cap̋ & ifti man̄
ptin& xl.iii foc̃ . t . r . e . 7 femp qui non potuerunt terras
fuas uend̃ . nec dare . 111 . car̋ . terræ . 7 . 1111 . ac̃ p̋ti . Tc̃ . x . car̋ .
modo . ix . Wiłłm̄ ten& . v . foc̋ Rainaldus . Balduinus 7 Helius.
Sup hos habuit . t . r . e . ẽps . vi . forisfacturas . fed hund̃ nec
uidit breue nec figillũ nec concefsũ regis ; Tc̃ totũ uał
vii . lib̃ . modo . viii . lib̃ . & . ħt . 1 . lḡ longi . & . 111 . qr̋ ; 7 in lato .
. 1 . lḡ . & . 1 . qr̋ . & de gelto . xxx . d̋ . ħ man̄ accep̋ Almar̋ cũ vxore
fua antequã efł& ẽps . & p̋ ea tenuit in epifcopatũ . m̄ ten̄ . W . ẽps.

⌐In plũmefteda . 1 . foc̋ eft additus ab eruafto . fed fuit ftigandi
. 111 . ac̃ . terræ . Semp arat . cũ . 11 . bouib₂ & reddit . v . d̃.

⌐*FLECWEST . H̃ .* Hemefbei ten& Algarus comes . t . r . e .
& Alwi̋ emit . ftigandus abftulit . & dedit Almaro fri fuo.
f7 hund̃ . nefcit quomodo . ex illo fuit in epifcopatũ . in dominio
. 111 . car̋ terræ . & femp . xxx . 111 . uiłł . & . xiii . bord̋ . Tc̃ . vi . fer̋ .
modo . 111 . Semp . 111 . car̋ in dominio . & . xi . car̋ hominũ .
. 1 . æcełia . xx . ac̃ . 7 uał . xv₂ . d̋.
& . xl ac̃ . p̋ti . & . 11 . falin̄ . m̄ . xii . porc̋ . 7 c 7 lx . oũs . & . 1111 .
foc̃ . de . lx . ac̃ terræ . 111 . ac̃ p̋ti . & . femp . 1 . car̋ . Ifti ma
n̄ pertin& . 1 . berewita marthã . 11 . car̋
terræ Semp . vii . uiłł . & . 111 . bord̋
& . 1 . ferù . Semp . 11 . car̋ in dñio.
& . 1 . car̋ hom̄ . & . l . ac̃
prati.

BLOFIELD Hundred

28 In BLOFIELD Bishop A(e)lmer held 2 c. of land before 1066.
Always 9 villagers; 2 slaves.
Always 2 ploughs in lordship; ½ men's plough. Woodland, 8
pigs; meadow, 4 acres. Always 2 cobs; 2 head of cattle.
Now 11 pigs; 3 goats.   195 a
To this manor belonged 43 Freemen before 1066 and always,
who could not sell or grant their lands.
3 c. of land; meadow, 4 acres.
Then 10 ploughs, now 9.
William holds 5 Freemen. Reynold, Baldwin and Eli. Before
1066 the Bishop had the 6 forfeitures over these but the Hundred
has seen neither the King's writ nor seal nor grant.
Value of the whole then £7; now £8.
It has 1 league and 3 furlongs in length and 1 league and 1
furlong in width, tax of 30d.
A(e)lmer received this manor with his wife before he was
Bishop, and later held it in the Bishopric. Now Bishop William
holds.

29 In PLUMSTEAD 1 Freeman was added by Erfast, but he was
Stigand's. 3 acres of land. He has always ploughed with 2 oxen.
He pays 5d.

WEST FLEGG Hundred

30 Earl Algar held HEMSBY before 1066 and A(i)lwy bought it.
Stigand took it away and granted it to his brother A(e)lmer, but
the Hundred does not know how. From that (time) it was in the
Bishopric. In lordship 3 c. of land.
Always 33 villagers; 13 smallholders. Then 6 slaves, now 3.
Always 3 ploughs in lordship; 11 men's ploughs.
Meadow, 40 acres; 2 salt-houses.
1 church, 20 acres;
value 16d.
Now 12 pigs; 160 sheep.
Also 4 Freemen, at 60 acres of land; meadow, 3 acres; always
1 plough.
To this manor belongs 1 outlier, MARTHAM, 2 c. of land.
Always 7 villagers; 3 smallholders; 1 slave.
Always 2 ploughs in lordship; 1 men's plough.
Meadow, 50 acres.

Ricardus ſuꝑ·xxx·ſol.

Adhuc jacent huic mañ. xx . vii . ſoc . xxx ać . terræ . & . v.

ać ꝓti. ſemp. iii . car . 7 in Wintretuna . ii . ſoc . x . ać . & ſemp

dim. car . Tc uał xxvi . lib . modo . xxix . lib . ħt totū . i . lg

7 dim in longo . 7 . x . qr in lato . 7 de gelto . xxx . d . 7 marthā

ħt . i . leug . 7 dim . & . in lato . i . leug . & . de gelto . xxx . d . ſed plu-

res ibi tenent . In eſcou . ii . bord . de . de . vi . ać . terræ . & ꝑ

tinent ad heimeſbei.

ⅤHEINESTEDE HVNDRET. In Rokelunda . W . de-

noers 7 ſutherlingaham . ii . uiłt . de . xvi . ać . & . ii . ać ꝓti.

Semp tc dim . car . modo . ar . cū . ii . boū . ptin& in Langale.

ⅤDIM . Ħ . herſam . ⅤIn mendahā . W . de noers . teñ . i . pſbit . Al-

gar . xl . iii . ać . eccliaſtice terræ . m̄ ſub . W . denoiers . Semp . iii .

bord . Semper inter ſe 7 hoes . i . car . Silua . xv . porc . 7 . iii .

ać. ꝓti . Semp uał . x . ſoł

ⅤLOTNINGA . Ħ . North langale tenent Anant lib ho

ſub . rege . e . ꝑ . iii . car terræ . Tc & ꝑ. ii . uiłt . modo . i . Semp

viii . bord . Tc . ii . car & dim . ꝑ . i . & dim . modo . i . car in dñio.

Semp . i . car hom . Silua . xx . porc . 7 viii . ać ꝓti . & . i.

moliñ . Tc . vii . eq . modo . ᵭᵫ . vi . Tc . iiii . añ . m̄ . i.

. xx . porc . modo . xiiii . modo . lxxxxv . ous

7 xxv . ſoc . anant . de . i . car terræ.

Tc & poſt . iiii . car . m̄ . iii.

& . iii . libi homines ejđe cōm̄đ . xl . ać 7 ſota regis . Tc . i.

car & dim . ꝑ & modo . i . In eađ . i . ꝑbr mteger . & . ii . dim.

tenent . c . ać . libæ terræ . & . jacent m̄ ecł̄ia ſc̄e andree.

Tc & ſemp uał . iiii . lib . ħt . ꓺ . lg in longo . & . i . in lato.

& de gelto . xi . d . In tꝑr . r . e . habuit Almar tr̄a iłti anant

& ſocii fueī 7 ſubita morte fuit morteus.

Further 27 Freemen appertain to this manor—Richard against   195 b
   30s—30 acres of land; meadow, 5 acres.
In WINTERTON 2 Freemen; 10 acres; always ½ plough.
Value then £26; now £29.
   The whole has 1½ leagues in length and 10 furlongs in width;
tax of 30d. Martham has 1½ leagues [in length] and in width 1
league; tax of 30d, but more hold there.
   In SCO 2 smallholders, at 6 acres of land; they belong to
Hemsby.

HENSTEAD Hundred
31 In ROCKLAND (St. Mary) and SURLINGHAM William of Noyers
(holds) 2 villagers, at 16 acres; meadow, 2 acres.
   Then always ½ plough; now they plough with 2 oxen.
They belong in Langley.

EARSHAM Half-Hundred
32 In MENDHAM William of Noyers holds 1 priest, Algar, 43 acres of
ecclesiastical land; now under William of Noyers.
   Always 3 smallholders.
   Always 1 plough between himself and the men. Woodland,
      15 pigs; meadow, 3 acres.
Value always 10s.

LODDON Hundred
33 Anand, a free man, held LANGLEY under King Edward, as 3 c. of
land.
   Then and later 2 villagers, now 1; always 8 smallholders.
   Then 2½ ploughs, later 1½, now 1 plough in lordship.
      Always 1 men's plough; woodland, 20 pigs; meadow, 8 acres;
      1 mill. Then 7 horses, now 6. Then 4 cattle, now 1; [then]
      20 pigs, now 14. Now 95 sheep.
   Also 25 Freemen of Anand's, at 1 c. of land.
   Then and later 4 ploughs; now 3.
   Also 3 free men under the patronage of the same, 40 acres.
   The King's jurisdiction.   196 a
     Then 1½ ploughs, later and now 1.
In the same 1 whole priest and 2 halves. They hold 100 acres
of free land and (their lands) appertain in the church of St.
Andrew.
Value then and always £4.
   It has 1 league in length and 1 in width, tax of 11d.
   Before 1066 A(e)lmer had the land of this Anand; they were
joint-tenants. (Anand) died a sudden death.

xv . aᴄ̄ terræ & dim . car . 7 . I . aᴄ̄ . p̃ti . Tᴄ̄ silua . v . porc . Et in
grege fete . II . foᴄ . de . II . aᴄ . Tota uᵬl . tᴄ̄ . x . lib . 7 modo . XIII
lib . & . VIII . fol . 7

¶ I Helmingehã ten& Renoldus . I . lib homo . xxx . aᴄ̄
terre . de q̃ habuit ẽps Almar cõmdationẽ tantũ . femp
. II . uiᵬt . & . III . borᵭ . Tᴄ̄ . II . car int fe . & hom . m̃ . I . femp uaᵬ
x . fol . 7 ḫt . I . lᵹ 7 dim in longo . 7 . I . in lato . & reddit . XL . d .
de gelto regis . quicũq̃ ibi tẽneat.

*HVNDRET . DE TAVER*ham ; In Tauerham teñ . I . liba
fem̃ . t . r . e . dim . car terræ . Tᴄ̄ . III . uiᵬt . & . II . borᵭ . femp
. I . car in dominio . Tᴄ̄ 7 p̃ dim car ho ninũ . 7 . v . aᴄ̄ p̃ti . filua
II . porc . Tᴄ̄ . III . foᴄ . XIII . aᴄ̄ . terræ . modo . I . foᴄ . Tᴄ̄ dim car
Tᴄ̄ uaᵬ . XII . fol . modo . xx . fol.

¶ In Atebruge ten& Gosfridus . I . lib homo . XVI . aᴄ̄ terre
& . I . borᵭ . femp . dim . carr . & . II . aᴄ̄ . p̃ti . 7 uaᵬ
. VI . fol . & . VIII . d . I . æcclia VI . aᴄ̄ . & . uaᵬ . VI . d .

¶ *ERPINCHAM SUD . HVNDRET* . Blielinga

tenuit heroldus . t . r . e . III . car terræ . & . dim . fẽp xII . uiᵬli .
& xVI . borᵭ . & . I . feru . femp . II . car . in dominio . & . VI . car hom .
. x . aᴄ̄ p̃ti . Tᴄ̄ filua . cc . porc . modo . c . femp . I . moᵬ . & . I . rñc .
7 xVI . porc . Tᴄ̄ uaᵬ . VI . lib . modo . VIII . & ḫt . I . longo . & . I .
in lato . & . IIII . d . & oᵬolũ de gelto . huic mañ jacent in ſtriñ -
cham . II . foᴄ . femp . LX . aᴄ̄ terræ . & xIIII . borᵭ . femp . I . car & d .
& . II . aᴄ . & dim p̃ti . filua de . XVIII . porc . & . II . part . alti
& . VII . partes molini . Tᴄ̄ uaᵬ . xv . fol . modo . xxv ;

The Hundred of EYNSFORD
34 Also in THURNING 1 free man; 15 acres of land; ½ plough.
Meadow, 1 acre; then woodland, 5 pigs.
Value 8s. *And in GUIST 2 Freemen, at 2 acres. Value of the whole
then £10; now £13 8s.*

35 In HELMINGHAM Reynold, 1 free man, holds 30 acres of land, of
whom Bishop A(e)lmer had the patronage only.
Always 2 villagers; 3 smallholders.
Then 2 ploughs between himself and the men; now 1.
Value always 10s.
It has 1½ leagues in length and 1 in width, it pays tax of 40d,
whoever holds there.

Hundred of TAVERHAM
36 In TAVERHAM 1 free woman before 1066 held ½ c. of land.
Then 3 villagers; 2 smallholders.
Always 1 plough in lordship. Then and later ½ men's plough.
Meadow, 5 acres; woodland, 2 pigs.
Then 3 Freemen; 13 acres of land; now 1 Freeman. Then ½ plough.
Value then 12s; now 20s.

37 In ATTLEBRIDGE Geoffrey, 1 free man, holds 16 acres of land,
1 smallholder;
always ½ plough. Meadow, 2 acres.
Value 6s 8d.
1 church; 6 acres;
value 6d.

SOUTH ERPINGHAM Hundred
38 Harold held BLICKLING before 1066; 3½ c. of land.   196 b
Always 12 villagers; 16 smallholders; 1 slave.
Always 2 ploughs in lordship; 6 men's ploughs; meadow, 10
acres. Then woodland, 200 pigs, now 100. Always 1 mill;
1 cob; 16 pigs.
Value then £6; now 8.
It has 1 [league] in length and 1 in width, tax of 4½d.
2 Freemen appertain to this manor in Hevingham; always 60
acres of land.
14 smallholders.
Always 1½ ploughs; meadow, 2½ acres; woodland at 18 pigs;
two-thirds of another and seven-eighths of a mill.
Value then 15s; now 25.

In bnincham . i . car terre . & . L . ac . & . iii . uill . & . xi . bord .
semper . ii . car . & . dim . & . v . ac . pti . Silua de . xx . viii .
porc . Tc . i . mol . que modo ten& . Godric ad feudu
regis . Tc ual . xii . fot . m . xx . ii . hoc jac& in blieliga .

Marsam ten& heroldus . iiii . car . terræ . femp . vi . uill
& xxix . bord . & . femp . ii . car in dnio . & . iiii . car hom .
vi . ac pti . filua . de . c . porc . & . iiii . foc ten& . Rogrus .
. i . car terræ . & . iii . bord . & . ii . car . & . i . runc . & . ii .
an . 7 xii . porc . 7 xxvi . cap . 7 . vi . uafa apu . Tc ual
vi . lib . modo . ix . Et ht . i . leug in long . 7 . iii . qr 7 . vii .
qr in longo . 7 . xi . d . de gefto .

In Stratuna . i . foc . xxx . ac . ad marsa . & dim car . .
& ual . ii . fot .

HVND DE HAPINGA . In horfeia

ten& . W . de noers . i . lib homo Almari . epi comd tantu
xxv . ac . & . iii . bord . & dim car . & . x . ac . pti . 7 ual

197 a

ii . fot . Rex & coms foca .

In ead . ii . lib hoes . A . epi . comd de . xvii . ac . & . v . ac . pti . & ual .
xxx . d .

39 In (Little) BARNINGHAM 1 c. of land and 50 acres.
    3 villagers; 11 smallholders.
    Always 2½ ploughs; meadow, 5 acres; woodland at 28 pigs. Then
        1 mill, which now Godric holds as part of the King's Holding.
    Value then 12s; now 22.
    This appertains in Blickling.

40 Harold held MARSHAM; 4 c. of land.
    Always 6 villagers; 29 smallholders.
    Always 2 ploughs in lordship; 4 men's ploughs.
        Meadow, 6 acres; woodland at 100 pigs.
    Also Roger holds 4 Freemen; 1 c. of land; 3 smallholders;
        2 ploughs.
    1 cob; 2 head of cattle; 12 pigs; 26 goats; 6 beehives.
    Value then £6; now 9.
    It has 1 league 3 furlongs in length, and 7 furlongs in width;
    tax of 11d.

41 In STRATTON (Strawless) 1 Freeman; 30 acres as part of (the lands
    of) Marsham; ½ plough.
    Value 2s.

    The Hundred of HAPPING
42 William of Noyers holds in HORSEY (what) 1 Freeman under the
    patronage only of Bishop A(e)lmer (held), 25 acres.
        3 smallholders.
        ½ plough; meadow, 10 acres.
    Value 2s.   197 a
        The King and the Earl (have) the jurisdiction.
        In the same 2 free men under the patronage of Bishop A(elmer)
    at 17 acres; meadow, 5 acres.
    Value 30d.

In Scroutebei. vii . ſoc

xx. aċ. ſemp. i . car . & ual xxxii . đ . 7 iſti ſoc . jacent in hameſbei.

. i . ecċlia xxxvi. aċ . & . ual . iii . ſol . In eadē . x . libi homines

de. Ħ. habuit Ailmarus eps . comđ . t . r . e . & hnt . ii . car terræ

& . v . aċ . ſemp . v . car . & . iii . aċ. pti . Tc ual . xx. ſol . m . xxx.

hos oms tenuit Ailmarus eps . t . r . e . & arfaſtus . m . Wiłł. eps. & tam

ex uno habuit Abbas de olmo comđcione tantu . t . r . e . Et

ex łi libis hominibʒ ten& Ricardus fili alann. vi . de epo. & idē eps

alios.

𝖵 In Oſmeſbei . ii . libi homines . Guend . xl . aċ. ſemp. i . car.

& . ii . aċ pti. & ual . viii . ſol . hetia ten& idē Ricardus.

𝖵 In trikebei . i . lib hō . xii . aċ . terræ . ſub. alm . epo . comdatione

tantu . ſemp . dim. car . & ual. xii . đ. & hit dim łg in longo

& . dim in lato. 7 xiiii . đ. & obolu . de gelto ;

HVNĐ . DEPWADE . In Stratuna . xii . libi homines de ꝗbʒ

. A . eps. habuit comđ tant . t . r . e . cc. iii . aċ. & . x . borđ & dim.

& . iii . car . & . vi . aċ. pti. Tc ual xx. ſol . m . xl.

𝖵 Clauelinga. *HVNĐ*. In Rauincħa . i . lib hō . Ailmari

epi comđ . xxx . aċ. & . ii . borđ. & . dim car . & . ual& . iii . ſol.

The Hundred of (East) FLEGG

43 In SCRATBY 7 Freemen, 20 acres. Always 1 plough.
Value 32d.
   These Freemen appertain in Hemsby.
   1 church, 36 acres;
value 3s.
   In the same 10 free men. Bishop A(e)lmer had the patronage
of these before 1066. They have 2 c. of land and 5 acres. Always
5 ploughs. Meadow, 3 acres.
Value then 20s; now 30.
   Bishop A(e)lmer held all these before 1066, and Erfast; now
Bishop William. And yet the Abbot of Holme had the patronage
only of one before 1066. Out of these free men Richard son of
Alan holds 6 from the Bishop, and this Bishop (holds) the others.

44 In ORMESBY 2 free men of Gyrth's, 40 acres. Always 1 plough;
   meadow, 2 acres.
Value 8s.
   The same Richard also holds this.

45 In THRIGBY 1 free man, 12 acres of land, under Bishop A(e)lmer—
in patronage only. Always ½ plough.
Value 12d.
   It has ½ league in length and ½ in width; tax of 14½d.

DEPWADE Hundred

46 In STRATTON 12 free men of whom Bishop A(e)lmer had the
patronage only before 1066, 203 acres.
   10 smallholders and a half.
   3 ploughs; meadow, 6 acres.
Value then 20s; now 40.

CLAVERING Hundred

47 In RAVENINGHAM 1 free man under the patronage of Bishop
A(e)lmer; 30 acres.
   2 smallholders;
   ½ plough.
Value 3s.

*HVNDRET . DE GRENE*hou : de INUASIONIBVS

EJVSDÉ FEVDI. In gresingahā inuasit. Raď . hō eƥi de tedfort
quendā libū hoem . cū , i . car̄ . terræ qui erat in socha regis de cres-
-singahā . &. de . ii . hoibƺ deten& sochā ; 7 ual̄ . xx . sol̄.

*In cressingahā . vi . libi . hŏes . Eduini . iii . car̄ terre . Tc̄ . vi . car̄ . m̄ . ii.
7 . iiii . ac̄ . ƥti . i . mol̄ . Tc̄ ual̄ . lx . sol̄ . m̄ . xxx . sol̄.

HVND̄ . DE FREDREBRVGE. In meltinga . xv . libi homines
xl . ac̄ terræ . semp . dim̄ . car̄ . &. vi . borď ; 7 ual̄ . xxx . sol̄ . de his habuit
sui . antec̄ com̄d tantū . Stigandus socā.

*In . H̄ . de Smetheduna . hunestanestuna . ten̄ . i . soc̄ . Stigandi
t . r . e . i . car̄ . terre . &. i . car̄ . Tc̄ . iii . borď . m̄ . ii . 7 . ii . 7 đ . ac̄ ƥti .
dim̄ mol̄ . silu xx . iiii . porc̄ . Tc̄ . i . piscar̄ . Totū ual̄ . x . sol̄.

HVNDRET . DE grimeshou . In estanforda . i . lib hō . de lx .
ac̄ . Tc̄ & ƥ . i . car̄ . modo nichil . Semp . i . uill̄ . ii . ac̄ ƥti . Semp
ual̄ . vi . sol̄ . &. viii . đ . de hoc habuit . antecessor ej . W . com̄d
tantū 7 Rex soc̄ . 7 W . eƥs ten& eum.

HVNDRET LAWENDIC. In Gatelea . i . lib̄ hō vi . ac̄ . terræ .
& ual̄ . vi . đ . quē tenuit Bonde lib hō ante c̄ hug de montfort .
t . r . e . ƥ ea effectus ē homo erfasti . eƥi . & idō . ten& . Willm̄.
Soca in mulehā.

48   In (Great) CRESSINGHAM Ralph, the Bishop of Thetford's man, annexed a certain free man with 1 c. of land who was in the King's jurisdiction of (Great) Cressingham, and he detains the jurisdiction of 2 men.
Value 20s.

49   In (Great) CRESSINGHAM 6 free men of Edwin's, 3 c. of land.
    Then 6 ploughs, now 2. Meadow, 4 acres; 1 mill.
Value then 60s; now 30s.

The Hundred of FREEBRIDGE

50   In MINTLYN 15 free men, 40 acres of land. Always ½ plough.
    6 smallholders.
Value 30s.
    Of these his predecessor had the patronage only. Stigand (had) the jurisdiction.

In the Hundred of SMETHDON

51   1 free man of Stigand's held HUNSTANTON before 1066, 1 c. of land. 1 plough.
    Then 3 smallholders, now 2.
    Meadow, 2½ acres; ½ mill; woodland, 24 pigs. Then 1 fishery.
Value of the whole 10s.

The Hundred of GRIMSHOE

52   In STANFORD 1 free man, at 60 acres.
    Then and later 1 plough, now nothing.
    Always 1 villager.
    Meadow, 2 acres.
Value always 6s 8d.
    Of this the predecessor of the same W(illiam) had the patronage only, and the King the jurisdiction. Bishop William holds him.

LAUNDITCH Hundred

53   In GATELEY 1 free man, 6 acres of land.
Value 6d.
    Bondi, a free man, the predecessor of Hugh of Montfort, held him before 1066. Later he was made Bishop Erfast's man, and thus William holds.
The jurisdiction (is) in Mileham.

HVND DE BRODERCOS. În colekirka inuaſit Ærefaſtus
ſiluā de fatigeham. & eſt in longo. LX. ac̄.

HVNDRET. DE GALGOV. In ſexelingahā ten̄. heroldus. II.
libi homines. de. I. car̄. terræ. & dim̄. modo ten̄ eos. Wiſtmus ep̄s

198 a

7 Sēp. VII. bord̄. Tc̄. II. car̄. modo. II. & dim̄. V. ac̄. p̄ti. 7 đ. moł.
Tc̄ uał. xx. ſoł. modo. xxx. Adhuc ten&. h. in eađ uilla. xxx. ac̄.
_{Lagaā. I. lib h̄}
&. I. bord̄. Semp. I. car̄. II. ac̄ p̄ti. Tc̄ uał. V. ſoł. modo. VII. ſoł.

HVNDRET. DE HOLT. In ſnuterlea. ten̄ Edricus ſub rege. e.
_{W. de noert. de ep̄). W.}
libe heroldo. II. car̄. terræ. Semp. II. uiłti. 7 xxv. bord̄. &. I. feru̇. Sēp̄
in dominio. II. car̄. 7 hom̄. II. car̄. III. ac̄ p̄ti. I. molin̄. 7. IIII. ſoc̄. de.
xx. IIII. ac̄. 7 dim̄. car̄. Totū uał. t. r. e. xL ſoł. modo. IIII. lib̄. I. æcclia
xxx. ac̄. vał xvi. đ.

In burningahā. IIII. libi ho̅es heroldi. de. II. car̄. terræ & dim̄. q̄s ten&
Roger Lungus enſis de. W. ep̄o. Semp. IX. uiłt. Tc̄. XIII. bord̄. mòdo. xvII.
Tc̄. in dn̄io. III. car̄. modo. II. & đ. 7 dim̄. poſſet reſtaurari; Tc̄. hom̄.
II. car̄. & dim̄. modo. IIII. Silua ad xxx. porc̄. VI. ac̄ p̄ti. I. molin̄. Tc̄
II. runc̄. modo. ſimiliſ̄. Tc̄. IIII. porc̄. modo. VIII. Tc̄. IX. o̅ūs. m̄. c. 7. IIII.
m̄. V. uas apū. 7 III. ſoc̄. de. xII. ac̄. 7 dim̄. car̄. Tc̄ uał. L. ſoł. m̄. IIII. lib̄.
7 ħt. I. lḡ. in longo. &. VIII. qr̄. in lato. 7 xIII. đ de gelto. I. æcclia. xII. ac̄.
& uał. xII. đ.

The Hundred of BROTHERCROSS

54 In COLKIRK Erfast annexed woodland from Fakenham. It is 60 acres in length.

The Hundred of GALLOW

55 Harold held in SAXLINGHAM; 2 free men, at 1½ c. of land. Now Bishop William holds them.

    Always 7 smallholders.   198 a

    Then 2 ploughs, now 2½. Meadow, 5 acres; ½ mill.

Value then 20s; now 30.

Further H(arold) held in the same village LANGHAM, 1 free man, 30 acres.

    1 smallholder.

    Always 1 plough. Meadow, 2 acres.

Value then 5s; now 7s.

The Hundred of HOLT

56 In BLAKENEY W(illiam) of Noyers (holds) from Bishop W(illiam); Edric held under King Edward freely (from) Harold, 2 c. of land.

    Always 2 villagers; 25 smallholders; 1 slave.

    Always 2 ploughs in lordship; 2 men's ploughs.

        Meadow, 3 acres; 1 mill.

    Also 4 Freemen, at 24 acres; ½ plough.

Value of the whole before 1066 40s; now £4.

    1 church; 30 acres;

value 16d.

57 In BRININGHAM 4 free men of Harold's, at 2½ c. of land whom Roger Longsword holds from Bishop William.

    Always 9 villagers. Then 13 smallholders, now 17.

    Then 3 ploughs in lordship, now 2½; ½ could be restored.

        Then 2½ men's ploughs, now 4.

    Woodland for 30 pigs; meadow, 6 acres; 1 mill. Then 2 cobs, now the same. Then 4 pigs, now 8. Then 9 sheep, now 104. Now 5 beehives.

    Also 3 Freemen, at 12 acres; ½ plough.

Value then 50s; now £4.

    It has 1 league in length and 8 furlongs in width, tax of 13d.

    1 church, 12 acres;

value 12d.

⌐In mæltuna . IIII . libi homines heroldi . m̂ . W . eṗs . & . Roḡ Lungus enſis
de eo . 7 anſchetellus ꝓpoſitus . & Roḡ . 7 . III . caŕ terræ . Semp . II . uilt.
7 xxx.II. borđ . 7 ineos . VII . caŕ & dim̂ . Silua ad LX . porc̄ . VI . ac̄
p̂ti . Sēp . II . runc̄ . Tc̄ . & modo VIII . an̂ . Tc̄ . v . porc̄ m̂ . x.
. I . æcclia . de . VI . ac̄ . 7 ual . v . đ . Tc̄ ual . xxx . ſot . m̂ . xL . ſot.
7 h̄t . I . leug in long . & dim̂ in lato . & x . đ . de gelto.
⌐In bruningahā ten̄ & Roḡ Longus enſis . VI . ac̄
        . I . æcclia . de . XII . ac̄ . uaĺ . XII . đ.
quas . R . com̄s ten̄ & . 7 P⁹ . A . comes & hoc
            |teſtatur . hunđ.

198 b

HVNDRET . GRENAHOGA . Hindringahā . ten̄ . A . eṗs . t.
r . e . modo . W . eṗs . VIII . libi homines . III . caŕ terre . XIIII . borđ . ſēp
ſilua . x . porc̄ . v . ac̄ p̂ti . Tc̄ . v . caŕ . modo . III . Tc̄ ual . xL . ſot . m̂
reddit . L . ſot . 7 de hac terra ten̄ & . Wiltm̂ . denuers dimidietatē.
⌐In hindringahā . ten̄ drogo . de beuraria . & an . I . hom̂ . de . I . ac̄
terræ & ante ceſſor ej . & p̄ ſaiſiū eū q̄dā ꝓpoſitus Wilti . eṗi
& ten̄ & eū q̄ dr̂ ſeolf.
⌐In torp . II . libi homines . m̂ ten̄ & . uiltm̂ denuers eos . de . W.
eṗo . c . ac̄ . træ . đ . ac̄ . p̂ti . ſemp . I . caŕ . 7 đ . t . r . e . ual . xx . ſot.
modo xxx.
⌐*ERPINGEHĀ NORTH . HVNDRET.*
⌐In hottune . ten̄ . almarus eṗs . I . libū hom̂ . ꝑ comd̄ . de xv.
ac̄ terræ . 7 Wiltm̂ denoiers ten̄ & . W . eṗo . 7 h̄t . dim̂ borđ.
Silua . ad . II . porc̄ . dim̂ caŕ . Tc̄ ual . II . ſot . modo . xVI . đ.

58 In MELTON (Constable) 4 free men of Harold's; now Bishop
W(illiam) (holds) and Roger Longsword from him, and (so do)
Ansketel the Reeve and Roger; 3 c. of land.
    Always 2 villagers; 32 smallholders.
    Between them 7½ ploughs.
    Woodland for 60 pigs; meadow, 6 acres; always 2 cobs. Then
       and now 8 head of cattle. Then 5 pigs, now 10.
    1 church, at 6 acres;
value 5d.
    Value then 30s, now 40s.
    It has 1 league in length and ½ in width, tax of 10d.

59 In BRININGHAM Roger Longsword holds 6 acres which Earl R(alph)
held.
    1 church, at 12 acres;
value 12d.
    Later Count Alan (held). The Hundred testifies to this.

(North) GREENHOE Hundred   198 b
60 Bishop A(elmer) held HINDRINGHAM before 1066, now Bishop
William; 8 free men, 3 c. of land.
    14 smallholders.
    Always woodland, 10 pigs; meadow, 5 acres.
    Then 5 ploughs, now 3.
Value then 40s; now it pays 50s.
    William of Noyers holds a half of this land.

61 In HINDRINGHAM Drogo of Beuvriere held; 1 man, at 1 acre of land.
His predecessor also (held). Later a certain reeve of Bishop
William's took possession of him and holds him, who is called
Saewulf.

62 In (Cock)THORPE 2 free men; now William of Noyers holds them
from Bishop W(illiam); 100 acres of land;
    meadow, ½ acre.
    Always 1½ ploughs.
Value before 1066, 20s; now 30.

NORTH ERPINGHAM Hundred
63 In *HOTTUNE* Bishop A(e)lmer held 1 free man for patronage, at 15
acres of land. William of Noyers holds from Bishop W(illiam); he
has ½ smallholder.
    Woodland for 2 pigs.
    ½ plough.
Value then 2s; now 16d.

ꝉIn b̄nigehā . ı . liƀ hō quē teñ Wiulfus . t . r . e . de . xv . ac̄
tr̄e modo teñ W . de noiers ab ep̄o . W . Semp . đ . car̓ . Sēp
uaꝉ xvı . đ.

ꝉIn becchehā . teñ . ı . liƀ hō ep̄i Almari c̓omdatione lxxx . ac̄
terræ . Semp . ıı . uiꞁꞁi . & . v . borđ . Silua ad . v . porc̓ . & . ı . ſoc̓.
de . ıı . ac̄ . & dim̓ terræ . ſemp . ıı . car̓ . ı . æcclia . de . ıı . ac̄
& dim̓ . Et ē addita b̄wita ad blikelinges . Tc̄ uaꝉ
vıı . ſoꝉ . & m̊ . xıı . & ħt dim̓ leuga in longo . &
. ıııı . qr̓ in lato . & . ıııı . đ & obolū.

199 a
ꝉWALESSAM . HVND̃ . In hemelintuna . ıı . liƀi
homines đ lx . ac̄ terræ Raſtalre . t . r . e . cū ſoca & ſaca ſed
de uno habuit Almar ep̄s c̓omđ tantū m̊ ten& unū . W . ep̄s
& alterū Com̄s . R . & uaꝉ . ıı ; ſoꝉ.

HVNDREꞱ . DE BLAFELDA . In plumm̄eſteda . ten& god-
winus . ı . liƀū hoēm gerti . ı . car̓ terræ . modo teñ . W . ep̄s . Sēp
. v . borđ . Semp̓ . ı . car̓ in dominio . Semp̓ dimidia . car̓ hom̓.
Silu̓ . vııı . porc̓ . ı . ac̄ . p̓ti . Semp̓ . ıı . an̓ . & . ibi s̄ . x . liƀi homines
đ . xxx . ac̄ terræ c̓omdati tantū goduin . Sēp . ı . car̓ . & . ı . ac̄.
p̓ti . Tc̄ uaꝉ . x . ſoꝉ . m̊ . xl . & pꝗ rex . W . uenit in hanc terr̄a
inuaſit Almarus ep̄s ꝑ foris factura . quia mulier que tenuit
nupſit intra annū ꝑ mortē uiri.

64 In (North) BARNINGHAM 1 free man whom Wigulf held before 1066, at 15 acres of land; now W(illiam) of Noyers holds from Bishop W(illiam). Always ½ plough.
Value always 16d.

65 In (East) BECKHAM 1 free man under the patronage of Bishop A(e)lmer held 80 acres of land.
 Always 2 villagers; 5 smallholders.
 Woodland for 5 pigs.
 Also 1 Freeman, at 2½ acres of land.
  Always 2 ploughs.
 1 church, at 2½ acres.
It was added as an outlier to Blickling.
Value then 7s; now 12.
 It has ½ league in length and 4 furlongs in width, [tax of] 4½d.

WALSHAM Hundred   199 a
66 In HEMBLINGTON 2 free men, at 60 acres of land. Ralph the Constable (held them) before 1066 with the full jurisdiction, but Bishop A(e)lmer had the patronage only of 1. Now Bishop W(illiam) holds 1 and Earl R(alph held) the other.
Value 2s.

The Hundred of BLOFIELD
67 In PLUMSTEAD Godwin held 1 free man of Gyrth's, 1 c. of land. Now Bishop W(illiam) holds.
 Always 5 smallholders.
 Always 1 plough in lordship. Always ½ men's plough; woodland, 8 pigs; meadow, 1 acre; always 2 head of cattle.
 There are 10 free men at 30 acres of land under the patronage only of Godwin. Always 1 plough; meadow, 1 acre.
Value then 10s; now 40.
 After King W(illiam) came into this land Bishop A(e)lmer annexed it for a forfeiture because the woman who held it married within a year after the death of her husband.

In ƀlungeham ten&.ɪɪ.caꞃ́ terræ.xv.liƀi.hoḗs Almaꞃi
eꝓi comdationeꜩtantū.Semꝓ.ɪx.borđ.vɪɪɪ.aꞇ ꝓti.Semꝓ.
vɪɪɪ.caꞃ́.Tꞇ uaɫ.xx.ſoɫ.&.m̅.xxvɪ.ſoɫ..ɪ.æcclia.xxx.aꞇ.7.uaɫ
ɪɪ.ſoɫ.&.vɪɪɪ.đ.M̅ ten̅.W.de noiers. Ad huc in plumeſteda.ɪɪ.liƀi
hoḗs gerti.7 ſtigandi qđ eruaſtus.eꝑs inuaſit.ʟ.aꞇ terræ.&.ɪɪ.
aꞇ ꝓti.Semꝓ.ɪɪ.borđ.Semꝓ.ɪ.caꞃ́.hos tenuit.R.coms.quando
ſe forisfecit.&.R.blundus ad censū.Tꞇ uaɫ.v.ſoɫ.modo.ɪɪɪ.
In plumeſteda.ten&.ɪ.liƀ hō Almari comdatione tantū.xvɪ.
aꞇ terræ.Tꞇ dim̅ caꞃ́.modo.ɪɪ.boūs.Tꞇ.uaɫ.ɪɪ.ſoɫ.modo.xvɪ.đ.
In frietorp.ɪ.liƀ hō Alſi sub.R.Comite.xvɪ.aꞇ.terræ.Seꝑ
dim̅.caꞃ́.ɪ.aꞇ.ꝓti.Semꝓ.uaɫ.ɪɪ.ſoɫ.Hꞇ tenuit balduin
ꝓpoſit eꝓi comđ tantū ſ7 ne comđtus

199 b
eſt Godrico in manu regis.
In Letha.vɪɪ.liƀi hoḗs Almari comdatione tantū.t.r.e.m̅ ten̅ Re﹣
noldus.ɪ.caꞃ́ terræ.7 dim̅.Semꝓ.ɪɪɪ.caꞃ́.7.femꝓ.ɪɪɪɪ.borđ.Silu.
ɪɪɪɪ.porꞇ.&.xɪɪ.aꞇ ꝓti.Tꞇ uaɫ.x.ſoɫ.&.ɪɪɪɪ.đ.ɪ.æcclia.v.aꞇ.uaɫ.
v.đ.&.h̅ɪ.ɪ.lg̅ in longo.&.v.qꞃ́.in lato.qcūq̄ ibi teneat.& de gelto
vɪ.den̅.&.obolū.

68 In (North) BURLINGHAM 15 free men under the patronage of
Bishop A(e)lmer held 2 c. of land.
    Always 9 smallholders.
    Meadow, 8 acres; always 8 ploughs.
Value then 20s; now 26s 8d.
    1 church; 30 acres;
value 2s 8d.
    Now W(illiam) of Noyers holds.

69   Further in PLUMSTEAD 2 free men of Gyrth's and Stigand's.
Bishop Erfast annexed this. 50 acres of land;
    meadow, 2 acres.
    Always 2 smallholders.
    Always 1 plough.
    Earl R(alph) held these when he forfeited, and R(obert) Blunt
(has them) at tribute.
Value then 5s; now 3.

70 In PLUMSTEAD 1 free man holds in the patronage only of A(e)lmer
held 16 acres of land. Then ½ plough; now 2 oxen.
Value then 2s; now 16d.

71 In FREETHORPE 1 free man, Alsi, under Earl R(alph), 16 acres of
land. Always ½ plough; meadow, 1 acre.
Value always 2s.
    Baldwin, the Bishop's reeve, held him in patronage only but
now he is in the patronage of Godric and in the King's hand.   199 b

72 In *LETHA* 7 free men in the patronage only of A(e)lmer before
1066, now Reynold holds; 1½ c. of land.
    Always 3 ploughs.
    Always 4 smallholders.
    Woodland, 4 pigs; meadow, 12 acres.
Value then 10s; now 10s 4d.
    1 church; 5 acres;
value 5d.
    It has 1 league in length and 5 furlongs in width, whoever holds
there, tax of 6½d.

⫟In ƀlungehā . III . liƀi hŏes Almari comdatione tantū . t . r . e . m̄ ten̄
helius XL.VI.aē . terræ . & . IIII . aē . p̄ti . Semp . I . cař . 7 femp . ual . IIII . fol.

⫟In ead . I . liƀ hō Almari ep̄i comdatione tantū . t . r . e . m̄ . ten̄ id helius
de . LX . aē terræ liƀæ . 7 . XL . que p̄tinent cuidā æccliæ . VII . aē p̄ti . Tē
IIII . bord . i liƀa . modo . V . & . II . bord . intra quæ append& . æcclie . Tē . I . cař.
& dim̄ . p̄ 7 modo . II . cař . & fub fe . I . æcclia . de . X . aē . ual . X . đ . & fub fe
VII.s̄ . liƀi hŏes comdatione tantū . de . XL . aē terræ . & . III . aē p̄ti.
Semp . I . cař . Sēp ual . XIII . fol .

⫟In eadē . II . liƀi homines Almari comdatione tantū . t . r . e . m̄ . ten̄
. W . de noers . de . L . aē . terræ . femp . I . uilł . 7 . IIII . bord . 7 XII . aē . p̄ti.
Semp . I . cař . & dim̄ . 7 dim̄ fal . Tē ual . L . đ . modo reddit . X . fol.
& ead uilla ħt . X . g̃ qr in longo . & . VI . in lato . 7 de gelto . XX . đ .

⫟In Sutƀlingehā . VIII . liƀi homies almari ep̄i . comdatione tantū
modo ten& . W . ep̄s de noiers . de . C . XL . aē . terræ . Semp . XI . bord . & . VIII.
aē p̄ti . Tē . III . cař . p̄ 7 modo . II . & dim̄ . Semp ual& . XX . fol . dim ecclia
XV . aē . ual . XV . đ .

73 In (North) BURLINGHAM 3 free men in the patronage only of
A(e)lmer before 1066, now Eli holds; 46 acres of land.
   Meadow, 4 acres; always 1 plough.
Value always 4s.

In the same 1 free man in the patronage only of Bishop A(e)lmer
before 1066, now the same Eli holds; at 60 acres of free land and
40 which belong to a certain church;
   meadow, 7 acres.
   Then 4 smallholders in the free [land], now 5; 2 smallholders
on land which appertains to the church.
   Then 1½ ploughs, later and now 2 ploughs.
   Also under him 1 church, at 10 acres;
value 10d.
   Also under him are 7 free men in patronage only, at 40 acres
   of land; meadow, 3 acres. Always 1 plough.
Value always 13s.

In the same 2 free men in the patronage only of A(e)lmer before
1066, now W(illiam) of Noyers holds, at 50 acres of land.
   Always 1 villager; 4 smallholders.
   Meadow, 12 acres. Always 1½ ploughs; ½ salt-house.
Value then 50d; now it pays 10s.
   The same village has 10 furlongs in length and 6 in width;
tax of 20d.

74 In SOUTH BURLINGHAM 8 free men in the patronage only of Bishop
A(e)lmer, now W(illiam) of Noyers holds; at 140 acres of land.
   Always 11 smallholders.
   Meadow, 8 acres. Then 3 ploughs, later and now 2½.
Value always 20s.
   ½ church, 15 acres;
value 15d.

𝖥 In ead̄ . ii . libi hões . Almari . epī com̄datione.

modo ten̄ id̄ . W . i . car̄ terræ . Sep̄ . vi . bord̄ . Semp . i . car̄ . & dim̄ . 7 . iiii.

ac̄ p̄ti . 7 . iiii . libi homines . sub eis . viii . ac̄ terræ

200 a

& . i . ac̄ p̄ti . Semp dim̄ . car̄ . semp ual̄ x . sot̄ . & ħt blingaham

. i . lḡ in longo . & dim̄ in lato . sed plures ibi tenent . & de gelto . xx . đ.

𝖥 In Leta . i . lib̄ homo . almari ep̄i com̄d . & ten& . xvi . ac̄ terræ . 7 . i . ac̄

& dim̄ . prati . Semp ual& . v . đ.

𝖥 In bregestuna . i . lib̄ hō . edricus . rector nauis . Reḡ . e . i . ac̄ car̄

terræ . Semp . iiii . uilt̄ . & . i . bord̄ . & . ii . serū . & . iii . ac̄ . p̄ti . Semp

. i . car̄ in dominio . & dim̄ . car̄ hom . Silua . ii . porc̄ . 7 semp i . runc̄.

& . vi . an̄ . 7 lx . ōus . m̄ . 7 xvi . porc̄ . 7 xvi . cap̄ . i . æcclia . de . x . ac̄ . 7

ual̄ . x . đ . Et isti p̄tinent . x . libi hões & dim̄ . com̄dat tantū ante-

cessore . de . lxxx . ac̄ terræ . iii . ac̄ . p̄ti . Semp . ii . car̄ . 𝖥 Et in blinga-

ħā . iiii . ac̄ . & dim̄ træ p̄tinentes in brerestuna . Tc̄ ual̄ . x . sot̄ . 7 p̄ simt̄.

modo . xxx . sot̄ . Et p̄q rex W . uenit in angliā fuit iste edric̄ exlex.

indaciā & ep̄s almar̄ inuasit terrā . M̄ ten̄ . W . de noiers.

𝖥 In catuna . i . lib̄ hō Gerti com̄d tantū . t . r . e . đ lx . ac̄ . terræ . qn̄do

eruastus uen̄ ad episcopatū dedit cuidā suo hōi . Reinaldo . Tc̄ . v . bord̄.

modo . iiii . Tc̄ . i . car̄ in dominio . & semp & dim̄ car̄ hom . Silua . v . porc̄.

7 . i . runc̄ . & . xii . porc̄ . vii . ac̄ p̄ti . Tc̄ ual̄ . 7 semp . xv . đ.

In the same 2 free men in the patronage of Bishop A(e)lmer, now
W(illiam) also holds; 1 c. of land.
   Always 6 smallholders.
   Always 1½ ploughs; meadow, 3 acres.
   Also 4 free men under them, 8 acres of land.
      Meadow, 1 acre; always ½ plough.   200 a
Value always 10s.
   (South) Burlingham has 1 league in length and ½ in width, but
more hold there; tax of 20d.

75 In *LETA* 1 free man under the patronage of Bishop A(e)lmer; he
holds 16 acres of land; meadow, 1½ acres.
Value always 5d.

76 In BRADESTON 1 free man, Edric, steersman of King Edward's ship;
1 c. of land.
   Always 4 villagers; 1 smallholder, 2 slaves.
   Meadow, 3 acres.
   Always 1 plough in lordship; ½ men's plough;
   woodland, 2 pigs. Always 1 cob; 6 head of cattle. Now 60
      sheep; 16 pigs; 16 goats.
   1 church, at 10 acres;
value 10d.
   To this 10 free men and a half belong under the patronage only
of E(dric's) prdecessor, at 80 acres of land;
      meadow, 3 acres. Always 2 ploughs.

77 In (South) BURLINGHAM he also (holds), 4½ acres of land belonging
in Bradeston.
Value then 10s; later the same; now 30s.
   After King W(illiam) came into England that Edric was an
outlaw in Denmark and Bishop A(e)lmer annexed the land. Now
W(illiam) of Noyers holds.

78 In CATTON 1 free man under the patronage only of Gyrth before
1066, at 60 acres of land; when Erfast came to the Bishopric he
granted it to one of his men, Reynold.
   Then 5 smallholders, now 4.
   Then 1 plough in lordship. Always ½ men's plough;
   woodland, 5 pigs; 1 cob; 12 pigs; meadow, 7 acres.
Value then and always 15d.

⊽In buchā . ɪɪ . liƀi hŏes . 7 . in caȷtuna . ɪ . 7 almar habuit comđ . ʟᵛᴵᴵ . ač.
terræ . 7 . vɪ . ač . p̃ti . Tč . ɪ . car . & dim . m̃ ; Tč uał . vɪ . soł . 7 vɪɪɪ . đ . modo
. v . & de oĩbʒ his fup̃dictis ħt rex 7 coms̃ facā & focā.

⊽BLAFELDA . HVNDRET . ⊽In brundala . ɪ . liƀ hŏ . Almari
ep̃i comđtione tantū . fed foca fuit . R . ftalre . modo ten . W . ep̃s . de .
xxx . ač terræ . & . vɪ . ač p̃ti . Semp . ɪ . uiłł . & . ɪɪ . borđ . Tč . dim . car .

200 b

Modo arat cū ɪɪ . bouibʒ Tč uał . ɪɪɪ . foł . modo . ɪɪ . foł . ⊽Adhuc in brundala . ɪ . liƀ hŏ Almar . comđ tantū . xɪ . ač . terræ . & dim . Tč dim . car .
Modo nichil . Tč uał xɪɪ . đ . p̃ & modo . vɪ . modo ten . W . ep̃s.

⊽In Witona . xvɪɪɪ . liƀi hŏes almar comđ . cc . ač terræ . & . v . borđ . & . xɪ.
ač p̃ti . Semp . ɪɪɪ . car . ʜelius ten . ɪɪ . hes . ɪ . car . terræ . & . v . borđ . & . xɪ.
ač p̃ti . Tč uał . x . foł . modo . reddit . xxx . & ħt Witona . xɪ . qr̃ in longo.
& . v . qr̃ in lato . & de gelto . vɪɪ . đ . Rex ħt focā.

⊽In eadē . ɪ . liƀ hŏ gerti . t . r . e . com tantū dim xxvɪ . ač terræ . &
Godric tenuit fub comite Rađ . & helewis neptis eruafti ep̃i tenuit
ab eruafto . & modo . Ã . W . ep̃o . Semp arat . cū . ɪɪ . bouibʒ Tč uał
xvɪ . đ . 7 femp.

200 a, b

79 In BUCKENHAM 2 free men—Eli—and in CATTON 1—Reynold. A(e)lmer had the patronage. 57 acres of land; meadow, 6 acres. Then 1 plough, now ½.
Value then 6s 8d; now 5.
The King and Earl (have) the full jurisdiction of all the above-mentioned.

BLOFIELD Hundred

80 In BRUNDALL 1 free man in the patronage only of Bishop A(e)lmer, but the jurisdiction was of R(alph) the Constable. Now Bishop W(illiam) holds, at 30 acres of land;
 meadow, 6 acres.
 Always 1 villager; 2 smallholders.
 Then ½ plough, now he ploughs with 2 oxen.   200 b
Value then 3s; now 2s.

Further in BRUNDALL 1 free man under the patronage only of A(e)lmer; 11½ acres of land.
 Then ½ plough, now nothing.
Value then 12d; later and now 6.
 Now Bishop W(illiam) holds.

81 In WITTON 18 free men under the patronage of A(e)lmer; 200 acres of land.
 5 smallholders.
 Meadow, 11 acres. Always 3 ploughs.
Eli holds 2 men, 1 c. of land.
 5 smallholders.
 Meadow, 11 acres.
Value then 10s; now it pays 30.
 Witton has 11 furlongs in length and 5 furlongs in width, tax of 7d. The King has the jurisdiction.

In the same 1 free man under the patronage only of Gyrth before 1066, half (Gyrth's) 26 acres of land. Godric held under Earl Ralph, and Heloise, niece of Bishop Erfast, held from Erfast, and now from Bishop W(illiam).
 He has always ploughed with 2 oxen.
Value then 16d and always.

HVNDRET . FLECWEST . In Wintretuna . i . liƀ homo
sɔ̄i beñ de holmo cōm tantū . LX . aɔ̄ terræ . III . aɔ̄ p̃ti . Semp . ỿ .
. borđ . & dim̃ . ſalina . Semp . i . car̃ . & ſub.eo . i . liƀ hō . de . IIII . aɔ̄ tr̃æ
Tɔ̄ ual . II . ſot . modo . IIII .

ᚃ In Somertuna . III . liƀi hoẽs . t . r . e . ſed p̃q̃ toſtius exiit de anglia.
fuit . I . æccłia ſ . be꞉de holmo tenæñt . c . VI . aɔ̄ terræ . IX . aɔ̄ p̃ti . Sẽp
IX . borđ . Semp . I . car̃ & dim̃ . Semp ual . IIII . ſot . & . VIII . đ .

ᚃ In aſchebei . II . liƀi hoies ſɔ̄i . ƀ . de holmo . XVI . aɔ̄ . terre . & . II . aɔ̄ p̃ti꞉
Semp dim̃ car̃ . Tɔ̄ ual . XII . đ . & modo . XVI . đ .

ᚃ In Wintretuna . VIII . liƀi hoẽs Almari cōmđ tantū . XIIII . aɔ̄ .
terræ . ſemp dim̃ car̃ . Tɔ̄ ual . VIII . đ . m̃ . XXIIII .

ᚃ In marthā . XXXVI . liƀi hoẽs Almari comdation tantū . v . car̃ .

201 a
terræ . & x . aɔ̄ . modo ten& . W . ep̃s . 7 . L . aɔ̄ p̃ti . Semp XVI . car̃ .
Tɔ̄ ual . VI . liƀ . M̃ . VIII . liƀ . & x . ſot . I . æccłia . L . aɔ̄ . 7 ual . L . đ .

ᚃ In rolueſbi . I . liƀ hō comdatus erat . Ailmari ep̃i LXXX . aɔ̄ terræ
II . aɔ̄ p̃ti . & . v . borđ . & . x . liƀi homines . Semp . II . car̃ . 7 . In burh
II . liƀi homines . de . L . aɔ̄ . teræ . Semp ual . x . ſot .

WEST FLEGG Hundred

82 In WINTERTON 1 free man under the patronage only of St. Benedict of Holme, 60 acres of land;
     meadow, 3 acres.
     Always 5 smallholders.
     ½ salt-house; always 1 plough.
     Also under him 1 free man, at 4 acres of land.
Value then 2s; now 40.

83 In SOMERTON 3 free men before 1066 but after Tosti went from England, Berard (had them). There was 1 church of St. Benedict's of Holme. They hold 106 acres of land;
     meadow, 9 acres.
     Always 9 smallholders.
     Always 1½ ploughs.
Value always 4s 8d.

84 In ASHBY 2 free men of St. Benedict's of Holme, 16 acres of land;
     meadow, 2 acres. Always ½ plough.
Value then 12d; now 16d.

85 In WINTERTON 8 free men under the patronage only of A(e)lmer, 14 acres of land. Always ½ plough.
Value then 8d; now 24.

86 In MARTHAM 36 free men in the patronage only of A(e)lmer;   201 a
5 c. of land and 10 acres. Now Bishop W(illiam) holds.
     Meadow, 50 acres; always 16 ploughs.
Value then £6; now £8 10s.
     1 church; 50 acres;
value 50d.

87 In ROLLESBY 1 free man was under the patronage of Bishop A(e)lmer; 80 acres of land;
     meadow, 2 acres.
     5 smallholders; 10 free men.
     Always 2 ploughs.
In BURGH (St. Margaret) 2 free men, at 50 acres of land.
Value always 10s.

⨍Adhuc in ead̃ roluesbei . i . lib̃ hõ . de . lxxx . ac̄ terræ . Almar⁊
ep̃i 7 aluuoldi Ab̃bis com̃d̃ tantũ . 7 . hic hõ erat ita in mo-
naſterio qd ñ pot̃at dare tr̃a ſuã nec uend̃e . Semp . i . bord̃ .
ii . ac̄ p̃ti . 7 ſub ipſo xii . lib̃i homines . de . xl . ac̄ tr̃æ . & . iii . ac̄⁊
& dim̃ p̃ti . Sẽp . in̄t eos . ii . car̃ . & dim̃ . Tc̄ . ual̃ . x . ſol̃ .
m̃ redd̃ . xxx . ſol̃.

⨍In baſtuuuic . i . lib̃ hõ almari ep̃i . com̃d̃ tantũ & ſub ipſis
ali⁹ lib̃ hõ . & hñt xxx . ac̄ terræ . & . ii . ac̄ p̃ti . Tc̄ . dim̃ . car̃⁊
7 m̃ . Tc̄ ual̃ . ii . ſol̃ . modo xxii . d̃.

⨍In eſco . i . lib̃ hõ . almari ep̃i com̃d̃ . tantũ . de . xv . ac̄ . terræ
& dim̃ . car̃ . dim̃ . ac̄ . p̃ti . 7 ual̃ xvi . d̃.

⨍In bitlakebei tẽn̄ ketel . i . lib̃ hõ dim̃⁊ fuit almari ep̃i co⁊
m̃dtion f7 tota terra ſua fuit ita . in monaſtr̃ ſc̄i bened
de holmo . ad uic̃tũ qd nec dare nec uend̃e potuit . lvii . ac̄ . terræ
x . ac̄ . p̃ti . Eruaſtus inuaſit . m̃ ten̄ Wilt ep̃s . & b̃nar ſub eo . Sẽp
. i . car̃ in dominio . & . ſub eo viii . lib̃i hões xl . v . ac̄ . terræ . vii .
ac̄⁊ p̃ti . Sẽp . i . car̃ . & dim̃⁊ . Tc̄ ual̃ . x . ſol̃ . p̃⁹ 7 modo . xx . ſol̃ .
due parteſ æcclie . vii . ac̄ . 7 ual̃ . v . d̃ . ħt . v . q⁊r in longo . 7 . iii .
& dim̃ in lato 7 de gelto xx . d̃ . & obolũ ;

Further in this ROLLESBY 1 free man, at 80 acres of land, under the patronage only of Bishop A(e)lmer and Abbot Alfwold. This man was in the monastery to the extent that he could not grant or sell his land.

Always 1 smallholder.

Meadow, 2 acres.

Also under him 12 free men, at 40 acres of land;
meadow, 3½ acres.

Always 2½ ploughs between them.

Value then 10s, now it pays 30s.

88 In BASTWICK 1 free man under the patronage only of Bishop A(e)lmer. And under them another free man. They have 30 acres of land; meadow, 2 acres. Then ½ plough, and now.
Value then 2s; now 22d.

89 In SCO 1 free man under the patronage only of Bishop A(e)lmer, at 15 acres of land. ½ plough; meadow, ½ acre.
Value 16d.

90 In BILLOCKBY Ketel holds. He was half Bishop A(e)lmer's in patronage, but all his land was in the monastery of St. Benedict's of Holme for supplies to the extent that he could neither grant nor sell it; 57 acres of land;

meadow, 10 acres.

Erfast annexed it; now Bishop William holds and Bernard under him.

Always 1 plough in lordship.

Also under him 8 free men, 45 acres of land;
meadow, 7 acres.

Always 1½ ploughs.

Value then 10s; later and now 20s.

Two-thirds of a church, 7 acres;
value 5d.

It has 5 furlongs in length and 3½ in width, tax of 20½d.

ᚹIn clepeſbei . IIII . liƀi homineſ . II . ex his Almari eṗi . coṁḋ . & . I.
alſi . I . s . b . de . c . aᷓc . terræ . modo ten̄ . W . eꝑs . x . aᷓc ṗti . & ſub eis . VI.
borḋ . Semper dim̄ . cař . & . I . cař . Tᷓc . ual . v . ſol . ꝑ 7 modo . xx . ſol.
ħt . VII . qř . in longo . & . v . in lato . & . de gelto . XII . ḋ.

HVNḊ . DE HEINESTEDE . In ſutherlingahā . I . liƀ hō elmari.
coṁḋ . t . r . e . ḋ . x . aᷓc . terræ . 7 . II . aᷓc . ṗti . & . II . borḋ . Semp ař
cū . II . boũ . Semp ual xvI . ḋ . modo ten̄ & . W . eꝑs

ᚹIn teueteſſalla . I . liƀ hō . xL . aᷓc terre . t . r . e . teſte hund̄ . 7 pti -
nuit pars uiri ad ſᷓca aldridā . & pars feṁe . xx . aᷓc . ad ſcm̄ edmundū.
Semp dim̄ . cař . & . II . borḋ . Eruaſtus inuaſit . modo ten̄ . W . eꝑs ab
antec̄ . 7 Reinaldus de perapund . ſub eo . Tᷓc ual . v . ſol . m̂ . xx ;

TERRÆ SᷓCJ MICHAHELIS DE NORWIC ;

HVDRET . DE TAVERHĀ . In tauerhā . I . cař . terræ . tenuit
Sᷓcs . M̄ . t . r . e . 7 Stigandus ſub eo . ſemp . IIII . uilt . & . II . borḋ . ſemp
. I . cař in dominio . & . I . cař hom̄ . & . IIII . ſoc̄ . xII . aᷓc . terræ . ſemp
vIII . aᷓc ṗti . ſilua xII . porc̄ . & ual xx . ſol.

91 In CLIPPESBY 4 free men, 2 of these under the patronage of   201 b
     Bishop A(e)lmer, and 1 of Alsi and 1 of St. Benedict, at 100
     acres of land. Now Bishop W(illiam) holds.
          Meadow, 10 acres.
          And under them 6 smallholders.
          Always ½ plough; 1 plough.
     Value then 5s; later and now 20s.
          It has 7 furlongs in length and 5 in width, tax of 12d.

     The Hundred of HENSTEAD
92 In SURLINGHAM 1 free man under the patronage of A(e)lmer
     before 1066, at 10 acres of land;
          meadow, 2 acres.
          2 smallholders.
          He has always ploughed with 2 oxen.
     Value always 16d.
          Now Bishop W(illiam) holds.

     [DISS Half-Hundred]
93 In TIVETSHALL 1 free man, 40 acres of land before 1066, as the
     Hundred testifies, and the man's part, 20 acres, belonged to St.
     Etheldreda and his wife's part, 20 acres, belonged to St. Edmund.
          Always ½ plough.
          2 smallholders.
          Erfast annexed it. Now Bishop W(illiam) holds from his
     predecessor, and Reynold of Pierrepont under him.
     Value then 5s; now 20.

10a   LANDS OF ST. MICHAEL OF NORWICH

     Hundred of TAVERHAM
1   In TAVERHAM St. M(ichael) held 1 c. of land before 1066, and
     Stigand under him.
          Always 4 villagers; 2 smallholders.
          Always 1 plough in lordship; 1 men's plough.
          4 Freemen, 12 acres of land.
               Meadow, always 8 acres; woodland, 12 pigs.
     Value 20s.

TERRE OSBERNI EPI . *GILDECROS* . *HVND* .

In benham tenuit Aluric lib hō . t . r . e . ı . car̄ . terræ . ſemp . ııı .
uiłłi . 7 . v . bord . Tc̄ . ı . ſeru̅ . & . x . ac̄ . p̄ti . ſemp . ı . car̄ in dominio.

202 a

& dim̄ cat̄ hom . Silua . de . c . porc̄ . & . ııı . ſoc̄ . v . ac̄ . modo . ı . runc̄ .
ſemp . ııı . an̄ . Tc̄ . vı . porc̄ . mòdo . xxvıı . Tc̄ . vı . oūs . modo xxx . Tc̄
. v . cap̄ . modo . xxx . Tc̄ ual̄ xx . ſol̄ . modo . xL .

 In Wica . ten̄ . ı . lib hō . ı . car̄ terræ . t . r . e . Tc̄ & p̄ . vıı . uiłł . m̄ .
vııı . ſemp . v . bord . & . ı . ſeru̅ . 7 . ıııı . ac̄ . p̄ti . Tc̄ 7 p̄ . ı . car̄ in dn̄io .
modo . ıı . ſemp . ııı . car̄ . hom̄ . Tc̄ ual̄ . xx . ſol̄ . modo . xL . 7 . x . li -
bi hoēs 7 dim̄ . ı . car̄ . tr̄e . 7 dim̄ ac̄ p̄ti . ſemp . ıı . car̄ . & . ual̄
x . ſol̄ . tota ſoca in keninchala .

H̄ . de grenehoga . Hindringahā ten̄ . ııı . libi hoēs . t . r . e . ııı . libi
hoēs . t . r . e . xxxıı . ac̄ . terræ . ſemp . ı . car̄ . ſemp . x . ſol̄ . t . r . e . 7 ſēp
h̄t rex & coīns ſacā . 7 hos . tres hoēs q̄s . berardus ten̄& caluͤpniantur
hoēs drogonis . ad feudū dn̄i ſui .

HVND . *DEPEWADE* . Taſeburc tenuit Torolf lib hō Stigandi
xxx . ac̄ Semp . ı . bord . & . ı . car̄ in dn̄io . 7 . ıııı . ac̄ . p̄ti . vııı . pars
mol̄ . 7 vı . libi homines . x . ac̄ . coīnd tantū . t . r . e . & . ſemp dim̄ car̄ .

 In foneſeta . ı . lib hō . Stigandi . xxx . ac̄ . ſemp . ıı . bord Tc̄ & . poſt
. ı . car̄ . modo dim̄ . ıııı . ac̄ . p̄ti . Tc̄ . ıı . molin̄ . P̄ . ı . modo . n̄ . & . ıı .
libi hoēs . ıı . ac̄ . Tc̄ ual̄ . xx . ſol̄ . P̄ 7 m̄ . xxx . Tota taſeburc . h̄t
x . qr̄ in longo . & . vıı . in lato . & . ıx . đ . de gelto .

LANDS OF BISHOP OSBERN

GUILTCROSS Hundred

1 In BANHAM Aelfric, a free man, held before 1066, 1 c. of land.
    Always 3 villagers; 5 smallholders. Then 1 slave.
    Meadow, 10 acres.
    Always 1 plough in lordship; ½ men's plough;   202 a
      woodland at 100 pigs.
    Also 3 Freemen, 5 acres.
    Now 1 cob, always 3 head of cattle. Then 6 pigs, now 27.
      Then 6 sheep, now 30. Then 5 goats, now 30.
  Value then 20s; now 40.

2 In WICK 1 free man held 1 c. of land before 1066.
    Then and later 7 villagers, now 8. Always 5 smallholders;
      1 slave.
    Meadow, 4 acres.
    Then and later 1 plough in lordship, now 2; always 3 men's
      ploughs.
  Value then 20s; now 40.
    Also 10 free men and a half, 1 c. of land.
      Meadow, ½ acre. Always 2 ploughs.
  Value 10s.
    The whole jurisdiction (is) in Kenninghall.

The Hundred of (North) GREENHOE

3 3 free men held HINDRINGHAM before 1066, 32 acres of land.
    Always 1 plough.
  Value always 10s before 1066.
    The King and the Earl always had the jurisdiction. Drogo's
  men claim these 3 men whom Berard holds as part of the Holding
  of their lord.

DEPWADE Hundred

4 Thorulf, a free man of Stigand's, held TASBURGH, 30 acres.
    Always 1 smallholder.
    1 plough in lordship. Meadow, 4 acres; one-eighth of a mill.
    Also 6 free men, 10 acres in patronage only before 1066.
      Always ½ plough.

5 In FORNCETT 1 free man of Stigand's, 30 acres.
    Always 2 smallholders.
    Then and later 1 plough, now ½. Meadow, 4 acres. Then 2 mills,
      later 1, now none.
    Also 2 free men, 2 acres.
  Value then 20s; later and now 30.
    The whole of Tasburgh has 10 furlongs in length and 7 in
  width, tax of 9d.